T0394733

Doing Justice to a Wronged Literature

Islamic History and Civilization

STUDIES AND TEXTS

VOLUME 194

The titles published in this series are listed at *brill.com/ihc*

Portrait of Thomas Bauer
PHOTO BY NATALIE KRANEISS

Doing Justice to a Wronged Literature

Essays on Arabic Literature and Rhetoric of the 12th–18th Centuries in Honour of Thomas Bauer

Edited by

Hakan Özkan
Nefeli Papoutsakis

BRILL

LEIDEN | BOSTON

Cover illustration: Fol. 1b of Ibn Nubāta's autograph of *Muntaḫab al-hadiyya*, MS Köprülü 1379. Courtesy of the Süleymaniye Library, Istanbul, Turkey.

The Library of Congress Cataloging-in-Publication Data is available online at https://catalog.loc.gov
LC record available at https://lccn.loc.gov/2022031939

Typeface for the Latin, Greek, and Cyrillic scripts: "Brill". See and download: brill.com/brill-typeface.

ISSN 0929-2403
ISBN 978-90-04-52177-3 (hardback)
ISBN 978-90-04-52178-0 (e-book)

This book is printed on acid-free paper and produced in a sustainable manner.

Contents

Editors' Introduction

In 2013, Thomas Bauer was awarded the prestigious German Leibniz Award, with which he founded and funded ALEA (abbreviation for Arabische Literatur und Rhetorik Elfhundert bis Achtzehnhundert), a research group based at the Department of Arabic and Islamic Studies of the University of Münster, with a view to promoting the study of Arabic literature and rhetoric dating from the sixth/twelfth to the twelfth/eighteenth centuries—an area of Arabic studies notoriously neglected and maligned by earlier scholarship. The idea of producing a Festschrift for Thomas's sixtieth birthday in September 2021, originated in this group. With it, we wished to express our gratitude to him as well as celebrate his long and outstanding career as a researcher and university teacher that has established him as a leading academic in our field. Thomas's latest great success gave us additional reason to celebrate and honour him: In December 2019, in collaboration with Syrinx von Hees, Thomas Bauer won a twelve-year research grant from the DFG (Deutsche Forschungsgemeinschaft) to produce an open-access, online critical edition of the complete works of Ibn Nubāta al-Miṣrī (686–768/1287–1366), the most acclaimed Arab poet of the Mamluk era. This project employs five senior researchers, two doctoral students and a Digital Humanities expert. It thus secured the positions of all members of the ALEA group for at least twelve years (four of us obtained tenure), which shows Thomas's care for the staff of the Department he runs.

Thomas Bauer is not only an Arabist but also an Islamicist and has produced several ground-breaking studies in a number of different areas, including classical Arabic lexicography, early Arabic poetry, Abbasid literature, Arabic literature and rhetoric of the Ayyubid, Mamluk and Ottoman periods, and the cultural history of Islam more generally. It is fair to say that his work has brought the field forward in all these areas by offering a fresh and imaginative thorough reading of the sources that challenges well-established views and opens up new perspectives for future research. Thanks to a series of critical studies produced over the last two decades in particular, he has succeeded in debunking the decline narrative by calling attention to the quality, interest and vitality of the Arabic literature dating from the sixth/twelfth to the twelfth/eighteenth centuries and to its complex and diverse aesthetics. Apart from founding the ALEA group to boost research in this undeservedly neglected area, he also supported and inspired other colleagues, too, to work on this domain. This is why we decided to give the Festschrift the thematic focus "Arabic literature and rhetoric from the sixth/twelfth to the twelfth/eighteenth centuries," although this by no means covers the wide range of topics, on which Thomas Bauer has worked. Thirty-odd years ago, when ʿUmar Mūsā Bāshā, an Arab scholar much admired by Thomas and a pioneer in the study of this area, described Ottoman-era Arabic literature as *al-adab al-maẓlūm* (the wronged literature),[1] this characterisation held true for the literature of the Ayyubid and Mamluk periods as well. Meanwhile Thomas Bauer's work has done much to rehabilitate this literature and do justice to it.

The present volume is a collection of case studies on individual literary authors, texts, themes and rhetorical figures dating from the said period. A number of scholars who either have worked closely with the ALEA group since its foundation or are long-time friends of Thomas have joined us in producing it. Due to pandemic-related restrictions and inconveniences, however, some colleagues who had initially agreed to contribute to the Festschrift have regrettably been obliged to withdraw. Emil T. Homerin, a dear friend of the ALEAs, who had very much wanted to participate, sadly passed away in December 2020. Others were willing to contribute but felt that the volume's thematic focus lay beyond their area of expertise and thus could not participate. We would like to thank them all for their readiness to join us in honouring Thomas and thank especially all contributors for their kind cooperation. We also cordially thank Hinrich Biesterfeld and Sebastian Günther for accepting the volume for publication in the Islamic History and Civilization series of Brill and are grateful to Teddi Dols for her assistance throughout the process of production.

The contributions are preceded by a short academic curriculum vitae and a list of publications of Thomas Bauer and have been arranged very roughly chronologically, but the *adab* principle of delectable variation has also been observed—all the more so as several articles take a diachronic perspective and cover several centuries.

The work of Usāma Ibn Munqidh (488–584/1095–1188), a sixth-/twelfth-century Arab intellectual and politician who is primarily known for his memoirs, the *Kitāb al-Iʿtibār* (Book of instruction by example), has long attracted attention for the insights it offers into contemporary Muslim attitudes towards the Crusaders. In this connection Ewald Wagner revisits a topic that has for some time been debated between Paul Cobb and Robert Irwin, namely, Usāma's attitude towards *jihad*. Adducing new evidence from Usāma's poetry, a source untapped by the two scholars, he shows that Usāma was not unfavourably disposed towards *jihad*, as Irwin had claimed, thus supporting Cobb's

1 ʿUmar Mūsā Bāshā, *Taʾrīkh al-adab al-ʿarabī: al-ʿAṣr al-ʿUthmānī*, Damascus 1989, 7.

views on the subject. Wagner also offers additional evidence against Irwin's contention that Usāma was a Shiite, another point in which he agrees with Cobb.

In the context of a long-term ongoing project of his that aims at tracing the changes observed over time in the use of rhetoric in pre-modern Arabic poetry, Ali Hussein analyses the rhetorical fabric (the sum total of rhetorical devices used) of a poem by ʿAfīf al-Dīn al-Tilimsānī (d. 690/1291), a Sufi poet of the early Mamluk period, and compares it to the rhetorical fabric of three pre-Mamluk poems. Besides bearing witness to the great variety of figures employed in the poems, the study documents the enhanced importance of certain rhetorical devices in specific periods and genres and brings out some stylistic peculiarities of Sufi poetry.

The son of ʿAfīf al-Dīn al-Tilimsānī, Shams al-Dīn Muḥammad (661–88/1263–89), nicknamed al-Shābb al-Ẓarīf (the Elegant Youth), was likewise a fine poet, albeit a secular one. Apart from poetry, al-Shābb is also known to have composed a collection of *maqāmāt* entitled *Maqāmāt al-ʿushshāq* (The Lover's *Maqāma*s), some of which have been preserved in manuscript. In their jointly written contribution Bilal Orfali and Maurice Pomerantz offer an *editio princeps* of a beautiful *maqāma* by al-Shābb al-Ẓarīf entitled *Faṣāḥat al-mashūq fī malāḥat al-maʿshūq* (The Eloquence of the Lover Concerning the Elegance of the Beloved) and briefly summarise its contents.

The Syrian poet Ibn Muqātil (664 or 674–761/1266 or 1276–1359) was one of the most important and influential *zajjāls* (composers of *zajal*s, strophic poems in vernacular Arabic) of the early Mamluk period. In a contest organised by the Mamluk Sultan al-Malik al-Nāṣir Muḥammad b. Qalāwūn (r. 693–4/1293–4, 698–708/1299–1309, 709–41/1310–41), himself a *zajal* dilettante, to decide whether Ibn Muqātil or his opponent, the Damascene al-Amshāṭī (d. 725/1325), was the best *zajjāl*, Ibn Muqātil won the day with his *zajal* beginning *qalbī yuḥibb tayyāh* (My heart loves an haughty person), a *zajal* that several poets subsequently tried to imitate and surpass. Hakan Özkan, an expert on the Eastern *zajal*,[2] offers a new edition and a translation of this poem and examines which features of it account for its success.

Ibn Nubāta al-Miṣrī (686–768/1287–1366) was, as said earlier, the most acclaimed poet of the Mamluk era. As such he has attracted Thomas's attention since the early 2000s and figures prominently in at least a dozen of his studies.

2 H. Özkan, *Geschichte des östlichen zağal: Dialektale arabische Strophendichtung aus dem Osten der arabischen Welt—von den Anfängen bis zum Ende der Mamlukenzeit*, Baden-Baden 2020, is the revised version of Hakan's Habilitationsschrift. Hakan was mentored by Thomas Bauer.

Ibn Nubāta was also a preeminent prose writer. The official letters he composed during the short period he served in the Chancery at Damascus (743–5/1342–5) and which he collected in three volumes, testify to this preeminence. Andreas Herdt, who has already published two selections of Ibn Nubāta's correspondence[3] and is currently editing the three volumes, edits here one of Ibn Nubāta's official letters concerning the recovery of the reigning Sultan from an illness and translates and analyses the very demanding text introducing the reader to the intricacies of chancery writing and demonstrating its importance for the history of Arabic literature.

As opposed to Ibn Nubāta, a representative of the literary high culture, Ibrāhīm al-Miʿmār ("the builder") (d. 749/1348–9) was, as his name indicates, a craftsman poet. His talent was, however, such that elite authors "raided," as a contemporary put it, the ideas and motifs of his poetry. Thomas Bauer, who first called attention to this master poet in 2002, has recently published al-Miʿmār's *Dīwān* (collected poetry) in collaboration with Anke Osigus and Hakan Özkan.[4] In his contribution, Gregor Schoeler presents, translates and analyses one of al-Miʿmār's *zajal*s—a most demanding and intriguing poem that al-Miʿmār put in the mouth of a young artiste and prostitute, a monologue that she addresses to her mother, who had presumably tried to persuade her to mend her ways.

Manuscripts of *Kalīla wa-Dimna*, a famous collection of fables of Indian origin that reached the Arab world via a middle-Persian version thanks to the translation-redaction of Ibn al-Muqaffaʿ (d. ca. 139/757) in the second/eighth century, start proliferating from the seventh/thirteenth century onwards. Ibn al-Muqaffaʿ's exact version is irretrievable because of multifarious alterations and accretions due to the copyist-redactors of the text in later centuries, as the work became increasingly popular and reached wider audiences. Beatrice Gruendler, who directs the Berlin-based project *Kalīla and Dimna—AnonymClassic*, investigates what these later alterations and accretions tell us about the tension between oral and written media by examining closely a story found in Ibn al-Muqaffaʿ's preface, on rote memorisation as opposed to understanding based on thorough reading.

Geert Jan van Gelder's paper describes and analyses the history of *ibdāʿ*, a technical term in *ʿilm al-badīʿ*, the science of the various figures of speech and stylistic embellishments collectively known as *badīʿ*, which is a branch of premodern Arabic rhetoric. With the lexical meaning "creating something novel,"

3 A. Herdt, Kitāb zahr al-manṯūr *and* Min tarassul Ibn Nubātah: *A critical edition of two prose works by Ibn Nubātah al-Miṣrī*, Baden-Baden 2019.

4 T. Bauer, A. Osigus and H. Özkan, *Der Dīwān des Ibrāhīm al-Miʿmār (gest. 749/1348–49): Edition und Kommentar*, Baden-Baden 2018.

the word has often been used as a general term for stylistic excellence. Nevertheless, thanks to Ibn Abī l-Iṣbaʿ (d. 654/1256), an author on *badīʿ* who claims to have invented this "figure," *ibdāʿ* came to mean specifically "accumulating several rhetorical figures in one line of verse or one prose period." The term was duly adopted and discussed by later writers on *badīʿ* and the "figure" (by definition an accumulation of several figures) regularly occurs in *badīʿiyyāt* (poems illustrating the various *badīʿ* figures and embellishments usually taking the form of a eulogy on the Prophet) in subsequent centuries.

Ibn Abī Ḥajala (725–76/1325–75), a talented poet and prose writer, who authored several anthologies and *maqāmāt*, is another Mamluk-era littérateur whom we now know better thanks to Thomas Bauer. In 2015, in collaboration with Syrinx von Hees, Thomas organised a congress on Ibn Abī Ḥajala at Münster. This resulted in the publication of a volume comprised of thirteen studies on various aspects of Ibn Abī Ḥajala's work.[5] In his contribution, Werner Diem edits, translates and analyses all the extant excerpts from Ibn Abī Ḥajala's lost epistle *al-Sajʿ al-jalīl fī-mā jarā min al-Nīl* (Splendid rhymed prose on what happened because of/[over]flowed from the Nile), concerning the disastrous flooding of the Nile in 761/1360.

Verena Klemm explores the special manuscript culture that the Syrian Ismaʿilis, a relatively isolated and secretive Shiite community, practised in their mountainous retreat in Jabal Bahrāʾ, not far from Hama, over the centuries. There, away from the cultural centres of the region, religious experts compiled various texts of interest to the community in composite manuscripts (*majmūʿāt*) that were and are even today kept in private collections inaccessible to research. As an example, she presents a few manuscripts containing, among other things, *Manāqib al-mawlā Rāshid al-Dīn*, a collection of hagiographic tales about Rāshid al-Dīn Sinān (d. ca. 589/1193), the leader of the community at the time of Saladin. The tales, which were initially transmitted orally, were written down at the time of Hama's efflorescence under al-Malik al-Muʾayyad (r. 710–31/1310–31) and sharply contrast with the literary high culture that thrived at his court.

Pigeons are one of the most important bird species in the cultural history of the Arab peoples and have over the centuries been part of their daily life in various ways. Besides, pigeons and doves are perhaps the most popular bird with Arabic littérateurs and feature prominently in various poetic genres, especially in nature and love poetry and in the elegy, poets often projecting their feelings

5 N. Papoutsakis and S. von Hees, (eds.), *The sultan's anthologist: Ibn Abī Ḥağalah and his work*, Baden-Baden 2017.

on them. They therefore also figure prominently in several pre-modern Arabic anthologies. How and in what context are they then presented in literary anthologies of the Mamluk era? How have anthologists selected their material from the plethora of earlier and contemporary texts featuring pigeons and which topoi and motifs were important to them? These are the questions that Anke Osigus addresses in her study.

The Arabic popular epic thrived especially in Mamluk and later times. Transmitted in a mixed oral and written way, it at first sight seems to have little in common with the literature of the cultural elite. On closer inspection, however, the interaction between the two literary spheres becomes obvious. A good case in point is the role that books play in the epics, which is what Remke Kruk set out to examine. Do the epics contain references to extant literary works, book titles and authors? If so, what is the narrative function of these references? Are any fictional books mentioned, and if so, what is their role in the stories? As Kruk shows, fictional books, usually imparting supernatural knowledge, are a major motif in the epics, even though their role differs from *sīra* to *sīra*.

Inspired by Thomas's interest in and work on Arabic rhetoric and its development over time, Syrinx von Hees investigates the reception of al-Khaṭīb al-Qazwīnī's (666–739/1268–1338) two famous compendia on rhetoric, the *Talkhīṣ al-Miftāḥ* and the *Īḍāḥ fī ʿulūm al-balāgha*, by the later Mamluk littérateur and critic Ibn Ḥijja al-Ḥamawī (767–837/1366–1434) in the *Khizānat al-adab*, his commentary on his own *badīʿiyya*. She looks into Ibn Ḥijja's treatment of *ṭibāq* (antithesis) as an example of how he relates to the work of his predecessors and shows that rhetorical theory did not cease to develop after al-Qazwīnī, that later authors did not hesitate to challenge al-Qazwīnī's views and that important theoretical issues were discussed freely and productively in *badīʿiyyāt* commentaries as well.

Who was ʿAbd ar-Raḥīm al-Buraʿī and when did he live? The name may sound familiar to those who are knowledgeable about Arabic religious poetry, especially praise poetry on the prophet Muḥammad. For al-Buraʿī's beautiful and moving poems are in this day and age commonly sung in religious ceremonies all over the Arab world. But the dates of the Yemenite poet and religious scholar (d. 803/1400–1) had long been uncertain and so were his other details, too. Ines Weinrich has therefore embarked on a thorough inspection of all the available material—numerous prints and manuscripts of al-Buraʿī's collected poems and other work and references in the sources and the secondary literature—and succeeded in dispersing many of the legends and uncertainties surrounding him.

The tale of *Sūl and Shumūl* is one of the most moving love stories in the Thousand and One Nights. It has appositely been described as "the Arab 'Orpheus in the Underworld,'" as it offers an intriguing insight into an Arabic-Islamic underworld of sorts and singing and poetry recitation are crucial elements of the plot. Claudia Ott, who has recently published a German translation of *Sūl and Shumūl*, discusses the state of the art concerning the tale and draws attention to the unique interfaith (Muslim-Christian) interaction that takes place in it. In addition, she allows us a rare glimpse into her work as a translator and the problems associated with it.

Epigrammatic poetry reached an apogee in the Mamluk period but epigrams remained popular in Ottoman times, too. Very often epigrams ended with a punch line in which a figure of speech was employed, *taḍmīn* (quotation of another poet's verse or hemistich) and *iqtibās* (quotation from the Quran or *ḥadīth*) being among the commonly used figures. Incorporating Quranic quotations in prose or poetry was a common, albeit controversial practice that enhanced the literariness of a text and enriched and complicated its meaning. Alev Masarwa discusses the use of *iqtibās* in the poetry and especially the epigrams of Māmayh al-Rūmī (d. ca. 987/1579), an acclaimed early-Ottoman Arabic poet of Circassian origin.

Ibrāhīm Ibn al-Mullā (d. 1032/1623) is a little-known Arabic littérateur, the scion of a scholarly family of Aleppo. Among his surviving works is *Ḥalbat al-mufāḍala wa-ḥilyat al-munāḍala* (The Racecourse of Competition and the Ornament of Contest), a selection of his correspondence with contemporary littérateurs and religious scholars, family members and Ottoman dignitaries. The bulk of this correspondence consists of riddle exchanges. Nefeli Papoutsakis traces briefly the history of Ibrāhīm's family, surveys his life and oeuvre and focuses on *Ḥalbat al-mufāḍala* with a view to assessing its importance as a source for the history of the Arabic literary riddle.

This being a volume written by many hands, contributors were allowed to write in British or American English and, those writing in German, to follow their spelling preferences.

Last but not least, we would like to cordially thank Elida Vrajolli, a BA student at the Department of Arabic and Islamic Studies of the University of Münster, for assisting us in preparing the list of Thomas Bauer's publications. The list includes only a few select pieces of Thomas's numerous articles and interviews that have appeared in newspapers. We also thank Noralyne Maranus and the team of TAT Zetwerk for setting and preparing the volume for the press.

Thomas Bauer: Short Academic Curriculum Vitae

When Thomas Bauer finished school in 1980, he intended to study law and become a judge. Luckily for him and, above all, our field, however, a pure coincidence prevented him from taking that road and completely changed the course of his life. Without a doubt he would have become an excellent judge and may have written numerous outstanding books in the field of law, but Arabic and Islamic studies would have lost one of its most original, enthusiastic and dedicated scholars of the last decades. What was this lucky coincidence? He simply forgot or, one should rather say, subconsciously neglected to enrol in time. Hence, he was forced to change plans.

As he had already shown interest in Arabic during his high school years, the decision what to do next came naturally and he matriculated at the University of Erlangen to read Islamic studies, Semitic philology, and German linguistics. He graduated in 1987 with a Magister thesis on the *Kitāb al-Nabāt* (Book of Plants) by Abū Ḥanīfa al-Dīnawarī (d. 282/895), an extraordinary Arabic work that combines lexicography, botany and Arabian folklore. Thomas's excellent thesis on it, entitled *Das Pflanzenbuch des Abū Ḥanīfa ad-Dīnawārī*, was published by Harrassowitz in the following year. A book publication at this stage of one's career is not a small feat and it portended what was about to come. More importantly, however, this study shows that for Thomas—just as for Abū Ḥanīfa—philology is a holistic endeavour—it is not simply concerned with language and literary texts but also with their referents, the wide world around us, and especially human culture. This explains the thoroughness with which Thomas studied Abū Ḥanīfa's book and which is typical of all his other work.

From 1987 to 1990 Thomas pursued his doctoral studies in Erlangen supervised by Wolfdietrich Fischer, the renowned German Arabist and author of the *Grammatik des klassischen Arabisch*, who had also supervised his Magister thesis and was later to mentor his post-doctoral degree (habilitation), too. Thomas's doctoral thesis *Altarabische Dichtkunst: Eine Untersuchung ihrer Struktur und Entwicklung am Beispiel der Onagerepisode* (published by Harrassowitz in 1992) is a deeply researched study of a theme recurrent in early Arabic poetry: the comparison of the poet's camel to the onager. Again, taking a wider view of this theme and its function and development over time, the study broke with earlier scholarship and offered new insights into the structure, meaning, and *Sitz im Leben* of the early Arabic ode as a whole.

Having spent a year as a research associate at the University of Heidelberg, in 1991 Thomas returned to Erlangen, took up a position as a research assistant and started working on his habilitation, besides teaching various classes on Arabic and other Semitic languages. His habilitation thesis *Liebe und Liebesdichtung in der Abbasidenzeit: Eine literatur- und mentalitätsgeschichtliche Studie des arabischen Ġazal im 9. und 10. Jahrhundert* (submitted in 1997, published by Harrassowitz in 1998), is the first thorough study of Abbasid love poetry viewed in the broader context of cultural history and the history of mentalities, and uses approaches from gender studies and sociology.

After a three-year period as an associate professor at the University of Erlangen (1997–2000), Thomas was appointed full professor at the University of Münster in February 2000. There he received a rather peculiar welcome: The rector, in whose presence he was sworn in as the then youngest professor at the university, advised him to be prepared and look for other universities in the state that have a department of Arabic and Islamic studies, as his own department might sooner or later be closed like other small departments of the Faculty of Philology. We do not know how this advice influenced Thomas in his first years in Münster. What we do know, however, is that he did not only keep in existence the department of Arabic and Islamic studies, then manned by himself, a secretary and an Arabic tutor, but also enlarged it exponentially. Thanks to his efforts the department has been endowed with four more professorships (Islamic history, Islamic law, Arabic literature and rhetoric, and Modern Arabic literature), two permanent positions of post-doctoral assistants, a further secretary and a second Arabic tutor, in addition to the ALEAs and several doctoral and post-doctoral researchers employed on a temporal basis.

In 2002–3 Thomas co-founded and directed (until 2005) the Centrum für Religiöse Studien (Centre for Religious Studies), an umbrella institution aiming at coordinating and strengthening the study of religion and especially comparative religion at the University of Münster. In this context he also co-founded the Zentrum für Islamische Theologie (Centre for Islamic Theology), which is now about to become a Faculty of Islamic Theology and where confessional Islamic theology and religious education are taught—a fact that shows his commitment to interfaith dialogue and the integration of Muslims in Germany. Apart from serving on several university boards at Münster, incl. those of the Centre for Eastern Mediterranean Studies and of the Excellence Cluster "Religion and Politics in Pre-modern and Modern Cultures," in 2012 Thomas was elected as the then youngest member (another record!) of the North Rhine-Westphalian Academy of Sciences, Humanities and the Arts. In addition, he is sectional editor of the *Encyclopaedia of Islam Three* for pre-modern Arabic literature and serves in the editorial boards of three scholarly journals.

Through his research agenda in the last twenty-one years at Münster, he inspired, as said, many colleagues to work on Mamluk and Ottoman-era Arabic literature, arguably being the first Arabist to emphatically highlight its value and importance, debunking the concept of the decline of Islamic culture after the fifth/eleventh century and exposing it as a colonialist construct. He also drew special attention to the Arabic rhetorical tradition and its remarkable achievements in the fields of linguistics and stylistics. In more recent years he has researched extensively on ambiguity and ambiguity tolerance in premodern Islamic societies as well as generally in the modern world. His two books on these and related issues, *Die Kultur der Ambiguität: Eine andere Geschichte des Islams* (published by Insel Verlag in 2011; English translation: *A culture of ambiguity: An alternative history of Islam*, published by Columbia University Press in 2021), and *Die Vereindeutigung der Welt: Über den Verlust von Mehrdeutigkeit und Vielfalt* (on the lack of ambiguity tolerance and the loss of diversity in the modern world; published by Reclam in 2018) have made him widely known not only to the academic but also to the general public. *Die Vereindeutigung der Welt* won him the Tractatus award of the Austrian philosophical society Philosophicum Lech. Another recent work of his, *Warum es kein islamisches Mittelalter gab: Das Erbe der Antike und der Orient* (Beck, 2018), on 'Middle Ages' being a misnomer when applied to Islamic history, won the "WISSEN! Sachbuchpreis," a renowned German award for non-fiction books of the wbg (Wissen. Bildung. Gesellschaft) in 2019. The three last-named books have been translated into several languages (Arabic, English, Turkish, Swedish, Russian, Greek, Slovene, and Spanish). Like the numerous interviews Thomas has given in newspapers, radio features and TV broadcasts, these works also aim at, and have contributed to, eliminating prejudices against Islam in public opinion.

Thomas's numerous publications and especially his books for the wider public testify to his remarkable ability to develop new ideas by bringing together his broad general knowledge and his expertise in Arabic and Islamic studies. Thorough philological analysis and sound argumentation that draws on such diverse fields as science and the arts thus lead to novel and intriguing insights of broad historical and anthropological significance.

On behalf of the undersigned friends and colleagues, we warmly congratulate Thomas on his sixtieth birthday and his multifarious achievements and wish him long life and good health. May he always succeed in his endeavours and never cease to inspire us.

Hakan Özkan and Nefeli Papoutsakis

Tabula Gratulatoria

Abdo Abboud
Hinrich and Heika Biesterfeldt
Noureddine Boulouh
Werner Diem
Jens Fischer
Beatrice Gruendler
Sebastian Günther
Jaakko Hämeen-Anttila
Fereshte Hedjazi
Andreas Herdt
† Emil Homerin
Ali Hussein
Verena Klemm
Remke Kruk
Abdelkarim Lardi
Alev Masarva
Samir Mubayd
Norbert Oberbauer
Bilal Orfali
Anke Osigus
Claudia Ott
Hakan Özkan
Nefeli Papoutsakis
Maurice Pomerantz
Sabine Prätor
Kristina Richardson
Luca Rizzo
Everett Rowson
Gregor Schoeler
Marco Schöller
Tilman Seidensticker
Iyad Shraim
Monika Springberg
Ulrike Stehli-Werbeck
Adam Talib
Stephan Tölke
Manfred Ullmann
Geert Jan van Gelder
Syrinx von Hees
Elida Vrajolli
Ewald Wagner
Ines Weinrich
Robert Wieczorek
Barbara Winckler
Vildan Yaşar

Publications of Thomas Bauer

1985

Review of Bernd Heine, Thilo C. Schadeberg and Ekkehard Wolff (eds.), *Die Sprachen Afrikas*, Hamburg, 1981, in *Zeitschrift für Arabische Linguistik* 14/1 (1985), 96–100.

1988

Das Pflanzenbuch des Abū Ḥanīfa ad-Dīnawarī: Inhalt, Aufbau, Quellen, Wiesbaden: Harrassowitz, 1988.

Review of A.F.L. Beeston, *Sabaic grammar* (Journal of Semitic Studies, Monograph No. 6), Manchester, 1984, in *Zeitschrift für Arabische Linguistik* 19/2 (1988), 93–5.

Review of Jacqueline Pirenne (ed.), *Corpus des inscriptions et antiquités sud-arabes, Tome II: Le musée d'Aden, Fasc. 1: Inscriptions; Fasc. 2: Antiquités*, Louvain, 1986, in *Zeitschrift für Arabische Linguistik* 19/2 (1988), 95–7.

1991

Review of Tilman Seidensticker, *Das Verbum sawwama: Ein Beitrag zum Problem der Homonymenscheidung im Arabischen* (Sitzungsberichte der Bayerischen Akademie der Wissenschaften, philosophisch-historische Klasse; Beiträge zur Lexikographie des klassischen Arabisch 6), München, 1986, in *Der Islam* 68/1 (1991), 168–9.

1992

Altarabische Dichtkunst: Eine Untersuchung ihrer Struktur und Entwicklung am Beispiel der Onagerepisode, 2 vols., Wiesbaden: Harrassowitz, 1992.

Review of Ewald Wagner (ed.), *Der Dīwān des Abū Nuwās, Teil III* (Bibliotheca Islamica 20c), Stuttgart and Beirut, 1988, in *Zeitschrift der Deutschen Morgenländischen Gesellschaft* 69/1 (1992), 121.

1993

Formel und Zitat: Zwei Spielarten von Intertextualität in der altarabischen Dichtung, in *Journal of Arabic Literature* 24 (1993), 117–38.

Wie fängt man eine Qaṣīde an? Formelhafte und nichtformelhafte Nasīb-Einleitungsverse, in *Zeitschrift für Arabische Linguistik* 25 (1993), 50–75.

1994

Die Pflanzensystematik der Araber, in Cornelia Wunsch (ed.), *XXV. Deutscher Orientalistentag vom 8. bis 13.4.1991 in München: Vorträge* (Zeitschrift der Deutschen Morgenländischen Gesellschaft. Suppl. 10), Stuttgart: Steiner, 1994, 108–17.

Muzarrids Qaṣīde vom reichen Ritter und dem armen Jäger, in Wolfhart Heinrichs and Gregor Schoeler (eds.), *Festschrift Ewald Wagner zum 65. Geburtstag, Band 2: Studien zur arabischen Dichtung* (Beiruter Texte und Studien 54), Beirut: Steiner, 1994, 42–71.

1995

al-Samaw'al b. ʿĀdiyā, in P.J. Bearman et al. (eds.), *The Encyclopaedia of Islam: New Edition, viii*, Leiden: Brill, 1995, 1041–2.

1996

Arabic Writing, in Peter T. Daniels and William Bright (eds.), *The world's writing systems*, New York: Oxford University Press, 1996, 559–64.

Das arabische Schriftsystem, in Hartmut Günther and Otto Ludwig (eds.), *Schrift und Schriftlichkeit: Ein interdisziplinäres Handbuch internationaler Forschung*, Vol. 2, (Handbücher zur Sprach- und Kommunikationswissenschaft 10.2), Berlin and New York: De Gruyter, 1996, 1433–6.

Die schriftliche Sprache im Arabischen, in Hartmut Günther and Otto Ludwig (eds.), *Schrift und Schriftlichkeit: Ein interdisziplinäres Handbuch internationaler Forschung*, Vol. 2, (Handbücher zur Sprach- und Kommunikationswissenschaft 10.2), Berlin and New York: De Gruyter, 1996, 1483–90.

Abū Tammām's contribution to ʿAbbāsid ġazal poetry, in *Journal of Arabic Literature* 27 (1996), 13–21.

Raffinement und Frömmigkeit: Säkulare Poesie islamischer Religionsgelehrter der späten Abbasidenzeit, in *Asiatische Studien* 50 (1996), 275–95.

Review of Andras Hamori, *The composition of Mutanabbī's panegyrics to Sayf al-Dawla* (Studies in Arabic Literature 14), Leiden, 1992, in *Zeitschrift der Deutschen Morgenländischen Gesellschaft* 146/2 (1996), 561–2.

Review of Arie Schippers, *Spanish Hebrew poetry and the Arabic literary tradition* (Medieval Iberian Peninsula 7), Leiden, 1994, in *Zeitschrift der Deutschen Morgenländischen Gesellschaft* 146/2 (1996), 563–4.

Review of Gerard Wiegers, *Islamic literature in Spanish and Aljamiado*, Leiden, 1994, in *Zeitschrift der Deutschen Morgenländischen Gesellschaft* 146/2 (1996), 564–6.

1997

Review of R.B. Serjeant and R.L. Bidwell (eds.), *Arabian Studies* (University of Cambridge Oriental Publications 42), Cambridge, 1990, in *Der Islam* 74/1 (1997), 190–1.

1998

Liebe und Liebesdichtung in der arabischen Welt des 9. und 10. Jahrhunderts: Eine literatur- und mentalitätsgeschichtliche Studie des arabischen Ġazal (Diskurse der Arabistik 2), Wiesbaden: Harrassowitz, 1998.

Al-ʿAbbās ibn al-Aḥnaf: Ein literaturgeschichtlicher Sonderfall und seine Rezeption, in *Wiener Zeitschrift für die Kunde des Morgenlandes* 88 (1998), 65–107.

The following articles in Julie Scott Meisami and Paul Starkey (eds.), *Encyclopedia of Arabic Literature*, 2 vols., London and New York: Routledge, 1998:

ʿAbīd ibn al-Abraṣ (sixth century CE), i, 52,
ʿAlqama ibn ʿAbada (mid-sixth century CE), i, 83,
ʿĀmir ibn al-Ṭufayl (c. 570–c. 10/632), i, 87,
ʿAmr ibn Maʿdīkarib (d. after 16/637), i, 88,
ʿAntara ibn Shaddād al-ʿAbsī (second half of sixth century CE), i, 94,
al-Aʿshā Maymūn ibn Qays (before 565 CE–c. 7/629), i, 107,
Aʿshā Bāhila (sixth century CE), i, 107–8,
Bishr ibn Abī Khāzim (d. between 210–26/825–40), i, 153,
Durayd ibn al-Ṣimma (d. 8/630), i, 198,

Ḥātim al-Ṭāʾī (late sixth century CE), ii, 276,
Hind bint al-Khuṣṣ, i, 287–8,
Jāhiliyya, i, 406–7,
Jirān al-ʿAwd al-Numayrī (first/seventh century), i, 415,
Kaʿb ibn Zuhayr (first/seventh century), ii, 421–2,
Labīd ibn Rabīʿa al-ʿĀmirī (d. c. 41/661), ii, 460–1,
Mālik ibn Nuwayra (d. 11/632), ii, 500,
Muʿallaqāt, ii, 532–4,
al-Muhalhil ibn Rabīʿa (fifth century CE), ii, 538,
al-Munakhkhal al-Yashkurī (sixth century), ii, 550,
al-Muraqqish al-Akbar (sixth century CE), ii, 552–3,
al-Muraqqish al-Aṣghar (sixth century CE), ii, 553,
al-Mutalammis (sixth century CE), ii, 557–8,
Mutammim ibn Nuwayra (first/seventh century), ii, 558,
Qays ibn al-Khaṭīm (d. before 1/622), ii, 636,
Rabīʿa ibn Maqrūm (d. shortly after 16/672 in advanced age), ii, 643,
al-Rāʿī al-Numayrī (d. c. 96/714), ii, 645,
al-Samawʾal (sixth century CE), ii, 685–6,
al-Shamardal (fl. c. 101/720), ii, 703,
al-Shammākh (first/seventh century), ii, 703,
Ṭarafa ibn al-ʿAbd (middle of the sixth century), ii, 759,
Umayya ibn Abī l-Ṣalt (d. c. 9/631), ii, 793.

Review of Udo Gerald Simon, *Mittelalterliche Sprachbetrachtung zwischen Grammatik und Rhetorik*, Heidelberg, 1993, in *Zeitschrift für Arabische Linguistik* 35 (1998), 90–1.

1999

Verben und Textpartikeln in altarabischen narrativen Texten, in Norbert Nebes (ed.), *Tempus und Aspekt in den semitischen Sprachen: Jenaer Kolloquium zur semitischen Sprachwissenschaft* (Jenaer Beiträge zum Vorderen Orient 1), Wiesbaden: Harrassowitz, 1999, 9–22.

Todesdiskurse im Islam, in *Asiatische Studien* 53 (1999), 5–16.

al-Taṣawwur al-minhajī li-l-nabāt ʿinda l-ʿArab al-qudamāʾ, in *al-ʿAqīq* (al-Madīna) 25/26 (1999): 119–32 (Arabic translation of Die Pflanzensystematik der Araber, 1994).

Review of Manfred Ullmann, *Das Motiv der Kreuzigung in der arabischen Poesie des Mittelalters*, Wiesbaden, 1995, in *Zeitschrift für Arabische Linguistik* 37/2 (1999), 94–6.

Review of Majd al-Afandī, *al-Ghazal fī l-ʿasr al-Mamlūkī al-awwal*, Damascus, 1994, in *Mamlūk Studies Review* 3 (1999), 214–8.

2000

al-Ṣīġa wa-l-iqtibās: Lawnān min al-tanāṣṣ fī l-shiʿr al-ʿarabī al-qadīm, in *al-Bayān* (al-Kuwayt) 362 (2000), 17–34 = Fuʾād Naʿnāʿ, *Buḥūth almāniyya fī l-adab al-ʿarabī al-qadīm*, Damascus: Dār al-Bashāʾir, 1429/2008, 79–116 (Arabic translation of Formel und Zitat: Zwei Spielarten von Intertextualität in der altarabischen Dichtung, 1993).

ʿUrwa b. Ḥizām, in P.J. Bearman et al. (eds.), *The Encyclopaedia of Islam: New Edition*, x, Leiden: Brill, 2000, 908–9.

Review of Wolfhart Heinrichs and Gregor Schoeler (eds.), *Festschrift Ewald Wagner zum 65. Geburtstag. Band 1: Semitische Studien unter besonderer Berücksichtigung der Semitistik*, Beirut and Stuttgart, 1994, in *Zeitschrift für Arabische Linguistik* 38 (2000), 94–7.

Review of Firdaws Nūr ʿAlī Ḥusayn (ed.), *Ibn Ḥajar al-ʿAsqalānī: Dīwān Shaykh al-Islām Ibn Ḥajar al-ʿAsqalānī*, Cairo, 2000, in *Mamlūk Studies Review* 4 (2000), 267–8.

Review of George Bohas and Bruno Paoli, *Aspects formels de la poésie arabe. 1: La métrique classique*, Toulouse, 1997, in *Zeitschrift der Deutschen Morgenländischen Gesellschaft* 150/2 (2000), 663–5.

Review of Gertrud and Helmut Denzau, *Wildesel* (Thorbecke Species 3), Stuttgart, 1999, in *Wiener Zeitschrift für die Kunde des Morgenlandes* 90 (2000), 368–70.

Review of Navid Kermani, *Gott ist schön: Das ästhetische Erleben des Koran*, München, 1999, in *Wiener Zeitschrift für die Kunde des Morgenlandes* 90 (2000), 370–3.

Review of James E. Montgomery, *The vagaries of the qaṣīdah: The tradition and practice of early Arabic poetry* (Gibb Literary Studies 1), Cambridge, 1997, in *Wiener Zeitschrift für die Kunde des Morgenlandes* 90 (2000), 373–7.

2001

Fremdheit in der klassischen arabischen Kultur und Sprache, in Brigitte Jostes and Jürgen Trabant (eds.), *Fremdes in fremden Sprachen* (Übergänge 43), München: Wilhelm Fink, 2001, 85–105.

Review of Pierre Cachia, *The arch rhetorician or the schemer's skimmer: A hand-*

book of late Arabic badīʿ drawn from ʿAbd al-Ghanī an-Nābulsī's Nafaḥāt al-azhār ʿalā nasamāt al-asḥār, *summarized and systematized*, Wiesbaden, 1998, in *Zeitschrift der Deutschen Morgenländischen Gesellschaft* 151/1 (2001), 214–7.

Review of Wen-chin Ouyang, *Literary criticism in medieval Arabic-Islamic culture: The making of a tradition*, Edinburgh, 1997, in *Zeitschrift für Arabische Linguistik* 40/2 (2001), 94–6.

2002

Islamische Totenbücher: Entwicklung einer Textgattung im Schatten al-Ġazālīs, in Stefan Leder et al. (eds.), *Studies in Arabic and Islam: Proceedings of the 19th Congress, Union Européenne des Arabisants et Islamisants, Halle 1998* (Orientalia Lovaniensia Analecta 108), Leuven: Peeters, 2002, 421–36.

Ibrāhīm al-Miʿmār: Ein dichtender Handwerker aus Ägyptens Mamlukenzeit, in *Zeitschrift der Deutschen Morgenländischen Gesellschaft* 152 (2002), 63–93.

ʿIfrīt, in Jane Dammen McAuliffe (ed.), *The Encyclopedia of the Qurʾān*, ii, Leiden and Boston: Brill, 2002, 486–7.

Insanity, in Jane Dammen McAuliffe (ed.), *The Encyclopedia of the Qurʾān*, ii, Leiden and Boston: Brill, 2002, 539–41.

Review of Manfred Ullmann, *Der Neger in der Bildsprache der arabischen Dichter*, Wiesbaden, 1998, in *Zeitschrift für Arabische Linguistik* 41 (2002), 92–4.

Review of Maḥmūd Sālim Muḥammad, *Ibn Nubāta: Shāʿir al-ʿaṣr al-Mamlūkī* (Silsilat al-Aʿlām), Damascus and Beirut, 1999, in *Mamlūk Studies Review* 6 (2002), 219–23.

Review of Albert Arazi and Salmān Muṣālaḥa (eds.), *al-ʿIqd al-thamīn fī dawāwīn al-shuʿarāʾ al-sitta al-jāhiliyyīn*, Jerusalem, 1999, in *Zeitschrift der Deutschen Morgenländischen Gesellschaft* 152/1 (2002), 197–201.

Review of Gert Borg, *Mit Poesie vertreibe ich den Kummer meines Herzens: Eine Studie zur altarabischen Trauerklage der Frau*, Leiden and Istanbul, 1997, in *Der Islam* 79/1 (2002), 195–7.

2003

Die Dichter Hārūn ar-Rašīds, in Wolfgang Dreßen et al. (ed.), *Ex Oriente: Isaak und der weisse Elefant; Bagdad—Jerusalem—Aachen: Eine Reise durch drei Kulturen um 800 und heute; Katalogbuch in 3 Bd. zur Ausstellung in Rathaus,*

Dom und Domschatzkammer Aachen, Vol. 1: Die Reise des Isaak: Bagdad, Mainz: von Zabern, 2003, 168–81.

Die Leiden eines ägyptischen Müllers: Die Mühlen-Maqāme des Ibrāhīm al-Miʿmār (st. 749/1348), in Anke I. Blöbaum, Jochem Kahl und Simon D. Schweitzer (eds.), *Ägypten—Münster: Kulturwissenschaftliche Studien zu Ägypten, dem Vorderen Orient und verwandten Gebieten* (*Festschrift Erhart Graefe*), Wiesbaden: Harrassowitz, 2003, 1–16.

Literarische Anthologien der Mamlukenzeit, in Stephan Conermann and Anja Pistor-Hatam, *Die Mamluken: Studien zu ihrer Geschichte und Kultur. Zum Gedenken an Ulrich Haarmann (1942–1999)* (Asien und Afrika 7), Schenefeld: EB-Verlag, 2003, 71–122.

Communication and emotion: The case of Ibn Nubātah's *Kindertotenlieder*, in *Mamlūk Studies Review* 7 (2003), 49–95.

Vom Sinn der Zeit: Aus der Geschichte des arabischen Chronogramms, in *Arabica* 50 (2003) 501–31.

Review of Ibn Ḥajar al-ʿAsqalānī, *Dhayl al-Durar al-kāmina fī aʿyān al-miʾa al-thāmina*, ed. Aḥmad Farīd al-Mazīdī, Beirut, 1419/1998; Ibn Ḥajar al-ʿAsqalānī, *Dhayl al-Durar al-kāmina fī aʿyān al-miʾa al-thāmina*, ed. ʿAdnān Darwīsh, Cairo, 1412/1992; Ibrahīm b. Muḥammad Ibn Duqmāq, *Nuzhat al-anām fī tārīkh al-Islām*, ed. Samīr Tabbāra, Beirut, 1420/1999, in *Mamlūk Studies Review* 7/1 (2003), 257–61.

Review of Arnoud Vrojlik, *Bringing a laugh to a scowling face: A study and critical edition of the "Nuzhat al-nufūs wa-muḍḥik al-ʿabūs" by ʿAlī Ibn Sūdūn al-Bašbuġāwī*, Leiden, 1998; ʿAlī Ibn Sūdūn al-Yashbaghāwī, *Nuzhat al-nufūs wa-muḍḥik al-ʿabūs*, ed. Maḥmūd Sālim, Damascus, 1421/2001, in *Mamluk Studies Review* 7/1 (2003), 267–72.

2004

(Co-edited with Lamya Kaddor and Katja Strobel), *Islamischer Religionsunterricht: Hintergründe, Probleme, Perspektiven* (Veröffentlichungen des Centrums für Religiöse Studien Münster 1), Münster: Lit, 2004.

Das Centrum für Religiöse Studien der Universität Münster, in Thomas Bauer, Lamya Kaddor and Katja Strobel (eds.), *Islamischer Religionsunterricht: Hintergründe, Probleme, Perspektiven* (Veröffentlichungen des Centrums für Religiöse Studien Münster 1), Münster: Lit, 2004, 7–13.

Shāʿir (Poet): From the ʿAbbāsid period to the Nahḍa, in P.J. Bearman et al. (eds.), *The Encyclopaedia of Islam: New Edition*, xii (Supplement), Leiden: Brill, 2004, 717–22.

2005

(Co-edited with Ulrike Stehli-Werbeck), *Alltagsleben und materielle Kultur in der arabischen Sprache und Literatur: Festschrift für Heinz Grotzfeld zum 70. Geburtstag* (Abhandlungen für die Kunde des Morgenlandes LV, 1), Wiesbaden: Harrassowitz, 2005.

(Co-edited with Angelika Neuwirth), *Ghazal as world literature I: Transformations of a literary genre* (Beiruter Texte und Studien 89), Beirut: Orient-Institut, 2005.

(Co-edited with Thorsten Gerald Schneiders), *„Kinder Abrahams": Religiöser Austausch im lebendigen Kontext; Festschrift zur Eröffnung des Centrums für Religiöse Studien* (Veröffentlichungen des Centrums für Religiöse Studien Münster 2), Münster: Lit, 2005.

Das Nilzaǧal des Ibrāhīm al-Miʿmār: Ein Lied zur Feier des Nilschwellenfestes, in Thomas Bauer and Ulrike Stehli-Werbeck (eds.), *Alltagsleben und materielle Kultur in der arabischen Sprache und Literatur: Festschrift für Heinz Grotzfeld zum 70. Geburtstag* (Abhandlungen für die Kunde des Morgenlandes LV, 1), Wiesbaden: Harrassowitz, 2005, 69–88.

(Co-authored with Angelika Neuwirth) Introduction, in Thomas Bauer and Angelika Neuwirth, *Ghazal as world literature I: Transformations of a literary genre* (Beiruter Texte und Studien 89), Beirut: Orient-Institut, 2005, 9–31.

Ibn Ḥajar and the Arabic Ghazal of the Mamluk Age, in Thomas Bauer and Angelika Neuwirth (eds.), *Ghazal as world literature I: Transformations of a literary genre* (Beiruter Texte und Studien 89), Beirut: Orient-Institut, 2005, 35–55.

Die Sprachlosigkeit überwinden: Grußwort zur Eröffnung des Centrums für Relogiöse Studien, in Thomas Bauer and Thorsten Gerald Schneiders (eds.), *„Kinder Abrahams": Religiöser Austausch im lebendigen Kontext; Festschrift zur Eröffnung des Centrums für Religiöse Studien* (Veröffentlichungen des Centrums für Religiöse Studien Münster 2), Münster: Lit., 2005, 19–25.

„Abraham ist mein Väterchen": Eine Auswahl aus den „Dichtungen des Morgenlandes" von Georg Friedrich Daumer, in Thomas Bauer and Thorsten Gerald Schneiders (eds.), *„Kinder Abrahams": Religiöser Austausch im lebendigen Kontext; Festschrift zur Eröffnung des Centrums für Religiöse Studien* (Veröffentlichungen des Centrums für Religiöse Studien Münster 2), Münster: Lit., 2005, 97–138.

Vertraute Fremde: Das Bild des Beduinen in der arabischen Literatur des 10. Jahrhunderts, in Stefan Leder and Bernhard Streck (eds.), *Shifts and drifts in nomad-sedentary relations* (Nomaden und Sesshafte 2), Wiesbaden: Reichert, 2005, 377–400.

Rhetorik: Arabische Kultur, in Gert Ueding et al. (eds.), *Rhetorik: Begriff, Geschichte, Internationalität*, Tübingen: Niemeyer, 2005, 283–300 = Gert Ueding et al. (eds.), *Historisches Wörterbuch der Rhetorik Band 8*, Tübingen: De Gruyter, 2007, 111–37.

Mamluk literature: Misunderstandings and new approaches, in *Mamlūk Studies Review* 9/2 (2005), 105–32.

2006

The Arabic ghazal: Formal and thematic aspects of a problematic genre, in Angelika Neuwirth et al. (eds.), *Ghazal as world literature II: From a literary genre to a great tradition* (Istanbuler Texte und Studien 4), Würzburg: Ergon, 2006, 3–13.

Die badīʿiyya des Nāṣīf al-Yāziǧī und das Problem der spätosmanischen arabischen Literatur, in Angelika Neuwirth and Andreas C. Islebe (eds.), *Reflections on reflections: Near Eastern writers reading literature; dedicated to Renate Jacobi* (Literaturen im Kontext 23), Wiesbaden: Reichert, 2006, 49–118.

Religion und Klassisch-Arabische Literatur, in Andreas Pflitsch and Barbara Winckler (eds.), *Poetry's voice—society's norms: Forms of interaction between Middle Eastern writers and their societies; dedicated to Angelika Neuwirth* (Literaturen im Kontext 24), Wiesbaden: Reichert, 2006, 13–29.

Review of Yaḥyā ibn ʿAbd al-ʿAẓīm al-Jazzār, Dīwān al-Jazzār, ed. Muḥammad Zaghlūl Sallām, Alexandria, 2001; ʿUmar ibn Masʿūd al-Maḥḥār, *Dīwān Sirāj al-Dīn al-Maḥḥār*, ed. Aḥmad Muḥammad ʿAṭā, Cairo, 1422/2001, in *Mamlūk Studies Review* 10/1 (2006), 206–13.

2007

The Dawādār's hunting party: A Mamluk *muzdawija ṭardiyya*, probably by Shihāb al-Dīn Ibn Faḍl Allāh, in Arnoud Vrolijk and Jan P. Hogendijk (eds.), *O ye gentlemen: Arabic studies on science and literary culture in honour of Remke Kruk* (Islamic philosophy, theology and science 74), Leiden: Brill, 2007, 291–312.

Anthologies: Arabic Literature, Post-Mongol Period, in Gudrun Krämer et al. (eds.), *The Encyclopaedia of Islam, Three*, fasc. 2007–1, Leiden and Boston: Brill, 124–8.

Abū Ḥafṣ al-Shiṭranjī, in Gudrun Krämer et al. (eds.), *The Encyclopaedia of Islam, Three*, fasc. 2007–2, Leiden and Boston: Brill, 43.

Abū Misḥal, in Gudrun Krämer et al. (eds.), *The Encyclopaedia of Islam, Three*, fasc. 2007–2, Leiden and Boston: Brill, 57–8.

Abū l-Ṭayyib al-Lughawī, in Gudrun Krämer et al. (eds.), *The Encyclopaedia of Islam, Three*, fasc. 2007–2, Leiden und Boston: Brill, 60–1.

Abū Ziyād al-Kilābī, in Gudrun Krämer et al. (eds.), *The Encyclopaedia of Islam, Three*, ii, fasc. 2007–2, Leiden and Boston: Brill, 64–5.

In search of "post-classical literature": A review article, in *Mamlūk Studies Review* 11/2 (2007), 137–67.

2008

„Was kann aus dem Jungen noch werden!": Das poetische Erstlingswerk des Historikers Ibn Ḥabīb im Spiegel seiner Zeitgenossen, in Otto Jastrow, Shabo Talay and Herta Hafenrichter (eds.), *Studien zur Semitistik und Arabistik: Festschrift für Hartmut Bobzin zum 60. Geburtstag*, Wiesbaden: Harrassowitz, 2008, 15–56.

How will the Treaty of Lisbon impact the European Union's foreign, security and defense policy?, in Christian-Peter Hanelt and Almut Möller (eds.), *Bound to cooperate—Europe and the Middle East II*, Gütersloh: Bertelsmann Stiftung, 2008, 32–49.

Ibn Nubātah al-Miṣrī (686–768/1287–1366): Life and works. Part 1: The life of Ibn Nubātah, in *Mamlūk Studies Review* 12/1 (2008), 1–35.

Ibn Nubātah al-Miṣrī (686–768/1287–1366): Life and works. Part 2: The *Dīwān* of Ibn Nubātah, in *Mamlūk Studies Review* 12/2 (2008), 25–69.

Kayfa yabdaʾu l-shāʿiru l-qaṣīda?, in Fuʾād Naʿnāʿ, *Buḥūth almāniyya fī l-adab al-ʿarabī al-qadīm*, Damascus: Dār al-Bashāʾir, 1429/2008, 117–63 (Arabic translation of Wie fängt man eine Qaṣīde an? Formelhafte und nichtformelhafte Nasīb-Einleitungsverse, 1993).

Qaṣīdat Muzarrid b. Ḍirār al-lāmiyya bayna l-fāris al-ġanī wa-l-ṣayyād al-faqīr, in Fuʾād Naʿnāʿ, *Buḥūth almāniyya fī l-adab al-ʿarabī al-qadīm*, Damascus: Dār al-Bašāʾir, 1429/2008, 165–99 (Arabic translation of Muzarrids Qaṣīde vom reichen Ritter und dem armen Jäger, 1994).

al-ʿAmīdī, in Gudrun Krämer et al. (eds.), *The Encyclopaedia of Islam, Three*, fasc. 2008–1, Leiden and Boston: Brill, 138–9.

al-Azharī, Zayn al-Dīn, in Gudrun Krämer et al. (eds.), *The Encyclopaedia of Islam, Three*, fasc. 2008–1, Leiden and Boston: Brill, 176–8.

2009

Jamāl al-Dīn Ibn Nubātah, in Joseph E. Lowry and Devin J. Stewart (eds.), *Essays in Arabic literary biography 1350–1850*, Wiesbaden: Harrassowitz, 2009, 184–202.

Al-Nawājī, in Joseph E. Lowry and Devin J. Stewart (eds.), *Essays in Arabic literary biography 1350–1850*, Wiesbaden: Harrassowitz, 2009, 321–31.

al-Qālib al-ṣīġī wa-l-iqtibās: Nawʿān min al-laʿb al-tanāṣṣī fī l-shiʿr al-jāhilī, in Mūsā Rabābiʿa, *Marāyā l-istishrāq al-almānī al-muʿāṣir*, Amman, 1429/2009, 39–70 (Arabic translation of Formel und Zitat: Zwei Spielarten von Intertextualität in der altarabischen Dichtung, 1993).

Kayfa tubdaʾu l-qaṣīda?, in Mūsā Rabābiʿa, *Marāyā l-istishrāq al-almānī al-muʿāṣir*, Amman, 1429/2009, 73–110 (Arabic translation of Wie fängt man eine Qaṣīde an? Formelhafte und nichtformelhafte Nasīb-Einleitungsverse, 1993).

ʿAmr ibn Maʿdīkarib, in Gudrun Krämer et al. (eds.), *The Encyclopaedia of Islam, Three*, fasc. 2009–2, Leiden and Boston: Brill, 83–4.

al-Āthārī, in Gudrun Krämer et al. (eds.), *The Encyclopaedia of Islam, Three*, fasc. 2009–2, Leiden and Boston: Brill, 119–20.

Review of Helmut Werner (ed.), *Das islamische Totenbuch: Jenseitsvorstellungen des Islam*, Bergisch Gladbach, 2002, in *Zeitschrift der Deutschen Morgenländischen Gesellschaft* 159 (2009), 185–90.

2010

The relevance of early Arabic poetry for Qurʾanic studies including observations on *kull* and on Q 22:27, 26:225, and 52:31, in Angelika Neuwirth, Nicolai Sinai and Michael Marx (eds.), *The Qurʾān in context: Historical and literary investigations into the Qurʾānic milieu* (Texts and Studies on the Qurʾān), Leiden: Brill, 2010, 699–732.

2011

Die Kultur der Ambiguität: Eine andere Geschichte des Islams, Berlin: Verlag der Weltreligionen im Insel Verlag, 2011.

„Der Fürst ist tot, es lebe der Fürst!“: Ibn Nubātas Gedicht zur Inthronisation al-Afḍals von Ḥamāh (732/1332), in Ulrich Marzolph (ed.), *Orientalistische Studien zu Sprache und Literatur: Festgabe zum 65. Geburtstag von Werner Diem*, Wiesbaden: Harrassowitz, 2011, 285–315.

Normative Ambiguitätstoleranz im Islam, in Nils Jansen and Peter Oestmann (eds.), *Gewohnheit, Gebot, Gesetz: Normativität in Geschichte und Gegenwart: Eine Einführung*, Tübingen: Mohr Siebeck, 2011, 155–80.

Die Poesie des Terrorismus, in Andreas K.W. Meyer (ed.), *Siebenjahrbuch Deutsche Oper Berlin MMIV–MMXI*, Berlin: Nicolaische Verlagsbuchhandlung, 2011, 123–7.

2012

Grußwort im Namen des Instituts für Arabistik und Islamwissenschaft, in Mouhanad Khorchide and Marco Schöller (eds.), *Das Verhältnis zwischen Islamwissenschaft und Islamischer Theologie: Beiträge der Konferenz Münster, 1.–2. Juli 2011* (Masāʾil 1), Münster: Agenda, 2012, 16–21.

Musterschüler und Zauberlehrling: Wie viel Westen steckt im modernen Islam?, in *Rottenburger Jahrbuch für Kirchengeschichte* 31 (2012), 73–83.

Review of Ewald Wagner, *Abū Nuwās in Übersetzung: Eine Stellensammlung zu Abū Nuwās-Übersetzungen vornehmlich in europäischen Sprachen*, Wiesbaden, 2012, in *Wiener Zeitschrift für die Kunde des Morgenlandes* 102 (2012), 408–9.

Review of Luise Ossenbach, *Vermaß des Glaubens: Ein arabisches Gedicht zum Lob des Propheten von ʿAlam ad-Dīn as-Saḫāwī (st. 1245)*, Würzburg, 2009, in *Orientalistische Literaturzeitung* 107 (2012), 41–2.

2013

(Co-edited with Bertold Höcker, Walter Homolka, Klaus Mertens and Jan Feddersen), *Religion und Homosexualität: Aktuelle Positionen* (Hirschfeld-Lectures 3), Göttingen: Wallstein, 2013.

Islam und „Homosexualität,“ in Thomas Bauer et al. (eds.), *Religion und Homosexualität: Aktuelle Positionen* (Hirschfeld-Lectures 3), Göttingen: Wallstein, 2013, 71–89.

Mamluk literature as a means of communication, in Stephan Conermann (ed.), *Ubi sumus? Quo vademus? Mamluk studies—State of the art* (Mamluk Studies 3), Göttingen: V&R unipress, 2013, 23–56.

“Ayna hādhā min al-Mutanabbī!”: Toward an aesthetics of Mamluk literature, in *Mamlūk Studies Review* 17 (2013), 5–22.

Adab and Islamic scholarship after the “Sunnī revival,” in Gudrun Krämer et al. (eds.), *The Encyclopaedia of Islam, Three*, fasc. 2013–3, Leiden and Boston: Brill, 38–42.

2014

Kultura dvoumnosti: drugačna zgodovina islama, Ljubljana: Krtina, 2014 (Slovene translation of *Die Kultur der Ambiguität*, 2011).

Dignity at stake: *Mujūn* epigrams by Ibn Nubāta and his contemporaries, in Adam Talib, Marlé Hammond and Arie Schippers (eds.), *The rude, the bad and the bawdy: Essays in honour of Professor Geert Jan van Gelder*, Cambridge: Gibb Memorial Trust, 2014, 160–85.

How to create a network: Zaynaddīn al-Āṯārī and his Muqarriẓūn, in Stephan Conermann (ed.), *Everything is on the move: The Mamluk empire as a node in (trans-)regional networks* (Mamluk Studies 7), Göttingen: V&R unipress, 2014, 205–21.

The Islamization of Islam, in Joanna Witkowska and Uwe Zagratzki (eds.), *Ideological battlegrounds—Constructions of us and them before and after 9/11*, Vol. 1: *Perspectives in literatures and cultures*, Newcastle upon Tyne: Cambridge Scholars Publishing, 2014, 1–15.

Male-male love in classical Arabic poetry, in E.L. McCallum and Mikko Tuhkanen (eds.), *The Cambridge history of gay and lesbian literature*, Cambridge: Cambridge University Press, 2014, 107–24.

2015

Der Islam im europäischen Gedächtnis, in Claudia Schmidt-Hahn (ed.), *Islam verstehen—Herausforderung für Europa* (Disputationes 2014), Innsbruck: Studienverlag, 2015, 26–32.

2016

Ambiguität in der klassischen arabischen Rhetoriktheorie, in Oliver Auge and Christiane Witthöft (eds.), *Ambiguität im Mittelalter* (Trends in Medieval Philosophy 30), Berlin and Boston: De Gruyter, 2016, 21–47.

al-Ḥammāmī, in Gudrun Krämer et al. (eds.), *The Encyclopaedia of Islam, Three*, fasc. 2016–2, Leiden and Boston: Brill, 144–5.

al-Jazzār, in Gudrun Krämer et al. (eds.), *The Encyclopaedia of Islam, Three*, fasc. 2016–4, Leiden and Boston: Brill, 141–3.

2017

Thaqāfat al-iltibās: Naḥw taʾrīkh ākhar li-l-Islām, Beirut: Manshūrāt al-Jamal, 2017 (Arabic translation of *Die Kultur der Ambiguität*, 2011).

"Extremely beautiful and extremely long": Al-Qīrāṭī's exuberant letter from the year 761/1360, in Joseph E. Lowry and Shawkat M. Toorawa (eds.), *Arabic humanities, Islamic thought: Essays in honour of Everett K. Rowson* (Islamic History and Civilization 141), Leiden: Brill, 2017, 338–60.

The micro-qaṣīdah: A formal experiment from the 8th/14th century, in Nefeli Papoutsakis and Syrinx von Hees (eds.), *The sultan's anthologist—Ibn Abī Ḥağalah and his work* (Arabische Literatur und Rhetorik Elfhundert bis Achtzehnhundert 3), Baden-Baden: Ergon, 2017, 45–70.

Methoden zum Verständnis des Korans am Beispiel eines Speisegebots, in Willi Steul (ed.), *Koran erklärt: Ein Beitrag zur Aufklärung*, Berlin: Suhrkamp, 2017, 32–4.

Ibn al-Qaysarānī, in Gudrun Krämer et al. (eds.), *The Encyclopaedia of Islam, Three*, fasc. 2017–2, Leiden and Boston: Brill, 139–41.

Ibn Daftarkhwān, in Gudrun Krämer et al. (eds.), *The Encyclopaedia of Islam, Three*, fasc. 2017–5, Leiden and Boston: Brill, 109–10.

Review of Konrad Hirschler, *Medieval Damascus: Plurality and diversity in an Arabic library: The Ashrafīya library catalogue* (Edinburgh Studies in Classical Islamic History and Culture), Edinburgh, 2016, in *Bulletin of the School of Oriental and African Studies* 80/1 (2017), 142–4.

2018

Die Vereindeutigung der Welt: Über den Verlust an Mehrdeutigkeit und Vielfalt, Ditzingen: Reclam, 2018.

Warum es kein islamisches Mittelalter gab: Das Erbe der Antike und der Orient, München: Beck, 2018.

(Co-edited with Anke Osigus and Hakan Özkan), *Der Dīwān des Ibrāhīm al-Miʿmār (gest. 749/1348–49): Edition und Kommentar* (Arabische Literatur und Rhetorik Elfhundert bis Achtzehnhundert 4), Baden-Baden: Ergon, 2018.

ʿIzz al-Dīn al-Mawṣilī, in Gudrun Krämer et al. (eds.), *The Encyclopaedia of Islam, Three*, fasc. 2018–3, Leiden and Boston: Brill, 110–1.

Review of Perry Anderson and Suleiman Mourad, *Das Mosaik des Islam*, Berlin: Berenberg Verlag, 2018, in *Frankfurter Allgemeine Zeitung*, 21.03.2018, 10.

Was den Blick verstellt, in *Frankfurter Allgemeine Zeitung*, 23.08.2018, 12.

2019

Müphemlik kültürü ve İslâm: Farklı bir İslâm tarihi okuması, Istanbul: İletişim, 2019 (Turkish translation of *Die Kultur der Ambiguität*, 2011).

Förlusten av mångfald—när världen görs enfaldig, Ludvika: Dualis, 2019 (Swedish translation of *Die Vereindeutigung der Welt: Über den Verlust an Mehrdeutigkeit und Vielfalt*, 2018).

(Co-edited with Dominik Höink and Clemens Leonhard), *Musik und Religion* (Religion und Politik 20), Baden-Baden: Ergon, 2019.

Ambivalent beauty: The beard in classical Arabic love poetry, in Youri Volokhine, Bruce Fudge and Thomas Herzog (eds.), *Barbe et barbus: Symboliques, rites et pratiques du port de la barbe dans le Proche-Orient ancient et moderne*, Bern: Peter Lang, 2019, 131–41.

Auf der Suche nach Eindeutigkeit: Wie die Flucht vor Ambiguität Religion und Kultur verändert, in Martin Dürnberger (ed.), *Die Komplexität der Welt und die Sehnsucht nach Einfachheit*, Innsbruck: Tyrolia, 2019, 51–69.

L'Islamisation de l'Islam, in *Hespéris-Tamuda* 54, 1 (2019), 229–40 (French translation of The Islamization of Islam, 2014).

Ibn Munīr al-Ṭarābulusī, in Gudrun Krämer et al. (eds.), *The Encyclopaedia of Islam, Three*, fasc. 2019–2, Leiden and Boston: Brill, 54–6.

Zwischentöne: Das deutsche Kunstlied des 19. Jahrhunderts zwischen Religion und Bürgerlichkeit, in Thomas Bauer, Dominik Höink and Clemens Leonhard (eds.), *Musik und Religion* (Religion und Politik 20), Baden-Baden: Ergon, 2019, 97–127.

Wie Salome in den Orient kam, in Miron Hakenbeck and Malte Krasting (eds.), *Programmbuch zur Neuinszenierung der* Salome *von Richard Strauss, Premiere am 27. Juni 2019*, München: Bayerische Staatsoper, 2019, 90–101.

The following entries in Rainer Falk and Sven Limbeck (eds.), *Casta Diva: Der schwule Opernführer*, Berlin: Querverlag, 2019:

Friedrich von Flotow, 230–1,
Martha oder Der Markt zu Richmond, 232–4,
Peter Cornelius, 301–2,
Der Barbier von Bagdad, 303–5,
Hans Pfitzner, 456–7,
Palestrina, 458–60,
Ermanno Wolf-Ferrari, 469–70,
I quattro rusteghi, 71–3.

Alternativlosigkeit ist Zukunftslosigkeit, in *Frankfurter Allgemeine Zeitung* (Feuilleton), 06.06.2019.

2020

Kul'tura neodnoznačnosti i pljuralizma: k drugomu obrazu islama, Moscow-Berlin: Directmedia Publishing, 2020 (Russian translation of *Die Kultur der Ambiguität*, 2011).

Ο μονοσήμαντος κόσμος, Αθήνα: Αντίποδες, 2020 (Greek translation of *Die Vereindeutigung der Welt: Über den Verlust an Mehrdeutigkeit und Vielfalt*, 2018).

Limāḏā lam tūjad ʿuṣūr wusṭā islāmiyya? al-Sharq wa-turāth al-ʿuṣūr al-ʿatīqa, Beirut: Manshūrāt al-Jamal, 2020 (Arabic translation of *Warum es kein islamisches Mittelalter gab*, 2018).

Nearer, my prophet, to thee: Šamsaddīn an-Nawāǧī's supplicatory poem in the metre *mutadārik*, in Alev Masarwa and Hakan Özkan, *The racecourse of literature: An-Nawāǧī and his contemporaries* (Arabische Literatur und Rhetorik Elfhundert bis Achtzehnhundert 8), Baden-Baden: Ergon, 2020, 193–212.

Wann war die klassische Periode der islamischen Kultur?, in Bacem Dziri and Merdan Güneş (eds.), *Niedergangsthesen auf dem Prüfstand / Narratives of decline revisited* (Reihe für Osnabrücker Islamstudien, vol. 39), Berlin: Peter Lang, 2020, 159–73.

Review of Mouhanad Khorchide, *Gottes falsche Anwälte: Der Verrat am Islam*, Freiburg, 2020, in *Theologische Revue* 116/5 (2020), 372–5.

Klug durch Fortschritt?, in *Hohe Luft: Philosophie-Zeitschrift; Für alle, die Lust am Denken haben* 6/2020, 44–5.

2021

A culture of ambiguity: An alternative history of Islam, New York: Columbia University Press, 2021 (English translation of *Die Kultur der Ambiguität*, 2011).

Neden İslam'ın Orta Çağı Yoktu?—Antik Çağ'ın Mirası ve Doğu, Istanbul: Runik Kitap, 2021 (Arabic translation of *Warum es kein islamisches Mittelalter gab*, 2018).

Editorial Work

Editorial Boards: *Al-Masāq: Islam and the medieval Mediterranean* (until 2016); *Journal of Arabic Literature*; *Der Islam*.

Sectional Editor: *The Encyclopaedia of Islam, Three*

Prizes and Awards

2013: Gottfried Wilhelm Leibniz-Preis
2018: Tractatus-Preis of the Philosophicum Lech for *Die Vereindeutigung der Welt: Über den Verlust an Mehrdeutigkeit und Vielfalt*
2019: "WISSEN! Sachbuchpreis" for *Warum es kein islamisches Mittelalter gab: Das Erbe der Antike und der Orient*

1

Usāma b. Munqiḏ (488–584/1095–1188) und der *ǧihād*

Ewald Wagner

Vorbemerkung: Als die Herausgeber bei mir anfragten, ob ich einen Beitrag zu der Festschrift für Thomas Bauer liefern könnte, hat mich das sehr gefreut, und ich wollte der Aufforderung gerne nachkommen. Da ich aber bereits zu den *muʿammarūn* gehöre und seit einigen Jahren nicht mehr aktiv wissenschaftlich tätig sein kann, bleibt mir nichts anderes übrig, als einen Ladenhüter hervorzukramen. Es handelt sich um einen Aufsatz, den ich zu einer Zeit, als er noch aktueller war, für eine nicht-orientalistische Zeitschrift (deshalb fehlen die arabischen Texte zu den übersetzten Gedichten) geschrieben hatte, mich dann aber mit der Redaktion nicht über die Gestaltung hatte einigen können. Ich hoffe, dass der Jubilar die *niyya* anerkennt und sich über den Beitrag seinerseits freut.

Im Jahre 2007 veröffentlichte Paul M. Cobb einen Aufsatz mit dem Titel „Infidel Dogs: Hunting Crusaders with Usama ibn Munqidh." Dem eigentlichen Thema stellte er ein Kapitel: Usama and Holy War voran.[1] Grund dafür war, dass einige Jahre zuvor Robert Irwin in einem Aufsatz[2] aus der angeblichen Tatsache, dass in Usāmas Autobiographie, dem *Kitāb al-Iʿtibār*,[3] das Wort *ǧihād* nicht vorkäme, geschlossen hatte, dass Usāma dem *ǧihād* negativ gegenübergestanden hätte. Cobb konnte nachweisen, dass sich das Wort zweimal in dem *Kitāb al-Iʿtibār* nachweisen lässt, einmal allerdings nur als substantiviertes Adjektiv *muǧāhid* „Glaubenskämpfer," auf einen Panther bezogen, der einen Kreuzfahrer getötet hatte. Außerdem konnte er weitere Argumente vorbringen, die gegen Irwins These sprechen. Cobb hat bei seiner Argumentation nicht auf die Poesie Usāmas zurückgegriffen. Im Folgenden soll das nachgeholt werden, indem die Erwähnungen des *ǧihād*, die sich in der Dichtung Usāmas finden, wiedergegeben werden, und somit Cobbs These gestärkt wird.

1 Cobb, Dogs 58–63.

2 Irwin, Usamah.

3 Hg. von Hitti, P.K., *Usāmah's memoirs entitled Kitāb al-Iʿtibār*, Princeton 1930; u.a. übers. von Hitti, P.K., *Memoirs of Usāma Ibn Munqidh: An Arab-Syrian gentleman and warrior in the period of the Crusades*, New York 1929.

 | DOI:10.1163/9789004521780_003

Da die Kontroverse Irwin-Cobb schon einige Jahre zurückliegt, seien hier, um den Leser in die Problematik einzuführen, die Argumente beider Seiten kurz rekapituliert und durch einige neue Fakten und Gedanken ergänzt.

Irwins erstes Argument war, dass sich Usāma bei seiner diplomatischen Tätigkeit oft im Land der Franken aufhielt, mit ihnen im Auftrage von Muʿīn ad-Dīn Unur von Damaskus Verträge abschloss und sogar fränkische Freunde hatte.[4] Cobb weist darauf hin, dass Verträge zwischen Kreuzfahrern und muslimischen Herrschern üblich waren und auch nicht der Lehre vom *ǧihād* widersprachen, die temporäre Waffenstillstände zulässt.[5] Man könnte hinzufügen, dass ein erklärter Befürworter des *ǧihād*, der spanische Reisende Ibn Ǧubayr, durchaus Kreuzfahrerland bereiste und sich bei Hin- und Rückfahrt genuesischer Schiffe bediente.

Etwas komplizierter wird es bei dem zweiten Argument von Irwin. Er nimmt an, dass Usāma Šīʿit war und dass nach šīʿitischer Lehre bis zur Wiederkehr des verborgenen Imāms kein *ǧihād* möglich sei, weil nur er den *ǧihād* anführen dürfe. Wie schon Cobb festgestellt hat,[6] war diese Doktrin zu Usāmas Zeit schon aufgeweicht und zumindest ein defensiver *ǧihād* auch ohne Imām verdienstvoll. Und als defensiv betrachteten die Muslime ihren *ǧihād*, da die Kreuzfahrer ja in ihr Land eingedrungen waren.

Cobb bezweifelt aber auch, dass Usāma überhaupt Šīʿit war. Das schwerwiegendste Argument für Usāmas Šīʿitentum ist eine Stelle in der Usāma-Biographie von aḏ-Ḏahabī (gest. 748/1348 oder 753/1352), in der es heißt: „Er war ein rechtgläubiger Imāmit (Zwölferšīʿit), nur dass er seine Einstellung verbarg und seinen Glauben geheim hielt (*taqiyya* übte). Er war überaus wohltätig und pflegte die Šīʿa zu unterstützen. Er beschenkte ihre Armen und gab den Šarīfen (Prophetennachkommen).“[7] Das Problem an dieser Stelle ist allerdings, dass aḏ-Ḏahabī hier aus der verlorenen Geschichte der Šīʿa von Yaḥyā Ibn Abī Ṭayyiʾ (gest. 627/1230) zitiert, dessen Vater Usāma getroffen haben will. Ich habe mit Cobb Zweifel am Wahrheitsgehalt dieser Geschichte. Šīʿitische Autoren neigen dazu, bekannte Persönlichkeiten für ihre Religion in Anspruch zu nehmen. So wurde auch der alles andere als šīʿitisch orientierte Dichter Abū Nuwās (gest. um 198/814) bis ins 20. Jahrhundert hinein auf Grund offensichtlich gefälschter Gedichte in šīʿitischen biographischen und bibliographischen Werken aufgeführt.[8]

---

4 Irwin, Usamah 77–8.

5 Cobb, Dogs 59.

6 Cobb, Dogs 61. Kurz zuvor hatte Cobb seine Thesen zu Usāmas angeblichem Šīʿitentum in ähnlicher Weise in seiner Monographie über Usāma dargelegt: Cobb, *Warrior-poet* 73–4.

7 Arabischer Text u.a. bei Derenbourg, *Vie* 602; übers. Cobb, Dogs 60.

8 Wagner, *Abū Nuwās* 115–6.

Einen Hinweis auf Usāmas Zugehörigkeit zur Šīʿa erblickte Irwin auch darin, dass Usāma zeitweilig den Fāṭimiden diente. Dem hielt Cobb zu Recht entgegen, dass die meisten Hofleute der Fāṭimiden Sunniten waren.

Hier seien noch zwei von Irwin und Cobb nicht berücksichtigte Fakten genannt, die eventuell für eine šīʿitische Gesinnung Usāmas sprechen könnten. Usāma pflegte eine poetische Korrespondenz mit zwei prominenten Šīʿiten, dem Adelsmarschall (*naqīb*) der Šīʿiten von Mossul Abū ʿAbdallāh Zayd b. Muḥammad al-Ḥusaynī,[9] und mit al-Malik aṣ-Ṣāliḥ Ṭalāʾiʿ b. Ruzzīk, der 549–56/1154–61 Wesir der Fāṭimiden war. Er war armenischer Herkunft und hatte sich im Irak zur Imāmiyya bekehrt.[10] Falls diese Verbindung zu führenden Šīʿiten auf eigene šīʿitische Gesinnung hindeuten sollte, würde sie auf alle Fälle bedeuten, dass man sie nicht zu verheimlichen brauchte (keine *taqiyya* zu üben brauchte). Eher ist anzunehmen, dass die Korrespondenz auch einen Sunniten nicht kompromittierte, so dass Usāma sie ohne weiteres in seinen *Dīwān* aufnehmen konnte.

In seinem *Kitāb al-ʿAṣā* gibt Usāma zwei Anekdoten wieder, in denen der erste Kalif der Umayyaden Muʿāwiya eine Rolle spielt.[11] Seinem Namen folgt die Formel *laʿanahū llāhu taʿālā* „Gott – er ist erhaben – verfluche ihn." Da Muʿāwiya ʿAlīs Gegner in der Schlacht von Ṣiffīn war, steht er natürlich zusammen mit den drei ersten Kalifen Abū Bakr, ʿUmar und ʿUṯmān auf der schwarzen Liste der Šīʿiten. Allerdings waren die Umayyaden mit Ausnahme von ʿUmar b. ʿAbd al-ʿAzīz seit der ʿabbāsidischen Revolution auch bei den Sunniten nicht sehr angesehen, so dass die Fluchformel auch von einem Sunniten stammen könnte. Gegen die Zugehörigkeit des Verfassers zur Šīʿa spricht auch, dass er die ersten drei Kalifen mit der Eulogie *raḍiya llāhu ʿanhu* „Gott möge Wohlgefallen an ihm finden" versehen hat.[12] Bei einem Šīʿiten hätten sie auch die Fluchformel verdient. Schließlich besteht auch die Möglichkeit, dass die Formeln von Usāma aus seiner Quelle übernommen wurden oder später von einem Abschreiber eingefügt wurden.

---

9 Ibn Munqiḏ, *Dīwān* 139–41 = Nr. 259–60 Brief mit Antwort und Rückantwort; 143 = Nr. 263 Brief mit Anfang der Antwort.

10 Bianquis, Ṭalāʾiʿ b. Ruzzīk. Zu Usāmas poetischer Korrespondenz mit ihm s. Ibn Munqiḏ, *Dīwān* 136–7 = Nr. 254 Brief des Wesirs mit Antwort Usāmas; 140–1 = Nr. 260 Brief des Wesirs mit Antwort; 213–7 = Nr. 338 Brief des Wesirs mit Antwort; 220–7 = Nr. 343 Brief des Wesirs mit Antwort; 174–8 = Nr. 304 Lobgedicht Usāmas auf den Wesir mit dessen Antwort. Teilweise weisen meine Stellenangaben nur auf Teile der Briefe hin, weil Usāma seine Gedichte auseinandergerissen hat, um die Teile thematisch verschiedenen Kapiteln zuzuordnen. Die Hinweise der Herausgeber in den Anmerkungen führen die Gedichte wieder zusammen.

11 Ibn Munqiḏ, *al-ʿAṣā* 98–9 und 261. Zu dem Buch vgl. Cobb, Book of the Staff.

12 Ibn Munqiḏ, *al-ʿAṣā* 241 und 296: Abū Bakr; 296: ʿUmar; 240: ʿUṯmān.

Cobb nennt noch zwei Hinweise auf Usāmas Zugehörigkeit zur Sunna: Erstens beruft er sich in seinem *Kitāb Lubāb al-ādāb*[13] mehrfach auf die ersten drei Kalifen.[14] Zweitens hat Usāma eine als Handschrift erhaltene Kurzfassung (*talḫīṣ*) eines Werkes des berühmten sunnitischen Gelehrten Ibn al-Ǧawzī (gest. 597/1200) verfasst, das dem Lobe der beiden ʿUmar (des zweiten Kalifen ʿUmar b. al-Ḫaṭṭāb und des Umayyadenkalifen ʿUmar b. ʿAbd al-ʿAzīz) gewidmet war.[15] Ich möchte als Drittes noch hinzufügen, dass Usāma einen Sohn Abū Bakr, also nach dem ersten Kalifen, benannte. Das scheint mir bei einem Šīʿiten undenkbar. Der Sohn verstarb früh, und Usāma verfasste mehrere Trauergedichte auf ihn.[16] So blieb uns der Name erhalten.

Cobb stellt zu Recht fest, dass man aus seiner religiösen Einstellung keine Rückschlüsse auf ein negatives Verhältnis Usāmas zum *ǧihād* ziehen kann. Er gibt weitere Gründe, die für eine positive Einstellung sprechen. Außer den beiden oben genannten Stellen enthält das *Kitāb al-Iʿtibār* indirekte Hinweise auf den *ǧihād*. So bezeichnet Usāma seinen 547/1152 im Kampf gegen die Franken gefallenen Bruder ʿIzz ad-Dīn und andere Personen als *šahīd* (Märtyrer).[17] Den Rang eines Märtyrers konnte man nur im *ǧihād* erwerben. Im *Kitāb Lubāb al-ādāb* zitiert Usāma mehrere Koranverse und Prophetentraditionen, die zum *ǧihād* auffordern.[18]

Diese etwas spärlichen Hinweise auf den *ǧihād* in den Werken Usāmas möchte ich im Folgenden durch Zitate aus seiner Dichtung vermehren. Ich führe dabei auch *ǧihād*-Erwähnungen in den Antwortversen an, die Usāma auf seine poetischen Briefe erhielt und die er in seinen von ihm selbst redigierten *Dīwān* aufnahm. Ein Gegner des *ǧihād* hätte solche Verse unterdrückt.

Ein Lobgedicht Usāmas ist dem Emir Muʿīn ad-Dīn Unur, gewidmet, der 534–44/1140–9 als Atabeg für den Būriden Muǧīr ad-Dīn in Damaskus herrschte. Unur hatte bei einem Zusammentreffen mit den Franken diese in die Flucht geschlagen:[19]

---

13 Ibn Munqiḏ, *Lubāb al-ādāb*. Zu dem Werk vgl. Cobb, *Lubāb al-ādāb*.

14 Stellennachweise bei Cobb, Dogs 60, Anm. 13. Übrigens erhält al-Muʿāwiya im *Lubāb al-ādāb* keine Fluchformel, sondern die Eulogie für normale Verstorbene *raḥimahu llāh* „Gott erbarme sich seiner," z.B. 35; 87; 123.

15 Cobb, Dogs 61; vgl. auch GALS i, 553.

16 Ibn Munqiḏ, *Dīwān* 297–300 = Nr. 509–10; 301–2 = Nr. 515; 302–4 = Nr. 518–20.

17 Cobb, Dogs 61–2.

18 Cobb, Dogs 58, Anm. 4.

19 Ibn Munqiḏ, *Dīwān* 170 = Nr. 298, Z. 3–8 und 12–3; französische Übersetzung bei Derenbourg, *Vie* 210.

> Bei dir bewahrheitet sich die Beschreibung (durch deine Namen). Du bist (in der Tat) ein Muʿīn ad-Dīn (Helfer der Religion). Beschreibungen sind eben Omen und Augurium.
>
> Du bist wirklich das Schwert des Islam; denn das Schicksal macht deine Schneiden, oh Schwert, nicht schartig.
>
> Durch dich, oh du sein scharfes Schwert, mehrte sich die Macht des Islam, und Polytheismus und Unglaube wurden erniedrigt.
>
> Vertraue auf das, was du dir erhofftest! Gott vergilt den Dienern auch geheime Pläne.
>
> Immer hast du im Verborgenen den Glaubenskrieg (*ǧihād*) geplant. Dann proklamiertest du ihn offen, als Offenheit möglich war.
>
> Alle Schätze der Könige vergehen, aber deine beiden Schätze bleiben: (jenseitiger) Lohn und (diesseitige) Dankbarkeit.

Usāma befand sich damals gerade im Frankenland, so dass er nicht am Glaubenskrieg teilnehmen konnte. Im gleichen Gedicht bedauert er das einige Zeilen später:

> Ist es gerecht, dass ich der Teil von uns beiden war, der sich im Lande des Unglaubens befand und du allein auf dem Kriegszug warst?
>
> Mein Teil an dieser Angelegenheit wird schändliches Andenken sein, und meiner wird man nicht zusammen mit den Glaubenskämpfern (*fī man yuǧāhidu*) gedenken.

Der oben genannte imāmitische Wesir al-Malik aṣ-Ṣāliḥ vertraute Usāma in einem Handschreiben Glaubenskriegspläne an und forderte ihn auf, auch den Zangiden Nūr ad-Dīn (gest. 565/1174) zu beeinflussen, am Glaubenskrieg teilzunehmen:[20]

> Wir vertrauen dir wichtige Angelegenheiten an, denn du bist würdig, dass sie dir vorgetragen werden.
>
> Die wichtigste Angelegenheit ist die des Glaubenskrieges (*ǧihād*) gegen den Unglauben. Höre, denn wir werden ihn durchführen.

Es folgt ein Bericht über die Kriegsvorbereitungen und dann das, was Usāma Nūr ad-Dīn sagen soll:

20 Ibn Munqiḏ, *Dīwān* 136, vor Nr. 254, Vers 4–5 und 12–3; französische Übersetzung bei Derenbourg, *Vie* 287–8.

Du bist derjenige, von dem man die Beendigung der Krankheit der Tyrannei durch die Ungläubigen erhofft und auf den man blickt.

Darum erbeute durch den Glaubenskrieg (*ǧihād*) deinen (himmlischen) Lohn, damit man dich als seinen (des *ǧihād*) Genossen findet! Welch trefflicher Genosse!

In Usāmas Antwort heißt es auf al-Malik aṣ-Ṣāliḥ bezogen:[21]

Die Aufforderung zum Glaubenskrieg (*ǧihād*) ließ von sich hören. Da sagte ein König, der für die edlen Taten geschaffen war: „Hier bin ich!"

Ein gerechter König, durch den die Religion erleuchtet wurde und dessen Leuchten den Islam umspannte.

Er hat keine (andere) Beschäftigung, die ihn von seinem Glaubenskrieg (*ǧihād*) gegen die Ungläubigen, von Gerechtigkeit und von guten Taten abhielte.

In einem anderen Brief fordert al-Malik aṣ-Ṣāliḥ Usāma zum direkten oder wenigstens verbalen *ǧihād* auf:[22]

Bei meinem Leben, derjenige, der in Religionsangelegenheiten guten Rat gibt, dem wird bei Gott (himmlischer) Lohn angerechnet.

Der Glaubenskrieg (*ǧihād*) gegen den Feind in Tat und Wort ist für jeden Muslim vorgeschrieben.

Du hast einen hohen Rang in beiden, seit du, wenn es zu Kriegen kam,

Dich in ihnen als Held erwiesest. Du hattest nie jemanden, der dir beim Stechen und Schlagen gleich kam.

Wenn du anstachelst, bist du in dem, was du sagst, ein Meisterdichter und ein Prediger.

Und wenn du (zum *ǧihād*) aufforderst, dann kann deine Entschlossenheit nicht verhehlen, dass deine Pläne das Ziel erreichen.

Auch an den Kalifen richtet Usāma die Aufforderung zum *ǧihād*:[23]

Du bist der Schatten Gottes auf Erden. Du weist die Tyrannen und Unterdrücker in ihre Schranken.

21 Ibn Munqiḏ, *Dīwān* 188–9 = Nr. 311, Vers 9–11.

22 Ibn Munqiḏ, *Dīwān* 165 = Nr. 293, Vers 16–20.

23 Ibn Munqiḏ, *Dīwān* 193 = Nr. 318, Vers 10–1.

Keine Sünde möge sich unter den Lohn des Glaubenskrieges (*ǧihād*) mischen, den du dir vor allen Menschen erworben hast!

In einem langen Auftragsgedicht, das die Siege des Auftraggebers über die Franken schildert, heißt es:[24]

Unter den muslimischen Königen gibt es keinen Glaubenskämpfer (*muǧāhid*), der uns gleicht, den weder Hitze noch Kälte (vom *ǧihād*) abhalten können.

Wir machten den Glaubenskrieg (*ǧihād*) zu unserem Streben und unserer Beschäftigung. Weder Gesang noch Wein erfreuten uns.

Bei uns war das Blut der Feinde begehrenswerter als der Wein und der Schlag der Schwerter auf sie begehrenswerter als die Flöte und die Saiten (der Laute).

Wir begegnen ihnen wie dem Geliebten. Sie sind nämlich Feinde, durch deren Besuch sich die Last (der Sünden) für uns verringert.

Zum Lobe Saladins verfasste Usāma die folgenden Zeilen, die nicht im *Dīwān* stehen, aber von ʿImād ad-Dīn al-Kātib al-Iṣfahānī in seiner *Ḫarīdat al-qaṣr* überliefert werden:[25]

Du gabst das Geld der Schatzkammern, nachdem es hinter den Siegeln der Schatzmeister alt geworden war, aus

Für eine Truppe von lauter Glaubenskämpfern (*muǧāhid*), Kriegern, Streitern, die es mit Ebenbürtigen aufnehmen,

Die mit weißen, scharfen Schwertern in den Krieg ziehen und blutroten zurückkommen,

Die eintauchen in das Feuer des Kampfgetümmels, wie der Durstige sich auf die Tränken des Teichs stürzt.

Drei weitere Gedichte, in denen der *ǧihād* erwähnt wird, die aber gleichfalls im *Dīwān* fehlen, werden in Abū Šāmas *Kitāb ar-Rawḍatayn* überliefert. Im ersten lobt Usāma Nūr ad-Dīn aus Anlass des Weihnachtsfestes (*laylat al-mīlād*):[26]

---

24 Usāma, *Dīwān* 201 = Nr. 324, Vers 8–11.

25 Al-Iṣfahānī, *Ḫarīdat al-qaṣr* 532, Vers 32–5. Der arabische Text nach der *Ḫarīda* auch bei Derenbourg, *Vie* 144, und die französische Übersetzung 372–3.

26 Abū Šāma, *Rawḍatayn* i, 2, 584, Vers 1–2. Die Herausgeber der Festschrift machten mich freundlicherweise darauf aufmerksam, dass Kapstein, *Muḥammad's birthday festival* 32,

> Die Geschöpfe haben jedes Jahr eine Nacht, in der das Feuer entzündet wird.
>
> Aber Nūr ad-Dīn hat im Gegensatz zu der übrigen Menschheit zwei Feuer: das Feuer der Gastfreundschaft und das Feuer des Glaubenskrieges (*ǧihād*).

Die beiden anderen Gedichte, in denen sich *ǧihād*-Belege finden, loben Saladin:[27]

> Du führtest den Glaubenskrieg (*ǧāhadta*) gegen die Schar der Ungläubigen, so dass du sie beschämt werden ließest. Auf ihnen lastet jetzt die Enttäuschung über die Erniedrigung und der Rückschlag.

Und:[28]

> (Du verdienst) Lohn und Andenken. Dazu gehört Dank in dieser Welt und morgen das Paradies.
>
> Was du tatest, ist nicht gering zu schätzen: Du erfülltest eifrig die Pflicht des Glaubenskrieges (*qumta bi-farḍi l-ǧihādi muǧtahidā*).

Ich hoffe, mit den vorangegangenen Zeilen es über Cobbs Argumente hinaus etwas wahrscheinlicher gemacht zu haben, dass Usāma Sunnit war, und durch die Zitate aus seinen Gedichten gezeigt zu haben, dass Usāma nicht nur kein Gegner, sondern ein Befürworter des *ǧihād* war.

---

die Zeilen bereits übersetzt hat und *mīlād* auf den Geburtstag Muḥammads bezieht, „because it cannot be expected that Nūr al-Dīn, who during his entire career made efforts to restore the Sunnite orthodoxy, would have been associated in a poem of praise with any other mawlid than that of the prophet.“ Ich bin mir da nicht so sicher. Im Orient wurden Feste häufig religionsübergreifend gefeiert. Vielleicht lag Nūr ad-Dīn ein orientchristliches Fest doch näher als die Übernahme einer *bidʿa* der šīʿitischen Fāṭimiden. Aṯ-Ṯaʿālibī (gest. 961/1038), der allerdings gut hundert Jahre vor Einführung der *laylat mawlid an-nabī* lebte, bezieht *laylat al-mīlād* eindeutig auf Jesus, vgl. sein *Ṯimār al-qulūb* 633: *laylatu l-mīlādi hiya l-laylatu llatī wulida fīhā ʿĪsā*. Danach übersetzt Manfred Ullmann im WKAS, Bd. 2, T. 4, 2029a mit „Heiligabend, die Weihnachtsnacht“. Für den *ǧihād*-Beleg ist es letztlich gleichgültig, wessen Geburtstag Nūr ad-Dīn feierte. Wir feiern mit dieser Festschrift auf alle Fälle den Geburtstag des Jubilars.

27 Abū Šāma, *Rawḍatayn* i, 2, 395, Vers 1–2. Französische Übersetzung Derenbourg, *Vie* 349.

28 Abū Šāma, *Rawḍatayn* i, 2, 605, Vers 2–3. Französische Übersetzung Derenbourg, *Vie* 355.

Bibliographie

Quellen

Abū Šāma, ʿAbd ar-Raḥmān b. Ismāʿīl, *Kitāb ar-Rawḍatayn fī aḫbār ad-dawlatayn an-nūriyya wa-ṣ-ṣalāḥiyya*, Hg. M. Ḥilmī M. Aḥmad, Ğuzʾ 1, Qism 1. 2, Kairo 1951–62.

Ibn Munqiḏ, Usāma, *Dīwān*, Hgg. A.A. Badawī und Ḥ. ʿAbd al-Mağīd, Kairo 1953.

Ibn Munqiḏ, Usāma, *Kitāb al-ʿAṣā*, Hg. Ḥ. ʿAbbās, Alexandria 1978.

Ibn Munqiḏ, Usāma, *Usāmah's memoirs entitled Kitāb al-Iʿtibār*, Hg. P.K. Hitti, Princeton 1930.

Ibn Munqiḏ, Usāma, *Memoirs of Usāma Ibn Munqidh: An Arab-Syrian gentleman and warrior in the period of the Crusades*, übers. von P.K. Hitti, New York 1929.

Ibn Munqiḏ, Usāma, *K. Lubāb al-ādāb*, Hg. A.M. Šākir, Kairo 1987.

al-Iṣfahānī, ʿImādaddīn al-Kātib, *Ḫarīdat al-qaṣr wa-ğarīdat al-ʿaṣr: Qism šuʿarāʾ aš-Šām*, T. 1, Hg. Š. Fayṣal, Damaskus 1375/1955.

aṯ-Ṯaʿālibī, *Ṯimār al-qulūb fī l-muḍāf wa-l-mansūb*, Hg. M.A. Ibrāhīm, Kairo 1965.

Sekundärliteratur

Bianquis, T., Ṭalāʾiʿ b. Ruzzīk, in EI², x, 149–51.

Cobb, P.M., Infidel dogs: Hunting Crusaders with Usama ibn Munqidh, in *Crusades* 6 (2007), 57–68.

Cobb, P.M., Usāma Ibn Munqidh's *Lubāb al-ādāb* (*The Kernels of Refinement*): Autobiographical and historical excerpts, in *Al-Masāq: Islam and the Medieval Mediterranean* 18 (2006), 67–78.

Cobb, P.M., *Usamah ibn Munqidh: Warrior-poet in the age of the Crusades*, Oxford 2006.

Cobb, P.M., Usamah ibn Munqidh's *Book of the Staff*: Autobiographical and historical excerpts, in *Al-Masāq: Islam and the Medieval Mediterranean* 17 (2005), 105–22.

Derenbourg, H., *Ousâma Ibn Mounḳidh: Un émir syrien au premier siècle des croisades (1095–1188)*, P. I: *Vie d'Ousâma*, Paris 1889.

Irwin, R., Usamah ibn Munqidh: An Arab-Syrian gentleman at the time of the Crusades reconsidered, in J. France und W.G. Zajac (Hgg.), *The Crusades and their sources: Essays presented to Bernard Hamilton*, Farnham 1998, 71–87.

Kapstein, N.J.G., *Muḥammad's birthday festival: Early history in the central Muslim lands and development in the Muslim West until the 10th/16th century*, Leiden 1993.

Wagner, E., *Abū Nuwās: Eine Studie zur arabischen Literatur der frühen ʿAbbāsidenzeit*, Wiesbaden 1965.

2

The Rhetorical Fabric of a Seventh/Thirteenth-Century Sufi Poem by ʿAfīf al-Dīn al-Tilimsānī

Ali Ahmad Hussein

One way of understanding the development of pre-modern Arabic poetry is by tracing the development of its rhetoric. Rhetorical development is traced by examining the rhetorical elements in poetry and analysing their use in different poems during different periods—a lengthy and demanding undertaking, far beyond the scope of a single study. Rather than emphasising rhetorical elements that beautify the text or elevate its literacy, I focus on every rhetorical element found in a poem and then compare that poem's complete rhetorical fabric with those of other poems. Deciding which rhetorical elements to stress in a study depends on the scholar's reading of the poem, regardless of whether the elements play a large or small role. The aim is to elucidate all rhetorical components which comprise the poem's language. This is the only way to understand which rhetorical elements are central to a specific text in a specific period compared with others from the same or other eras.

This article is a step forward in this lengthy and challenging process. It analyses the rhetorical fabric of a seventh/thirteenth-century Sufi poem by ʿAfīf al-Dīn Sulaymān b. ʿAlī al-ʿĀbidī al-Kūmī. ʿAfīf al-Dīn was an early Mamluk poet from Tilimsān, today a western Algerian town, widely known as ʿAfīf al-Dīn al-Tilimsānī or al-ʿAfīf al-Tilimsānī. A descendant of the Berber tribe al-Kūmiya, which was settled on the coast near Tilimsān, he was born in 610/1213, lived for some years in Cairo and then moved to Damascus, where he died in 690/1291. He was accused by some contemporaries of heterodox views, the famous theologian and jurisconsult Ibn Taymiyya (d. 695/1296) being among those who attacked him.[1]

The poem considered here comprises 14 verses in the metre *khafīf* rhyming in *hamza* (*-āʾū*).[2] Structurally it can be divided into two sections, both serving one central theme: the relationship between the individual and God. Verses

1 Al-Tilimsānī, *Dīwān* 11–22; Krenkow and Yalaoui, al-Tilimsānī; Bell, *Love theory* 89–90; Schimmel, *As through a veil* 45.

2 Al-Tilimsānī, *Dīwān* 65–7. There is another, slightly different version of the poem in *Dīwān*, ed. al-Kayyālī, 17–8. Due to restrictions of space, these differences are not addressed here.

 | DOI:10.1163/9789004521780_004

1–7 speak of a symbolic love affair with a woman named Asmāʾ and verses 8–13 depict a symbolic wine session. The final verse refers to the love affair.

The Arabic text of the poem and an English translation are given below, followed by a verse-to-verse commentary clarifying ambiguities and, most importantly, discussing the rhetorical elements in each verse (all of which are explained in the glossary at the end of the article). This is followed by a feature analysis of the poem's rhetorical elements and their statistical evaluation. The article ends with a brief comparison between these and the rhetorical features in three pre-Mamluk poems.

The Poem

1 مَنَعَتْهَا الصِّفَاتُ والأَسْمَاءُ   أَنْ تُرَى دُونَ بُرْقُعٍ أَسْمَاءُ

[Her] epithets and appellations barred Asmāʾ from appearing unveiled.

2 قَدْ ضَلَلْنَا بِشَعْرِهَا وَهْوَ مِنْهَا   وَهَدَتْنَا بِهَا لَهَا الأَضْوَاءُ

We marched astray within Her hair, which is a part of Her [= Asmāʾ], but the lights guided us to Her through Her.

3 كَيْفَ بِتْنَا مِنَ الظَّمَا نَتَشَاكَى   يَا لَقَوْمِي وَفِي الرِّحَالِ المَاءُ

O, my people! Why bemoan our thirst when we have water in our saddlebags?

4 كَمْ بَكَيْنَا حُزْنًا بِمَنْ لَوْ عَرَفْنَا   كَانَ مِنْ شِدَّةِ السُّرُورِ البُكَاءُ

How many tears of grief we have shed for the One for whom, had we but known [Her], we would have wept from great joy!

5 نَحْنُ قَوْمٌ مِتْنَا وَذَلِكَ شَرْطٌ   فِي هَوَاهَا فَلْيَيْئَسِ الأَحْيَاءُ

We are a people who have perished. This is a prerequisite for Her love! Let the living languish in despair.

6 وَأَقَامَتْ نُفُوسَنَا فِي حِمَاهَا لَا بِنَا بَلْ بِهَا لِيَصْفُو الصَّفَاءُ

She permitted our souls to dwell in Her protected abode, so that purity becomes yet purer—through Her, not through us!

7 فَالمُلَبِّي إِذَا دَعَتْ هِيَ مِنَّا وَمُجِيبُونَهَا[3] بِهَا الأَصْدَاءُ

When she calls, it is She who obeys from us. It is through Her that [our] echoes answer Her call.

8 يَا أَبَا الخَيْرِ قُمْ لَكَ الخَيْرُ فَاطْرِبْ مَسْمَعَ الفَقْرِ مِنْكَ ذَاكَ الغِنَاءُ

O Abū l-Khayr (“Father of Good”)—may good befall you! Arise and rouse with your [voice] the ears of poverty (or: the place where poverty is found). That is [true] chanting!

9 لَا تَفُتْ كَاسَكَ الَّتِي مِنْ لَمَاهَا هِيَ فِيهَا تَنَافَسَ النُّدَمَاءُ

Do not forgo your cup which is taken from Her dark [lips]!—the cup for which the companions compete.

10 لَمْ أَقُلْ قَدْ عَدَتْكَ كَأْسُكَ لَكِنْ رُبَّمَا طَوَّحَتْ بِكَ الصَّهْبَاءُ

I do not say that you have forsaken your cup, but perhaps white [wine] will fell you.

11 إِنَّمَا يَشْرَبُ الَّتِي تَسْلُبُ العَقْـ ـلَ نَدَامَى هُمُ لَهَا أَكْفَاءُ

Only worthy companions can drink [a wine] such as this, which steals all reason.

12 أَسْكَرُوهَا بِهِمْ كَمَا أَسْكَرَتْهُمْ فِي ابْتِدَاهُمْ بِهَا فَتَمَّ الوَفَاءُ

They intoxicated it [the wine] through themselves, just as it intoxicated them through itself when they began imbibing it. Thus was loyalty forged between the two.

3 In the printed vesion of the poem, the word is وَمُجِيبُوهَا, which is unmetrical. I have adopted the reading وَمُجِيبُونَهَا from the manuscript facsimile on p. 51 of the *Dīwān*. Al-Tilimsānī, *Dīwān*, ed. al-Kayyālī, 17, has وَيُجِيبُونَهَا.

13 فَجَزَاءٌ مِنْهَا وَمِنْهُمْ وِفَاقٌ   وَوِفَاقٌ مِنْهَا وَمِنْهُمْ جَزَاءُ

It is recompense from Her and assent from them. It is assent from Her and recompense from them.

14 قَدْ تَسَمَّتْ بِهِمْ وَلَيسُوا سِوَاهَا   فَالْمُسَمَّى أُولِئكَ الأَسْمَاءُ

She was named after them as they are not different from Her. The one named is identical with the names.

Commentary

Verse 1

Probably the most famous Asmāʾ is the beloved of the pre-Islamic poet Muraqqish the Elder (d. ca. 552 CE). There are different versions of their story. In brief, Muraqqish falls in love with his cousin, Asmāʾ. Her father exploits his absence to marry her to a wealthy man from Yemen, and Muraqqish is falsely told that his beloved has died. When he discovers the truth, he follows her to Yemen, but falls ill shortly before reaching her campsite. Asmāʾ, aware that he has come, hurries to meet him, allowing him one last glance of her before he dies.[4]

The verse is rooted in a symbolic analogy based on a metaphor. The quest for knowledge of the truth or that of the divine essence is expressed through a human love-image, in which the beloved (symbolising truth or divine essence) veils Her face, while the lover endeavours to remove the veil and relate to what is hidden behind it. This veiling-unveiling dichotomy is a well-known Sufi theme.[5]

Apart from the obvious common denominator between love for Asmāʾ vs. the Sufi urge to reveal the truth or divine essence, there is a second equivalence. For Muraqqish, Asmāʾ is unattainable: he must undertake an exhausting journey, only to catch a glimpse of her just moments before his death. The Sufi makes a similar journey towards the divine essence, but only after an electrify-

4 Al-Iṣfahānī, *al-Aghānī* vi, 93–8; Pellat, Muraḳḳish.

5 Various terms, semantically and historically developed over the centuries, have been used by Sufi scholars to describe the veiling-unveiling dichotomy; mainly *kashf* or *mukāshafa* ("unveiling/divine irradiation"), *mushāhada* ("witnessing") and *tajallī* ("appearing") vs. *satr*, *istitār* ("concealment") and *ḥijāb* ("veil"). See Gardet, Kashf; Geoffroy, Tadjallī.

ing symbolic voyage does he manage to remove the veil that covers the face of his beloved, as seen at the poem's end.

The face of the Sufi Asmāʾ is veiled not with fabric but metaphorically with Her "epithets and appellations." This reflects the Sufi belief that the wondrous names of God, including His epithets, necessarily bear other mysterious and deeper meanings, along with more names, as yet unrevealed.[6] The arcane meanings of these names can be comprehended only through spiritual meditation.[7] Knowledge of their true essence leads to the divine Himself.

In addition to the symbolic analogy, the verse includes other rhetorical figures. (1) The intellectual trope (*majāz ʿaqlī*) in the expression *manaʿathā l-ṣifātu wa-l-asmāʾu* ("appellations and epithets barred Asmāʾ from appearing"). The verb 'to bar' is attributed not to its true referent—Asmāʾ—but to an alternative (the appellations and epithets). (2) Echo (*radd al-aʿjāz ʿalā l-ṣudūr*): the verse ends and opens with the same word, i.e. Asmāʾ. (3) Paronomasia (*jinās* or *tajnīs*) in the two occurrences of the word Asmāʾ ("appellations" vs. "the beloved").

Verse 2

This verse describes the poet being led astray by Asmāʾ's dense hair, and seeking light to guide him. The notion of being led astray by the hair of the beloved is hyperbolic. The word *shaʿr* (hair) possibly refers not only to the hair itself but, as a synecdoche, to its blackness and denseness—an alluring female feature in classical Arabic poetry.[8] Three separate metaphors in this verse combine to produce one complete image: the black hair of the beloved, the light and the march. The Sufi resembles the imaginary lover, covered totally by the hair of his beloved, while attempting to uncover Her face. Asmāʾ's thick dark hair engulfs Her lover, causing him to lose his way, so he lights his path, attempting to find the way towards his beloved's face. This is a symbolic [metaphoric] image for the Sufi on his journey towards knowledge of the divine essence. The Sufi is prevented from seeing, encountering or uniting with the divine by divine obscurities that make him feel that he is travelling along a dark path. He seeks help in reaching his goal—help that may include meditation, as mentioned above, or other Sufi practices and knowledge that will enable him to perceive the divine essence. This combination of metaphors into a single image is a type of compound [symbolic] metaphor.

---

6 Al-Sharqāwī, *Muʿjam* 42–5.

7 Al-Ghazzālī, *al-Maqṣad* 46; Gardet, Al-Asmāʾ al-ḥusnā; Geoffroy, Tad̲j̲allī. See also Gardet, D̲h̲ikr, on the role of *dhikr* ("the tireless repetitions of the word Allah") in these meditations.

8 Lichtenstädter, *Nasīb* 43.

Contained in this same metaphor is a multi-antithesis or two contradictory images: marching astray within black hair juxtaposed to finding the right path with the help of light.

Another rhetorical feature observed here and repeatedly in the next verses is wordplay with prepositions and pronouns—multiple use of several, successive (or nearly successive) pronouns suffixed to prepositions. In this verse, the expression *minhā* ("from Her") appears in the first hemistich, followed by the two successive constructions—*bihā* ("by means of Her") and *lahā* ("to Her") in the second. "We marched astray within *Her* hair, which is a part of *Her* [= Asmāʾ], but the lights guided us to *Her* through *Her*." Wordplay like this leads to a semantic vagueness: it delays immediate grasp of the verse's message by distracting the reader from its content, as he attempts to decode the referents of each pronoun. Such stylistic play must be intended. The Sufi poem intentionally places the reader in the complexity and confusion experienced in the attempt to perceive the divine.

Verse 3

The meaning of *riḥāl*—'saddles'—relates the verse to the second section of the multi-thematic traditional *qaṣīda*: the poet-protagonist's trip in the desert after leaving the deserted campsite of his departed beloved (the *aṭlāl*).[9] The verse thus hints at the Sufi's journey towards his symbolic, as yet unattained beloved and depicts a group of travellers complaining of thirst. They are calmed by the poet-protagonist, who reminds them that they have water in their saddlebags and thus no reason for concern. To the Sufi, drinking reflects the intake of true knowledge, poured directly from the divine into the heart/reason.[10] Complaining of thirst is a metaphorical analogy to the Sufi's protest of possessing insufficient knowledge. The poet-protagonist calms his companions by reminding them that they do have water: that is, although they do not know all they desire to know, they possess knowledge that others (perhaps non-Sufis) do not. Further, they alone have the means of acquiring knowledge of the truth and the divine, for which they yearn. As well as this metaphoric analogy, the verse includes antithesis between the notions of thirst (*ẓamaʾ*) and possessing water (*fī l-riḥāli l-māʾu*, "water in our saddlebags").

9 See Jacobi, The camel-section.

10 Al-Sharqāwī, *Muʿjam* 169. The notion of "drinking the knowledge" appears on several occasions in Sufi writings, see al-Yūsuf, *al-Fikr al-ṣūfī* 213.

Verse 4

The companions are sad, weeping. The reason is clear from the preceding verses and from the phrase *bi-man law ʿarafnā* ("for the One for whom, had we but known"). They are eager to see as much as they can of the true essence of the divine or—metaphorically—of the beautiful face of Asmāʾ. This same verse states that, once they perceive the essence of that which causes them sadness, the tears of grief will turn to tears of joy.

Another figure of speech adds imagery to verse 4: periphrasis (*kināya*). It is used in the phrase *bi-man law ʿarafnā* ("for the One for whom, had we but known")—that is, the divine essence, and metaphorically, the face of Asmāʾ. The verse also has an antithesis between the notions of sadness (*ḥuzn*) and great joy (*shiddat al-surūr*), as well as an acoustic feature in *radd al-aʿjāz ʿalā l-ṣudūr*, which depends on repetition of two words derived from the same root (*bakaynā* and *bukāʾ*).

Verse 5

The notion of death interweaves through the two layers of the poem: literal death (in human love) and metaphoric death (in divine knowledge). In classical Arabic culture, unrequited true love often leads to the death of the lover.[11] For the Sufi, death has a different, metaphorical meaning: suppression of the desires of the self. This helps the Sufi leave the materialism of earthly life behind him and move towards a more spiritual existence, closer to the divine.[12] When the Sufi's soul departs his body, he does not perish, but moves on to immortal life in the presence of the divine.[13] In other words, for the Sufi, death is to leave behind earthly, material life and to approach immortal, heavenly life. In light of the main idea of this poem, to the Sufi, death means complete removal of the veil.

Two verb metaphors (and two antitheses) are included in this verse: the ideas of death vs. life. As opposed to the Sufi, who experiences metaphorical death, others are still "living." The living nourish their material desires and widen their separation from the divine. It is, therefore, not the dying but the living who should experience total despair. Verses 3 and 5 repeat the word *qawm* ("people").

11 Samḥāt, *Martyrs of love*.
12 Al-Kāshānī, *Muʿjam* 110–3.
13 Al-Sharqāwī, *Muʿjam* 267–8.

Verse 6

The lover is focused on Asmāʾ and feels that his soul (emotions and thoughts) lives with Her (in Her *ḥimā*, i.e., Her protected abode). For the Sufi, this is a metaphorical expression (an analogy based on metaphor) of the belief that his soul resides in the prohibited abodes of the divine. These prohibited places may be the different *maqāmāt* (pl. of *maqām*)—the spiritual stages on the long path traversed by the Sufi until he perceives and witnesses the divine. At every stage, he strives to purify himself of the world, preparing himself to reach still higher—although not everyone is permitted, or capable, of approaching the higher stages.[14]

There are two semantic layers in this verse. The first refers to the human love affair: the lover's soul resides in Asmāʾ's abodes. A metaphor occurs in the verb "to reside" (*aqāmat*) with reference to the "souls". The abstract notion of the soul is concretised into a body residing in a physical space. The second layer is the metaphorical expression for the soul of the Sufi residing in the abodes (i.e. the proximity) of the divine or for what the Sufi experiences in the different *maqāmāt*. This type of metaphorical expression can thus be termed a multi-layered metaphor.

The second hemistich is somewhat vague. The phrase *li-yaṣfū* (for *li-yaṣfuwa*) *l-ṣafāʾ* is hyperbolic: "purity becomes purer" or "purity is purified." For the Sufi, purity has two meanings. The first relates to the Sufi who purifies himself at every *maqām* in order to reach a higher spiritual level. The second is the one discussed by Yūsuf Zaydān, editor of al-Tilimsānī's *dīwān*, namely, the primordial covenant (*al-mīthāq*, cf. Q 7:172), the first attestation of the souls, before God created the bodies, that there is only one God.[15] This does not, however, fit the poem's context, and the first meaning is more suitable. Accordingly, the verse means that purity will be further purified or made purer by the divine, not by the Sufi. This can be interpreted in two ways. It either means that purity acquired by the Sufi at every level cannot be compared with that of the divine, which is a "pure purity;" or that it is an idealised purity, acquired by the Sufi at the *maqāmāt*, as he ascends from one level of purity to the next, the purest being the last, when he removes the veil that separates him from the divine.[16]

14 Affeich and Azzam, Sufi terms 38.

15 Al-Tilimsānī, *Dīwān* 66, footnote 3.

16 The idea of such a multiple purification of the souls occurs in non-Sufi Muslim philosophers as well, e.g., in the *Epistles* of the Brethren of Purity (*Ikhwān al-Ṣafāʾ*), though with slight differences from the Sufi belief. See Mattila, Philosophical worship 23–6; see also, mainly, Epistle 45 in Ikhwān al-Ṣafāʾ, *Rasāʾil* iv, 41–3; and Epistle 3, ibid. i, 138.

Other rhetorical features in this verse are: (1) intellectual trope in the phrase *li-yaṣfū l-ṣafāʾu*, where the verb *li-yaṣfū* ("to become purer") is attributed to "purity" itself instead of more logically to the Sufi, or to the divine, who purifies the souls. (2) A derivative relationship between words *yaṣfū* and *ṣafāʾ*. (3) Most importantly, a type of wordplay that involves repetition of preposition plus pronominal suffix in the phrase *lā binā bal bihā* ("through Her, not through us!"). Both this specific derivation and the repetition of preposition plus pronominal suffix increase the verse's ambiguity—which effect seems intended both in this and other Sufi poems.[17]

Verse 7

The call of the Sufi by the divine (metaphorically expressed by the call of Asmāʾ to her lover—an analogy based on metaphor) hints at the intimate relationship between the two. The divine invites all people, but only the Sufi obeys. He answers the call of the divine by *aṣdāʾ* (pl. of *ṣadā*). *Ṣadā* has several meanings, two of which fit the context—brain and echo.[18] In the former case, the Sufi responds to the call of the divine with his brain (that is, intellectually and spiritually, without words). This call-response motif may refer not only to the prayer of the Sufi (the movement between the different *maqāmāt*) but also, specifically, to its highest level or final destination, where he at last perceives, discovers or unites with the divine. There, the divine calls the Sufi and he answers.

Understood as echo, *ṣadā* also expresses a level of non-verbal communication between the Sufi and the divine. Here, again, there are two possible interpretations. It either refers to the stage after the divine has been revealed to the Sufi, when there is non-verbal, possibly telepathic communication; or it may be explained by the philosophy of the late fourth/tenth-century Iraqi school known as Brethren of Purity (*Ikhwān al-Ṣafāʾ*). According to the Brethren, the believer purifies his soul through ascetic practices and acquiring knowledge, elevating it to higher levels. In doing so, he endeavours to imitate or resemble in his soul the divine essence.[19] Like in the *Ikhwānian* idea of the resemblance of the individual to the divine, the "echo" in this poem may refer to a resemblance or imitation by the Sufi of his creator. The Sufi obeys the divine calls on people to follow Him, by imitating His attributes through ascetic behaviour.

Wordplay is observed in this verse, too, in the three subsequent pronouns / prepositions plus suffixed pronouns: *hiya* ("She" [Asmāʾ/the divine]), *minnā*

17 Semantic ambiguity in general is a characteristic that differentiates the poetic from the non-poetic. See Hoffmann, Agonistic poetics 46.

18 Lane, *Lexicon* iv, 1671.

19 Epistle 15 in Ikhwān al-Ṣafāʾ, *Rasāʾil* iii, 41; see also Epistle 31, ibid. iii, 143.

("from us" [the lover/Sufi]) and *bihā* ("through Her" [Asmāʾ/the divine]). Here again this inhibits a grasp of the intended meaning and perplexes the reader. The difficulty is in understanding how the Sufi answers Her *through Her*. (As discussed above, they answer Her through echoing or imitating Her non-verbal utterances or attributes.)

Verse 8

This verse and those that follow depict a gathering of Sufis listening to a singer and imbibing metaphoric or symbolic wine.[20]

Abū l-Khayr is explained by Zaydān as the sobriquet of the chanter. Through his songs, "the souls of the Sufi listeners are led towards the lands of joy" (*taḥdū bi-l-arwāḥi ilā bilādi l-afrāḥ*).[21] The sobriquet (lit. "father of good") may have been inspired by the Sufi notion of Good (*khayr*). Some Sufi schools believe that existence (*wujūd*) is utterly good and its counterpart *sharr* or evil has no real existence, being only the absence of good. The divine is considered to be "the absolute pure good" (*khayr maḥḍ muṭlaq*).[22] The "father of good" may, therefore, be a periphrasis (family-periphrasis) which means "the chanter who brings good, or is responsible for leading the listeners to goodness." Since the singer was intensely spiritual, his chanting led the Sufis to higher mystical levels; it led them towards the absolute goodness.

The *masmaʿ* (lit. "the place/organ where one listens") is a pheriphrastic expression referring either to the "ear" or to the space where Sufis gathered.[23] The phrase *fa-ṭrib masmaʿa l-faqri* can thus be translated either as "rouse with your voice the place where poverty is found" or "rouse the ears of poverty". Both versions contain a multi-layered synecdoche: the word *faqr* ("poverty") should be used for "poor people;" the new phrase *masmaʿa l-fuqarāʾi* should simply indicate only the *fuqarāʾ*, not their ears nor their gathering place.

		Synechdoche 1		Synechdoche 2
fa-ṭrib masmaʿa l-faqri	⟶	*fa-ṭrib masmaʿa l-fuqarāʾi*	⟶	*fa-ṭribi l-fuqarāʾa*
stir the ears/the place of poverty	⟶	*stir the ears/place of the poor people*	⟶	*stir the poor people*

20 Al-Sharqāwī, *Muʿjam* 176–7.

21 Al-Tilimsānī, *Dīwān* 66, footnote 5.

22 For a detailed discussion of the philosophical Sufi notion of *khayr* vs. *sharr*, see al-Ḥakīm, *al-Muʿjam* 442–6.

23 See Lane, *Lexicon* iv, 1428–9.

The Sufi concept of poverty rejects all private property so as to live only for the Lord and give everything to Him—an essential principle for the Sufi aspiring to gnosis (*maʿrifa*).[24]

Dhāka l-ghināʾu ("That is [true] chanting!") is a periphrasis for the fine quality of Abū l-Khayr's singing: this is what the Sufi loves to listen to!

Further rhetorical elements in the verse are: (1) the paranomasia between the two words *khayr* in Abū l-Khayr (part of the sobriquet) and the phrase *laka l-khayru* ("may good befall you!"); and (2) wordplay in repeating the construction of preposition plus pronominal suffix—*laka* ("for you") and *minka* ("from you").

Verse 9

To the Sufi, wine is an expression of divine love. The Sufi asks (himself or a comrade?) not to forgo the cup. This wine, he says, is taken from the dark lips of the beloved. This is an image derived from classical love poetry, in which the lips of the beloved (hence her kiss) are likened to wine because of their sweet taste and the deep feeling for the lover whom they kiss.[25] Here the image is reversed: wine is compared with the lips of the beloved and is expressed via a new symbolic metaphor: the love of the divine is substituted by the cup of wine. In Sufi poetry, as shown in the following verses, the experience of the Sufi in seeking divine love is expressed metaphorically through the image of drinking wine.

There is a periphrasis in this metaphor. "Do not forgo the cup!" is a periphrastic expression for "drink the whole cup!" Using the periphrasis rather than direct speech hints at the great value of this wine. Such wine should not be forgone! The sense of its value is enhanced by the phrase *fīhā tanāfasa l-nudamāʾu* ("the cup for which the companions compete")—a second periphrasis conveying its worth.

As stated earlier, to the Sufi, wine is a new symbolic metaphor for the love of the divine. The image as a whole—that drinking this precious wine is as delectable as kissing the lips of the beloved, for which the companions compete—is a prolongation of the metaphor. It symbolises an order or quest of the Sufi for passionate enjoyment and love of the divine.

Other rhetorical elements in this verse are: (1) Synecdoche, which is used twice: firstly, in "cup," meaning "wine"; secondly, in *lamā*, which literally refers to the "black colour [of the lips]", meaning the lips themselves. Dark lips are a captivating female characteristic in classical Arabic poetry. (2) Wordplay with

24 Nizami, Faḳīr.

25 Hussein, Majāz ʿaqlī 438.

pronouns and prepositions, similar to the instances mentioned above. The pronoun *hiya* ("it/Her") is followed by the construction *fīhā* ("in it"). Both refer to the cup.

Verse 10

This verse is built on a compound rhetorical figure—a periphrasis whose meaning produces a metaphor. The phrase *rubbamā ṭawwaḥat bika l-ṣahbāʾu* ("but perhaps white [wine] will fell you") is a periphrastic expression that hints at a state of intoxication. Nada Saab defines intoxication (*sukr*) in Sufism as a metaphorical expression. She explains: "[It] refers to a Ṣūfī [...] experience of ecstasy that is often characterised by bewilderment and perplexity. It describes the state of a Ṣūfī who has lost awareness of all except God, the sole object of his adoration."[26] Saab summarises the philosophical dispute between two main Sufi doctrines: that of the Persian mystic Abū Yazīd al-Biṣṭāmī (d. ca. 261/875), founder of Drunken Sufism, who favoured intoxication over sobriety (*ṣaḥw*, an antithetical Sufi metaphor), since intoxication eliminates or deconstructs the human attributes that constitute the veil between God and man; and that of the Baghdadi Sufi al-Junayd (d. 297/910), which is known as the school of Sober Sufism. Saab briefly mentions the idea of intoxication as described by the Nishapuri mystic ʿAbd al-Karīm al-Qushayrī (d. 465/1073): a state of absence from oneself because of strongly experiencing God (*wārid*), with the attributes of God's beauty revealed in their full splendour. This is followed by sobriety and the return to consciousness. Al-Qushayrī describes the intoxication resulting from the "cups of love" and the closeness it creates to the divine. On the first level, the Sufi behaves like a drunk, on the second he is truly drunk, but on the third level his thirst is quenched and he achieves sobriety.[27]

Bearing in mind these ideas, this verse is a call by the Sufi to someone undefined (the poet-protagonist? another companion?) to experience divine love more intensely, in a way that enables him to perceive the beauty of the divine or experience God strongly (*wārid*), and to reach this through intoxication. Since the Sufi state of intoxication is ephemeral and elusive, the poet-protagonist charges that those whom he addresses, while drinking the wine, are not drinking it in sufficient quantities.

Other rhetorical elements in the verse are: (1) *kaʾsuka* ("your cup"), a synecdoche which refers to the wine in the cup; (2) *ʿadatka kaʾsuka* (lit. "your cup [did not] forsake you"), a mental trope meaning "you [have not] forsaken the cup;"

26 Saab, Intoxication.

27 Saab, Intoxication.

(3) *ṭawwaḥat bika l-ṣahbāʾu* ("white [wine] felled you"), another intellectual trope, meaning "you fell because you drunk the wine"; (4) *ṣahbāʾ* (lit. "having redness intermixed with its whiteness"), a linguistic periphrasis referring to wine—that is, [*khamrun*] *ṣahbāʾ*;[28] (5) wine itself as a new symbolic metaphor describing the experience of the Sufi in seeking divine love; and finally (6) repetition of the word *kaʾsuka/kaʾsaka* in this and the previous verse.

Verse 11

This verse comprises multiple metaphors and periphrases. *Allatī taslubu l-ʿaqla* ("the one that steals reason") refers both to the wine (an object-periphrasis) and contains a verb metaphor, in which the verb "to steal" metaphorically describes the state of intoxication when reason is absent.[29] Another metaphor—the image of the companions (*nadāmā*) drinking wine until they become intoxicated—is an analogy based on a metaphor expressing the Sufi's growing love for the divine.

A second periphrasis is contained in the phrase *humū lahā akfāʾū* ("only worthy companions [can drink it]"). The first periphrasis refers to the value of the wine. This one is about the worth of the drinkers: only they can drink a wine like this. Such periphrases appear in earlier poems, although not symbolically.[30] Lastly, there is a derivation relationship between the word *nadāmā* in this verse and *nudamāʾ* in v. 9.

Verse 12

The feminine pronoun here apparently refers to the wine, not to Asmāʾ or to the divine. The verse presents a hyperbolic image of the drinkers: intoxicated at the beginning, they then cause the wine itself to become inebriated. Describing the wine itself as drunk (a verb metaphor) conveys the stirring feeling that such a wine experiences. Since wine expresses the love for the divine, an intoxicated wine articulates the moments of intense love that the Sufi experiences in his ascent towards the divine. The love increases gradually until it makes the lovers metaphorically intoxicated. It then grows still greater until it becomes hyperbolically intoxicated by itself.

Once the companions and the wine are both intoxicated, a contract of loyalty is forged between them. The use of the word "loyalty" to describe the relationship between wine and drinkers is metaphorical (a verb metaphor). The wine is personified and assigned the same feelings as the lovers.

---

28 Hussein, Hudhalī wine poetry 30.

29 For more on the theft metaphor, see Ullmann, *Der verstohlene Blick*.

30 Hussein, Majāz ʿaqlī 437–41.

Another, less convincing, explanation of this verse is offered by Zaydān: *ibtidāʾ* ("the beginning") refers to the time when God created the souls but had not yet created the bodies. The souls were intoxicated with love for their creator and declared their loyalty to Him and belief in His unity (reference to Q 7:172). Since the poem makes no reference to the creation of souls, this interpretation seems forced.

Other rhetorical features in the verse are: (1) Repetition of the verb *askara* ("to intoxicate"). (2) Two intellectual tropes. The first is in the phrase *askarat-hum* ("it intoxicated them"). According to classical Muslim understanding of *majāz ʿaqlī*, wine has no power to affect people by itself. The true subject is the drinkers who become intoxicated. The second trope is in *fa-tamma l-wafāʾu* (lit. "loyalty accomplished"), where the subject should be the two loyal sides. (3) A synecdoche in the phrase *fī btidāhum bihā* ("when they began it [that is, the wine"] = "when they began imbibing it"). *Bihā* may also depend on *askarathum*, not on *ibtidāhum*. Accordingly, the verse's word order is slightly changed to: *ka-mā askarathum bi-hā* ("as it intoxicated them through itself"). The synecdoche is preserved since wine is mentioned but refers to the drinking process ("it intoxicated them through itself" = "it intoxicated them through drinking it"); (4) Lastly, the wordplay with prepositions plus suffixed pronouns: *askarūhā bihim* followed by *askarathum … bihā*.

Verse 13

The love relationship is fruitful at the poem's end. It is a state of complete harmony between "Her" and "them." Asmāʾ/the divine compensates Her lovers satisfactorily. The beloved is replete with what Her lovers have offered: sincerity, loyalty, devotion and great love. This is expressed through an analogy based on metaphor: the successful love affair with Asmāʾ = the success of the Sufi in reaching the divine.

There are clear acoustic elements in this verse: (1) Reversion (*ʿaks*) in the order of words in the two hemistiches. (2) Repetition of *jazāʾ* ("recompense"), *minhā wa-minhum* ("from Her and from them"), and *wifāq* ("assent"). (3) Wordplay in prepositions and suffixed pronouns (*minhā wa-minhum*). And (4) *radd al-aʿjāz ʿalā l-ṣudūr*: *fa-jazāʾun* and *jazāʾun*. So intense a dependence on acoustic elements in this verse may reflect the state of joy within the Sufi/lover. He is jubilant and seems to dance with the words, tossing a single word from side to side. This musical affectation accompanied by the repetition of words is undeniable.

The use of the feminine pronoun in this verse introduces a certain ambiguity. Given that another feminine subject (*khamr* or wine) appears in earlier verses, the reader first thinks of this as the pronoun's referent. A second reading, however, shows this is erroneous, as the pronoun refers to Asmāʾ/the divine.

Verse 14

There is irregular use of the masculine plural pronominal suffixes in this verse: *tasammat bi-him* ("She was named after *them*") and *laysū siwāhā* ("*They* are not different from Her"). The masculine plural suffix is normally used to reference people only, whereas the feminine singular is used for the nonhuman as well. Here, however, the masculine plural suffixes refer to the nonhuman, that is, the "appellations and epithets" of the divine. The Sufi discovers these true appellations of the divine only at the end of his striving/journey. They are not mentioned in the poem, and the Sufi often keeps them secret.[31] This irregular use of the masculine plural pronominal suffixes, in place of the feminine singular, is misleading. The reader may mistakenly take the pronoun to refer to the people in this verse—the Sufis (who discover that the divine is basically nothing other than themselves) rather than to the appellations. The second hemistich, however, makes this interpretation less likely. It asserts that the "one named" is identical with "these appellations" (*fa-l-musammā ulāʾika l-asmāʾu*). Here, the poet uses the demonstrative plural pronoun *ulāʾika* (it, too, normally signifies people), instead of a feminine singular demonstrative pronoun such as *hādhihi* ("these") or *tilka* ("those"), to refer to the appellations. The use of human-associated pronouns to describe the nonhuman in this verse is apparently intentional, aiming to elevate the nonhuman to human level. That is, these most elevated of names are referenced differently.

The divine names revealed are identical with the divine. This may indicate that the appellations of the divine express His true essence. Once the Sufi knows them, he has discovered the true, hidden essence of the divine.

Rhetorically, the verse depends on acoustic rather than semantic elements. Since the perplexing issue (the veiled identity of the divine or the veiled face of Asmāʾ) is already solved, reliance on semantic rhetoric is less helpful here, at the poem's end. Acoustic or musical elements, which may reflect, as mentioned previously, joy and jubilation in the lovers/Sufis are more useful. Acoustics in this verse are expressed in a play on three words deriving from the same root—*radd al-aʿjāz*: *tasammat* ("is named"), *musammā* ("the named") and *asmāʾ* ("names/appelations"). As indicated in verse 1, the names were the main obstacle to the lover's seeing Asmāʾ's beautiful face, and, metaphorically, to the Sufi's perceiving the true essence of the divine. Maybe the importance of the notion of "names/appellations" is the reason for repeating this word in its different derivations in closing the poem.

31 Al-Sharqāwī, *Muʿjam* 43.

The Rhetorical Fabric in al-Tilimsānī's Poem—a Statistical Analysis

The poem comprises 66 rhetorical elements, averaging 4.71 per verse.

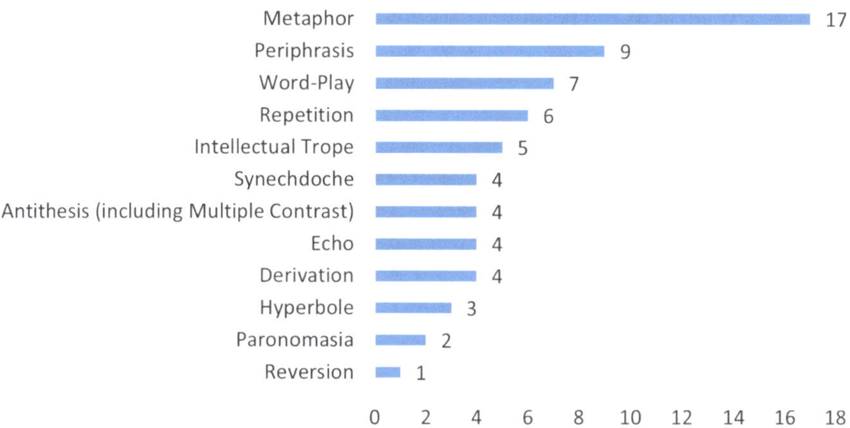

FIGURE 1 Rhetorical elements in al-Tilimsānī's poem

The poem depends mainly on metaphor, which has the lion's share of featured rhetorical elements (a ratio of 25.79 %). Next is periphrasis and then wordplay and repetition, which occur almost equally. The simile plays no role.

There are many types of metaphor in this poem. Most of them (10 out of 17, about 59 %) are symbolic, which makes, in my view, the greatest difference between the use of metaphor in Sufi and non-Sufi poetry:

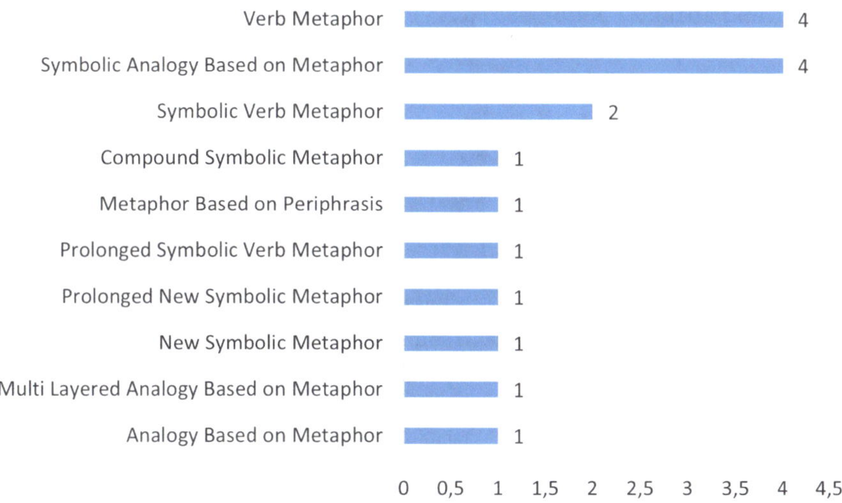

FIGURE 2 Metaphor in al-Tilimsānī's poem

If we subsume these types into the main forms of metaphor used in earlier periods of classical Arabic poetry, the verb metaphor and the analogy based on metaphor remain the two most prominent forms, used in virtually the same ratio. The wide use of verb metaphor is the norm in earlier classical Arabic poems. The present poem, however, is characterised by heavy use of analogy based on metaphor, which is also possibly a feature of ʿAbbasid and post-ʿAbbasid Arabic poetry.[32]

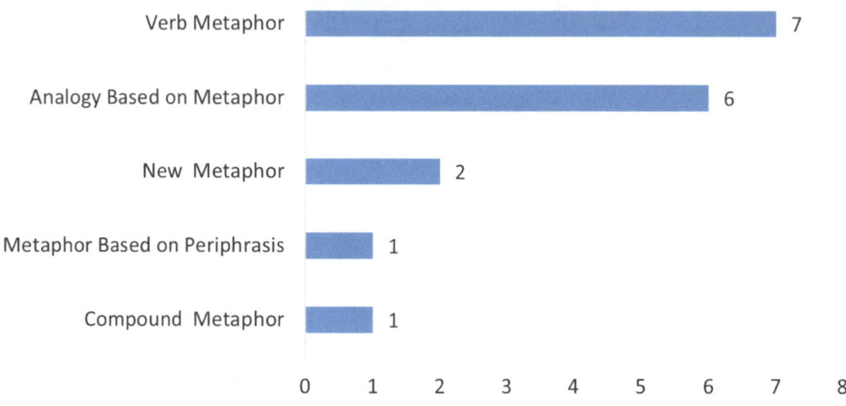

FIGURE 3 Main types of metaphor in al-Tilimsānī's poem

Periphrasis also plays a major role in this poem (used nine times, 13.66%), although a far more modest one than in pre-Islamic poetry and even in the early ʿAbbasid period.[33] The two most prominent types of periphrasis in this poem are the object- and attribute-periphrases, which are used equally. Linguistic and attribute-periphrases usually occur more often in pre-Islamic and early ʿAbbasid poetry than object-periphrases (see figure 4).[34]

The high percentage of wordplay is also a characteristic of this poem. Its function has been discussed; its development in classical Arabic poetry in general is of interest. The multi-layered metaphor and the synecdoche, though used only marginally here, have not been noted in previous comparative studies on rhetoric.

If the rhetorical elements in this poem that relate solely to sense (metaphor, periphrasis, synecdoche, antithesis, hyperbole and intellectual trope) are separated from those that contribute to sound in addition to sense, the ratio would be 42 (64%) to 24 (36%) in favour of the former. The latter percentage, however, is not small, demonstrating that sound in this poem is far from insignificant.

32 This is supported by the conclusion in Hussein, *Rhetorical fabric* 253.

33 Hussein, *Rhetorical fabric* 253.

34 Hussein, *Rhetorical fabric* 253.

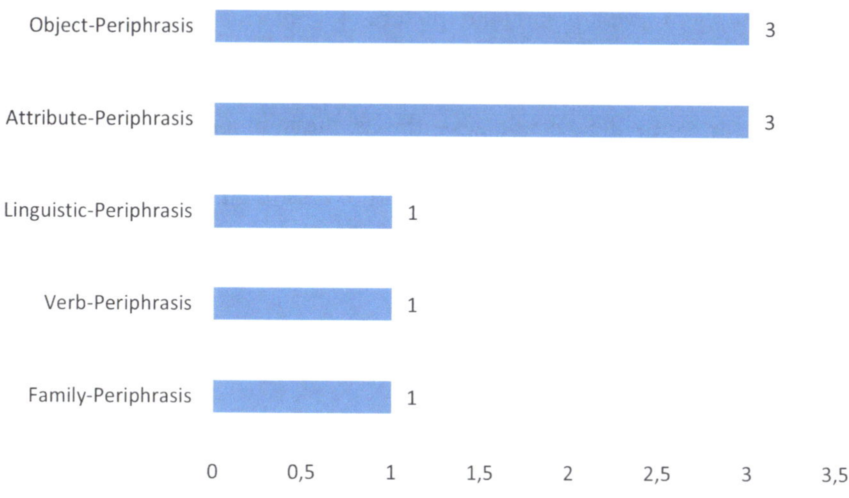

FIGURE 4 Periphrasis in al-Tilimsānī's poem

A Preliminary Comparison with Other pre-Mamluk Poems

As part of a larger project studying the development of rhetoric in classical Arabic poetry, I have analysed 109 poems dating from different periods. These poems have also been analysed in a web programme (https://arabic-rhetoric.haifa.ac.il/, access restricted). Together with colleagues from the Department of Information Systems at the University of Haifa, we are developing a programme capable of automatically analysing several rhetorical elements in an existing corpus of some 26,000 poems. (Some early successes are described in a forthcoming article.[35])

Given that detailing the rhetorical development in these 109 poems is not possible within the limits of an article, I randomly selected three poems to compare with al-Tilimsānī's *qaṣīda*. My only criterion in selecting them was their length, which I wanted to be similar to that of al-Tilimsānī's text. The three poems are by the pre-Islamic poet al-Nābigha al-Dhubyānī (fl. 570–600 C.E.),[36] the Umayyad Jarīr (d. ca. 110/728–9)[37] and the ʿAbbasid Abū Tammām (d. ca. 231/845).[38] I am aware of the shortcomings of such a comparison and the peculiarities of Sufi poetry and its greater dependence on symbolism. My aim

35 Abd Alhadi, Hussein, and Kuflik, Automatic identification.

36 Poem 6, rhyming in *-bī*, *basīṭ* metre, 16 verses, in al-Nābigha al-Dhubyānī, *Dīwān* 35–7.

37 Poem 11, rhyming in *-jī*, *kāmil* metre, 21 verses, in Jarīr, *Dīwān* i, 136–9.

38 Poem 21, rhyming in *-bū*, *ṭawīl* metre, 16 verses, in Abū Tammām, *Dīwān* i, 150–2.

here is simply to give a preliminary picture of similarities and discrepancies in the various genres as represented in these four poems. This picture must be adjusted, refined and completed by future studies. In the statistical comparisons, I use only the percentages—that is, the number of times a specific rhetorical element occurred in a poem divided by the sum of all the rhetorical elements of that poem. A comparative chart of these elements appears below, followed by a discussion of the main features that differentiate the rhetorical fabric of the poems in question.

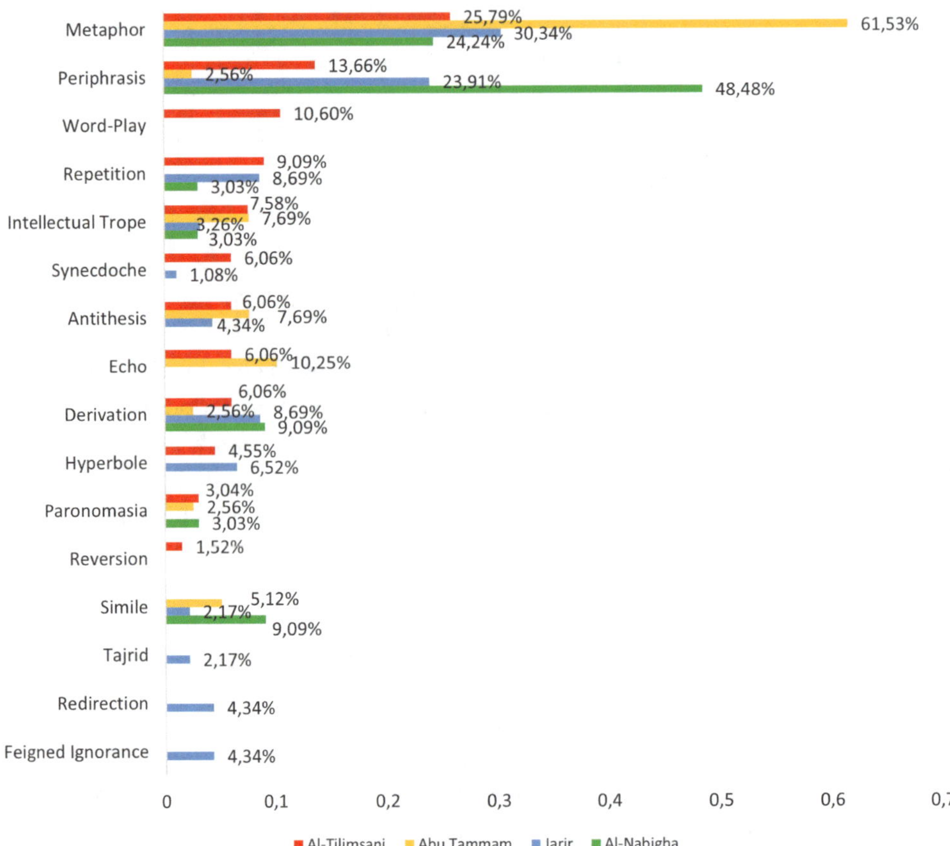

FIGURE 5 Percentages of rhetorical figures in the four poems

The use of the metaphor in al-Tilimsānī's poem is closer, percentage-wise, to that in the pre-Islamic poem than to that in the Umayyad and ʿAbbasid poems (26%, 24%, 30% and 62% respectively). In the Umayyad poem, the use of the metaphor increases in comparison with the pre-Islamic poem—an increase which doubles in Abū Tammām's poem, then drops in that of al-Tilimsānī to a statistical level close to that of the pre-Islamic ode.

Periphrasis moves in the opposite direction. It is widely used in the pre-Islamic poem (48%), its role statistically decreasing thereafter. It falls to the half of that percentage in the Umayyad poem (24%) and is almost ignored in the poem by Abū Tammām (3%). Its role grows in al-Tilimsānī's Mamluk work, but fails to reach the same proportion as in the pre-ʿAbbasid poems.

Repetition is used similarly in the poem of al-Tilimsānī and that of the Umayyad period. It is almost ignored in the pre-Islamic poem and totally absent from that of Abū Tammām. The same is true of derivation. Wordplay, on the other hand, is characteristic only of the Mamluk poem (11%). Echo is the sole element characterising the ʿAbbasid and post-ʿAbbasid poems but not used at all in the two pre-ʿAbbasid poems. It is almost twice as common in Abū Tammām's poem as in that by al-Tilimsānī (10 vs. 6%).

The statistical decrease in the role of the simile is of interest. From 9.09% in the pre-Islamic poem, its percentage decreases drastically in the Umayyad poem, then increases somewhat in that by Abū Tammām, but is reduced to nil in al-Tilimsānī's poem.

Conclusions

Two main conclusions emerge. Firstly, in the four works compared in this study, poetry evolved from being largely periphrastic in the pre-Islamic *qaṣīda*, to metaphoric in the Umayyad and ʿAbbasid periods, to symbolic and multilayered (symbolising different types of rhetorical feature, mainly the metaphor; and the use of compound and multilayered figures of speech) in al-Tilimsānī's poem. The use of symbolism is unsurprising since it is characteristic of Sufi poetry, but the development of symbolism in pre-modern Arabic poetry in general and its comparison with symbolism in Sufi literature in particular, must be studied further. Secondly, this Sufi-Mamluk poem by al-Tilimsānī is closer in its general rhetorical fabric to the pre-ʿAbbasid poems than to that of Abū Tammām. Whether this reflects the overall development of rhetoric in the poetry of these four periods cannot, however, be answered without further analyses of larger corpora.

Glossary

For the sake of brevity, the sources from which the following definitions are taken are omitted. They can be found in my previous publications on rhetoric and the references given there.[39] Some of these definitions reflect my own understanding of a rhetorical feature. Rhetorical elements that are not described in pre-modern sources but have been identified and named by me are asterisked. Most examples come either from al-Tilimsānī's poem or from poems analysed in https://arabic-rhetoric.haifa.ac.il/. Each term is followed by its Arabic name in brackets.

Analogy based on metaphor (*istiʿāra tamthīliyya*): Always a complete metaphorical sentence; the omission of any part of this sentence drastically changes the intended meaning. Example: "He is **drawing on water**" describes useless work (such as a hopeless study). Omitting "drawing" or "water" alters the meaning.

Antithesis (*ṭibāq*): Two words with contradictory meanings, which both relate to a common context. Example: "**happiness**" and "**sadness**" both describe the condition of the Sufi lovers [al-Tilimsānī's verse 4].

Attribute-periphrasis (*kināya ʿan ṣifa*): I previously translated this type of periphrasis as "epithet-periphrasis."[40] Other translations, such as "attribute-periphrasis" or even "quality-" or "properity-" periphrasis, may fit better.[41] The periphrastic sentence is used as an indirect hint at a certain attribute or quality. Example: "**I ate the whole meal**" is a periphrasis indicating that the food was delicious and/or that the eater was very hungry. Neither "delicious" nor "hungry" appears in the phrase. The whole meal was eaten, and at least one of the two attributes apply.

Branching (*tajrīd*): An individual addressing him/herself in the second person. Example: "**Do not remain** at the deserted campsite of **your** beloved, but **mount your** camel and **move** on!" There are several different forms of this rhetorical element.[42]

***Compound metaphor (*istiʿāra murakkaba*):** This term, in its present definition, is mine and not included in my previous studies. Two different metaphors are combined to produce one harmonious image. Example: "During that battle, **falling stars flashed above** our heads **into the dark night**." This image describes the gleaming spears/swords thrust above the heads of the warriors on a battlefield covered by dense dust. The "falling stars" is a new metaphor that describes the "gleam-

39 Hussein, *Rhetorical fabric* 42–59 (Chapter Three, "Terminology"); *idem*, Hudhalī wine poetry; *idem*, Majāz ʿaqlī.

40 Hussein, *Rhetorical fabric* 44.

41 I am grateful to Professor Geert Jan van Gelder for suggesting these translations.

42 See, e.g., Ibn Jinnī, *al-Khaṣāʾiṣ* ii, 473–6.

ing spears/swords." The "dark night" is a second new metaphor for the "dusty sky." Together they produce a congruent image of stars falling during the dark night.

Derivation (*ishtiqāq*): Two words derived from the same root with the same meaning. Example: ***kataba*** ("he **wrote**") and ***kitāba*** ("**writing**").

Echo (or echoing the rhyme at the beginning of the line) (*radd al-aʿjāz ʿalā l-ṣudūr*): The last word of a verse is repeated (either in its entirety, or as another word derived from the same root, or as a paronomasia) in the first hemistich or in the first word of the second hemistich. Example: repetition of the word **Asmā'** (two different meanings) in verse 1.

***Family-periphrasis (*kināyat ʿā'ila*):** Intimately related to the metaphor, this is an expression that uses a word indicating a family member—such as *abū* ("father"), *akhū* ("brother"), *bint* ("daughter")—together with a certain attribute or quality. Example: "**brother of bravery (*akhū l-shajāʿati*)**" meaning a brave individual. While this construction is logically a metaphor, classical scholars always refer to it as a periphrasis. In a previous publication, I proposed the term "family-metonymy."[43]

Feigned ignorance (or aporia) (*tajāhul al-ʿārif*): A rhetorical question, sometimes asked as if the answer is unknown. Example: "**Do horses also cry at the abandoned campsite?**"

Hyperbole (*mubālagha*): An exaggerated description to emphasise an attribute or action. Example: "**I spent the whole night and all day talking** to him, but he was not convinced". The speaker talked a great deal trying to convince his interlocutor, but not 24 hours nonstop. (Were this the case, the phrase would not be a hyperbole.)

Intellectual trope (*majāz ʿaqlī*): Attributing an action not to its real subject but to another that appears in the sentence. Example: ***nāma laylī*** ("**my night slept**"). The action of "**sleeping**" is attributed to the **night**, whereas the actual sleeper is "**I.**"

Linguistic periphrasis (*kināya lughawiyya*):** Related to the object-periphrasis, this is a grammatical construction comprising an omitted qualified noun (*manʿūt*) and a qualifier/adjective (*naʿt*). Example: ***ḥusām (lit. "**cutting**") is often used in Arabic to indicate a "**sword**," from the original construction *sayfun ḥusāmun* ("a cutting sword").

Metaphor (*istiʿāra*): A word or sentence taken from a certain semantic field and attributed figuratively to another 'alien' field.

***Metaphor based on periphrasis (*istiʿāra bi-l-kināya*):** A phrase used as a periphrasis in one context, but metaphorically in another. Example: *yaduhu maghlūlatun* ("his hand is shackled") is a periphrasis that expresses misery when describing a person, but a metaphor when it refers to God—who, according to some Muslim doctrines, has no hands, as in the Quranic expression *yadu llāhi maghlūlatun* ("God's hand is

43 Hussein, *Rhetorical fabric* 47.

shackled") [Q 5:67]. Additional example: "I was **laid on the ground** because of drinking wine" [cf. v. 10] is a periphrasis for "I was **drunk**." "Wine will fell you" in this poem refers to "drunkenness" as a metaphor for the Sufi state of ecstasy.

***Multi-layered metaphor (*isti'āra muta'addidat al-ṭabaqāt*):** A phrase is used metaphorically to express a certain meaning (metaphor A1). This meaning is, in turn, understood as a further metaphor expressing, by analogy, another meaning (metaphor A2). Example: **"The lover's soul resides in the prohibited abodes of the beloved"** (metaphor A1) → **"The Sufi resides in the prohibited abodes of the divine"** (metaphor A2) = **"The Sufi experience in the different *maqāmāt*"** (metaphor A2, verse 6).

Multiple contrast (*muqābala*): Antithesis is sometimes found between sentences. Sentence A contains words, each of which is antithetical to words contained in sentence B. Example: "We were **happy** and **enthusiastic** but our comrades were **sad** and **lazy**." In this article, no separation between Antithesis and Multiple Contrast is made.

New metaphor (*isti'āra ḥadītha*, or *isti'āra taṣrīḥiyya*): The attributed word is a noun, which is used in place of another similar noun which does not appear in the sentence. Example: "I saw a **lion**" meaning "I saw a **brave man**." While a brave man can never be a lion (an animal), the two share the quality of courage.

Object-periphrasis (*kināya 'an mawṣūf*): The translation of the term is mine. By object I mean 'a described object'—a person, animal or object (bodily organ, stone) that is not named in the phrase but alluded to through description or through its characteristic/s or virtue/s. Example: "The warrior was stabbed **in that part of the body where hatred accumulates**." This is a periphrastic phrase, which indicates that the warrior was stabbed in the "heart/chest," the place where, according to classical belief, love and hate are experienced.

Old metaphor (*isti'āra qadīma*, or *isti'āra makniyya*): The attributed word is a noun, which is used with a second noun from a different 'alien' field. Example: "The **claws of death**." Death, of course, has no claws.[44]

Paronomasia (or pun) (*jinās* or *tajnīs*): Two acoustically similar words that have different meanings. Example: **Asmā'** in verse 1 is a woman's name, but also has the meaning "names/appellations" (pl. of *ism*). Different types of paronomasia are described in classical and modern books on rhetoric.

Periphrasis (*kināya*): A phrase used to convey another meaning or another object (see explanation of "object" under Object-Periphrasis). The two parts of the periphrasis (the phrase itself and the meaning/object at which it hints) are related to

44 This is what classical authors term *isti'āra bi-l-kināya*: see Cachia, *Arch rhetorician* no. 122. The term "old metaphor" (based on analogy, *tamthīl*) was coined by W. Heinrichs to distinguish it from "new metaphor" (based on simile, *tashbīh*).

one another, or, in the phraseology used to define the metaphor, the relationship between them must actually exist. Example: "**I ate the whole meal**" is a periphrasis. The eating of the whole meal actually happened, in contrast to a phrase such as: "I encountered a lion", which means "I encountered a brave man." A brave man can never be a lion and the phrase is thus metaphoric, not periphrastic.

*__Prolonged new metaphor__ (***istiʿāra ḥadītha/taṣrīḥiyya murashshaḥa***): A new metaphor followed by some form of related prolongation—a word, phrase or sentence. The added word/s only specify or distinguish the metaphor. Their omission does not change its intended meaning. Example: "I met a **lion roaring**" or "I met a **lion lying in his den**" both tell of meeting a brave man, though in the first example he is perhaps talking loudly, and in the second the meeting occurs in his home or village.[45]

Redirection (*iltifāt*): Diverse pronouns refer to a single referent. Example: "I could not talk to **her**. O my beloved, if **you** decide to part, please do so gently." Both pronouns—"her" and "you"—refer to the same referent: the beloved.

Reversion (*ʿaks*): The word order of one sentence is reversed in the next. Example: "He **criticises everything**; although **everything about him** should be **criticized**."

Simile (*tashbīh*): When A is likened to B. There are two main forms of simile. "A is similar to B" and "A is B". Example: "**He looks like a lion**" and "**He is a lion**."

*__Symbolic metaphor__ (***istiʿāra ramziyya***): The attributed noun/verb/sentence has no direct relationship with the context in which it is used. There is no direct similarity between Asmāʾ, the female beloved, for example, and the divine essence—contrary to a non-symbolic metaphor, such as "I met the **lion**," where man and beast share certain qualities. Rather, Asmāʾ becomes a symbol that must be decoded to be understood.

Synecdoche (*majāz mursal*): One noun replaces another. Unlike the new metaphor, there is no similarity between the two nouns. Their relationship is best described as 'adjacent.' Both are found in the same spatial arenas, one of the nouns often being part of the other, or an instrument of it, and so on. Either noun can replace the other. Example: ***samāʾ*** (lit. "**sky**") is used to refer to "**rain**." Rain is part of (or spatially neighbours) the sky, even though the sky can never be rain nor vice versa.

Verb metaphor (*istiʿārat fiʿl*): The metaphorically attributed word is a verb or one having the meaning of a verb, such as an infinitive. Example: "Wine becomes **intoxicated**" [verse 12].

*__Verb-periphrasis__ (***kināya ʿan fiʿl***): The periphrastic sentence is used to intimate a certain action. Example: "**He was late in saddling his horse**" indicates that the

45 The term is asterisked because it is an amalgam of the pre-modern *istiʿāra murashshsaḥa* and "new metaphor" as dubbed by W. Heinrichs.

horseman **set out late.** Verb-periphrasis is sometimes combined with attribute-periphrasis (where the same phrase is used to describe an attribute: "he was late"). Both sentences are factual: the horseman started out late and he saddled his horse late.

Bibliography

Abd Alhadi, H., A. Hussein and T. Kuflik, Automatic identification of rhetorical elements in classical Arabic poetry, forthcoming.

Abū Mūsā, M., *al-Taṣwīr al-bayānī: Dirāsa taḥlīliyya li-masāʾil al-bayān*, Cairo 1993.

Abū Tammām, *Dīwān*, commentary by al-Khaṭīb al-Tibrīzī, ed. R. l-Asmar, Beirut ²1994.

Affeich, A. and M. Azzam, Sufi terms and their translation from Arabic to English. Diwân al-Ḥallâž as a case study, in *Terminàlia* 19 (2019), 28–38.

Bell, J.N., *Love theory in later Hanbalite Islam*, New York 1979.

Cachia, Pierre, *The arch rhetorician, or the schemer's skimmer: A handbook of late Arabic badīʿ drawn from ʿAbd al-Ghanī an-Nābulsī's* Nafaḥāt al-azhār ʿalā nasamāt al-asḥār, *summarized and systematized*, Wiesbaden 1998.

Gardet, L., Al-Asmāʾ al-ḥusnā, in *EI*², i, 714–7.

Gardet, L., Dhikr, in *EI*², vii, 223–7.

Gardet, L., Kashf, in *EI*², iv, 696–8.

Geoffroy, E., Tadjallī, in *EI*², x, 61.

al-Ghazzālī, *al-Maqṣad al-asnā fī sharḥ maʿānī asmāʾ Allāh al-ḥusnā*, ed. B.ʿA. al-Jābī, Cyprus 1987.

al-Ḥakīm, S., *al-Muʿjam al-ṣūfī: al-Ḥikma fī ḥudūd al-kalima*, Beirut 1981.

Hoffmann, Th., Agonistic poetics in the Qurʾān: Self-referentialities, refutations, and the development of a Qurʾanic self, in S. Wild (ed.), *Self-referentiality in the Qurʾān*, Wiesbaden 2006, 39–57.

Hussein, A.A., *The rhetorical fabric of the traditional Arabic qaṣīda in its formative stages. A comparative study of the rhetoric in two traditional poems by ʿAlqama l-Faḥl and Bashshār b. Burd*, Wiesbaden 2015.

Hussein, A.A., The rhetoric of Hudhalī wine poetry, in *Oriens* 43 (2015), 1–53.

Hussein, A.A., Majāz ʿaqlī 'intellectual trope' and the description of wine in a poem by Abū Dhuʾayb al-Hudhalī, in *AO* 71/4 (2018), 429–42.

Ibn Jinnī, *al-Khaṣāʾiṣ*, ed. M.ʿA. al-Najjār, 3 vols., [n.p.] 1952–57.

Ikhwān al-Ṣafāʾ, *Rasāʾil*, 4 vols., Qom 1405 AH [1985].

al-Iṣfahānī, Abū l-Faraj, *Kitāb al-aghānī*, eds. I. ʿAbbās, I. al-Saʿāfīn, and B. ʿAbbās, 25 vols., Beirut 2002, ³2008.

Jacobi, R. The camel-section of the panegyrical ode, in *JAL* 13 (1982), 1–22.

Jarīr, *Dīwān*, commentary by Muḥammad b. Ḥabīb, ed. N.M.A. Ṭāhā, 3 vols., Cairo ³1986.

al-Kāshānī, *Muʿjam iṣṭilāḥāt al-ṣūfiyya*, ed. ʿA. Shāhīn, Cairo 1992.
Krenkow, F., and M. Yalaoui, al-Tilimsānī: 3. Sulaymān b. ʿAlī b. ʿAbd Allāh, in EI², x, 499–500.
Lane, E., *An Arabic-English lexicon*, 8 vols., London and Edinburgh 1863.
Lichtenstädter, I., Das Nasīb der altarabischen Qaṣide, in *Islamica* (1932), 17–96.
Mattila, J., The philosophical worship of the Ikhwān al-Ṣafā, in JIS 27/1 (2016), 17–38.
al-Nābigha al-Dhubyānī, *Dīwān*, ed. ʿA. ʿAbd al-Sātir, Beirut 1996.
Nizami, K.A., Faḳīr, in EI², ii, 757–8.
Pellat, Ch., Muraḳḳish, in EI², vii, 603.
Saab, N., Intoxication in Ṣūfism, in EI³, first published online: 2018; first print edition: 2019–1.
Samḥāt, D., *Martyrs of love in Arabic literature:* al-Wāḍiḥ al-mubīn fī dhikr man ustushhida min al-muḥibbīn *as an example*, M.A. thesis, University of Haifa 2012, unpublished.
Schimmel, A., *As through a veil: Mystical poetry in Islam*, New York 1982.
al-Sharqāwī, Ḥ., *Muʿjam alfāẓ al-ṣūfiyya*, Cairo 1987.
al-Tilimsānī, ʿAfīf al-Dīn, *Dīwān*, ed. Y. Zaydān, Cairo 2008.
al-Tilimsānī, ʿAfīf al-Dīn, *Dīwān*, ed. ʿĀ.I. al-Kayyālī al-Ḥusaynī, Beirut 2013.
Ullmann, M., *Der verstohlene Blick: Zur Metaphorik des Diebstahls in der arabischen Sprache und Literatur*, Harrassowitz 2017.
al-Yūsūf, ʿA., *al-Fikr al-ṣūfī fī ḍaw' al-Kitāb wa-l-sunna*, Kuwait ³1986.
al-Zamakhsharī, *al-Kashshāf*, ed. ʿA.A. ʿAbd al-Mawjūd and ʿA.M. al-Muʿawwaḍ, 6 vols., Riyadh 1998.

3

"You Have Become the *amīr* of My Heart": An Edition of the *Faṣāḥat al-mashūq fī malāḥat al-maʿshūq* or the *Maqāma Iqṭāʿiyya* of al-Shābb al-Ẓarīf al-Tilimsānī (d. 688/1289)

Bilal Orfali and Maurice Pomerantz

Introduction

Thomas Bauer's landmark article "Mamluk literature: Misunderstandings and new approaches" of 2005, opens with the following observation:

> We live in hard times for pioneers and discoverers. There are no more blank spots on the map of our globe, there are no undiscovered continents, no unexplored jungles, and no unknown tribes to be found. But still there is Mamluk literature.[1]

This article provides an *editio princeps* of a *maqāma* entitled "The Eloquence of the Lover Concerning the Elegance of the Beloved" (*Faṣāḥat al-mashūq fī malāḥat al-maʿshūq*) composed by the well-known Damascene poet Shams al-Dīn Muḥammad b. Sulaymān b. ʿAlī al-Tilimsānī (d. 688/1289) known as al-Shābb al-Ẓarīf. We offer this brief article and edition in honor of our dear colleague Thomas Bauer, who is without doubt one of the great pioneers of the field of Mamluk literature who has encouraged us to explore this particular area of uncharted territory.

The *Maqāmāt* of al-Shābb al-Ẓarīf

The poet al-Shābb al-Ẓarīf (d. 688/1289) was not famed during his life as a prose writer. However, he composed a group of *maqāma*s, several of which have been preserved in manuscript. Ḥājjī Khalīfa (d. 1067/1657) in his *Kashf al-ẓunūn*

1 Bauer, Mamluk literature: Misunderstandings and new approaches 105.

 | doi:10.1163/9789004521780_005

notes that al-Shābb al-Ẓarīf was the author of a collection of *maqāmas* known as the *Maqāmāt al-ʿushshāq*.[2] While such a title is fitting for a collection of his *maqāmas* which concern love and passion, it is not mentioned in any of the preserved manuscripts.

The *maqāmāt* of al-Shābb al-Ẓarīf have been preserved in four manuscripts:

1. MS Istanbul Aya Sofya 3843
2. MS Paris Arabe 3947
3. MS Berlin Sprenger 85
4. MS Berlin Wetzstein 1847

MS Istanbul Aya Sofya 3843 (undated) is the largest collection and contains the following three titles:

1. *Faṣāḥat al-mashūq fī malāḥat al-maʿshūq* (ff. 169b–171a)
2. *al-Maqāma al-iqṭāʿiyya* (ff. 171a–172b)
3. *al-Maqāma al-thālitha* (ff. 172b–176a)

Maqāmas number 1 and 2 in MS Aya Sofya 3843 ff. 169b–172a correspond to one long *maqāma* without a title in ff. 1b–8b of MS Paris Arabe 3947. MS Berlin Sprenger 85 f. 6b, identifies itself as containing excerpts from a *maqāma* by al-Shābb al-Ẓarīf entitled, *Faṣāḥat al-mashūq fī malāḥat al-maʿshūq*.[3] The same manuscript reproduces several poems found in section one of MS Aya Sofya 3843 (ff. 169b–171a), and a large section from section 2 (ff. 171a–172b) suggesting that the unnamed copyist believed this to be one *maqāma*.

The *maqāmas* 1 and 2 of MS Aya Sofya 3843 are conjoined in narrative, such that the words "this is a copy of his letter of investiture" (*hādhihi nuskhatu taqlīdihi*) are followed directly by a copy of said letter. We believe that *al-Maqāma al-iqṭāʿiyya* rather than being a separate *maqāma* is an alternate name for the entire *maqāma*. The name of the *maqāma* refers to the chancery document of investiture (*taqlīd iqṭāʿī*) which stands at the center of this work. Supporting this hypothesis is the fact that when al-Ṣafadī cites verses from *al-Maqāma al-iqṭāʿiyya* by al-Shābb al-Ẓarīf in *al-Wāfī* he does so by citing verses that are found in the section prior to the chancery document, ff. 171a–172b, suggesting that he also thought the title referred to the entire *maqāma* (viz. ff. 169b–172b).[4]

The *maqāma* entitled *al-Maqāma al-thālitha* found in MS Aya Sofya 3843 ff. 172b–176a has been published on several occasions in the late 19th and early

2 Kâtip Çelebi, *Kashf al-ẓunūn* ii, 1786.

3 Ahlwardt, no. 8549 has *Faṣāḥat al-masbūq fī malāḥat al-maʿshūq*.

4 al-Ṣafadī, *al-Wāfī bil-wafayāt* iii, 134.

20th century.[5] A further *maqāma* can be found in MS Berlin Wetzstein 1847 with the title, *al-Maqāma al-Hītiyya al-Shīrāziyya* which we have recently edited.[6]

"The Eloquence of the Lover Concerning the Elegance of the Beloved"

The *maqāma* opens with an *isnād*, which alleges that the events were related to the author by a reliable transmitter. The unnamed narrator describes how he has entered a garden where there was a festive scene of drinking. One of the drinking companions whom he finds there (*nadīm*) extolls the virtues of reciting poetry to others, and encourages members of the collective to compose verses. As they contemplate, a man appears. He mysteriously refuses to drink from their cup and join them. Instead, he recites a poem about his love which they read as divulging the extent of his passion and madness. The audience members apprehend the man suffers from lovesickness, and attempt to calm him. The men state that not every love union is permitted, attempting to assuage his grief. The man is still caught in the snares of love, is drowning in tears. He offers them another poem, even more powerful than the last, describing the beauty of his beloved. However, his passion reaches an even more fevered pitch and he composes a letter of investiture (*taqlīd*) which humorously emphasizes the power that the beloved has obtained over him. He then offers a poem of praise for the beloved, which again delights the audience, and he exits the scene.

Notes on the Edition

The edition is based on MS Istanbul Aya Sofya 3843 (أ) and MS Paris Arabe 3947 (ب), with the first as the *aṣl* providing the preferred readings. Since the aim of this scholarly edition is not to produce a critical text, we opted to omit minor variants between these two manuscripts. When the Paris manuscript offers a preferred reading or a plausible alternative reading, we indicate this in the footnotes. Thus, we preferred not to include variants such as missing hamzas, obvious mistakes, lacunae, wrong diacritic marks, masculine and feminine agreements, or reversed phrases. The manuscript includes ancillary signs

5 al-Talla'farī, *Dīwān*, where the *maqāma* appears as an appendix.

6 Pomerantz, A *maqāma* on same-sex marriage in the thirteenth century. For this work, see *GAL* i, 300.

indicating the parallelism in rhyme, which we tried to duplicate. Some signs were consistently added to the Arabic text, such as the doubling sign over a consonant (*tashdīd*). The *tashdīd* was omitted, however, in liaison for the definite article in case of "sun letters." The sign of nunation (*tanwīn*) was added regularly in the accusative and, when helpful, in the genitive and nominative. Meters have been added in square brackets, preceding the verses of poetry in the Arabic text. The beginning of each page of MS Aya Sofya is given in square brackets in the text. The footnotes include some minor explanations and refer to the *Dīwān* of al-Shābb al-Ẓarīf.

المقامة الأولى وتُعرف بفصاحة المشوق في ملاحة المعشوق

أنشأ الأستاذ الرئيس البارع البليغ الأوحد شمس الدين أبو عبد الله محمّد بن الشيخ المحقّق العارف عفيف الدين التلمسانيّ رحمه الله قال رحمه الله تعالى:[7]

حكى بعض رواة الأخبار * ومن يوثق به في الإخبار * قال كنت أنهض فأهزّ عطف الزهو[8] والفرح * وأركض فألزّ[9] طِرف اللهو والمرح * إن عطا مهفهف تغزّلت * وإن سطا مثقّف تعزّلت * أكون طورًا لكواكب المسرّات[10] شرقًا * وتارةً لسحائب[11] المبرّات برقًا * لا أفْرَقُ من الخطب لباس * ولا أبرز من الهمّ في لباس * فكنت مع فتية يطلعون من شمس الكؤوس[12] شُعاعًا * ويجمعون من شمل النفوس شعاعًا * وساق ينظم سلك السرور في اتّساق:[13] [من المجتثّ]

7 أ: أنشأ الأستاذ الرئيس البارع البليغ الأوحد شمس الدين أبو عبد الله محمّد بن الشيخ المحقّق العارف عفيف الدين التلمسانيّ رحمه الله قال رحمه الله تعالى، ب: بسم الله الرحمن الرحيم صلّى الله على سيّدنا محمّد وآله وسلّم قال الصدر الإمام الأوحد الفاضل شمس الدين أبو عبد الله محمّد بن الشيخ الإمام الأوحد عفيف الدين سليمان التلمسانيّ رحمهما الله تعالى.

8 أ: الزهو، ب: الزهر.

9 ألزّ الشيء شدّه وألصقه (اللسان).

10 أ: المسرّات، ب: المسيرت.

11 أ: لسحائب، ب: كسحائب.

12 أ: الكؤوس، ب: الكؤش.

13 ديوان الشابّ الظريف، حقّقه وأعدّ تكملته وفسّر ألفاظه شاكر هادي شكر، النجف: مطبعة النجف، 1967، 149.

يُنوِّلُ الطَرْفَ كَيسا　　إنْ ناولَ الكفَّ كَاسا
وإنْ تقـدّمَ حيًّـا　　وإنْ تحـدّثَ كاسـا

ونحن في نعيم مقيم ونديم[14] اللذّات يديم:[15] [من الخفيف]

إنْ شَكَوْنا لَهُ ظَمانا[16] وَجَدْنا　　مِنهُ للريِّ بالحديثِ ظَمانا[17]
ما سَبَانا لينُ المَعاطِـفِ مِنْـهُ　　إذْ[18] تَثَنّى إلّا وقَدْ مَاسَ بَانَا

ونغمة تنطق بها الأوتار * ونعمة تحقّق بها الأوطار * والخمر تفتق لنا عرفًا[19] ينقل عبؤه[20] * والسكر يرفق بنا لطفًا فلا يثقل عِبؤه[21] * في ليلة ما غاب لها بدر * ولا كتم أتراب[22] أنجمها خدر * فتقدّم[23] من الجماعة نديم* قد رقّ[24] في الخلاعة أديم * وقال يا معشر الندماء * ومشرع[25] الكرماء * إنّ أحقّ بالمناظرة النسيب * وأدقّ[26] في المحاضرة النسيب * وإن كان الشعر قد قلّ حافظه * ومُلّ لافظه * بعد أن كان نشره ضائعًا إذ ينشد * فأصبح ذكره ضائعًا لا ينشد * لكنّه روح ينشئ من رمق الكلام جسمًا * ويُوحُ توشّى في أفق الظلام وسمًا * فمن نزلت الكأس بساحة راحته * فليجعل قراها سماحة

14 ب: ونديم، أ: بنديم.

15 أ: ونحن في نعيم مقيم بنديم اللذّات يديم، ب: ونديم اللذّات يديم ونحن في نعيم مقيم.

16 أ: ظمانا، ب: ظماءً.

17 أ: ظمانا، ب: صمانا.

18 أ: إذ، ب: مذ.

19 سقطت من ب: تفتق لنا عرفًا.

20 أ: ينقل عبؤه، ب: نقل عباه.

21 أ: يثقل عِبؤه، ب: نقل عباه.

22 أ: كتم أتراب، ب: ثم أشراب.

23 أ: فتقدم، ب: فقدم.

24 أ: رق، ب: رق منه.

25 أ: ومشرع، ب: ومعشر.

26 أ: وأدق، ب: وأرق.

فصاحته * فأضرمنا نار الفكر فاتّقدت * [170أ] وأيقظنا أعين القرائح فما رقدت * فبينا نحن نقسم النظم[27] نصفين * ونجعل للساقي والخمر وصفين[28] * إذ قدم علينا رجل * سريع الخطو عجل * مروّع الخطب وجل * يظهر عليه للوله إشارات * وللخبل أمارات * فلمّا خوطب صدّ * ولمّا قُدّم إليه[29] الكأس ردّ * ثمّ أنشد:[30] [من البسيط]

إليكُمُ خَمْرَكُم عنّي مَع الوَتَرِ — ليسَ المُدامةُ والألحانُ مِنْ وَطَرِي
فما تُقِرُّ سرورًا عِنْدَ ذي حَزَنٍ — ولا تُسِرُّ فؤادًا[31] عندَ ذي فكَرِ
لو أنّ بالأفقِ ما لاقيتُ مِنْ حُرَقٍ — إذًا لفرّقَ شَمْلَ الأنجُمِ الزُّهَرِ
إنْ رُمتموني نديمًا فارفعوا كَمَدي — واستنجِدوا جَلدي واستوقِفوا سَهَري[32]
لا أستلذُّ كُؤوسَ الخمرِ دائرةً — إلّا إذا كان كأسُ الحبِّ لم يدُرِ

قال:[33] فعلمنا أنّ كؤوس المحبّة أترعت له فعبّها * وأنّ خدع الأماني في نيل الوصل أبدت عليه غِبّها * فأخذنا في تسكين روعه * وتهوين جنسه عليه ونوعه * وسألناه عن حاله فأرشد * إلى[34] ما أوضح شرح حال غرامه وأنشد:[35] [من الطويل]

أرى نارَ وَجْدي أطفأَتني ولا تُطفى — وسرَّ غَرامي قد خَفَيْتُ ولا يَخْفى
كأنَّ الصَّبا أهدَتْإليَّ تحيّةً — تُعرِّفُها نَشْرًا وتَنْشُرُها عَرْفا

27 ب: نقسم النظم، أ: نقسم.

28 أ: ونجعل للساقي والخمر وصفين، ب: ونجعله للخمر وساقي وصفين.

29 أ: قدم إليه، ب: قدمت له.

30 سقطت من ب: ثمّ أنشد.

31 أ: فؤادًا، ب: قرار.

32 أ: سهري، ب: سحري.

33 سقطت من ب: قال.

34 سقطت من ب: إلى.

35 الأبيات الثلاثة الأولى في ديوان الشابّ الظريف 179.

وَبيـنَ بيُـوتِ النازليـنَ عَلـى الحِمـى غزالٌ أبى أنْ يعرفَ الوَصْلَ والعَطْفا
وقـلّ وفـاءٌ يرتجيـهِ متيّـمٌ بمختلـفٍ خلقًـا ومختلـقٍ خلفـا

فقلنا له إنّ كنه الأماني لا يقرب أمنها فيُوق[36] من سحرها * وإنّ لجج المطامع يصعب سقيها فترق[37] عن بحرها * فما كلّ وصلٍ[38] حلال * ولا كلّ صدٍّ دلال * فعرق حتّى غرق * ورشف الدمع حتّى شرق * وأنشد:[39] [من الطويل]

أسيرُ لحاظٍ كيفَ يَنجو مِنَ الأَسْرِ وعاشـقُ ثَغـرٍ كيـفَ يَصحـو مِـنَ السُّكْـرِ
ولا سِيَّما صَبٌّ يـذوبُ صَبابـةً[40] بما جلَّ عَنْ حَصْرٍ وما دَقَّ مِنْ خَصْرِ [170ب]
يهـدُّه الواشـي فيبكـي صبابـةً فيفـرَقُ مِـنْ نَهْـرٍ ويغـرَقُ فـي نَهْـرِ
تعلّـقَ في أُفـقِ الملاحـةِ كوكبًـا تألّـقَ دريًّـا وضاحـكَ عَـنْ دُرِّ
ففي كلِّ جوٍّ مِنْهُ وَقْعٌ مِنَ الهوى وفـي كـلِّ قُطْـرٍ منْـهُ وَقْـعٌ[41] مِـنَ القَطـرِ

ثمّ قال: لقد نطقتم نصحًا * ولفظتم فصحًا[42] * فلو كان الحبّ[43] نصفين * والحكم لاثنين * لجاملت الودّ بالودّ * وعاملت الضدّ[44] بالصَدّ * ولكنّ الهوى أغلب * والجوى أسلب * والقلق أطول * والفرق

36 أ: فيوق، ب: فتوق.

37 أ: فترق، ب: فتوق.

38 أ: وصل، ب: وصال.

39 ديوان الشابّ الظريف 138-139.

40 أ: صَبابةً، ب: من الهوى.

41 أ: وقع، ب: نقع.

42 أ: نطقتم نصحًا ولفظتم فصحًا، ب: نهضتم نصحًا ونطقتم فصحًا.

43 أ: الحبّ، ب: الجواب.

44 أ: الضد، ب: الصد.

أجول * والكمد أمدّ[45] * والسُّهد أشدّ[46] * والحبّ لا يحسن منعه * ولا يخشن[47] صنعه * قوله قاضٍ * وسيفه ماضٍ * سرت ببدره وصُبحه * وصبرت لخسره وربحه * فالجسدُ يخلّ وينحل * والجلدُ يضمحلّ ويرحل * والدمع يعيث * والصبر لا يغيث * والجسم يتعب * والصبر[48] ينعب * واللحظ أسير * والحظّ يسير * والجرح جُبار * والبَرح جبّار * وشرح الشجون يطول * ورشح العيون يهول[49] * والسقام يغير بركب من بني الأصفر * فلا يرجع من الجسم إلّا بالحظّ الأوفر * فقلنا لله درّك[50] ما أحسن وصفك وصفتك[51] * وألذّ عرفك ومعرفتك * ملكت اللبّ وأنت اللبيب * وذكرت الحبّ فمن الحبيب * فأنشد:[52] [من الرجز]

مِثْـلُ الغَـزالِ نَظْـرَةً ولَفْتَـةً　　مَـنْ ذا رآهُ نظـرةً ولا افتتَـنْ
أعـذَبُ خَلْـقِ اللهِ ثغراً وفمًا　　إنْ لَمْ يَكُنْ أحَقَّ بالحُسْنِ[53] فَمَـنْ
قَدْ سَنَّ في شَرْعِ الهَوى تسهُّدي　　وأحرَمَ الأجفانَ والعينَ الوسَنْ[54]
عـذارُهُ وخـدُّهُ وريقُـهُ[55]　　الماءُ والخُضْرَةُ والوجهُ الحَسَـنْ

وأنا تارةً أظهر[56] الرفعة والعلوّ * والرجعة عن الحبّ والسلوّ * فآونةً ألبس للصبر حلّة * وأنشد تعلّة: [من الخفيف]

---

45 أ: أمدّ، ب: أمرّ.

46 أ: أشدّ، ب: أسرّ.

47 في أ وب: يحسن، تصحيف.

48 أ: والصبر، ب: والجسم.

49 أ: يهول، ب: حمول.

50 سقطت من أ: درّك.

51 سقطت من ب: وصفتك.

52 البيتان الأوّلان والرابع في ديوان الشابّ الظريف 280 باختلاف.

53 أ: بالحسن، ب: بالحب.

54 سقط البيت من ب.

55 أ: عذاره وخده وريقه، ب: في جسمه وصدغه وشكله.

56 أ: وأنا تارةً أظهر، ب: وتارة أبدي.

وإذا ما الحبيبُ حَقَّقَ ما يَنْ سُبُ للظبي[57] من صفاتِ النفورِ
فاعذِرَنْه واصبرْ عليه فلا بُدَّ د لصبـر المحـبّ مـن تأثيـر

ثمّ قال إنّه في الملاحة أمير قلبها * ومالك خِلبها: [171أ] [من السريع]

ظبيٌ له في كلِّ قلبٍ هوًى قدْ حَكَمَ اللهُ بتَخْليدِهِ
قلّدَهُ الحُسن الذي يَشْتَهي وهذه نُسخةُ تقْليدِهِ[58]

﴿هَذَا عَطَاؤُنَا فَامْنُنْ أَوْ أَمْسِكْ بِغَيْرِ حِسَابٍ﴾[59]

الحمدُ لله الذي شرّفَ مراتب الحُسن وعرّفها* وزيّن جنانه وزخرفها* وأقام لواءه* وأدام ولاءه* وجعل ذكره غير ذي دثور * ورسمه غير دَثور * وصيّر النفوس متملّكةً لشيطانها[60] * وجعل القلوب متمسّكةً بأشطانها * نحمده حمدًا مقترنًا بأكمل شكر * مقتربًا بأجمل ذكر * ونشهد أن لا إله إلّا الله وحده لا شريك له شهادة نرجو بها لدولتنا بقاءً * وللظفر بأملنا لقاءً * وصلّى الله على سيّدنا محمّد المبعوث لأكرم أمّة * المنعوت بأعظم همّة * صلّى الله عليه ما لطفت نسيم لناشقها * وحلت[61] صفات حبيب في عين عاشقها * وعلى آله وصحبه غيوث الجود وسحبه * ما أنار من وجه المحبوب[62] قمر أرضيّ سمائيّ * ودار في[63] طرف المحبّ فلك هوائيّ مائيّ * وبعد: فلمّا منحنا الله فيما له ظهرنا[64] * وأصلحنا فيما فيه[65] أشرنا * وجب علينا إتحاف من بذل في نصحنا اجتهادًا * وإسعاف من أحسن في مواقفنا وجهادنا

57 أ: للظبي، ب: بلظى.

58 ويليه في أ زائدة: المقامة الثانية وتُعرف بالإقطاعيّة، انظر مقدّمة التحقيق.

59 سورة ص: 39.

60 أ: لشيطانها، ب: لسلطانها.

61 أ: وحلت، ب: وحليت.

62 أ: المحبوب، ب: الحبيب.

63 أ: في، ب: من.

64 أ: فيما له ظهرنا، ب: ما ذكرنا.

65 أ: فيه، ب: إليه.

مواقفًا[66] وجهادًا * ولمّا كان مجلس أمير الملاحة ذي الأسيلين الصقيلين * والكحيلين الكليلين[67] * فلان الدين نصر الله رايات ذوائبه وظفرها * ووفى لها حقوق النصر[68] بالسواد الأعظم ووفرها * ممّن حسن سافرًا ونافرًا * ومفاصلًا ومواصلًا * وأخلص لنا نيّته * وأسس على محافظتنا بنيته * وحمدت[69] حظوته * وشهدت في عاشقيه سطوته * في معرك لا يُصطلى فيه للخدود بنار * ولا يؤخذ فيه لقتيل القدود بثار * طبعت سيوف أجفانه من رقاد * ورشقن سهامًا لسن[70] هُمومًا ولا[71] يخطرن إلّا في فؤاد * فتقت لأصداغه ريح الجلّاد بعَنْبر * وأمدّه من محيّاه بفلق الصباح المسفر * [171ب] وجنى من القلوب ثمر الوقائع بالنصر يانعًا * وتحكّم في النفوس فلم يلقَ مانعًا * برز مرسومنا الكريم أنفذه الله تعالى أن يُفاض عليه الإنعام * ويُضاف إليه من القلوب الإحكام[72] * وأن يطلق لخاصّه * وأتباعه وخواصّه * ما يقوّي جيش الغرام[73] * ويعين[74] مرامي اللحظ على المرام * فلخاصّه القُليب ولشعره[75] المحلول من السواد * ولأعينه السويداء ولثغره قرية يبرواد[76] * ولجبينه جميع الهلالي من الوضّاحية * وللكنية طيبة الاسم ولواشيه المعرّة * ولعاشقيه نوًى مُضافًا إلى ما لشفتيه من الرقّة * ولوجنتيه من ضارج وذلك لأوّل سنة تكامَلَ حسنه من فعل السنة الشمسيّة * غير منازع فيما نوّلناه * ومُشارك فيما

66 أ: مواقفا، ب: موافقا.

67 سقطت من ب: الكليلين.

68 أ: حقوق النصر، ب: جفون الظفر.

69 أ: وحمدت، ب: وعدّت في المحبّين.

70 أ: لسن، ب: لبّسن.

71 أ: ولا، ب: فلا.

72 أ: أن يُفاض عليه الإنعام ويُضاف إليه من القلوب الإحكام، ب: أن تسبغ النعماء وتفاض عليه وأن يناط به الحكم على أمراء البلاغة ويفاض عليه.

73 أ: الغرام، ب: البلاغة على الدوام.

74 ب: ويعين، أ: معين.

75 أ: فلخاصه القليب ولشعره، ب: فللخاصة القليب ولشعره.

76 أ: بيرواد، ب: بيرود.

خوّلناه * فليوضح لمعاطفه[77] أنّنا أطلقنا هذا الخبز خاصًّا لدقيقها * وليفصح[78] لمراشفه أنّا جعلنا أحرار الهوى ملكًا لرقيقها * وليتلقَّ ذلك برضًا تُعشب به أرض ضارج من خدّه * وقبول يَسْري ببيارقه[79] ركب الهيف من سروات قدّه * ويهزّ عطفه * ويُبدي لطفه[80] * كتب برسالة الصدغ الأجلّ بهاء[81] الحسن خضر الزرّادي * والاعتماد على خطّ العارض البادي[82] *

قال فملك بجوهر لفظه إذ عرضه * جوهر كلّ فتى من القوم وعَرَضَه * وشغلنا بتقليد[83] أميره * عن تقييد أموره * وقلنا له[84] من الذي ألقت البلاغة إليه المقاليد * حتّى رتّب هذا التقليد * فقال عبدٌ[85] جعله ابن الأثير[86] سيّدًا[87] * ومعدوم معدم[88] أوجده وأمدّه فصار لمباني العليا مشيّدًا * الذي انتسب[89] إلى التاج * واقتدى بمعاني المنهاج * قلنا فبما مدح من حيّاه[90] * وأظهر في لمح[91] الملاحة

77 ب: فليوضح لمعاطفه، أ: فليوضح.

78 أ: ليفصح، ب: يفصح.

79 ب: بارقه.

80 ويليه في ب زائدة: غير مشارك فيما نولناه ومنازع فيما خولناه.

81 أ: بهاء، ولعلّ الصواب ما أثبتناه.

82 أ: البادي، ب: البادي والسلام.

83 ب: بتقليد، أ: بتقيّد.

84 أ: وقلنا له، ب: وقلنا.

85 أ: عبد، ب: عبد الله.

86 لعلّه ابن الأثير الحلبي أبو الفداء إسماعيل بن أحمد الفقيه المؤرّخ (ت 699 هـ)، انظر ديوان الشابّ الظريف 233.

87 ويليه في ب زائدة: وأيده حتى صار المعالي العليا مشيدًا.

88 سقطت من ب: معدم.

89 أ: انتسب، ب: الشب.

90 أ: حيّاه، ب: حباه.

91 أ: لمح، ب: ملح.

محيّاه * فلولا أحمد بن سعيد[92] * لم تنظر الفصاحة إلّا[93] من بعيد * ثمّ قال للمكارم شارحًا[94] * وقام كالحمائم صادحًا وأنشد:[95] [من الطويل]

بلا غيبـةٍ للبـدرِ وجهُـكَ أجمـلُ   وما أنـا فيمـا قُلْتُـه مُتَجمّـلُ
ولا عَيْبَ عِنْدي فيكَ لَوْلا صيانةٌ[96]   لديـكَ بهـا كُـلُّ امرِئٍ يتبـذّلُ
وحُبُكَ حتّى لَوْ عَنِ الحُجْبِ نَلْتَقي   حِجابًا وما تَبدو[97] لها كنتَ تَفْعَلُ [172أ]
لِحاظُكَ أَسْيافٌ ذكورٌ فما لها   كَما زَعَموا مِثْلَ الأَرامِلِ تَغْزِلُ
وما بالُ بُرْهانِ العِذارِ مُسَلَّمًا   ويَلْزَمُه دورٌ وفيه تَسَلْسُلُ
وعَهْدي أنّ الشمسَ بالصَّحْوِ أذِنَتْ   فما بالُ سُكْري مِن مُحَيّاكَ يُقْبِلُ[98]
كأنَّكَ لَمْ تُخْلَقْ لغيرِ نواظرٍ   تُسَهِّدُها وَجْدًا وقَلْبٍ[99] تُعَلِّلُ
لدَيْكَ قلوبُ العاشقينَ وإنْ تَجُرْ   عَلَيْها إلى سُلْوانِها ليسَ تَعْدِلُ
حبيبي لِيَهْنَ الحُسْنُ أنَّكَ حُزْتَهُ   ويَهْنَ فُؤادي أنّهُ لكَ مَنْزِلُ
ويَهْنَ امتداحي ابنَ الأثيرِ فإنّهُ   يشرّفُهُ ممدوحُهُ ويُجمِّلُ
وبُشْرى لآمالي الصَّوادي فإنَّها   لَدَيْهِ مِنَ النُّعمى تُعَلُّ وتُنْهَلُ
فتى لم يَفُتْهُ في المكارِمِ منزلٌ   ولا شذَّ في وِرْدِ العُلى عَنْهُ مَنْهَلُ
ولا رامَ من في[100] جُودِهِ مُتطاوِلٌ   ولا حازَ أدْنى مجدِهِ مُتطوِّلُ

92 لعلّه الشاعر أبو جعفر أحمد بن عبد الملك بن سعيد بن خلف بن سعيد، ولد في قلعة بني سعيد بالقرب من غرناطة ونشأ فيها وانتقل إلى غرناطة، كان محبًّا للأدب والشعر وله حظّ بارع في كتابة الأدب ونظم الشعر، كان شاعرًا ووزيرًا عند الخليفة عبد المؤمن، ت 559 هـ.

93 أ: إلا، ب: ولا.

94 أ: للمكارم شارحًا، ب: للملاحة مادحًا.

95 الأبيات التسعة الأولى في ديوان الشابّ الظريف 199-200.

96 ب: صيانة، أ: صبابة.

97 ب: تبدو، أ: يبدو.

98 أ: يقبل، ب: مقبل.

99 أ: وقلب، ب: وقلبا.

100 أ: من في، ب: من ما، ولعلّ الصواب: مرمى.

ولا شَكَّ في إحسانِهِ متأوِّلٌ — ولا ارتابَ في حُسنٍ لهُ مُتأمِّلُ

أيادٍ يَراعُ الجَودُ مِن فَيْضِ نَيْلِها — وأيدٍ يَراعُ الجُودِ عَنْهُنَّ يَنْقُلُ

يُنَوِّلُ جانٍ ثَمْرَهُنَّ فيَجْتَني — ويُهمِلُ جانٍ عندَهُنَّ وتهمِلُ[101]

لهُ درُّ ألفاظٍ ودَرُّ مواهبٍ — يُحدِّثُ عنها الفاضِلُ المُتَفَضِّلُ

أقَمْتُ زَمانًا ليس[102] أنظِمُ مدحَةً — ولا ليَ هَمٌّ أنَّني أتغَزَّلُ

وما الناسُ إلّا اثنانِ[103] عاشٍ وعاشقٍ — مَعَ اثنَيْنِ ذا يَجْني وذلك يقبلُ[104]

فلمّا تراءى بارقُ الجُودِ وانتشَتْ — سحائبُ إنْعامٍ بها الغيثُ مُسبِلُ

تعرَّضتُ بالمدحِ الذي أنا عالِمٌ — بتَصْريفِه إذْ كانَ في الناسِ يُجْهَلُ

فصُنْتُ قَريضي[105] عَنْ سِواكَ فَبَحْرُهُ — لبَحرِ نَداكَ اليومَ يا حِبرُ[106] مُبْذَلُ

قال فمالَ القوم طربًا * وقضوا من شكر المادح والممدوح أربًا * ثمّ نهض الفتى ووثب * ولم ندرِ كيف ذهب * ونظرنا فإذا الجوّ قد لطم خدّ الليل بكفّ صبحه * وكسرَ جناح [172ب] النسر الطائر في جنحه * ونشقنا أرواح الصبح الوضّاح * فرفعنا ما اجتمعنا بسببه خشية الافتضاح * وهذا أعجب ما رأيت ووعيت * وأغرب ما وعيت وأوعيت.[107]

101 أ: ينوِّلُ... ويهمل ... وتهمل، ب: تنول ... وتمهل ... ويهمل.

102 أ: ليس، ب: لست.

103 أ: إلّا اثنانِ، ب: غير اثنين.

104 أ: وذلك يقبلُ، ب: وذا يتقبل.

105 أ: قريضي، ب: قديحي، وهو تصحيف.

106 أ: حبر، ب: خير.

107 أ: وأوعيت، ب: ورعيت، تمّت المقامة بحمد الله وعونه وحسن توفيق وصونه.

Appendix

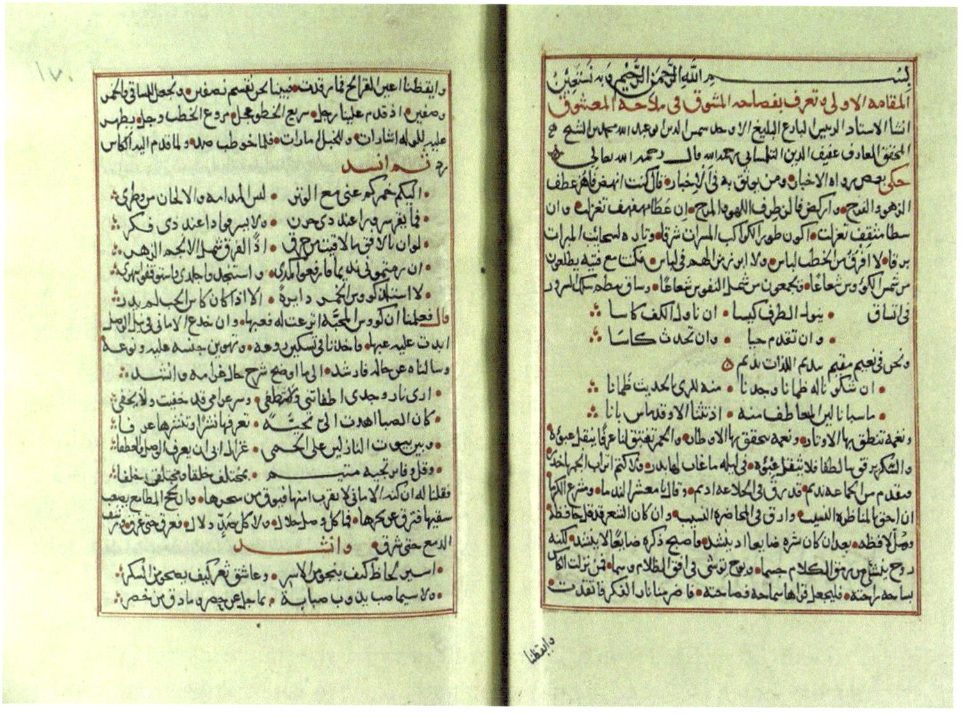

FIGURE 1 MS AYA SOFYA 3843, 169b–170a

Bibliography

Bauer, T., Mamluk literature: Misunderstandings and new approaches, in *MSR* 9 (2005), 105–30.

Kâtip Çelebi, *Kitāb Kashf al-ẓunūn ʿan asāmī al-kutub wa-l-funūn*, Beirut 1990.

Pomerantz, M., A *maqāma* on same-sex marriage in the thirteenth century, in *Intellectual History of the Islamicate World* (2021), 1–27.

al-Ṣafadī, Khalīl b. Aybak, *Al-Wāfī bil-wafayāt*, ed. H. Ritter et al., 30 vols., Wiesbaden 1962–2013.

al-Shābb al-Ẓarīf, *Dīwān al-Shābb al-Ẓarīf*, ed. Sh.H. Shukr, Najaf 1967.

al-Tallaʿfarī, *Dīwān al-Tallaʿfarī*, Beirut 1310[/1892–3].

4

Die Kunst der *zaǧal*-Dichtung von Ibn Muqātil am Beispiel seines *qalbī yuḥibb tayyāh*

Hakan Özkan

Thomas Bauer habe ich zum Anlass der Edition des Diwans des großen Handwerkerdichters aus der Mamlukenzeit Ibrāhīm al-Miʿmār (gest. 749/1348–9) im Jahr 2007 in Berlin kennengelernt.[1] Ich hatte mich damals um die Mitarbeit an eben jener Edition beworben, als der Jubilar am Wissenschaftskolleg den Grundstein für eines seiner wichtigsten Werke der letzten Jahrzehnte legte: *Die Kultur der Ambiguität*. Wichtige Dinge bespricht Bauer nicht selten am Mittagstisch; das war mir nicht bewusst, so war ich einigermaßen erstaunt, als ich beim Spaziergang nach dem Mittagessen fast schon beiläufig erfuhr, dass das Bewerbungsgespräch erfolgreich verlaufen ist, und ich noch im gleichen Jahr mit der Arbeit an der Edition beginnen könnte.

Ein Gedichttyp, für den al-Miʿmār berühmt war, hat es mir seit jener Zeit angetan: das *zaǧal*. Das *zaǧal* ist ein Strophengedicht in einem stilisierten, vereinfachten Dialekt, welches ursprünglich aus al-Andalus stammt und sich auch im Osten des arabischsprachigen Raums großer Beliebtheit erfreute. Als ich dann sieben Jahre später vor der Frage stand, welches Thema ich für meine Habilitationsschrift auswählen soll, habe ich nicht lange gezögert. Das östliche *zaǧal* sollte es sein. Es war eine Bauchentscheidung, doch je mehr ich mich damit beschäftigte, desto mehr wurde mir bewusst, was ich mir da eingehandelt habe. Die Schwierigkeiten, die sich aus schlechter Quellenlage, fehlenden Informationen zu dieser Gedichtform und v.a. ihrer Lexik ergeben, haben mich vor ungeahnte Schwierigkeiten gestellt. In der *Geschichte des östlichen zaǧal* habe ich einige dieser Probleme gelöst, andere waren nicht so leicht aufzuklären.[2] Die Korpusanalyse, in der ich die bedeutendsten Dichter und ihre Gedichte herausarbeite, gehört zu den besser aufgeklärten Aspekten der Geschichte des *zaǧal*. Bei einem dieser berühmten Dichter handelt es sich um den Syrer Ibn

1 Bauer, Osigus, Özkan, *Dīwān al-Miʿmār*. Vor dem Erscheinen des Diwans hat Bauer mehrmals über al-Miʿmār und seine Dichtung publiziert: Bauer, Handwerker, Leiden, und Nilzaǧal.

2 Özkan, *Geschichte*.

 | DOI:10.1163/9789004521780_006

Muqātil (664 oder 674–761/1266 oder 1276–1359). Ähnlich wie der große *zağal*-Meister aus al-Andalus, Ibn Quzmān (gest. 555/1160), versuchte sich Ibn Muqātil zuerst an hochsprachlichen Gedichten, bis er sich dem Abfassen von *zağals* verschrieb. Ebenso wie Ibn Quzmān brachte er es in dieser Disziplin zu großem Ruhm, sowohl in den Augen von *zağal*-Spezialisten als auch von gelehrten Dichtern und sogar dem *zağal*-dichtenden Mamlukensultan al-Malik an-Nāṣir Muḥammad b. Qalāwūn (reg. 693–4/1293–4, 698–708/1299–1309, 709–41/1310–41). In einschlägigen Anthologien und *zağal*-Poetiken sticht Ibn Muqātil regelmäßig an prominenter Stelle hervor. Zu seinen *zağals* wurden zahlreiche Kontrafakturen (*muʿāraḍāt*) verfasst – weitaus die meisten überhaupt. Am Beispiel eines seiner berühmtesten Gedichte *qalbī yuḥibb tayyāh* („Mein Herz liebt einen Eitlen") will ich in diesem Beitrag untersuchen, welche ästhetischen und stilistischen Kriterien bei der Wertschätzung seiner *zağals* eine Rolle gespielt haben könnten und kurz besprechen, wie sich die Kontrafakturen im Verhältnis zu Ibn Muqātils Vorlage ausnehmen.

Ibn Muqātil (664 oder 674–761/1266 oder 1276–1359) – Leben und Werk

Mit vollem Namen heißt der Dichter ʿAlī (oder ʿAlāʾ ad-Dīn) Ibn Muqātil b. ʿAbd al-Ḫāliq al-Ḥamawī at-Tāǧir („der Kaufmann"). Über sein frühes Leben ist kaum etwas bekannt. Nach Ibn Ḥağar al-ʿAsqalānīs (773–852/1372–1449) *ad-Durar al-kāmina* wurde er in Ḥamāh geboren, daher seine Nisbe al-Ḥamawī; eine zweite Nisbe, ad-Dimašqī, deutet darauf hin, dass seine Familie aus Damaskus stammt oder dass er dort lebte. In Anerkennung seiner Meisterschaft im *zağal*-Dichten stellt der Polyhistor aṣ-Ṣafadī (696–764/1297–1363) fest, dass Ibn Muqātil erst relativ spät in seinem Leben berühmt wurde. Wahrscheinlich war es in dieser Zeit, dass er Zugang zum Hof des ayyubidischen Herrschers von Ḥamāh, ʿImād ad-Dīn Abū l-Fidāʾ al-Malik al-Muʾayyad (672–732/1273–1331), erhielt.[3] Aṣ-Ṣafadī, welcher auch *zağals* verfasste, traf Ibn Muqātil mehrmals sowohl in Damaskus als auch in Ḥamāh. Ibn Muqātil soll ihm einige seiner *zağals* und andere Gedichte vorgetragen haben. Bei einem dieser Treffen in Damaskus präsentierte ihm aṣ-Ṣafadī wiederum seine *muʿāraḍa* zu dem in diesem Beitrag zu behandelnden *zağal*.[4] Nach Angaben mehrerer Biographen sammelte Ibn Muqātil seine *zağals* in einem eigens dieser Gedichtform gewidmeten Diwan, der aus zwei Bänden bestanden haben soll, welcher jedoch nicht überliefert ist.

3 Ibn Faḍlallāh al-ʿUmarī, *Ḏahabiyya* 177.

4 Aṣ-Ṣafadī, *Aʿyān* 3:556.

Nicht nur die Bedeutung Ibn Muqātils als eines berühmten *zaǧal*-Dichters seiner Zeit, sondern auch die Wichtigkeit dieser dichterischen Form auf der höchsten Ebene des Mamlukenreichs wird aus einem Vorfall ersichtlich, der sich in Syrien während der Herrschaft des Sultans al-Malik an-Nāṣir Muḥammad b. Qalāwūn ereignete: Zwei Städte, die für ihre Vorliebe für *zaǧals* besonders bekannt waren, Ḥamāh (vertreten durch Ibn Muqātil) und Damaskus (vertreten durch al-Amšāṭī, gest. 725/1325, den großen Rivalen von Ibn Muqātil), stritten sich über die Frage, wer von den beiden Dichtern das beste *zaǧal* verfasst hat. Al-Malik al-Nāṣir, der selbst ein leidenschaftlicher *zaǧal*-Dichter war, beschloss, den Streit zu schlichten, indem er eine Jury einberief, die aus drei berühmten Literaten der damaligen Zeit bestand: Ibn Nubāta (gest. 768/1366), Ibn Sayyid an-Nās (gest. 734/1334), und Abū Ḥayyān al-Ġarnāṭī (gest. 745/1345). Die Jury entschied zu Gunsten von Ibn Muqātil und seines hier zu besprechenden *zaǧals*.[5]

Das *zaǧal* – *qalbī yuḥibb tayyāh*

Die hier vorgestellte Edition des *zaǧals* von Ibn Muqātil beruht auf drei gedruckten und neun handschriftlichen Quellen. Als Grundversion dient die edierte Version des Gedichts im *ʿUqūd al-laʾāl* an-Nawāǧīs, welche die besten Varianten zu enthalten scheint. Varianten aus anderen Quellen werden bevorzugt, sofern sie sinnvoller und metrisch passender erscheinen. Der Text inklusive des kritischen Apparats findet sich im Anhang dieses Beitrags. Die Vokalisierung von *zaǧals* kann ein Problem darstellen, insbesondere wenn darin tatsächlich dialektale Formen vorkommen. In diesem Gedicht und vielen anderen Gedichten hält sich dieser Einfluss sehr in Grenzen. Doch selbst wenn eindeutig aus einem Dialekt stammende Ausdrücke vorkommen würden, wäre damit noch nicht gesagt, wie diese ausgesprochen bzw. vokalisiert wurden. Daher verwende ich grundsätzlich die hochsprachliche Vokalisierung. Der fehlende *iʿrāb* und die weiter unten zu besprechenden Hilfsvokale sind von dieser Regel natürlich ausgenommen.[6]

وقال أيضا والتزم الجناس المقلوب في جميع خرجاته

Und er sagte weiterhin, dabei erlegte er sich auf, in allen Gemeinreimversen den *ǧinās maqlūb* anzuwenden.

5 Ibn Ḥiǧǧa, *Bulūġ* 129.

6 Genaueres zur Schreibung, Vokalisierung und Aussprache von *zaǧals*, s. Özkan, *Geschichte* 305–9, sowie 408–12 und *passim*.

1. Strophe

قَلْبِي يِحِبّ تَيَّاهْ

Mein Herz liebt einen Eitlen,

لَيْسْ يَعْشَقِ ٱلَّا إِيَّاهْ

es liebt nur ihn.

فَازْ مَنْ وَقَفْ وَحَيَّاهْ

Es gewinnt, wer Halt macht und ihn grüßt,

يَرْصُدْ عَلَى مُحَيَّاهْ

auf seinem Antlitz beobachtet

بَدْرَ السَّمَا ويُطْبَعْ   مَنْ رَامْ وِصَالُو يَعْطَبْ

den Vollmond des Himmels und beeindruckt [zurückbleibt]. / Wer ihn begehrt, der geht zugrunde.

2. Strophe

صَغِيرْ نِحَيرْ فِي أَمْرُو

Ein Kleiner, der mich ratlos zurücklässt.

غَزَالْ قَهَرْ بِشَمْرُو

Eine Gazelle, die dich durch ihre Widerspenstigkeit überwältigt.

لَيْثِ الهَوَى وَنِمْرُو

Ein Löwe der Leidenschaft, ein Leopard.

فَاعْجَبْ لِصُغْرِ عُمْرُو

Und das in seinem zarten Alter!

رِيمِ ٱبْنِ عَشْرِ وَٱرْبَعْ   أَرْدَى الأُسُودْ وَأَرْعَبْ

Eine Antilope von 14 Jahren, / welche die Löwen hinstreckt und in Angst versetzt.

3. Strophe

أَذْكُرْ نَهَارْ تَبَعْتُو

Ich erinnere mich an den Tag, als ich ihm folgte

وَرُوحِي كُنْتُ بِعْتُو

und meine Seele an ihn verkaufte,

خَيَّبْ مَا فِيهْ طَمِعْتُو

enttäuschte er, was ich von ihm begehrte,

وَقَالْ وَقَدْ سَمِعْتُو

und ich hörte ihn tatsächlich sagen:

إِرْجَعْ وَلِي لَا تَتْبَعْ   نَخْشَى عَلَيْكْ لَا تَتْعَبْ

„Gehe zurück, folge mir nicht / [denn] ich fürchte, du mühst dich [umsonst] ab."

4. Strophe

كَمْ قُدَّامُو وَخَلْفُو

Wie oft bin ich vor und hinter ihm hin- und

مَشَيْتْ مُطِيعْ لِخُلْفُو

hergelaufen, beugte mich seiner Widerspenstigkeit

وَرَدْتُ لَثْمِ كَفُّو

und wollte [nur] seine Handfläche küssen.

قَالْ دَعْ مُنَاكْ وَكُفُّو

[Doch] er sagte: „Lass es sein mit dem Wünschen, hör auf!

فَإِنَّ لَثْمِ إِصْبَعْ   مِنَ الثُّرَيَّا أَصْعَبْ

Denn nur einen [meiner] Finger zu küssen ist schwerer / als die Plejaden zu erreichen."

5. Strophe

مَا زِلْتِ لُو نُدَارِي

[Doch] ich umwarb ihn weiter.

حَتَّى حَصَلْ فِي دَارِي

Bis er bei mir zu Hause landete.

نَادَيْتْ وَدَمْعِي جَارِي

Ich schrie [vor Freude] unter strömenden Tränen.

إِشْ لَوْ تَكُونْ يَا جَارِي

„Wie wäre es denn, mein Lieber,

تَدَعْنِي مِنْ فِيكَ ٱشْبَعْ　　قَالْ إِشْ يَكُونْ لَكَ ٱشْعَبْ

wenn du mich an deinen Lippen sattküssen ließest?“ / Er erwiderte: „Was ist schon Ašʿab[7] im Vergleich zu dir!“

6. Strophe

مَنْ حَازْ فِي حُسْنُو حَدُّو

Einer, der in der Schönheit das Äußerste erreicht hat.

لَحْظُو لِقَتْلِي حَدُّو

Sein Blick ist die Klinge, mit der er mich tötet.

وَوَرْدِ خَدُّو نَدُّو

Die Rose seiner Wange riecht wie Räucherwerk.

مَا فِي الرِّيَاضْ شِي نِدُّو

In den Gärten gibt es nichts, das ihr gleicht.

رَوْضْ بِالْحَيَا مُبَرْقَعْ　　عَلَيْهْ سِيَاجْ مُعَقْرَبْ

Ein Garten, der mit Schamhaftigkeit verschleiert ist / versehen mit verschlungenen Hecken.

7 Sprichwörtlich gewordener Name eines besonders habgierigen Mannes, vgl. Rosenthal, *Humor*.

7. Strophe

مَنْ فِي الجَمَالْ فَرِيدُو

Einer, dessen Schönheit einzigartig ist,

لِلصَّبّْ مِنْ وَرِيدُو

er schlachtet den leidenschaftlich Liebenden an der Halsschlagader

يَذْبَحْ وَهُوَ يُرِيدُو

mit dessen voller Zustimmung

وَكَمْ ذَا شَيْخْ مُرِيدُو

Manch ein alter Herr/*šayḫ* wurde zu seinem Schüler,

خَلَّاهْ دُمُوعُو يبَلَّعْ   وَهُوَ بِعَقْلُو يلَعَّبْ

er ließ ihn dessen Tränen schlucken / und spielte dabei mit dessen Verstand.

8. Strophe

كَمْ خَصْمٍ فِي المَقَاتِلْ

Manch einen Gegner an den tödlichen Körperstellen

صَابُو إِبْنْ مُقَاتِلْ

traf Ibn Muqātil.

وَكَمْ ذَا فِي المَحَافِلْ

Wie oft hat er auf Zusammenkünften

قَدْ أَنْشَا غُصْنٍ حَافِلْ

gefeierte Sonderreimverse hervorgebracht,

مِنْ كُلِّ بَيْتْ مُرَبَّعْ   مَلْحُونْ بِأَلْفِ مُعْرَبْ

in jeder Strophe vier an der Zahl / im *laḥn* und mit tausend flektierten Formen.

Typologie, Reim und Metrum

Es handelt sich bei diesem Gedicht um ein *zaǧal aqraʿ*, wörtlich übersetzt, ein „kahles *zaǧal*," d.h. ein *zaǧal* ohne Eingangsvers bzw. -verse (*maṭlaʿ*). Es enthält neun Strophen, die jeweils aus vier Sonderreimversen (*aġṣān*, Plur. von *ġuṣn* = wörtl. „Zweig") und einem Gemeinreimvers, *simṭ* (wörtl. „Schnur") bzw. *ḫarǧa* (wörtl. „Ausgang" bzw. freier übersetzt „Kehraus") bestehen. Sonderreimverse weisen innerhalb der jeweiligen Strophe das gleiche Reimschema auf, Gemeinreimverse teilen sich dasselbe Reimschema über das ganze Gedicht, in unserem Fall *-ab*. Viele *zaǧals* weisen Metren auf, die teilweise stark von den sechzehn kanonischen Metren abweichen. In diesem Fall ist das nicht so: hier haben wir es mit einem *raǧaz* zu tun, ein einfaches und eingängiges Metrum, das oft und gerne für *zaǧals* verwendet wurde, die kurze und rhythmisch akzentuierte Verse aufweisen.[8]

Aufbau, Themen und Erzählerisches

Das *zaǧal* beginnt mit dem Vers *qalbī yuḥibb tayyāh*, mit dem der Dichter das Hauptthema des Gedichts – die Liebe zu einem eitlen Jungen – setzt. Das Gedicht besteht aus drei thematisch-strukturellen Teilen. Den dritten Teil kann man thematisch und strukturell leicht abgrenzen. Es handelt sich um die letzte Strophe, in der sich der Dichter mit Namen vorstellt und seine dichterischen Fähigkeiten in der *zaǧal*-Dichtung preist. Dieser Teil setzt sich nicht nur durch seine Stellung am Ende des Gedichts ab, sondern auch durch seine Thematik. Die ersten beiden Teile sind strukturell nicht gänzlich voneinander zu trennen, zumindest nicht strophenweise bis einschließlich der fünften Strophe. Sie sind vielmehr miteinander verschränkt. Bei diesen Teilen handelt es sich einmal um die Narration des persönlichen Verhältnisses zwischen dem Dichter und dem Jungen und den allgemeinen Beschreibungen des Jungen. Diese Beschreibungen werden mehrmals mit Relativsätzen verbunden, die mit *man* („wer" bzw. „der") anfangen, so zum Beispiel in Strophe eins, Vers drei: *man waqaf wa-ḥayyāh*, oder zu Beginn der Strophen sechs (*man ḥāz fī ḥusnū ḥaddū*) und sieben (*man fī l-ǧamāl farīdū*).

Die Erzählung der Entwicklung des persönlichen Verhältnisses zwischen den beiden spielt sich vor allen Dingen in den Strophen eins bis einschließlich

8 *Zaǧals* besitzen einige Eigentümlichkeiten, was Vokallänge im Wortauslaut, Hilfsvokale und anderes betrifft. Bei Berücksichtigung dieser kommt man auf das Versmaß, hier *raǧaz*, vgl. hierzu Özkan, *Geschichte* 216 Fn. 7, 232, 242, 306–9.

fünf ab. Die erste Strophe ist zweigeteilt: einerseits stehen dort die einleitenden Verse mit der Liebeserklärung des Dichters, andererseits sehen wir die allgemeine Beschreibung der Schönheit und Anziehungskraft des Jungen in den letzten zwei Sonderreimversen und dem abschließenden Gemeinreimvers. Die Strophen drei bis fünf hingegen handeln vorrangig von den persönlichen Erfahrungen mit dem Jungen, die in dem Erfolg gipfeln, ihn erobert zu haben, bzw. wenigstens ihn bis zu sich nach Hause gelockt zu haben. Strophe zwei und die Strophen sechs und sieben sind wiederum vorrangig der Beschreibung des Jungen und seiner Wirkung auf das lyrische Ich und Männer, insbesondere ältere Männer, gewidmet.

Gehen wir zuerst auf den vorrangig narrativen Teil des Gedichts ab der zweiten Strophe ein. Diese Strophe ist zum größten Teil der Beschreibung des Jungen gewidmet. Wir sehen jedoch, dass hier der Blick und die Perspektive des Dichters präsenter ist (*ṣaġīr naḥīr fī amrū*). Der Geliebte sei noch ganz klein (*ṣaġīr*) bzw. jung. Er wird körperlich mit einer Gazelle verglichen, in der Liebesleidenschaft, die er auslöst, ist er aber ein Löwe und ein Leopard, selbst in jenem zarten Alter. Im letzten Vers hebt der Dichter dessen Alter (vierzehn Jahre) und Schönheit hervor, aber auch dessen Gefährlichkeit. In der nächsten Strophe wechselt die Szenerie – Strophen werden im *zaǧal* häufig als größere, abgegrenzte semantische bzw. narrative Einheiten verwendet: Der Dichter ruft sich einen Tag in Erinnerung, an dem er dem Jungen folgte. Seine Seele hatte er zu dem Zeitpunkt bereits unwiederbringlich an ihn verkauft. Doch wird sein Begehren enttäuscht. Der Geliebte lässt ihn abblitzen und mahnt ihn, nicht weiter hinter ihm herzulaufen. Die vierte Strophe knüpft an die vorherige an: Wie oft schon sei er hinter dem Geliebten hergelaufen, wie oft schon habe er sich seiner Koketterie ergeben, wie oft wollte er schon seine Handflächen küssen; doch auch dies lässt der sich zierende Junge nicht zu. Die fünfte Strophe stellt ebenfalls eine zeitlich nachgeschaltete Folge dar. Der Dichter lässt nicht locker, bis der Junge schließlich bei ihm zuhause landet. Die Freude darüber lässt den Dichter in Tränen ausbrechen. Sich sattküssen will er nun. Die letzte Antwort des Jungen auf dessen Begehren ist nun nicht mehr so kategorisch ablehnend: Mit dem Satz „Was ist schon Ašʿab im Vergleich zu dir!“ lässt er das Ganze nun etwas hoffnungsvoller für seinen Freier klingen, er solle nicht so gierig sein …

Da die Geschichte ihr Ende und einen wohl erfolgreichen Ausgang schon in der fünften Strophe gefunden hat – konkret lässt uns der Dichter das nicht wissen – verlegt er sich in den folgenden zwei Strophen sechs und sieben auf die Erhöhung der Qualitäten des Jungen. Dadurch wird auch die wahrscheinliche Eroberung desselben ungleich bemerkenswerter und wertvoller: Dessen Schönheit ist etwas ganz Besonderes und sein Blick tötet die Verliebten, ja sie ergeben sich freiwillig, um von dem Geliebten geschlachtet zu werden; sein Duft betört und übertrifft alles, was es an exquisiten Düften in den Gärten gibt. Insbesondere älteren Herren, bzw. den *šayḫs* (d.h. verehrten Lehrern bzw. Sufilehrern) hat er es angetan, in ihrer Verliebtheit lässt er sie so sehr weinen, dass sie ihre Tränen verschlucken. Schließlich müssen sie auch um ihren Verstand bangen.

In der letzten, selbstbezüglichen Strophe prahlt Ibn Muqātil mit seinen Fähigkeiten: So manchen Gegner habe er (im übertragenen Sinn natürlich) an todbringenden Stellen am Körper (*maqātil*, Sg. *maqtal*) getroffen.[9] In den nächsten Versen wird deutlich in welchem Bereich er seine Überlegenheit zeigt – im *zağal*-Dichten. Der Gemeinreimvers gibt schließlich an, wie die Strophen des Gedichts aufgebaut sind (*min kullə bayt murabbaʿ* = „jede vier (Sonderreim-)Verse enthaltende Strophe") und wie es sich mit der Sprache des Gedichts verhält – nämlich *malḥūn bi-alfə muʿrab* = „im *laḥn* verfasst mit tausend flektierten Formen" – eine für das *zağal* besonders geeignete Sprachform, nämlich die, in der man unflektierte mit flektierten Formen vermischt.

Stilistik

Ibn Muqātil ist ein Meister der Klangfiguren. Insbesondere Paronomasien haben es ihm angetan. Wie in seinem anderen berühmten und oft zitierten Gedicht *inna maʿ maʿšūqī ǧufūn wa-liḥāẓ* („Mein Geliebter hat [solche] Lider und Augenwinkel"), stellt die Paronomasie auch in diesem Gedicht das Hauptmerkmal dar. Dass es das Hauptmerkmal ist, erkennt man umgehend an der Überschrift, die dem Gedicht in den meisten Textzeugen vorangestellt ist (*wa-qāla ayḍan wa-ltazama l-ǧināsa l-maqlūba fī ǧamīʿi ḫarǧātih* = „und er sagte weiterhin, dabei erlegte er sich auf, in allen Gemeinreimversen den *ǧinās maqlūb* anzuwenden"). Es handelt sich hier nicht um eine homonymische Paronomasie (*ǧinās lafẓī*) wie in dem Gedicht *inna maʿ maʿšūqī ǧufūn*, sondern um eine metathetische.[10] Die Metathese betrifft jeweils zwei Buchstaben der Wörter, die jeweils am Ende der beiden Hälften der Gemeinreimverse stehen.

Außer der metathetischen Paronomasie wendet Ibn Muqātil in diesem *zağal* auch andere Arten von Paronomasien an, die jeweils am Ende der Verse zum Tragen kommen. Darunter zählen u.a. die konsonantische Paronomasie (*ǧinās*

9 Eine konsonantische Paronomasie, die sich hier wegen seines Namens Ibn Muqātil anbietet, s. folgenden Abschnitt zu Paronomasien.

10 Vgl. Cachia, *Skimmer* 26 (metathetic paronomasia).

muḥarraf), wo sich Wörter nur durch die Vokalzeichen unterscheiden wie zum Beispiel in Strophe vier, Vers eins und zwei: *ḫalfū/ḫulfū*; Strophe fünf, Vers drei und vier: *kaffū/kuffū*; Strophe sieben, Vers drei und vier: *naddū/niddū*;[11] Strophe acht, Vers eins und zwei: *maqātil/muqātil*.[12] Ein weiterer Typ von Paronomasie ist das *ǧinās mustawfī* oder in der Übersetzung von Cachia „incongruent paronomasia," nach der zwei graphisch und phonetisch gleiche Begriffe verschiedenen Wortarten zuzuordnen sind wie zum Beispiel *ǧārī* „fließend"/*ǧārī* „mein Nachbar" in Strophe fünf, Vers drei und vier.[13] Schließlich sei noch eine weitere von Ibn Muqātil gerne verwendete Paronomasie genannt: *ǧinās muṭarraf* bzw. *nāqiṣ* oder *murdaf* („tipped, prosthetic or prefixed paronomasia"). In diesem Fall ist eines der Wörter am Anfang länger als das andere. Diese Paronomasie findet sich u. a. in Strophe eins, Vers drei und vier: *ḥayyāh/muḥayyāh*; Strophe fünf, Vers eins und zwei: *nudārī/dārī*; Strophe acht, Vers drei und vier: *maḥāfil/ḥāfil*. Auch über die Paronomasien hinaus besticht dieses *zaǧal* durch seine klangliche Gestaltung. Insbesondere lässt sich das an den kurzen, jeweils aus sieben Silben bestehenden Versen festmachen, die durch die schnelle Abfolge von Endreimen einen bewegten Rhythmus erzeugen.

Ibn Muqātil scheint einzelne Strophen nicht nur wie oben dargestellt narrativ-strukturell als abgeschlossene Einheiten zu betrachten, sondern auch stilistisch bieten viele Strophen spezifische Merkmale auf, die in übrigen Strophen nicht zu sehen sind. So zum Beispiel in Strophe zwei, das vor den Buchstaben ر und غ nur so strotzt (Vers eins: *ṣaġīr naḥīr fī amrū*; Vers zwei: *ġazāl qahr bi-šamrū*; Vers drei: *layṭə l-hawā wa-nimrū*; Vers vier: *fa-ʿǧab li-ṣuġrə ʿumrū*; Vers fünf: *rīmə bnə ʿašrə wa-rbaʿ / ardā l-usūda wa-rʿab*). D. h. jeder Vers enthält mindestens einmal einen dieser Buchstaben, zumeist jedoch zwei oder mehr. Ähnlich sieht es in Strophe sechs aus, wo der Buchstabe ح in den ersten beiden Versen gehäuft vorkommt.

Wie auch in seinem *zaǧal inna maʿmaʿšūqī ǧufūn wa-liḥāẓ* zieht Ibn Muqātil Klangfiguren den semantisch operierenden Figuren wie *tawriyah* und *istiḫdām* (in der Mamlukenzeit beliebte Stilfiguren des Doppelsinns) vor, die Dichter wie Ibn Ḥiǧǧa, Ibn Nubāta und Ibrāhīm al-Miʿmār wesentlich häufiger verwendeten.

11 Hier könnte man auch *niddū/niddū* lesen.

12 Vgl. Cachia, *Skimmer* 25–6 (consonantal paronomasia).

13 Vgl. Cachia, *Skimmer* 21.

Sprachliche Besonderheiten

Der stilisierte Dialekt bzw. die stilisierte Umgangssprache, die *zağals* eigen ist, wird vor allem durch die fehlende Desinentialflexion als Hauptmerkmal gekennzeichnet. Auch das *zağal* Ibn Muqātils ist hier keine Ausnahme. Kennzeichnend für die fehlende Flexion sind die vielen Wörter in Pausa wie *fāz, waqaf, yurṣad* etc. (Beispiele aus Strophe eins). Ein weiteres Erkennungsmerkmal von *zağals* ist die Schreibung *-ū* für *-hu*, das Ibn Muqātil in diesem Gedicht sehr häufig einsetzt wie beispielsweise *amrū, bi-šamrū, nimrū, ʿumrū* (Beispiele aus Strophe zwei). Weiterhin typisch für die Sprache des *zağals* ist der Hilfsvokal *ə*, wie in *li-ṣuġrə* in Vers vier von Strophe zwei. Dieser Hilfsvokal überbrückt die Juxtaposition von zwei Konsonanten zwischen zwei Wörtern. Im Allgemeinen habe ich diesen Laut hier mit *kasra* wiedergegeben wie in *yuḥibbə* (Strophe eins, Vers eins), *laytə* (Strophe zwei, Vers drei) usw., auch wenn der Syntax nach eine andere Flexion, also eine Vokalisierung mit *ḍamma* oder *fatḥa*, angezeigt ist. Dass es sich bei *zağals* nicht um „dialektale" Gedichte handelt, sieht man auch in diesem Gedicht. Keine der von Ibn Muqātil verwendeten Formen kann man ohne weiteres einem Dialekt als solchem zuordnen – selbst Wörter wie das *quddāmū*[14] (Strophe vier, Vers eins), das beispielsweise im heutigen Levantinischen und Ägyptischen als *ʾəddām* bzw. *ʾuddām* ausgesprochen in der Bedeutung „vor" (örtlich) verwendet wird, sind ebenso in der Form *quddāma* aus der Hochsprache bezeugt. Dennoch dürften solche Wörter bei der Zuhörerschaft einen Anflug von Dialektalität bzw. besser gesagt Umgangssprache vermittelt haben, da sie in der Hochsprache seltener in dieser Bedeutung anzutreffen sind.

Kontrafakturen

Es ist unmöglich, an dieser Stelle eine ausreichend umfängliche Diskussion der drei bekannten Kontrafakturen zu diesem *zağal* anzustellen. Stattdessen begnüge ich mich damit, die Kontrafakturen von aṣ-Ṣafadī, al-Muqaddasī und al-Banawānī zusammenfassend mit der Vorlage zu vergleichen und im Fall von aṣ-Ṣafadī auch den begleitenden Paratext etwas genauer zu analysieren.

---

14 Das *-ā-* in *quddāmū* wird zwar lang geschrieben, jedoch kurz ausgesprochen bzw. skandiert; langes *-ā* in offenen Silben können im *zağal* generell kurz skandiert werden, vgl. Özkan, *Geschichte* z. B. 251, 308; vgl. auch die Schreibung als قدّمه bzw. قدّموا im Variantenapparat zu dieser Stelle im Anhang.

Nachdem er das oben übersetzte *zağal* zitiert hat, schreibt aṣ-Ṣafadī folgendes in seiner Biographie zu Ibn Muqātil:

فأعجبني هذا الذي فيه من قلب البعض في أغصانه وبعد حين خطر لي نظم شيء في هذا فقلت أنا وجعلت جميع قوافيه مقلوب البعض.[15]

Mir gefiel, was hier an partiellen metathetischen Paronomasien in den Gemeinreimversen vorliegt.[16] Nach einer Weile kam ich darauf, etwas in dieser Art zu dichten. Und so habe ich folgendes vorgetragen, wobei ich jeden Reim mit einer partiellen metathetischen Paronomasie ausstattete.

Wie seine Vorlage ist auch aṣ-Ṣafadīs Kontrafaktur ein *zağal aqraʿ*, steht aber im abweichenden Versmaß *muǧtaṯṯ*. Doch fängt er wie angekündigt schon zu Beginn in den Sonderreimversen an, die metathetische Paronomasie in den Reimwörtern anzuwenden: *qalbī li-waṣlū taraqqab / wa bi-l-ḫuḍūʿ lū taqarrab*. Neben den genannten Gemeinsamkeiten (*zağal aqraʿ*, metathetische Paronomasie) ist das einleitende *qalbī* im ersten Vers ein Hinweis darauf, dass es sich um eine Kontrafaktur auf das Gedicht von Ibn Muqātil handelt. Anders als Ibn Muqātil erzählt aṣ-Ṣafadī in seinem *zağal* jedoch keine konsistente Geschichte, wie dies Ibn Muqātil tut. Auch scheint ihm die Leichtigkeit des Vorbilds etwas abzugehen, da er sich zu sehr von dem Zwang zur metathetischen Paronomasie in jedem einzelnen Vers leiten lässt. Nach dem Gedicht verweist aṣ-Ṣafadī auf diesen Umstand und erklärt unumwunden die Überlegenheit seines *zağals* gegenüber dem *zağal* von Ibn Muqātil:

ولما نظمت هذا الزجل كان في دمشق في أوائل سنة ست وخمسين وسبع مئة وسمع بي لجاء إليّ وطلب الوقوف عليه فأوقفته فبهت له وأنشدني له أشياء من هذا النوع ولكنه لم يلتزم ذلك في جميع القوافي.

Als ich dieses *zağal* dichtete, befand er (Ibn Muqātil) sich in Damaskus, zu Anfang des Jahres 756/1355. Er hörte von mir [dass ich mich auch in Damaskus befand] und kam. Er fragte mich, ob ich ihm das Gedicht zeigen könnte, was ich auch tat. Es verschlug ihm die Sprache, und er trug mir etwas in dieser Art vor, doch hielt er sich nicht an die besagte Vorgabe in allen Reimen.

---

15 Aṣ-Ṣafadī, *Aʿyān* 3:560.

16 Eigentlich bedeutet *aġṣān* Sonderreimverse, hier scheint aṣ-Ṣafadī jedoch die Gemeinreimverse zu meinen, was ein Hinweis darauf sein kann, dass die Terminologie nicht absolut feststand, vgl. Özkan, *Geschichte* 18.

Aṣ-Ṣafadī möchte uns also weismachen, dass er der bessere *zaǧǧāl* ist und der viel gerühmte *zaǧal*-Meister Ibn Muqātil trotz Versuchen es nicht geschafft hätte, in jedem Reim eine metathetische Paronomasie unterzubringen.[17] Aber meint aṣ-Ṣafadī im Ernst, er habe Ibn Muqātil übertroffen, indem er eine formale Komplikation hinzufügt? Es ist kaum möglich, ein Urteil darüber zu fällen. Diese Prahlerei und diese wettkampfartigen Überbietungen kennen wir schon von Ibn Ḥiǧǧa und anderen Dichtern. Die Rezeptionsgeschichte zeichnet jedoch ein anderes Bild, das eindeutiger nicht sein könnte. Es ist nicht aṣ-Ṣafadīs *zaǧal*, das Jahrhunderte überdauerte und seine Wirkung hat entfalten können, sondern jenes von Ibn Muqātil.

Auch der Dichter ʿĪsā al-Muqaddasī bzw. al-Maqdisī (geb. vor 858/1454, gest. nach 878/1473) verfasste eine Kontrafaktur zu Ibn Muqātils Gedicht, woraus er die Eingangsverse und die erste Strophe zitiert.[18] Er beschreibt das *zaǧal* als *mašhūr ʿinda ahl al-adab* („berühmt unter den Literaten“). Bevor er seine Kontrafaktur *ḥibbī kašaf liṯāmū* anführt, die er im Jahr 878/1473 verfasst hat, schildert er, wie ihm ein Freund diese *muʿāraḍa* aufgetragen hat – ein verbreiteter Topos.[19] Sein *zaǧal* folgt den Vorgaben seines Vorbilds: *zaǧal aqraʿ*, Versmaß *raǧaz*, metathetische Paronomasien in den Gemeinreimversen. Soweit ich es beurteilen kann, kommt die Kontrafaktur al-Muqaddasīs auch nach dem Rhythmus, der Beschwingtheit und nicht zuletzt nach den sonstigen klanglichen Eigenschaften an ihr Vorbild heran, wobei Ibn Muqātil eine größere Vielfalt an Paronomasien zu präsentieren scheint.

Der genauso wie al-Muqaddasī mehr als ein Jahrhundert später lebende ägyptische Dichter und Theoretiker ʿAbd al-Wahhāb b. Yūsuf al-Banawānī (gest. ca. 860/1456) schuf auch eine *muʿāraḍa* auf dieses *zaǧal*.[20] Ebenso wie al-Muqaddasī fängt er sein Gedicht nicht mit *qalbī* an. Die metathetischen Paronomasien, die er im Gedicht verwendet, unterscheiden sich nicht von der Art wie sie Ibn Muqātil verwendet: Al-Banawānī bringt nicht wie aṣ-Ṣafadī in jedem Vers eine metathetische Paronomasie unter. Er richtet sich vielmehr an Ibn Muqātils *zaǧal* aus, indem er diese Art von Paronomasien nur in den Gemeinreimversen einsetzt. Al-Banawānī verwendet auch Wörter, die bereits in Ibn Muqātils *zaǧal* vorkommen, u.a. als Reimwörter, so wie *ḫalfū*/*ḫilfū* (Strophe drei, Vers eins). Aus der – zugegeben – subjektiven und zeitlich verrückten

17 Um die Qualität seines eigenen *zaǧals* zu unterstreichen, zitiert aṣ-Ṣafadī sogar eine Kontrafaktur von Muǧīr al-Dīn Muḥammad b. aš-Šahrazūrī, aṣ-Ṣafadī, *Aʿyān* 3:562–4.

18 Hs. Escorial árabe 459, fol. 79r.

19 Hs. Escorial árabe 459, fols. 79v–81r.

20 Al-Qurayšī, *Funūn* 2:46.

Perspektive des heutigen Betrachters scheint al-Banawānīs Gedicht eine gelungene Kontrafaktur zu sein, sowohl in seinem Aufbau als auch in seiner klanglichen Gestaltung.

Fazit

Was macht nun das *zaǧal* von Ibn Muqātil so besonders? Warum ist es zu *dem* Aushängeschild von Ibn Muqātil und der östlichen *zaǧal*-Dichtung überhaupt geworden, welches noch für lange Zeit nachfolgende Dichtergenerationen inspirieren sollte? Ein Erklärungsansatz könnte sein, dass es sich wie auch sein anderes berühmtes *zaǧal* (*inna maʿ maʿšūqī ǧufūn wa-liḥāẓ*) vor allem durch seine vielen schillernden Paronomasien auszeichnet, darunter eben jenen metathetischen Paronomasien, die trotz ihrer formalen Schwierigkeit nicht überstrapaziert wirken. Doch es sind nicht allein die Paronomasien. Auch darüber hinaus glänzt es durch seine Klangwirkung im allgemeinen sowie dem Rhythmus seiner kurzen Verse. Aber auch die einfache Sprache, die leichtfüßige, geradezu heiter-liebliche Art der Beschreibung des Verhältnisses vom Dichter zu dem eitlen Jungen machen das Gedicht zu einem Kleinod in der Geschichte des *zaǧals*, und es scheint, als ob eben diese Leichtigkeit und Einfachheit verbunden mit den Klangfiguren seinen Ruhm ausgemacht haben. Möglicherweise haben es wir hier mit *sahl wa-mumtaniʿ* zu tun, also mit einem Gedicht, das zwar leicht daherkommt, aber unerreichbar schwer zu komponieren ist. Anders lässt es sich kaum erklären, warum es so viel Anerkennung genoss und mehrere *zaǧal*-Liebhaber und -Dichter versucht haben, es ihm gleichzutun oder sogar es zu übertreffen.

Anhang – *zaǧal* (*qalbī yuḥibb tayyāh*) inkl. kritischem Apparat

Siglen der Quellen:

ع) an-Nawāǧī, *ʿUqūd* 277–80.

ف) an-Nawāǧī, *ad-Durr an-nafīs fīmā zāda ʿalā ǧinān al-ǧinās wa-aǧnās at-taǧnīs*, Hs. Kairo Dār al-Kutub 296 *balāġa*, fols. 243r–244r.

ص) aṣ-Ṣafadī, *Aʿyān* 3:559–60.

ش) Ibn Mubārakšāh, *Safīna*, Hs. Istanbul Feyzullah 1612, fols. 3r–4r.

د) Ibn Iyās, *ad-Durr al-maknūn fī s-sabʿ funūn*, Hs. Kairo Dār al-Kutub *šiʿr* 724, fols. 173v–174r.

خ) Ibn Ḥiǧǧa, *Ḫizāna* 1:94.

Al-Ḥiǧāzī, *Rawḍ*:

غ) Hs. Gotha 400, fols. 80ᵛ–81ʳ.
آ) Hs. Istanbul Ayasofya 4017, fol. 101ʳ–101ᵛ.
س) Hs. Istanbul Ayasofya 4018, fol. 156ʳ–156ᵛ.
ق) Hs. Kairo Maʿhad 429, fols. 105ᵛ–106ʳ.
م) Hs. Kairo Maʿhad 1764, fol. 105ʳ–105ᵛ.
ن) Hs. Mossul 44/8, fols. 78ᵛ–79ʳ.
ط) Hs. Bagdad Maktabat al-Matḥaf al-ʿIrāqī 12, fols. 175ᵛ–176ʳ.

وقال أيضا والتزم الجناس المقلوب في جميع خرجاته:[21]

قَلْبِي يِحِبّ تَيَّاهْ[22]
لَيْسْ يَعْشَقِ ٱلَّا إِيَّاهْ[23]
فَازْ مَنْ وَقَفْ وَحَيَّاهْ
يَرْصُدْ عَلَى مُحَيَّاهْ

بَدْرَ السَّمَا وَيُطْبَعْ مَنْ رَامْ وِصَالُو يَعْطَبْ[24]

21 وقال ... خرجاته] قال الشيخ علاء الدين بن مقاتل الحموي هذا الزجل الذي سارت به الركبان وهو من الجناس اللفظي المقلوب د؛ علي بن مقاتل زجل ش؛ وللشيخ علاء الدين بن مقاتل زجل غريب في هذا النوع التزم فيه الجناس المقلوب في جميع خرجاته ف؛ وأنشدني لنفسه بحماه زجلاً وهو ص؛ وللشيخ علاء الدين بن مقاتل الحموي أيضاً زجل في هذا النوع، سارت به الركبان أنشده المصنف في حماة بحضرة الملك المؤيد والشيخ صفي الدين والشيخ جمال الدين بن نباتة حاضرين فوقع في المجلس شيء أقوله إذا استوعبت الزجل كتابة وأوّله خ؛ وله والتزم الجناس المقلوب غ آس ق م ن ط.

22 يِحِبّ] معجب د؛ بجب خ س | تَيَّاهْ] تياهو ق

23 لَيْسْ] لس ش | يَعْشَقِ] نعشق ش ف غ آس م ن ط

24 وَيُطْبَعْ] لويطبع خ؛ ويطيع ق | رَامْ] راد ش ص | يُعْطَبْ] يعطف ق

صَغِيرْ نَحِيرْ فِي أَمْرُو[25]
غَزَالْ قَهَرْ بِشَمْرُو[26]
لَيْثِ الهَوَى وَنِمْرُو[27]
فَاعْجَبْ لِصُغْرِ عُمْرُو[28]

رِيمِ ٱبْنِ عَشْرِ وَٱرْبَعْ   أَرْدَى الأُسُودْ وَأَرْعَبْ

أُذْكُرْ نَهَارْ تَبْعْتُو[29]
وَرُوحِي كُنْتُ بِعْتُو[30]
خَيَّبْ مَا فِيهْ طَمَعْتُو[31]
وَقَالْ وَقَدْ سَمِعْتُو[32]

إِرْجَعْ وَلِي لَا تِتْبَعْ   نَخْشَى عَلَيْكْ لَا تِتْعَبْ[33]

25 نَحِيرْ] يحير ع؛ بحير خ ص | أَمْرُو] أموروا م

26 قَهَرْ] قمر ص | بِشَمْرُو] بشحرو ص؛ بسمرو خ؛ يشمرو ق

27 لَيْثِ] ليت م | وَنِمْرُو] ويمرو ق

28 فَاعْجَبْ] واعجب ط

29 أُذْكُرْ] نذكر ص

30 وَرُوحِي] والروح م (في الهامش) | وَرُوحِي ... بِعْتُو] يبدل هذا البيت بالبيت التالي في ط

31 خَيَّبْ] وخيب خ؛ حيب آ؛ حسب س؛ وحيث ق | خَيَّبْ مَا] حيثما ن؛ حي ما ط | فِيهْ] كان ش ص

32 وَقَالْ] فقال خ | وَقَدْ] كما ش؛ كلام ما ص

33 نَخْشَى] أخشى خ ف ع؛ يخشى ن

كَمْ قُدَّامُو وَخَلْفُو[34]
مَشَيْتْ مُطِيعْ لِخَلْفُو[35]
وَرَدْتُ لَثْمْ كَفُّو[36]
قَالْ دَعْ مُنَاكْ وَكُفُّو[37]

فَإِنَّ لَثْمِ إِصْبَعْ مِنَ الثُّرَيَّا أَصْعَبْ[38]

مَا زِلْتِ لُو نُدَارِي
حَتَّى حَصَلْ فِي دَارِي[39]
نَادَيْتْ وَدَمْعِي جَارِي[40]
إِشْ لَوْ تَكُونْ يَا جَارِي[41]

تَدَعْنِي مِنْ فِيكَ ٱشْبَعْ قَالْ إِشْ يَكُونْ لَكَ ٱشْعَبْ[42]

34 كَمْ ... ٢٠ أَصْعَبْ] لا يرد هذا الدور في ش | قُدَّامُو] قدّمه د، قدّموا غ آس ق م ن ط | وَخَلْفُو] وحلفوا غ

35 لِخَلْفُو] لحلفو ق

36 وَرَدْتُ] وقصدي ص، ورمت د خ، ورحت ن | لَثْمِ] لتم آم

37 قَالْ] وقال ق

38 فَإِنَّ لَثْمِ] فلثم كل ص | أصعب] أصعف ق

39 حَصَلْ] حضر ق

40 وَدَمْعِي] ودمع د

41 إِشْ] أيش ص خ ق، آش آ | لَوْ] لم ق | لَوْ تَكُونْ] كان يصيب خ | تَكُونْ] يكون ش، تكن ع غ آس ق م ن ط | يَا] لي ن

42 تَدَعْنِي] لو كنت خ، دعني س | مِنْ] لا ترد في غ | مِنْ فِيكَ] منك آ ق ن ط، فيك م | إِشْ] إيش ص خ س ق م ط | يَكُونْ] يكن خ غ ق، نكون آم

مَنْ حَازْ فِي حُسْنُو حدُّو[43]
لَحْظُو لِقَتْلِي حَدُّو[44]
وورْدِ خَدُّو نَدُّو[45]
مَا فِي الرِّيَاضْ شِي نِدُّو[46]

رَوْض بِالْحَيَا مُبَرْقَعْ عَلَيْه سِيَاجْ مُعَقْرَبْ[47]

مَنْ فِي الْجَمَالْ فَرِيدُو[48]
لِلصَّبّ مِنْ ورِيدُو
يَذْبَحْ وَهُو يرِيدُو[49]
وَكَمْ ذَا شَيْخْ مُرِيدُو[50]

خَلَّاهْ دُمُوعُو يَبْلَعْ وَهُو بِعَقْلُو يَلْعَبْ[51]

43 مَنْ ... ٣٥ مُعَقْرَبْ] يبدل هذا الدور بالدور التالي في ش ص | حاز] جاز ش ف | في] لا ترد في خ | حُسْنُو] حسن ن | حدُّو] خدّوع ص د خ ن

44 لَحْظُو] لحضي ن | لقتلي] لقتل د

45 خَدُّو] خد د | نَدُّو] وندو م

46 شِي] لا يرد ف د

47 بِالحيَا] الحيا خ | سِيَاجْ] ساج خ

48 الجَمَالْ] الحمال آس

49 يَذْبَحْ] ندبح م | وَهُويرِيدُو] ولويزيدوخ | يُرِيدُو] مريده د

50 وكَمْ ... مُرِيدُو] كم شيخ خدا مريدو ن | مُرِيدُو] يريدو آ؛ سريدوا ق

51 خَلَّاهْ] حلاه غ | خَلَّاهْ ... ٣٩ حَافِلْ] تنقص هذه الأبيات ف د | دُمُوعُو] دموع ش؛ ودمعو ص | يَبْلَعْ] يبلغ ص م | يَلْعَبْ] بلعب ن

كَمْ خَصْمِ فِي المَقَاتِلْ[52]
صَابُو إِبْنْ مُقَاتِلْ
وَكَمْ ذَا فِي المَحَافِلْ
قَدِ انْشَا غُصْنِ حَافِلْ[53]

مِنْ كُلِّ بَيْتْ مُرَبَّعْ مَلْحُونْ بِأَلْفِ مُعْرَبْ[54]

Bibliographie

Quellen

al-Ḥiğāzī, Abū ṭ-Ṭayyib (oder Abū l-ʿAbbās) Šihābaddīn Aḥmad, *Rawḍ al-ādāb*, Hs. Gotha 400.

al-Ḥiğāzī, Abū ṭ-Ṭayyib (oder Abū l-ʿAbbās) Šihābaddīn Aḥmad, *Rawḍ al-ādāb*, Hs. Istanbul Ayasofya 4017.

al-Ḥiğāzī, Abū ṭ-Ṭayyib (oder Abū l-ʿAbbās) Šihābaddīn Aḥmad, *Rawḍ al-ādāb*, Hs. Istanbul Ayasofya 4018.

al-Ḥiğāzī, Abū ṭ-Ṭayyib (oder Abū l-ʿAbbās) Šihābaddīn Aḥmad, *Rawḍ al-ādāb*, Hs. Kairo Maʿhad 429.

al-Ḥiğāzī, Abū ṭ-Ṭayyib (oder Abū l-ʿAbbās) Šihābaddīn Aḥmad, *Rawḍ al-ādāb*, Hs. Kairo Maʿhad 1764.

al-Ḥiğāzī, Abū ṭ-Ṭayyib (oder Abū l-ʿAbbās) Šihābaddīn Aḥmad, *Rawḍ al-ādāb*, Hs. Mossul 44/8.

al-Ḥiğāzī, Abū ṭ-Ṭayyib (oder Abū l-ʿAbbās) Šihābaddīn Aḥmad, *Rawḍ al-ādāb*, Hs. Bagdad Maktabat al-Matḥaf al-ʿIrāqī 12.

Ibn Faḍlallāh al-ʿUmarī, Aḥmad b. Yaḥyā, *Ḏahabiyyat al-ʿaṣr*, Hg. I. Ṣāliḥ, Beirut 1983.

Ibn Ḥağar al-ʿAsqalānī, *ad-Durar al-kāmina fī aʿyān al-miʾa aṯ-ṯāmina*, Hg. ʿA. Darwīš, 4 Bde., Beirut 1993.

Ibn Ḥiğğa al-Ḥamawī, *Bulūġ al-amal fī fann az-zağal*, Hg. R.M. al-Qurayšī, Damascus 1974.

52 كَمْ] لا ترد في م

53 اَنْشَا] أبداغ م، أبد ق | غُصْنِ] لوخ، عصرغ | غُصْنِ حَافِلْ] لا ترد في س، قد أنشا لو بحافل ن | حَافِلْ] جحافل خ

54 مُرَبَّعْ] في مربع ش ص ف غ آس ق ط م

Ibn Ḥiǧǧa al-Ḥamawī, *Ḫizānat al-adab wa-ġāyat al-arab*, 2 Bde., Hg. ʿI. Šaʿītū, Beirut 1987.

Ibn Iyās, Muḥammad b. Aḥmad, *ad-Durr al-maknūn fī s-sabʿ funūn*, Hs. Kairo Dār al-Kutub 724 Šiʿr Taymūr.

Ibn Mubārakšāh, Šihābaddīn Aḥmad, *Safīna*, Hs. Istanbul Feyzullah Efendi 1612.

al-Muqaddasī (oder al-Maqdisī), ʿĪsā, *al-Ǧawhar al-maknūn fī s-sabʿat funūn*, Hs. Escorial árabe 459.

an-Nawāǧī, *ad-Durr an-nafīs fīmā zāda ʿalā ǧinān al-ǧinās wa-aǧnās at-taǧnīs*, Hs. Kairo Dār al-Kutub 296 *balāġa*.

an-Nawāǧī, Šamsaddīn Muḥammad b. Ḥasan, *ʿUqūd al-laʾāl fī l-muwaššaḥāt wa-l-azǧāl*, Hg. A.M. ʿAṭā, Kairo 1999.

aṣ-Ṣafadī, Ṣalāḥaddīn b. Ḫalīl b. Aybak, *Aʿyān al-ʿaṣr wa-aʿwān an-naṣr*, Hgg. ʿA. Abū Zayd et al., 6 Bde., Damaskus 1997–8.

Sekundärliteratur

Bauer, T., Ibrāhīm al-Miʿmār: Ein dichtender Handwerker aus Ägyptens Mamlukenzeit, in ZDMG 152 (2002), 63–93.

Bauer, T., Das Nilzaǧal des Ibrāhīm al-Miʿmār. Ein Lied zur Feier des Nilschwellenfestes, in T. Bauer und U. Stehli-Werbeck (Hgg.), *Alltagsleben und materielle Kultur in der arabischen Sprache und Literatur: Festschrift für Heinz Grotzfeld*, Wiesbaden 2005, 69–88.

Bauer, T., Die Leiden eines ägyptischen Müllers: Die Mühlen-Maqāme des Ibrāhīm al-Miʿmār (st. 749/1348), in A.I. Blöbaum, J. Kahl und S.D. Schweitzer (Hgg.), *Ägypten – Münster: Kulturwissenschaftliche Studien zu Ägypten, dem Vorderen Orient und verwandten Gebieten ... donum natalicum ... Erharto Graefe ... oblatum*, Wiesbaden 2003, 1–16.

Cachia, P., *The arch rhetorician or the schemer's skimmer: A handbook of late Arabic badīʿ drawn from ʿAbd al-Ghanī an-Nābulsī's Nafaḥāt al-azhār ʿalā nasamāt al-asḥār*, Wiesbaden 1988.

Özkan, H., *Geschichte des östlichen zaǧal: Dialektale arabische Strophendichtung aus dem Osten der arabischen Welt – von den Anfängen bis zum Ende der Mamlukenzeit*, Baden-Baden 2020.

Özkan, H., Ibn Muqātil, in *EI*^{3}, first published online: 2019; first print edition: 2020–1 (1–2).

Rosenthal, F., *Humor in early Islam*, Leiden ^{2}2011.

5

Offizielle mamlukenzeitliche Schreiben und ihre Aussagekraft am Beispiel einer Frohbotschaft aus der Feder Ibn Nubātas

Andreas Herdt

Ibn Nubāta al-Miṣrī (686–768/1287–1366) fand nach einem langen und kargen Leben als Literat im fortgeschrittenen Alter von 57 Jahren endlich eine Anstellung in der Kanzlei von Damaskus als Sekretär.[1] Zum Zeitpunkt der Aufnahme dieser Beschäftigung hatte er bereits mehrere maßgebende literarische Werke verfasst und seinen bleibenden Ruhm als vielseitig gebildeter und sowohl in Reim als auch in Prosa höchst versierter *adīb* begründet.

Nach dem ersten Jahr im Staatsdienst veröffentlichte Ibn Nubāta die offiziellen Dokumente, die er im Auftrag seiner Dienstherren verfasst hatte, in einem Band. Dieser trägt den schlichten Titel *Taʿlīq ad-dīwān aš-šarīf li-sanat 743 min kalām Ibn Nubāta* und hat den Untertitel *at-tawāqīʿ, al-mukātabāt, al-adʿiyya*.[2] Wie es bereits aus dem Untertitel hervorgeht, folgt der Band einer dreiteiligen Struktur. Der erste Teil umfasst Ernennungsschreiben, deren Überschriften – in vielen Fällen zumindest andeutungsweise – die Namen der ernannten Personen und immer die Funktion, die ihnen übertragen wurde, enthalten. Im zweiten Teil findet man offizielle Mitteilungen sowie Schreiben, die den Charakter privater Angelegenheiten zu haben scheinen. Die beiden genannten Teile umfassen insgesamt sechsunddreißig Schriftstücke. Den dritten und abschließenden Teil dieses Bandes bildet eine Sammlung von zahlreichen kurzen und elaborierten Einleitungsformulierungen, die aus den Briefen Ibn Nubātas exzerpiert wurden. Auf *Taʿlīq ad-dīwān aš-šarīf li-sanat 743 min kalām Ibn Nubāta* ließ Ibn Nubāta im darauffolgenden Jahr eine gleichgeartete Sammlung – diesmal von achtundvierzig Dokumenten – mit dem fast identischen Titel *Taʿlīq ad-dīwān li-sanat 744 min kalām Ibn Nubāta* und mit dem sehr ähn-

1 Einen guten und gründlich recherchierten Überblick über das Leben und Wirken dieses Autors bieten folgende Beiträge von Bauer, *Jamāl al-Dīn Ibn Nubātah* ii, 184–202; Bauer, *Ibn Nubātah al-Miṣrī*.

2 Dieser Text ist in zwei Handschriften erhalten, nämlich Hs. Berlin 8640 und Hs. Tübingen M a VI 70.

 | DOI:10.1163/9789004521780_007

lichen Untertitel *at-tawāqīʿ, al-kutub, aṣ-ṣudūr*[3] folgen. Allerdings unterscheidet sich der Band des Jahres 744 von seinem Vorgänger insofern, als in ihm, erstens, keine aus dem jeweiligen ursprünglichen Textzusammenhang ausgesonderten und zu einer eigenständigen Gruppe zusammengefügten einleitenden Formulierungen (*aṣ-ṣudūr*) vorkommen und als, zweitens, Ernennungen (*at-tawāqīʿ*) und offizielle Schreiben zu sonstigen Anlässen (*al-kutub*) in ihrer Anordnung keinem formalen Prinzip zu folgen scheinen. Diese Reihe wird abgerundet durch eine dritte – und soweit unsere Kenntnis reicht letzte – Sammlung von einundsiebzig Dokumenten mit dem Titel *Taʿlīq ad-dīwān li-sanat 745 min kalām Ibn Nubāta* mit dem Untertitel *at-tawāqīʿ ṯumma al-kutub ṯumma al-adʿiyya wa-ṣ-ṣudūr*.[4]

Dem vorliegenden Beitrag liegt die Frohbotschaft über die Genesung des amtierenden mamlukischen Sultans aus dem handschriftlichen Band *Taʿlīq ad-dīwān aš-šarīf li-sanat 743 min kalām Ibn Nubāta* zu Grunde. Der Text dieses Schreibens wird nachfolgend ediert, übersetzt und im Hinblick auf einige seiner formalen wie inhaltlichen Merkmale besprochen. Dies geschieht mit dem Ziel, zum einen, Ibn Nubāta als Autor näher kennenzulernen und, zum anderen, in einige Aspekte der in der Vormoderne üblichen Kommunikationskultur Einblicke zu gewinnen.

Anmerkungen zur Edition

Taʿlīq ad-dīwān aš-šarīf li-sanat 743 min kalām Ibn Nubāta ist nach heutigem Kenntnisstand in zwei Handschriften überliefert: Hs. Berlin 8640 und Hs. Tübingen M a VI 70. Bei der Tübinger Handschrift handelt es sich um eine Sammelhandschrift, und darin stellt *Taʿlīq ad-dīwān aš-šarīf li-sanat 743 min kalām Ibn Nubāta* lediglich einen kleinen Teil (Fol. 151[a]–169[a]) dar. Der Edition des hier behandelten Schreibens wurde die Tübinger Handschrift als Leithandschrift (Sigle: تو) zu Grunde gelegt, und die Berliner Handschrift diente als Sekundärhandschrift (Sigle: بر). Die Tübinger Handschrift bietet einen vollständigeren, allerdings nur rudimentär diakritisch punktierten und weitgehend unvokalisierten Text, dessen *rasm* in den meisten Fällen viel genauer als derjenige der Berliner Handschrift ist. Die Berliner Handschrift ist zwar einerseits größtenteils – wenn auch nicht immer eindeutig – punktiert, bietet aber andererseits

3 Dieser Text ist in einer einzigen Handschrift erhalten, nämlich Hs. University of Cambridge Add. 3533.

4 Dieser Text ist in einer einzigen Handschrift erhalten: Hs. Leiden Acad. 186.

einen unvollständigen Text und enthält viele offensichtliche und gravierende Verschreibungen.

Im edierten Text[5] wurden einige im handschriftlichen Text ursprünglich nicht vorkommende Zeichen verwendet, um dem Leser die Erschließung dieses mamlukischen Schriftzeugnisses zu erleichtern. Aufgrund der Tatsache, dass offizielle Schreiben der mamlukischen Epoche in gereimter Kunstprosa verfasst sind, wurde das Zeichen ، zur Markierung der Grenze zwischen den Kola gebraucht; in den beiden genannten Handschriften wurde zu diesem Zweck ein dicker Punkt nach dem jeweiligen Kolon verwendet.[6] Darüber hinaus wurde von weiteren folgenden Zeichen, die im handschriftlichen Text in keiner Weise angedeutet sind, Gebrauch gemacht, um eindeutige intertextuelle Zusammenhänge hervorzuheben sowie den edierten Text inhaltlich zu ordnen. Koranische Zitate bzw. Fragmente wurden mit ﴿ ﴾, Versfragmente sowie idiomatische Wendungen mit ( ) eingeklammert. Mit [ ] wurde der Editionstext in seine Sinnabschnitte gegliedert: [1] steht für die Einleitung, [2x] für den Hauptteil und dessen Untergliederungen und [3] für den Abschluss. Dem nachfolgend edierten Text ist ferner ein textkritischer Apparat beigefügt, in dem einige den Sinn des Textes in wesentlicher Weise betreffende handschriftliche Varianten erfasst sind.

Abschließend sei noch kurz auf eine überlieferungsgeschichtliche Besonderheit hingewiesen. Das berühmte mehrbändige Kanzleihandbuch *Ṣubḥ al-aʿšā fī ṣināʿat al-inšā* von Šihābaddīn Aḥmad al-Qalqašandī (756–821/1355–1418) enthält u.a. zahlreiche Schreiben Ibn Nubātas.[7] Ein beträchtlicher Teil dieser Dokumente ist auch in den Bänden *Taʿlīq ad-dīwān aš-šarīf li-sanat 743*, *Taʿlīq ad-dīwān li-sanat 744* und *Taʿlīq ad-dīwān li-sanat 745* überliefert. Aufgrund der Tatsache, dass es sich um offizielle Schriftstücke handelt, könnte man meinen, Fassungen von gleichen Dokumenten, die sich sowohl in einem der *Taʿlīq*s als auch in *Ṣubḥ al-aʿšā fī ṣināʿat al-inšā* finden, sollten eigentlich einen weitgehend identischen Wortlaut bieten. Doch diese Annahme erweist sich in keinem einzigen Fall als zutreffend. Die jeweiligen Fassungen stimmen nur im Großen und Ganzen miteinander überein, weichen jedoch in zahlreichen – meistens

5 Fol. 163^{b}–164^{a} der Tübinger Handschrift.

6 Hinsichtlich der Markierung der Grenze zwischen einzelnen Kola der in arabischer Reimprosa verfassten Texte gab es in der vormodernen handschriftlichen Tradition keine Einheitlichkeit. Hierfür konnte auch ein merklich größerer Abstand zwischen den Kola dienen.

7 Nach erster Sichtung konnte eine erkleckliche Zahl von ca. 97 offiziellen Schreiben ermittelt werden, die sich eindeutig Ibn Nubāta zuordnen lassen. Diese Zahl könnte allerdings auch höher liegen, da al-Qalqašandī nicht immer den Autor der von ihm zitierten offiziellen Dokumente explizit nannte.

hinsichtlich einzelner Wörter – Details voneinander ab.[8] Dies gilt auch für die Frohbotschaft über die Genesung des Sultans, die auch in *Ṣubḥ al-aʿšā fī ṣināʿat al-inšā* überliefert ist und in der dortigen Fassung bei einigen Wörtern wesentliche Abweichungen aufweist.[9] Nur solche textlich bedeutsamen Abweichungen werden im kritischen Apparat erfasst (Sigle: صبح), und auf die Angabe weiterer geringfügiger Unterschiede wird verzichtet.

كتاب البشارة بالعافية الشريفة السلطانية[10]

[1] أورد اللهُ عليه من الهناء كلّ سريّ يسرّه ، وكلّ سَنيّ يقرّ[11] أمام ناظره الكريم ويُقرّه ، وكلّ وفيّ إذا طلع على آفاق حلب قيل (لله دَرّه) ، ولا زالت البشائرُ تلقاه بكلّ وجه جميل ، وكلّ جليّ جليل[12] ، وكلّ خبرٍ[13] تصحّ الدنيا بصحّة مقتضيه[14] فليس بها غير النسيم عليل ، تقبيلًا يُزاحم به عقود الثغور ، ويلائم بمبسمه سينات[15] هذه السطور[16] ، ويكاد يمنع من ضمّ الشفتَيْن للثم طول الابتسام للسرور ، [2a] ويُنهي بعد رفْع اليد بدُعائه ، وضمّ الجوانح على ولائه ، وجزْم الهناء المشترك بنصيب مسرّته لمسرّة[17] مولانا وهنائه ، أنّ المثال الشريف زاده الله شَرَفا ، وزاد[18] فضل سلطانه على العباد سَرَفا

8 Manche Unterschiede könnten dadurch erklärt werden, dass der nur partiell punktierte *rasm* der handschriftlichen Originale dieser Dokumente beim Abschreiben zu Missverständnissen seitens der Kopisten und daher zu manchen ursprünglich nicht intendierten Schreibvarianten geführt hat. Auf diese Weise könnte ein Großteil der betreffenden Textvarianten entstanden sein.

9 In drei Fällen wurde bemerkenswerterweise jeweils ein ganzes Kolon ausgelassen.

10 وردتْ نسخة هذه البشارة في صُبح الأعشى في صناعة الإنشا (جزء 8، صفحة 366 وما يليها).

11 يقرا بر.

12 السجعة „وكلّ جليّ جليل" لم ترد في بر.

13 خير بر.

14 بدلًا من „بصحّة مقتضيه" ورد في صبح „بصِحَّتِهِ".

15 سنيّات تو، سنيات بر، ورجّحْنا ما أثبتناه.

16 السجعة „ويلائم بمبسمه سينات هذه السطور" لم ترد في صبح.

17 بدلًا من „بنصيب مسرّته لمسرّة" ورد في صبح „بمسرة".

18 وازاد بر.

، ورد[19] بالبشارة العُظمى ، والنعمى التي ما ضاهتْها الأيّامُ قبْلُ بنُعمى ، والمسرّة التي يأكل حديثُها أحاديث المسرّات ﴿أكلًا لمّا﴾ ، ويُحِبّه[20] الإسلامُ والمسلمون ﴿حبًّا جمًّا﴾ ، وسلامةِ[21] جوهر الجسد الشريف من ذلك العَرَض[22] ، وشفائه الذي في عيون الأعداء منه شفًا[23] يطعن و﴿في قلوبهم مرض﴾ ، وأنّ مادّة الأدواء بحمد الله قد انحسمَتْ[24] ، والواردة من الافتقاد[25] بالأجر والعافية قد اتّسمت[26] ، وثغور المماليك التي تصبح ثغورُ الممالك مِثلَها قد ابتسمت[27] ، وأنّ ظنون الإشفاق قد اضمحلّت ، ونسمات الروض قد فدت[28] الجسد الشريف فاعتلّت ، وأخبار الهناء يُغنّيها[29] كلُّ بريد[30] نشوان من الفرح أُسائلها[31] (أيّ المواطن حلّت) ،[2b] فيا لها بشارةً خصّت الإسلام وعمّت بنيه ، وسارت فوق الأرض وسرّت تحتها أسلاف الملك ومُبتنيه ، وشملت البلاد وعبادها ، والسلطنةَ وقد حجب الله عمادها عمّا دهى ، والملك السليماني وقد ثبّت الله به على الدنيا من السماء خيمتها ومن الجبال أوتادها ، والطير وقد حملت وُرقه أوراق بطائق[32] السرور ، والوحش وقد قالت مهاه على عيني أتحمّل ذلك السقام أو ذلك الفتور ، ﴿ذلك الفضلُ من الله وكفى بالله عليما﴾ ، والألطاف الراحم بها المؤمنين من خلقه ﴿وكان بالمؤمنين رحيما﴾ ،[2c] وكان ورود هذا المثال الشريف على يد فلان

19 وزاد تو، ورد بر.

20 ويُحِبُّها صبح.

21 بسلامة صبح.

22 العوض بر.

23 شِفَاراً صبح.

24 انجسمت بر.

25 الانقياد بر.

26 انسمت بر، ابتسمت صبح.

27 السجعة „وثغور المماليك التي تصبح ثغورُ الممالك مِثلَها قد ابتسمت" لم ترد في صبح.

28 فدّت تو، فدت بر.

29 يعسها تو، بعينها بر، يُعيِّنها صبح.

30 يريد بر.

31 سايلها بر.

32 هذه الكلمة لم ترد في صبح.

فيا له مِن واردٍ لَمشارع الأمن أوْرَد ، ولروائع البأس[33] عن القلوب حجب أو ردّ ، وقد جهّزه المملوك بالمثال الشريف المختصّ بمولانا وبهذه الخدمة بعد أنْ ضُربت البشائر متنوّعة[34] في كلّ ضربٍ من التهاني ، وزيّنت البلد زينةً ما نظمت[35] فيها غير العقود أيدي الغواني ،[3] فيأخذ مولانا[36] حظّه من هذه البشرى ، ونصيبه من هذا الوجه الذي ملأ الوجوه بِشْرا ، وشطره[37] من الهناء المخصوص الذي تعجّل منه المملوك شطرا ، والذي ألزمها[38] وألزم الخلق شكران الفرح فاجتمعوا عليه والحمد لله شكرا[39] ، والله تعالى يسرّه بكلّ خيرٍ تُشرق زواهِرُه ، وتعبق في كمائم الدروج أزاهِرُه ، ويتألّق على يد بريده من المخلّقات[40] كلّ كوكب صبح تملأ الدنيا بشائرُه.

Übersetzung der frohen Kunde von der Genesung des Sultans

[1] Gott möge aus der Menge der Glückwünsche, die es gibt, bei ihm [d.h. beim Adressaten] alle erlesenen ankommen lassen, damit sie ihn erfreuen, die allerbesten, damit sie vor seinem hochgeachteten Blick festgegründet stehen (*yaqarru*) und ihn erquicken (*wa-yuqirruhu*), und alle überfließend vollen (*wa-kulla wafiyy*), die so beschaffen sind, dass man sagt, wenn sie am Horizont von Aleppo[41] (*Ḥalab*)[42] aufscheinen: Wie wunderbar sind sie (*li-llāhi darruhu*)![43] Mögen die Freudennachrichten ihm immer mit einem schönen

33 الناس صبح.

34 مسوغةً صبح.

35 نطمت بر، لطمت بر.

36 هذه الكلمة لم ترد في صبح.

37 وسطره تو، وشطره بر.

38 الزمها بر.

39 السجعة „والذي ألزمها وألزم الخلق شكران الفرح فاجتمعوا عليه والحمد لله شكرا" لم ترد في صبح.

40 المحلقات تو، المخلقات بر وصبح.

41 Die Nennung dieses Stadtnamens deutet darauf hin, dass das vorliegende Schreiben an den Statthalter in Aleppo ergangen ist.

42 *Ḥalab* bedeutet neben „Aleppo" auch „frischgemolkene Milch," und diese zweite, vordergründig nicht gemeinte Bedeutung korrespondiert mit *darruhu*, wörtl. „seine Milch," in der den Satz abschließenden idiomatischen Wendung.

43 Idiomatische Wendung, die wörtl. „für Gott bzw. Gottes ist seine Milch" bedeutet.

Gesichtsausdruck begegnen,[44] mit eindeutigen gewaltigen Geschehnissen[45] und ihm Nachrichten solchen Inhalts verkünden, dass nach der Genesung der Bezugsperson dieser Nachrichten die diesseitige Welt genest und außer dem [sanft wehenden] Luftzug niemand mehr matt ist (*fa-laysa bi-hā ġayra n-nasīmi ʿalīl*).[46] [Er küsst die Hand des Empfängers][47] mit solchen Küssen, welche den [vorzüglich aufgereihten] Halsperlenketten der vorderen Zähne gleichen (*taqbīlan yuzāḥimu bihi ʿuqūda ṯ-ṯuġūr*),[48] welche aufgrund ihres freudigen Lächelns zu den *sīn*-Buchstaben dieser Zeilen (*sīnāti hāḏihī s-suṭūr*)[49] passen[50] und welche die geöffneten Lippen sich nicht schließen lassen zum Kuss wegen des andauernden Lächelns, das diese Freude hervorgebracht hat.

[2a] Der Absender, nach der Erhebung (*rafʿ*)[51] seiner Hände [gen Himmel] zum Bittgebet [für den Adressaten], nach der Umschließung (*ḍamm*)[52] der tiefempfundenen Ergebenheit mit seinen Rippen und nach der nachdrücklichen Beteuerung (*ǧazm*)[53] des gemeinsamen Wohlseins, das er [mit dem Empfänger] durch die Teilhabe an unseres Herrn Freude und Wohlsein genießt, [nach

44 Eigentlich: Mögen die Freudennachrichten von sämtlichen Gesichtern, die diesen Freudennachrichten zur Verfügung stehen, für die Begegnung mit ihm nur schöne Gesichter auswählen.

45 Wörtl. „mit Eindeutigem, Gewaltigem“.

46 Hier spielt Ibn Nubāta mit dem doppelten Sinn des Adjektivs *ʿalīl*, das zum einen „krank“ und zum anderen „sanft, leicht (von einer Brise)“ bedeutet. Das hier verwendete Stilmittel der *tawriya* im Zusammenhang mit dem erwähnten Adjektiv wurde von Ibn Nubāta häufig entweder so oder in ähnlicher Form verwendet.

47 Diese Hinzufügung ist spekulativ, aber sie wird durch den anschließend gebrauchten inneren Akkusativ *taqbīlan* bedingt, der die vorhergehende Verwendung *yuqabbil* voraussetzt. Da die einleitende Formel der mamlukenzeitlichen Briefe oft lautete *al-mamlūku yuqabbilu l-yada llatī* [usw.] bzw. *al-mamlūku yuqabbilu l-arḍa llatī* [usw.], wurde die Hinzufügung daran sinngemäß angelehnt.

48 Wörtl. „mit dem Küssen, mit dem er die Halsketten der vorderen Zähne abdrängt“. Die Rang- bzw. Qualititätsgleichheit wurde in der Vormoderne häufig durch das Bild des Gedränges zwischen den Wettstreitenden ausgedrückt.

49 Die Tübinger Leithandschrift hat an dieser Stelle eindeutig die Lesart *saniyyāti hāḏihī s-suṭūr*, die Berliner Handschrift scheint auch diese Lesart zu bieten. Die Editionsentscheidung unsererseits für *sīnāt* liegt darin begründet, dass zum einen Ibn Nubāta das gleiche Bild, mindestens einmal, an einer anderen Stelle in seinen Werken verwendet hat (Ibn Nubāta, *Zahr* 265) und dass zum anderen das Adjektiv *saniyy* hier inhaltlich nicht zu passen scheint.

50 Wörtl. „[mit dem Küssen], mit dessen Lächeln er diesen Zeilen entspricht.“

51 Abgesehen von der allg. Bedeutung „auf-, hochheben“ wird auch in der arab. Grammatik in der Bedeutung verwendet „ein Wort in den Nominativ setzen.“

52 Abgesehen von der allg. Bedeutung „sammeln, ernten; eingliedern“ wird auch in der arab. Grammatik in der Bedeutung verwendet „einen Konsonanten mit dem Vokal *u* aussprechen.“

53 Abgesehen von der allg. Bedeutung „abschneiden; beschließen“ wird auch in der arab.

alledem] setzt er den Empfänger darüber in Kenntnis, dass das oberherrscherliche Schreiben (*al-miṯāl aš-šarīf*),[54] Gott möge die Hochachtung ihm gegenüber steigern und seine übergroße Macht über seine [bzw. Seine] Knechte über alles Maß hinaus mehren (*wa-zāda faḍla sulṭānihi sarafan*),[55] eingetroffen ist. Dieses enthält die erfreulichste aller Botschaften, die größte Wohltat, der keine der Wohltaten, die in den verstrichenen Zeiten erwiesen worden sind, gleicht, und die Freude, deren Ausspruch alle übrigen Aussprüche bezüglich der Freuden „vollständig aufzehrt" [Q 89:19];[56] und der Islam und die Muslime „lieben über alles" [Q 89:20] diesen Ausspruch. Dieses Schreiben verkündet die Erlösung der Substanz des Körpers des Sultans vom Akzidens der Krankheit und die Genesung dieses Körpers (*šifāʾihi*), und infolge dieser Genesung stecken in den Augen der Feinde schneidende Kanten fest (*minhu šafan yaṭʿanu*) und „in ihrem Herzen haben sie eine Krankheit" [Q 2:10]. Dieses Schreiben verkündet, dass, Gott sei Preis dafür, die Krankheit geheilt wurde (*anna māddata l-adwāʾi bi-ḥamdi Llāhi qad-i nḥasamat*),[57] dass die [dem Sultan] erwiesene [göttliche] Güte (*al-wāridata mina l-iftiqādi*)[58] ihm vor allen Dingen [jenseitigen] Lohn

Grammatik in der Bedeutung verwendet „ein Verb in den Apokopatus oder Imperativ setzen". Es ist offensichtlich, dass Ibn Nubāta mit der Nennung der drei grammatischen Begriffe neben der eigentlich gemeinten eine grammatische Sinnebene geschaffen hat. Es ist allerdings nicht auf Anhieb ersichtlich, ob diese zusätzliche Sinnebene einen tiefer liegenden Sinn für den damaligen Leser ergeben sollte oder ob sie hier lediglich eine *nukta*, bestehend in der Verwendung der rhetorischen Figur *at-tawǧīh*, darstellt.

54 Der Begriff *al-miṯāl aš-šarīf* taucht u.a. oft in den Nilbriefen auf und bezeichnet dort Briefe, die im Namen des jeweils amtierenden mamlukischen Sultans in Kairo mit der Nachricht über den *wafāʾ* des Nils ergingen. Das Adjektiv *šarīf*, abgesehen von seiner Bedeutung im religiösen Kontext, drückte häufig einen Bezug zum mamlukischen Sultan aus und wurde synonym zum Adjektiv *sulṭānī* verwendet. Aus diesem Grunde wurde in den Fällen, in welchen der Bezug zum mamlukischen Sultan in Kairo eindeutig war, das Adjektiv *šarīf* mit „oberherrscherlich" übersetzt; damit sollte eine etwaige Unklarheit vermieden werden, wenn z.B. der Adressat des vorliegenden Schreibens als *mawlānā* „unser Herr" angesprochen wird.

55 Auch die Übersetzung ist möglich „und die Großherzigkeit seines [bzw. Seines] Sultans gegenüber seinen [bzw. Seinen] Knechten alle Maße sprengend mehren."

56 Die Übersetzung der Koranzitate wurde entweder wörtlich aus der Koranübersetzung Rudi Parets übernommen oder, wo es erforderlich war, daran angelehnt.

57 Diese Formulierung lässt sich nur sinngemäß wiedergeben. Die Wendung *ḥasm al-mādda* wurde im vormodernen Sprachgebrauch nicht selten im Kontext von Rebellionen, Aufständen u.Ä. im Sinne „hart durchgreifen, bekämpfen; unterbinden, ein Ende setzen" verwendet.

58 Das Wort *al-iftiqād* kommt bei Ibn Nubāta in den Briefen vor, in denen man Dank für empfangene Geschenke ausdrückt. Es scheint dort die Bedeutung zu haben „Akt der Freundlichkeit, eine Liebenswürdigkeit (bestehend in der Übersendung von Wassermelonen z.B.)."

und körperliches Wohl beschert hat, dass die Vorderzähne der Untertanen (*ṯuġūr al-mamālīk*), und hierin werden die Grenzstädte der mamlukischen Provinzen (*ṯuġūr al-mamālik*) es ihnen gewiss gleichtun, im beglückten Lächeln sichtbar geworden sind, dass die Sorge [um den Sultan] nun ein Ende gefunden hat, dass die Duftzüge der Wiesen, nachdem sie den Sultanskörper ausgelöst hatten, selbst schwach geworden sind und dass alle freudetrunkenen Postboten den Nachrichten dieses Wohls [den überlieferten Vers] vorsingen:[59] „Ich frage sie, welchen Ort sie als ihr Zuhause auserkoren haben."[60]

[2b] Welch wunderbare frohe Botschaft ist diese Nachricht, die den Islam und die Gesamtheit der Muslime betrifft,[61] die oberhalb der Erdoberfläche dahineilt und unter der Erde Freude bereitet den Vorvätern des Königtums und dessen Erbauern, die sämtliche Landstriche mit all ihren Bewohnern umfasst sowie auch das Sultanat, dessen Pfeiler (*ʿimādahā*)[62] Gott nun erlöst (wörtl. abgeschirmt) hat von dem Übel, das ihn heimgesucht hat; diese Nachricht umfasst das Königtum des Salomo, durch welches Gott das Zelt dieser Welt, nämlich den Himmel, und die Pflöcke dieser Welt, nämlich die Berge, unverrückbar gefestigt hat, [sie umfasst] die Vögel, deren Tauben die Blätter der Benachrichtigungen dieser Freude verbreiten, und die wilden Tiere, deren Antilopen sagen: Ich [übernehme und] trage auf meinem Auge diese Krankheit oder diese Kraftlosigkeit.[63] „Derart ist Gottes Huld, und Gott weiß gut genug Bescheid." [Q 4:70] Und derart sind Zeugnisse der Güte Gottes, mit welchen Er den Gläubigen unter Seinen Geschöpfen Seine Barmherzigkeit erzeigt und „Er verfährt barmherzig mit den Gläubigen." [Q 33:43]

59 Der *rasm* dieses Wortes ist in der Tübinger Handschrift nicht punktiert; die Berliner Handschrift bietet den gleichen *rasm*, dessen unklare Punktierung die beiden Lesarten *yuʿīnuhā* oder *yuʿayyinuhā* erlaubt. Ausgehend von der Tendenz Ibn Nubātas, den von ihm eingeflochtenen Versen bzw. Versfragmenten bestimmte Signalwörter voranzustellen, erschien hier *yuġannīhā* als sinnvoll.

60 Hierbei handelt es sich um ein Versfragment des bekannten Dichters der abbasidischen Epoche Abū Tammām (gest. 232/845), wobei der betreffende Vers den Anfang seines Lobgedichts bildet. Ibn Nubāta hat häufig in die von ihm verfassten Texte, seien es offizielle oder private Schreiben gewesen, Verse bzw. Versfragmente der für ihn damals klassischen Zeit eingeflochten; sein persönlicher Favorit scheint Abū ṭ-Ṭayyib al-Mutanabbī (gest. 354/965) gewesen zu sein, doch auch auf Abū Tammāms Verse griff er häufig zurück.

61 Auch die beiden Übersetzungen sind möglich: „die den Islam im Einzelnen und die Muslime im Allgemeinen betroffen hat" bzw. „die den Islam ausgezeichnet und sämtliche Muslime umfasst hat."

62 Eine Anspielung auf den amtierenden mamlukischen Sultan al-Malik aṣ-Ṣāliḥ ʿImād ad-Dīn Ismāʿīl b. Muḥammad b. Qalāwūn (reg. 743–746/1342–1345).

63 Hier benutzt Ibn Nubāta ein in der vormodernen arabischen Dichtung häufiges Bild, wobei der schmachtvolle Blick mit Krankheit assoziiert wird.

[2c] Die Überbringung dieses oberherrscherlichen Schreibens ist durch den Soundso erfolgt. Welch wunderbarer Ankommender ist er, der [uns] bei den Wassertränken der Geborgenheit ankommen [und laben] ließ und der die Herzen von den schaudererregenden Hieben des Kampgetümmels erlöst bzw. [die Hiebe] abgewehrt hat. Der Untertan hat ihn [diesen Überbringer], versehen mit dem oberherrscherlichen Schreiben, das für unseren Herrn bestimmt war, sowie mit diesem vorliegenden Schreiben, auf den Weg [zu ihm] geschickt, nachdem diese Frohbotschaft feierlich so gewürdigt wurde, als hätte sie die Frohbotschaften zu sämtlichen Anlässen, zu denen beglückwünscht wird, in sich getragen (*baʿda an ḍuribati l-bašāʾiru mutanawwiʿatan fī kulli ḍarbin mina t-tahānī*),[64] und nachdem die Stadt [anlässlich dieser Frohbotschaft] mit einem Schmuck verziert wurde, den die Hände der Frauen von natürlicher [betörender] Schönheit ausschließlich aus Halsperlenketten zusammengefügt haben.

[3] Unser Herr [der Adressat] nehme seinen Anteil an dieser frohen Botschaft entgegen, seinen Teil von diesem erquickenden Ereignis [wörtl. Gesicht], dank welchem die Gesichter in überschwänglicher Freude erstrahlen,[65] und [er nehme] die für ihn bestimmte Hälfte dieser Beglückwünschung,[66] deren andere Hälfte der Untertan bereits empfangen hat und die den Untertan und seinen Adressaten sowie auch alle Geschöpfe zum Dank für diese Freude verpflichtet, sodass sie allesamt zum Zwecke der Danksagung, und Gott sei Preis dafür, sich zusammenfinden. Gott, erhaben sei Er, wird gewiss den Adressaten mit allen Wohl bringenden Nachrichten erquicken, deren glänzende Sterne hell aufscheinen, deren Blumen in den Kelchen der Papierbögen ihren Duft verströmen und die so sind, dass durch die Überbringung mittels [ausschwärmender] Postboten der Morgenstern dieser duftenden Botschaften (*al-muḫallaqāt*)[67] glänzt, dessen Frohbotschaften die ganze Welt erfüllen.

---

64 Eine sinngemäße Wiedergabe, die hoffentlich den hier gemeinten Sinn einigermaßen trifft.

65 Wörtl. „das die Gesichter mit Freude erfüllt hat."

66 Wörtl. „seine Hälfte der [für ihn] bestimmten [bzw. der ausgezeichneten] Beglückwünschung."

67 Wörtl. bedeutet *muḫallaq* „das, was mit *ḫalūq*, einer Paste aus Moschus und Safran, bestrichen wurde". Dieses Wort war beim mamlukenzeitlichen Leser am ehesten mit dem Brauch assoziiert, der als *taḫlīq* bekannt war und der in der Bestreichung der im Nilometer von Kairo befindlichen Messsäule sowie der Wände des Schachtes des Nilometers mit der erwähnten Paste bestand. (Diem, *Nilbriefe* 97) Dieser Brauch bildete einen wichtigen Bestandteil der Zeremonie, die mit dem Fest der Nilschwemme einherging, und er findet häufige Erwähnung in den Nilbriefen. Wohlgerüche wurden darüber hinaus u.a. mit erfreulichen Nachrichten assoziiert.

Analyse

Der Adressat

Die Frohbotschaft setzt unvermittelt und buchstäblich mitten im Satz ein, denn das Verb, auf das sich der innere Akkusativ *taqbīlan* der Einleitung bezieht, ist nicht erwähnt. Der zu erwartende Satzanfang müsste vermutlich wie folgt klingen: *al-mamlūku yuqabbilu l-yada l-karīmata*. Es werden weder Angaben zum Datum der Versendung noch zur Identität des Adressaten gemacht noch lassen sie sich aus dem Text erschließen. Was den zeitlichen Aspekt betrifft, so kann der Leser ausgehend vom Titel des Bandes nur so viel schlussfolgern, dass das geschilderte Ereignis irgendwann im Laufe des Jahres 743/1342 stattgefunden haben muss. Der Adressat ist, wie vorher erwähnt, nicht explizit genannt. In den mamlukenzeitlichen Briefen war es üblich, den Namen bzw. den Ehrentitel des Adressaten in den ersten Reimprosakola der Einleitung anzudeuten. Dies geschah dadurch, dass die konstituierenden Nomen des Namens bzw. des Ehrentitels des Empfängers einzeln aufgegriffen und in neuem Sinnzusammenhang zusammengesetzt wurden.[68] Ibn Nubāta setzte dieses Mittel in den von ihm verfassten Ernennungen konsequent ein. Doch im vorliegenden Fall scheinen keine Anhaltspunkte vorzuliegen, die Rückschlüsse auf den Namen bzw. den Ehrentitel des Empfängers erlauben könnten. Lediglich der Ort seiner Amtsausübung, Aleppo, ist genannt, aber nur – so scheint es –, um ausgehend von seinem wörtlichen Sinn eine idiomatische Wendung einzuweben.

Der Empfänger wird mit *mawlānā* „unser Herr“ angesprochen. Dies ist eine weit verbreitete Anrede im mamlukenzeitlichen offiziellen und im privaten Schrifttum gewesen. Der Absender bezeichnete sich selbst in solchen Fällen entsprechend als *mamlūk* „Sklave“. Beide Begriffe haben eine eigene Entwicklungsgeschichte, in deren Verlauf sie auf gesellschaftlich gesehen sehr unterschiedliche Personengruppen bezogen wurden, und sind hier nicht in ihrem wörtlichen Sinn zu verstehen.[69] Mit deren Verwendung sollte – theoretisch

---

68 So lautet z.B. das erste Kolon der Ernennung von Tāǧ ad-Dīn ʿAbd ar-Raḥīm, dem Sohn des berühmten Rhetorikers und Predigers Ǧalāl ad-Dīn al-Ḫaṭīb al-Qazwīnī (666–739/1268–1338), zum Prediger der Omayyadenmoschee in Damaskus wie folgt: *al-ḥamdu li-llāhi llaḏī rafaʿa li-l-manābiri raʾsan bi-stiqrāri tāǧihā* „Preis sei Gott, Der die Köpfe der Kanzeln erhoben hat durch das Festsitzen ihrer Krone“ (Fol. 151ᵃ). In dieser Ernennung wird der Bezug zum erwähnten Tāǧ ad-Dīn ʿAbd ar-Raḥīm dadurch hergestellt, dass das Wort *tāǧ*, das in seinem Ehrentitel enthalten ist, aufgegriffen und im Kontext der Personifikation von Kanzeln in einer neuen Zusammensetzung gebraucht wird.

69 Siehe zur kurzen Übersicht der Entwicklungsgeschichte der beiden Begriffe samt einigen Verwendungsbeispielen: al-Baqlī, *at-Taʿrīf* 330–1, 336.

zumindest – der hohe Respekt gegenüber dem Empfänger und die ehrerbietige, diensteifrige Haltung des Absenders ausgedrückt werden. Es ist bemerkenswert, dass diese beiden Begriffe auch in der Korrespondenz von Personen gebraucht wurden, die auf der gleichen hierarchischen Stufe standen. Im vorliegenden Fall stand der namenlose Statthalter von Damaskus, in dessen Namen die Frohbotschaft erging, sogar auf einer höheren administrativen Stufe als der namenlose Statthalter von Aleppo, an den die Frohbotschaft adressiert war.

Formale Merkmale

In der Überschrift des hier betrachteten Schreibens kommt das Wort *bišāra* „frohe Botschaft, erfreuliche Kunde" vor. In allen konstituierenden Schreiben von *Taʿlīq ad-dīwān aš-šarīf li-sanat 743 min kalām Ibn Nubāta* gibt es lediglich drei, deren jeweilige Überschrift *bišāra* explizit enthält: *Kitāb al-bišāra bi-s-salṭana aš-šarīfa aṣ-ṣāliḥiyya ilā nāʾib Ḥamāh ʿan al-ḥāǧib*,[70] *Kitāb al-bišāra bi-wafāʾ an-Nīl*[71] und *Kitāb al-bišāra bi-l-ʿāfiya aš-šarīfa as-sulṭāniyya*.[72] Wohlgemerkt sind zum Thema der Nilschwemme in *Taʿlīq ad-dīwān aš-šarīf li-sanat 743* zwei Schreiben überliefert. Nur das erste hat den eben erwähnten Titel, das zweite folgt im Anschluss daran und trägt die Überschrift *Kitāb āḫar fī l-maʿnā*.[73] Es wurde weiter oben im Abschnitt *Anmerkungen zur Edition* darauf hingewiesen, dass zahlreiche offizielle Schreiben aus der Feder Ibn Nubātas auch in *Ṣubḥ al-aʿšā fī ṣināʿat al-inšā* überliefert sind. Dies trifft auch in besonders bemerkenswerter Weise auf die vier eben erwähnten Frohbotschaftsbriefe zu. Sie alle – und nur sie allein – werden nämlich von al-Qalqašandī im Kapitel zitiert, das davon handelt, auf welche Weise die Briefe des mamlukischen Sultans an bestimmte Statthalter verschickt und dann von den Letzteren an den Rest der Statthalter weiter versendet werden. Dieses Kapitel eröffnet al-Qalqašandī mit der folgenden aufschlussreichen Einleitung:

> Wisse, dass dies üblich ist: wenn ein oberherrscherliches Schreiben, das von der Pforte des Sultans abgeschickt wurde, beim Statthalter in Damaskus ankommt [unklar],[74] verkündet der Statthalter von Damaskus schriftlich den anderen Statthaltern die frohe Botschaft der Ankunft des ober-

70 Fol. 159ᵇ–160ᵃ. Die Folienangaben hier und im Folgenden beziehen sich auf die Tübinger Handschrift.

71 Fol. 161ᵃ–161ᵇ.

72 Fol. 163ᵇ–164ᵃ.

73 Fol. 161ᵇ.

74 Die Passage hier ist unklar.

> herrscherlichen Schreibens. Er verschickt an jeden Statthalter zusammen mit dem oberherrscherlichen Schreiben, das für jeden einzelnen von ihnen bestimmt ist, sein eigenes Begleitschreiben, in dem er sinngemäß das bei ihm eingetroffene oberherrscherliche Schreiben wiedergibt. Allerdings stellt seine sinngemäße Wiedergabe eine Nacherzählung des eingegangenen oberherrscherlichen Schreibens dar, und er beschränkt sich auf die Rolle des Wiederholers.[75]

Mit anderen Worten, die hier behandelte Frohbotschaft Ibn Nubātas ist ein Begleitschreiben gewesen, das zusammen mit dem oberherrscherlichen Schreiben diesbezüglich aus Kairo an den Statthalter von Aleppo ergangen ist.

Intertextualität

Über den berühmten Dichter der abbasidischen Epoche Abū Nuwās (gest. 198/813) wird folgende Anekdote überliefert. Er soll einmal einen der wichtigsten Überlieferer der vor- wie frühislamischen Dichtung namens Ḫalaf al-Aḥmar (gest. 180/796), bei dem er in die Lehre gegangen ist, um Erlaubnis gebeten haben, eigene Verse dichten zu dürfen. Dieser soll bereit gewesen sein, ihm diese Erlaubnis nur dann zu gewähren, wenn Abū Nuwās zuvor tausend Gedichte früherer Dichter auswendig gelernt habe. Nach einer gewissen Zeit der Abwesenheit sei Abū Nuwās wieder zu Ḫalaf al-Aḥmar gekommen und habe im Laufe der nächsten Tage die memorierten Verse wortgetreu vorgetragen. Nach erfolgreich bestandener Prüfung habe er erneut die gleiche Erlaubnis erbeten. Doch diesmal habe sein Lehrer von Abū Nuwās verlangt, die gelernten Verse so gründlich zu vergessen, als hätte er sie nie gewusst. Nach einiger Zeit der Abwesenheit sei der junge Dichter imstande gewesen, auch diese Herausforderung zu meistern, und erst danach habe sein Lehrer ihm die Befähigung zugesprochen, eigene Gedichte zu reimen.[76] Soweit wir informiert sind, musste sich Ibn Nubāta einer solchen Prüfung nicht unterziehen. Nichtsdestoweniger gewährt die erwähnte Anekdote einen erhellenden Einblick in die in der Vormoderne unter den arabischen Literaten herrschende Mentalität. Auch Ibn Nubāta muss sich immer wieder vergegenwärtigt haben, in einer jahrhundertelangen literarischen Tradition zu stehen, und er muss sich seiner Pflicht bewusst gewesen sein, sich dieses kulturellen Erbes als würdig zu erweisen und es fortzuschreiben. Und so nimmt es nicht wunder, dass im Korpus seiner Schriften die herausragenden Vertreter der für ihn damals maßgebenden Zeit

---

75 al-Qalqašandī, *Ṣubḥ* viii, 363. Vgl. Diem, *Nilbriefe* 82.

76 Ibn Manẓūr, *Aḫbār* 55.

der arabischen Literatur immer im Hintergrund mehr oder minder gegenwärtig sind. Eine Art, den Bezug zu den einstigen Koryphäen herzustellen, bestand darin, diese direkt namentlich zu nennen. Diese Art kommt besonders in den mamlukenzeitlichen Ernennungsschreiben vor und Ibn Nubāta hat davon häufig Gebrauch gemacht. Namhafte Vertreter einer bestimmten wissenschaftlichen Disziplin, die für die Ausübung des jeweiligen Amtes von unmittelbarer Relevanz war, wurden darin häufig genannt und in Beziehung zu der ernannten Person gesetzt, um die fachliche Kompetenz dieser Person vor diesem illustren Hintergrund zur Geltung zu bringen. Eine andere, subtilere Art bestand darin, eingeflochtenen Versen bzw. Versfragmenten der Altvorderen spezifische Merkwörter voranzustellen und sie so kenntlich zu machen. So wurde die Aufmerksamkeit des kundigen Lesers entsprechend gelenkt; andererseits entschärfte Ibn Nubāta auf diese Weise etwaige Plagiatsvorwürfe. Hierbei wurden für dichterische Zitate vorwiegend das Verb *anšada* „[Gedichtverse] rezitieren“ bzw. dessen Ableitungen und für koranische Zitate das Verb *talā* „[Koranverse] rezitieren“ bzw. dessen Ableitungen verwendet. In vielen anderen Fällen wiederum wurden eingewobene Zitate auf gar keine Weise kenntlich gemacht, und es ist anzunehmen, dass Ibn Nubāta sie als kulturelles Allgemeingut verstanden haben muss.[77] Abgesehen von Zitaten – seien diese nun wie oben beschrieben markiert oder nicht –, die sich nach einem gewissen Aufwand doch meistens erkennen und eindeutig zuordnen lassen, hat Ibn Nubāta eine noch subtilere und daher schwerer zu fassende Form von Anleihen eingesetzt. Diese bestand darin, klassische *maʿānī*[78] entweder in seine Texte einzuweben oder auf diese anzuspielen. Solche Anleihen sind besonders schwer zu eruieren, weil sie eine immense innige Vertrautheit mit dem kulturellen Erbe der vormamlukischen Zeit voraussetzen. Bei der Sichtung der oben erwähnten *Taʿlīq*-Bände Ibn Nubātas konnte beobachtet werden, dass Ibn Nubāta an einigen Stellen entweder einen überlieferten dichterischen *maʿnā* übernimmt oder aber ihn in dessen Gegenteil kehrt. Der Umfang dieser letztgenannten Spielart von Anleihen kann aktuell nicht eingeschätzt werden, wir begnügen uns an dieser Stelle lediglich mit dem Hinweis darauf, dass ein solches Phänomen stattgehabt hat.

77 In der hier behandelten Frohbotschaft betrifft dies kurze Koranzitate und eine idiomatische Redewendung.

78 Die Übersetzung dieses Kernbegriffs der arabischen Poetik, Literaturkritik und Rhetorik ist nicht einfach, weil er je nach der wissenschaftlichen Disziplin unterschiedliches meinen kann. Hier ist „Ideeninhalt; literarisches Motiv“ damit gemeint.

Geschichtlicher Gehalt

Der Überschrift der Frohbotschaft lässt sich lediglich nur soviel entnehmen, dass der namentlich nicht genannte amtierende Sultan wieder gesund geworden ist. Weder die Überschrift noch der Wortlaut der Frohbotschaft enthalten konkrete Details hinsichtlich der Identität des Sultans, der Art seiner Erkrankung oder des Zeitpunktes seiner Genesung. Zwecks Eruierung dieser Angaben muss externes Quellenmaterial herangezogen sowie der Text des Schreibens nach impliziten Hinweisen durchforscht werden. Hierbei erlaubt der Titel der Handschrift *Taʿlīq ad-dīwān aš-šarīf li-sanat 743* im ersten Schritt eine grobe zeitliche Einordnung dieses Ereignisses und bietet somit einen guten Ausgangspunkt für weiterführende Recherche.

Wollten wir dabei nur davon ausgehen und uns ausschließlich auf den Text der Frohbotschaft beschränken, so sind wir durch Zuhilfenahme des annalistisch strukturierten Geschichtswerkes *as-Sulūk li-maʿrifat duwal al-mulūk* von Taqī ad-Dīn Aḥmad b. ʿAlī al-Maqrīzī (766–845/1364–1441) imstande, die Identität des im besagten Jahr amtierenden Sultans zu bestimmen. Es muss sich um den mamlukischen Sultan Ismāʿīl b. Muḥammad b. Qalāwūn (reg. 743–6/1342–5) gehandelt haben, der im Monat *Muḥarram*, dem ersten Monat des islamischen Kalenders, des Jahres 743/1342 inauguriert wurde.[79] Im Text der Frohbotschaft selbst ist bei genauerem Hinsehen ein wichtiger, wenn auch vage gehaltener impliziter Hinweis auf die Identität des Sultans enthalten, der allerdings in seinem eigentlichen Sinn erst vor dem Hintergrund der betreffenden Angaben al-Maqrīzīs über die Geschehnisse des Jahres 743/1342 verstanden werden kann. An einer Stelle heißt es bei Ibn Nubāta nämlich:

> Welch wunderbare frohe Botschaft ist diese Nachricht, die den Islam und die Gesamtheit der Muslime betrifft, die oberhalb der Erdoberfläche dahineilt und unter der Erde Freude bereitet den Vorvätern des Königtums und dessen Erbauern, die sämtliche Landstriche mit all ihren Bewohnern umfasst sowie auch das Sultanat, dessen Pfeiler (*ʿimādahā*) Gott nun erlöst (wörtl. abgeschirmt) hat von dem Übel, das ihn heimgesucht hat.

Mit *ʿimādahā* wird die Aufmerksamkeit des Lesers auf den *laqab* „Ehrentitel" des Sultans gelenkt, nämlich *al-Malik aṣ-Ṣāliḥ ʿImād ad-Dīn*, und mit diesem Vorwissen gewappnet kann der Leser die Ambiguität um *ʿimādahā* auflösen und den eigentlich gemeinten Sinn dieses Wortes verstehen. Wohlgemerkt war

79 al-Maqrīzī, *as-Sulūk* iii, 376.

Ibn Nubāta dank seiner umfassenden Bildung versiert darin, Namens- bzw. Ehrentitelbestandteile von Personen in seine Texte subtil einzuweben und sie somit auf diese Art zu adressieren bzw. zu erwähnen. Trug z.B. jemand einen koranischen Namen wie Ismāʿīl, Dāwūd oder Ibrāhīm, so bestand eine hohe Wahrscheinlichkeit, dass Ibn Nubāta die jeweilige Person aus dem Kontext eines Koranzitats heraus, in dem dieser Name vorkommt, adressierte. Auf Ismāʿīl wurde mit Vers 39 der 14. Sure, auf Dāwūd mit Vers 20 der 38. Sure und auf Ibrāhīm mit Vers 37 der 53. Sure verwiesen. Neben dem Koran stand Ibn Nubāta auch das immense Korpus des arabisch-islamischen Schrifttums in seinen vielfältigen Ausprägungen zur Verfügung, aus dem er sich je nach Bedarf bedienen konnte und bedient hat.[80]

Was den mamlukischen Sultan betrifft, so enthalten zwar einige biographische Lexika wie *Kitāb al-wāfī bi-l-wafayāt* von Ṣalāḥ ad-Dīn Ḫalīl b. Aybak aṣ-Ṣafadī (gest. 764/1363),[81] *ad-Durar al-kāmina* von Aḥmad b. ʿAlī b. Ḥağar al-ʿAsqalānī (773–852/1372–1449)[82] oder *al-Manhal aṣ-ṣāfī wa-l-mustawfī baʿd al-Wāfī* von Yūsuf b. Taġrībirdī (812–74/1410–70)[83] grundlegende, allgemeine Angaben über ihn und seine Herrschaft, allerdings sind diese nicht detailliert genug, um den Inhalt der Frohbotschaft auf irgendeine Art widerzuspiegeln. Somit sind wir darauf angewiesen, das gesamte von al-Maqrīzī für das Jahr 743/1342 zusammengetragene Material in der Hoffnung zu sichten, dort einen historiographischen Niederschlag des in der Frohbotschaft geschilderten Ereignisses zu finden. Und tatsächlich verzeichnet dieser Autor für das betreffende Jahr zwei Ereignisse, die nähere Betrachtung verdienen.

Im Monat *Rabīʿ al-Āḫir*, dem 4. Monat des islamischen Kalenders, habe der Sultan auf einmal permanentes Nasenbluten (*ruʿāf mustamirr*) gehabt. Einige Zeit später sei er gesund geworden und zu diesem Anlass seien Feierlichkeiten veranstaltet worden; danach sei der Sultan wieder daran erkrankt und kurze Zeit später wieder gesund geworden.[84] Nach al-Maqrīzī hat sich diese Abfolge im Monat *Rabīʿ al-Āḫir* zugetragen.

Im Monat *Ǧumādā al-Āḫira*, dem 6. Monat des islamischen Kalenders, sei der Sultan für mehrere Tage erkrankt, und infolgedessen habe ihn die Schlaffheit am ganzen Körper befallen (*mariḍa ayyāman ḥattā starḫat aʿḍāʾuhu*).[85]

80 Wohlgemerkt hätte Ibn Nubāta genauso gut eine entsprechende koranische Referenz auf *aṣ-Ṣāliḥ* verwenden können, wie er es andernorts gemacht hat.

81 aṣ-Ṣafadī, *al-Wāfī* ix, 131.

82 Ibn Ḥağar, *ad-Durar* i, 380.

83 Ibn Taġrībirdī, *al-Manhal* ii, 425–7.

84 al-Maqrīzī, *as-Sulūk* iii, 381.

85 al-Maqrīzī, *as-Sulūk* iii, 384.

Erst im Monat *Rağab*, dem 7. Monat des muslimischen Jahres, sei die Körperkraft wieder zu ihm zurückgekehrt.[86] Anlässlich dieser Genesung berichtet al-Maqrīzī allerdings von keinen Feierlichkeiten.

Im Text der Frohbotschaft über die Genesung des Sultans finden sich keine Anhaltspunkte dafür, wann genau der Sultan erkrankt und genesen ist und welcher Art seine Erkrankung war. Wenn man versucht, aus den Formulierungen Ibn Nubātas konkrete Hinweise darauf zu gewinnen, welche Krankheit genau den Sultan befallen hat, so stellt man fest, dass diese Formulierungen sich stark an literarischen Topoi orientieren; sie scheinen ferner in dieser Hinsicht keine historische Substanz zu beinhalten, die über die bloße allgemeine Feststellung hinausginge, dass der Sultan im besagten Jahr krank und dann gesund geworden sei. Wenn z. B. Ibn Nubāta davon spricht, dass Antilopen sich bereit erklären, die Krankheit bzw. die Kraftlosigkeit des Sultans zu übernehmen und auf ihren Augen zu tragen, so verwendet er hier einen Topos, der auch an anderen Stellen in seinen Briefen nachweislich vorkommt. Damit wird der Wunsch ausgedrückt, die wie auch immer geartete Krankheit, welche häufig als ein Zustand der Schwäche und Trägheit aufgefasst wurde, möge von ihrem Träger, dem Kranken, auf die Augenlider von Antilopen übergehen, wobei in diesem neuen Kontext Schwäche und Trägheit sinnbildlich für einen schmachtenden bzw. halb gesenkten Blick stehen. Es möge an dieser Stelle nur ein Hinweis darauf genügen, dass Ibn Nubāta diesen Topos auch an manch anderer Stelle aufgriff und ihn entweder in exakt dieser oder in einer ähnlichen Form gebrauchte.[87]

Abschließend sei hervorgehoben, dass die Schilderung der Krankheit in der Frohbotschaft keine Schlüsse darauf erlaubt, auf welche der beiden von al-Maqrīzī für das Jahr 743/1342 verzeichneten Krankheitsfälle des Sultans Ibn Nubāta sich beziehen könnte.

Fazit

Bevor wir uns abschließend der eingangs gestellten Frage bezüglich der Aussagekraft der mamlukenzeitlichen Schreiben zuwenden, seien nachfolgend die oben einzeln angesprochenen Merkmale der Frohbotschaft zusammengefasst.

1. Der behandelte Text der Frohbotschaft konkretisiert keine Namen: der Adressat, der Sultan und der Absender sind anonym. Es findet sich darin lediglich eine vage Anspielung auf den Namen des Sultans.

86 al-Maqrīzī, *as-Sulūk* iii, 386.

87 Ibn Nubāta, *Zahr* 106, 416, 444.

2. Abgesehen von Aleppo, der Stadt, an welche die Frohbotschaft versandt wurde, werden keine weiteren Orte genannt.
3. Weder die Krankheit, von welcher der Sultan genesen ist, noch ihre Dauer werden spezifiziert.
4. Die Frohbotschaft enthält kein Datum.

Da die Frohbotschaft in ihrer gegenwärtig überlieferten Form nicht vollständig ist, kann nicht ausgeschlossen werden, dass die unter den Punkten 1, 2 und 4 genannten fehlenden Angaben ursprünglich – zumindest theoretisch – in einem Teil der Frohbotschaft enthalten gewesen sind, der nicht mitüberliefert wurde. Dies trifft allerdings definitiv nicht auf die Krankheit zu, denn diese selbst wird in einem Teil des Schreibens beschrieben, der vollständig erhalten ist. Daraus kann geschlussfolgert werden, dass die abstrakten sich auf die Krankheit beziehenden Formulierungen durchaus vom Verfasser intendiert waren. Es ist ferner fraglich, ob der Adressat fortlaufend über den Verlauf der Krankheit unterrichtet wurde oder ob er lediglich über das Ergebnis des positiven Krankheitsverlaufs informiert wurde. Wir wissen auch nicht, wie die Frohbotschaft der breiten Öffentlichkeit bekanntgegeben wurde; sollte dies z.B. im Rahmen eines Gottesdienstes von der Kanzel herab erfolgt sein, dann hätte der figurative Stil seine Wirkung auf die Zuhörer sicherlich nicht verfehlt. Die Frohbotschaft enthält zweifelsohne einen geschichtlichen Kern, aber sie kann erst durch die Heranziehung externer Quellen in ihren geschichtlichen Kontext eingeordnet werden.

Mamlukenzeitliche offizielle Verlautbarungen stellen ein eigenartiges literarisches Genre dar. Die Bezeichnung „offiziell“ weckt beim heutigen Leser die Erwartung eines sachlichen und an Fakten orientierten Stils, der nicht nur frei von rhetorischen Figuren und Einflüssen der schöngeistigen Literatur, sondern auch von der persönlichen Akzentsetzung des Schreibers sei. Doch diese Erwartung bewahrheitet sich nicht. Offiziell sind diese Schreiben insofern, als sie einer vorgegebenen Struktur[88] folgen und einige Wendungen beinhalten, die zum unabdingbaren Formular[89] der offiziellen Korrespondenz gehört haben. Ansonsten scheint der mamlukenzeitliche Sekretär eine gewisse Freiheit gehabt zu haben, bei der sprachlichen Ausgestaltung der von ihm verfassten Dokumente rhetorische Figuren zu verwenden und auf das klassische literarische Erbe zurückzugreifen. Die Frohbotschaft über die Genesung des Sultans ist ein Beispiel dafür. Sie weist zwar wesentliche Elemente des Formu-

88 Damit ist hier in Anlehnung an W. Diem die Gliederung der Briefe in inhaltliche Blöcke verstanden (Diem, *Nilbriefe* 419).

89 Damit ist hier in Anlehnung an den eben erwähnten Autor die formelhafte Gestaltung des Rahmens der Briefe verstanden (Diem, *Nilbriefe* 419).

lars der offiziellen mamlukenzeitlichen Schreiben auf und ist entsprechend strukturiert, doch gleichzeitig hatte Ibn Nubāta bei der sprachlichen Ausgestaltung einen großen Spielraum, den er nicht nur mit literarischen Motiven füllte, sondern auch dafür nutzte, dieser offiziellen Mitteilung sein eigenes unverkennbares stilistisches Gepräge zu geben.[90]

Literaturverzeichnis

al-Baqlī, M.Q., *at-Taʿrīf bi-muṣṭalaḥāt Ṣubḥ al-aʿšā*, Kairo 1983.

Bauer, T., Jamāl al-Dīn Ibn Nubātah, in J.E. Lowry und D.J. Stewart (Hgg.), *Essays in Arabic Literary Biography 1350–1850*, Wiesbaden 2009, 184–202.

Bauer, T., Ibn Nubātah al-Miṣrī (686–768/1287–1366): Life and Works, *in MSR* 12,1 (2008), 1–35, und 12,2 (2008), 25–69.

Diem, W., *Arabische amtliche Nilbriefe: Ein Beitrag zur arabischen Kulturgeschichte, Epistolographie und Stilgeschichte des 12.–15. Jahrhunderts*, Baden-Baden 2020.

Ibn Ḥaǧar al-ʿAsqalānī, *ad-Durar al-kāmina fī aʿyān al-miʾa aṯ-ṯāmina*, 4 Bde., Hyderabad 1929–31.

Ibn Nubāta al-Miṣrī, *Taʿlīq ad-dīwān aš-šarīf li-sanat 743 min kalām Ibn Nubāta*. Hs. Berlin 8640 und Hs. Tübingen M a VI 70.

Ibn Nubāta al-Miṣrī, *Kitāb zahr al-manṯūr* and *Min tarassul Ibn Nubāta. A critical edition of two prose works by Ibn Nubāta al-Miṣrī*, A. Herdt (Hg.), Baden-Baden 2019.

Ibn Manẓūr al-Miṣrī, *Aḫbār Abī Nuwās. Taʾrīḫuhu, nawādiruhu, šiʿruhu, muǧūnuhu*, Hgg. M.ʿA. Ibrāhīm [u. a.], [Kairo] 1924.

Ibn Taġrībirdī, Abū l-Maḥāsin, *al-Manhal aṣ-ṣāfī wa-l-mustawfī baʿd al-Wāfī*, Hg. M.M. Amīn, 13 Bde., [Kairo] 1984–2009.

al-Maqrīzī, Taqī ad-Dīn, *as-Sulūk li-maʿrifat duwal al-mulūk*, Hg. M.ʿA. ʿAṭā, 8 Bde., Beirut 1997.

al-Qalqašandī, Aḥmad b. ʿAlī, *Ṣubḥ al-aʿšā fī ṣināʿat al-inšā*, Hg. M.Ḥ. Šamsaddīn, 15 Bde., Beirut 1988.

aṣ-Ṣafadī, Ṣalāḥ ad-Dīn Ḫalīl b. Aybak, *Kitāb al-wāfī bi-l-wafayāt*, Hgg. A. al-Arnāʾūṭ [u. a.], 29 Bde., Beirut 2000.

90 Das bevorzugte und wohl am häufigsten benutzte Stilmittel Ibn Nubātas war *ǧinās*, und dieses kommt sowohl in der hier besprochenen Frohbotschaft als auch in zahlreichen anderen Schreiben dieses Autors mit bemerkenswerter Häufigkeit vor.

6

Ein Hetärengespräch aus dem Kairo des 8./14. Jahrhunderts: al-Miʿmār: *Dīwān*, Gedicht Nr. 540

Gregor Schoeler

Der mamlukenzeitliche ägyptische Handwerkerpoet Ibrāhīm al-Miʿmār („der Baumeister") (gest. 749/1348–9), der bis vor nicht allzu langer Zeit noch so gut wie unbekannt war,*[1] darf heute als einer der bedeutendsten arabischen Dichter der Mamlukenzeit gelten. Die Entdeckung verdanken wir hauptsächlich dem Jubilar, der vor kurzem zusammen mit Anke Osigus und Hakan Özkan eine mustergültige Edition des *Dīwān*s vorgelegt hat.[2] Schon vorher hatte er eine umfassende einführende Studie über Leben und Werk al-Miʿmārs[3] sowie zwei Aufsätze über einzelne Werke von ihm veröffentlicht.[4] Thomas Bauer hat mithin einen beachtlichen Teil seiner neueren Forschungen dem mamlukenzeitlichen Handwerkerpoeten gewidmet. Ausserdem hat er Kollegen und

* Bei der Wahl des Begriffs „Hetäre" bin ich mir der Problematik bewusst, die mit der Übertragung eines Begriffes aus einer Kultur auf eine andere verbunden ist. Doch habe ich für den Titel des Aufsatzes keine griffigere Bezeichnung für eine junge Frau finden können, deren Erwerbstätigkeit – einerseits – sich auf höherem Niveau abspielt (Unterhaltung durch Musizieren, Singen, Tanzen usw.) und – andererseits – mit dem erotischen Element unlösbar verbunden ist (fliessender Übergang zur Prostitution) (s. auch Anm. 32 und 44). – Ebenso möglich wie „Hetäre," dabei aber mit derselben Problematik verbunden, wäre für den Titel des Aufsatzes wohl das Wort „Geisha," der Name der ebenfalls musisch ausgebildeten traditionellen japanischen Unterhaltungskünstlerin gewesen (s. Schuller, *Hetären* 27–8 und 244–5). – Zur Eignung der von mir gewählten Bezeichnung „Hetären*gespräch*" sei bemerkt, dass sich unter Lukians von Samosata (st. um 200 in Alexandrien) klassischem Werk *Hetairikoi dialogoi* („Hetärengespräche") zwei Dialoge finden, die zwischen Mutter und Tochter geführt werden (III und VII).

1 Weder in der *EI*[2] noch in der *Encyclopedia of Arabic Literature* (EAL) noch in den *Essays in Arabic Literary Biography 925–1350* (EALB) findet sich ein Artikel über ihn. In dem Band *Arabic Literature in the Post-Classical Period* aus der Cambridge History of Arabic Literature (CHAL) wird er in zwei Artikeln insgesamt drei Mal beiläufig erwähnt (83, 211, 212); im Kapitel „Arabic Religious Poetry" wird er fälschlich als „court poet" (83) bezeichnet. Alle Miʿmār-Zitate in diesen Werken sind nicht dem *Dīwān*, sondern der Sekundärüberlieferung entnommen.

2 Siehe Literaturverzeichnis.

3 Bauer, Ibrāhīm al-Miʿmār.

4 Bauer, Die Leiden; ders., Das Nilzağal.

Schüler zur Bearbeitung von Werken dieses und anderer Dichter aus der Epoche angeregt.[5]

Ein Anteil an dem Verdienst der Entdeckung al-Miʿmārs kommt auch der Arbeit an dem Projekt „Katalogisierung der orientalischen Handschriften in Deutschland“[6] zu. Im Rahmen dieser Arbeit war eine Berliner Handschrift des *Dīwāns* dieses Dichters zum Vorschein gekommen.[7] Auf welche Weise die Kenntnis von dieser Entdeckung dann zu dem Jubilar gelangt ist, hat er selbst im Vorwort zu seiner Edition beschrieben (D 8). Und schon vorher hatte Ewald Wagner in der Besprechung einer wichtigen Buchveröffentlichung, die ebenfalls aus der „Katalogisierung“ hervorgegangen ist, diese „Entdeckungsgeschichte“ einem interessierten Fachpublikum bekannt gemacht.[8]

Von den Erkenntnissen, die der Jubilar über die Mamlukenzeit und deren Literatur, insbesondere auch über al-Miʿmār, gewonnen und in Veröffentlichungen bekannt gemacht hat, seien nun einige besonders wichtige hervorgehoben und wörtlich zitiert, die zum Verständnis des im Folgenden zu behandelnden Themas entscheidend beitragen können:

> Die Mamlukenzeit [...] zeichnet sich [..] durch grössere Durchlässigkeit zwischen Hoch- und Volksliteratur[9] aus. In dieser Zeit nun wird es möglich, die Welt der städtischen Mittelschichten literarisch ausführlicher zu thematisieren. Al-Miʿmār betrachtet die Welt ganz und gar aus der Perspektive eines Angehörigen der Mittelschicht [...]. [Die Gedichte] werfen mehr Licht als das Werk jedes anderen Literaten dieser Zeit auf die Gefühle, Erfahrungen und das Weltbild der Angehörigen der Handwerkerschicht dieser Zeit. Für die sozial- und mentalitätsgeschichtliche

5 Zum Beispiel Biesterfeldt, Mizr; Özkan, Drugs.

6 Sie ist ein 1957 von Wolfgang Voigt begründetes, bis 1989 von der Deutschen Forschungsgemeinschaft finanziertes Forschungsprojekt. Es wird seit 1990 von der Akademie in Göttingen fortgeführt. Derzeitiger Leiter ist Tilman Seidensticker.

7 Schoeler, *Arabische Handschriften* ii, 301–2, Nr. 276. – Die *šuhra* (Name, unter dem eine Persönlichkeit bekannt ist) des Dichters ist dort (und auch im Index des Bandes) nach Brockelmann *GAL* ii, 10, und Suppl. ii, 3, aber fälschlich, als *al-Ḥāʾik* („der Weber“) angeführt.

8 Wagner, [Rez.:] Sobieroj 461: „Die kurze Inhaltsangabe der Berliner Handschrift des *Dīwāns* des dichtenden Handwerkers Ibrāhīm al-Miʿmār in Gregor Schoelers Katalog von 1990 (hat) Thomas Bauer veranlasst, sich ab 2002 näher mit dem Dichter und der Mamlūkendichtung insgesamt zu beschäftigen und damit ein allgemeines Interesse für eine ganze, bisher vernachlässigte Periode der arabischen Literaturgeschichte zu erwecken.“

9 Über die Berechtigung, al-Miʿmār als „Volksdichter“ zu bezeichnen, handelt Bauer in seinem Aufsatz Ibrāhīm al-Miʿmār 63–4, 90–3.

> Erforschung der Mamlukenzeit stellen sie damit eine Quelle ersten Ranges dar.[10]

Al-Miʿmār hat ausser Gedichten mit Monoreim (in *qaṣīd*-Versmassen und im *rağaz*), die die grosse Menge seiner poetischen Produktion ausmachen, seltener auch solche in Strophenform verfasst (*mawāliyās*, *zağals*, ein *muwaššaḥ*). Von den umgangssprachlichen *zağals* sind 11 vollständig erhalten. Al-Miʿmārs *zağals* erfreuten sich schon zu seinen Lebzeiten grosser Berühmtheit (D Einleitung 33–4; Ö 103–6) und sind auch für uns von besonderem Interesse. Denn durch ihre Thematik fallen sie aus dem heraus, was man sonst von arabischer Dichtung gewohnt ist. (Dies gilt allerdings auch für viele Gedichte der *qaṣīd*-Gattungen.) Einige der Themen der *zağals* sind: Drogen,[11] u. zw. je ein Gedicht auf Wein (Nr. 535) und Bier (Nr. 536),[12] drei auf den Haschisch (Nrn. 537, 538, 543), eine Satire auf einen „Hamsterer" (das „Nilzağal," Nr. 533),[13] die Klage einer jungen Frau, die sich über ihren Ehemann nach der Hochzeit beklagt (Nr. 539), Klage eines Mannes, der Liebhaber und Frau nicht befriedigen kann (Nr. 541).

Das *zağal*, das im Folgenden behandelt werden soll, reiht sich in diese Gruppe ein. Protagonistin in unserem Gedicht ist allerdings nicht eine Angehörige der Mittelschicht, zu der al-Miʿmār zählte, sondern ein junges Mädchen oder, wahrscheinlicher, eine junge erwachsene Frau aus der Unterschicht; wir erfahren nicht, ob sie Freie, Freigelassene oder Sklavin ist.

Ira Lapidus nennt in seinem Buch *Muslim cities in the later Middle Ages* unter jenen, die zur Unterschicht gehörten und ohne feste Anstellung herumzogen: „Unterhaltungskünstler, […] Ringer, Clowns, Spieler, Geschichtenerzähler und Sängerinnen, die das gemeine Volk auf den Strassen und um die Zitadellen herum unterhielten." (83). Unter mehrere der von Lapidus aufgezählten Kategorien fällt die junge Frau, die der Dichter in dem Gedicht sprechen lässt: Sie ist eine äusserst vielseitige Unterhaltungskünstlerin, kann singen, tanzen, mehrere Instrumente spielen, Gedichte vortragen und lustige Geschichten erzählen; ausserdem arbeitet sie als Prostituierte. Offensichtlich will sie sozial aufsteigen – gegen Ende des Gedichts betont sie, dass Emire und Wesire zu ihrer Kundschaft zählen.

10 Bauer, Die Leiden 1–2.
11 Siehe hierzu Özkan, Drugs.
12 Siehe hierzu Biesterfeldt, Mizr.
13 Siehe hierzu Bauer, Das Nilzağal.

al-Miʿmār, *Dīwān* Nr. 540 (*zaǧal*)

0. *yā mmī anā fī l-ḥurriyya*
mā lī niyya

1. *tuʿaqqilīnī mā ǧannik*
ayš fī ḏihnik
lā tušġilīnī fruġ ʿannik
bi-l-kulliyya

Mutter, ich bin frei,
ich beabsichtige nicht (deinen Ratschlägen zu folgen)!

Willst du mich vernünftig machen/festhalten? Du bist ja wahnsinnig!
Was geht in deinem Kopf vor?
Belästige mich nicht, sonst trenne ich mich von dir
ganz und gar.

Kommentar: … *anā fī l-ḥurriyya mā lī niyya*. Die Rede der jungen Frau setzt die Situation voraus, dass die Mutter sie kurz zuvor bedrängt und ihr geraten hat, das lockere, ungebundene Leben aufzugeben. Vielleicht hat sie ihr empfohlen, einer arrangierten Ehe zuzustimmen. – Dass die junge Frau mit *anā fī l-ḥurriyya* meinen könnte, dass sie eine freie Frau (also keine Sklavin) ist, was theoretisch durchaus möglich wäre, ist nach der Rede, die folgt, unwahrscheinlich. – *mā ǧannik* = *mā aǧannaki*. – *tuʿaqqilīnī*. *ʿaqqala* (II. Stamm) hat zwei ganz unterschiedliche Bedeutungen: „he rendered him *ʿāqil*, i.e. intelligent, etc.;" und „he withheld him, or restrained him … *ʿan ḥāǧatihī* from the object of his want" (s. Lane, s.v. *ʿQL*). Die erste Bedeutung gilt heute auch im Äg.-Ar.: „to teach sense to, make reasonable" (Badawi-Hinds, s.v. *ʿQL*). Beide Bedeutungen ergeben hier einen Sinn; dies wird vom Dichter beabsichtigt sein (Stilmittel der *tawriya*, „Doppelsinnwitz"). In der zweiten Bedeutung, „vernünftig (machen)," ergibt das Wort eine wirkungsvolle Antithese (*ṭibāq*) zu „verrückt." Eine Quasi-Antithese enthält auch die letzte Zeile („zu schaffen machen – sich trennen"). – *lā tušġilīnī fruġ ʿannik*. Ungewöhnlich ist die Präposition *ʿan* statt *min* nach *fariġa*. Nach der Deutung von Y. Faḫraddīn (s. den Kommentar zu Strophe 13) wäre die Zeile wie folgt zu verstehen: „Belästige mich nicht, sonst decke ich auf, wie es mir dir steht." – Zu der Drohung in den beiden letzten Zeilen s. ebd.

2. *yā maymatī ḫallīnī lʿab*
ākul wa-šrab

wa-unšid al-ašʿār wa-ṭri/ab
ḏā lī ġiyya.

Mütterchen, lass mich spielen,
essen, trinken,
Gedichte aufsagen und durch Gesang erfreuen,
das ist meine Leidenschaft.

Kommentar: *mayma*, „Mütterchen," dialektales Diminutiv von *umayma*. – Das Nomen *ṭarab*, „(Unterhaltung) durch Musik, Musik," bezieht sich im ägyptisch-arabischen Dialekt speziell auf Vokalmusik, „delight or pleasure derived from singing; vocal entertainment;" das Verb *ṭarab* I (i) bedeutet „to affect pleasurably with song" (Badawi-Hinds, s.v. ṬRB). – *ġiyya* heisst im Äg.-Ar. auch „hobby" (Badawi-Hinds, s.v. ĠWY); diese Bedeutung trifft wohl hier zu.

3. *urquṣ wa-ḫāyil wa-tmasḫar*
arḍī l-maḥḍar
wa-fī d-duḫūl ḥulwa sukkar
lī ṭaʿmiyya.

Ich tanze, unterhalte (die Leute) und spotte,
ich mache die versammelte Gesellschaft froh.
Wenn ich hereinkomme, ist da „Süsse" und „Zucker;"
ich bin eine „Leckere."

Kommentar: *ḫāyil*. 1. Pers. Sg. Impf. von *ḫāyala* (III. Stamm). Verschiedene Bedeutungen kommen in Frage: „to attract attention of, distract" (Badawi-Hinds, s.v. ḪYL); „to daze, dazzle the eyes" (Spiro, s.v. ḪYL) (Vorschlag von N. Papoutsakis). Gut würde hier auch die Bedeutung des VI. Stammes, *taḫāyala*, „umherstolzieren," passen (Vorschlag von D. Reynolds). – *itmasḫar*, „to become derisive, engage in mockery" (Badawi-Hinds, s.v. MSḪR). – *ḥulwa sukkar*, „Süsse und Zucker," hier natürlich im übertragenen Sinn. – *ṭaʿmiyya*, bedeutet hier wohl „Wohlgeschmack" („saveur": Dozy, s.v. ṬʿM); das Wort ist hier Synonym zu *ṭaʿm*, das auch „sweetness" heissen kann (s. Lane, s.v. ṬʿM). (Sicher meint es hier nicht das bekannte ägyptische Gericht dieses Namens.) – *fī d-duḫūl*, wörtlich „beim Eintreten, beim Eindringen," kann sich auch auf das Penetrieren beim Geschlechtsverkehr beziehen. Die Doppeldeutigkeit ist wahrscheinlich beabsichtigt.

4. *uġannī aw raqqiṣ bi-ṭ-ṭār*
ṣumm al-aḥǧār
ṭarrib w-in ḥarraktu awtār
ayš ʿūdiyya.

Ich singe, oder ich bringe zum Tanzen mit dem (Schlagen des) Tamburins
(sogar) die tauben Steine;
hoch erfreue ich (die Leute), und wenn ich die Saiten schlage:
welch gute Lautenspielerin bin ich doch!

Kommentar: Diese Strophe, in der Edition im Apparat (S. 318, Anm. 3) untergebracht, findet sich nur in zwei von insgesamt sieben zur Edition herangezogenen Handschriften. – Die meisten Sängerinnen begleiteten ihren Gesang mit der Laute (Farmer, *History* 154).

5. *aḥkī n-nawādir wa-z-zāyid*
ʿindī zāyid
wa-mzaḥ wa-hāriš wa-tġāyid
ġazāliyya.

Ich erzähle lustige Geschichten und anderes mehr,
ich kenne mehr als genug,
ich spasse und stichele (oder schäkere) und wiege mich in den Hüften
wie eine junge Gazelle (oder: verführerisch).

Kommentar: *hāriš*. 1. Pers. Sg. Impf. von *hrš* III, „he incited discord, dissension, [etc.] or animosity between, or among, the people" (Lane, s.v. HRŠ [II, III]); „quereller quelqu'un;" […] „batifoler, folâtrer [herumtollen, übermütig sein]" (Dozy, s.v. HRŠ); „streiten, schäkern, scherzen" (Wehr, s.v. HRŠ). – *gazāliyya.* Am nächsten liegt, das Wort von *ġazāl*, „(junge) Gazelle" abzuleiten, „to which the girl, or young women, is likened in the commencing of an ode" (Lane, s.v. ĠZL). Die Bedeutung wäre dann „gazellenartig," „wie eine junge Gazelle." Jedoch scheint mir diese Übersetzung nicht gut zu dem vorausgehenden *taġāyada*, „sich in den Hüften wiegen," zu passen. Vielleicht darf man annehmen, dass ein (nicht nachweisbares) Adjektiv aus dem Wortfeld von *ġazila*, „sich verliebt benehmen, flirten," mit der Bedeutung „kokett, verführerisch" vom Dichter (mit) intendiert ist.

6. *waǧhī l-malīḥ lammā tqannaʿ*
yā llāh mā bdaʿ
wa-mā-ḥsanū ḥīna tḫalaʿ
fī kūfiyya

Wenn mein schönes Gesicht verschleiert ist,
o Gott, wie einzigartig!
Und wie schön ist es, wenn es unverschleiert ist,
und ich eine kūfiyya trage.

Kommentar: *lammā tqannaʿ*, „wenn ... verschleiert ist." Gemeint ist wohl: „Selbst, wenn mein Gesicht verschleiert ist, sind die Leute entzückt." – *itḫalaʿ* (*ḪLʿ* VIII) „1. to be pulled out, be extracted." 2. „to be detached, dislocated" (Badawi-Hinds, *Dictionary*, s.v. *ḪLʿ*). – *maḥsanū* = *mā aḥṣanahū*. – *kūfiyya*. Die heute zumeist von Männern getragene Kopfbedeckung („viereckiges Tuch, diagonal zusammengelegt, unter dem *ʿiqāl* als Kopfbedeckung getragen," Wehr, s.v.) wurde früher auch von Frauen getragen. „... à l'époque de la rédaction des *Mille et une Nuits*, cette coiffure était portée par les femmes ..." (Dozy, *Vêtements*, s.v. *kūfiyya*). Das Tuch war aus Baumwolle, Seide oder Brokat und konnte kostbar bestickt sein. Möglicherweise wurde die Kūfiyya von den Frauen auch um den Kopf gerollt, wie ein kleiner Turban getragen (Dozy, ebd.). Wichtig ist für unseren Zusammenhang, dass die Kūfiyya offenbar nicht das Gesicht der Frauen verhüllte.

7. *bayna l-maġānī lī ma/u/ilḥa*
yawma ṣ-ṣubḥa
miṣriyya miṯl uḫtī Farḥa
aš-šāmiyya.

Unter den Sängerinnen geniesse ich Ansehen
am frühen Morgen (wenn wir gemeinsam zum Tanz [?] antreten);
(ich) eine Ägypterin, (ebenso) wie meine Schwester Farḥa,
die Syrerin.

Kommentar: *al-maġānī*, „Sängerinnen." Nach Dozy (s.v. *ĠNY*) ist „le pluriel du fém. *muġanniya* ... chez les vulgaires *maġānin*;" so auch ʿAbd ar-Rāziq, *La femme*, 79f. – Während das Wort *qayna*, das oft Synonym mit *muġanniya* gebraucht wird, einschliesst, dass es sich um eine Sklavin handelt, scheint dies bei *muġanniya* nicht der Fall zu sein. Wir wissen nicht, ob die Protagonistin unseres Gedichts eine Freie, eine Freigelassene oder eine Sklavin ist. – Die

Deutung des Wortes MLḤH (*mu/i/alḥa*) bereitet Schwierigkeiten. Von den fast unendlich vielen Bedeutungen kommen in Frage: *mulḥa*, normalerweise = „witzige Erzählung, Bonmot," aber auch = *mahāba*, „Ehrfurcht, Würde" (*al-Munǧid*, s.v. MLḤ); seltener auch „lieu agréable" und „objet joli, élégant" (Dozy, s.v. MLḤ); „a clear white colour" u.ä. (Lane, s.v. MLḤ); *milḥa* bedeutet „a sacred or inviolable bond, etc." (Lane, ebd.). Nimmt man letztere Bedeutung an, könnte der Sinn sein: „Unter den Sängerinnen habe ich Bindung" (d.h. gute Freundinnen, Kameradinnen) (Vorschlag von N. Papoutsakis). Vielleicht ist MLḤH aber hier gleich *malāḥa*, d.h. „gentillesse, grâce, agrément, élégance, beauté" (Dozy, s.v. MLḤ). – Da *maǧnā*, pl. *maǧānin*, auch „Wohnsitz, Aufenthaltsort," im ägyptischen und syrisch-libanesischen Dialekt auch „Villa" (Wehr, s.v.), bedeutet, könnte man die Zeile auch so verstehen: „Zwischen den Wohnsitzen (oder: Villen) habe ich einen schönen Ort." Vielleicht ist die Mehrdeutigkeit beabsichtigt. – *yawm aṣ-ṣubḥa*. Dozy (s.v. ṢBḤ) bemerkt zu *ṣubḥa/ṣabāḥiyya*: „On donne aussi ce nom à la danse qu'on exécute ce jour-là (sc. le lendemain de la noce) devant la maison de l'époux ou dans la cour." (Hinweis von N. Papoutsakis). – *uḫt*, „Schwester," kann ausser der leiblichen Schwester auch eine „Freundin," „Kameradin" sein. Nach einem Vorschlag von Y. Faḫraddīn handelte es sich hier um die Halbschwester der jungen Frau; deren Vater wäre der „Onkel," von dem in Strophe 13 die Rede ist (s. den Kommentar hierzu, unten).

8. *wa-šāši marfūʿ ḏāk dāʾim*
nasǧ al-qāʾim
ʿarīḍ silki abyaḍ nāʿim
šuġl aydiyya.

Jenes mein Musselintuch ist immer hochgezogen,
ein Gewebe des … (?).
(Das Musselin ist) weit, mit weissen, weichen Fäden,
die Arbeit meiner Hände.

Kommentar: *šāš*. Grundbedeutung ist „Musselin" (Dozy, s.v. ŠWŠ). Musselin ist ein weicher Stoff; er ist mehr oder weniger durchsichtig, die aus Baumwolle hergestellten Fäden sind locker miteinander verwoben. Nach Mayer, *Mamluk costume*, ist *šāš* als Kleidungsstück (a) „the length of muslin worn on the turban … (b) a shawl worn around the neck worn as a part of the *khilʿa*" (79). So auch Dozy (s.v. ŠWŠ); s. auch ders., *Vêtements*, s.v. *šāš*, S. 239 (Der *šāš* hat also auch eine ähnliche Bedeutung wie *kūfiyya*). – Möglicherweise ist hier „Nachtgewand aus Musselin" gemeint (Vorschlag von Y. Faḫraddīn). – *šāš* kann auch eine Kopfbedeckung meinen, die wie ein Kamelhöcker aussieht: „Sorte de coiffure que les femmes en Egypte inventèrent vers l'an 780 H/[1378] et qui ressemblait à une bosse de chameau. Elle prenait sur le front de la femme, et se terminait vers le dos" (Dozy, ebd.). Diese Kopfbedeckung galt als ungesetzliche Neuerung. Wenn sie, wie Dozy sagt, erst um 1378 aufkam, hat sie zu al-Miʿmars Lebzeiten noch nicht existiert, so dass diese Bedeutung in unserem Gedicht nicht zutreffen kann. – Für *al-qāʾim* finde ich keine hier passende Bedeutung.

9. *fī l-farši mā minnī arhaǧ*
wa-mā aġnaǧ
aḥfaẓ kalāmī wa-tlaǧlaǧ
qaḥūbiyya.

Im Bett gibt es keine, die wilder ist,
und keine, die mehr aufreizende Bewegungen macht;
ich halte meine Worte zurück und stöhne laut
(wie) eine Hure.

Kommentar: *arhaǧ*. Hierfür finde ich in den Wörterbüchern keine wirklich passende Bedeutung. Nach Dozy (s.v. RHǦ) heisst *rahǧa* „turbatio," also „Verwirrung, Unordnung." Lane (s.v. RHǦ) gibt an: *arhaǧū fī l-kalām*, „they raised tumult in talking and clamouring." Ich wähle als Verlegenheitslösung das Wort „wilder." – *aġnaǧ*. Nach Lane heisst *ġunǧ* „amorous … gesture or behaviour combined with coquettish boldness, and feigned coyness or opposition and an affecting of languor," „lascivious motion, or a wiggling of the body or hips, under the excitement of sexual passion, or to excite such passion" (s.v. ĠNǦ). Nach Badawi-Hinds heisst *ġanaǧ* „to utter sounds during sexual intercourse to indicate pleasure and enthusiasm (of a women)" (s.v. ĠNǦ).

10. *abkī wa-taǧrī lī damʿa*
sabʿa sabʿa
kaḏā yakūn hawnī/hūnī ṣ-ṣanʿa
w-illā š hiyya

Ich weine und meine Tränen strömen,
sieben zu sieben.
So wird mein bequemes Leben (oder: meine Schande) mein Gewerbe sein;
wenn nicht, was sonst?

Kommentar: *sabʿa sabʿa*. Vielleicht ist gemeint „eine Woche nach der anderen“ (Vorschlag von N. Papoutsakis). HWN kann als *hawn* („Ruhe, Bequemlichkeit“) oder *hūn* („Schande“) vokalisiert werden. Falls man *hawnī* liest, ist der Sinn des Satzes wohl: „Ich muss jetzt wohl mein unmoralisches Leben endgültig zu meinem Gewerbe machen;“ aber auch *hūnī* ergibt einen guten Sinn. Sehr wahrscheinlich ist die Doppeldeutigkeit beabsichtigt (rhetorische Figur der *tawriya*).

11. *arḍī l-ḥarīf mā itwānā*
fīmā tʿānā
wa-nāḍiǧā ḥarām anā
aṣlāniyya

Ich befriedige den Kunden, ohne zu ermatten,
während ich mich abmühe.
Ich bin eine Reife, (aber auch) eine ‚Verbotene‘ (oder ‚Heisse‘)
eine Echte!

Kommentar: *al-ḥarīf*, „der Kunde, Bursche,“ heisst nach Dozy (s.v. ḤRF) auch „amant“ (Freier, Liebhaber). – *nāḍiǧā*, „reif,“ wohl für *nāḍiǧa*. Das Wort hat auch die übertragene Bedeutung „in a perfect state of fitness for being used“ (Lane, s.v. NḌǦ). – *ḥarrāmānā* steht so im edierten Text; es ist wohl zusammengezogen aus *ḥarām anā*, „ich bin eine Verbotene,“ d.h. eine, die sich verbietet, weil sie sich für zu gut dafür hält, sich mit jedem einzulassen. Vielleicht ist zu emendieren *ḥarrā* (für *ḥarra*) *anā*, „ich bin eine Heisse.“ – *aṣlāniyya*. – *aṣlānī* = *aṣlī* (Dozy, s.v. ʾṢL). Das Wort kann auch von türkisch *aslan/arslan*, „Löwe,“ hergeleitet sein. Die Bedeutung wäre dann „mannstolle, geile Frau;“ vgl. das Schimpfwort *ibn al-labwa*, „Sohn einer Löwin“ (Vorschlag von H. Özkan und D. Reynolds).

12. *kam min wazīr qabbal kaffī*
yaʿšaq ṭarfī
w-āḫar amīr yaḫlaʿ ḫuffī
min riǧliyya.

Manch ein Wesir küsste meine Hand,
weil er meinen Blick liebte.
Und ein anderer, ein Emir, zog mir die Schuhe aus
von meinen Füssen.

13. *fī l-ḥuẓwa ǧā wāfir qismī*
yahnī ʿammī
wa-ntī fa-yūdiʿ lik yā mmī
fī l-maḥẓiyya

Gunst ist mir in reichem Mass erwiesen worden,
mein Onkel freut sich (an mir).
Und für dich, Mutter, wird er etwas hinterlegen
bei (oder: in) der Favoritin.

Kommentar: *ḥuẓwa* und sein Synonym *maḥẓiyya* bedeuten „bevorzugte Stellung, Gunst, Ansehen, Wertschätzung," und speziell auch „favourite women" (Badawi-Hinds, s.v. ḤḌY) bzw. „concubine" (Dozy, s.v. ḤẒW). – *haniʾa, yahnaʾ bihī* heisst „he rejoiced in him, or it" (Lane, s.v. HNʾ); dial. *hinī, yihnā*, bedeutet „to give pleasure or gratification" (Badawi-Hinds, s.v. HNY). –*ʿamm*, „Onkel," ist nicht nur der leibliche väterliche Onkel; *yā ʿammī* („mein Onkel") ist auch „respectful title of, and form of address and reference to, a man (usually) older than the speaker and of the lower social class" (Badawi-Hinds, s.v. ʿMM). In einem anderen *zaǧal* (Nr. 543), das von Sex mit einem Jungen handelt (hierzu s. Ö 337), lässt al-Miʿmār den Jungen ihn mit *yā ʿammī* anreden. – *awdaʿa li-* (Pers.) heisst „déposer entre les mains de" (Fagnan, s.v. WDʿ) (*wadīʿa* ist „das anvertraute Gut, Depositum"). Vielleicht ist hier gemeint „investieren in" oder „einen Schatz hinterlegen bei/in" (Vorschlag von Idris Kiwirra). Für die beiden letzten Zeilen, wohl die rätselhaftesten und schwierigsten des ganzen Gedichts, gebe ich hier die hypothetische Deutung nach einem Vorschlag von I. Kiwirra. Danach ist der Onkel ein Kunde oder Gönner (oder Besitzer, falls sie Sklavin ist) und gleichzeitig Liebhaber der jungen Frau; die in der letzten Zeile genannte *maḥẓiyya* („Favoritin, Konkubine") ist die Tochter, nicht die Mutter. Nach dieser Deutung verspricht die Tochter ihrer Mutter, dass das (nicht genannte) Depositum, das der Gönner „bei/in ihr hinterlegen" will, auch ihr, der Mutter zugute kommen wird. Es ist sehr wohl möglich, dass damit ein Kind gemeint ist, das der Liebhaber der jungen Frau angehängt hat (Vorschlag von D. Reynolds). – Eine ganz andere Deutung schlägt Y. Faḫraddīn vor. Diese Deutung, wonach der „Onkel" der derzeitige Partner oder Ehemann der Mutter und diese die „Favoritin" wäre, setzt einen Zusammenhang zwischen den Strophen 1, 7, 13 voraus. Die Drohung der Tochter in Strophe 1 bezöge sich darauf, dass sie ein in der vorliegenden Strophe 13 angesprochenes skandalöses inzestuöses Dreiecks-Verhältnis zwischen dem „Onkel" (dem gegenwärtigen Partner oder Ehemann der Mutter), ihr selbst und ihrer Mutter aufdecken will. Die in Strophe 7 genannte „Ägypterin," also die Tochter, die Protagonistin unseres

Gedichts, würde einer früheren Beziehung ihrer Mutter zu einem Ägypter entstammen; ihre „Schwester Farḥa, die Syrerin," wäre ihre Halbschwester; deren Vater, der „Onkel," ein Syrer, der gegenwärtige Partner der Mutter, hätte mit seiner Stieftochter ein geheimes Liebesverhältnis. Unsere Strophe 13 wäre demnach wie folgt zu übersetzen: „Gunst ist mir in reichem Mass erwiesen worden: Mein Onkel [dein jetziger Partner] vergnügt sich mit mir; aber dir, Mutter, wird er den Titel ‚Favoritin' lassen," d.h. nach aussen so tun, als ob du seine Favoritin wärest.

14. *min sa'dī anšā lī l-Mi'mār*
dār fīhā šǧār
bi-ġṣān wa-taṭla' ǧawwa d-dār
al-manšiyya.

Ich habe Glück gehabt: al-Mi'mār („der Baumeister," der Dichter des *zaǧal*)
hat mir gebaut
ein Haus, in dem Bäume sind
mit Zweigen; und diese wachsen im Inneren des Hauses,
des neu errichteten.

Kommentar: „ein Haus, in dem Bäume sind," also ein Atriumhaus. – *al-manšiyya.* Das Wort heisst nach Badawi-Hinds „recently built village or suburb," nach Fagnan „enceinte d'une ville," „nouveau quartier" (in beiden Fällen s.v. *nš'*). Hier ist es wohl Adjektiv und bezieht sich auf das Haus, „das neugebaute Haus." – Ich halte für sicher, dass mit *dār,* „Haus" hier auf die Strophe, oder, *pars pro toto,* auf das Gedicht ‚versteckt' angespielt wird, das al-Mi'mār auf/für die junge Frau verfasst hat; *dār* ist ein Synonym von *bayt,* und *bayt* hat zwei Bedeutungen: „Haus, Zelt" *und* „Strophe;" *aġṣān* kann „Zweige" (am Baum) und „Sonderreimzeilen" (im Strophengedicht) bedeuten; *anšā,* „er hat gebaut," kann sich auch auf ein Schriftstück beziehen (= „er hat verfasst"). Zwar liegt hier keine *metaphora continuata* vor, bei der sämtliche Elemente des Gemeinten konsequent metaphorisiert sind (es fehlt z.B. eine Entsprechung des Elements „Gemeinreimzeilen" (*asmāṭ*), die das Strophengedicht ausser den Sonderreimzeilen auch hat), aber m.E. reichen die doppeldeutigen Elemente aus, um annehmen zu können, dass hier eine Anspielung auf das Gedicht vorliegt.

Sprache, Form, Struktur und Versmass des Gedichts

Wir haben ein *zaǧal* vor uns.[14] Das *zaǧal* ist eine vulgärsprachliche strophische Gedichtgattung. Die *zaǧal*-Poetiken schreiben vor, dass die Wörter in den Gedichten keine Flexionsendungen (*iʿrāb*) haben sollen.

Die Sprache unseres Gedichts ist „eine stilisierte Form der Umgangssprache" des 14. Jhs. (D Einl. 22). Manche östliche *zaǧal*s verwenden Andalusismen (Ö 149, 230, 241, 274, 281 u. ö.), gewissermassen eine *hommage* an die Dichter des Urprungslandes des *zaǧal*, vor allen anderen an den grössten von ihnen, Ibn Quzmān (st. 555/1160).[15] In unserem Gedicht finden sich, so weit ich sehe, keine Andalusismen; sie scheinen bei al-Miʿmār überhaupt selten zu sein (Ö 241).

Seiner strophischen Struktur nach ist das vorliegende *zaǧal* ein aus 14 Strophen bestehendes „eigentliches *zaǧal*," d. h. die Strophen haben das Reimschema: *aa* bbb*a* ccc*a* ddd*a* usw. Das Gedicht beginnt mit zwei miteinander reimenden Zeilen (sog. Gemeinreimzeilen). Dieses Element ist der *maṭlaʿ* („Eingang," „Vorspiel"), die „Überschrift" (im eigentlichen Sinne des Wortes), in der das Thema des folgenden Gedichts angeschlagen wird (Ablehnung des Vorschlags der Mutter). Es folgen, in der ersten Strophe, zunächst drei miteinander reimende Zeilen, die einen neuen Reim haben (*aġṣān*, wörtlich „Zweige," meist mit „Sonderreimzeilen" übersetzt); die Strophe wird abgeschlosssen durch eine Zeile, die den Reim des „Vorspiels" aufnimmt (ar. *simṭ*, wörtlich „Schnur der Halskette," meist mit „Gemeinreimzeile" wiedergegeben). Entsprechend sind alle folgenden Strophen gebaut.

Die Zeilen mit Gemeinreim bestehen – mit einer Ausnahme – alle aus 4 Silben; die Ausnahme ist die erste Zeile des Vorspiels, die zugleich die erste Zeile des Gedichts ist; sie hat 8 Silben. Von den Zeilen mit Sonderreim (d. h. den Zeilen 1–3 jeder Strophe) besteht die erste und dritte immer aus 8 Silben, die zweite aus 4 Silben.

Das Versmass ist nicht-ḫalīlisch; die meisten Zeilen bestehen oft nur aus langen Silben (– – – –); jedoch können die erste und die dritte Silbe auch kurz sein (o – o –).[16]

14 Hierzu s. Schoeler und Stoetzer, Zaǧal.

15 Siehe Colin, Ibn Ḳuzmān.

16 Genaueres zum Versmass s. D 133–4 (zu Nr. 540) und Özkan, Why stress does matter.

Exkurs: Zur Problematik literarhistorischer Deutungen. Mögliche Fehldeutungen

Der folgenden Interpretation des Gedichts sei aus gegebenem Anlass eine Betrachtung über die Problematik kunst- und literarhistorischer Deutungen vorausgeschickt. Wir gehen dabei von einer Erörterung des Kultursoziologen Arnold Hauser (1892–1978) aus, der sich seinerseits auf den Soziologen und Philosophen Karl Mannheim (1893–1947) beruft. Nach Hauser müssen die Schöpfungen der Kunst immer von neuem interpretiert werden.[17] Es gibt nicht *die* Interpretation eines Kunstwerks, sondern immer viele Interpretationen:

> Dies bedeutet freilich nicht, dass jede beliebige Deutung [...] möglich und ohne weiteres akzeptierbar sei. [...] Unsere Erklärung einer künstlerischen Schöpfung muss einerseits so beschaffen sein, dass sie in sich keinen Widerspruch enthalte und dass jeder wahrnehmbare Zug des Gegenstandes sich in den Deutungsversuch einfügen lasse; andererseits muss sie mit den dokumentarisch oder sonstwie objektiv feststellbaren historischen Umständen der Entstehung des Gegenstandes in Übereinstimmung gebracht werden können. Wie verschieden die möglichen Interpretationen eines Kunstwerks sonst auch sein mögen, diesen beiden Forderungen werden sie entsprechen müssen.[18]

Die erste Forderung, besonders deren erster Teil (keine inneren Widersprüche), leuchtet unmittelbar ein. Was den zweiten Teil dieser ersten Forderung betrifft: Im Falle unseres Gedichts liegt die Schwierigkeit weniger darin, den Erklärungsversuch so zu gestalten, dass alle wahrnehmbaren Züge in ihn sich einfügen lassen, als die zum Verständnis notwendigen, aber unserem Wissen (noch) sich entziehenden Züge des Gegenstandes richtig zu erkennen. Das führt uns zu der zweiten Forderung.

Um dieser Forderung – die Deutung muss mit den objektiv feststellbaren Umständen der Entstehung in Einklang gebracht werden können – zu genügen, ist zum einen die Kenntnis des historischen und gesellschaftlichen Hintergrundes des Gegenstandes erforderlich. Im Falle der Interpretation unseres Gedichtes ist die Erlangung dieser Kenntnis dank der günstigen Quellenlage und der (allerdings nicht in allzu grosser Zahl vorliegender) Forschungen hierzu weitgehend möglich.

17 Hauser, *Methoden* 269.
18 Ebd. 268.

Jedoch stellt das Gedicht den Übersetzer und Interpreten in anderer Hinsicht vor besondere Herausforderungen. Der Grund hierzu ist ganz trivial: Er liegt zunächst einmal in der Schwierigkeit der Sprache, in der der Text abgefasst ist – nämlich des in einer besonderen Form des Arabischen geschriebenen Gedichts. Zu welch eklatanten Fehldeutungen, auch auf anderen Gebieten als bei der Interpretation von Dichtung, etwa in der Geschichtsforschung, falsche Übersetzungen geführt haben, hat sich in der Islamwissenschaft in der letzten Zeit gezeigt.[19] Den Aspekt der Fehldeutung bei der Interpretation eines sprachlichen Kunstwerks durch eine falsche Übersetzung hat Hauser verständlicherweise in seiner Erörterung nicht berücksichtigt; man könnte ihn vielleicht in seiner ersten Forderung unterbringen und diese dadurch ergänzen.

Fehler können bei der Edition von Texten z.B. durch falsch gelesene Schriftzüge entstehen; in Übersetzungen können sie sich, einerseits, durch falsch oder nicht genau verstandene Wörter, grammatische Konstruktionen und – vor allem – Phrasen, andererseits durch eine schwerverständliche poetische Sprache und einen schwierigen Stil einstellen und so zu Fehldeutungen führen.[20] Was die lexikalischen Hilfsmittel für unser Gedicht betrifft, so liegen für die nicht-klassische Sprache zwar Dozys *Supplément aux dictionnaires arabes* und Fagnans *Additions* hierzu vor; und für den modernen ägyptischen Dialekt gibt es Badawi-Hinds' *Dictionary*. Diese Wörterbücher helfen oft, können aber nicht ein (m.W. noch nicht existierendes) Wörterbuch der ägyptischen Umgangssprache der mamlukischen und osmanischen Zeit ersetzen.

Eine mindestens ebenso grosse Fehlerquelle ist in unserem Fall aber die stellenweise schwierige poetische Sprache und der Stil des Dichters. Schwer verständliche Anspielungen, Mehrdeutigkeit von Ausdrücken (Stilfigur der *tawriya*, „double entendre," „Doppelsinnwitz"), und, wie sich gezeigt hat, auch Doppel- oder Mehrdeutigkeit von ganzen Sätzen sind Stilmittel, die al-Miʿmār häufig verwendet und bewusst sucht; er ist in der Anwendung der *tawriya* ein wahrer Meister. Das hat Thomas Bauer in seinen Forschungen mehrfach betont; und er hat die *tawriya*, die er „als Lieblingsstilmittel seiner (al-Miʿmārs)

19 Siehe etwa Hagen und Seidensticker, Reinhard Schulzes Hypothese.

20 Man denke an das „dunkle Dichten" (*trobar clus*) der Trobadors (Marcabru, Arnaut Daniel; 12. Jh.) oder die Oden Friedrich Hölderlins (1770–1843), die die Übersetzer und Interpreten vor grosse Schwierigkeiten stellen. Ein aufschlussreiches Beispiel hierfür ist eine Stelle in der an sich guten und verdienstvollen arabischen Übersetzung einer Auswahl Hölderlinscher Gedichte (*Muḫtārāt min šiʿrihī*) von Fu'ād Rifqa. In der Übersetzung der Ode „An die Hoffnung" (S. 80) wird die „liebliche Zeitlose (= Herbstzeitlose)" zur *al-lā-zamanī al-ḥabīb*, „die liebe Zeitlosigkeit," eine Fehldeutung, die dem Übersetzer-Dichter Rifqa, der ein Schüler des Existenzphilosophen Friedrich Bollnow (1903–91) war, leicht unterlaufen konnte.

Zeit" bezeichnet, zugleich auch als „Stilmittel der Ambiguität schlechthin" erkannt;[21] jenes Phänomens also, das in seiner Deutung der vormodernen Kultur des Islams eine so entscheidende Rolle spielt. Es kann leicht vorkommen, dass man eine *tawriya* oder die Doppel- oder Mehrdeutigkeit eines ganzen Satzes nicht erkennt; dann muss das nicht unbedingt zu einer falschen, aber doch zu einer unvollständigen Interpretation führen. Dass in der letzten Strophe unseres Gedichts mit dem „Haus" (*dār* = *bayt*) das vorliegende Gedicht selbst (oder eine bestimmte Strophe [*bayt*] daraus) gemeint sein kann, ist leicht zu übersehen; doch würde einem in diesem Fall – vorausgesetzt, dass unsere Interpretation richtig ist – die Schlusspointe des Gedichts entgehen.

Um nun ein konkretes Beispiel für eine mögliche Fehldeutung in unserer Interpretation anzuführen: Ein Rätsel bleibt die Deutung und Erklärung der Figur des „Onkels" in der vorletzten Strophe. Ich habe unterschiedliche Erklärungen dafür angeboten, die auf Vorschlägen von hervorragenden Arabisten, darunter auch Muttersprachlern, beruhen. Die Deutungen schliessen einander aus. Eine von beiden mag richtig sein, aber es wird wohl weitere Deutungen, vielleicht noch bessere, geben. Oder hat der Dichter bewusst Worte und Formulierungen gewählt, die mehrere Deutungen zulassen?

Es kann also nicht ausgeschlossen werden, dass in der Übersetzung des vorliegenden Gedichts Fehler und Mängel sind, die zu falschen oder sonst irgendwie angreifbaren Interpretationen geführt haben. Ich bin aber zuversichtlich, dass meine Gesamtdeutung, die weitgehend nicht auf den kritischen Stellen beruht, den genannten Forderungen an die Diskutierbarkeit literaturhistorischer Deutungen entspricht.

Sängerinnen, Kurtisanen, Edelprostituierte im vormodernen Islam, insbesondere im Mamlukenreich der ersten Hälfte des 8./14. Jahrhunderts

„Professionelle Musikerinnen, oft Sängerinnen, waren immer führend im musikalischen Leben in der Geschichte der arabischen Welt."[22] Sehr gut sind wir über die Musikkultur der Abbasidenzeit unterrichtet, wo Musiker(innen) und

21 Bauer, Ibrāhīm al-Miʿmār 82; ders., *Die Kultur* 260–1.

22 Danielson, Artists 292. – Die Verfasserin behandelt das musikalische Leben in Kairo im 19. und im ersten Viertel des 20. Jhs. Die Sängerinnen hiessen *ʿawālim* (Sg. *ʿālima*), „Wissende" (295).

Sänger(innen) am Abbasidenhof eine grosse Rolle spielten.[23] Aber auch Berichte über Sängerinnen und Sänger der Ayyubidenzeit liegen vor (G 58), und in der Mamlukenzeit fliessen Quellen, die Angehörige dieser Berufsgruppe behandeln, besonders reichlich. Die meisten Sängerinnen in der vormodernen Zeit waren geborene Sklavinnen.[24]

Schon in vorislamischer Zeit gab es Sängerinnen und Musikerinnen; sie traten bei Festen und Weingelagen auf. Nach Ch. Pellat[25] hat man hier je nach der gesellschaftlichen Stellung dieser Frauen zwei Kategorien zu unterscheiden: Die Rolle der einen Kategorie von Sängerinnen, wohl alle Sklavinnen, „die einem hoch stehenden Städter oder Beduinen gehörten, war es, ihren Herrn, allein oder in der Gesellschaft von Gästen, zu unterhalten, unbeschadet anderer Beziehungen, die sie mit ihm haben konnten." Die andere, die niedrigere Kategorie „war mit der Weinbude verbunden oder folgte wandernden Weinhändlern; man kann sich gut vorstellen, dass sie sich einer Art von Prostitution hingeben konnten." Für die Mamlukenzeit, auf die wir nun näher eingehen wollen, unterscheidet A. ʿAbd ar-Rāziq in ähnlicher Weise ebenfalls zwei Gruppen von Sängerinnen:

1. Diejenigen, die der Elite – das ist in der Mamlukenzeit: der Militärkaste – dienten (A 55, 66–7). Sie waren alle geborene Sklavinnen.[26] Die Sultane und höheren Offiziere (Emire) hielten Musikkapellen (A 55); die ‚Orchester' der letzteren bestanden aus 10–15 Sklavenmädchen. Im 8./14. Jh. waren diese Musikkapellen ein Statussymbol der mamlukischen Militärhaushalte (R 9, 13–4).
2. Die volkstümlichen Sängerinnen, die das einfache Volk, besonders beim Feiern von Hochzeiten, Beschneidungs- und anderen Festen unterhielten (A 66–8). Viele von ihnen (alle?) waren Sklavinnen (A 68).

---

23 Für die vor- und frühabbasidische Zeit s. Neubauer, *Musiker*, und ST 86; für das 4./10. Jh. s. M 154.

24 Siehe sogleich unten.

25 Pellat, Ḳayna 821.

26 In den knapp drei Jahrhunderten, da Mamluken, also (Ex-)Sklaven, Ägypten, Syrien/Palästina, den Ḥiǧāz und Südwestanatolien beherrschten (648–922/1250–1517), spielten nicht nur die männlichen Sklaven eine zentrale Rolle, aus denen sich die Elite des Staates, darunter sogar der Sultan, rekrutierte. Eine notwendige Ergänzung zur Institution des „männlichen Sklaventums" war „die Institution des weiblichen Sklaventums" (R 8–9). Von grosser Bedeutung war die Rekrutierung von Sklavinnen, insbesondere solcher, die als Konkubinen/Kurtisanen des Sultans und der Emire (= die höheren Offiziere) dienen sollten. Die Elite betrachtete die Konkubinen vornehmlich als Mittel, die hohe Rate der Kindersterblichkeit zu überwinden (R 9). – Eine wichtige und hoch angesehene Stellung nahmen die Sängersklavinnen ein.

Die Sängersklavinnen (Sing. *muġanniya;* als Pl. wird meist dialektal *maġānī* gebraucht)[27] der mamlukischen Elite hatten eine besondere Stellung inne. Vergleichbare Phänomene sind die japanischen Geishas (im 17.–19. Jh.) und das antike Hetärenwesen.[28]

Die ‚Berufe' der Sängersklavin und der Kurtisane fielen häufig in einer Person zusammen (ST 17 ff., bes. 34; G 73). Entsprechend war die Grenze zwischen einer volkstümlichen Sängerin und einer Liebesdienerin oft nicht scharf.[29] Ein Beispiel ist die Protagonistin in unserem Gedicht.

Die meisten Sängerinnen hatten eine Ausbildung hinter sich. Bei hervorragenden und schönen Sängerinnen, die der Militärelite dienten, war die Ausbildung besonders gründlich und sehr teuer, und dementsprechend hoch war der Preis, der für die Mädchen bezahlt wurde (R 10, 11; A 66–7; vgl. auch M 154). In Kairo und in den Provinzhauptstädten wurde der Unterricht für Elite-Sängerinnen von grossen Musikern erteilt (R 9). Gegenstand der Ausbildung waren Gesang und Lautenspiel, oft aber dazu auch Dichtkunst und die Literatur der feinen Bildung (*adab*). Es kam vor, dass Herrscher grosse Musiker und Sänger aus dem Ausland holten, damit diese ihre Kunst den Sängerinnen des Sultans beibrachten (A 67).

Bei den volkstümlichen Sängerinnen konnte die Ausbildung in der Provinz, bei der dortigen Zunftvorsteherin (*ḍāminat al-maġānī*) erfolgen (R 11). Sie hatten eine hohe Steuer zu bezahlen (*ḍamān al-maġānī*), die von der Zunftvorsteherin, bei der sie auch gemeldet sein mussten, eingezogen wurde (A 79–80). Ausserdem ist anzunehmen, dass die Mädchen, wenn sie Sklavinnen waren, einen Teil ihres Einkommens ihrem Besitzer oder ihrer Besitzerin abgeben mussten.[30] Die *ḍamān al-maġānī* galt auch für Prostituierte (A 45–6), deren Tätigkeit dadurch quasi legalisiert wurde.[31]

Sängerinnen sowie auch andere volkstümliche Unterhaltungskünstlerinnen – die beiden Tätigkeiten konnten, wie das Beispiel in unserem Gedicht zeigt, zusammenfallen – hatten bedeutend mehr Freiheiten als die ‚ehrbaren' freien Frauen (Beeston, *Epistle* 2; W 163, 166; ST 91, G 73).[32] Vor allem waren

---

27 Eine andere häufige Bezeichnung für „Sängerin" ist *qayna*. Dieser Begriff schliesst ein, dass die Sängerin Sklavin ist (s. den Kommentar zu Strophe 7).

28 Siehe unten Anm. 32. – Siehe auch die *-Anmerkung zum Titel des Aufsatzes.

29 Lapidus, *Muslim cities* 83; für die frühe Abbasidenzeit s. Beeston, *Epistle* 21, 34–5.

30 Ich kann dies allerdings bisher nur für die Abbasidenzeit belegen (M 159).

31 Siehe sogleich unten mit Anm. 34.

32 Hier drängt sich ein Vergleich mit dem antiken Hetärenwesen auf, und zwar mit jenem der hellenistischen Zeit. Während das Hetärentum in der klassischen Epoche ein aristokratisches Phänomen war, fand in der hellenistischen Epoche eine „Verbürgerlichung des Hetärenwesens" statt; es wurde eine städtische Erscheinung (Schuller, *Hetären* 111).

sie nicht den strengen Regeln der Sexualgesetze unterworfen, die für die verheiratete Frau galten. „Das *Gros* war eher offenherzig veranlagt, hatte man sie doch von Beginn ihrer Ausbildung an ein Benehmen und eine Ausdrucksweise gelehrt, die es gerade darauf anlegte, neben dem Part als Sängerin und Gesellschafterin den einer Geliebten zu übernehmen." (G 74, vgl. auch G 71, 73, 48). Da sie eine Steuer, die *ḍamān al-maġānī*, bezahlten, war es ihnen – auch solchen, die einer höheren Kategorie angehörten – nicht verboten, Prostitution auszuüben (A 45–6). Das juristische Prinzip, auf Grund dessen die Prostitution nicht mit Körperstrafen geahndet werden musste, war die *šubha*, d. h. die „Ähnlichkeit," nämlich mit gesetzlich erlaubten vergleichbaren Handlungen oder Institutionen.[33] Denn da Prostitution mit Geld entlohnt wird, gleicht sie den gesetzlichen Institutionen Ehe bzw. Konkubinat, bei denen ja Kauf oder etwas Ähnliches (bei der Ehe die Morgengabe) involviert ist. Dieses Prinzip war allerdings bei den Rechtsgelehrten nicht immer unumstritten; in der Osmanenzeit setzte es sich aber allgemein durch.[34]

Zahlreiche gute Sängerinnen aller Zeiten sind namentlich bekannt; ihnen sind Artikel in den biographischen Werken gewidmet worden. Dies gilt für beide Kategorien, die Elite- und die volkstümlichen Sängerinnen.[35] Wie die

---

Die volkstümlichen Sängerinnen und Unterhalterinnen im mamlukenzeitlichen Ägypten – und im Besonderen auch die Protagonistin in unserem Gedicht – kommen dem Hetärentyp der hellenistischen Epoche recht nahe. Eine Gemeinsamkeit zwischen diesen beiden Frauentypen ist der gesellschaftliche Stand: Sie waren meist Angehörige der städtischen Unterschicht, Sklavinnen oder Freigelassene, die aber gesellschaftlich aufsteigen und sogar berühmt werden konnten (s. Schuller, *Hetären* 37). Die Protagonistin in unserem Gedicht ist zu dem Zeitpunkt, da sie die Auseinandersetzung mit ihrer Mutter hat, *noch* eine Unterhaltungskünstlerin, die sich in Kreisen der Unterschicht bewegt; sie unterhält das einfache Volk. Allerdings ist ihr fester Entschluss und ihr Ziel, zur Elite aufzusteigen. Schullers Charakterisierung einer Hetäre aus der hellenistischen Zeit könnte auch auf die junge Frau in unserem Gedicht passen: „Eine Hetäre konnte eine ehemalige Sklavin sein, die zunächst für ihren Eigentümer als käufliche Dirne tätig war, nach ihrer Freilassung aber sozusagen auf eigene Rechnung und in gesellschaftlich höherstehenden Kreisen ein selbständiges Leben führte. Sie wechselte ihre Liebhaber, aber es konnte auch vorkommen, dass ernsthafte Liebesverhältnisse entstanden." (Schuller, *Hetären* 37).

33 Erlaubt ist einem Mann nach dem islamischen Recht nicht nur der Verkehr mit seinen Ehefrauen (bis zu vier), sondern zusätzlich auch mit einer beliebigen Zahl von Sklavinnen, die er rechtmässig durch Kauf erworben hatte. Für die freie Braut wird bei der Eheschliessung vom Bräutigam der *mahr* (das Brautgeld, die Morgengabe) bestimmt und bezahlt. – Siehe Baldwin, Prostitution 125–7; *EI*[2] Ed., Bighāʾ, und Rowson, Shubha.

34 „The Ottoman jurists I consulted were unanimous in excluding prostitutes and their clients from the fixed penalties. To do this they appealed to the legal concept of *shubha* which translates as ambiguity." (Baldwin, Prostitution 125).

35 Für die Mamlukenzeit s. z. B. R 10–1; A 285 Nr. 98, A 68 und 269–302 („Dictionnaire biographique").

Konkubinen hatten die Sängersklavinnen grosse Aussichten, freigelassen zu werden (A 54). Hervorragende Künstlerinnen wurden sehr oft reich und konnten eine Traumkarriere machen: „Ebenso wie ein männlicher Mamluk hoffen konnte, Sultan zu werden, so konnte eine Sängerin niedriger Herkunft hoffen, Sultanin zu werden.“ (R 11). Wohl zu allen Zeiten hatten reiche Sängersklavinnen eigene Dienerinnen oder Sklavinnen (M 160, W 164, ST 29).

Einzigartig ist die Karriere einer schwarzen Sängersklavin namens Ittifāq, die in der ersten Hälfte des 14. Jhs. lebte (A 285, R 10–1). Die Voraussetzungen, die sie mitbrachte, waren nicht einmal günstig. Sie war eine Sklavin in der zweiten Generation,[36] war nicht besonders schön, und ihre erste Ausbildung war nur in der Provinz, bei einer *ḍāminat al-maġānī*, erfolgt. Jedoch konnte sie danach in Kairo, u.a. bei einem berühmten Lautenspieler, studieren. Ihre Stimme muss wundervoll gewesen sein. Sie wurde Gattin dreier aufeinanderfolgender Sultane, dann eines Wesirs und schliesslich eines maghrebinischen (merinidischen) Sultans, der sie bei einer Reise durch Kairo kennen lernte. Es ist kein Wunder, dass Ittifāq deshalb in westlicher Literatur der Übername „die Lola Montez ihres Zeitalters“ gegeben wurde (R 11, Anm. 37).

∴

In den folgenden beiden Abschnitten soll nun der Versuch einer Interpretation unseres *zaǧal*s unternommen werden. Sie erfolgt in zwei Ansätzen: zuerst verknüpft mit einer analytischen Inhaltsangabe, dann in Verbindung mit einer Darstellung der Redeweise und der Stilmittel des Gedichts.

Thema des Gedichts und interpretierende Inhaltsangabe

Der Dichter unseres *zaǧal*, der Kairener al-Miʿmār, war ein Zeitgenosse Ittifāqs, und man kann sicher sein, dass er deren Traumkarriere in seiner Stadt Kairo miterlebt hat. Sein Geschöpf, die junge Frau, die er in dem Gedicht eine heftige Auseinandersetzung mit der Mutter haben lässt, ist eine volkstümliche Unterhaltungskünstlerin, die sich auch der Prostitution hingibt. Wir erfahren nicht, ob sie Freie, Freigelassene oder Sklavin ist[37] (vielleicht Sklavin der zweiten Generation wie Ittifāq?). Sie ist vielseitig begabt, kann singen, tanzen, Gedichte

36 Sklaventum war erblich, wenn beide Eltern des Kindes Sklaven waren.

37 Das *anā fī-ḥurriyya* in der ersten Strophe darf man wohl nicht so verstehen, dass sie eine freigeborene Frau war; s. oben im Kommentar zu Strophe 1.

rezitieren und zwei Instrumente spielen, und hat mit ihrer Kunst und ihren Darbietungen, aber auch durch ihre Schönheit und Reize, schon einen gewissen Erfolg beim Publikum, insbesondere natürlich bei Männern, gehabt; dies geht aus ihren Berichten und Schilderungen klar hervor. Für sie muss ein beruflicher Aufstieg, wie Ittifāq ihn hatte, höchstes Lebensziel gewesen sein.

Die Mutter hat versucht, die Tochter zu überreden, ihr bisheriges lockeres Leben aufzugeben. Dies wird zwar nirgendwo ausdrücklich gesagt, denn die Mutter selbst kommt in dem Gedicht gar nicht zu Wort. Was sie von der Tochter erwartet, kann aber weitgehend aus deren Gegenrede erschlossen werden; diese Rede füllt das ganze Gedicht aus.

Die Tochter weist den Vorschlag der Mutter in aller Schärfe zurück, droht sogar für den Fall, dass diese sich ihren Plänen widersetzt, mit einem Bruch. Damit beginnt das Gedicht. Die Tochter führt daraufhin aus: Sie ist jung und lebenslustig, isst und trinkt gern, sie ist schön und verführerisch; durch ihr Verhalten und ihre Kleidung zieht sie die Blicke der Männer auf sich. Sie ist nicht nur eine vielseitige Künstlerin und eine gute Unterhalterin, sondern hat auch handwerkliche Fähigkeiten: sie kann die vorteilhaften Kleider, die sie trägt, selbst anfertigen. Ausserdem, und vor allem, ist sie eine gute Liebesdienerin.[38] Aber die Aussicht, nur oder hauptsächlich durch Prostitution ihren Lebensunterhalt verdienen zu müssen, macht sie traurig; sie bricht in Tränen aus. Trotz ihrer grossen Fähigkeit, Männer zu befriedigen, will sie sich nicht mit jedem beliebigen einlassen; dafür ist sie sich zu schade. Bisher hat sie wohl meistens mit Männern der Unter- und Mittelschicht verkehrt. So sucht sie eine Alternative. Sie berichtet, dass hochgestellte Leute, Angehörige der Elite, Wesire und Emire, ihr den Hof gemacht haben. Sie will gesellschaftlich aufsteigen, d.h. wohl, Kurtisane bei einem Emir, einem Wesir, oder sogar (das sagt sie aber nicht), wie Ittifāq, beim Sultan werden. Schon jetzt hat sie mehrfach Glück gehabt: Ein Gönner – offenbar ein älterer Mann, denn sie nennt ihn „Onkel" – verkehrt mit ihr. Vielleicht wird er sie bei hervorragenden Musikern weiter ausbilden lassen. Auch einen weiteren Gönner hat sie bereits gefunden: einen Baumeister, der auch ein bekannter Dichter ist. Er hat, wie sie sagt, ein Haus für sie gebaut. Sie hat nun alles, um ihr Glück zu machen.

38 Die Zahlung der Steuer (*ḍamān al-maġānī*) ermöglichte es selbst Frauen, die einer hohen gesellschaftlichen Schicht angehörten, die Prostitution auszuüben (A 45).

Interpretation des Gedichts auf der Grundlage der Redeweise und der verwendeten Stilmittel

Das ganze Gedicht besteht aus der Rede *einer* Person, einer jungen Frau; es ist eine Gegenrede, in der sie auf die Rede ihrer Mutter, die ihr einen ‚guten Rat' gegeben hat, reagiert. Die Mutter hat wohl verlangt, dass die Tochter ihre Lebensweise grundlegend ändere. Diesen Rat weist die Sprecherin in einer rhetorisch glänzenden Gegenrede mit aller Heftigkeit und Leidenschaft zurück. Um die Mutter von ihrem Standpunkt zu überzeugen,[39] verwendet sie vor allem *Argumente*, und zwar vor allem *Beispiele*, dazu setzt sie auch das Mittel der Erregung von Emotionen (Pathos) der Zuhörerin (der Mutter) ein. Aspekte der Lobrede (Epideiktik) werden häufig herangezogen, vor allem in den preisenden Beschreibungen der eigenen Schönheit und Fähigkeiten der Sprecherin (arab. *faḫr*).

Was den Stil betrifft, so beginnt das Gedicht – in der Anrede an die Mutter – mit einer stark emphatischen Rede. In der ersten Strophe werden bereits Hauptmittel des rhetorischen Stils eingesetzt: Ausruf, rhetorische Frage, und, am Schluss der Strophe, sogar Drohung. Eine wirkungsvolle Antithese (vernünftig machen – wahnsinnig sein) akzentuiert die gegensätzlichen Standpunkte von Mutter und Tochter noch. In der zweiten Strophe setzt sich dieser Stil zunächst fort: Der Anruf wird zu Beginn wiederholt (Redefigur der Distanzwiederholung; *takrīr*), dann folgt eine Rede, in der die Sprecherin über sich selbst berichtet, indem sie ihre Tätigkeiten, Leidenschaften und Wünsche nennt und erläutert. Diese Rede setzt auch sich in den folgenden Strophen fort. Immer wieder ergibt sich für die Sprecherin die Gelegenheit, ihre Vorzüge hervorzuheben. Die preisenden Schilderungen sind oft bildlos; auffällig ist das mehrfach auftretende Schema des schlichten Aufzählens verschiedener Tätigkeiten. Nur wenige schlagende Metaphern und starke rhetorische Mittel kommen vor. Stark ist die Hyperbel in Strophe 4 (das Spiel der Sängerin bringt selbst die stummen Steine zum Tanzen). Die Tropen (feiner Geschmack und Süssigkeiten für körperliche Reize und Genüsse) in Strophe 3 sind konventionell, wirken aber durch ihre Häufung. In Strophe 4 und dann in Strophe 6 mischt

39 Im Folgenden verwende ich Begriffe der Systematik der aristotelischen Rhetorik. Diese waren arabischen Gelehrten bekannt (Schoeler, *Grundprobleme* 73–81; ders., Berichtigungen und Nachträge *80* zu 75), jedoch dürfte diese Kenntnis nicht ausserhalb der Kreise von Gelehrten mit philosophischer Bildung vorhanden gewesen sein. Obwohl al-Miʿmār für einen Angehörigen der Mittelschicht eine beträchtliche Bildung besass (D Einl. 23–4), sind solche theoretischen Kenntnisse bei ihm natürlich nicht vorauszusetzen; er wird den rhetorischen Stil mit allen seinen Finessen aufgrund seiner Vertrautheit mit entsprechender Dichtung von Vorgängern und seiner poetischen Intuition folgend verwendet haben.

sich rhetorischer Stil in die Beschreibung ein: Durch die Ausrufe („Welch gute Lautenspielerin bin ich doch!“, „O Gott, wie einzigartig,“ usw.) wird der Selbstpreis belebt und gesteigert. In Strophe 6 findet sich zudem noch eine wirksame rhetorische Figur: die Antithese „verschleiert sein – unverschleiert sein.“ Dadurch wird die geschilderte Schönheit des Gesichts selbst für eine der Schönheit ungünstige Situation behauptet. In den folgenden Strophen 7 bis 9 werden die dem Selbstlob dienenden Schilderungen fortgesetzt. Sie beziehen sich jetzt zunächst auf die besondere Stellung der Sängerin unter ihren Gefährtinnen (Strophe 7, 1–2), bei denen auch eine rätselhafte „Schwester,“ eine Syrerin, genannt wird; dann auf Art ihrer Kleidung (Strophe 8) und schliesslich auf ihre sexuellen Fähigkeiten und Praktiken (Strophe 9). Eine ihrer Verhaltensweisen hierbei, das Stöhnen beim Verkehr, setzt sie sogar mit der einer Hure gleich; der Begriff scheint zunächst sogar positiv konnotiert zu sein. Tatsächlich ist damit jedoch ein Stichwort gefallen, das einen (vorübergehenden) Umschwung in der Stimmung der Sprecherin bringt und damit auch eine Änderung des Stils ihrer Rede (Strophe 10). Die preisenden Schilderungen werden unterbrochen von dem Ausdruck einer tiefen Traurigkeit, die von der Erwähnung einer vermeintlich düsteren beruflichen Zukunftsperspektive ausgelöst worden ist. Die Trauer äussert sich im Weinen; die Wiederholung (*takrīr*) des Wortes sieben (die eine Distributivzahl ergibt: sieben zu sieben) in der Beschreibung der Tränen drückt deren unterbrochene Folge und die Heftigkeit des Tränenergusses aus. Hier kommt das Überzeugungsmittel der Erregung von Emotionen (bei der Zuhörerin) ins Spiel. Für den kritischen Betrachter ist allerdings unmöglich zu entscheiden, ob dies alles echt oder gespielt ist; wenn es „Theater“ ist, ist es aber gut gespielt (Überzeugungsmittel der ‚kunsthaften Aufführung‘, *hypokrisis*). Es kommt ja nur darauf an, die Mutter zu überzeugen (Strophe 10). Aber sehr bald, noch in derselben Strophe, in der letzten Zeile, kommt erneut ein Umschwung; dieser wird mit einer Frage eingeleitet, die die Sprecherin an sich selbst richtet und sich auf eine mögliche Alternative zu der düsteren Zukunftsvision bezieht. Die Antwort darauf (in den folgenden Strophen 11–12) führt wiederum zu Berichten und Schilderungen ihrer Qualitäten und Fähigkeiten, insbesondere der sexuellen (sie nennt letztere ausdrücklich in Strophe 11 noch einmal). Alle diese Fähigkeiten prädestinieren sie geradezu zum sozialen Aufstieg, und bereits gemachte Erfahrungen bestätigen dies. In Strophe 12 dringt dadurch, dass diese mit einem wirksamen Ausruf („Gar mancher Wesir …!“) eingeleitet wird, wiederum rhetorischer Stil in die Rede ein. Was folgt, sind kurze Berichte von Erfolgserlebnissen. Darin hebt sie die Zeichen der Wertschätzung hervor (Handküsse, Schuheausziehen), die ihr von hohen Persönlichkeiten – Wesiren und Emiren – entgegengebracht worden sind. In den letzten beiden Strophen (13–14) zeigt die junge Frau durch Beispiele auf, dass diese Zukunftsvision keine blosse Fantasie ist, sondern bereits angefangen hat, Wirklichkeit zu werden. Dazu nennt sie zwei Gönner, die sie jetzt schon gefunden hat, und nennt die Leistungen, die diese bereits für sie erbracht haben und noch künftig erbringen wollen. Wirkungsvoll, auch inhaltlich, ist in der vorletzten Strophe (13), die mit einer Anrede beginnende, an die Mutter gerichtete Rede (Zeile 3–4), wodurch gegen Ende des Gedichts noch einmal der rhetorische Stil zur Geltung kommt. Die Rede der jungen Frau, wie man sie auch versteht, enthält das für ihre Überzeugungsarbeit so wichtige Argument, dass auch ihre Mutter an ihrem neuen Glück teilhaben wird. Da die Tochter sich nur in geheimnisvollen Andeutungen darüber ergeht, was der „Onkel" bei – oder in – der Favoritin hinterlegen wird, erregt sie die Neugierde der Mutter. – Das auffällige Wortspiel (*ǧinās*) *ḥazwa* (Vorzugsstellung) und *maḥẓiyya* (Favoritin, Kurtisane; heisst aber ebenfalls auch Vorzugsstellung) verstärkt hier die intendierte positive Wirkung der Rede noch.

Das auffälligste Stilmittel in der letzten Strophe ist, dass der Verfasser hier die Nennung seines Dichternamens, der zugleich seinen Beruf bezeichnet, verbunden mit der Beschreibung der Leistung, die er in Ausübung seines Berufs für die junge Frau erbracht hat, in deren Rede einbaut. Die Vorgehensweise, den Dichternamen am Schluss zu nennen, und damit sozusagen die Unterschrift unter das Gedicht zu setzen, haben gelegentlich schon frühere arabische Dichter, z. B. Abū Nuwās (st. ca. 198/813),[40] befolgt; ein vorgeschriebenes Stilmittel ist sie im späteren persischen *ġazal* geworden (dort wird es *taḫalluṣ* genannt).[41] Al-Miʿmār verfährt in dieser Schluss- und „Ego-Strophe"[42] äusserst geschickt: Er stellt sich selbst samt seiner Leistung in eine Reihe mit dem vorher genannten Gönner, den er die Sprecherin erwähnen lässt, so dass diese „Ego-Passage" nicht als Fremdkörper in dem Gedicht wirkt. Dabei erscheint seine, des Dichters, Leistung dennoch in besonderer Weise hervorgehoben: Sie wird an prominenter Stelle, am Schluss, genannt, wo die Erwähnung und Beschreibung eines Hauses mit Bäumen, das der Baumeister für die junge Frau behauptet gebaut zu haben, das Gedicht mit einer ansprechenden, fast idyllischen Schilderung zu Ende gehen lässt.

Aber das ist noch nicht alles. Für den Schluss des Gedichts hat sich al-Miʿmār ein ganz besonderes Kunstmittel aufgehoben: Es ist eine versteckte Anspielung, ein doppelter Sinn, der sich dem Hörer nicht unmittelbar erschliesst. Mit „Bauen" (*anšā*) kann nämlich auch das Verfassen von Dichtung, mit „Haus"

40 Abū Nuwās, *Dīwān* iv, 228–9, Nr. 120; 232, Nr. 122.

41 De Bruijn, Takhalluṣ (2.).

42 „Ego-Passagen" (so Özkan), besonders in der letzten Strophe, finden sich öfter in den östlichen *zaǧal*s, s. Ö. Index, s. v. „Ego-Passage," 559.

(*dār* = *bayt*) auch die vorliegende Strophe (*bayt*), oder *pars pro toto* das ganze Gedicht, gemeint sein.[43] Das „Haus," das al-Miʿmār der jungen Frau gebaut hat, ist also wohl nichts anderes als das vorliegende Gedicht, das er ihr gewidmet hat. In diesem Fall wird die fiktive Sprecherin gar keinen Wert darauf legen, dass die angesprochene Person, ihre Mutter, die Anspielung versteht; sie, die ja überzeugt werden soll, dass das geschilderte freie Leben der Tochter das beste für sie beide ist, kann ruhig bei dem Glauben bleiben, dass es sich um ein wirkliches prächtiges Haus handelt.

Abschliessende Betrachtung. Hypothese über ein mögliches Vorbild des Gedichts

Die Sprecherin in unserem *zaǧal* ist eine junge Frau aus der ersten Hälfte des 8./14. Jahrhunderts; sie ist eine Volksunterhalterin und Liebesdienerin, die der gesellschaftlichen Unterschicht angehört. Jedoch ist bei jeder weitergehenden Aussage, die auf der Grundlage des Gedichts das Geschlechterwissen über diese Zeit bereichern will, ein Vorbehalt geltend zu machen: Das *zaǧal* ist nicht, wie dies auch bei den mittelalterlichen europäischen Frauenliedern (galicisch-portugiesischen *cantigas de amigo*, romanischen *ḫarǧa*s in arabischen *muwaššaḥ*s, okzitanischen und deutschen Mädchenliedern, z. B., Marcabrus *A la fontana del vergier*, des Kürenbergers „Ich zoch mir einen valken," Walter von der Vogelweides „Under der linden" usw.) der Fall ist, von einer Frau, sondern von einem Mann gedichtet worden.[44] Wir haben also nicht den unmittelbaren Ausdruck der Gemütsbewegung einer Frau vor uns, sondern eine Rede, die von einem Mann in den Mund einer Frau gelegt worden ist. Dies muss uns immer bewusst sein. Wir dürfen aber annehmen, dass der Text des Dichters nicht blosser Fantasterei entsprungen ist, sondern auf genauen Beobachtungen beruht oder jedenfalls in guter Kenntnis der Situation der Unterhaltungskünstlerinnen/Edelprostituierten seiner Zeit verfasst ist.

Diese Feststellung bringt mich dazu, zum Schluss – mit aller gebotenen Vorsicht – eine Hypothese zur Diskussion zu stellen. Nach einer Theorie, die von dem Germanisten und Sprachgeographen Theodor Frings (1886–1968) aufge-

43 Siehe den Kommentar zu Strophe 14.

44 Eine ähnliche Feststellung ist zum antiken Hetärenwesen zu machen. Schuller bemerkt – und bedauert –, dass fast alle Berichte hierüber von Männern stammen: „Über fast keinen einzigen Sachverhalt hören wir auch nur ein Wort von weiblicher Seite, geschweige denn von einer Hetäre selbst" (*Hetären* 24, 139). Eine der beiden Ausnahmen, die Schuller anführt, sind ein paar kurze Verse von Sappho (a. a. O. 139–40).

stellt und von keinem Geringeren als dem bedeutenden Romanisten Leo Spitzer (1887–1960) unterstützt und weiterentwickelt wurde,[45] wäre das Frauenlied eine in zahlreichen verschiedenen antiken und mittelalterlichen bzw. vormodernen Literaturen verbreitete Gattung gewesen, die, ursprünglich in der volkstümlichen Dichtung beheimatet, auch zur hohen Literatur „aufgestiegen" ist. So liegt nach dieser Theorie der Trobadorlyrik eine volkstümliche Schicht zugrunde.[46] Es handelt sich nicht nur um Gedichte aus der Romania und dem deutschen Raum, von denen wir oben einige Beispiele angeführt haben, sondern auch um verwandte Lieder, u.a. aus Russland, Skandinavien, dem alten Griechenland, ja auch aus China und Ägypten (3.–2. Jahrtausend v. Chr.).[47] Zu den Themen der Lieder gehört auch das Gespräch des jungen Mädchens mit der Mutter.[48] Um nun auf unseren Dichter zu kommen: Man kann sich die Frage stellen, ob der Handwerkerpoet zu dem Gedicht, das er einer städtischen Volkssängerin und -unterhalterin in den Mund gelegt hat, vielleicht von einem volkstümlichen ägyptischen Frauenlied angeregt wurde, in dem die Sprecherin ein einfaches Mädchen aus Kairo oder dem Delta war? Wollte er vielleicht ein Gegenstück zu oder eine Parodie auf ein solches Mädchenlied dichten?[49] Dass al-Miʿmār für sein Gedicht die Gattung des *zaǧal* gewählt hat, ist vielleicht dadurch nahegelegt worden, dass auch das *zaǧal* eine ursprünglich volkstümliche, zur hohen Literatur „aufgestiegene" Gattung ist.

Danksagung

Mein herzlicher Dank gilt allen Kollegen, die mich bei dieser Arbeit unterstützt haben: Dr. Hakan Özkan (Münster) hat mir das Gedicht als geeignetes Thema dieses Festschriftbeitrages vorgeschlagen und eine erste Rohfassung meiner Übersetzung durchgesehen und korrigiert. Danach haben lic. phil. Idris Kiwirra (Basel), Dr. Yūsuf Faḫraddīn (Haifa), Prof. Dr. Dwight F. Reynolds (Santa Barbara) und Dr. Nefeli Papoutsakis (Münster) mir wertvolle Vorschläge zur Lösung vieler Rätsel, die der schwierige Text stellt, gemacht. Nefeli Papoutsakis und Hakan Özkan haben die abschliessende Redaktion des Textes über-

45 Spitzer, Die mozarabische Lyrik.

46 Ebd., 229.

47 Ebd., 199.

48 Ebd., 209, 211.

49 Jedenfalls hat unser Gedicht mit den „erzählerisch-kohärenten, mit Dialogen gespickten Abenteuer-*zaǧal*s, die [von Spielleuten] … zu bestimmten Anlässen auf öffentlichen Plätzen dargeboten wurden" (Ö 436; zur Gattung s. Voegeli, Manṣūbat, und Cachia, *Popular narrative ballads*) nicht das Geringste zu tun.

nommen. Wesentliche Beiträge aller Genannten zum Verständnis des Gedichts habe ich in den Kommentaren zu den betreffenden Stellen dokumentiert.

Literatur- und Abkürzungsverzeichnis

A = ʿAbd ar-Rāziq, A., *La femme au temps des Mamlouks en Egypte*, Thèse Université de Paris-I (Sorbonne), Paris 1975.

Abū Nuwās, al-Ḥasan b. Hāniʾ, *Dīwān* iv, Hg. G. Schoeler, Wiesbaden 1982.

Badawi, E. und Hinds, M., *A dictionary of Egyptian Arabic: Arabic-English*, Beirut 1986.

Baldwin, J.E., Prostitution, Islamic law and Ottoman societies, in *JESHO* 55/1, 117–52.

Bauer, T., Ibrāhīm al-Miʿmār: Ein dichtender Handwerker aus Ägyptens Mamlukenzeit, in *ZDMG* 152 (2002), 63–93.

Bauer, T., Die Leiden eines ägyptischen Müllers: Die Mühlen-Maqāme des Ibrāhīm al-Miʿmār (st. 749/1348), in A.I. Blöbaum, J. Kahl und S.D. Schweitzer (Hgg.), *Ägypten – Münster: Kulturwissenschaftliche Studien zu Ägypten, dem Vorderen Orient und verwandten Gebieten ... donum natalicum ... Erharto Graefe ... oblatum*, Wiesbaden 2003, 1–16.

Bauer, T., Das Nilzağal des Ibrāhīm al-Miʿmār: Ein Lied zur Feier des Nilschwellenfestes, in Th. Bauer und U. Stehli-Werbeck, unter Mitarbeit von Th.G. Schneiders (Hgg.), *Alltagsleben und materielle Kultur in der arabischen Sprache und Literatur: Festschrift für Heinz Grotzfeld zum 70. Geburtstag*, Wiesbaden 2005, 69–88.

Beeston, A.F.L., *The epistle on singing-girls of Jāḥiẓ*, ed. with transl. and comm., Warminster 1980.

Biesterfeldt, H., *Mizr fī Miṣr*. Ein Preisgedicht auf das Bier aus dem Kairo des 14. Jahrhunderts, in H. Biesterfeldt und V. Klemm (Hgg.), *Differenz und Dynamik im Islam: Festschrift für Heinz Halm zum 70. Geburtstag*, Würzburg 2012, 383–98.

Cachia, P., *Popular narrative ballads of modern Egypt*, Oxford 1989.

CHAL = Allen, R. und D.S. Richards (Hgg.), *Arabic literature in the post-classical period* (The Cambridge History of Arabic Literature), Cambridge 2006.

Colin, G.S., Ibn Ḳuzmān, in *EI*², iii, 849–52.

D = al-Miʿmār, Ibrāhīm, *Der Dīwān* (s. d.).

Danielson, V., Artists and entrepreneurs: Female singers in Cairo during the 1920s, in N.R. Keddie and B. Baron (Hgg.), *Women in Middle Eastern history: Shifting boundaries in sex and gender*, New Haven 1992, 292–309.

de Bruijn, J.T.P., Takhalluṣ (2.), in *EI*², x, 123.

Dozy, R.A., *Dictionnaire détaillé des noms de vêtements chez les Arabes*, Amsterdam 1845.

Dozy, R.A., *Supplément aux dictionnaires arabes*, 2 Bde., Leiden 1881.

EAL = Meisami, J.S., und P. Starkey (Hgg.), *Encyclopedia of Arabic Literature*, 2 Bde., London-New York 1988.

EALB = De Young, T., und M. St. Germain (Hgg.), *Essays in Arabic Literary Biography 925–1350*, Wiesbaden 2011.
Ed., Bighāʾ, in EI², xii, 133–4.
Fagnan, E., *Additions aux dictionnaires arabes*, Algier 1923.
G = Gökpinar, Y., *Höfische Musikkultur im klassischen Islam: Ibn Faḍlallāh al-ʿUmarī (gest. 749/1349) über die dichterische und musikalische Kunst der Sängersklavinnen*, Leiden-Boston 2020.
Hagen, G. und T. Seidensticker, Reinhard Schulzes Hypothese einer islamischen Aufklärung: Kritik einer historiographischen Kritik, in ZDMG 148 (1998), 83–110.
Hauser, A., *Methoden moderner Kunstbetrachtung*, München 1958.
[Hölderin, F.] Hildarlin, *Muḫtārāt min šiʿrihī, waḍaʿahā fī l-ʿarabīya* F. Rifqa, Beirut 1974.
Kazimirski, A. de Biberstein, *Dictionnaire arabe-français*, 2 Bde., Paris 1960.
Lane, E.W., *Madd al-qāmūs: An Arabic-English lexicon*, 8 Bde., London 1863–93.
Lapidus, I.M., *Muslim cities in the later Middle Ages*, Cambridge 1984.
Mayer, L.A., *Mamluk costume: A survey*, Genf 1952.
al-Miʿmār, Ibrāhīm, *Der Dīwān*, Ed. und Komm.: Th. Bauer, A. Osigus und H. Özkan, Baden-Baden 2018.
M = Mez, A., *Die Renaissance des Islams*, Heidelberg 1922 (Nachdruck Hildesheim 1968).
Neubauer, E., *Musiker am Hof der frühen ʿAbbāsiden*, Diss. Frankfurt/M. 1965.
Ö = Özkan, *Geschichte* (s.d.).
Özkan, H., The drug *zajals* in Ibrāhīm al-Miʿmār's *dīwān*, in MSR 17 (2013), 213–48.
Özkan, H., *Geschichte des östlichen* zaǧal: *Dialektale arabische Strophendichtung aus dem Osten der arabischen Welt – von den Anfängen bis zum Ende der Mamlukenzeit*, Baden-Baden 2020.
Özkan, H., Why stress does matter: New material on metrics in *zajal* poetry, in MSR 19 (2016), 101–14.
Pellat, Ch., Ḳayna, in EI², iv, 820–4.
R = Rapoport, Y., Women and gender in Mamluk society: An overview, in MSR 11/2 (2007), 1–47.
Rowson, E.K., S̲h̲ubha, in EI², ix, 492–3.
Schoeler, G., *Arabische Handschriften*, Teil 2, Unter Mitarbeit von H.-C. Graf von Bothmer, T. Duncker Gökcen und H. Jenni (Verzeichnis der orientalischen Handschriften in Deutschland. Arabische Handschriften. Bd. XVII, B, 2), Stuttgart 1990.
Schoeler, G., *Einige Grundprobleme der autochthonen und der aristotelischen arabischen Literaturtheorie* (Abhandlungen für die Kunde des Morgenlandes XLI, 4), Wiesbaden 1975.
Schoeler, G., Berichtigungen und Nachträge zu meiner Abhandlung *Einige Grundprobleme ...*, in ZDMG 126 (1976), *78*–*81*.
Schoeler, G., und W. Stoetzer, Zaǧal, in EI² xi, 373–7.
Schuller, W., *Die Welt der Hetären: Berühmte Frauen zwischen Legende und Wirklichkeit*, Stuttgart 2008.

Spiro, S., *Arabic-English vocabulary of the colloquial Arabic of Egypt*, Cairo-London 1895.

Spitzer, L., Die mozarabische Lyrik und die Theorien von Theodor Frings, in: R. Baehr (Hg.), *Der provenzalische Minnesang: Ein Querschnitt durch die neuere Forschungsdiskussion*, Darmstadt 1967, 198–230 ([dtsch. Übers.n von R. Baehr]: Spitzer, L., The Mozarabic lyric and Theodor Frings' theories, in *Comparative Literature* 4 [1952], 1–22).

ST = Stigelbauer, M., *Die Sängerinnen am Abbasidenhof um die Zeit des Kalifen Al-Mutawakkil: Nach dem Kitāb al-Aġānī des Abū l-Farağ al-Iṣbahānī und anderen Quellen dargestellt*, Diss. Wien 1975.

Voegeli, M., *Manṣūbat Ṣafā l-ʿaiš* – ein volkstümliches ägyptisch-arabisches *zağal* aus dem 17. Jahrhundert, in *Asiatische Studien* 50 (1996), 463–78.

W = Wagner, E., *Abū Nuwās. Eine Studie zur arabischen Literatur der frühen ʿAbbāsidenzeit*. Wiesbaden 1964.

Wagner, E., [Rez.:] Florian Sobieroj [Hrsg.]: *Die Responsensammlung Abū l-Qāsim al-Qušairī's über das Sufitum …*, Wiesbaden, Harrasssowitz 2012, in ZGAIW 20–21 (2012–14), 461–3.

7

Media in Flux: The Tale of the Yellow Folio from *Kalīla and Dimna*

Beatrice Gruendler

In the preface added by the translator-adaptor Ibn al-Muqaffaʿ (d. 157/756) to his (lost) Arabic version of the manual of statecraft packaged as parables, *Kalīla and Dimna*, much is said about reading books, interpreting parables, applying knowledge in life, and being an exemplary scholar.[1] As the full text of this work only resurfaces from the mists of history half a millennium later in the seventh/thirteenth century as a kaleidoscope of versions, we may never know the exact words he wrote. The text has become fluid, and over the centuries, copyist-redactors have added their overtones.[2] However, some of the embedded tales appear in all extant manuscripts. These, as the rest of the text, have diverged in their formulation, but as elements, they can be assumed to have existed since Ibn al-Muqaffaʿ's time.

In the Arabic preface, the sub-stories are well-fitted to the purpose they serve. This differs from sub-stories in later chapters, some of which become more complex and develop a dynamic of their own beyond the purpose they supposedly serve. In the Arabic preface, each sub-story belongs to a larger topic and is often introduced by a saying or analogy which the story then exemplifies. The topics are not clearly separated but rather merge into each other, with some items from one topic appearing elsewhere. General sayings on culture, life, or virtue and analogical images are interspersed at many places.

---

1 The *Kalīla and Dimna—AnonymClassic* project has received funding from the European Research Council, under the European Union's H2020-EU.1.1.—EXCELLENT SCIENCE program, Advanced Grant no. 742635. See the project website: https://www.geschkult.fu-berlin.de/en/e/kalila-wa-dimna/. I thank Ulrich Marzolph, the members of the *AnonymClassic* team, and the editors of the present volume for their feedback on an earlier draft of this article.

For an overview on *Kalīla wa-Dimna* and its textual history, see Gruendler et al., An interim report; Gruendler, Les versions arabes; de Blois, *Burzōy's voyage* (whose chapter abbreviations are used); Grotzfeld et al., Kalila und Dimna; and Brockelmann, Kalīla wa-Dimna. On Ibn al-Muqaffaʿ and his entire written oeuvre, see Kristó-Nagy, *La pensée d'Ibn al-Muqaffaʿ*.

2 On silent co-authorship in *Kalīla wa-Dimna*, see Gruendler, A rat and its redactors.

 | DOI:10.1163/9789004521780_009

The first topic is about knowledge acquired by reading books, and particularly this book, which is to be done thoroughly and conscientiously. The meaning of the parables is to be decoded with awareness of their outward and hidden meanings. Here appears the sub-story of the bequeathed treasure, which exemplifies things memorized when young and understood upon adulthood. Another sub-story (absent in Q-c)[3] concerns a man who loses a treasure he found by having it carried home by others who keep it for themselves. The reason for his loss is that he failed to reflect on the consequences of his actions. The third sub-story is about a man who mistakes reciting a text about grammar or rhetoric for knowing its contents (to be discussed in detail).

The second topic concerns the application of acquired knowledge in life. One sub-story tells of a man who is aware of a burglar in his house but falls asleep while the burglar robs everything, because the man failed to use his knowledge. Another sub-story compares a blind and a sighted man both of whom fall into a ditch, but the sighted one is to be blamed, for he should have been aware.

The third topic concerns how a scholar is to conduct himself, namely virtuously, without excessive ambition or harming others. This is illustrated by the merchant and his fraudulent partner who ends up stealing his own merchandise (placed under this topic in L-c). Another sub-story tells of a naked pauper (not in Q-c), who scares away a thief who is about to rob his last bit of food and who escapes leaving his garb behind. This makes the pauper gain from the failed theft. However, the tale is told to explain that one must not rely on such rare luck but instead strive toward the good like most people.

The fourth topic, that one must learn from others' experience but must check any received information, is not illustrated by any story.

Then follows a reprise of the first topic, and the preface ends here in one group of versions (L-c). Another group (P-c) places the sub-story of the merchant and his fraudulent partner here and follows it up with three further tales. The story of the thief and the two jars holds up a mirror to the fraudulent partner with another thief who errs in stealing grain rather than gold as he intended. The next tale has a fisher find a shell that turns out to be empty. Being quickly discouraged, he forgoes a second chance, and another fisher retrieves from the waters another shell that contains a pearl. His failure is lack of perseverance. Finally, a tale of three brothers (not in Q-c) describes how a younger brother reforms his two elder spendthrift siblings by sharing his part of the inheritance with them and guiding them to proper behavior and responsible management of their wealth.

3 These labels and the manuscript groups they refer to are explained in section 2.

1 The Sub-story of "The Yellow Folio"

The sub-story of the misguided reader speaks precisely to the topic of the preface, namely about using the written medium in order to acquire knowledge. It is the tale of "The Yellow Folio," and it describes the error of a man who reads something without knowing or understanding the contents. It is titled after an inscribed sheet the man receives *al-ṣaḥifatu l-ṣafrāʾ*. The colour may refer to yellowing from age but plays no particular role in the story. As is usually the case with embedded tales, the present one is meant to reinforce a point in the argument. It is placed among short wisdom sayings on proper reading, an exhortation on how to extract knowledge, an analogical image, and a further exhortation to seek knowledge, forming together a coherent block.

The tale proper ensues after two general statements about reading, the first that one should read slowly and carefully in order to properly understand the text (16.1 ImReaderToGraspAndReflect),[4] and the second, that the reader of a book must contemplate both its overt and hidden meanings to draw any benefit from it (16.2 ImSuperficialReadingFruitless). The statements are followed by the short analogy of a nut (17): one can get to the edible contents only by cracking the shell (P-c and L-c) and extracting these (only L-c). The sub-story then follows to illustrate more specifically what "cracking the nut" entails in the process of reading. After the tale, an exhortation to seek knowledge resumes the larger topic (20.1; see the synopsis on which units appear in which versions, Appendix 3.2).

The sub-story itself gives a counter example to "cracking the nut": it tells of a man who gets it all wrong and confuses owning a piece of writing and reciting its contents with penetrating the subject of what was written down. Beyond these basic facts, the versions contained in the manuscripts diverge. Ibn al-Muqaffaʿ's rendition has been overwritten, and the different ways of the man's failure as they are described can only be attributed to the copyist-redactors between the thirteenth and the nineteenth century, whose versions survive. Their various renditions will be compared in the following.

These no longer reflect the context of the Arabic adaptation, the time of the introduction of the book codex to Arabic-Islamic culture, when *Kalīla and Dimna* was one of the first books with prefaces and chapters, translated in the mid-second/eighth century from the Middle Persian version, itself combining

4 The serial numbers and labels refer to the segments into which the preface has been subdivided for alignment of corresponding passages in the digitized versions. For the full text of the present sub-story, see the Appendix 3.4 and 3.5.

elements from Sanskrit works. With its sophisticated structure, including multiple intercalated narrative frames, it stood out among the formats used for early Arabic books.[5] The preface under discussion originates from the Arabic adaptation, as do several other chapters of the book. *Kalīla and Dimna* is a book which reflects about its own medium. What does reading mean? Which ways of reading exist? And which purpose do they serve? The sub-story to be discussed heightens this self-reflexivity through inversion, dramatizing a failed performance of reading. Other prefaces (*Kalīla and Dimna* contains no less than four) speak on the topic of books too, but from different angles, such as on medical books as a scholarly reference (Bu), and on *Kalīla and Dimna* in specific as a source of rulers' knowledge (Sv, Lv) or memorialization (Az) and a treasured object (Sv, Lv), on the motive and process of its composition (Az), its importation to Persia (Sv, Lv, Bu), and its translation (Lv). But the Arabic preface focuses in particular on what one is to do with this book and how best to draw benefit from it. The tale of the Yellow Folio comes to stand in as a cameo of sorts for the usage of books, which forms a prominent topic of the Arabic preface. But the exact wording of what Ibn al-Muqaffaʿ wrote as a contemporary to the adoption of this medium into Arabic-Islamic culture is no longer retrievable. The book's surviving versions reflect a much later era. Meanwhile, the work had shifted from a model of secretarial prose to an "everyman's handbook" on practical ethics and popular philosophy. In this later period, the book as medium was no longer new, but the novelty was its widening use by individuals who were not scholars or members of the elite and nonetheless owned, read, and wrote books.[6]

Before delving into the tale, a short overview of the manuscripts' versions and how they relate to each other is in order. One can distinguish five different types, each of which plays a different role in the textual transmission. A majority of the manuscripts forms part of a continuum, that is, a group of versions among which much text is shared, but each witness differs from the other in an incremental way with a tendency towards accretion over time, but also with cuts and substitutions. Three continua have been identified, referred to as the Paris continuum, the London continuum, and the Queen continuum.[7]

5 On early Arabic book formats in general, see Gruendler, *The rise of the Arabic book*, 27–9, and on *Kalīla and Dimna*, ibid., 155–61.

6 For the increased readership in the middle period, see Hirschler, *The written word*, and for readership and authorship in the eleventh/seventeenth and twelfth/eighteenth centuries, see Hanna, *In praise of books*, Sajdi, *The barber of Damascus*, and Diyāb, *The book of travels*.

7 For a detailed discussion of this concept, its applicability and limitations, see Gruendler, The relation among manuscripts.

Outside of these fall several early manuscripts from the seventh/thirteenth and eighth/fourteenth century, which differ in a number of ways from the continua and from each other (group E). In a further type of versions, elements from all the previous are selectively combined; these are the so-called *cross-copied* versions.[8] Finally, few manuscripts are actually near-verbatim copies of others. It turns out that copyists of *Kalīla and Dimna* did not often "copy", and are therefore referred hereafter as copyist-redactors.

As it may have become clear at this point, reading *Kalīla and Dimna* is not a linear process. Rather one cannot look at one version without being aware of the rendition of the same passage in a number of others. For the present purpose, a synoptic edition has been composed of fifteen witnesses. Numerically speaking, these represent only ten percent of the work's ca. 140 extant manuscripts, but they have been selected in such a way as to represent a maximal variance across the first four of the above-described types (near-verbatim copies are excluded, as they do not contribute to the present analysis). Reading "parallel" across fifteen witnesses, as it were, is an unusual experience, and today, the juxtaposition of versions is a more common technique in filmmaking than in literature. The reader of early Arabic prose, however, is often presented with a number of versions of the same event in succession, be that in Prophetic *ḥadīth* or historical or literary accounts (*akhbār*). But these mostly short texts differ from a book like *Kalīla and Dimna* not only in length but also by the fact that, in *ḥadīth* and *akhbār*, transmission began orally and was then committed to writing, within a continued mixed written-oral tradition that lasted (at least) for the first four centuries of Arabic and Islamic culture. Conversely, *Kalīla and Dimna* began as a written work and changed through rewriting, without any sort of accompanying oral control of the transmission that would have reigned in the textual proliferation, and by the seventh/thirteenth century it had changed from a classic of *adab* to a popular book on ethics and practical philosophy. Thus the above given plot plays out in a number of versions, each penned at a different time and place, and the copyist-redactors are mostly anonymous or obscure. As it is, the modular structure of the book, subdivided into enframed tales and interspersed with self-contained sayings and analogical images, facilitates the kind of parallel reading required for comparison, as the text presents numerous points of junction that can easily be found in another version. In many manuscripts, the text is subdivided accordingly with paragraph symbols, rubrication, or overstrikes (which often coincide

8 The term was coined by Jean Dagenais, with reference to Old Castilian, see his *Ethics of reading*, 132.

with the borders of segments in the present analysis). This clear articulation of the work's different elements was probably an aid and incentive for the pre-modern cross-copyists who had several *Vorlagen* in front of them to create their own combined versions.

2 The Versions of the Sub-story Compared

The story analysed hereafter evolves in four phases (numbered 19.1–19.4). A man wants to acquire *faṣāḥa*, asks a scholar and friend of his for help, and receives what he desired in the form of an inscribed folio (19.1). He returns home and practices reading it (19.2). In a gathering he then speaks up, but one of those present opines that he made a mistake. The man disagrees, defending himself with owning the folio, which he keeps at his house (19.3). An appended comment declares that the man's insistence made his ignorance even more blatant (19.4). The tale is followed by the general saying that one is liable to seek knowledge (20.1).

The witnesses differ in length and wording in each phase. I will first contrast two larger groups, the Paris continuum and the London continuum (hereafter P-c and L-c; the Queen continuum, Q-c, aligns in this chapter with P-c), then discuss the early group and the cross-copied versions, and finally touch upon a few witnesses that show substantial individual rewriting.[9]

2.1 *Continua*

(19.1) The narrative bifurcates from the beginning between the two continua. In L-c, the man's goal is to acquire "some knowledge of *faṣāḥa*" (*shay'an min ʿilm al-faṣāḥa*). He brings a folio with him and asks a friend and scholar to fill it with writing about the discipline (*ʿilm*), or basics (*aṣl*), of the *ʿarabiyya*. The term refers to the written form of Arabic that had been codified since the second/eighth century, as opposed to urban Arabic colloquials. *Faṣāḥa* has two nuances, articulateness, in the sense of correct and clear expression, and eloquence, i.e., artful expression. Here the former meaning of correctness is implied.[10]

---

9 For a list of the manuscripts and their abbreviations, see Appendix 3.1. Regarding Q-c, though it first aligns with P-c and then switches to L-c, it retains a number of its own characteristics, for which see Khalfallah, What the chapter of "The King and His Dreams" reveals.

10 For the synoptic digital edition that has facilitated this analysis, LERA, see the home page: https://lera.uzi.uni-halle.de/. See also Schütz and Pöckelmann, LERA. On its adaptation to

In P-c, the man communicates his need without bringing along any writing material, and it is the friend who chooses to impart his knowledge using a folio on which he sketches out (*rasama*) eloquent speech. This version paraphrases *faṣāḥa* as belonging to people's speech (*faṣīḥ al-kalām, min kalām al-nās*) with its varieties (*taṣārīf*) and facets (*wujūh*).[11] Not correctness but eloquence is the kind of knowledge desired here. In some later witnesses, the term *wujūh* is reread as *jawhar* "substance" (Riyadh 2407, P3473).[12] This is a reinterpretation of the consonantal skeleton (*rasm*), here by separating and reanalyzing the first radical as the conjunction *wa-* and adding a *rāʾ* at the end. Such free rereading of the *rasm* occurs frequently in *Kalīla and Dimna* with more or less logical, or creative, results. The present rereading generally fits, though what the "essence of eloquence" precisely refers to is uncertain.

To compare: L-c is about the correct usage of Arabic as codified, whereas the P-c aims at rhetorical elegance. The man in L-c is more modest, he simply desires a piece (*shayʾan*), and he wants to have it in written form and not acquire it, as would have been the way in the second/eighth century by reading out a text with a scholar (*samāʿ*) in many sessions, resulting in a written copy afterwards, whose reading has been commented and corrected. The imparting of written knowledge in scholarship (*munāwala*) exists but ranks lower than oral transmission, because personal interaction with a scholar conveyed authority, and moreover the Arabic script does not regularly record the full pronunciation of each word. This might be done by adding all vowels signs, but their use was rare and at the discretion of the writer, even though in early lexical texts vocalization does appear. The way in which the request is uttered in the story characterizes an amateur who is not interested in truly becoming versed in the linguistic sciences. In the next part (19.2), he will then reuse this knowledge as if he had learned it orally, so he is not really aware of how to deal with the written medium.

(19.2) When the man has returned home to internalize the knowledge from the sheet, he does so in L-c by treating it like the transcript of something heard; he reads it without realizing that he does not know the meaning (*yaqraʾuhū*

Arabic, see the contribution of Mahmoud Kozae and Marwa M. Ahmed in Gruendler et al., An interim report 272–6. The cross-analysis tool has been created by Mahmoud Kozae, and the graphs of the present analysis are included in the Appendix 3.3–3.4.

11 The non-technical meaning is intended by the plural here, as opposed to the grammatical meaning of the singular *taṣrīf*, "conjugation, declension." But for the latter meaning, see BnT 2281, p. 138 below.

12 Together with Berlin We II 672, these manuscripts form the Wetzstein subgroup (We) of P-c.

wa-lā yadrī maʿnāhu).[13] The verb *qaraʾa* may variously mean to read silently or aloud or to recite by heart; the context implies that he is reading it out aloud. His error is to see reading and knowing as coinciding, which leads him to think that mere reading conveys mastery of the contents (*ẓanna annahū bi-l-qirāʾati qad aḥkama mā fīhi*). He is aware of knowledge to be gained, so his focus is epistemic, but he is mistaken about how to get there.

In P-c, the man's misplaced effort is emphasized. He rehearses reading out the folio aloud (*jaʿala yukthiru min qirāʾatihī*) but does not spend any time trying to grasp its contents (*wa-lā yaqifu ʿalā maʿānīhi*). This continuum then adds the man's eagerness to display his knowledge and he joins a gathering of scholars and literati (*ahl al-adab wa-l-ʿilm*). His error consists in not bothering with the content at all and thinking that reading itself constitutes knowledge (*ẓanna annahū ktafā bimā qaraʾahū*). His focus is performative, he wants to show other people what he has learned, and those to whom he wants to display his knowledge are also people of *adab* (a multifaceted concept that one may summarize as "applied culture," as it is selective knowledge prepared for display as opposed to in-depth scholarship).

(19.3) In L-c, the man then applies in speech (*takallama*) what he thinks he knows but commits a linguistic mistake (*laḥanta/alḥanta*).[14] This is pointed out to him by another person. The fact that this occurs in a gathering of scholars is only given as an aside in L-c (*ahl al-ʿilm wa-l-faṣāḥa*); literati (*ahl al-adab*) are not included. The focus is the man's linguistic error, *laḥn*, a technical term and a topic that was treated since the second/eighth century in numerous treatises on the rectification of speech. His incredulous counter-question repeats the same term, "Did I commit/Am I accused of a language error?" (*alḥanu/ulaḥḥanu*), implying that this cannot be since he owns a folio containing the rules of the *ʿarabiyya*. In L-c this ends the sub-story. The man's foolish question is enough to show his confusion between reading and knowing.

---

13 The transcription with full case endings is historically debatable, since many versions exhibit moderate forms of Middle Arabic, i.e. relaxed grammar but few pseudo-corrections and little or no dialectal features (on the former phenomenon, see Blau, *On pseudo-corrections*, 11–22, for a definition, and 56–109, for a list of Arabic examples). The pronunciation of what is written cannot be completely restored due to the nature of the Arabic *abgad*-alphabet. For practical purposes, a classical Arabic phonetic transcription has been chosen, except for such cases when a Middle Arabic feature clearly appears in the *rasm*, which is then rendered accordingly.

14 The fourth verbal form is not attested in this meaning in classical Arabic, but the substitution of the fourth for the first form is frequent in Middle Arabic; this register is used to various degrees in many manuscript versions of *Kalīla wa-Dimna*. For a list of Middle Arabic features, see Fudge, *A hundred and one nights*, Introduction, xxxvi–vii.

In P-c the encounter is formulated as a dialogue (*muḥāwaratuhum*), and the error is remarked upon in a non-technical way (*akhṭaʾta*) but specified to be one of pronunciation (*fīmā naṭaqta*) in some versions (We group). In his retort the man adds that he not only keeps the folio at home but has also read it, continuing his misunderstood equation of knowing and performing. P-c adds to the public embarrassment by having the interlocutor correct the man, "The correct way is different from what you said/pronounced" (*al-wajhu ghayru mā takallamta/naṭaqta*).

(19.4) Only in P-c, the events of the sub-story receive a commentary, namely that the man's offering of a defense rather than silently conceding his (obvious) mistake makes his ignorance (*jahl*) and his lack of *adab* even more blatant.

(20.1) In L-c (here only A4095 and L4044) the resuming text brings the sub-story back to the general argument, stressing that what is called for is the opposite of what the man in the story attempted, namely to seek knowledge (*fa-l-marʾu ḥaqīqun an yaṭluba l-ʿilm*), for which books are a means that must be used in the way proper to it. L-c makes most clear that a written text is an instrument of knowledge and not a means for oral performance.

2.2 *Early Group*

(19.1–19. 4) The versions of the sub-story in the early group align partially with P-c (I344, Pococke 400), whereas P3475[15] remains close to the L-c with minor differences and an addition in the resuming statement (20.1). In (19.1) the former two versions define the topic of the man's ignorance as "the definitions of speech" *ḥudūd al-kalām*. This term, less technical in appearance, denotes nonetheless correct speech and appears in a number of book titles since the third/ninth century, simply as *al-Ḥudūd* or *Ḥudūd al-naḥw*. It is possible that the phrase *ḥudūd al-kalām* was at the root of the bifurcation between the continua, with L-c elaborating the component of *ḥudūd* into *aṣl/ʿilm al-ʿarabiyya* with the focus on grammar, whereas P-c developed the component of *kalām* into eloquence (*faṣīḥ al-kalām*), with the focus on rhetoric.

(19.2) In the second segment I344 and Pococke 400 share phrases that appear in neither continuum, namely the man's lack of interpreting the folio's written content (*taʾwīl mā fīhi*), which is more precise than not grasping (*lā yaqifu ʿalā,*

15 P3475, dated 1175/1761, is a near verbatim copy of the partially damaged BRR 3566, dated to c. 663–679/1265–80, and is used for the Im chapter missing in the older *Vorlage*.

P-c) or not knowing (*lā yadrī*, L-c) the content. The man's complete ignorance is then contrasted in syntactic parallelism with his perfect recitation (*māhiran bi-qirāʾatihī jāhilan bi-taʾwīlihī*). His hubris is also accentuated; not only does he think mere memorization suffices (*iktafā*, P-c) or equates mastery (*aḥkama*, L-c), but he assumes himself to have risen to the level of true scholars and to be their match (*ahl al-ʿilm ... wa-ẓanna annahū qad kāfaʾahum fī ʿilmihim*).

(19.3) In the third segment, a member of the gathering (here no scholar) commenting on his speech and pointing the error out to him also mentions the correct way (*innamā huwa/innahū kadhā wa-kadhā*). A further addition, absent in both continua, has those present test the man, and his correct recitation of the sheet (I344 clarifies this as being recited by heart *ḥafiẓa*, not read off the page) with his complete disregard for the content. The phrase "He recited the contents with apparent perfection" (*qaraʾa mā fīhā ẓāhiran māhiran*) echoes the parallelism of the previous segment.

(19.4) The commenting segment includes a phrase emphasizing that the embarrassment was in public (*ʿinda l-nās*) and both versions add a further subject of his ignorance: besides *adab*, he also lacks understanding (*fahm*, I344) or knowledge (*ʿilm*, Pococke 400).

2.3 *Versions with Substantial Rewriting*

BnT 2281

Among the versions with substantial rewriting is BnT 2281. It belongs to the Paris continuum but reformulates the text freely in many passages. The substory is spiced with much technical vocabulary, mostly from the linguistic sciences. When approaching his friend (19.1), the man formulates his request in rhyming theological jargon, desiring "what deserves priority" on the subject (*al-ʿilm al-faṣīḥ bi-mūjib al-tarjīḥ*).[16] He wants to be given this in the form of a fascicle, not just a folio (*an yutḥifahū bi-juzʾin*) and he then details the elements as "the finer points of lexicon and inflection in speech" (*fuṣūl* (sic) *tatanāwalu daqāʾiqa l-lughati wa-taṣrīfa l-kalām*).

Back at home (19.2), BnT 2281 describes the man's study of the written words as not being based upon unravelling their meanings (*akhadha fī l-dirāsati li-alfāẓihā wa-lam yuʿawwil ʿalā ḥalli maʿānīhā*), and spells out his conviction that repetition is the key to becoming an articulate speaker (*fa-zaʿama annahū nāla*

16 This version tends to add rhyming phrases, as also at the end of the preface in describing the book's first goal as *fa-yudriku l-iltifāta ilā ẓāhiri fuṣūlihī bi-nawādirin kathīratin wa-fiṭanin ghazīratin* (124.2).

bi-dhālika l-tikrāri wa-ṣāra faṣīḥan). The false self-perception is repeated in the next segment (19.3) before he joins the gathering (*fa-jāwazahum ẓannan minhu annahū ʿārif*). The final comment simply states the man's own exposure of his pathetic deficiency (*wa-zādahū dhālika hanatan wa-ntiqāṣan*), rather than his lack of *adab* as elsewhere in P-c.

This version's rewriting has sharpened the contrast between delusion and fact: the man's own usage of scholarly jargon and the narrative's linguistic details make the story's outcome even more grotesque.

We II 672

Another version, We II 672, differs in its way of rewriting; rather than constantly rephrasing as in BnT 2281, this copyist-redactor adds periodically entire passages to the text. He identifies himself in the colophon as Aḥmad al-Rabbāṭ (d. 1830).[17] At the beginning (19.1) the man expresses the wish to learn something under the direction of his scholar friend (*yataʿallamu bi-qaṣdihī*), and what the friend then gives him in writing is described in general terms as "something of the system" (*shay*ʾ (sic) *mina l-niẓām*).

At home (19.2) this version likewise has him repeat the written folio until he knows it by heart (*jaʿala yukarriruhā … ilā an ḥafiẓahā*).

The comment (19.4) receives a long addition further explaining the man's failure by his lack of awareness of his shortcomings. Had he been conscious of it, he could have researched what he did not know, or asked someone who did, and thereby not only remedied his lack of knowledge but might also even have been counted among the scholars or literati.

There is some irony in the fact that the most creative versions, while narrating a failure in the usage of the Arabic language, do not use the accusative (*rasama lahū … fuṣul*, BnT 2281; *kataba lahū … shay*ʾ, We II 672) in keeping with the Middle Arabic idiom. In We II 672 the amount and degree of such features are higher, including pseudo-corrections and colloquial terms. It is uncertain whether the redactor of We II 672, a known bibliophile, amateur scholar, composer, and author of several works, among them a *Dīwān* of popular poetry, knew the *ʿarabiyya*. Even if so, the Middle Arabic idiom may have been a choice, as it had become standard in many popular genres, and it dominates over classical Arabic in manuscript versions of *Kalīla and Dimna*.[18] It happens that this particular story clashes with the style in which it is imparted. One hypothesis is that P-c, whose versions proliferate more and exhibit an increase of Middle

17 On him and his library, see Liebrenz, The library of Aḥmad al-Rabbāṭ.

18 This does not apply to those manuscripts that are copied from early modern printed editions of *Kalīla and Dimna*.

Arabic features shifts the topic therefore to rhetoric (rather than grammar as in L-c). We may never know whether the effect of irony in BnT 2281 and We II 672 was intended.

2.4 *Cross-Copied Versions*

P3471

To turn to the versions that combine models, P3471 remains in this narrative within P-c. In the Arabic preface, it relies mainly on P3466, but fills in certain elements from other P-c versions, as is visible here only in one phrase in the first segment.[19]

P5881

In P5881 in turn, one can observe a fine-grained interlinking of all facets of the narrative from different versions. In the first segment (19.1), portions of L-c are chosen, in the following (19.2–19.3) parts of P-c are folded into the narrative structure of L-c with the additional elements only present in the early group: *wa-nṭalaqa* (L-c) *bihā ilā manzilihī* (all versions) *wa-jaʿala yaqraʾuhā* (L-c) *wa-yadrusuhā* (E) *wa-lā yaqifu ʿalā* (P-c) *maʿnāhā* (all versions) *wa-lā yaʿrifu taʾwīla mā fīhā* (E) etc., and the segment ends with a unique phrase about the man, who thought "that he equaled them in scholarship" (*wa-sawāhum fī l-maʿrifa*, 19.2). The man's critic addresses him with "You erred and committed a solecism" (*akhṭaʾta wa-laḥanta*, 19.3) combining the formulation of P-c and L-c. In the final comment (19.4), only present in P-c and the early group, their elements are again combined, and "scholarship" (*maʿrifa*, repeated from 19.1) is added only here to the things he lacks. P5881 thus merges the aspects of both continua and the early group, carefully intercalating their phrases at each step of the narrative. This skilled collage is the most rounded version of all.[20]

To summarize, common to all versions is that a piece of scholarly, or literary, writing has led to wrong assumptions and public chastisement. According to the story and the context of sayings into which it is embedded, to simply treat such writing as a transcript of oral text to be reproduced by recitation is the wrong way to go about it. Reading requires more, for it must unlock a text's meaning. Nor does any kind of reading suffice, rather, proper reading demands

19 In other chapters of P3471, such as Lv, Oc, and Mc (abbreviations by de Blois), a wider variety of models are combined.

20 This being said, the full credit cannot be given to the copyist-redactor of P5881, as this is a near verbatim copy of A4214, datable by a reader's note to before 761/1360. The practice can indeed be documented since that century.

conscientious effort and reflection. Writing needs to be approached in a different way from something heard and requires a second step of cogitation and comprehension to get to the content. Beyond this, the continua differ; L-c is in general shorter and speaks about scholarly knowledge, here linguistic knowledge, which is an established discipline whose terminology is deployed in the narrative (*laḥn, ʿarabiyya*). P-c is longer and places the event within a social context, making it more dramatic. Here the focus lies on the performance of culture (*adab*; qualified further in some versions as *ʿilm*, Pococke 400 and P5881; *fahm* I344; *ʿaql*, P3473; or *maʿrifa*, P5881; 19.4), which in this case grandiosely fails and results in shame and embarrassment of the ignoramus.

It is not possible here to do justice to the context of each version's genesis, as they cover too large a span of time, and much about their creators and geographic provenance is unknown. The manuscripts differ in quality (and material value) between professionally produced and illustrated copies, such as Pococke 400, and plain versions made for the copyist-redactor's personal use, such as We II 672, thus serving various social layers of readers.[21]

It is not surprising, that the present story incurred such interference through rewriting, because *Kalīla and Dimna* was the kind of book with which misunderstandings could occur. Straddling the boundary between high and popular literature, it gave amateurs access to what they regarded as scholarship.[22] Being popular but overtly claiming at the same time to belong to philosophy, *Kalīla and Dimna* played a particular role in the increased readership among common people in the middle period. The insistence of the man in the story that he keeps the folio in his home (absent in E and added in L-c and P-c but not Q-c) might reflect a new kind of owner's pride among a wider audience. It is interesting to note that in the sole illustration of this tale, in the early manuscript Pococke 400, the man holds the sheet in his hand while reciting it, as is the case in this version, which lacks the phrase about keeping it at home.[23]

21 In general, the rare early manuscripts from the seventh/thirteenth to ninth/fifteenth century are luxury copies, most of them illustrated, whereas the more numerously preserved manuscripts from the eleventh/seventeenth century onward include both professionally executed and plain codices, but less valuable copies of the earlier periods may have been lost; an exception of an early plain specimen is the manuscript of Dayr al-Shīr, dated 739/1339, which was edited by Louis Cheikho.

22 On the difficulty of assigning *Kalīla and Dimna* to a particular genre, see Keegan, Its meaning lies elsewhere.

23 Gruendler, *Rise of the Arabic book*, 160. As to the motifs of the illustrations, the burglary tales are those mostly illustrated within the Arabic preface, as it is usually the embedded stories that receive illustrations throughout *Kalīla and Dimna*. One must concede, however, that some images contain graphic detail that is not contained in the stories to which they belong. On the illustrations and legends and their relationship to the text, see Redwan, Illustrations in Arabic *Kalīla wa-Dimna* manuscripts.

Due to its fluid status, *Kalīla and Dimna* represents an interactive textual tradition that makes it possible for copyist-redactors to argue out points of interest, such as the usage of books. Being not scholars in the narrow sense, they treated it freely and actualized the narrative according to their own perceptions. In particular from the twelfth/eighteenth century onward, book ownership and readership as well as book-writing increased among craftspeople and professionals, even if only for their own use in the forms of diary chronicle, travelogue, and autobiography. The same era saw the evolution of the lending library, and one manuscript (London BL Add. 7413) bears circa thirty readers' notes, many more than ownership notes, which were most likely borrowers. The more invasive rewriting of two later manuscripts (BnT 2281 and We II 672) may be a reflection of this, as is also the increased self-description of *Kalīla and Dimna* as a book of philosophy (*falsafa*)—the frequency of this term grows with time—of a kind in which people who were at best amateur scholars could have a share.

3 Appendix

3.1 *List of Manuscripts Used in the Article*

Early Group

- I344 = Istanbul, Archaeological Museum, EY 344 (dated to eleventh/seventeenth century), very similar to Riyadh, King Faisal Center, MS 2536 (dated 747/1346)
  Poc. 400 = Oxford, Bodleian Library, Pococke 400 (755/1354)
- P3475 = Paris, Bibliothèque nationale de France, arabe 3475 (dated 1175/1761), a near verbatim copy of BRR 3566 = Rabat, Bibliothèque royale de Rabat, 3655 (dated to c. 663–679/1265–80)
- CCCP 578 = Cambridge Corpus Christi College, Parker Library, 578, dated to the eighth/fourteenth century

Paris Continuum (P-c)

P3465 subgroup

- P3465 = Paris, Bibliothèque nationale de France, arabe 3465 (dated to c. 616–617/1220)
- P2789 = Paris, Bibliothèque nationale de France, arabe 2789 (MTM, first part dated 1008/1599–1600)
- H170 = Hamburg, Staats- und Universitätsbibliothek, cod. orient. 170 (undated)

Wetzstein subgroup (We)
- Riyadh 2407 = Riyadh, King Faisal Center, 2407 (dated 1103/1692)
- P3473 = Paris, Bibliothèque nationale de France, arabe 3473 (dated 1110/1699)
- We II 672 = Berlin, Staatsbibliothek, Wetzstein II 672 (dated 1246/1830)

Queen-continuum (*Q-c*) (aligns with P-c from beginning to Rd, incl. Im)
- P3466 = Paris, Bibliothèque nationale de France, arabe 3466 (before 854/1450)
- BnT 2281 = Tunis, Bibliothèque nationale de Tunisie, 2281 (dated 1070/1660)
- USJ 0022(2) = Beirut, Université Saint-Joseph, 0022(2) (dated 1263/1847)

London Continuum (L-c)
- A4095 = Istanbul, Ayasofya, 4095 (dated 618/1221)
- L8751 = London, British Library, Or. 8751 (dated 799/1369)
- L4044 = London, British Library, Or. 4044 (dated to ninth/fifteenth century)

Queen continuum (aligns with L-c from Oc to the end, incl. Mc)
- P3466, BnT 2281, USJ 0022(2) see above

Cross-Copied Versions (CC)
- P3471 = Paris, Bibliothèque nationale de France, arabe 3471 (dated 1053/1643)
- P5881 = Paris, Bibliothèque nationale de France, arabe 5881 (dated 1092/1681), a near verbatim copy of A4214 = Istanbul, Ayasofya 4214, datable before 761/1360.

3.2 *Segments of the Digital Edition according to Their Presence in the Manuscripts*

Label	P-c	Q-c	L-c	E	CC
16.1 ImReaderToGraspAndReflect			x	x	P5881
16.2. ImSuperficialReadingFruitless	x		x	x	P5881
17. ImNutCrackedForBenefit	x		x	x	P5881
18 ImExtractHiddenKnowledge			x	x	P5881
19.1 ImManWithYellowFolio	x	x	x	x	P3471/P5881
19.2 ImManMemorizes	x	x	x	x	P3471/P5881
19.3 ImManErrs	x	x	x	x	P3471/P5881
19.4 ImYellowFolioComment	x	x		x	P3471/P5881
20.1 ImOneToSeekKnowledge			x	x	

3.3 *Graphs Showing the Cross-Analysis of Segments 19.1–19.4*

Explanation of the graphs: manuscripts are arranged along the horizontal axis in the order of the marked up edition below, and the analyzed phrases form the vertical axis. Regarding the colors, P-c is shaded in yellows and browns, L-c in blues, E in greens, phrases appearing in every group in grey, and unique parts in magenta. The colors are identical in the marked-up edition below.

[ ] marks words not counted in the analysis and given for the context.
( ) marks words not present in all marked versions.

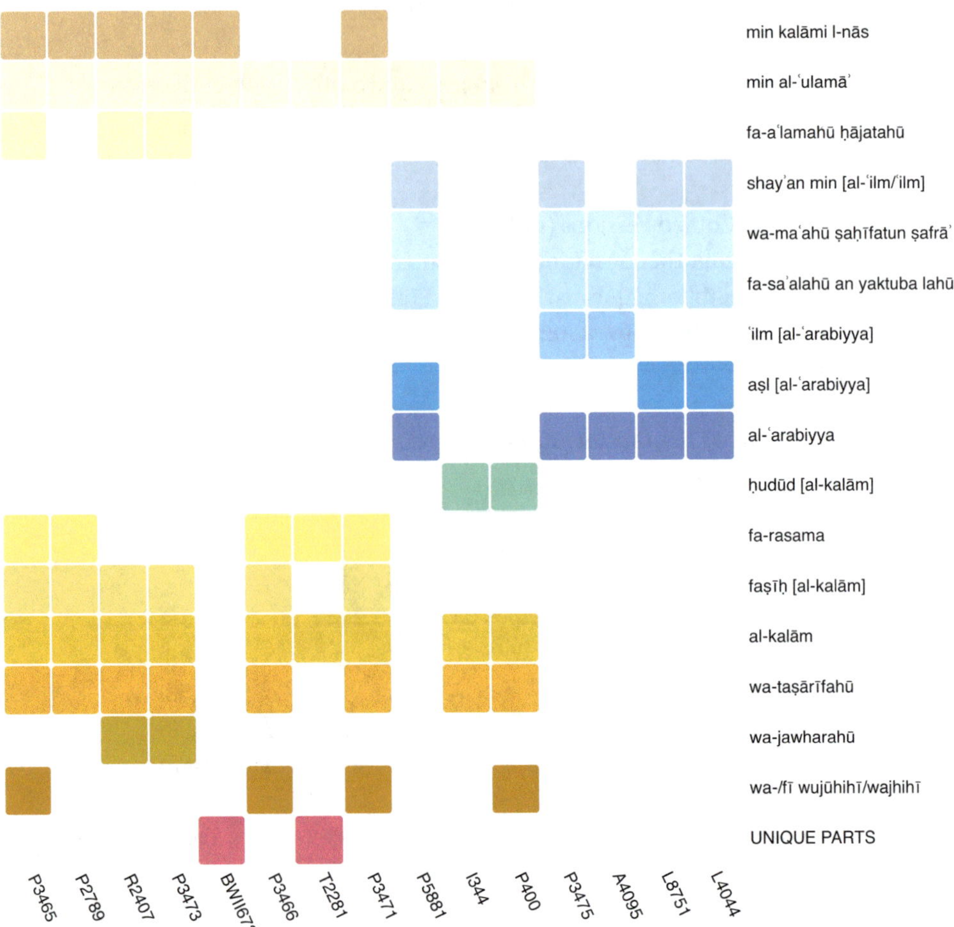

19.1 ImManWithYellowFolio

19.2 ImManMemorizes

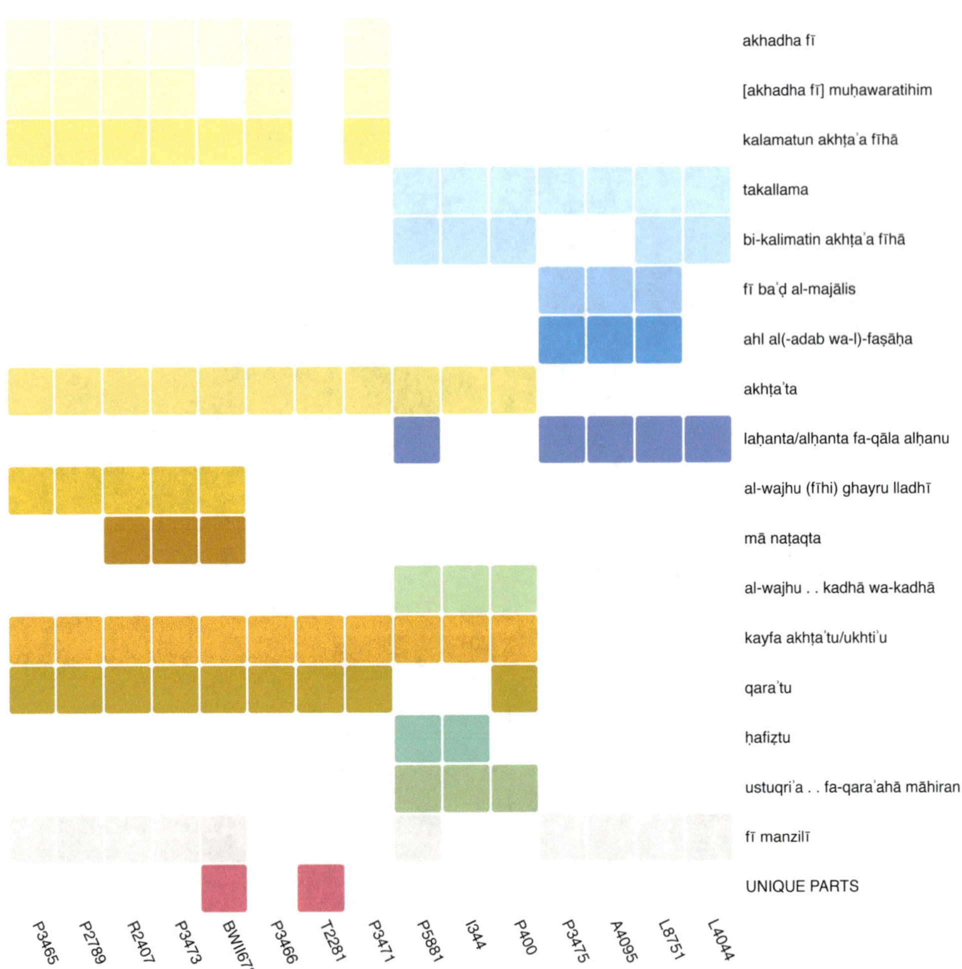

19.3 ImManErrs

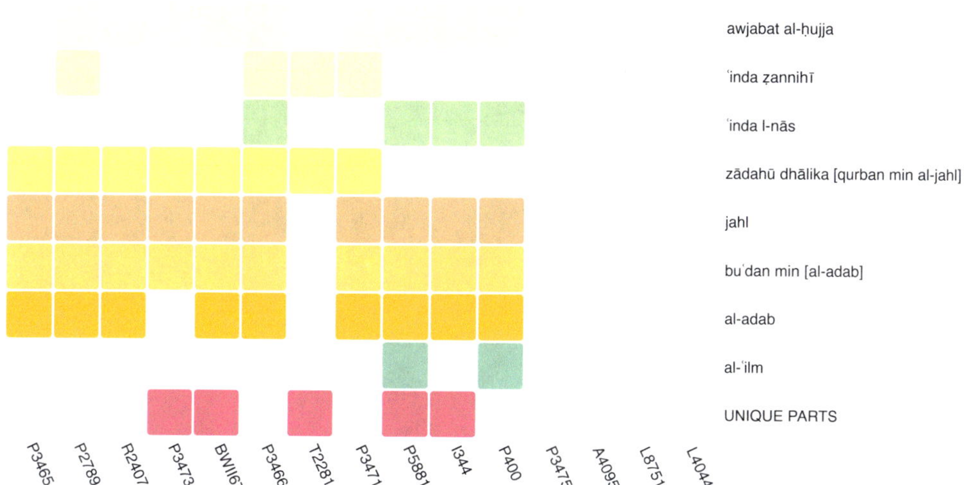

19.4 YellowFolioComment

3.4 *Cross-Analysis in the Digital Edition of "The Yellow Folio"*

Manuscripts	P3465 A	P2789 B	R2407 C	P3473 D
[19.1] ImManWithYellowFolio	وكان أيضًا كالرجل الذي طلب علم الفصيح من كلام الناس فأتى صديقًا له من العلماء له علم بالفصاحة فأعلمه حاجته إلى علم الفصيح فرسم له صديقه في صحيفة رصفها له فيها فصيح الكلام وتصاريفه ووجوهه	وكان أيضًا يكون كالرجل الذي طلب علم الفصاحة من كلام الناس فأتى صديقًا له من العلماء له علم بالفصاحة فرسم له صديقه في صحيفة وضعها له فيها فصيح الكلام وتصاريفة	وكان كالرجل الذي طلب علم الفصيح من كلام الناس فأتى صديقًا له من العلماء فأعلمه حاجته إلى ذلك ومعرفته فكتب له صديقه في صفيحة صفراء فصيح الكلام وتصاريفه وجوهره	وكان كالرجل الذي طلب علم الفصيح من كلام الناس فأتى صديقًا له من العلماء فأعلمه حاجته إلى ذلك وإلى معرفته فكتب له صديقه في صحيفةٍ صفراء فصيح الكلام وتصاريفه وجوهره
[19.2] ImManMemorizes	فانصرف المتعلّم إلى منزله فجعل يكثر قراءتها ولا يقف على معانيها ثمّ إنّه جلس ذات يوم في محفل من أهل العلم والأدب	فانصرف المتعلّم إلى منزله وجعل يكثر قراءتها ولا يقف على معانيها ولا يعرف ما فيها ثمّ جلس ذات يوم بين أهل العلم والأدب والفطنة وهو يظنّ أنّه قد اكتفى ممّا قرأه من تلك الصحيفة	فانصرف المتعلّم بها إلى منزله وجعل يكثر من قراءتها وهو لا يقف على معانيها ولا يعرف ما فيها ثمّ إنّه جلس ذات يوم في محفلٍ من أهل الأدب والعلم وهو يظنّ أنّه قد اكتفى بما قرأه من الصحيفة	فانصرف المتعلّم بها إلى منزله فجعل يُكثر من قراءتها ولا يفهم معانيها ولا يعرف ما فيها ثمّ أنّه جلس ذات يوم في محفلٍ من أهل الأدب والعلم والفطنة وهو يظنّ بأنّه قد اكتفى بما قرأه من تلك الصحيفة
[19.3] ImManErrs	فأخذ في محاورتهم فجرت له كلمة أخطأ فيها فقال له بعض الجماعة إنّك قد أخطأت والوجه غير ما تكلّمت به فقال كيف أخطئ وقد قرأت الصحيفة الصفراء وهي في منزلي	فأخذ في محاورتهن فجرت له كلمة أخطأ فيها فقال له بعضهم أخطأت والوجه غير ما تكلّمت فقال كيف أخطأت وقد قرأت الصحيفة الصفراء وهي في منزلي	فأخذ في محاورتهم فرّت له كلمة أخطأ فيها فقال له بعضهم إنّك قد أخطأت فيما نطقت به والأوجه فيه غير ما نطقت فقال كيف أخطئ وأنا قرأت الصحيفة الصفراء وهي في منزلي	فأخذ في محاورتهم فرّت له كلمةُ أخطأ فيها فقال بعضهم إنّك أخطأت فيما تكلّمت به والوجه فيه غير ما نطقت به فقال كيف أخطئ وقد قرأت الصحيفة الصفراء وهي في منزلي
9.4] ImYellowFolioComment	فكانت مقالته لهم أوجبت الحجّة عليه وزاده ذلك قربًا من الجهل وبعدًا من الأدب	فكانت مقالته لهم أوجب الحجة عليهم عند ظنّه وزادة ذلك قربًا من الجهل وبعدًا من الأدب	وكانت قراءته لها لتوجب عليه الحجّة <وزاده> ذلك قربًا من الجهل وبعدًا من الأدب	فكانت قراءته لها أوجب الحجّة عليه وزاده ذلك قربًا من الجهل وبعدًا من العقل

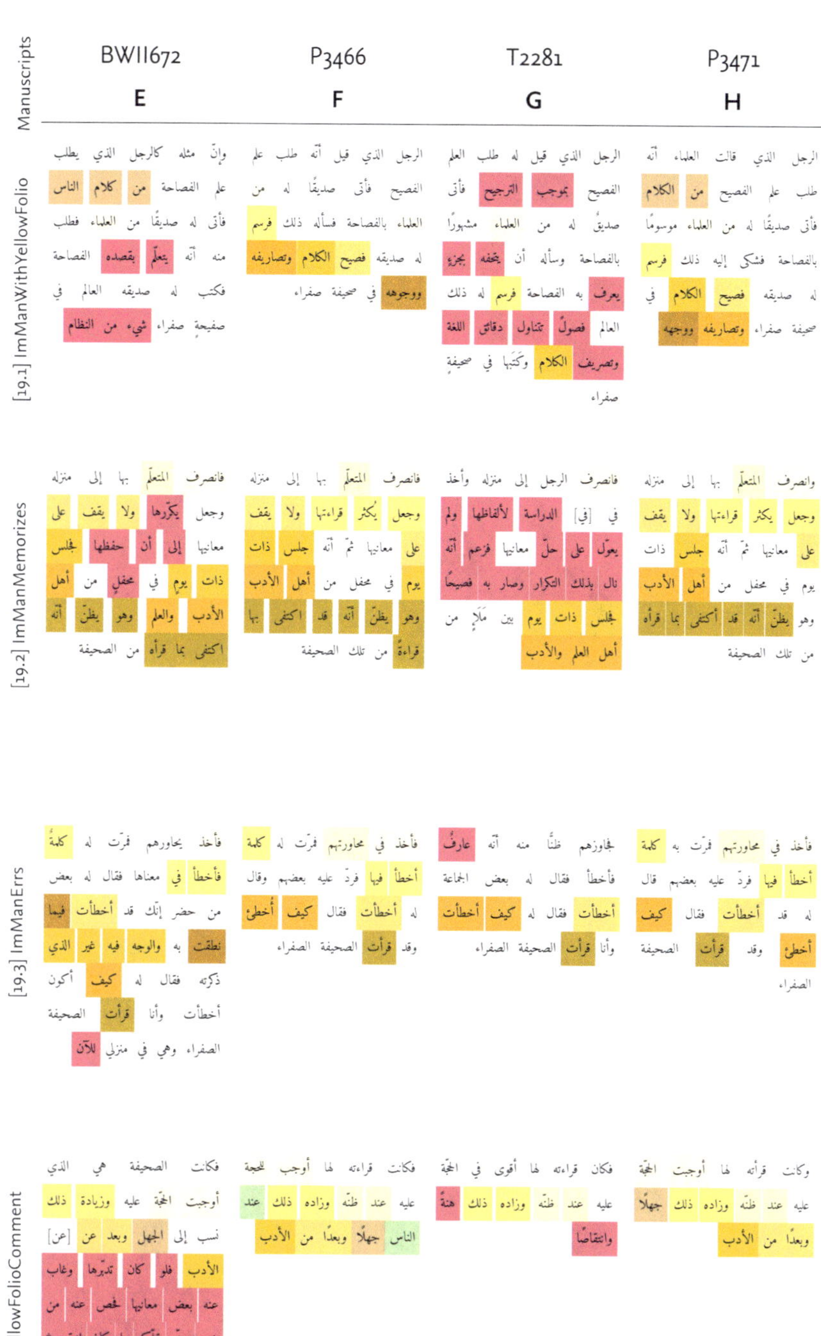
Manuscripts
BW11672
E
P3466
F
T2281
G
P3471
H
[19.1] ImManWithYellowFolio
[19.2] ImManMemorizes
[19.3] ImManErrs
[19.4] ImYellowFolioComment

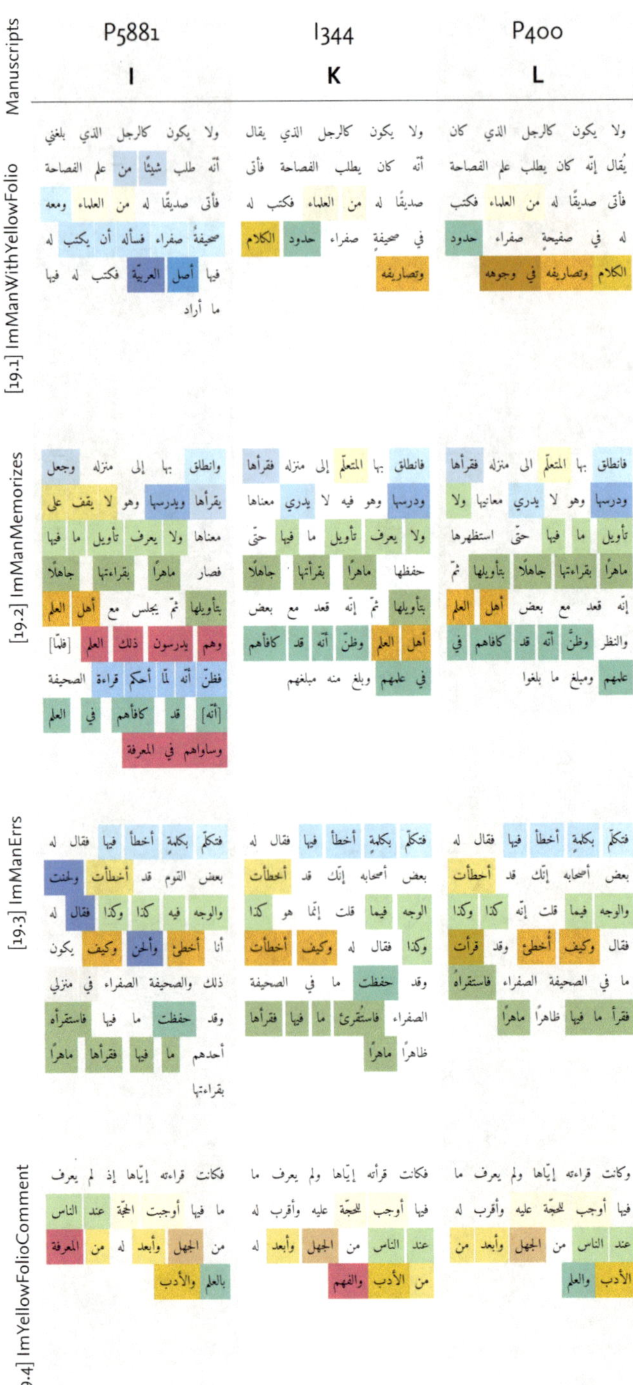
Manuscripts
P5881
I
I344
K
P400
L
[19.1] ImManWithYellowFolio
ولا يكون كالرجل الذي بلغني
أنّه طلب شيئًا من علم الفصاحة
فأتى صديقًا له من العلماء ومعه
صحيفةٌ صفراء فسأله أن يكتب له
فيها أصل العربيّة فكتب له فيها
ما أراد
ولا يكون كالرجل الذي يقال
أنّه كان يطلب الفصاحة فأتى
صديقًا له من العلماء فكتب له
في صحيفةٍ صفراء حدود الكلام
وتصاريفه
ولا يكون كالرجل الذي كان
يُقال إنّه كان يطلب علم الفصاحة
فأتى صديقًا له من العلماء فكتب
له في صفيحةٍ صفراء حدود
الكلام وتصاريفه في وجوهه
[19.2] ImManMemorizes
وانطلق بها إلى منزله وجعل
يقرأها ويدرسها وهو لا يقف على
معناها ولا يعرف تأويل ما فيها
فصار ماهرًا بقراءتها جاهلًا
بتأويلها ثمّ يجلس مع أهل العلم
وهم يدرسون ذلك العلم [فلمّا]
فظنّ أنّه لمّا أحكم قراءة الصحيفة
[أنّه] قد كافأهم في العلم
وساواهم في المعرفة
فانطلق بها المتعلّم إلى منزله فقرأها
ودرسها وهو فيه لا يدري معناها
ولا يعرف تأويل ما فيها حتّى
حفظها ماهرًا بقرأتها جاهلًا
بتأويلها ثمّ إنّه قعد مع بعض
أهل العلم وظنّ أنّه قد كافأهم
في علمهم وبلغ منه مبلغهم
فانطلق بها المتعلّم الى منزله فقرأها
ودرسها وهو لا يدري معانيها ولا
تأويل ما فيها حتّى استظهرها
ماهرًا بقراءتها جاهلًا بتأويلها ثمّ
إنّه قعد مع بعض أهل العلم
والنظر وظنّ أنّه قد كافاهم في
علمهم ومبلغ ما بلغوا
[19.3] ImManErrs
فتكلّم بكلمةٍ أخطأ فيها فقال له
بعض القوم قد أخطأت ولحنت
والوجه فيه كذا وكذا فقال له
أنا أخطئ وألحن وكيف يكون
ذلك والصحيفة الصفراء في منزلي
وقد حفظت ما فيها فاستقرأه
أحدهم ما فيها فقرأها ماهرًا
بقراءتها
فتكلّم بكلمةٍ أخطأ فيها فقال له
بعض أصحابه إنّك قد أخطأت
الوجه فيما قلت إنّما هو كذا
وكذا فقال له وكيف أخطأت
وقد حفظت ما في الصحيفة
الصفراء فاستُقرئ ما فيها فقرأها
ظاهرًا ماهرًا
فتكلّم بكلمةٍ أخطأ فيها فقال له
بعض أصحابه إنّك قد أخطأت
والوجه فيما قلت إنّه كذا وكذا
فقال وكيف أُخطئ وقد قرأت
ما في الصحيفة الصفراء فاستقراهُ
فقرأ ما فيها ظاهرًا ماهرًا
[19.4] ImYellowFolioComment
فكانت قراءته إيّاها إذ لم يعرف
ما فيها أوجبت الحجّة عند الناس
من الجهل وأبعد له من المعرفة
بالعلم والأدب
فكانت قرأته إيّاها ولم يعرف ما
فيها أوجب للحجّة عليه وأقرب له
عند الناس من الجهل وأبعد له
من الأدب والفهم
وكانت قراءته إيّاها ولم يعرف ما
فيها أوجب للحجّة عليه وأقرب له
عند الناس من الجهل وأبعد من
الأدب والعلم

Manuscripts	P3475 **M**	A4095 **N**	L8751 **O**	L4044 **P**
[19.1] ImManWithYellowFolio	ولا يكون كالرجل الذي بلغني عنه أنه طلب شيئا من العلم فأتى صديقًا له ومعه صحيفة صفراء فسأله أن يكتب له فيها علم العربيّة فكتب له فيها	ولا يكن كالرجل الذي بلغني أنّه طلب علم الفصاحة فأتي صديقًا له ومعه صحيفةُ صفراء فسأله أن يكتب له فيها علم العربيّة فكتب له في الصحيفة ما أراد	ولا يكن كالرجل الذي بلغني أنّه طلب شيئًا من علم الفصاحة فأتى صديقًا له ومعه صحيفة صفراء فسأله أن يكتب له فيها أصل العربيّة فكتب له في الصحيفة	ولا يكون مثل الرجل صاحب الصحيفة الصفراء بلغني أنه طلب شيئا من علم الفصاحة فأتى صديقا له ومعه صحيفة صفراء فسأله أن يكتب له أصل العربيّة في تلك الصحيفة فكتب له شيئًا من ذلك
[19.2] ImManMemorizes	وانطلق إلى منزله وجعل يقرأها وهو لا يدري مغاناها وظنّ أنّه بالقراءة قد أحكم ما فيها	فانطلق الرجل إلى منزله وجعل يقرأها ولا يدري ما معناها وظنّ أنّه قد أحكم ما في الصحيفة	فانطلق الرجل بها الي منزله لجعل يقرأها لا يدري ما يقرأ فظنّ أنّه قد أحكم مَا في الصَّحيفه	فأخذ الرجل الصحيفة فانطلق بها إلى منزله وجعل يقرأها وهو لا يدري ما معنى الذي يقرأه إلا أنه يقرأ الذي يرى في الصحيفة وجعل يقعد مع القوم وهو يظن أنّه قد أحكم أحكم ما في الصحيفة
[19.3] ImManErrs	ثم أنّه تكلّم في بعض المجالس وفيه علماء أهل الأدب والفصاحة فقال له بعضهم لحنّت فقال ألحن والصحيفة الصفراء في منزلي	وأنّه تكلّم في بعض المجالس وفيه جماعةٌ من أهل الأدب والفصاحة فقال له بعضهم ألحنت فقال ألحن والصحيفة الصفراء في منزلي	فتكلّم بكَلمة أخطأ فيها في بعض المجالس وفيه جماعة مِن أهل الفصَاحَة وَالأَدَب فقال له بغض القوم لحنت فقال أنا ألحن والصفيحة الصفراء في منزلي	فتكلّم بكلمة أخطأ فيها فقال له بعض من عنده من القوم لحنّت أيها الرجل فقال ألحن والصحيفة الصفراء في منزلي
[19.4] ImYellowFolioComment	Absent	Absent	Absent	Absent

3.5 *Full text of "The Yellow Folio"*

Im_P3465	Im_P2789	Im_H170	Im_R2407	Im_P3473	Im_BWII6	Im_P3466	Im_T2281	Im_P3471	Im_P5881	Im_I344	Im_P400	Im_P3475	Im_A4095	Im_L8751	Im_L4044
وكان أيضًا كالرجل الذي طلب علم الفصيح من كلام الناس فأتى صديقًا له من العلماء له علم بالفصاحة فأعلمه حاجته إلى علم الفصيح فرسم له صديقه في صحيفة رصفها له فيها فصيح الكلام وتصاريفه ووجوهه	وكان أيضًا يكون كالرجل الذي طلب علم الفصاحة من كلام الناس فأتى صديقًا له من العلماء له علم بالفصاحة فرسم له صديقه في صحيفة وضعها له فيها فصيح الكلام وتصاريفة	وكان كالرجل الذي طلب العلم الفصيح فرسم له بعض أصدقائه فصيحةً فيها فصيح الكلام وتصاريفه ووجوهه	وكان كالرجل الذي طلب علم الفصيح من كلام الناس فأتى صديقًا له من العلماء فأعلمه حاجته إلى ذلك ومعرفته فكتب له صديقه في صفيحة صفراء فصيح الكلام وتصاريفه وجوهره	وكان كالرجل الذي طلب علم الفصيح من كلام الناس فأتى صديقًا له من العلماء فأعلمه حاجته إلى ذلك وإلى معرفته فكتب له صديقه في صحيفةٍ صفراء فصيح الكلام وتصاريفه وجوهره	وإنّ مثله كالرجل الذي يطلب علم الفصاحة من كلام الناس فأتى له صديقًا من العلماء فطلب منه أنّه يتعلّم بقصده الفصاحة فكتب له صديقه العالم في صفيحةٍ صفراء شيء من النظام	الرجل الذي قيل أنّه طلب علم الفصيح فأتى صديقًا له من العلماء بالفصاحة فسأله ذلك فرسم له صديقه فصيح الكلام وتصاريفه ووجوهه في صحيفة صفراء	الرجل الذي قيل له طلب العلم الفصيح بموجب الترجيح فأتى صديقٌ له من العلماء مشهورًا بالفصاحة وسأله أن يتحفه بجزءٍ يعرف به الفصاحة فرسم له ذلك العالم فصولٌ تتناول دقائق اللغة وتصريف الكلام وكتَبها في صحيفةٍ صفراء	الرجل الذي قالت العلماء أنّه طلب علم الفصيح من الكلام فأتى صديقًا له من العلماء موسومًا بالفصاحة فشكى إليه ذلك فرسم له صديقه فصيح الكلام في صحيفة صفراء وتصاريفه ووجهه	ولا يكون كالرجل الذي بلغني أنّه طلب شيئًا من علم الفصاحة فأتى صديقًا له من العلماء ومعه صحيفةٌ صفراء فسأله أن يكتب له فيها أصل العربيّة فكتب له فيها ما أراد	ولا يكون كالرجل الذي يقال أنّه كان يطلب الفصاحة فأتى صديقًا له من العلماء فكتب له في صحيفةٍ صفراء حدود الكلام وتصاريفه	ولا يكون كالرجل الذي كان يُقال إنّه كان يطلب علم الفصاحة فأتى صديقًا له من العلماء فكتب له في صفيحةٍ صفراء حدود الكلام وتصاريفه في وجوهه	ولا يكون كالرجل الذي بلغني عنه أنه طلب شيئا من العلم فأتى صديقًا له ومعه صحيفة صفراء فسأله أن يكتب له فيها علم العربيّة فكتب له فيها	ولا يكن كالرجل الذي بلغني أنّه طلب علم الفصاحة فأتي صديقًا له ومعه صحيفةً صفراء فسأله أن يكتب له فيها علم العربيّة فكتب له في الصحيفة ما أراد	ولا يكن كالرجل الذي بلغني أنّه طلب شيئًا من علم الفصاحة فأتى صديقًا له ومعه صحيفة صفراء فسأله أن يكتب له فيها أصل العربيّة فكتب له في الصحيفة	ولا يكون مثل الرجل صاحب الصحيفة الصفراء بلغني أنه طلب شينا من علم الفصاحة فأتى صديقا له ومعه صحيفة صفراء فسأله أن يكتب له أصل العربيّة في تلك الصحيفة فكتب له شيئًا من ذلك

Im_P3465	Im_P2789	Im_H170	Im_R2407	Im_P3473	Im_BWII6	Im_P3466	Im_T2281	Im_P3471	Im_P5881	Im_I344	Im_P400	Im_P3475	Im_A4095	Im_L8751	Im_L4044
يكثر	يكثر	يكثر	يكثر من	يُكثر من	يكرّرها	يُكثر	[في]	يكثر	يقرأها	ودرسها	ودرسها	وهو لا	يقرأها ولا	يقرأها لا	بها إلى
قراءتها	قراءتها	قراءتها	قراءتها	قراءتها	ولا يقف	قراءتها	الدراسة	قراءتها	ويدرسها	وهو فيه	وهو لا	يدري	يدري ما	يدري ما	منزله
ولا يقف	ولا يقف	فلا يقف	وهو لا	ولا يفهم	على	ولا يقف	لألفاظها	ولا يقف	وهو لا	لا يدري	يدري	مغاناها	معناها	يقرأ فظنّ	وجعل
على	على	على	يقف على	معانيها	معانيها	على	ولم يعوّل	على	يقف على	معناها ولا	معانيها	وظنّ أنّه	وظنّ أنّه	أنّه قد	يقرأها
معانيها ثمّ	معانيها	معانيها	معانيها	ولا يعرف	إلى أن	معانيها ثمّ	على حلّ	معانيها ثمّ	معناها ولا	يعرف	ولا تأويل	بالقراءة	قد أحكم	أحكم ما	وهو لا
إنّه جلس	ولا يعرف	ولا يعرف	ولا يعرف	ما فيها ثمّ	حفظها	أنّه جلس	معانيها	أنّه جلس	يعرف	تأويل ما	ما فيها	قد أحكم	ما في	في	يدري ما
ذات يوم	ما فيها ثمّ	ما فيها ثمّ	ما فيها ثمّ	أنّه جلس	فجلس	ذات يوم	فزعم أنّه	ذات يوم	تأويل ما	فيها حتّى	حتّى	ما فيها	الصحيفة	الصّحيفه	معنى
في محفل	جلس ذات	إنّه جلس	إنّه جلس	ذات يوم	ذات يومٍ	في محفل	نال بذلك	في محفل	فيها	حفظها	استظهرها				الذي يقرأه
من أهل	يوم بين	ذات يومٍ	ذات يوم	في محفلٍ	في محفلٍ	من أهل	التكرار	من أهل	فصار	ماهرًا	ماهرًا				إلا أنه
العلم	أهل العلم	في محفلٍ	في محفلٍ	من أهل	من أهل	الأدب	وصار به	الأدب	ماهرًا	بقرأتها	بقراءتها				يقرأ الذي
والأدب	والأدب	من أهل	من أهل	الأدب	الأدب	وهو يظنّ	فصيحًا	وهو يظنّ	بقراءتها	جاهلًا	جاهلًا				يرى في
	والفطنة	العلم	الأدب	والعلم	والعلم	أنّه قد	فجلس	أنّه قد	جاهلًا	بتأويلها ثمّ	بتأويلها ثمّ				الصحيفة
	وهو يظنّ	والأدب	والعلم	والفطنة	وهو يظنّ	اكتفى بها	ذات يوم	أكتفى بما	بتأويلها ثمّ	إنّه قعد مع	إنّه قعد مع				وجعل
	أنّه قد	والفطنة	وهو يظنّ	وهو يظنّ	أنّه اكتفى	قراءةً من	بين مَلإٍ	قرأه من	يجلس مع	بعض أهل	بعض أهل				يقعد مع
	اكتفى ممّا	وهو يظنّ	أنّه قد	بأنّه قد	بما قرأه	تلك	من أهل	تلك	أهل العلم	العلم وظنّ	العلم				القوم وهو
	قرأه من	أنّه قد	اكتفى بما	اكتفى بما	من	الصحيفة	العلم	الصحيفة	وهم	أنّه قد	والنظر				يظن أنّه
	تلك	اكتفى بما	قرأه من	قرأه من	الصحيفة		والأدب		يدرسون	كافأهم في	وظنّ أنّه				قد أحكم
	الصحيفة	قرأه من	الصحيفة	تلك					ذلك العلم	علمهم	قد كافاهم				أحكم ما
		تلك		الصحيفة					[فلمّا]	وبلغ منه	في علمهم				في
		الصحيفة							فظنّ أنّه	مبلغهم	ومبلغ ما				الصحيفة
									لمّا أحكم		بلغوا				
									قراءة						
									الصحيفة						
									[أنّه] قد						
									كافأهم في						
									العلم						
									وساواهم						
									في						
									المعرفة						

Im_P3465	Im_P2789	Im_H170	Im_R2407	Im_P3473	Im_BWII6	Im_P3466	Im_T2281	Im_P3471	Im_P5881	Im_I344	Im_P400	Im_P3475	Im_A4095	Im_L8751	Im_L4044
فأخذ في محاورتهم فجرت له كلمة أخطأ فيها فقال له بعض الجماعة إنّك قد أخطأت والوجه غير ما تكلّمت به فقال كيف أخطئ وقد قرأت الصحيفة الصفراء وهي في منزلي	فأخذ في محاورتهم ن فجرت له كلمة أخطأ فيها فقال له بعضهم أخطأت والوجه غير ما تكلّمت فقال كيف أخطأت وقد قرأت الصحيفة الصفراء وهي في منزلي	فأخذ في محاورتهم فجرت له كلمةٌ أخطأ فيها فقال له بعضهم قد أخطأت فيها والوجه غير ما تكلّمت به فقال كيف أخطئ وقد قرأت الصحيفة الصفراء وهي في منزلي	فأخذ في محاورتهم فمرّت له كلمة أخطأ فيها فقال له بعضهم إنّك قد أخطأت فيما نطقت به والأوجه فيه غير ما نطقت فقال كيف أخطئ وأنا قرأت الصحيفة الصفراء وهي في منزلي	فأخذ في محاورتهم فمرّت له كلمةٌ أخطأ فيها فقال بعضهم إنّك أخطأت فيما تكلّمت به والوجه فيه غير ما نطقت به فقال كيف أخطئ وقد قرأت الصحيفة الصفراء وهي في منزلي	فأخذ يحاورهم فمرّت له كلمةٌ فأخطأ في معناها فقال له بعض من حضر إنّك قد أخطأت فيما نطقت به والوجه فيه غير الذي ذكرته فقال له كيف أكون أخطأت وأنا قرأت الصحيفة الصفراء وهي في منزلي للآن	فأخذ في محاورتهم فمرّت له كلمة أخطأ فيها فردّ عليه بعضهم وقال له أخطأت فقال كيف أُخطئ وقد قرأت الصحيفة الصفراء	فجاوزهم ظنًّا منه أنّه عارفٌ فأخطأ فقال له بعض الجماعة أخطأت فقال له كيف أخطأت وأنا قرأت الصحيفة الصفراء	فأخذ في محاورتهم فمرّت به كلمة أخطأ فيها فردّ عليه بعضهم قال له قد أخطأت فقال كيف أخطئ وقد قرأت الصحيفة الصفراء	فتكلّم بكلمةٍ أخطأ فيها فقال له بعض القوم قد أخطأت ولحنت والوجه فيه كذا وكذا فقال له أنا أخطئ وألحن وكيف يكون ذلك والصحيفة الصفراء في منزلي وقد حفظت ما فيها فاستقراه أحدهم ما فيها فقرأها ماهرًا بقراءتها	فتكلّم بكلمةٍ أخطأ فيها فقال له بعض أصحابه إنّك قد أخطأت الوجه فيما قلت إنّما هو كذا وكذا فقال له وكيف أخطأت وقد حفظت ما في الصحيفة الصفراء فاستُقرئ ما فيها فقرأها ظاهرًا ماهرًا	فتكلّم بكلمةٍ أخطأ فيها فقال له بعض أصحابه إنّك قد أخطأت والوجه فيما قلت إنّه كذا وكذا فقال وكيف أخطئ وقد قرأت ما في الصحيفة الصفراء فاستقراة فقرأ ما فيها ظاهرًا ماهرًا	ثم أنّه تكلّم في بعض المجالس وفيه علماء أهل الأدب والفصاحة فقال له بعضهم لحنّت فقال ألحّن والصحيفة الصفراء في منزلي	وأنّه تكلّم في بعض المجالس وفيه جماعةٌ من أهل الأدب والفصاحة فقال له بعضهم ألحنت فقال ألحن والصحيفة الصفراء في منزلي	فتكلّم بكلمة أخطأ فيها في بعض المجالس وفيه جماعة مِن أهل الفصَاحَة وَالأَدب فقال له بغض القوم لحنت فقال أنا ألحن والصفيحة الصفراء في منزلي	فتكلّم بكلمة أخطأ فيها فقال له بعض من عنده من القوم لحنّت أيها الرجل فقال ألحن والصحيفة الصفراء في منزلي

Im_P3465	Im_P2789	Im_H170	Im_R2407	Im_P3473	Im_BWII6	Im_P3466	Im_T2281	Im_P3471	Im_P5881	Im_I344	Im_P400	Im_P3475	Im_A4095	Im_L8751	Im_L4044
فكانت مقالته لهم أوجبت الحجّة عليه وزاده ذلك قربًا من الجهل وبعدًا من الأدب	فكانت مقالته لهم أوجب الحجة عليهم عند ظنّه وزادة ذلك قربًا من الجهل وبعدًا من الأدب	فكان مقالته أوجبت الحجّة عليه وزاده ذلك قربًا من الجهل وهذا من الأدب	وكانت قراءته لها لتوجب عليه الحجّة <وزاده> ذلك قربًا من الجهل وبعدًا من الأدب	فكانت قراءته لها أوجب الحجّة عليه وزاده ذلك قربًا من الجهل وبعدًا من العقل	فكانت الصحيفة هي الذي أوجبت الحجّة عليه وزيادة ذلك نسب إلى الجهل وبعد عن [عن] الأدب فلو كان تدبّرها وغاب عنه بعض معانيها فحص عنه من غيره حتّى تملّكه ما كان †أنتقص بين الناس بل كان عُدّ من العلماء أو الأدباء	فكانت قراءته لها أوجب للحجة عليه عند ظنّه وزاده ذلك عند الناس جهلًا وبعدًا من الأدب	فكان قراءته لها أقوى في الحجّة عليه عند ظنّه وزاده ذلك هنةً وانتقاصًا	وكانت قرأته لها أوجبت الحجّة عليه عند ظنّه وزاده ذلك جهلًا وبعدًا من الأدب	فكانت قراءته إيّاها إذ لم يعرف ما فيها أوجبت الحجّة عند الناس من الجهل وأبعد له من المعرفة بالعلم والأدب	فكانت قرأته إيّاها ولم يعرف ما فيها أوجب للحجّة عليه وأقرب له عند الناس من الجهل وأبعد له من الأدب والفهم	وكانت قراءته إيّاها ولم يعرف ما فيها أوجب للحجّة عليه وأقرب له عند الناس من الجهل وأبعد من الأدب والعلم				

Bibliography

Anonymous, *A hundred and one nights*, ed. and trans. by Bruce Fudge, New York 2016.

Blau, J. *On pseudo-corrections in some Semitic languages*, Jerusalem, 1970.

Brockelmann, C. Kalīla wa-Dimna, in *EI*², iv, 503–6.

Cheikho, L. (ed.), *La version arabe de Kalîlah et Dimnah*, Beirut 1905.

Dagenais, J., *The ethics of reading in manuscript culture*, Princeton 1994.

de Blois, F., *Burzōy's voyage to India and the origin of the book of Kalīlah wa Dimnah*, London 1990.

Diyāb, Ḥanna, *The book of travels*, ed. by Elias Muhanna and transl. by Johannes Stephan, New York, 2021.

Grotzfeld, H., S. Grotzfeld and U. Marzolph, Kalila und Dimna, in R.W. Brednich and K. Ranke (eds.), *Enzyklopädie des Märchens*, vol. 7, Berlin 1993, 888–95.

Gruendler, B., The relation among manuscripts of *Kalīla and Dimna* as continua, in B. Gruendler and I. Toral (eds.), *An unruly classic: Kalīla and Dimna and its Syriac, Arabic, and early Persian versions*, Leiden (forthcoming).

Gruendler, B., A rat and its redactors: Silent co-authorship in *Kalīla wa-Dimna*, in A. Vernay-Nouri and E. Brac de la Perrière (eds.), *The journeys of Kalila and Dimna: Fables in the literature and arts of the Islamic world*, Leiden and Boston, 3–42.

Gruendler, B., *The rise of the Arabic book*, Cambridge, Mass. and London, 2020.

Gruendler, B., Les versions arabes de *Kalīla wa-Dimna*: Une transmission et une circulation mouvantes, in M. Ortola (ed.), *Énoncés sapientiels et littérature exemplaire: Une intertextualité complexe*, Nancy 2013, 387–418.

Gruendler, B. et al., An interim report on the editorial and analytical work of the AnonymClassic Project, *Medieval Worlds: Comparative and Interdisciplinary Studies* 11 (2020), 241–79: http://dx.doi.org/10.1553/medievalworlds no11 2020s241

Hertel, J. (ed.), *Tantrākhyāyika: Die älteste Fassung des Pañcatantra nach den Handschriften beider Rezensionen*, 2 vols., Berlin 1909.

Hanna, N., *In praise of books: A cultural history of Cairo's middle class, sixteenth to eighteenth century*, Syracuse, New York 2003.

Hirschler, K., *The written word in the medieval Arabic lands: A social and cultural history of reading practices*, Edinburgh 2012.

Keegan, M.L., Its meaning lies elsewhere: The vagaries of *Kalila and Dimna*, *Poetica* 52 (2021), 13–40.

Khalfallah, Kh., What the chapter of "The King and His Dreams" reveals about the variety of versions of *Kalīla wa-Dimna*, in B. Gruendler and I. Toral (eds.), *An unruly classic: Kalīla and Dimna and its Syriac, Arabic, and early Persian versions*, Leiden (forthcoming).

Kristó-Nagy, I., *La pensée d'Ibn al-Muqaffaʿ: «Un agent double» dans le monde persan et arabe*, Paris 2013.

Liebrenz, B., The library of Aḥmad al-Rabbāṭ: Books and their audiences in 12th to 13th/18th to 19th-century Syria, in U. Pietruschka and R. Elger (eds.): *Marginal perspectives on early modern Ottoman culture: Missionaries, travelers, booksellers*, Halle 2013, 17–59.

Redwan, R., Illustrations in Arabic *Kalīla wa-Dimna* manuscripts: What is their story? in B. Gruendler and I. Toral (eds.), *An unruly classic: Kalīla and Dimna and its Syriac, Arabic, and early Persian versions*, Leiden (forthcoming).

Sajdi, D., *The barber of Damascus: Nouveau literacy in the eighteenth-century Ottoman Levant*, Stanford, California 2013.

Schütz, S., and M. Pöckelmann, LERA—Explorative Analyse komplexer Textvarianten in Editionsphilologie und Diskursanalyse, in *Book of Abstracts of the Third Annual Conference of Digital Humanities for German-Speaking Regions*, 2016, 239–43: http://dhd2016.de/ and https://dhd-blog.org/?p=6779

8

Al-Ibdāʿ, a Tour de Force of Rhetoric: The History of an Arabic Rhetorical Term

Geert Jan van Gelder

In the second Sura of the Quran (al-Baqara 2:117) God is called *badīʿ al-samāwāt wa-l-arḍ*, "the Originator of the heavens and the earth." More often, *badīʿ* is used, in post-Quranic Arabic, as an adjective, with the sense of "novel, original" or more generally "wonderful, singular." Derived of the same lexical root, *ibdāʿ* means "creating something novel;" it is used in theological and philosophical discussions as "creation ex nihilo" or "primordial innovation," contrasted with *khalq*, "creation of something from an existing thing."[1] In literary criticism, *al-badīʿ* became the collective noun for a number of figures of speech and stylistic embellishments, since the seminal treatise *al-Badīʿ* by the prince, poet, and critic ʿAbdallāh ibn al-Muʿtazz (d. 296/908). The number of these figures and embellishments grew steadily and became a discipline eventually called *ʿilm al-badīʿ*.

The word *ibdāʿ* was occasionally used in a vague and general sense for "producing stylistic excellence and originality." Ibn Ṭabāṭabā (d. 322/934) says in his *ʿIyār al-shiʿr*:[2]

> A skilful poet mingles these motifs in comparisons (…) and he will take care not to limit himself to using motifs that he steals from others instead of being original (*dūna l-ibdāʿ fīhā*).

In a chapter entitled *Bāb al-mukhtaraʿ wa-l-badīʿ* in his *al-ʿUmda*, an encyclopaedic work on poetry, Ibn Rashīq (d. 456/1065 or 463/1071) distinguishes—though none too clearly—between *ikhtirāʿ*, defined as *khalq al-maʿānī llatī lam yusbaq ilayhā* ("inventing motifs without precedent") and *ibdāʿ*, defined as *ityān al-shāʿir bi-l-maʿnā l-mustaẓraf wa-lladhī lam tajri l-ʿāda bi-mithlihi* ("when a

1 See al-Tahānawī (d. after 1158/1745), *Kashshāf iṣṭilāḥāt al-funūn* 134–5 for the several meanings of *ibdāʿ*; also Gardet, Ibdāʿ.

2 Ibn Ṭabāṭabā, *ʿIyār al-shiʿr* (ed. al-Māniʿ) 32. The edition by Ṭāhā al-Ḥājirī and Muḥammad Zaghlūl Sallām 32 has, surely incorrectly, *al-īdāʿ* instead of *al-ibdāʿ*.

 | DOI:10.1163/9789004521780_010

poet produces a charming motif that is not customary"). But, he adds, it has become customary to consider the former as referring to the *maʿnā*, the sense or content, the latter to the *lafẓ*, the way it is expressed in words.[3] Ḥāzim al-Qarṭājannī (d. 684/1285), uses *ibdāʿ* several times in the same general sense in his *Minhāj al-bulaghāʾ wa-sirāj al-udabāʾ* (The Path of the Eloquent and the Lamp of the Lettered).[4]

Among the many works that contain lists of stylistic embellishments (*badīʿ*), always illustrated with poetry and often prose as well, there are several that are written in Persian, for Persian authors began to adopt Arabic terminology and concepts in order to apply them to Persian. The earliest extant work of this kind is *Tarjumān al-balāgha* (The Interpreter of Eloquence) by Muḥammad b. ʿUmar al-Rādūyānī, who wrote his book at some time between 481/1088 and 507/1114.[5] One of the 73 sections of the book introduces *ibdāʿ*, as one of the various stylistic embellishments or figures of speech.[6] Unfortunately, due to a lacuna in the only known manuscript, the term *ibdāʿ* and its definition or description are missing there, but the chapter heading is found on the contents page (7, facsimile p. 156): *faṣl fī l-ibdāʿ fī l-maʿānī*, "section on creating novel motifs". There are examples from Persian poetry. Although al-Rādūyānī states that he was inspired by an Arabic precursor, *Maḥāsin al-kalām* (The Beauties of Speech) by Naṣr b. al-Ḥasan al-Marghīnānī,[7] he did not take the "figure" of *ibdāʿ* from that work, nor from any other Arabic or Persian treatise as far as can be ascertained. The examples that al-Rādūyānī quotes, without commentary, as illustrations of *ibdāʿ* do not reveal any special characteristics and it seems that *ibdāʿ* has its general sense of "creating a novel motif."[8] It is odd to find such a "figure" with a vague and broad meaning as a specific section in a list of *badīʿ*. Nevertheless, al-Rādūyānī was followed by Rashīd al-Dīn Waṭwāt (d. 573/1177) in his *Ḥadāyiq al-siḥr fī daqāyiq al-shiʿr* (Gardens of Magic: On the Subtleties of Poetry), a work written in Persian but, unlike *Tarjumān al-balāgha*, with examples taken from

3 Ibn Rashīq, *al-ʿUmda* i, 265. In modern Arabic literary criticism, *ibdāʿ* is used in the sense of "creativity"; see e.g. the special issue of *Fuṣūl* 10:1–2 (1991) entitled *Qaḍāyā l-ibdāʿ* (*Issues of Creativity*).

4 Al-Qarṭājannī, *Minhāj al-bulaghāʾ* 69, 121, 215, 297, 308, 311, 317, 319, 346.

5 Heinrichs, al-Rādūyānī; Chalisova, Persian rhetoric 144–51 ("Râduyâni's *Tarjomân al-balâgha*").

6 Al-Rādūyānī, *Tarjumān al-balāgha* 131–3.

7 Al-Marghīnānī's treatise was published in Van Gelder, *Two Arabic Treatises on Stylistics*. On the author (who lived in the first half and perhaps well into the second half of the 5th/11th century) and for a summary of the contents, see the Introduction, 4–5, 14–26.

8 I am grateful to Anna Livia Beelaert (Leiden), who greatly helped me with the interpretation of these and other Persian passages.

Arabic as well as Persian literature.[9] It is there that one finds a definition of *ibdāʿ*:[10]

این صنعت را ارباب بیان کفته اند که معانی بدیع باشذ بالفاظ خوب نظم داذه و از تکلّف نکاه داشته و من می کویم کی این از جملهٔ صنعت نیست بل کی سخن عقلا و فضلا در نظم و نثر جنین می باید و هرج برین کونه نباشذ سخن عوام بوذ ومجمع مردم را نشایذ ...

> Of this figure of speech those who are knowledgeable in eloquence have said that it means original ideas (*maʿānī*) arranged in beautiful words and avoiding affectation (*takalluf*). I say that it does not belong to the figures of style, but that the language of those who are intelligent and learned, both in prose and poetry, should be like this, and whatever language which is not like this, is the language of the common people, and not proper for social gatherings ... [tr. Anna Livia Beelaert]

Rashīd al-Dīn Waṭwāṭ, while incorporating *ibdāʿ* in his list of *badīʿ*, clearly finds its inclusion unwarranted. The examples that he gives, Persian verses by Rūdakī, ʿUnṣurī, and Manṭiqī, show a variety of regular figures, notably *mubālagha* ("hyperbole"), and the line by Manṭiqī contains the figure called *murāʿāt al-naẓīr*, mentioning several words that belong to the same semantic field, in this case three limbs *tan* ("body"), *dast* ("hand"), and *dil* ("heart"). An Arabic example, by al-Mutanabbī, a verse in praise of both Kāfūr and Sayf al-Dawla (*firāqun wa-man fāraqtu ghayru mudhammamī* | *wa-ammun wa-man yammamtu ghayru muyammamī*)[11] illustrates several forms of *tajnīs* (paronomasia), parallelism, and internal rhyme. The Persian line by ʿUnṣurī contains an adjective, *maḥmūd* ("praiseworthy") that refers at the same time to the ruler called Maḥmūd. It is this figure that is mentioned in some later Persian treatises that include *ibdāʿ* in their lists of *badīʿ*: Sharaf al-Dīn Rāmī (middle of 8th/14th century), in his *Ḥaqāʾiq al-ḥadāʾiq*, explains *ibdāʿ* as "attributing to a patron who is praised a quality shared with his name."[12] A similar explanation of the term is found in *Badāʾiʿ al-afkār fī ṣanāʾiʿ al-ashʿār* by Ḥusayn Wāʿiẓ Kāshifī

9 See de Blois, Rashīd al-Dīn (...) Waṭwāṭ; Chalisova, Persian rhetoric 151–8 ("Vatvât's *Hadâʾeq al-sehr*").

10 Waṭwāṭ, *Ḥadāyiq al-siḥr* 83–4. I follow the edition in writing *Ḥadāyiq* and *daqāyiq* instead of the standard Arabic forms *Ḥadāʾiq* and *daqāʾiq*.

11 Al-Mutanabbī, *Dīwān* 649.

12 Rāmī, *Ḥaqāʾiq al-ḥadāʾiq* 125. I owe this and the following reference to Anna Livia Beelaert.

(d. 910/1504–5),[13] who adds, however, that "the older authorities (*muqaddimān*) said that *ibdāʿ* is when a poet clothes an original motif (*maʿnā-yi badīʿ*) with a mantle of eloquent words (*kiswat-i lafẓī-yi jazl*)."

In Arabic treatises on *badīʿ* the term *ibdāʿ* is never listed in the vague sense introduced by al-Rādūyānī. It appears, however, with a more specific sense, in *Taḥrīr al-taḥbīr* (approx. The Record of Elegant Style), a large compendium of *badīʿ* listing 125 figures, by the Egyptian author Ibn Abī l-Iṣbaʿ (d. 654/1256).[14] It is one of the figures which the author proudly claims to have introduced first.[15] The editor, Ḥifnī Muḥammad Sharaf, rejects this claim in a note, referring to Waṭwāṭ's *Ḥadāyiq al-siḥr*, but Ibn Abī l-Iṣbaʿ is justified in his claim because he provides a different definition of *ibdāʿ*:

باب الإبداع وهو أن تكونَ مفردات كلمات البيت من الشِّعر، أو الفصل من النَّثر، أو الجملة المفيدة، متضمّنة بديعا بحيث تأْتي في البيت الواحد والقرينة الواحدة عدة ضروب من البديع بحسب عدد كلماته أو جملته، وربما كان في الكلمة الواحدة المفردة ضربان فصاعدا من البديع، ومتى لم تكن كل كلمة بهذه المثابة فليس بإبداع

> *Ibdāʿ*: This is when the individual words of a line of poetry, or of a colon of prose, or of a meaningful sentence, contain *badīʿ*, such that in one line of verse or in one prose segment there are several kinds of *badīʿ*, according to the number of words in it or in the sentence. One single word may in fact contain two or more kinds. When not every word shows this, it does not count as *ibdāʿ*.[16]

The section is the penultimate one, followed only by *ḥusn al-khātima*, "beautiful conclusion," and it seems to serve as a kind of culmination or summation of what went before. *Ibdāʿ* is clearly an anomalous "figure,"[17] but it struck a chord with many subsequent authors who adopted it, as the following will demon-

---

13 Kāshifī, *Badāʾiʿ al-afkār* 147.

14 Ibn Abī l-Iṣbaʿ, *Taḥrīr al-taḥbīr* 611–5; also in his *Badīʿ al-Qurʾān* 340–3, a work excerpted from the larger volume.

15 Ibn Abī l-Iṣbaʿ, *Taḥrīr al-taḥbīr* 525.

16 He clearly means that the number of figures must equal or surpass the number of words in the verse or sentence. Al-Tahānawī, though quoting Ibn Abī l-Iṣbaʿ, gives a less stringent definition of *ibdāʿ*: "when an utterance contains several kinds of *badīʿ*" (*Kashshāf iṣṭilāḥāt al-funūn* 135).

17 As Aḥmad Ibrāhīm Mūsā says (*al-Ṣibgh al-badīʿī* 299), it is a strange "figure" and the difference with *tamzīj*, "mixing" (*Taḥrīr al-taḥbīr* 536–9) and *muqārana*, "yoking together" (603–6) is not altogether clear.

strate. Translating it as "originality" or "creativity" will not do here, and Pierre Cachia aptly rendered it as "Cumulation—Tour de Force" in his summary and partial translation of a late work on *badīʿ*, *Nafaḥāt al-azhār ʿalā nasamāt al-asḥār fī madḥ al-nabī al-mukhtār* (Odours of Flowers on the Breezes of Dawn: In Praise of the Chosen Prophet) by ʿAbd al-Ghanī al-Nābulusī (d. 1143/1731).[18] Even better, because more accurate, is Thomas Bauer's German translation of *ibdāʿ* as *Stilformhäufung*.[19]

To illustrate the figures listed in *Taḥrīr al-taḥbīr* Ibn Abī l-Iṣbaʿ quotes examples from poetry as well as prose. He takes pains to include examples from the Quran wherever possible (some figures, such as those concerning poetic rhyme, only apply to poetry). It is a Quranic example that makes up the bulk of the discussion of *ibdāʿ*; it is followed by one line of poetry by the author himself. The Quranic passage is one *āya* ("verse") from Sura Hūd 11:44, describing the end of the Flood when Nūḥ/Noah's ark settles on a mountain called al-Jūdī:[20]

﴿وَقِيلَ يَا أَرْضُ ٱبْلَعِي مَاءَكِ وَيَا سَمَاءُ أَقْلِعِي وَغِيضَ ٱلْمَاءُ وَقُضِيَ ٱلْأَمْرُ وَٱسْتَوَتْ عَلَى ٱلْجُودِيِّ
وَقِيلَ بُعْدًا لِلْقَوْمِ ٱلظَّالِمِينَ﴾

> And it was said, "Earth, swallow your water!" and "Sky, abate!". The water subsided and the matter was accomplished. It settled on al-Jūdī, and it was said, "Away with the wrong-doing people!"

In a chapter on poetic inspiration Ibn Rashīq reports that when some of the Prophet's most eloquent fellow tribesmen wanted to compose something to match the Quran, honing their inspiration with "fine wheat, choice wine, mutton, and solitude," they gave up when they heard this verse.[21] Ibn Rashīq gives no sources for this and I have not been able to find it in older works. His contemporary Ibn Sinān al-Khafājī (d. 466/1074) says that "people have always singled out Quranic passages of which they admire the eloquence (*balāgha*) and beautiful composition (*ḥusn al-taʾlīf*), among them God the Exalted's words 'And it

18 Cachia, *The arch rhetorician* 132 (no. 180). He often gives two renderings of a term, one of them being closer to the "literal" Arabic sense.

19 Bauer, Die *badīʿiyya* des Nāṣīf al-Yāziǧī 102.

20 The mountain is traditionally said to be "near Mosul," overlooking Jazīrat Ibn ʿUmar (modern Cizre in S.E. Turkey, to the east of which one finds Cudi Dağ or Mount Cudi); see Streck, Djūdī, and Monferrer-Sala, Ararat, where it is wrongly said that Yāqūt placed the mountain in Arabia.

21 Ibn Rashīq, *ʿUmda* i, 211; the same *āya* is also quoted as an excellent example of concision (*ījāz*), ibid. i, 253.

was said, Earth, swallow your water!'…"[22] But the verse does not figure prominently in early discussions of *badīʿ*,[23] of Quranic stylistic eminence, or in works on the inimitability of the Quran, such as al-Bāqillānī's *Iʿjāz al-Qurʾān*. Its prominence in such works is due to a contemporary of Ibn Rashīq and Ibn Sinān al-Khafājī, ʿAbd al-Qāhir al-Jurjānī (d. 471/1078), who dealt with it in his influential *Dalāʾil al-iʿjāz*.[24] He argues in some detail that its excellence does not lie in the individual words but in the way the words are connected (*irtibāṭ hādhihi l-kalim baʿḍihā bi-baʿḍ*). This passage obviously influenced al-Sakkākī (d. 626/1229), one of the systematisers of ʿAbd al-Qāhir's ideas, for he devoted several pages to the Quranic verse.[25] They come near the end of his book, before the appendixes on *badīʿ*, logic and prosody, as a kind of summary, illustrating literary excellence with one Quranic example, analysed in terms of figurative speech (*bayān*), syntactical stylistics (*maʿānī*), semantic purity (*faṣāḥa maʿnawiyya*), and phonetic purity (*faṣāḥa lafẓiyya*). He goes further than ʿAbd al-Qāhir and explicitly identifies several rhetorical figures such as metaphor (*istiʿāra*) and metonymy (*kināya*), but his main concern is not to list as many figures as possible but rather to demonstrate how the words and clauses hang together. Several authors on *ʿilm al-balāgha* follow in al-Sakkākī's footsteps by dedicating a passage to the analysis of Hūd 11:44 by way of summing up. Among them are Muḥammad b. ʿAlī al-Jurjānī (d. 729/1329) in his *al-Ishārāt wa-l-tanbīhāt fī ʿilm al-balāgha*[26] and al-Khaṭīb al-Qazwīnī (d. 739/1338) in his *al-Īḍāḥ*.[27]

Ibn Abī l-Iṣbaʿ does not seem to have known al-Sakkākī's *Miftāḥ*, but he mentions ʿAbd al-Qāhir al-Jurjānī's *Dalāʾil al-iʿjāz* among his sources.[28] He may also have seen the short passage on the verse in *al-Mathal al-sāʾir* by Ḍiyāʾ al-Dīn Ibn al-Athīr (d. 637/1239), which echoes ʿAbd al-Qāhir in stressing that its beauty lies not in the individual words but in their composition (*tarkīb*).[29] In the seventeen[30] words of the Quranic verse Ibn Abī l-Iṣbaʿ discovers twenty-one

22 Al-Khafājī, *Sirr al-faṣāḥa* 224.

23 It is listed as one of many examples of concision (*ījāz*) by Abū Hilāl al-ʿAskarī (d. *c.* 400/1010), *al-Ṣināʿatayn* 182.

24 ʿAbd al-Qāhir al-Jurjānī, *Dalāʾil al-iʿjāz* 44–5.

25 Al-Sakkākī, *Miftāḥ al-ʿulūm* 417–21.

26 Al-Jurjānī, *al-Ishārāt* 250–5.

27 Al-Qazwīnī, *al-Īḍāḥ* 470–4.

28 Ibn Abī l-Iṣbaʿ, *Taḥrīr al-taḥbīr* 89; *idem*, *Badīʿ al-Qurʾān* 5.

29 Ibn al-Athīr, *al-Mathal al-sāʾir* i, 214. Ibn Abī l-Iṣbaʿ mentions *al-Mathal al-sāʾir* among his sources, see *Taḥrīr al-taḥbīr* 91; *Badīʿ al-Qurʾān* 12.

30 *Sabʿ ʿashra* ("seventeen"), both in *Taḥrīr al-taḥbīr* 613 and *Badīʿ al-Qurʾān* 340, is not a copyist's or editor's error for *tisʿ ʿashra* ("nineteen"), because in Quranic orthography (not

kinds of *badīʿ* or "embellishments" (*maḥāsin*), some being specific and others more general and vague, and even far-fetched. It would take too much space to list and explain them all, but they include *munāsaba* (semantic and phonetic harmony) between (*i*)*blaʿī* ("swallow!") and *aqliʿī* ("abate!"); *majāz* (trope) in "heaven," because it stands for "rain from heaven"; *muṭābaqa* (antithesis) between "earth" and "heaven;" *istiʿāra* (metaphor) in "swallow" and "abate;" *ījāz* (concision); *insijām* (fluency); *ḥusn al-nasaq* (beautiful arrangement or sequence of the words). This last "figure" is of course his technical term for the quality discerned in the verse by ʿAbd al-Qāhir and others before him. It is in the section on *ḥusn al-nasaq* that Ibn Abī l-Iṣbaʿ already discusses it at some length.[31]

Ibn Abī l-Iṣbaʿ concludes his section of *ibdāʿ* in *Taḥrīr al-taḥbīr* with a verse of his own composition, taken from an ode on the Ayyūbid sultan al-Malik al-Ashraf. It aptly echoes the Quranic example by referring to rain, this time not in a destructive sense, and by alluding to the name of the mountain al-Jūdī by mentioning *jūd*, "generosity:"[32]

فَضَحْتَ الحَيَا والبَحْرَ جُودًا فقد بكى الـ حيا من حَياءٍ منك والْتطم البحْرُ

You put rain (*ḥayā*) and sea to shame with your generosity (*jūd*): the rain
weeps, ashamed (*ḥayāʾ*) on account of you, and the sea slaps its face.

The twelve words illustrate sixteen figures of speech, as the author proudly explains, including three counts of metaphor; two kinds of hyperbole (*mubālagha, ighrāq*); paronomasia; double entendre (*tawriya*) in the verb *iltaṭama*, which denotes slapping one's face as a sign of distress and the clashing of waves; the "sound distribution" (*ṣiḥḥat al-taqsīm*) of rain and sea, the two traditional Arabic metaphors for generosity; fantastic aetiology (*ḥusn al-taʿlīl*) in the "pathetic fallacy" of assigning an imagined cause to the falling of rain and the clashing of waves; and finally *ibdāʿ* itself, the cumulation or *tour de force* of combining all this in one verse.

---

normally followed in quotations in modern editions) *yā-arḍu* and *yā-samāʾu* are each written as one word.

31 *Taḥrīr al-taḥbīr* 425–6; *Badīʿ al-Qurʾān* 164–5. Ibn al-Naqīb (d. 698/1298), in his introduction to his *tafsīr*, also discusses the verse in the section on *ḥusn al-nasaq* (*Muqaddimat al-Tafsīr* 397–8).

32 *Taḥrīr al-taḥbīr* 614–5; with two more lines of the poem also quoted in al-Ṣafadī's biography of Ibn Abī Iṣbaʿ (al-Ṣafadī, *al-Wāfī* xix, 8). For the complete poem (61 lines) see Ibn al-Shaʿʿār, *Qalāʾid al-jumān* iii, 167–9.

Subsequent authors of treatises on stylistics follow Ibn Abī l-Iṣbaʿ and quote his words on *ibdāʿ*. Among them are Shihāb al-Dīn Maḥmūd b. Sulaymān al-Ḥalabī (d. 725/1325) in *Ḥusn al-tawassul*[33] and Najm al-Dīn Ibn al-Athīr (d. 736/1336) in his *Jawhar al-kanz*.[34] In his section on *badīʿ* in the Quran, al-Suyūṭī (d. 911/1505) does the same.[35] I have found only one later author who included *ibdāʿ* in a list of *badīʿ* without defining it as did Ibn Abī l-Iṣbaʿ. Ḥusayn b. Muḥammad al-Ṭībī (d. 743/1343) uses the term much as did al-Rādūyānī and Ibn Rashīq before him:[36]

> الإبداع وهو أن يخترع المتكلّم معانِيَ غيرَ مسبوق إليها (...) وهو ضربان: أحدهما ما يبتدع عند الحوادث المتجدّدة[37] (...) وثانيهما ما يبتدع من غير شاهد حالٍ

> *Ibdāʿ* is when a speaker invents motifs without anyone doing so before him (...). There are two kinds: one is to produce something novel (*yabtadiʿu*) on the occasion of new events (...); the second is to produce something novel without witnessing a situation.

Al-Ṭībī gives many examples of both kinds, such as lines from a poem by al-Mutanabbī on Sayf al-Dawla's large tent that was blown over in a storm,[38] and, as an example of the second kind, a distich about wine glasses that seem heavier when empty, just as bodies feel lighter when spirited.[39]

When Ibn Abī l-Iṣbaʿ supplied his own illustration of *ibdāʿ* he set a challenge that was taken up by some of the many authors who composed a *badīʿiyya*, a poem of some length, usually in praise of the prophet Muḥammad, each verse of which illustrates one or more kinds of *badīʿ*;[40] often they wrote a commentary on the poem.[41] The famous poet Ṣafī al-Dīn al-Ḥillī (d. 750/1349) had some

33 Shihāb al-Dīn al-Ḥalabī, *Ḥusn al-tawassul* 125–6.

34 Ibn al-Athīr, *Jawhar al-kanz* 231–3.

35 Al-Suyūṭī, *al-Itqān* iii, 330–1 (*ibdāʿ*) and see 316 (*ḥusn al-nasaq*).

36 Al-Ṭībī, *al-Tibyān* 305–9. His definition and illustrations of *ibdāʿ* are quoted by the much later Iraqi poet Ḥaydar al-Ḥillī (d. 1304/1887) in his *al-ʿIqd al-mufaṣṣal* iii, 376–80.

37 Instead of *al-mutajaddida* the edition has *al-mutaḥaddida*, clearly an error.

38 Al-Mutanabbī, *Dīwān* 445–7.

39 Al-Ṭībī, *Tibyān* 310, ascribing them to a westerner (*baʿḍ al-Maghāriba*). They have been attributed to various poets, see Ibn Abī Uṣaybiʿa, *ʿUyūn al-anbāʾ* II/i, 639; II/ii, 693–4.

40 On the genre see Van Gelder, Badīʿiyya. For a Christian Arabic example, see Bauer, Die *badīʿiyya* des Nāṣīf al-Yāziǧī.

41 A Persian example of a poem illustrating figures of speech in each verse is that by the 6th/12th-century poet Qiwāmī Ganjawī. The poem, a panegyric—not on the Prophet—of 101 lines, is quoted and translated in Browne, *A Literary history of Persia* ii, 47–96. Line 91

precursors when he composed his *badīʿiyya* but it was his poem and commentary that set a trend. In the commentary on vs. 122, on *ibdāʿ*,[42] he quotes Ibn Abī l-Iṣbaʿ, listing ten kinds of *badīʿ* in the Quranic verse, and he quotes Ibn Abī l-Iṣbaʿ's verse, adding that part of the latter's commentary is acceptable and part to be rejected (*fīhā l-maqbūl wa-l-mardūd*). His own verse, describing the Prophet's Companions, is as follows:

ذَلَّ النُّضارُ كما عَزَّ النَّظيرُ لهمْ　　بالبَذْلِ والفَضْلِ في علمٍ وفي كَرَمِ

Pure gold (*nuḍār*) is as lowly as the likes (*naẓīr*) of them are highly sought,
for spending freely and for excellence in knowledge and noble-mindedness.

Al-Ḥillī claims at least fourteen kinds of *badīʿ* for his own verse, "which is more than the number of its words" (twelve). Among the figures it contains he mentions antithesis (*dhalla*, "is lowly" and *ʿazza* "is dear, high"); paronomasia (*nuḍār* and *naẓīr*; *ḍ* and *ẓ* were and are often pronounced alike); internal rhyme (*tasjīʿ*, in *badhli*, "spending" and *faḍli*, "excellence"); "wrapping up and rolling out" (*laff wa-nashr*, enumerating terms followed by corresponding items, here "pure gold" and "likes," correlated—not wholly convincingly—with "spending freely" and "excellence"); hyperbole (in describing pure gold as lowly and cheap as a result of the Companions' generosity); metaphor (in calling gold "lowly" as if personified); *tamkīn* (easily fitting in the rhyme).[43] He thinks it possible that more figures may be extracted, mentioning six, including vague and general "figures" such as *insijām* ("fluency") and *ḥusn al-nasaq* ("beautiful arrangement"), but he has ignored them because, as he says, they are far-fetched (*baʿīdat al-taʾwīl*). One notes that unlike Ibn Abī l-Iṣbaʿ he does not include *ibdāʿ*; he has, after all, surpassed him already.

illustrates *ibdāʿ*. Browne (ii, 73–4) incorrectly says that it "means 're-originating,', 'reconstructing,' or 're-creating,' that is, expressing in similar but different form the thought of some previous poet or writer, while giving it a new meaning of application." The line illustrates various kinds of parallelism and internal rhyme as well as hyperbole and antithesis: *ḥazmash āwurda bād-rā bi-sukūn* | *ʿazmash afganda khāk-rā bi-madār* ("His resolve brings the wind to a standstill: his determination casts the dust into a whirl," tr. Browne). I thank Anna Livia Beelaert for reminding me of this poem.

42 Al-Ḥillī, *Sharḥ al-Kāfiya* 292–5.

43 Cachia calls it "dovetailing" (*The arch rhetorician* 111).

Only a few of the many *badīʿiyya*s composed in al-Ḥillī's wake can be discussed here.[44] Prominent among *badiʿiyya* authors is Ibn Ḥijja al-Ḥamawī (d. 837/1434), who set himself an extra constraint in his *badīʿiyya*, by paronomastically alluding to the term in each verse, following his predecessor ʿIzz al-Dīn al-Mawṣilī (d. 789/1387). He illustrates *ibdāʿ* with the following line, describing the Prophet:[45]

إبداعُ أخلاقِهِ إيداعُ خالقِهِ   في زُخْرُفِ الشُّعَرا فٱسْجَعْ بِهَا وَهِمِ[46]

> The novel features (*ibdāʿ*) of his character (*akhlāq*) were placed there (*īdāʿ*) by his Creator (*khāliq*),
> amidst the ornate speech of the poets: speak in rhymed prose of them and wander!

He seems to suggest (my translation is tentative) that poets and prose writers who describe the splendid qualities of the Prophet will necessarily fall short. The word *zukhruf*, "ornamentation, decoration," in connection with poets, probably alludes to Q al-Anʿām 6:112: *ka-dhālika jaʿalnā li-kulli nabiyyin ʿaduwwan shayāṭīna l-insi wa-l-jinni yūḥī baʿḍuhum ilā baʿḍin zukhrufa l-qawli ghurūran*, "Thus We have made for every prophet an enemy, devils of men and demons, who intimate ornate speech to one another, as a delusion." In English Quran translations *zukhruf al-qawl* has been rendered as "tinsel speech" (Bell), "tawdry speech" (Arberry), and "fancy speech" (Alan Jones), but the word *zukhruf* is not necessarily to be taken as negative, as seen in Q Yūnus 10:24: *idhā akhadhati l-arḍu zukhrufahā*, "When the earth has put on its finery." The last word of the verse, *wa-himī*, alludes to the well-known Quranic passage that condemns poets who "wander in every valley" (al-Shuʿarāʾ 26:224). Instead of reading it as the imperative of *hāma*, "to wander," it could also be taken as the imperative of *wahama*, "to imagine, fancy, have illusions, be mistaken."

The ten words of Ibn Ḥijja's verse contain thirteen kinds of *badīʿ* by his count, including two cases of double entendre (one with *ibdāʿ* and a second with *himī*);[47] graphic paronomasia (*ibdāʿ* and *īdāʿ* differ by merely one dot);

44 It was customary to use the same metre (*basīṭ*) and the same rhyme (*-mī*), following al-Ḥillī, who himself followed in this the very famous ode, called *al-Burda*, on the Prophet by al-Būṣīrī (d. *c.* 694/1294).

45 Ibn Ḥijja, *Khizānat al-adab* iv, 71–4.

46 The word *shuʿarāʾ* has lost it final *hamza* on account of the metre, which must count as a minor blemish.

47 The word *īdāʿ*, "depositing," is probably also meant as a pun, for it is also a form of literary

etymological paronomasia (*akhlāq* and *khāliq* are derived from the same root); semantic agreement, in alluding to poetry and rhymed prose; and various forms of parallelism. I cannot follow him in identifying all his alleged figures, for I fail to see a convincing example of *tarṣīʿ*, a form of syntactical and phonetic parallelism (*akhlāqihī* and *khāliqihī* do not form a good rhyme). Ibn Ḥijja moreover claims *suhūla* ("smoothness") and *insijām* ("fluency") for his verse,[48] and he does not hesitate to include, finally, *ibdāʿ*.

Ibn Ḥijja also quotes the example of *ibdāʿ* from the *badīʿiyya* of his predecessor, ʿIzz al-Dīn al-Mawṣilī:

كم أبدعوا روْضَ عدْلٍ بعدَ طَوْلِهِمِ   وأتْرَعوا حَوْضَ فضْلٍ قبلَ قَوِلِهِمِ

How many meadows of justice did they create, after their coming to power,
and how many cisterns of excellence did they fill, even before they spoke!

This line, says Ibn Ḥijja, allegedly contains sixteen kinds of *badīʿ*, but he feels unable, or unwilling, to list them all, which he leaves to other literary experts (*ḥudhdhāq al-adab*). ʿAbd al-Ghanī al-Nābulusī (d. 1143/1731), in the commentary on his own *badīʿiyya*, took the trouble to quote the line and explain that it contains paronomasia (*rawḍ—ḥawḍ, ṭawlihimī—qawlihimī*), antithesis (*baʿda—qabla*); metaphor (meadows of justice, cisterns of excellence); internal extended rhyme and parallelism, syntactical and phonetic (the two hemistichs match almost fully: *kam abdaʿū rawḍa ʿadlin baʿda ṭuwlihimī* | *wa-atraʿū ḥawḍa faḍlin qabla qawlihimī*). The verb *abdaʿū* alludes to *ibdāʿ*.[49]

In a *badīʿiyya* by the famous mystical poet ʿĀʾisha al-Bāʿūniyya (d. 923/1517), she modestly claims merely some eleven kinds for her own illustration of *ibdāʿ*:[50]

حَلّوا بقلبي وحَلّى جودُ مِنّتِهِمْ   جِيدي وشُكْرُ الأَيادي مسْمَعي وفَمي

borrowing and a form of *badīʿ* that has its own chapter in Ibn Ḥijja's *Khizānat al-adab* (iv, 106–61, together with *taḍmīn*, "quotation").

48 On these and related terms, see Van Gelder, Poetry for Easy Listening.

49 Al-Nābulusī, *Nafaḥāt al-azhār* 212.

50 ʿĀʾisha al-Bāʿūniyya, *al-Badīʿiyya* 80–1. The line is also quoted by al-Nābulusī, *Nafaḥāt al-azhār*, 213. In this poem she does not allude to the name of the figure in each line; apparently, she did so in another poem (Bauer, Die *badīʿiyya* 55 note 16).

They [viz., her loved ones] lodged (*ḥallū*) in my heart; the generosity (*jūd*) of their kindness
adorned (*ḥallā*) my neck (*jīdī*) and the gratefulness of their favours (adorned) my ears and mouth.

She mentions paronomasia (*ḥallū—ḥallā, jūd—jīd*); double entendre (*ḥallā* could mean "adorned" as well as "sweetened"); *ḥusn al-bayān*, "beauty of exposition," which Cachia translates as "articulateness;"[51] "smoothness (*suhūla*);" "fluency (*insijām*);" "harmony of expression and metre;" "harmony of metre and sense;" "semantic and phonetic harmony" (*munāsaba*)—but it is not clear what she means by it here—; "expansion" (*basṭ*, a kind of justified prolixity); and *ibdāʿ* itself. The text, incongruously, gives *mismaʿī* (or *masmaʿī*) *wa-famī*, "my ears and my mouth," as an example of paronomasia, but it would seem that the appropriate term, *murāʿāt al-naẓīr* ("semantic agreement"), was dropped in error.

Not every author of a *badīʿiyya* found it necessary to include *ibdāʿ*. Among those who do not mention it are the Andalusian Ibn Jābir (d. 780/1378)[52] and the Indian al-Bilgrāmī (d. 1200/1786).[53] Al-Suyūṭī lists it in his encyclopaedia of Quranic sciences, *al-Itqān*, as mentioned above, but in his *badīʿiyya*, entitled *Naẓm al-badīʿ fī madḥ khayr shafīʿ* (*Badīʿ* Versified: In Praise of the Best Intercessor), he ignores it.[54] Ibn Maʿṣūm (d. 1120/1708), however, includes it in his voluminous *Anwār al-rabīʿ fī anwāʿ al-badīʿ* (The Blossoms of Spring: On the Kinds of *Badīʿ*).[55]

He quotes the example of *ibdāʿ* by five predecessors and explains that his own verse contains fifteen kinds of *badīʿ*:

إبداعُ مدْحي لمن لم يبْقِ من بِدَعٍ   أفاد رِبْحي فإن أطنبْتُ لم أُلَمِ

The originality (*ibdāʿ*) of my praise for the one who left nothing novel (*bidaʿ*)
has given me profit. If I have been prolix, I will not be blamed.

51 Cachia, *The arch rhetorician* 112; Bauer, Die *badīʿiyya* 108: "Klarheit des Ausdrucks."

52 Ibn Jābir, *Badīʿiyyat al-ʿumyān*.

53 Al-Bilgrāmī, *Subḥat al-marjān*.

54 Al-Suyūṭī, *Naẓm al-badīʿ*. In the edition, the heading *al-ibdāʿ* (134) is an error for *al-īdāʿ*, as is the word *al-ibdāʿ* in the verse itself, as the explanation makes clear: it involves the quotation (*taḍmīn*) of a hemistich. On *īdāʿ* see above, note 47.

55 Ibn Maʿṣūm, *Anwār al-rabīʿ* v, 328–32.

The line contains two kinds of paronomasia (*ibdāʾ* and *bidaʿ*; *lam* and *ulamī*); *munāsaba* and internal rhyme (*madḥī* and *ribḥī*); *tašrīʿ*, because a new, shorter verse may be had by truncating parts: *ibdāʿū madḥī* | *afāda ribḥī* ("The originality of my praise | has given me profit");[56] metaphor (*afāda ribḥī*, presumably because its subject, "the originality of my praise," has been personified); *taʿlīl* ("fantastic or false aetiology," in making the "profit" ostensibly the reason for being prolix in his praise); *īghāl*, which consists of a final expression that is not essential but adds a finer point, here exemplified by "If I have been prolix I will not be blamed;"[57] double entendre (in using *ibdāʿ* in its common and its technical sense). Ibn Maʿṣūm also lists the usual vague terms: *musāwāh* ("equality," viz. between meaning and expression, the mean between concision and prolixity); two kinds of *iʾtilāf* ("harmony"), between expression and sense (as Ibn Maʿṣūm claims, "no single word can be exchanged for another") and between expression and prosody (there is no awkward word order caused by the metre); *insijām* (fluency, "which is evident"); *tahdhīb* ("polish," because "the words do not jar, are not repugnant, and the syntax is uncomplicated"). Finally, the verse illustrates *ibdāʿ*. "These are fifteen kinds, which exceeds the number of words of the verse. God knows best."

The same number is claimed by ʿAbd al-Ghanī al-Nābulusī in his *Nafaḥāt al-azhār* for his own example:[58]

محا الضلالَ بإثبات الهُدى وحَمى   حِمى شريعتِهِ بالسيْف والقَلَمِ

Pierre Cachia, in his partial translation and rearrangement of the book, places the section at the very end (in the original poem of 150 lines it is no. 84) and renders al-Nābulusī's line as follows:[59]

> He erased (*maḥā*) perdition[60] by affirming true guidance, and defended (*ḥamā*)
> The sanctuary (*ḥimā*) of His law by sword and pen.

The attentive reader should by now be able to discover most or all of the fifteen kinds of *badīʿ*. Of the more impressionistic features, al-Nābulusī leaves

56 Cachia, *The arch rhetorician* 12, translates the term as "Fission—(Trussing)".

57 Cachia, *The arch rhetorician* 57, translates the term as "The Royal Cubit—(Forcing the Pace)."

58 Al-Nābulusī, *Nafaḥāt al-azhār* 212–3.

59 Cachia, *The arch rhetorician* 132. I have added the parenthesized transliterations.

60 Instead of "perdition" I would translate *ḍalāl* as "error" or "going astray;" it is the antonym of *hudā*, "true guidance."

out “polish” (*tahdhīb*) but he claims for his verse both “fluency” (*insijām*) and “smoothness” (*suhūla*).

The *badīʿiyya* by Nāṣīf al-Yāzijī (d. 1287/1871) is the subject of Thomas Bauer’s study that has been cited several times above, a substantial article that also serves as an excellent introduction to the genre. Al-Yāzijī was not the only Christian who composed a *badīʿiyya*, adopting the customary metre and rhyme. Naturally it is not the prophet Muḥammad who is extolled in those poems. In some cases he is replaced with Christ, Mary, or the Apostles, but al-Yāzijī chose to omit explicit references to any named person or to any specific religion, limiting himself to the general themes of love and, in the concluding section, *dhamm al-dunyā*, the rejection of worldly things. The example of *ibdāʿ*, line 32 of its 114 lines, is part of the section in which the poet rebukes someone who blamed his passion:[61]

أَبْدَعْتَ فِي اللَوْمِ لُؤْمًا لَمْ يُلِمَّ بِهِ فَصْلٌ مِنَ الحُكْمِ أَو فَضْلٌ مِنَ الحِكَمِ

> You have invented new forms of blame, basely, which is unacquainted with either a wise decision or excellence of wisdom.

Since neither the poet nor Bauer provides a commentary on this line, one can only guess how many kinds of *badīʿ* the poet would have claimed. It contains double entendre (*abdaʿta*, alluding to *ibdāʿ*); various kinds of paronomasia (*lawm—luʾm—lam yulimm*; *faṣl—faḍl*; *ḥukm—ḥikam*); syntactic and semantic parallelism (*faṣlun mina l-ḥukmi—faḍlun min al-ḥikamī*); and of course *ibdāʿ*. No doubt some of the more impressionistic categories could be added.

Qāsim b. Muḥammad al-Bakrajī composed his *badīʿiyya* with commentary in 1293/1876.[62] The line illustrating *ibdāʿ* should ring a bell:[63]

إبداعُ أوصافِهِ إيداعُ واصفِهِ محى الضلالَ حِمى الأبطالِ بالخَذَمِ

> The novel features (*ibdāʿ*) of his attributes (*awṣāfihī*) were placed there (*īdāʿ*) by his Attributor (*wāṣifihī*).

61 Al-Yāzijī, *Dīwān* 24, Bauer, The *badīʿiyya* 96 (Arabic). His German translation (102) reads better than my more literal English: “Schimpf und Schande, ungekannte, hast du ersonnen, weisheitslos, Lügen bloß!”

62 Al-Bakrajī, *Ḥilyat al-badīʿ*; GALS iii, 342.

63 Al-Bakrajī, *Ḥilyat al-badīʿ* 242–4.

> The sanctuary (*ḥimā*) of the heroes erased (*maḥā*) error with cutting sword.

The first hemistich is obviously based on Ibn Ḥijja's verse and the second hemistich on that of al-Nābulusī. This is freely acknowledged since he quotes both lines in his commentary. Thus helped by his models he is able to enumerate fifteen kinds of *badīʿ*, adding that "if you look closely at the verse you may extract more; God knows best." He also quotes Ibn Abī l-Iṣbaʿ, al-Ḥillī, al-Mawṣilī, and ʿĀʾisha al-Bāʿūniyya, *al-shaykh* Abū l-Wafā, and al-Nābulusī. Altogether it is a good example of the intertextuality that is such a prominent feature of the genre.[64] Abū l-Wafāʾ is another Aleppine author of a *badīʿiyya* with commentary, Abū l-Wafāʾ b. ʿUmar b. ʿAbd al-Wahhāb al-ʿUrḍī (d. 1071/1660), the author of *Fatḥ al-badīʿ fī ḥall al-Ṭirāz al-badīʿ fī imtidāḥ al-shafīʿ*.[65] His verse deserves being quoted because al-Bakrajī says that he deserves first prize (*qad aḥraza l-shaykhu qaṣaba l-sabqa ʿalā ghayrihi*):[66]

أَبْدِعْ وأَوْدِعْ بعقْدِ الحمْدِ من مِدَحٍ بنُورِ تنزيلِ ما في نون والقَلَمِ

> Be original (*abdiʿ*) and deposit (*awdiʿ*), with a deed[67] of praise (*ḥamd*), eulogies (*midaḥ*)
> with the light (*nūr*) of the Revelation that is in the letter N (*nūn*) and the Pen.

The verse alludes to Sura 68, called *al-Qalam* ("the Pen"), which begins "*Nūn*. By the Pen and what they write," *Nūn* (N) being one of the letter names that open a number of Suras, the origin and meaning of which are contested. Among the figures in this line are different forms of paronomasia (*abdiʿ—awdiʿ, ḥamd—midaḥ, nūr—nūn*); metaphor (*ʿaqd*, here rendered "deed," literally "binding" or "knotting;" and *nūr*, "light"), and semantic agreement (*murāʿāt al-naẓīr*, in

64 See Bauer, The *badīʿiyya* 59–60, "Die Intertextualität der *badīʿiyya*," concluding (my translation): "All in all, one can state that it is hardly possible to find a comparable genre in world literature that is as intertextually 'loaded' as the *badīʿiyya*."

65 Al-ʿUrḍī, *Fatḥ al-badīʿ*, 459 (with thanks to Nefeli Papoutsakis for providing me with a scan of the passage). See *GAL* ii, 292, *GALS* ii, 402. The translation of the title is difficult, literally "The Victory of the Original One (but also 'God's Revelation' or 'The Opening of *Badīʿ*'): The Prose Commentary on the Novel Embroidery (also 'the novel model'), in Praise of the Intercessor (viz., the prophet Muḥammad)."

66 Al-Bakrajī, *Ḥilyat al-badīʿ* 244, after quoting part of Abū l-Wafā's commentary.

67 Instead of reading *bi-ʿaqdi l-ḥamdi* one could consider reading *bi-ʿiqdi l-ḥamdi*, "in the necklace of praise." But the context (depositing, a letter, a Pen) suggests a legal deed.

"praise" and "eulogies"). There are also said to be forms of allusion (*ishāra*, *talmīḥ*). I fail to see the "suggestion of double entendre" (*īhām al-tawriya*) said to be in *nūr tanzīl* (the light of the Revelation), but one could detect double entendre in *abdiʿ* and *awdiʿ* (alluding to the "figures" *ibdāʿ* and *īdāʿ*) and in *ʿaqd*, which is also the term for "versification of prose" and a kind of *badīʿ*.[68] Together with the more general features, including concision (*ījāz*), smoothness (*suhūla*), fluency (*insijām*), polish (*taʾdīb wa-tahdhīb*), harmony (*iʾtilāf*) between wording and metre, fitting in the rhyme word easily (*tamkīn*), "strangeness" (*gharāba*, said in connection with the word *ʿaqd*),[69] and of course *ibdāʿ*, one arrives at an unspecified but impressive number of kinds of *badīʿ*.

One cannot but admire the ingenuity of the poets who studded their illustrations of *ibdāʿ* with much artfulness, even though most modern readers will probably not consider them great poetry. Even without a religious bias many (myself included) may well conclude that, after all, Ibn Abī l-Iṣbaʿ's main example, the Quranic verse about the subsiding waters, deserves pride of place from a literary point of view. Unlike the examples from poetry, the Quranic verse is not constrained by metre. It was precisely the constraints of metre and rhyme that made *ibdāʿ* into a challenge for poets. The definition of *ibdāʿ* by Ibn Abī l-Iṣbaʿ, quoted above, spoke of "a line of poetry, or of a colon of prose, or of a meaningful sentence," but his only prose example is the Quranic passage. It is the same in all subsequent works on *badīʿ* and the commentaries on *badīʿiyyāt*: all illustrations are taken from poetry, even though prose is still duly mentioned in the definition of *ibdāʿ*. The compact and well-defined nature of the traditional *bayt*, with its maximum of 30 syllables (28 in the *basīṭ* metre normally used for a *badīʿiyya*) is eminently suitable to forms of artifice that attempt to pack as many items in its limited compass. Several kinds of *badīʿ* lend themselves to competition in this manner. Ibn Ḥazm (d. 456/1064), having quoted a line from a love poem of his that contains three comparisons (rain, cloud, meadow, compared to tears, eyes, and cheek, respectively), outdoes himself with another line that contains five comparisons (the poet, the woman, the wine cup, the wine, the dark night, compared to the earth, the rain, pearls, gold, and jet), adding proudly that it will be impossible to surpass this.[70] In works on

68 Cachia, *The arch rhetorician* 124–125.

69 It is not clear to me what kind of "strangeness" is meant here and I have not found *gharāba* as a separate kind of *badīʿ* in other *badīʿiyyas*, even though the term is often used, in a positive or negative sense, in works of literary criticism and stylistics. See Kīlīṭū, *al-Adab wa-l-gharāba* and Harb, *Arabic Poetics*.

70 Ibn Ḥazm, *Ṭawq al-ḥamāma* 109–10. The pearls refer to the bubbles resulting from mixing wine with water. For an English translation see Ibn Hazm, *The Ring of the Dove* 40–1.

badīʿ this figure would be classified as an example of *laff wa-nashr*, "wrapping up and rolling out."[71] In al-Ḥillī's *badīʿiyya* he illustrates it with five nouns followed by five prepositions:[72]

وجْدي حَنيني أنيني فِكْرتي وَلَهي   منهمْ إليهمْ عليهمْ فيهِمُ بِهِمِ

My passion, my longing, my moaning, my thought, my distraction
is from them, for them, about them, of them, by them.

Other poets succeeded in outdoing predecessors in stuffing as many words as possible into one line. The nine imperative verbs in a verse by Diʿbil (d. 245/860) were surpassed by the ten imperatives of Abū l-ʿAmaythal (d. 240/854) and then by al-Mutanabbī (d. 354/965), who first composed a line in *ṭawīl* metre (28 syllables) containing fourteen imperatives, following this up with two more lines, one with sixteen and finally a line that crams a tongue-twisting 24 imperatives in 28 syllables.[73] Since an imperative is a complete sentence, one could also say that there are as many sentences as imperatives in such lines. Rhetoricians classified such lines that contain a succession of syntactically similar clauses or sentences as *tafwīf*, "producing a striped garment."[74]

The most recent *badīʿiyya-cum-*commentary I have looked at for this article is by the Damascene scholar Ṭāhir al-Jazāʾirī, who died in 1338/1920.[75] As its title

Al-ʿImād al-Iṣfahānī, *Kharīdat al-qaṣr, Qism shuʿarāʾ al-Shām* i, 575, says that Abū l-Thanāʾ Maḥmūd b. Niʿma al-Shayzarī (d. after 565/1169) fitted six comparisons in one line, but that line only lists the *secunda comparationis*, the *prima* being understood: "She took off the clouds [her niqab], revealing a full moon [face] and stars [jewels, earrings], and wiped the dew [perspiration] from roses [cheeks] with jujube berries [henna-stained fingers]." It is of course based on the more famous verse by al-Waʾwāʾ al-Dimashqī: "She rained pearls from daffodils, watering roses, and bit on jujube berries with hail-stones" (al-Waʾwāʾ, *Dīwān* 84), which in turn outdoes a verse by Abū Nuwās: "It [a moon, i.e. a girl] wept and scattered pearls from daffodils, slapping the roses with jujube fruits" (Abū Nuwās, *Dīwān* iv, 15). Not to be outdone, al-Ḥillī raised the number to seven (al-Ṣafadī, *al-Wāfī* xviii, 486; al-Ḥillī, *Dıwan* 473), with the *prima comparationis* in a preceding line.

71 See e.g. Cachia, *The arch rhetorician* 60–1, who calls it "Multiple Attribution—(Rolling and Unrolling);" in western rhetoric called *versus rapportati*.

72 Al-Ḥillī, *Sharḥ al-Kāfiya* 76.

73 Al-Mutanabbī's line is *ʿishi bqa smu sud qud jud muri nha ri fi sri nil* | *ghiẓi rmi ṣibi ḥmi ghzu sbi ruʿ zaʿ di li ṯni nul* (al-Mutanabbī, *Dīwān* 495). For details and translations of this and similar verses, see Van Gelder, *Sound and Sense* 234–7, where also a somewhat obscure line by al-Ḥillī is given that claims thirty imperatives.

74 See e.g. Cachia, *The arch rhetorician* 10–1, "Repeat Patterning—(Striping)," Ibn Maʿṣūm, *Anwār al-rabīʿ* ii, 308–17.

75 Al-Jazāʾirī, *Badīʿ al-Talkhīṣ* (lithograph ed. 1296 [/1897]; the edition by ʿAdnān ʿUmar al-

suggests, his *Badīʿ al-Talkhīṣ wa-talkhīṣ al-badīʿ*, published in 1897, is a modest work of a mere fifty pages. It lists most of the usual kinds of *badīʿ*, but *ibdāʾ* is not among them. This is, as the author explains in his introduction, because he limited himself to the kinds of *badīʿ* that are in that most popular of works on *ʿilm al-balāgha*, *Talkhīṣ al-Miftāh* by al-Khaṭīb al-Qazwīnī. This compendium is a rewriting and shortening of the sections on rhetoric from al-Sakkākī's *Miftāḥ al-ʿulūm*, but whereas in the latter book *ʿilm al-badīʿ* is little more than a short appendix, al-Qazwīnī expands it and lists more figures, even though their number is much smaller than in works specialising in *badīʿ*. Al-Jazāʾirī was no literary reformer,[76] yet one wonders if his reduction of the traditional *badīʿiyya* is a sign of the rapidly diminishing status of traditional rhetoric during his lifetime, when journalism and modern genres brought a new and simplified language and literary style.

Bibliography

Primary Sources

Abū Nuwās, *Dīwān*, iv, ed. Gregor Schoeler, Wiesbaden 1982.

ʿĀʾisha bt. Yūsuf b. Aḥmad al-Bāʿūniyya, *al-Badīʿiyya wa-sharḥuhā: al-Fatḥ al-mubīn fī madḥ al-amīn*, ed. ʿĀdil Kuttāb and ʿAbbās Thābit, Damascus 2009.

al-ʿAskarī, Abū Hilāl, *al-Ṣināʿatayn*, ed. ʿAlī Muḥammad al-Bajāwī, Cairo 1971.

al-Bakrajī, Qāsim—al-Ḥalabī, *Ḥilyat al-badīʿ fī madḥ al-nabī al-shafīʿ*, Aleppo 1293 [/1876].

al-Bilgrāmī, Ghulām ʿAlī Āzād, *Subḥat al-marjān fī āthār Hindustān*, ed. Muḥammad Faḍl al-Raḥmān al-Nadwī al-Sīwānī, Aligarh 1976.

al-Ḥillī, Ḥaydar, *al-ʿIqd al-mufaṣṣal fī qabīlat al-majd al-muʾaththal*, ed. Muḍar Sulaymān al-Ḥillī, 3 vols., Baghdad 2014.

al-Ḥillī, Ṣafī al-Dīn, *Dīwān*, Beirut n.d.

al-Ḥillī, Ṣafī al-Dīn, *Sharḥ al-Kāfiya al-badīʿiyya*, ed. Nasīb Nashāwī, Damascus 1982.

Ibn Abī l-Iṣbaʿ al-Miṣrī, *Badīʿ al-Qurʾān*, ed. Ḥifnī Muḥammad Sharaf, Cairo 1377/1957.

Ibn Abī l-Iṣbaʿ al-Miṣrī, *Taḥrīr al-taḥbīr fī ṣināʿat al-shiʿr wa-l-nathr wa-bayān iʿjāz al-Qurʾān*, ed. Ḥifnī Muḥammad Sharaf, Cairo 1383 [/1963].

Khaṭīb, Damascus 2012, was not accessible to me). The title could be translated as "A Novel Compendium and a Compendium on *Badīʿ*," but the first two words also mean "The *Badīʿ* of (al-Qazwīnī's) *Compendium*."

76 *GALS* iii, 383: "Während sich sonst überall wenigstens Ansätze zu einer Erneuerung des literarischen Lebens zeigten, hielt Ṭāhir b. Ṣāliḥ b. A. b. Mauhūb al-Waġlīsī al-Ǧazāʾirī (…) starr and den Traditionen des alten Wissenschaftsbetriebes fest."

Ibn Abī Uṣaybiʿa, *ʿUyūn al-anbāʾ fī ṭabaqāt al-aṭibbāʾ / A Literary History of Medicine*, ed. Emilie Savage-Smith et al., 3 vols. in 5, Leiden 2020.

Ibn al-Athīr, Ḍiyāʾ al-Dīn, *al-Mathal al-sāʾir fī adab al-kātib wa-l-shāʿir*, ed. Aḥmad al-Ḥūfī and Badawī Ṭabāna, 4 vols., Cairo 1959–73.

Ibn al-Athīr, Najm al-Dīn Aḥmad b. Ismāʿīl al-Ḥalabī, *Jawhar al-kanz: Talkhīṣ Kanz al-barāʿa fī adawāt dhawī l-yarāʿa*, ed. Muḥammad Zaghlūl Sallām, Alexandria, n.d.

Ibn Hazm, *The Ring of the Dove: A Treatise on the Art and Practice of Arab Love*, tr. A.J. Arberry, London 1953.

Ibn Ḥazm, *Ṭawq al-ḥamāma fī l-ulfa wa-l-ullāf*, ed. Iḥsān ʿAbbās, Beirut 1993.

Ibn Ḥijja, Taqī al-Dīn Abū Bakr b. ʿAlī al-Ḥamawī, *Khizānat al-adab wa-ghāyat al-arab*, ed. Kawkab Diyāb, 5 vols., Beirut 2001.

Ibn Jābir al-Andalusī, Shams al-Dīn Abū ʿAbd Allāh Muḥammad, *Badīʿiyyat al-ʿumyān al-musammāh al-Ḥulla al-siyarā fī madḥ khayr al-warā*, ed. al-Sayyid ʿAbdallāh Makhlaṣ, Cairo 1347[/1928–9].

Ibn Maʿṣūm, ʿAlī b. Aḥmad, *Anwār al-rabīʿ fī anwāʿ al-badīʿ*, ed. Shākir Hādī Shukr, 7 vols., al-Najaf 1968–9.

Ibn al-Naqīb, Abū ʿAbdallāh Jamāl al-Dīn Muḥammad b. Sulayman, *Muqaddimat al-Tafsīr*, ed. Zakariyyā Saʿīd ʿAlī, Cairo 1995.

Ibn Rashīq, Abū ʿAlī al-Ḥasan al-Qayrawānī al-Azdī, *al-ʿUmda fī maḥāsin al-shiʿr wa-ādābihi wa-naqdihi*, ed. Muḥammad Muḥyī l-Dīn ʿAbd al-Ḥamīd, 2 vols., repr. Beirut 1972.

Ibn al-Shaʿʿār, *Qalāʾid al-jumān*, ed. Kāmil Salmān al-Jubūrī, 9 vols., Beirut 2005.

Ibn Ṭabāṭabā, Abū l-Ḥasan Muḥammad b. Aḥmad, *ʿIyār al-shiʿr*, ed. ʿAbd al-ʿAzīz b. Nāṣir al-Māniʿ, Riyadh 1985.

Ibn Ṭabāṭabā, Abū l-Ḥasan Muḥammad b. Aḥmad, *ʿIyār al-shiʿr*, ed. Ṭāhā al-Ḥājirī and Muḥammad Zaghlūl Sallām, Cairo 1956.

al-Iṣfahānī, al-ʿImād, *Kharīdat al-qaṣr wa-jarīdat al-ʿaṣr, Qism shuʿarāʾ al-Shām*, i, ed. Shukrī Fayṣal, Damascus 1955.

al-Jazāʾirī, Ṭāhir b. Ṣāliḥ, *Badīʿ al-Talkhīṣ wa-talkhīṣ al-badīʿ*, lithograph ed. [Damascus] 1296 [/1897].

al-Jurjānī, ʿAbd al-Qāhir, *Dalāʾil al-iʿjāz*, ed. Maḥmūd Muḥammad Shākir, Cairo [1984, date of preface].

al-Jurjānī, Muḥammad b. ʿAlī, *al-Ishārāt wa-l-tanbīhāt fī ʿilm al-balāġa*, ed. ʿAbd al-Qādir Ḥusayn, Cairo 1982.

Kāshifī, Ḥusayn Wāʿiẓ, *Badāʾiʿ al-afkār fī ṣanāʾiʿ al-ashʿār*, ed. Mīr Jalāl al-Dīn Kazzāzī, Tehran 1369/1990.

al-Khafājī, Abū Muḥammad ʿAbdallāh b. Muḥammad Ibn Sinān, *Sirr al-faṣāḥa*, Beirut 1982.

al-Marghīnānī, *al-Maḥāsin fī l-naẓm wa-l-nathr*, see under *Secondary Sources:* Van Gelder.

al-Mutanabbī, Abū l-Ṭayyib, *Dīwān* (with commentary by al-Wāḥidī), ed. F. Dieterici, Berlin 1861.

al-Nābulusī, ʿAbd al-Ghanī, *Nafaḥāt al-azhār wa-nasamāt al-asḥār fī madḥ al-nabī al-mukhtār: Sharḥ al-Badīʿiyya al-muzriya bi-l-ʿuqūd al-jawhariyya*, Būlāq 1299 [/1882].

al-Qarṭājannī, Abū l-Ḥasan Ḥāzim, *Minhāj al-bulaghāʾ wa-sirāj al-udabāʾ*, ed. Muḥammad al-Ḥabīb b. al-Khawja (Belkhodja), Beirut 1966.

al-Qazwīnī, al-Khaṭīb, *al-Īḍāḥ fī ʿulūm al-balāgha*, ed. Muḥammad ʿAbd al-Munʿim Khafājī, Beirut 1971.

al-Rādūyānī, Muḥammad b. ʿUmar, *Tarjumān al-balāgha / Tarcumān al-balāġa*, ed. Ahmed Ateş, Istanbul 1949.

Rāmī, Sharaf al-Dīn, *Ḥaqāʾiq al-ḥadāʾiq*, ed. Sayyid Kāẓim Imām, Tehran 1341/1962.

al-Ṣafadī, Ṣalāḥ al-Dīn Khalīl b. Aybak, *al-Wāfī bi-l-Wafayāt*, 30 vols., Beirut-Wiesbaden-Berlin 1931–2005.

al-Sakkākī, Abū Yaʿqūb Yūsuf b. Abī Bakr, *Miftāḥ al-ʿulūm*, ed. Naʿīm Zarzūr, Beirut 1983.

Shihāb al-Dīn al-Ḥalabī, Abū l-Thanāʾ Maḥmūd b. Sulaymān, *Ḥusn al-tawassul ilā ṣināʿat al-tarassul*, Cairo 1315 [/1897–8].

al-Suyūṭī, Jalāl al-Dīn ʿAbd al-Raḥmān, *al-Itqān fī ʿulūm al-Qurʾān*, ed. Muḥammad Abū l-Faḍl Ibrāhīm, 4 vols., Cairo 1974–5.

al-Suyūṭī, Jalāl al-Dīn, *Naẓm al-badīʿ fī madḥ khayr shafīʿ*, ed. ʿAlī Muḥammad Muʿawwaḍ and ʿĀdil Aḥmad ʿAbd al-Mawjūd, Aleppo 1995.

al-Tahānawī, Muḥammad Aʿlā b. ʿAlī, *Kashshāf iṣṭilāḥāt al-funūn, A Dictionary of the Technical Terms used in the Sciences of the Musalmans*, ed. Aloys Sprenger et al., 2 vols., Calcutta 1862.

al-Ṭībī, Sharaf al-Dīn Ḥusayn b. Muḥammad, *al-Tibyān fī ʿilm al-maʿānī wa-l-badīʿ wa-l-bayān*, ed. Hādī ʿAṭiyya Maṭar al-Hilālī, Beirut 1987.

al-ʿUrḍī, Abū l-Wafāʾ, *Fatḥ al-badīʿ fī ḥall al-Ṭirāz al-badīʿ fī imtidāḥ al-shafīʿ*, ed. Ranā al-Daqqāq, Beirut 2012.

Waṭwāṭ, Rashīd al-Dīn Muḥammad ʿUmarī, *Ḥadāyiq al-siḥr fi daqāyiq al-shiʿr*, ed. ʿAbbās Iqbāl, Tehran [1929].

al-Waʾwāʾ al-Dimashqī, *Dīwān*, ed. Sāmī al-Dahhān, Beirut 1993.

al-Yāzijī, Nāṣīf, *Dīwān: al-Nubdha al-thāniya al-maʿrūfa bi-Nafḥat al-rayḥān*, Beirut 1898.

Secondary Sources

Bauer, Thomas, Die *badīʿiyya* des Nāṣīf al-Yāziǧī und das Problem der spätosmanischen arabischen Literatur, in Angelika Neuwirth and Andreas Christian Islebe (eds.), *Reflections on reflections: Near Eastern writers reading literature; dedicated to Renate Jacobi*, Wiesbaden 2006, 49–118.

Browne, Edward G., *A literary history of Persia*, 4 vols., Cambridge 1908–24, repr. 1956.

Cachia, Pierre, *The arch rhetorician, or the schemer's skimmer: A handbook of late Arabic badīʿ drawn from ʿAbd al-Ghanī an-Nābulsī's* Nafaḥāt al-azhār ʿalā nasamāt al-asḥār, *summarized and systematized*, Wiesbaden 1998.

Chalisova, N., Persian rhetoric: Elm-e badiʾ and elm-e bayan, in J.T.P. de Bruijn (ed.), *General introduction to Persian literature*, London 2009, 139–71.

de Blois, F.C., Rashīd al-Dīn (…) Waṭwāṭ, in *EI*² viii, 444–5.

Gardet, L., Ibdāʿ, in *EI*², iii, 663–4.

Harb, Lara, *Arabic poetics: Aesthetic experience in classical Arabic literature*, Princeton NJ 2020.

Heinrichs, W.P., al-Rādūyānī, in *EI*² viii, 383.

Kīlīṭū, ʿAbd al-Fattāḥ, *al-Adab wa-l-gharāba: Dirāsāt bunyawiyya fī l-adab al-ʿArabī*, Beirut 1983.

Monferrer-Sala, Juan P., Ararat, *EI*³, first published online: 2012; first print edition 2012–4.

Mūsā, Aḥmad Ibrāhīm, *al-Ṣibgh al-badīʿī fī l-lugha al-ʿarabiyya*, Cairo 1388/1969.

Streck, M., Djūdī, in *EI*², ii, 573–4.

van Gelder, Geert Jan, Badīʿiyya, in *EI*³, first published online: 2009; first print edition 2009–4 (94–6).

van Gelder, Geert Jan, Poetry for easy listening: *insijām* and related concepts in Ibn Ḥijjah's *Khizānat al-adab*, in *MSR* 7 (2003 [2002]), 31–48.

van Gelder, Geert Jan, *Sound and sense in Classical Arabic poetry*, Wiesbaden 2013.

van Gelder, Geert Jan, *Two Arabic treatises on stylistics: al-Marghīnānī's* al-Maḥāsin fī ʾl-naẓm wa-ʾl-nathr, *and Ibn Aflaḥ's* Muqaddima, *formerly ascribed to al-Marghīnānī*, Leiden 1987.

9

Das Nilhochwasser von 761/1360 und Ibn Abī Ḥağalas *as-Sağʿ al-ğalīl fī-mā ğarā min an-Nīl*

Werner Diem

1 Einleitung

Vor der Errichtung des Nasser-Staudamms war Ägypten von der jährlichen Nilschwemme abhängig. Als Nilstand, der eine ausreichende Ernte gewährleistete, galt herkömmlicherweise ein Stand von sechzehn Ellen (*wafāʾ*), gemessen im Nilometer (*miqyās*) auf der Nilinsel ar-Rawḍa bei Kairo. Blieb der Nilstand darunter, bedingte die unzureichende Bewässerung des Ackerlandes Teuerung und Hungersnot, und war er wesentlich höher, verursachte dies eine verspätete Aussaat und damit ebenfalls Teuerung und Hungersnot. In beiden Fällen wurden öffentliche Bittgebete abgehalten und sonstige gottgefällige Maßnahmen durchgeführt.[1]

Ein besonders katastrophales Nilhochwasser trat im Jahre 761/1360 ein, und diesem Nilhochwasser hat Ibn Abī Ḥağala (st. 776/1375) eine Schrift mit dem Titel *as-Sağʿ al-ğalīl fī-mā ğarā min an-Nīl* „Die prächtige Reimprosa bezüglich dessen, was seitens des Nils geschehen ist“ gewidmet. Diese Schrift wird zwar in der biographischen Literatur unter den Werken Ibn Abī Ḥağalas erwähnt, doch ist offenbar kein vollständiger Text überliefert. Erhalten sind, soweit mir bekannt, lediglich Auszüge, die von as-Suyūṭī (st. 911/1505)[2] und al-Minūfī[3] (st. 927/1521) zitiert werden. Da sich die Auszüge as-Suyūṭīs und al-Minūfīs nur zum geringsten Teil decken, muß ihnen die Schrift jeweils noch vollständig vorgelegen haben. Dies läßt sich für al-Minūfī auch aus der Art, wie er sich zu den Auszügen äußert, schließen.[4]

1 Siehe hierzu Diem, *Nilbriefe*, Abschnitt 1.1.2. „Nil und Nilschwemme.“

2 As-Suyūṭī, *Kawkab* 339–42 und *Muḥāḍara* ii, 308–10.

3 Al-Minūfī, *Fayḍ* 76–9, 83–5, 86, 95.

4 Zu Weiterem siehe Abschnitt 3.

 DOI:10.1163/9789004521780_011

2 Das Nilhochwasser von 761/1360

Das Nilhochwasser von 761/1360 wird von al-Maqrīzī (st. 845/1442), Ibn Taġrī Birdī (st. 874/1470), al-Ḥiǧāzī (st. 878/1474), as-Suyūṭī (st. 911/1505) und Ibn Iyās (st. 929/1523) erwähnt. Von diesen Autoren fassen sich Ibn Taġrī Birdī[5] und al-Ḥiǧāzī[6] sehr kurz. Die Fakten sind ihnen gemäß wie folgt:

> Ibn Taġrī Birdī: Altes Wasser[7] genau 12 Ellen. Höchststand 24 Ellen. Verwüstung vieler Örtlichkeiten.
>
> al-Ḥiǧāzī: Altes Wasser ungefähr 12 Ellen. *Wafā'* am 6. Misrā.[8] Bei Erreichen von 19 Ellen und 7[9] Fingerbreit Ausrufung der Zunahme eingestellt. Höchststand 24 Ellen. Verwüstung vieler Örtlichkeiten bis zum 5. Bābah.[10]

Ausführlicher äußert sich al-Maqrīzī,[11] der seinerseits von as-Suyūṭī[12] zitiert wird. (Von as-Suyūṭī ausgelassene Teile stehen in eckigen Klammern):

> Der Nil war in diesem Jahr zum Verwundern. Denn der Grund[13] belief sich auf ungefähr 12 Ellen. Der *wafā'* war am [Donnerstag, dem] 6. Mesori, worauf [die Sperre des Kanals[14] am Tag danach, (also) am Freitag, durchbrochen wurde[15] und] für ihn 9 Fingerbreit von 20 Ellen[16] ausgerufen wurden. Hierauf wurde das Ausrufen des Anstiegs eingestellt,[17] worauf er ungefähr 24 Ellen erreichte. Es wurde (durch ihn) eine Reihe von Wohngebäuden verwüstet, und er blieb bis zum 5. Bābah konstant.[18] Am Tag

5 Ibn Taġrī Birdī, *Nuǧūm* x, 338.

6 Al-Ḥiǧāzī, *Fihrist*, fol. 145ᵛ.

7 *Al-mā' al-qadīm.* – Es ist das vom Vorjahr im unteren Bereich des Nilometers verbliebene Wasser gemeint.

8 Koptischer Monat Mesori, der übliche Monat des *wafā'*.

9 وسبع ist sehr wahrscheinlich ein Versehen für وتسع al-Maqrīzīs und as-Suyūṭīs.

10 Koptischer Monat Paophi.

11 Al-Maqrīzī, *Sulūk* iv, 247.

12 As-Suyūṭī, *Kawkab* 339.

13 *Qā'*, der unterste Bereich des Schachtes des Nilometers.

14 Es ist der bei al-Fusṭāṭ nach Kairo abzweigende Kanal gemeint.

15 Zur Durchbrechung des Kanals – d.h. Beseitigung seiner Sperre – im Rahmen der Nil-Zeremonien siehe Diem, *Nilbriefe*, Abschnitt 1.1.8. „Begehung des *wafā'*-Festes."

16 Sc. 19 Ellen und 9 Fingerbreit.

17 Der Nilstand wurde täglich vom Aufseher des Nilometers ausgerufen. Das Einstellen der Ausrufung bei zu geringem oder zu hohem Nilstand diente dazu, die Bevölkerung nicht weiter zu beunruhigen.

18 Das Hochwasser hatte also genau zwei Monate gedauert.

> danach gingen die Leute hinaus[19] und beteten zu Gott, worauf er sofort um vier Fingerbreit fiel.

Das leicht gekürzte Zitat as-Suyūṭīs von al-Maqrīzīs Bericht wird von Ibn Iyās in seinen Annalen[20] mehr oder weniger in eigenen Worten referiert, allerdings nur bis zum Ende des Satzes, der vom Erreichen von 24 Ellen handelt. Er beschließt sein Referat mit den Worten „Dies führt Scheich Ǧalāl ad-Dīn ʿAbd ar-Raḥmān al-Asyūṭī in seinem *Kawkab ar-rawḍa* titulierten Buch nach al-Maqrīzī – Gott erbarme sich seiner! – an." Hierauf folgen Ausführungen zum weiteren Verlauf des Nilhochwassers:[21]

> Als sich diese Angelegenheit immer mehr verschärfte, befahl der Herrscher dem Nachfahren Abū r-Raddāds,[22] das Ausrufen des Anstiegs (des Nils) in diesen Tagen einzustellen. Der Nil blieb bei diesem seinem Stand bis zum 20. Bābah. Die Leute wurden wegen dieses Stands (des Nils) beunruhigt und begannen in den Moscheen und Wallfahrtsstätten zu Gott um Fallen (des Nils) zu beten. Es entstand den Leuten dadurch[23] außerordentlich viel Schaden, denn die Straßen waren für die Reisenden abgeschnitten, so daß sie am Reisen gehindert wurden. Es wurde Ǧazīrat al-Fīl[24] überschwemmt, das Wasser reichte bis an die Häuser von al-Ḥusayniyya,[25] und das Wasser sprudelte aus dem Reinigungsbecken[26] der Ḥākim-Moschee beim Bāb al-Futūḥ. Es kamen (außerdem) Nachrichten, daß der Deich von al-Fayyūm kollabiert sei und die Ländereien von al-Fayyūm überschwemmt worden seien. Es wurden (auch)

19 Bei Gebeten für das Steigen oder Fallen des Nils begaben sich die Einwohner von Kairo gewöhnlich vor die Stadt. Da nun aber Ibn Iyās von einem Bittgebet al-Bulqīnīs in der Azhar-Moschee berichtet, ist hier wohl gemeint, daß die Menschen ihre Häuser zum gemeinschaftlichen Gebet verließen.

20 Ibn Iyās, *Badāʾiʿ* i, 1, 569.

21 Ibn Iyās, *Badāʾiʿ* i, 1, 569–70.

22 Die Nachfahren Abū r-Raddāds, des ersten muslimischen Aufsehers des Nilometers, hatten dieses Amt traditionell inne. Siehe hierzu Diem, *Nilbriefe*, Abschnitt 1.1.8.9. „Die Nachfahren Abū r-Raddāds als Betreuer des Nilometers."

23 Sc. durch das Hochwasser.

24 Gebiet nordwestlich von Kairo außerhalb des damaligen Bāb al-Baḥr, ehemals eine Nilinsel, die an der östlichen Seite mit dem Festland verschmolzen war (al-Maqrīzī, *Mawāʿiẓ* iii, 590–1).

25 Stadtviertel außerhalb der nördlichen Stadtmauer hinter dem Bāb al-Futūḥ. – Ibn Iyās, *Badāʾiʿ* الحسينة.

26 *Mīḍaʾa*, Becken für die rituelle Waschung.

> Dār an-Nuḥās[27] und die Ländereien von ar-Rawḍa[28] überschwemmt, und das Wasser sprudelte am Großen Deich (al-Ǧisr al-Aʿẓam)[29] hervor, der sich in der Nähe von Qanāṭir as-Sibāʿ[30] befindet. Es war eine entsetzliche Angelegenheit, und die Leute dachten, daß Gott, der Erhabene, ihnen die Sintflut gesandt habe. Als die Beunruhigung der Leute wegen dieser Angelegenheit immer stärker wurde, zog Šayḫ al-Islām Sirāǧ ad-Dīn ʿUmar al-Bulqīnī[31] zur Azhar-Moschee und betete zu Gott, dem Erhabenen. Da fiel er in einer einzigen Nacht um vier Fingerbreit und nahm jeden Tag kontinuierlich ab, bis die Straßen wieder zum Vorschein kamen. Den Landwirten entstand dadurch außerordentlich viel Schaden, weil die Ländereien hoch überschwemmt worden waren und das Wasser auf ihnen stagnierte.

In seiner Schrift *Nubḏa laṭīfa fī ḏikr an-Nīl al-mubārak* „Feinsinniges Traktat über die Erwähnung des gesegneten Nils“[32] gibt Ibn Iyās einen zwar entsprechenden, im Detail aber doch etwas anderen Bericht über das Hochwasser von 761/1360. Er zählt zunächst kurz die Fakten auf: alter Stand 12 Ellen, *wafāʾ* am 6. Misrā, höchster Stand 24 Ellen „gemäß dem von al-Maqrīzī in *al-Ḫiṭaṭ* Überlieferten.“ Dies – d.h. den Stand von 24 Ellen – hätten, so fährt er fort, einige bestritten, doch werde die Angabe al-Maqrīzīs von den Ausführungen as-Suyūṭīs in *Kawkab ar-Rawḍa* und den Ausführungen al-Maqrīzīs „in der Herrschaft von an-Nāṣir Ḥasan b. Muḥammad b. Qalāwūn,“ womit er auf den oben zitierten Abschnitt in al-Maqrīzīs Annalen verweist, gestützt. Da as-Suyūṭī in *Kawkab ar-Rawḍa* al-Maqrīzī ohne weitere Angabe zur Quelle zitiert, war Ibn Iyās wohl auch die Vorlage as-Suyūṭīs in al-Maqrīzīs Annalen unmittelbar bekannt. Was hingegen Ibn Iyās' Verweis auf al-Maqrīzīs *Ḫiṭaṭ* angeht, so ist es mir jedenfalls nicht gelungen, dort einen solchen Bericht festzustellen.[33] Ibn Iyās' Bericht in *Nubḏa* über die Ereignisse nach der Erreichung von 24 Ellen lautet wie folgt:

27 Viertel in Munšaʾat al-Mahrānī, einem Gebiet nordwestlich von al-Fusṭāṭ (al-Maqrīzī, *Ḫiṭaṭ* ii, 164–6; Karte *Ḫiṭaṭ* ii, 37).

28 Nilinsel bei al-Fusṭāṭ, an deren südlicher Spitze sich der Nilometer befindet.

29 Der Deich erstreckte sich zwischen Birkat al-Fīl und Birkat Qārūn von al-Kabš bis Qanāṭir as-Sibāʿ (al-Maqrīzī, *Ḫiṭaṭ* iii, 444, 534, 552).

30 Gebiet nordwestlich von al-Fusṭāṭ (al-Maqrīzī, *Ḫiṭaṭ* iii, 450).

31 Sirāǧ ad-Dīn ʿUmar b. Raslān al-Bulqīnī al-Kinānī al-ʿAsqalānī (st. 805/1403), ein angesehener Religionsgelehrter.

32 Ibn Iyās, *Nubḏa*, fol. 140r–140v.

33 Ich habe hierfür u. a. sämtliche Stellen für النيل gemäß dem Index von *Ḫiṭaṭ* durchgesehen.

> Da befahl er[34] das Ausrufen des Anstiegs (des Nils) einzustellen, nachdem sich die Leute vor einer Überschwemmung fürchteten. Der Nil blieb bis zum 25. Bābah konstant, ohne zu fallen, so daß den Leuten außerordentlich viel Schaden entstand. Denn der Deich von al-Fayyūm wurde (durch ihn) durchbrochen, die Gärten von Ǧazīrat al-Fīl wurden überschwemmt und die Straße nach Šubrā und al-Minya[35] wurde überschwemmt. Das Wasser reichte bis an die Häuser von al-Ḥusayniyya, so daß es überschwemmt wurde. Es liefen die Brunnen über und das Wasser sprudelte (aus dem Boden), bis es ihr Gebiet[36] bedeckte. Die Straßen nach Būlāq wurden an einigen Stellen abgeschnitten, und es wurden einige Häuser verwüstet. Er blieb bis Ende Bābah konstant (24 Ellen hoch), was man weder in der Ǧāhiliyya noch im Islām erlebt hatte. Eine solche Zunahme war noch nie eingetreten, noch hatte man ihresgleichen vernommen. Da zogen die Leute hinaus in die Wüste und vollzogen Bittgebete, worauf das Wasser an jenem Tag um vier Fingerbreit fiel.

Ibn Iyās hat also zwei Schilderungen des Hochwassers geliefert, wobei er dessen Auswirkungen, von der Ǧazīrat al-Fīl und dem Viertel al-Ḥusayniyya abgesehen, an unterschiedlichen Lokalitäten veranschaulicht. Ein wesentlicher Unterschied betrifft Ibn Iyās' Angabe zum Zeitpunkt, da das Wasser zu sinken begann. In *Badāʾiʿ* ist es der 20. Paophi und in *Nubḏa* der 25. Paophi bzw. Ende Paophi, während es gemäß al-Maqrīzī der 5. Paophi war. Hiervon ist das Datum 25. Paophi unter überlieferungsgeschichtlichen Gesichtspunkten am plausibelsten, weil bei dieser Annahme die Daten 20. Paophi und 5. Paophi so erklärt werden können, daß jeweils ein Element der Zahl 25 entfallen ist. Ibn Iyās' Quelle für seine beiden zusätzlichen Berichte ist unbekannt.

Die Verbindung der Nilschwemme von 761/1360, wie sie von al-Maqrīzī, Ibn Taġrī Birdī, al-Ḥiǧāzī, as-Suyūṭī und Ibn Iyās geschildert wird, mit Ibn Abī Ḥaǧalas *as-Saǧʿ al-ǧalīl* geht aus Vermerken as-Suyūṭīs und Ibn Iyās' im Anschluß an ihre Beschreibung der Nilschwemme hervor.

> Über dieses Ereignis hat der Literat Šihāb ad-Dīn Ibn Abī Ḥaǧala einen Brief mit dem Titel *as-Saǧʿ al-ǧalīl fī-mā ǧarā min an-Nīl* verfaßt (as-Suyūṭī, *Kawkab*).

34 Sc. der Herrscher.

35 Šubrā al-Ḫayma grenzte nördlich und Minyat as-Sīraǧ östlich an Ǧazīrat al-Fīl an. Siehe die Karte in al-Maqrīzī, *Ḫiṭaṭ* iii, 591.

36 Sc. das Gebiet von al-Ḥusayniyya.

> Über dieses Ereignis hat Scheich Šihāb ad-Dīn Ibn Abī Ḥağala eine feinsinnige Maqāma verfaßt, die Poesie und Prosa über dieses Thema enthält (Ibn Iyās, *Badāʾiʿ*).
>
> Über dieses Ereignis hat Scheich Šihāb ad-Dīn Ibn Abī Ḥağala eine bewunderungswürdige Maqāma verfaßt, die er *as-Sağʿ al-ğalīl fī-mā ğarā min an-Nīl* nannte (Ibn Iyās, *Nubḏa*).

Nur in as-Suyūṭīs *Kawkab* folgen auf die zitierte Bemerkung Auszüge aus *as-Sağʿ al-ğalīl*, hingegen nicht in Ibn Iyās' *Badāʾiʿ* und *Nubḏa*. Wenn Ibn Iyās Ibn Abī Ḥağalas Schrift eine Maqāma nennt, so liegt dem vielleicht eine Verwechslung mit Ibn Abī Ḥağalas gemäß as-Suyūṭī[37] im Jahre 773/1371–2 verfaßten *al-Maqāma az-zaʿfarāniyya*[38] zugrunde, die ebenfalls eine Nilüberschwemmung zum Thema hat und zahlreiche Zitate aus *as-Sağʿ al-ğalīl* enthält.[39] Eine solche Verwechslung findet sich nachweislich in al-Ġuzūlīs *Maṭāliʿ al-budūr fī manāzil as-surūr*.[40] Dort ist von einem Auszug aus *as-Sağʿ al-ğalīl* über *qulqās* „Kolokasie" die Rede, während der Auszug in Wirklichkeit aus *al-Maqāma az-zaʿfarāniyya* stammt.

3 Auszüge aus *as-Sağʿ al-ğalīl fī-mā ğarā min an-Nīl*

Die Auszüge aus *as-Sağʿ al-ğalīl* finden sich, wie eingangs erwähnt, in as-Suyūṭī, *Kawkab*, 339–42/*Muḥāḍara*, 308–10 und in al-Minūfī, *Fayḍ* 76–9, 83–5, 86, 95. In *Kawkab* folgen sie auf die Nachricht al-Maqrīzīs über das Nilhochwasser von 761/1360, während sie in *Muḥāḍara* und *Fayḍ* ohne solchen Bezug zitiert werden.

Die Auszüge von *Kawkab/Muḥāḍara* und *Fayḍ* überschneiden sich nur in einem einzigen Abschnitt, der Beschreibung der Ankunft des Nils („Ankunft"). Hierauf folgt in *Kawkab/Muḥāḍara* ein Abschnitt über das Hochwasser in Hinblick auf diverse Lokalitäten („Hochwasser"), in *Kawkab* ohne Übergang, in *Muḥāḍara* eingeleitet mit *ilā an qāla*, während in *Fayḍ* ein Abschnitt über den Rückgang des Nils („Rückgang") folgt, eingeleitet mit *wa-qāla ayḍan*. Da der Abschnitt „Rückgang" logischerweise auf den Abschnitt „Hochwasser" folgen sollte, ist zu vermuten, daß die Reihenfolge wohl „Ankunft" – „Hochwasser" – „Rückgang" war. Auf den Abschnitt „Rückgang" folgen in *Fayḍ* Zitate Ibn Abī

37 As-Suyūṭī, *Kawkab* 344.

38 Ibn Abī Ḥağala, al-Maqāma az-zaʿfarāniyya, 275–89.

39 Siehe hierzu entsprechende Vermerke in Abschnitt 4.

40 Al-Ġuzūlī, *Maṭāliʿ* ii, 52–3.

Ḥağalas aus Nilbriefen von fünf Autoren, eingeleitet mit *ṯumma naqala* (*fīhi*) *ʿan* und einem sechsten Zitat aus einem eigenen Nilbrief („Prosazitate"). Die Art der Anknüpfung der Prosazitate zeigt, daß sie auf den Abschnitt „Rückgang" gefolgt waren. Schließlich werden in *Fayḍ* noch in anderen Kontexten zwei Gruppen poetischer Zitate – Distichen, daneben Gedichte mit drei oder vier Versen – angeführt, bei denen offen ist, wo ihr Platz in der Schrift gewesen ist. Da diese beiden Gruppen nur durch einen kurzen anderen Text getrennt aufeinander folgen, wird dies auch ihre Reihenfolge in der Schrift gewesen sein.

Wie aus der Formulierung der Abschnitte „Ankunft" und „Rückgang" hervorgeht, hatte *as-Sağʿ al-ğalīl* die Form eines Briefes. Der Adressat ist nicht bekannt, doch spielt dies keine Rolle, da der Text zwar Briefform hat, in Wirklichkeit aber, einem damaligen Usus folgend, sein Thema auf höchst literarische Weise behandelt. Vermutlich war der Text umfangreicher, als es die Auszüge vermuten lassen, da ihn al-Minūfī an einer Stelle als *Kitāb as-Sağʿ al-ğalīl* bezeichnet.[41] Im folgenden sollen die Abschnitte in der oben rekonstruierten Reihenfolge näher vorgestellt werden.

A. Beschreibung des Anstiegs des Nils (*Kawkab*, 339–40; *Muḥāḍara*, 308–9; *Fayḍ*, 76–7). Der Auszug beginnt mit „Was den Nil betrifft, auf dem der Titel dieses dienstfertigen Schreibens beruht, so frage nicht, was von ihm geschehen ist," woraus hervorgeht, daß der Titel der Schrift von Ibn Abī Ḥağala selbst stammt. Text und Übersetzung in Abschnitt 4.1.

B. Kontakt des Nils mit diversen Lokalitäten (*Kawkab*, 340–2; *Muḥāḍara*, 309–10).

a) Dayr aṭ-Ṭīn.[42]
b) al-Ğīza.
c) ar-Rawḍa. In diesem Textteil wird nach einem Kolonpaar und einem Vers die Reaktion bestimmter Arten von Menschen auf das Hochwasser geschildert. Text und Übersetzung in Abschnitt 4.2.
d) al-Ğazīra al-Wusṭā.[43]
e) al-Munšaʾa.[44]

---

41 Al-Minūfī, *Fayḍ* 86.

42 Am Ostufer des Nils südlich von al-Fusṭāṭ und westlich von Birkat al-Ḥabaš gelegener Ort (al-Maqrīzī, *Ḫiṭaṭ* iii, 396; iv, 4, 1031).

43 Nilinsel nördlich der Insel ar-Rawḍa, heute al-Ğazīra.

44 Munšaʾat al-Mahrānī, Gebiet zwischen Nil und Nilkanal nordwestlich von al-Fusṭāṭ (al-Maqrīzī, *Ḫiṭaṭ* ii, 164).

f) Būlāq.

g) al-Ḫalīǧ al-Ḥākimī.[45] Text und Übersetzung in Abschnitt 4.3.

Von diesen Lokalitäten sind Dayr aṭ-Ṭīn, al-Ǧīza, ar-Rawḍa, al-Ǧazīra al-Wusṭā und Būlāq in Süd-Nord-Richtung erwähnt. Hingegen zweigt der Nilkanal (al-Ḫalīǧ al-Ḥākimī), der nach al-Munša'a erwähnt ist, südlich von al-Munša'a ab, das seinerseits südlich von al-Ǧazīra al-Wusṭā liegt. Die Aufzählung der Örtlichkeiten folgt also nur teilweise dem Verlauf des Nils in Süd-Nord-Richtung. Mit den von Ibn Iyās in seinen beiden Beschreibungen der Nilschwemme genannten Örtlichkeiten überschneiden sich diese Örtlichkeiten nur in ar-Rawḍa und Būlāq. Ein Unterschied besteht auch darin, daß Ibn Iyās überwiegend Orte nördlich von Kairo anführt, während die in *as-Saǧʿ al-ǧalīl* angeführten Orte überwiegend südlich von Kairo liegen.

C. Beschreibung des Rückgangs des Nils (*Fayḍ*, 77). Der Auszug beginnt mit „Aber zur Stunde, da der Sklave dieses untertänige Schreiben verfaßt, hat er zu fallen begonnen." Text und Übersetzung in Abschnitt 4.4.

D. Prosazitate Ibn Abī Ḥaǧalas (*Fayḍ*, 75–9)

a) Zitat aus einem Brief Scheich Nūr ad-Dīns, Enkel von Scheich ʿUmar b. al-Fāriḍ,[46] an al-Qāḍī Muʿīn ad-Dīn, Nāẓir al-Ǧayš von Damaskus.[47]

b) Zitat aus einem Brief Ibn Nubātas. Ediert in Diem, *Nilbriefe*, als INub3 in Abschnitt 2.10.

c) Zitat nach Šams ad-Dīn Ibn al-ʿAfīf at-Tilimsānī.[48]

d) Zitat aus einem Brief as-Sayyid Šaraf ad-Dīns.[49]

e) Zitat aus einem Brief Ṣalāḥ ad-Dīn aṣ-Ṣafadīs. Das Zitat ist Teil eines Nilbriefes, der in anderen Quellen vollständiger überliefert ist. Ediert in Diem, *Nilbriefe*, als ṢṢaf2 in Abschnitt 2.9.

f) Zitat aus einem Brief Ibn Abī Ḥaǧalas an Ibn Nubāta.

45 Kanal, der gegenüber der Insel ar-Rawḍa bei al-Fusṭāṭ in Richtung Kairo abzweigte. Er wurde Ende des 19. Jahrhunderts zugeschüttet. Seinem Verlauf folgt die heutige Straße Šāriʿ Būr [Port] Saʿīd.

46 Ibn al-Fāriḍ (st. 632/1235), der berühmte Mystiker. Über seinen Enkel Nūr ad-Dīn, von dem hier die Rede ist, konnte ich nichts Näheres eruieren.

47 Hibat Allāh b. Masʿūd b. Abī l-Faḍā'il al-Qāḍī Muʿīn ad-Dīn b. Ḥašīš (st. 739/1338–9), in den Jahren 722–8/1322-1327-8 Nāẓir al-Ǧayš in Damaskus. Aus jener Zeit muß der an ihn gerichtete Brief Nūr ad-Dīns stammen. Siehe zu ihm aṣ-Ṣafadī, *Wāfī* xxvii, 326–8.

48 Muḥammad b. ʿAfīf ad-Dīn Sulaymān b. ʿAlī at-Tilimsānī (st. 688/1289). Siehe zu ihm aṣ-Ṣafadī, *Wāfī* iii, 129–36.

49 Nicht identifiziert.

E. Poetische Zitate Ibn Abī Ḥaǧalas

a) Zitate in *Fayḍ*, 83–5, Abschnitt *Ḏikru baʿḍi mā nuẓima fī z-ziyādati wa-l-wafāʾi wa-n-Nīli*
Zitierte Dichter: Ibn aṣ-Ṣāḥib (st. 788/1386), al-Miʿmār (st. 749/1348–9), Ḫalīl al-Hamdānī al-Kaftī,[50] Muḥammad b. al-Ḥusayn,[51] as-Sirāǧ al-Warrāq (st. 695/1296), Tamīm b. al-Muʿizz (st. 374/984), Ibn aṣ-Ṣāʾiġ (st. 720/1320), ʿUmar b. al-Wardī (st. 749/1349), zwei Anonymi. – Die Verse Ḫalīl al-Hamdānī al-Kaftīs sind auch in *Fayḍ*, 95, zitiert, eingeleitet mit *wa-qad taqaddama ʿani s-Saǧʿi l-ǧalīli qawlu l-Hamdāniyyi l-Kaftiyyi.*

b) Zitate in *Fayḍ*, 86, Abschnitt *Ḏikru mā qīla fī s-sufuni*
Zitierte Dichter: Ibn Abī Ḥaǧala, Ibn Tamīm (st. 684/1285), Abū l-Ḥusayn al-Ǧazzār (st. 679/1281). – Schlußbemerkung al-Minūfīs: „Ich sage: Das, auf dessen Erwähnung sich der Verfasser dieser Handschrift (*aṣl*) beschränkt, hat er dem vorhin erwähnten *Kitāb as-Saǧʿ al-ǧalīl* entnommen und es entsprechend der Anordnung der Handschrift zitiert.“

4 Edition und Interpretation ausgewählter Teile

Etliche Passagen und Verse von *as-Saǧʿ al-ǧalīl* sind in Ibn Abī Ḥaǧalas *al-Maqāma az-zaʿfarāniyya* (MaqZaʿf) zitiert. Die Stellen sind in den Editionstexten mit *…* markiert.

4.1 *Anstieg des Nils (Abschnitt A)*

Quellen: *Kawkab, Muḥāḍara, Fayḍ.*

Drei Stellen, hiervon die letzte ein Vers, sind in MaqZaʿf 280, 287, 276 zitiert.

وأمّا البَحْرُ[52] الذى بُنِيَ عليه عُنوانُ هذه العُبُوديّة فلا تسأل عمّا جرى منه،[53] وما نَقَلَت الرُّواةُ[54] من العجائب عنه، وذلك[55] أنّه عَمَّ[56] في أوّلِ[57] قدومه بالنفع[58] البِلاد، وساوَى

50 Nicht identifiziert.

51 Nicht identifiziert.

52 *Fayḍ* النيل.

53 *Fayḍ* عنه.

54 *Kawkab* الوراق.

55 *Kawkab* والذى.

56 *Fayḍ* علّم.

57 في أوّل fehlt in *Kawkab*.

58 *Kawkab* بنفع.

بين بُطُون الأودية وظُهُور[59] الوِهاد، وقَدِمَ المُفْرَدُ مبشِّرًا بوفائه في جَمْعٍ لا نظيرَ له في الآحاد، واحمرَّت[60] على من طَلَبَ الغَلاءَ عُيُونُه، وتكفَّل للمُعْسِر بأن تُوفَى[61] بعد وفائه[62] دُيُونُه، ونَزَلَ السِّعْرُ حين أَخَذَ منه الطالعُ[63] ⟨في⟩[64] الارتفاع، وأَحْدَقَ بالقُرَى فأصبح كأنّه سماواتٌ[65] كواكبُها الضِّياع، فلم يكن بعد ذلك ﴿إِلَّا كَلَمْحِ[66] البَصَرِ أَوْ هُوَ أَقْرَبَ﴾[67]، حتّى عَسَلَ في شوارعِ مِصْرَ كما عَسَلَ[68] الطريقَ الثعلب، وجاسَ خِلالَ ديارِها فأصبح على زَرابِيِّها[69] المبثوثةِ بَسْطَة، *وأحاط بمَرْكَزِ المقياس[70] إحاطةَ الدائرة بالنُّقْطَة*، ثمّ عَلَت أمواجُه واشتدّ اضطرابُه، وكاد يَمتزِج *بنَهْرِ المَجَرَّة الذي الغمامُ زَبَدُه والنجومُ حَبابُه* [من الطويل]

وَشَرَّقَ حَتَّى لَيْسَ لِلشَّرْقِ مَشْرِقٌ وَغَرَّبَ حَتَّى لَيْسَ لِلغَرْبِ مَغْرِبُ[71]

Was das Gewässer angeht, auf dem der Titel dieses dienstfertigen Schreibens beruht,[72] so frage nicht, was seitens seiner geschehen ist / und welch unerhörte Dinge die Überlieferer über ihn berichten. Und zwar ließ er zu Beginn seines Kommens dem ganzen Land seinen Nutzen zuteil werden / und behandelte die Bäuche der Täler und die Rücken der Anhöhen auf gleiche Weise,[73] / nachdem der Einzelbote[74] die frohe Botschaft seines *wafāʾ* in Form einer Addition, die nicht ihresgleichen unter den Einerzahlen hatte,[75] überbracht hatte.

---

59 *Muḥāḍara* ظهورها.

60 *Kawkab* واحمرّ.

61 *Muḥāḍara* يوفي.

62 بعد وفائه fehlt in *Fayḍ*.

63 *Kawkab* und *Muḥāḍara* طالع.

64 Die Ergänzung des in allen Quellen fehlenden *fī* – und nicht von *bi-* – orientiert sich an *aḫaḏa fī l-inḥiṭāṭ* von Abschnitt C „Rückgang des Nils“.

65 *Fayḍ* سموات.

66 Alle drei Quellen كلمح.

67 Q 16:77.

68 *Fayḍ* zweimal غسل; *Muḥāḍara* عسر statt des zweiten عسل.

69 *Muḥāḍara* زرائبها.

70 *Muḥāḍara* بالمقياس.

71 Vers nur in *Kawkab*/*Muḥāḍara*.

72 Sc. der Titel *as-Saǧʿ al-ǧalīl fī-mā ǧarā min an-Nīl*. Aus der Stelle ist zu schließen, daß bereits Ibn Abī Ḥaǧala seiner Risāla diesen Titel gegeben hatte.

73 Der Nil füllte die Täler und überstieg oder umfloß die Anhöhen.

74 Der Einzelbote (*mufrad*) überbrachte von Qūṣ die Nachricht der Nilschwemme nach Kairo. Siehe hierzu Diem, *Nilbriefe*, Abschnitt 1.1.4. „Nachricht aus Qūṣ über den Beginn der Nilschwelle“.

75 Addiert werden bei dieser mathematischen Metapher der Ausgangsstand des Nils zu Beginn der Nilschwelle (*al-māʾ al-qadīm* „altes Wasser,“ *al-qāʿ* „der Grund“ oder *al-qāʿida*

Es röteten sich seine Augen gegen die Spekulanten, / und er verbürgte sich gegenüber dem Bedürftigen, daß seine Schulden nach dem *wafā'* voll beglichen würden.[76] Es fielen die Preise, als sein Aszendent zu steigen begann,[77] / und er umgab die Dörfer, so daß es so wurde, als sei er Himmel, deren Sterne die Dörfer seien.[78] So war er denn danach geradezu (so schnell) ‚wie ein Augenblick oder (noch) schneller' [Q 16:177], / bis er schließlich sich hin- und herbewegend durch die Straßen von Kairo lief, ‚wie der Fuchs sich hin- und herbewegend auf dem Weg läuft.'[79] Er spähte zwischen den Häusern herum, so daß er zu weiter Ausdehnung auf ihren ausgebreiteten Teppichen wurde,[80] und er umgab das Zentrum, das der *miqyās* war, wie es ein Kreis mit einem Punkt tut.[81] Hierauf wurden seine Wellen höher und er kam in noch heftigere Bewegung, / und er vermischte sich beinahe mit dem Milchstraßen-Fluß, dessen Schaum die Wolken und dessen Blasen die Sterne sind.[82]

„die Basis") und der während der Nilschwelle erfolgte Anstieg (*ziyāda*). Diese Addition ergab den tatsächlichen Nilstand. Die „Addition" ergab eine Zahl höher als neun, also zehn Ellen oder mehr.

76 Das erste Kolon ist von Ibn Ḥiǧǧa (st. 837/1433) in seinem Nilbrief von 819/1416 aufgenommen worden: *wa-lākinnahu ḥmarrat ʿuyūnuhu ʿalā n-nāsi bi-ziyādatin* „Aber seine Augen röteten sich zunehmend gegen die Menschen" (Diem, *Nilbriefe*, IḤiǧǧ in Abschnitt 2.12.). Auf der realen Ebene sind mit den Augen des Nils seine Strudel und mit ihrer Rötung die Färbung des Nils mit rötlichem Schlamm gemeint. Zugleich drückt die Metapher der Rötung der Augen aus, daß der Nil vor Zorn entbrannte, was wiederum impliziert, daß er in turbulenter Zunahme begriffen war. Das zweite Kolon drückt aus, daß eine ausreichende Nilschwemme zu günstigen wirtschaftlichen Verhältnissen führen würde.

77 Der Nil stieg an, und dies war ein glückliches Zeichen.

78 Daß der Nil bei der Nilschwemme gleichsam ein Himmel und die Dörfer die Sterne darin sind, ist ein altererbtes Motiv. Siehe hierzu Diem, *Nilbriefe*, Abschnitt 1.1.2. „Nil und Nilschwemme".

79 *kamā ʿasala ṭ-ṭarīqa ṯ-ṯaʿlabu* ist, worauf der Editor von *Muḥāḍara* hinweist, das Zitat eines Verses Sāʿida b. Ǧuʾayyas (Hell, *Huḏailiten* ii, 14, Vers 61): „Eine (für die Hand) angenehme (Lanze), deren Schaft sich, wenn die Hand sie schüttelt, in ihr hin- und herbewegt (d.h. schwingt), wie der Fuchs sich (beim Laufen) auf dem Weg hin- und herbewegt."

80 *wa-ǧāsa ḫilāla diyārihā*, das eine Anspielung auf Q 17:5 ist, und *zarābiyyihā l-mabṯūṯati* sind Zitate eines Kolonpaares eines Nilbriefes Ibn ʿAbd aẓ-Ẓāhirs (st. 692/1293), das von diversen Autoren, darunter Ṣalāḥ ad-Dīn aṣ-Ṣafadī, Ibn Nubāta und Ibn Makānis, zitiert worden ist. Siehe hierzu einen Abschnitt in Diem, *Nilbriefe*, nach der Übersetzung von ṢṢafi in Abschnitt 2.9.

81 Bei *iḥāṭata d-dāʾirati bi-n-nuqṭati* ist im Doppelsinn „wie es ein Strudel mit einem Tropfen (Wasser) tut" mitgemeint.

82 Das Kolon zitiert die Stelle eines Nilbriefes Ṣalāḥ ad-Dīn aṣ-Ṣafadīs (st. 764/1363): „und er hatte zugenommen, bis er sich beinahe mit dem Fluß der Milchstraße vermischte" (Diem, *Nilbriefe*, ṢṢaf2 in Abschnitt 2.9.).

Er ging in den Osten, so daß der Osten keinen Sonnenaufgang, * und er ging in den Westen, so daß der Westen keinen Sonnenuntergang mehr hatte.[83]

4.2 *Insel Rawḍa einschließlich der Reaktion bestimmter Arten von Menschen* (*Abschnitt Bc*)

Quellen: *Kawkab* und *Muḥāḍara*.

Der Anfang einschließlich des Verses ist in MaqZaʿf 280 zitiert.

Die behandelten Menschen sind der Reisende, der Weber, der Astrologe, der Dichter, der Metriker und der Grammatiker. Die Aussagen über diese Personen enthalten, vom Reisenden abgesehen, Fachtermini, die der realen Ebene angehören, wie auch solche Wörter, die sowohl in ihrer Grundbedeutung wie auch in ihrer Funktion als Fachtermini gelesen werden können. Da das Unglück des Nilhochwassers im Vordergrund steht, werden in der Übersetzung Wörter, die im Doppelsinn interpretierbar sind, primär gemäß der normalen Bedeutung und sekundär gemäß der Bedeutung als Fachterminus aufgefaßt. Die sekundären Lesarten, die in die Anmerkungen verwiesen sind, ergeben zwar für sich genommen auf fachterminologischer Ebene durchaus Sinn, doch besteht kaum einen Bezug zur konkreten Situation auf der realen Ebene. Der besseren Übersichtlichkeit halber sind die Personen in der Übersetzung durchnumeriert.

وأما الروضة فقد *أحاط بها إحاطةَ الكِمام بزَهْرِه، والكأس بحَباب خَمْرِه [من الكامل]

فَكَأَنَّها فِيهِ بِساطٌ أَخْضَرٌ   فَكَأَنَّهُ فِيها طِرازٌ مُذْهَبُ*

فكم بها من متْهِمٍ ومُنْجِد، ومُسافرٍ مما حصل له من المُقيمِ المُقْعِد، وحائكٍ أصبح حول نوْلَه يَنِير، وجعل من غَزْلِه بل من غَيْظِه على أجيره يَحْمِلُ ويَسِير، ومنجِّمٍ وصل الماءُ من منزله إلى العتبة الخارجة فأصبح في أَنْحَس[84] تقويم، ودخل إلى بيّت أَمْراضه ﴿فَنَظَرَ نَظْرَةً فِي النُّجُومِ فَقَالَ إِنِّي سَقِيمٌ﴾،[85] فأصبح في الطريق وعليه كآبةٌ وصُفْرَةَ، ودُمُوعُه في المَحاجِر كالحَصَى لها اجتماع وحُمْرَةَ، وشاعرٍ أوقعه في الضَّرُورة بَحْرُه المَديد، واشتغل بهدم داره عن بيّت القَصِيد، وعَرُوضِيٍّ ضاقت عليه الدائرةُ فقال هذه[86] الفاصلةُ، وقلع من عَرُوض بيّته وَتَدًا أزعج بقلعه مَفاصِلَه، ونَحْوِيٍّ اشتغل عن زيد وعمرو ببَلِّ كُتُبِه، وذهل حين استوى الماءُ والخَشَبَةَ عن

83 Der Nil füllte die ganze Welt vollkommen aus; es war nichts mehr sichtbar außer ihm.

84 *Kawkab* أحسن.

85 Q 37:88–9.

86 *Kawkab* هي.

المفعول معه والمفعول بِهِ، وطار عقلُه لا سيّما عن تصانيف ابن عُصْفُور، وأُخْبِرَ أن البحر وأثاث بيته جارٌّ ومَجْرُور.

Was ar-Rawḍa betrifft, so hat er sie so umgeben, wie Blütenblätter die Blüte umgeben / und der Becher die Blasen des Weins umgibt.

> Es ist mit ihr so, als sei sie in ihm ein grüner Teppich, * und es ist mit ihm so, als sei er in ihr eine vergoldete Stickerei.[87]

1. Wie so manchen gibt es auf ihr, der sich (am liebsten) in die Tihāma oder den Naǧd begeben / und abreisen möchte, (dies) wegen dessen, was ihm seitens des zu einem Aufenthalt zwingenden Verweilenden geschehen ist,[88]
2. (wie so manchen) Weber, der um seinen Webstuhl herum den Saum (des Tuches) zu besticken begonnen hatte / und sich wegen seines Garns, nein vielmehr wegen seiner Gereiztheit auf seinen Angestellten loszugehen anschickt,[89]
3. (wie so manchen) Astrologen, bei dem das Wasser die Türschwelle seines Hauses erreichte, so daß er in unheilvollste astrologische Berechnung geriet[90] / und das ‚Haus seiner Krankheiten‘[91] betrat, ‚denn er warf einen Blick auf die Gestirne, worauf er sagte: Ich bin krank‘ [Q 37:88–9], so daß er sich auf den Weg machte, während er an Kummer litt und (im Gesicht) gelblich war[92] / und sich seine Tränen in den Augenhöhlen wie Kieselsteine in Steinbrüchen[93] sammelten und (von Blut) rot waren,[94]

87 „vergoldet“ ist eine Anspielung auf die rötliche Farbe des Nilwassers. In Nilbriefen ist des öfteren vom „Gold“ und „Goldstaub“ des Nils die Rede.

88 Der Nil, der „verweilt,“ d.h. dessen Hochwasser fortdauert, zwingt Menschen auf der Insel ar-Rawḍa, die abreisen möchten, zum Aufenthalt, d.h. er hindert sie an der Abreise. Tihāma und Naǧd stehen als Merismus für alle nur möglichen Reiseziele.

89 Vielleicht war dem Weber das Garn für den Saum des Tuches ausgegangen und konnte wegen des Nilhochwassers nicht beschafft werden, weswegen er gereizt war und seinen Zorn an seinem Angestellten ausließ.

90 Die Sterne stehen schlecht für den Astrologen, d.h. er befindet sich in einer sehr schlechten Lage.

91 Astrologische Konstellation von Widder und Mars, die verschiedene Erkrankungen bedingt. Der Astrologe kam durch das Hochwasser in eben diesen Zustand, der sich aber auch aus der Beobachtung der Sterne ergab, und in der Tat zeigte er, wie anschließend berichtet wird, Krankheitssymptome.

92 Erkrankung der Galle (*ṣafrā’*) gehört zu den Krankheiten des „Hauses der Krankheiten.“

93 *maḥāǧir* ist zunächst im Sinn von „Augenhöhlen“ gemeint, wird aber im Kieselsteine-Vergleich in der Bedeutung „Steinbrüche“ impliziert.

94 Das Weinen von Tränen von Blut vor Kummer ist ein übliches dichterisches Motiv.

4. (wie so manchen) Dichter, den sein[95] ausgedehntes Gewässer in Not stürzte,[96] / so daß er durch die Zerstörung seines Hauses vom ‚Hauptvers der Qaṣīda' abgelenkt wurde,[97]

5. (wie so manchen) Metriker, den der Schicksalsschlag (des Hochwassers) bedrückte, so daß er sagte: ‚Dies ist der Einschneidende (Schicksalsschlag),' / nachdem er[98] vom Mittelpfosten seines Zeltes einen Pflock weggerissen hatte, durch dessen Wegreißen er die Verbindungen dieses (Zeltes) in Unordnung gebracht hatte.[99]

6. und (wie so manchen) Grammatiker, der durch die Durchnässung seiner Bücher von *Zayd* und *ʿAmr*[100] abgelenkt wurde / und, als Wasser und Brett[101] gleich hoch waren, vor Verwirrung *al-mafʿūl maʿahū* und *al-mafʿūl bihī*[102] vergaß, und der verrückt wurde, so daß er die Werke Ibn

95 Bezug zunächst auf den Nil und in anderer Lesart auf den Dichter. Siehe die nächste Anmerkung.

96 Alternative Lesart: „(wie so manchen) Dichter, den sein Versmaß Madīd in (poetischen) Zwang (*ḍarūra*) stürzte". Mit *ḍarūra* ist Abweichung von der Norm aufgrund von Metrum oder Reim gemeint.

97 Es korrespondieren *dār* „Haus" und *bayt* von *bayt al-qaṣīd* „der Vers (schlechthin) der Qaṣīda," letzteres hier nicht in der etymologisch zugrundeliegenden Bedeutung „Zelt," sondern in der Bedeutung „Haus." Der Dichter wird also durch die Zerstörung seines Hauses vom „Haus der Qaṣīda" abgelenkt, d. h. er denkt nicht mehr an Dichten.

98 Sc. der Nil.

99 Der Nil hat das Zelt des Metrikers überschwemmt und einen Zeltpflock weggerissen, wodurch das Zelt instabil geworden ist. Die alternative metrische Lesart lautet: „(wie so manchen) Metriker, dem die *dāʾira* zu eng war, so daß er ‚Hier ist eine *fāṣila*' sagte / und aus dem *ʿarūḍ* seines Verses einen *watad* herausriß und damit dic *mafāṣil* dieses (Verses) störte." Bekanntlich bilden gemäß al-Ḫalīls metrischer Theorie jeweils Gruppen bestimmter Versmaße eine *dāʾira* „Kreis". Die *fāṣila* ist die Folge von (K = Konsonant; V = Vokal) KVKVKVK oder KVKVKVKVK, ein *watad* ein kurzes Element mit bestimmter Lautfolge und der *ʿarūḍ* der letzte Versfuß des ersten Halbverses. Mit den *mafāṣil* des Verses sind sehr wahrscheinlich, beeinflußt durch die reale Ebene des Satzes, die *maqāṭiʿ* gemeint, also die Versfüße des Verses. Dem Metriker bot die *dāʾira* nicht genügend Raum, d. h. sein Vers war für die betreffenden Metren zu lang. Er kürzte deshalb den letzten Versfuß des ersten Halbverses (*ʿarūḍ*) um das kurze Element eines *watad*, wodurch er aber eine metrische Störung hervorrief.

100 Sc. von der Beschäftigung mit Grammatik, deren syntaktische Regeln an *Zayd* und *ʿAmr* exemplifiziert werden.

101 Es ist in diesem Kontext wohl die Türschwelle oder der Fußboden des Hauses des Grammatikers gemeint. Allerdings handelt es sich um ein Grammatikerbeispiel; siehe hierzu die nächste Anmerkung.

102 *mafʿūl maʿahū* „das, mit dem zusammen etwas getan wird" bezeichnet den Akkusativ nach *wa-*, das deshalb *wāw al-maʿiyya* heißt, und das vorhergehende *istawā l-māʾu wa-l-ḫašabata* ist ein berühmtes Grammatikerbeispiel hierfür. – *al-mafʿūl bihī* „das, an dem etwas getan wird" bezeichnet das Objekt einer Handlung. Dieses Objekt ist hier der Grammatiker und sein Besitz.

ʿUṣfūrs nicht mehr verstand,[103] / nachdem man ihm berichtet hatte, daß das Gewässer und sein Hausrat Wegschleppendes bzw. Weggeschlepptes waren.[104]

4.3 *al-Ḫalīǧ al-Ḥākimī* (*Abschnitt Bg*)

Quellen: *Kawkab* und *Muḥāḍara*.

Eine Stelle ist in MaqZaʿf 281 zitiert.

وأمّا الخليجُ الحاكميّ فقد *خرج عسكرُ موجه بعد الكَسْر على حَمِيَّة، ومَرَقَ من قُسِيِّ قناطِره كالسَّهْم من الرَّمِيَّة*، وتَواضَعَ حِينَ قَبَّلَ بحارةِ زُوَيْلَةَ عتباتِ غُرَفِها العالية، وترك السقّائين في حالة يعجز عن وصفها صَرِيعُ الدِّلاء وحمَّادُ الراوية، فَأصبحوا من الكَساد وقد سئموا الإقامة، قائلين في شوارع مِصْرَ يا الله السلامة.

Was al-Ḫalīǧ al-Ḥākimī angeht, so zogen die Truppen seiner Wellen nach der Durchbrechung[105] voller Begeisterung los, / und wie ein Pfeil die Jagdbeute, so durchquerte er die Bogen seiner Gewölbebrücken.[106] Er tat demütig, als er im Zuwayla-Viertel[107] die Schwellen der Oberzimmer küßte, / und ließ die Wasserträger in einem Zustand, den zu beschreiben (selbst) Ṣarīʿ ad-Dilāʾ und Ḥammād ar-Rāwiya nicht vermocht hätten.[108] Denn sie fanden (für Wasser) keinen Absatz mehr und waren seiner Anwesenheit überdrüssig, / wobei sie in den Straßen Kairos sagten: ‚O Gott, Rettung!‘

---

103 Ibn ʿUṣfūr al-Išbīlī (st. 669/1270), der bekannte Grammatiker. – Wörtliche Übersetzung des Kolons „und sein Verstand flog insbesondere von den Werken Ibn ʿUṣfūrs weg.“ Hierbei korrespondiert *ṭāra* „er flog“ mit *Ibn ʿUṣfūr* „Sohn eines Sperlings.“ Damit ergibt sich die witzige Bedeutung, daß der Grammatiker nicht einmal mehr die Werke eines Sperlings, die naturgemäß unbedeutend sein mußten, verstehen konnte.

104 Der Nil hatte den Hausrat des Grammatikers mit sich fortgerissen. – *ǧārr* und *maǧrūr* sind zugleich grammatische Termini der Bedeutung „in den Genitiv versetzend“ bzw. „in den Genitiv versetzt.“ In dieser grammatischen Lesart setzte der Nil zwar den Hausrat nicht in den Genitiv, aber er übte zumindest eine Wirkung auf ihn aus.

105 Sc. nach der Durchbrechung der Sperre, die vorher aufgehäuft worden war. Siehe Diem, *Nilbriefe*, Abschnitt 1.1.8.5. „Sperre des Nilkanals.“

106 Das Kolon zitiert das Kolon *wa-maraqa ka-s-sahmi min qusiyyi qanāṭirihi l-mankūsati* eines Nilbriefes Ṣalāḥ ad-Dīn aṣ-Ṣafadīs, der hierbei einen Nilbrief Ibn ʿAbd aẓ-Ẓāhirs zitiert. Siehe einen speziellen Abschnitt in Diem, *Nilbriefe*, nach der Übersetzung von ṢṢafı in Abschnitt 2.9.

107 Viertel im Südosten des historischen Kairo.

108 Ṣarīʿ ad-Dilāʾ (st. 412/1021) war Lobdichter, und Ḥammād ar-Rāwiya (st. 155/771) ein bedeutender Sammler altarabischer Gedichte. Beide waren sicherlich sehr wortmächtig, aber darauf kam es Ibn Abī Ḥaǧala bei ihrer Erwähnung nicht an. Vielmehr ist ein Wortspiel mit ihren Namen intendiert, welches die Erwähnung der Wasserträger fortführt. Der Name

4.4 *Rückgang des Nils (Abschnitt C)*

Quelle: *Fayḍ*.

Fünf Stellen und damit ein Großteil des Textes sind in derselben Reihenfolge mehr oder weniger wörtlich in MaqZaʿf 287–8 zitiert.

لكنّه ساعةَ سَطَّرَ المملوكُ هذه العُبُودية *أَخَذَ في الانحطاط*، وبشّر المَلّاحون أنّ *بَسْطَةَ مقياسِه في انبساط، وشنّفوا المَسامِعَ بما وَرَدَ عن حَبابِه[109] الذي هو في حُلُقِ داراتِه كالأَقراط*، وأَقبل الأمنُ عليهم حِينَ شَرَعَ في رُجوعِه، ونصبوا بمِصْرَ صوارِيَ[110] قُلُوعِه، *وأصبحت أكنافُ الروضة بأنواع الأَزهار مُنَمَّقَة، ومُقَطَّعاتُ النيل بخَلِيج الزَّعْفران مُخَلَّقة وغيرَ مُخَلَّقَة[111]*، *وحصَلَ حِينَ غَيْضِ الماء السُّرُور، ودارَ بمِصْرَ ما انْهَمد من السّواقي التي على مثلِها كان الخِصْبُ[112] يَدُور*، وذلك بعد أن عَمَّ بطوفانه الحقيرَ والجليل، *وإن كان قَطَعَ الطريقَ بإحسانه فـ﴿ما على المُحْسِنِين مِنْ سَبِيل﴾.*[113]

Aber zur Stunde, da der Sklave dieses untertänige Schreiben verfaßt, hat er zu fallen begonnen, / und die Schiffer haben die gute Nachricht verkündet, daß sich die Ausdehnung (des trockenen Landes) um seinen *miqyās* herum weiter ausdehnt,[114] / und sie haben die Ohren (der Menschen) mit Nachricht über seine Blasen, die an den Kehlen seiner Strudel wie Ohrringe sind, erfreut.[115] Es hat sich ihnen jetzt, da er sich zurückzuziehen anschickt, Sicherheit genähert,[116] / und sie haben in Kairo die Masten seiner Segel[117] aufgestellt.[118] Das

Ṣarīʿ ad-Dilāʾ „Von Unglücksfällen zu Boden gestreckt" läßt sich nämlich auch als „Von Eimern zu Boden gestreckt" interpretieren, und der Laqab ar-Rāwiya „der bedeutende Überlieferer" kann auch als „der bedeutende Tränker" interpretiert werden.

109 *Fayḍ* جنابه.

110 *Fayḍ* صواوين.

111 MaqZaʿf مُخَلَّقة. Der Passus مُخَلَّقة وغيرَ مُحَلَّقة ist Anspielung auf ﴿مُخَلَّقَةٍ وَغَيْرِ مُخَلَّقَةٍ﴾ Q 22:5 und Variation hiervon, aber anders, als der Herausgeber annimmt, kein Zitat.

112 *Fayḍ* الخصيب.

113 Q 9:91.

114 Daß Schiffer diese Nachricht überbringen, ist wohl dadurch bedingt, daß sie allein über die Verhältnisse auf der Insel ar-Rawḍa Bescheid wissen.

115 Strudel können auch entstehen, wenn Wasser durch Engstellen abläuft. Da es sich um eine positive Nachricht handelt, muß dies hier gemeint sein.

116 Schiffahrt auf dem Nil war während des Hochwassers gefährlich gewesen.

117 „Die Masten seiner Segel": Die Schiffe mit ihren Segeln gehören gewissermaßen zum Nil, da sie auf ihm fahren. In einem Nilbrief Ibn ʿAbd aẓ-Ẓāhirs begegnet der Ausdruck *taḥta qulūʿihi* „unter seinen (sc. des Nils) Segeln" (Diem, *Nilbriefe*, IAẒāh6 in Abschnitt 2.5.).

118 Die Schiffe konnten wieder auslaufen. Hierfür wurden die umgelegten Masten wieder aufgestellt.

Gebiet von ar-Rawḍa wird nunmehr von verschiedenartigen Blumen geziert, / und die Kurzen (Wellen) des Nils[119] sind jetzt im Ḫalīǧ az-Zaʿfarān[120] mit *ḫalūq* parfümiert[121] und nicht (mehr) mit einem Kettenhemd bekleidet.[122] Es hat sich, als das Wasser abnahm, Freude eingestellt, / und es drehen sich in Kairo die zerstörten Wasserräder (wieder), (Wasserräder), um derengleichen sich in Hinblick auf Fruchtbarkeit alles dreht. Und dies, nachdem er mit seinem Hochwasser Niedrig und Vornehm umfaßt hatte. / Auch wenn er mit seiner Wohltat die Wege abgeschnitten hatte,[123] nun, ‚gegen Wohltäter ist nun einmal nichts einzuwenden' [Q 9:91].[124]

5 Nachwirkung von *as-Saǧʿ al-ǧalīl*

5.1 *Wirkung des Nils auf Lokalitäten*

Das in *as-Saǧʿ al-ǧalīl* angewandte Verfahren, die Überschwemmung des Nils anhand von Lokalitäten zu veranschaulichen, findet sich auch in einem Niltext al-Qīrāṭīs (st. 781/1379).[125] Da al-Qīrāṭī und Ibn Abī Ḥaǧala Zeitgenossen waren, läßt sich nicht entscheiden, wem der beiden hierbei Priorität zukommt. Ibn Abī Ḥaǧala hat aber jedenfalls sein Verfahren in seiner im Jahre 773/1371–2 verfaßten und später in sein Buch *Manṭiq aṭ-ṭayr* „Sprache der Vögel"[126] integrierten *al-Maqāma az-zaʿfarāniyya*, die ebenfalls über ein Nilhochwasser handelt,

119 Bereits Ibn ʿAbd aẓ-Ẓāhir spricht in einem Nilbrief von solchen kurzen Wellen: *kam ḥasunat muqaṭṭaʿātuhu ʿalā marri l-ǧadīdayni* „Wie schön sind doch seine Kurzen (Wellen) im Verlauf von Tag und Nacht" (Diem, *Nilbriefe*, IAẒāh4 in Abschnitt 2.5.).

120 Der Ḫalīǧ az-Zaʿfarān zweigte nordöstlich von Kairo von al-Ḫalīǧ al-Ḥākimī ab und verlief entlang der heutigen Straße Šāriʿ al-ʿAbbāsiyya (aš-Šištāwī, *Muntazahāt* 224–6). Der Ḫalīǧ az-Zaʿfarān wird auch am Anfang von Ibn Abī Ḥaǧalas *al-Maqāma az-zaʿfarāniyya* erwähnt, und zwar als Ort, an dem sich der fiktive Erzähler befindet (276, Zitat in Abschnitt 5.1.), wie auch als Ort der Überschwemmung (287).

121 Da die *ḫalūq*-Salbe rötlich ist, spielt das Kolon auf die durch den mitgeführten fruchtbaren Schlamm bedingte rötliche Farbe des Wassers an. Zugleich korrespondiert die (metaphorische) Parfümierung des Kanals mit *ḫalūq* mit dem Namen „Safran-Kanal" des Kanals, da der Hauptbestandteil von *ḫalūq* Safran ist.

122 Der Nil ist nunmehr friedlich und nicht mehr aggressiv wie ein Krieger.

123 Daß der Nil einerseits wie ein Wegelagerer die Wege abschneidet, sich aber hierbei wegen des fruchtbaren Wassers, anders als ein echter Wegelagerer, wohltätig verhält, ist ein altererbtes Motiv. Siehe hierzu Diem, *Nilbriefe*, Abschnitt 1.4.5.1. „Spezifische Ausdrücke" s. r. *qṭʿ* und Abschnitt 6.4.13. „Aggression" sub f) „Wegeabschneiden."

124 Ebensowenig wie man einem Wohltäter Vorwürfe machen kann, wenn er übertreibt, ist dies gegenüber dem Nil möglich.

125 Diem, *Nilbriefe*, Qīr in Abschnitt 2.11.

126 Siehe zu diesem Werk und seinen Bestandteilen Pomerantz, *Maqāmah* 181–2.

angewandt. Zu Beginn dieser Maqāma, die nach dem Ḫalīǧ az-Zaʿfarān ihren Namen hat, tritt Ibn Abī Ḥaǧala als Abū r-Riyāš auf, der dem fiktiven Erzähler as-Sāǧiʿ Ibn Ḥamām über die Nilflut berichtet:

> Während ich[127] beim Ḫalīǧ az-Zaʿfarān mit den anderen (durch das Wasser der Überschwemmung) watete / und mich nach Dayr aṭ-Ṭīn erkundete, war da unversehens unser Scheich Abū r-Riyāš, der Verfasser von ‚Die prächtige Reimprosa / bezüglich dessen, was seitens des Nils geschehen ist,' nachdem er von der Reise zurückgekehrt war, / wobei er gleichsam ein Bogen und sein Stock dessen Sehne war.

In diesem Werk werden zwölf Lokalitäten genannt, zu denen alle in *as-Saǧʿ al-ǧalīl* angeführten Lokalitäten gehören. Darüber hinaus enthält das Werk auch Zitate aus *as-Saǧʿ al-ǧalīl*, darunter etliche aus den hier edierten Teilen von *as-Saǧʿ al-ǧalīl*: drei Zitate aus Abschnitt A (4.1.), ein Zitat aus Abschnitt Bc (4.2.), ein Zitat aus Abschnitt Bg (4.3.) und fünf Zitate aus Abschnitt C (4.4.).

Das Verfahren al-Qīrāṭīs und Ibn Abī Ḥaǧalas, die Nilschwemme anhand von Lokalitäten entlang des Nils zu veranschaulichen, hat Ibn Ḥiǧǧa (st. 837/1433) in seinem 819/1416 verfaßten amtlichen Nilbrief[128] verfeinert. Ibn Ḥiǧǧa nennt mit insgesamt 19 Toponymen nicht nur mehr Lokalitäten als seine beiden Vorgänger, sondern die Lokalitäten decken in Form von drei Gruppen den Lauf des Nils vom Sudan bis zu seiner Mündung in das Mittelmeer bei Damietta ab. Eine stilistische Besonderheit ist hierbei, daß die Lokalitäten innerhalb der drei Gruppen so angeordnet sind, daß Lokalitäten, die gemäß ihren Bezeichnungen in welcher fiktiven Beziehung auch immer zueinander stehen, aufeinander folgen.

5.2 *Wirkung des Nils auf bestimmte Arten von Menschen*

Eine weitere Besonderheit von *as-Saǧʿ al-ǧalīl*, die wohl eine Neuerung Ibn Abī Ḥaǧalas war, besteht in der Beschreibung der Wirkung des Hochwassers auf bestimmte Arten von Menschen – den Reisenden, den Weber, den Astrologen, den Dichter, den Metriker und den Grammatiker –, die sich auf der Insel ar-Rawḍa aufhielten (Abschnitt 4.2.), wobei diese Beschreibung teilweise in der jeweiligen Fachterminologie geschieht. Dieses Verfahren hat Ibn Abī Ḥaǧala in *al-Maqāma az-zaʿfarāniyya* nicht aufgenommen, und auch Ibn Ḥiǧǧa hat sich dessen in seinem Nilbrief nicht bedient.

127 Sc. as-Sāǧiʿ b. Ḥamām.

128 Diem, *Nilbriefe*, IḤiǧǧ in Abschnitt 2.12.

Nachwirkung hat dieses Verfahren indes durchaus gehabt, und zwar in zwei Maqāmas as-Suyūṭīs: *al-Maqāma al-baḥriyya aw an-Nīliyya fī r-raḫāʾ wa-l-ġalā* „Fluß- oder Nilmaqāma über Wohlfeilheit und Teuerung,“[129] die die verzögerte Nilschwemme des Jahres 897/1492 betrifft, und *al-Maqāma ad-durriyya fī ṭ-ṭāʿūn wa-l-wabāʾ* „Perlenmaqāma über Pest und Seuche,“[130] die von der in jenem Jahr eingetretenen Pest handelt.

In *al-Maqāma al-baḥriyya* äußern sich 22 Vertreter geistiger Berufe jeweils vor der ausgebliebenen und, mit Ausnahme des Arztes, nach der schließlich doch noch eingetretenen Nilschwemme, wobei sich nach der Nilschwelle zusätzlich die „Stimme der unbelebten Natur“ (*lisān al-ḥāl*) erhebt. Die Berufsbezeichnungen sind teilweise mehr oder weniger fiktiv, wofür etwa *at-taṣrīfī* „Flexionsspezialist; ‚Flexionist‘“ ein Beispiel ist, denn einen solchen speziellen Beruf gab es wohl kaum. Die Personen sind[131] *muqriʾ* „Koranleser,“ *muḥaddiṯ* „Traditionarier,“ *faqīh* „Rechtsgelehrter,“ *faraḍī* „Pflichtteilspezialist,“ *uṣūlī* „Rechtsgrundlagenspezialist,“ *ǧadalī* „Dialektiker,“ *ṣūfī* „Mystiker,“ *naḥwī* „Grammatiker,“ *taṣrīfī* „Flexionist,“ *luġawī* „Lexikologe,“ *maʿnawī* „Motiviker,“ *bayānī* „Metaphoriker,“ *badīʿī* „Stilist,“ *ʿarūḍī* „Metriker,“ *šāʿir ʿarabī* „klassischer Dichter,“ *šāʿir muwallad* „moderner Dichter,“ *kātib* „Schreiber,“ *ṭabīb* „Arzt,“ *manṭiqī* „Logiker,“ *musīqī* „Musiker,“ *mīqātī* „Terminspezialist,“ *muʾaḏḏin* „Gebetsausrufer.“ Wie schon Ibn Abī Ḥaǧala spielt as-Suyūṭī mit Fachausdrücken der jeweiligen Tätigkeit. Von den in *as-Saǧʿ al-ǧalīl* für die Nilinsel ar-Rawḍa erwähnten Personen sind nur der Metriker und der Grammatiker vertreten.

In *al-Maqāma ad-durriyya* äußern sich ebenfalls diverse Vertreter geistiger Berufe, und zwar zuerst während der Pest und dann erneut nach ihrem Ende. Die Personen sind *muqriʾ* „Koranleser,“ *muḥaddiṯ* „Traditionarier,“ *faqīh* „Rechtsgelehrter,“ *uṣūlī* „Rechtsgrundlagenspezialist,“ *naḥwī* „Grammatiker,“ *ṣarfī* „Flexionist“ und *balīġ* „Beredter.“ Sowohl in *al-Maqāma al-baḥriyya* wie auch in *al-Maqāma ad-durriyya* treten die Personen also zweimal auf: zuerst in einer kritischen Phase und dann erneut nach gutem Ausgang. Schließlich hat as-Suyūṭī in *Rašf az-zulāl min as-siḥr al-ḥalāl* zwanzig Vertretern geistiger Berufe, die sich weitestgehend mit den eben erwähnten Berufsvertretern decken, jeweils eine Maqāma gewidmet.

Die von Ibn Abī Ḥaǧala eingeführte Erwähnung von Personen hat as-Suyūṭī aber nicht nur übernommen, sondern er hat sich in *al-Maqāma al-baḥriyya* bei der Erwähnung des Grammatikers und des Metrikers auch in Form von Zitaten

129 As-Suyūṭī, *Maqāmāt* 161–80.

130 As-Suyūṭī, *Maqāmāt* 194–216.

131 Die Übersetzungen fiktiver arabischer Berufsbezeichnungen sind wie jene ad hoc gebildet.

an *as-Sağʿ al-ğalīl* orientiert, während die Passagen zum Grammatiker in *al-Maqāma ad-durriyya* keine Gemeinsamkeit mit denen von *as-Sağʿ al-ğalīl* aufweisen. Im folgenden werden das letzte Kolonpaar der Erwähnung des Grammatiker von *as-Sağʿ al-ğalīl* und die erste Kolontriade der ersten Erwähnung des Grammatikers von *al-Maqāma al-baḥriyya* einander gegenüber gestellt. Für *as-Sağʿ al-ğalīl* wird die alternative Übersetzung zugrundegelegt, die mit dem Namen des Grammatikers Ibn ʿUṣfūr spielt.

as-Sağʿ al-ğalīl:

وطار عقلُه لا سيّما عن تصانيف ابن عُصْفُور، وأُخْبِرَ أن البحر وأثاث بيته جارٌّ ومَجْرُور

Und sein Verstand flog insbesondere von den Werken von ‚Sohn eines Sperlings' weg / nachdem man ihm berichtet hatte, daß das Gewässer und sein Hausrat wegschleppend bzw. weggeschleppt waren.

al-Maqāma al-baḥriyya:

وأصبح النحوي يلتقط الحبّ كأنّه ابن عُصْفُور، ويقول السعر ممدود والمال مقصور، وأنا
وكتبي للبيع جارٌّ ومَجْرُور

Und der Grammatiker begann Körner aufzulesen, als sei er der Sohn eines Sperlings, / und zu sagen: ‚Der Preis (der Waren) ist ausgedehnt, während das Geld beschränkt ist. / Ich und meine Bücher sind in Hinblick auf Verkauf wegschleppend bzw. weggeschleppt'.[132]

Wie der Passus von *as-Sağʿ al-ğalīl* spielt der Passus von *al-Maqāma al-baḥriyya* mit dem Namen des Grammatikers Ibn ʿUṣfūr und mit den syntaktischen Termini *ğārr* und *mağrūr*, wozu die morphologischen Termini *mamdūd* und *maqṣūr* kommen.

132 Der Grammatiker ist in Not geraten, so daß er Getreidekörner auflesen und seine Bücher verkaufen muß.

Quellen

al-Ġuzūlī, *Maṭāliʿ al-budūr fī manāzil as-surūr*, Hg. S.M. at-Tiǧānī, Beirut 2015.

Hell, Joseph, *Neue Huḏailiten-Diwane*, 2 Bde., Leipzig 1926–33.

al-Ḥiǧāzī, *Fihrist an-Nīl al-mubārak*, Hs. Bibliothèque Nationale de France, Département des manuscrits, Arabe 2261.

Ibn Abī Ḥaǧala, al-Maqāma az-zaʿfarāniyya (ar-Rīša al-ʿāšira), in Ibn Abī Ḥaǧala, *Kitāb manṭiq aṭ-ṭayr*, Hg. A.ʿA. Mašhadānī, Rabat 2018, 275–89.

Ibn Abī Ḥaǧala, *as-Saǧʿ al-ǧalīl*, in: as-Suyūṭī, *Kawkab* 339–42 / *Muḥāḍara* 308–10; al-Minūfī, *Fayḍ* 76–9, 83–5, 86, 95.

Ibn Iyās, *Badāʾiʿ az-zuhūr fī waqāʾiʿ ad-duhūr*, Bd. i, 1, Hg. M. Muṣṭafā, Istanbul/Wiesbaden/Kairo 1975.

Ibn Iyās, *Hāḏihī nubḏa laṭīfa fī ḏikr an-Nīl al-mubārak li-l-marḥūm aš-šayḫ Šams ad-Dīn Muḥammad Ibn Iyās al-Ḥanafī*, Hs. Paris 3513.

Ibn Taġrī Birdī, *an-Nuǧūm az-zāhira fī mulūk Miṣr wa-l-Qāhira*, Hg. F.M. Šaltūt et al., Kairo 1929–72.

al-Maqrīzī, *al-Mawāʿiẓ wa-l-iʿtibār fī ḏikr al-ḫiṭaṭ wa-l-āṯār*, 5 Bde., Hg. A.F. Sayyid, London 2002.

al-Maqrīzī, *Kitāb as-Sulūk li-maʿrifat duwal al-mulūk*, Hg. S.ʿA. ʿĀšūr, Kairo 1939–73.

al-Minūfī, *al-Fayḍ al-madīd fī aḫbār an-Nīl as-saʿīd*, Hg. M. az-Zāhī, Beirut 2018.

aṣ-Ṣafadī, *al-Wāfī bi-l-wafayāt*, Hg. H. Ritter et al., 30 Bde., Beirut/Berlin 1962–2010.

aš-Šištāwī, Muḥammad, *Muntazahāt al-Qāhira fī l-ʿaṣrayn al-mamlūkī wa-l-ʿuṯmānī*, Kairo 1999.

as-Suyūṭī, *Ḥusn al-muḥāḍara fī aḫbār Miṣr wa-l-Qāhira*, 2 Bde., [Kairo] o.J.

as-Suyūṭī, *Kawkab ar-rawḍa fī tārīḫ ǧazīrat Miṣr al-musammāh bi-r-Rawḍa*, Hg. M. aš-Šakʿa und M. ʿĀšūr, Kairo 2008.

as-Suyūṭī, *Maqāmāt as-Suyūṭī al-adabiyya wa-ṭ-ṭibbiyya*, Hg. M.I. Salīm, Kairo [ca. 1988].

as-Suyūṭī, *Rašf az-zulāl min as-siḥr al-ḥalāl*. Beirut 1997.

Sekundärliteratur

Diem, W., *Arabische amtliche Nilbriefe: Ein Beitrag zur arabischen Kulturgeschichte, Epistolographie und Stilgeschichte des 12.–15. Jahrhunderts*, Baden-Baden 2020.

Pomerantz, M.A., A *Maqāmah* on the Book Market of Cairo in the 8th/14th Century. The 'Return of the Stranger' of Ibn Abī Ḥaǧalah (d. 776/1375), in N. Papoutsakis und S. von Hees (Hgg.), *The Sultan's Anthologist – Ibn Abī Ḥaǧalah and His Work*, Baden-Baden 2017, 179–209.

10

Hidden Literary History—Isma'ili Tradition in Syria

Verena Klemm

Not far from the princely court of al-Malik al-Mu'ayyad (r. 710–31/1310–31), the vibrant meeting place of great poets and intellectuals in Hama,[1] lay the territory of the Isma'ilis. Here, in the craggy, fortress-fortified massif of the Jabal Bahrā' (today, Jabal al-Anṣāriyya), west of the Orontes, oral hagiographic tales about the venerable Rāshid al-Dīn Sinān (d. ca. 589/1193) were collected and written down by an anonymous compiler in that very period of Hama's efflorescence. In contrast to the blood-curdling Assassin legends that the Crusaders carried to Christian Europe, these texts depict a man of prophetic knowledge, enlightenment, and authority, who inspired fear and respect among friend and foe alike.

This collection, the *Manāqib al-mawlā Rāshid al-Dīn* (The virtues of lord Rāshid al-Dīn), which survives in a few manuscripts, remained in the area, circulating for centuries among the Isma'ilis, who revered their Shaykh al-Jabal, their Old Man of the Mountain, as a spiritual and political leader. It was not until 1848 that a manuscript of the *Manāqib* found its way to the Societé Asiatique in Paris, and in the late 1980s another textual witness reached the Institute of Ismaili Studies in London. These manuscripts, discussed in detail below, situate the compilation of the *Manāqib* in the year 724/1324—squarely in the time of al-Malik al-Mu'ayyad. Aside from these few witnesses, most of the manuscripts of the Isma'ilis of Syria remain preserved and protected in private libraries. Since the literary tradition of the small religious minority[2] is hidden and barely documented, it also might appear to be virtually non-existent.

This article provides insight into a heterodox literary history that occurred far away from Syria's cultural centres. We will draw here, albeit selectively, on the insight potential the tradition offers, particularly as seen through a group

1 Bauer, Ibn Nubātah 188–90.

2 According to Archbishop William of Tyre (1130–86), the Isma'ilis numbered 60,000 or more in the region; they possessed 10 castles (cited in Daftary, *Assassin legends* 82; idem, *The Ismāʿīlīs* 350). By the mid-19th century, their numbers appear to have declined: Douwes, Modern history 24. In 1964, the community was estimated at 56,000 people, comprising about 1% of the population of the state of Syria (Halm, *Die Schia* 229).

 | DOI:10.1163/9789004521780_012

of multiple-text and composite manuscripts (*majmūʿāt*) now preserved at the Institute of Ismaili Studies—and focus on its "Sitz im Leben." To this end, we will also return to the aforementioned *Manāqib* work found in one of these manuscripts. However, it was not only indigenous literature that was produced and received in the Jabal Bahrāʾ, but diverse prose and poetry also arrived there from afar; accordingly, the transcontinental dimension of the Ismaʿiliyya is a defining feature of the literature.

1 Ismaʿili Traditions from a Bird's-Eye View: A Widely Stretched Net with Holes

With their doctrine of salvation rooted in Neoplatonic and Gnostic concepts of late antiquity, the Ismaʿilis represented a radical and revolutionary alternative to the Sunni caliphate. The emergence, development, and differentiation of Ismaʿili doctrine was accompanied by schisms, which led to special regional developments giving rise to new literatures and genres. The two greatest schisms occurred during the reign of the Fatimids (297–567/909–1171).

One of these schisms, resulting from a succession conflict following the death of the Fatimid imam-caliph al-Mustanṣir (d. 487/1094), gave rise to the eastern, Nizāri branch of the Ismaʿiliyya, named after al-Mustanṣir's son Nizār, who was, according to the belief of his followers, denied succession to the throne. The Nizāri sphere extends from Iran to Central Asia and north-western India. From the northern Iranian Assassin state of Alamūt, a small Ismaʿili territorial state was established in Syria beginning in 525/1130 through the acquisition and conquest of castles; it gained doctrinal and political independence from Alamūt under Rāshid al-Dīn Sinān.

After the abrupt break with Cairo, the seat of Fatimid power, the production and transmission of literature in this branch of the Ismaʿiliyya—which again split several times—took place under conditions of political pressure and persecution that continued until well into the 19th century. After the Mongol storm (654/1256), the Ismaʿilis of Iran survived, scattered and politically oppressed, with *taqiyya* (dissimulation) practices as well as a Sufism-transformed doctrine and literature. It was not until the flight of the first Agha Khan, Imam Ḥasan ʿAlī Shāh Maḥallatī (1804–81), from Iran to the protectorate of the British Empire in Bombay, that massive transcontinental modernisation and institutionalisation became possible. The Nizāri community in northwest India, the Khojas, had emerged centuries earlier through the conversion of a wealthy Hindu merchant caste. Khoja communities also exist in Pakistan's northwest frontier province of Chitral, on the upper Indus River in the Karakoram Mountains, and in the western Tarim Basin in China's Xinjiang region. The head of the Nizāri branch today is Karīm Agha Khan IV (born 1936 in Geneva).

Unlike the Nizāri *daʿwa*—that is, the religious mission in all its manifestations—the vassal kingdom of the Sulaihids in Yemen remained connected to the Fatimid empire by an abundant and undisturbed stream of literary transmission for nearly 100 years, between the mid-5th/11th and mid-6th/12th centuries, which spread from there further into India. The Ṭayyibi branch, which the Sulaihids embraced, was based on the claim that the Imamate rightfully belonged to the vanished child al-Ṭayyib, son of the Fatimid imam-caliph al-Āmir (d. 526/1132). The teaching also reached by sea to the north-western coastal regions of the Indian subcontinent (Sind, Gujarat, Maharashtra). Thus, the core of the tradition that was received by the Bohra-Ismaʿili community of merchants consists of a Fatimid corpus of literature augmented by literature written in the Ṭayyibi *daʿwa* in Yemen and India. A split in the 10th/16th century produced a Sulaimāni branch, predominantly present in Yemen and Najrān, and a numerically much larger Dāwūdi branch, whose religious centre remains in Bombay/Mumbai today.[3]

Ismail K. Poonawala, author of the *Biobibliography of Ismaili Literature*, basically divides Ismaʿili literature into *ẓāhir*, "external," or exoteric knowledge, and *bāṭin*, "internal," or esoteric knowledge. In exoteric knowledge he includes the large categories of law, historiography, and (non-religious) sciences,[4] which can be subdivided again formally and thematically. Esoteric, secret knowledge includes the *taʾwīl* (the decoding and allegorical interpretation of the *sharīʿa* and Quran) and the *ḥaqāʾiq*, which contain the cosmological and eschatological truths unlocked by the imams and their authorised representatives in the *taʾwīl*.[5] These are also transmitted in various literary forms. We encounter some of them in the Ismaʿili anthologies from Syria, as discussed below.

Poonawala's 1977 *Biobibliography* is the most authoritative reference work in Ismaʿili studies to date, albeit one that is decidedly in need of supplementation;[6] it explicitly follows Carl Brockelmann's *Geschichte der Arabischen Litteratur* in terms of its guiding categories of author, work, and manuscript. Between 1971 and 1973, Poonawala's broad research and surveys uncovered 1300

3 For the spread and differentiation of the Ismaʿiliyya, see Halm, *Die Schia* 224–43, in concise form; in full detail: Daftary, *The Ismāʿīlīs*, chapters 5–7.

4 Walker, *Exploring an Islamic empire* 131–85.

5 Poonawala, *Biobibliography* 19–20.

6 Most certainly, the new edition of this work, which Ismail Poonawala has been preparing for years, in collaboration with the Institute of Ismaili Studies, will be able to present a far greater number of manuscripts and titles.

titles of works, 1000 of them in Arabic, 200 in Persian, and 100 in Gujarati and Urdu. Poonawala did not include the Jināns, the religious poetry of the syncretic Satpanth, which were handed down in Indian dialects.[7]

Poonawala draws from a remarkably large number of historical and modern resources, such as bibliographies, catalogues, original sources, and specialised literature. By far his richest source of information on the manuscript record, however, is the private collections of Bohra scholars in Gujarat. In that urban and populous region, Poonawala documented around 1500 manuscripts, with some multiple copies of the same title. He estimates that thousands more heretofore unrecorded manuscripts could be found there in the future.[8] On the other hand, far fewer titles and manuscripts than those identified in the Ṭayyibi tradition comprise Poonawala's documentation of Nizāri literature. In Syria, for example, he was able to list only 44 titles of works (including poetry), each of which is represented by one or more manuscripts.[9]

The multitude, heterogeneity, and linguistic diversity of Poonawala's resources, as well as the fact that the overwhelming majority of the manuscripts he documented came from Bohra libraries, reflect two other defining characteristics of Ismaʿili literature: its wide geographical distribution and the disproportionate nature of its transmission. The latter seems to result from not only the differing avenues available for transmission, but also a lack of documentation, especially of the Nizāri textual witnesses.[10] In what follows, we now move to Syria, a region that lies off the far-flung, often transcontinental axes of the Ismaʿili literary tradition.

2 Historical and Literary Traditions in and from the Jabal Bahrāʾ

What can be said about a literary history whose evidence, as in the case of the Syrian Ismaʿilis, is largely hidden, unrecorded, and, in the worst case, destroyed

7 Poonawala, *Biobibliography* 19.

8 Ibid, XIII–XV, chapter "Sources of Ismāʿīlī works."

9 Ibid, 287–97, 348–50. At times, Poonawala's information does not include the precise number of textual witnesses. He also does not document whether some of the works listed are found together in multiple-text and composite manuscripts. Poonawala's primary sources for titles and manuscripts are the editions and works of the Syrian Ismaʿili scholars Muṣṭafā Ghālib and ʿĀrif Tāmir.

10 Shafique Virani, whose work *The Ismailis in the Middle Ages* is based on post-Mongol Nizāri sources in Iran, Central Asia, and northern India, draws on quite a few previously unrecorded manuscripts in Arabic, Persian, Sindhi, Siraiki, Hindustani, Punjabi, and Gujarati: ibid. 12.

and lost?[11] Which texts circulated here, and can we gain insights into their history, the conditions and forms of their transmission, their reception, or their loss?[12]

First, on the historical conditions: In the seventh of the stories compiled in the *Manāqib*, the invisible Rāshid al-Dīn sneaks past the guards into the tent of the sleeping Sultan Saladin (Ṣalāḥ al-Dīn). He thrusts a poisoned dagger next to the sultan's head and retreats unnoticed to his main castle of Maṣyaf. According to the story, when Saladin discovered this threat, a great shock seized him, which resulted in the historically attested, lasting truce between the two. As the story goes on to state, Saladin allowed the propagation of Isma'ili doctrine in Hama, Aleppo, Damascus, and Cairo. Moreover, he—who had just put an end to the Fatimid dynasty in 567/1171—made a guarantee of protection for the Isma'ilis a condition for later treaty partners.[13]

After Rāshid al-Dīn's death, at first nothing changed in the status of the small Isma'ili state in the mosaic of political-military topography.[14] Thanks to the successful resistance of the Mamluks, in 659/1260 the small community survived the onslaught of the advancing Mongols, who a few years earlier had brought destruction and expulsion upon their coreligionists in Iran with the storming of Alamūt (654/1256). It was quiet in the small Isma'ili enclave in Syria when the Mamluk sultan Baibars finally subjugated it in 672/1273. He, and after him the Ottomans, recognised the area with its Isma'ili name *Qilāʿ al-daʿwa*, the castles of the *daʿwa*, and allowed it partial autonomy. The Mamluks occupied the castle of Maṣyaf, from which they controlled the region. In return for tribute payments, they enabled the Isma'ilis to reoccupy several of their fortresses and to maintain their traditions. At that time, a shrine to Rāshid al-Dīn was built

11 This overarching problem, which is of central methodological relevance for literary historiography, is addressed in the essay by Arnold Esch, Überlieferungs-Chance.

12 These are the questions posed by the research approach of the "history of literary transmission" (Überlieferungsgeschichtliche Forschung) developed in Medieval German Studies: Klein, *Überlieferungsgeschichte*. The preface and the introductory contribution by Löser, Überlieferungsgeschichte(n) schreiben, in ibid. 1–19, offer a definition and presentation of the research paradigm. For research on the reasons and patterns of the loss of tradition, see Haye, *Verlorenes Mittelalter* 1–4.

13 Guyard, Grand maître, story 7, 398–408; story 8, 408–12. Saladin besieged Maṣyaf in 571/1176. On the historical contexts, ibid. 366–70; on the possible reasons for his withdrawal from the siege of Maṣyaf Castle and his henceforth good relationship with Sinān, see e.g. Willey, *Eagle's nest* 47–8; Hodgson, *The secret order* 188–9.

14 Its complexity is described on the basis of Latin and Arabic sources in Böhme, *Außenbeziehungen* 250–66. Thorau, Burgen, also on the basis of Arabic and Latin sources, traces the military conflicts and the struggle for the castles from the first third of the 6th/12th century until the conquest of the Isma'ili state by Baibars.

on the hill opposite Maṣyaf, from which he is said to have once threatened and defied Saladin.[15] Two years after the *Manāqib* under discussion was compiled, the traveller Ibn Baṭṭūṭa passed through the area from North Africa (727/1326). He confirmed that the Ismaʿilis lived peacefully in their ancient castles. Upon request, and in exchange for payment and material guarantees for their possible survivors, they sometimes rendered assistance to the Mamluk sultans by sending their *fidāʾī*s to kill their enemies.[16]

The Ottomans also left the small minority alone for the most part until late in the thirteenth/nineteenth-century Tanzimat period. They favoured them over the numerically stronger Nuṣairis and protected them in bloody family conflicts and land disputes.[17] The Nuṣairis, as we learn from the fate of one of the rare unearthed manuscripts,[18] did not spare the libraries of the Ismaʿilis in their frequent raids. In 1265/1848, the Ottoman sultan ʿAbd al-Majīd I (1255–77/1839–61) granted the Nizaris the right to settle in the city of Salamiyya, the long-abandoned place of origin of the Fatimids, and to cultivate the fertile surrounding land. This process continued until the 1920s and led to a partial exodus from the mountains.[19]

Violence and oppression instigated by the state power began when the majority of the Ismaʿilis of Syria switched their allegiance from the extinct Muʾmin-Shāhī-line to the Qāsim-Shāhī line of the Agha Khans in India around 1890. Their regular payments of *zakāt* to the 48th Imam, Sir Sultan Muhammad Shah Agha Khan III (1877–1957, designated in 1885), himself under the protection of the British in Bombay, were judged by the Ottomans to be high treason and they responded in a series of court cases (1902–8) with imprisonments and executions of Ismaʿili leaders and scholars.[20]

---

15 Guyard, Grand maître, story 7, 400.

16 Ibid. 376–7.

17 The centuries-long hostility of the Nuṣairis (from the early 20th century: ʿAlawīyūn/Alawites) towards the Syrian Ismaʿilis has its origins in the Ismaʿili immigration after the end of the Fatimid dynasty in 564/1171. At that time, the Ismaiʿlis gradually withdrew from the coastal cities of Syria to the mountainous region inhabited by the Nuṣairis. Dussaud, *Histoire* 23–4; Douwes, Modern history 21–4.

18 Guyard, Fragments relatifs à la doctrine des Ismaélîs, 178–83: the manuscript came into the hands of the French consul in Aleppo, Jean-Baptiste Rousseau (1780–1831), after the Nuṣairi invasion of Maṣyaf in 1809. It was collated, according to Guyard's description, in 1220/1805 (p. 180). Rousseau, *Mémoire* 57–8, gives a detailed account as a contemporary witness to this attack by the Nuṣairis on the Ismaʿili Amīr Muṣṭafā Idrīs, which was followed by a devastating massacre of the population and the almost complete destruction of their property. This event, according to Rousseau, plunged the Nizari Ismaʿilis of Syria into lasting misery and poverty.

19 Douwes, Modern history 28–9; Amīn, *Salamiyya* 142–73.

20 Douwes and Lewis, The trials; Merali, Fear and violence 62–6.

European travellers of the 18th and 19th centuries unanimously testify to the absolute secrecy the Ismaʿilis maintained when asked by outsiders about their literature.[21] It was not until the late 19th century that a hesitant editing of mostly smaller extracts (from multiple-text and composite manuscripts) was begun by E. Salisbury, J.B.L.J. Rousseau, and M. Stanislas Guyard.[22] In the 20th century, the research and editions of ʿĀrif Tāmir (1921–98) and Muṣṭafā Ghālib (1923–81) from Salamiyya brought to light an extremely limited corpus of doctrinal and philosophical texts that had circulated among the Ismaʿilis of Syria.[23] *In no case* did the aforementioned editors categorise according to type or describe in detail the manuscripts they used. This narrow base of texts and undocumented manuscripts thus represents as much as we know so far of the literary tradition of this small religious community in Syria.

2.1 *Ismaʿili Anthologies*

This meagre collection can now be enriched by the *majmūʿāt* mentioned at the beginning of this article—the multi-text and composite manuscripts[24] that Muṣṭafā Ghālib acquired from his own Ismaʿili community in Salamiyya and in the region. The manuscripts considered here came to the Institute of Ismaili Studies in 1988, several years after Ghālib's death.[25] There they were catalogued by Delia Cortese, together with Ismaʿili manuscripts from other regions.[26]

From this catalogue, I was able to identify ten multiple-text and composite manuscripts with clear connections to Syria, and copies of four of these manuscripts were kindly given to me.[27] Codicologically, three of these are

21 Niebuhr et al. in Guyard, Fragments 177–8, incl. footnote 2; Guyard, Grand maître 379.

22 Guyard, Fragments 177–8.

23 E.g. Tāmir, *Arbaʿ rasāʾil Ismāʿīliyya* contains doctrinal writings by Abū Firās Shihāb al-Dīn (see below), Ḥamīd al-Dīn al-Kirmānī (d. after 411/1020–1), and Shams al-Dīn b. Aḥmad al-Ṭayyibī (see below), and a *qaṣīda* by ʿĀmir b. ʿĀmir al-Baṣrī (see below).

24 See the definition and conceptualisation in Friedrich and Schwarke, *One-volume libraries*, Introduction 1–26. See also Hirschler, Development 277–9.

25 Kind communication from Dr. Farhad Daftary and Dr. Wafi Momen.

26 Cortese, *Manuscripts*, IX and 94–129 (chapter "Majmūʿāt-Collected Works"). For reasons of discretion, the country of origin and further information on former ownership were not documented in the catalogue. Nevertheless, I identified ten manuscripts with a clear connection to Syria, recognisable by the names of authors and scribes. These are: Ms. 154/994; ms. 155/1033; ms. 156/1018; ms. 157/1038; ms. 159/999; ms. 160/1039; ms. 170/1036; ms. 171/1017; ms. 175/1030; ms. 176/1031.

27 In February 2020. These are microfilm copies of ms. 154/994, ms. 155/1033, ms. 156/1018; ms. 176/1031. The oldest is ms. 156/1018, which bears dates of 1241/1826–7 and 1242/1827 (ibid. 99–101; see the more detailed description of the manuscript below p. 11). Ms. 154/994 and ms. 155/1033 (ibid. 94–6; 96–9) are dated 1310/1892. The year 1210 mentioned in

composite manuscripts, which were bound together from previously existing manuscripts to form a new unit. Since the manuscripts preserve traces of their transmission history, they promise far better insight into the literary culture of the Jabal Bahrāʾ than the previously mentioned edited individual texts, which were separated from their material context.

Each of the leather-bound[28] writings forms a "one-volume library" (Franz Rosenthal)[29] containing a compilation of diverse pieces in prose and poetry. It is quickly apparent that selected works from the spheres of religion, religious philosophy, cosmology, and ritual are united here. Several authors and poets from the region of Jabal Bahrāʾ and northern Syria are represented, and also included is the small work on the virtues of the Old Man of the Mountain, which will be discussed below.

The name given to these compilations by one of their former owners provides a clue as to their function: Two manuscripts (mss. 154/994 and 155/1033) come from the library of Muṣṭafā Tāmir Mīrzā, who held the high office of treasurer (*kamadia*) to the still very young Agha Khan III, in Syria around 1305/1887, when most of the Ismaʿilis of the region had shifted their allegiance to the Qāsim-Shāhī line.[30] The scholar immortalised himself by name in both manuscripts, referring to his two collections of texts as *al-kashkūl*.

This designation is revealing, albeit figuratively: A *kashkūl* is an often elaborately crafted bowl in the shape of a small ship. Dervishes carry these bowls on a chain over the shoulder to collect alms and gifts. *Kashkūl* is also known to be the title of the famous anthology by the Shiʿi scholar and mystic Bahāʾ al-Dīn al-ʿĀmilī (953–1031/1546–1622). Other works with this title are found primarily in Persian Sufi and Shiʿi literature.[31] Possibly the owner chose the term *kashkūl* to indicate the function of his two books as repositories of "miscellanea" and to express his esteem and appreciation for them. In fact, each of these two collections of texts takes on its own character through the specifics of its composition, which obviously goes back to a careful individual selection and the "handicraft" of the Ismaʿili scholar.[32]

---

the catalogue should be corrected to 1310. Ms. 176/1031 (ibid. 125–7) is a multiple-text manuscript inscribed in the first half of the 20th century in a single hand.

28 Douwes, Modern history 24.

29 Cited in Friedrich and Schwarke, *One-volume libraries*, Introduction 1.

30 Information kindly provided by his great-grandson Ismail Tamir (Duncan, BC).

31 Brockelmann, *Handbook*, Suppl. 3.2. (Indices). Numerous works by Iranian and Turkish authors that contained compilations on various topics bear the name *el-Keşkûl* or *Mecmûʿa Keşkûliyye*, in reference to ʿĀmilī's work: Elmalı, *el-Keşkûl* 324–5 (reference kindly provided by Prof. Dr. Hülya Çelik).

32 See also the contribution by Jan Schmidt, Ottoman multiple-text manuscripts, which

All ten of the Isma'ili *majmūʿāt* identified as clearly connected to Syria can be defined as thematic anthologies.[33] Each manuscript is unique: in each, excerpts of religious and philosophy of religion texts alternate with *qaṣīdas* and religious hymns (*anāshīd dīniyya*). The latter is a local genre, examples of which have been produced sporadically up to the present day, recited on religious occasions and at gatherings of Ismaʿili families, written in either formal, ceremonial language or in dialect.[34]

Unlike the poetry and hymns, the prose texts are predominantly *ḥaqāʾiq*, secret writings assigned to the sphere of *bāṭin*, reserved for the religious experts, the *shuyūkh*, and the community members who have been initiated by them. The manuscripts were used until the 20th century in subterranean premises called *bāsiṭiyya* (pl. *basāṭiyyāt*) for purposes of teaching and communal reading.[35] The owners of the *majmūʿāt* were thus the *shuyūkh*, who organised, received, transmitted, and preserved the religious and spiritual heritage of the Ismaʿiliyya in their personal *one-volume libraries*.

In this contribution, which is oriented mainly towards the history of transmission, I will not delve further into the structure and content of the surviving texts or the possible added value of their respective compilations. An investigation and specification of Ismaʿili anthologies to this end is still pending. For this reason, I will only briefly list the spectrum of literary forms and exemplary themes in the ten *majmūʿāt* from Syria considered here, based on Delia Cortese's catalogue.[36]

Among the prose texts are exclusively doctrinal texts and religious discourse: One encounters philosophical treatises (*rasāʾil*) on body, soul, and science; on multi-layered spiritual and physical worlds and eschatology; on interpretations and allegorical interpretations (*tafsīr, taʾwīl*) of exoteric and esoteric doctrines;

---

reflects on the astonishing boom in multiple-text and composite manuscripts in the late Ottoman period (pp. 208–9) and, following Christoph K. Neumann, praises them as "treasure troves of Ottoman intellectual history" (p. 210).

33 I am guided by a general definition of "anthology" in the *Metzler Lexikon Literatur*, as the collection and selection of texts carried out under various rubrics: ibid, s.v. Anthology. Proposals and reflections on the thematic typology can be found in Bauer, Literarische Anthologien, and, regarding Ottoman studies, in Schmidt, Ottoman multiple-text manuscripts. See also Procházka-Eisl and Çelik, *Texts* 7–8; Friedrich and Schwarke, *One-volume libraries*, Introduction 1–26.

34 Douwes, Modern history 39. Meetings for the recitation of the *anāshīd* exclusively for women were led in the 19th and early 20th centuries by female experts, who are still known by name (information kindly provided by Ismail Tamir).

35 Information kindly provided by Ismail Tamir, according to which there are still archaeological remains of several *basāṭiyyāt* in Salamiyya. The meaning of the name is uncertain.

36 Cortese, Manuscripts 94–129.

on the seven cycles of prophecy, a central motif of Ismaʿili salvation doctrine; and on faith and ethics. The spiritual and secular hierarchy of the *daʿwa* is listed, and the text of the vow (*ʿahd*) taken on the occasion of initiation is reproduced. We find traditions (*kalām, ḥadīth, riwāyāt*) of the first six imams as well as traditions of the Prophet related in the form of question-and-answer dialogues (*masāʾil*), which are attributed to the Prophet's comrades Salmān al-Fārisī and Jābir b. ʿAbdallāh al-Anṣārī, who are particularly revered by the Shiʿites. The speech formats also consist of excerpts from teaching sessions (*majālis*) and sermons (*khuṭab*). Alternating with these texts are blocks of doctrinally or mystically influenced *qaṣīda*s and *anāshīd* (hymns, see above), more rarely, also prayers and invocations. The quantitative proportion of prose and poetic formats varies; in most manuscripts, prose texts predominate.

The ten *majmūʿāt* contain a total of around 49 prose texts, often by anonymous authors. Several texts are reproduced in excerpts. In terms of their doctrinal character and the textual formats they contain, they are comparable to the Ismaʿili *majmūʿāt* from other (unnamed) regions catalogued by Cortese in the same chapter. In Poonawala's *Biobibliography*, in which, however, multiple-text and composite manuscripts are not identified or itemised, there is a much broader repertoire of Ismaʿili literature from both esoteric and exoteric spheres.

The themes collected in the anthologies from Syria can thus be categorised as exclusively religious or doctrinal. Moreover, the origin of the authors and poets testifies to a strongly Syrian-regional tradition, which gives the Ismaʿili anthologies a specific local colour: we encounter texts by or about *daʿwa* heroes such as Rāshid al-Dīn Sinān; al-Muʿaddil (born in Qadmūs, d. 658/1259–60), a poet and author of philosophical treatises, who was head of the *daʿwa* in Syria;[37] and Shams al-Dīn al-Ṭayyibī (b. 592/1195 near Aleppo, d. 652/1254 in Maṣyaf), who, as a *dāʿī* and philosophical poet, moved from Syria to Alamūt to join Imam ʿAlāʾ al-Dīn Muḥammad III (618–653/1221–55).[38]

In the ten manuscripts, a total of three authors of the Fatimid period (Aḥmad b. Ibrāhīm al-Naysābūrī, al-Qāḍī al-Nuʿmān, and Ḥamīd al-Dīn al-Kirmānī) are represented by one or at most two of their works. Likewise, excerpts from al-Masʿūdī's (d. 346/957) *Murūj al-dhahab wa-maʿādin al-jawhar*, as well as a *Zubd Rasāʾil Ikhwān al-Ṣafā*, attributed to the Brethren of Purity, indicate a transregional tradition. *Qaṣīda*s by Abū Firās al-Ḥamdānī (d. 357/968), the didactic, mystical *qaṣīda* titled *al-Tāʾiyya* by ʿĀmir b. al-ʿĀmir al-Baṣrī (d. after 700/1300–1),[39] and poems by Muḥyī l-Dīn Ibn al-ʿArabī (d. 636/1240) are also found among the texts.

37 Cortese, *Manuscripts* 98.

38 Ibid. 72.

39 On this poem and its author, see Poonawala, ʿĀmir b. ʿĀmir.

The predominantly Syrian-regional orientation stands in marked contrast to the trans-regional literary tradition of the Ṭayyibi *daʿwa*, which (as described above) had a continuous "chance of transmission" (A. Esch), beginning in Fatimid Cairo and extending through Yemen and into India. The Nizāri Ismaʿilis of Syria, on the other hand, according to the anthologies, remained only sporadically involved in an Ismaʿili flow of tradition. This also applies to the period of the religio-political alliance with Alamūt before and even a few decades after the autonomous rule of Rāshid al-Dīn Sinān in the 6th/12th century. Thus, there are also a few testimonies in the anthologies that refer to this relationship.[40]

From a codicological point of view, the collected works in the form of composite manuscripts have been referred to as "frozen libraries."[41] From a literary-historical perspective, however, the texts that were compiled in this type of book can rather be regarded as mobile, as they were on the move through various manuscripts and owners' hands and joined other texts in *one-volume libraries* from station to station. This process of circulation and transmission, which composite manuscripts undergo along with their contents, is, generally speaking, a rich treasure trove for literary historians. In the case of Ismaʿili anthologies, centuries-old religious, philosophical, and ritual texts are reproduced, received, and transmitted anew through the production act of assembling formerly independent units of manuscripts. In the process, as we will see below with the example of the aforementioned *Manāqib* work, meaningful textual variants also come to light.

As an anthology, the Ismaʿili anthology is as far removed as possible from a literary *adab* anthology in terms of content and structure. As Thomas Bauer has explained, the *adab* anthology is based on very specific cultural concepts and social functions.[42] Judged on the basis of the ten multiple-text and composite manuscripts under discussion, however, the Ismaʿili anthologies are inscribed with a completely different function: Each of these books preserves and transmits an identity-forming religious heritage which, because of external distress and danger, requires the very special and personal protection afforded by a religious authority who safeguards it in his own collection. On the initiative of a

40 Cortese, *Manuscripts* 125, ms. 176/1031: Shams al-Dīn al-Ṭayyibī, *Dustūr al-mawlā ʿAlāʾ al-Dīn* is a rare and as yet unstudied work on the regulations of the *daʿwa* under Imam ʿAlāʾ al-Dīn Muḥammad III of Alamūt. Ms. 154/994 (ibid. 95) contains the *qaṣīda al-mīmiyya* by Qays b. Manṣūr al-Dādīḫī (597–655/1200–1257) from Aleppo, who presumably died during the Mongol siege of Alamūt.

41 Friedrich and Schwarke, *One-volume libraries* 21; Schmidt, Ottoman multiple-text manuscripts 211.

42 Bauer, Literarische Anthologien 85–94.

religious authority, this preserved heritage occasionally finds application in the fields of education, teaching, and ritual.

In the following, we will turn our attention first to the manuscripts and then to the text and content of the work *Manāqib mawlānā Rāshid al-Dīn*, in order to draw further insights into the tradition of the Syrian Ismaʿilis.

2.2 *Three Witnesses of Tradition*

We know of three manuscripts in which the small *Manāqib* work survived:[43]

One of them was given to the Societé Asiatique in Paris by M. Catafago, Dragoman of the Prussian Consul General in Beirut. More detailed circumstances are unknown. In 1848 Catafago himself published a translation of the introduction to the work based on this manuscript, entitled *Faṣl min al-lafẓ al-sharīf* [—] *hādhihī manāqib al-mawlā Rāshid al-Dīn*.[44] In 1877, M. Stanislas Guyard published an edition of the same manuscript in the journal of the Societé, with a detailed historical introduction and translation, in which he drew attention to the manuscript's very poor condition.[45]

Muṣṭafā Ghālib,[46] however, based his edition on two other manuscripts. Among them is the oldest of the known textual witness (Siglum A of the edition): the manuscript was found, the editor informs us, in a *majmūʿa* from the collection of a *shaykh* he names, a well-known Ismaʿili scholar from the village of Khirbat al-Faras, near the coastal city of Tartus. According to Ghālib, the colophon of the manuscript bears the year 1078/1668,[47] which would make it more than 150 years older than the second manuscript included in his edition.

This second manuscript (Siglum B) Ghālib borrowed, as he writes, from a man in the small town of Maṣyaf, on the access side of the castle of the same name, the former headquarters of Sinān. Practicing *taqiyya*, the owner did not want to give his name.[48] The manuscript apparently came into Ghālib's possession and is now part of the *majmūʿāt* group in the Institute of Ismaili Studies in London. There it was recorded as ms. 156/1018[49] and a copy was given to me.[50] It is a composite manuscript, foliated throughout, consisting of three parts:

43 Poonawala, *Biobibliography* 290. See also Cortese, *Manuscripts* 100–1.

44 Catafago, Lettre 485–93. The manuscript is not recorded in Georges Vajda's catalogue of the manuscript collection of the Société Asiatique (1950).

45 Guyard, Grand maître 451.

46 Ghālib, Sinān Rāshid al-Dīn 165–214. This is not so much a critical edition as an editing with obvious cuts.

47 Ghālib, Sinān Rāshid al-Dīn 23–4.

48 Ibid.

49 Cortese, *Manuscripts* 99–101.

50 See footnote 27 above. On the basis of the microfilm copy available, it is not possible to check the materiality.

The first part comprises 187 folia.[51] The *Manāqib* work opens the second part of the composite (fol. 189[a]), which still has its original separate foliation of 68 folia. Varying slightly from the Catafago-Guyard manuscript, it is entitled *Manāqib al-mawlā Rāshid al-Dīn minhu l-salām*. The references in general terms to Ismaʿili warrantors at the beginning of each story are highlighted in red ink. At the end of the *Manāqib* text (fol. 223[a]) a large and multi-coloured floral star has been applied. Below this is the colophon listing the names of the compiler[52] and the scribe. The date of the copy is given as a Friday in Rajab 1242/January 1827. This part is followed by six hymns addressed to Rāshid al-Dīn. At the end of these hymns is a decorative leaf with the first lines of the Fātiḥa and a slightly different date, 1241/1826–7 (fol. 230[b]). Unlike the Catafago-Guyard manuscript, which, according to Guyard's brief description, is a simple, partially incorrectly transcribed, utilitarian manuscript intended for everyday use rather than for display, the *Manāqib* contained in this composite manuscript is an aesthetically decorated object transcribed by a single hand in predominantly correct Arabic.

The individual biography of a manuscript can be vividly compared to a life cycle with different stages and phases.[53] Accordingly, we can say that ms. 156/1018 saw the light of day when the two older parts were bound together in leather and united by a new foliation (230 folia). The inner binding was decorated with an arabesque rectangle, which has since been dyed deep black. Presumably it contained the name of the first owner, who was consigned to oblivion. On the opposite folio one can read that the book was given as a gift (*rizq*) from a father to his son. Underneath that notice, the later owner, Muṣṭafā Ghālib, imprinted his own stamp before it was sent on the journey to London in the late 1980s with other manuscripts that came to the Institute after Ghālib's death.

2.3 *Variants*—Two Versions of *Manāqib al-mawlā Rāshid al-Dīn minhu l-salām*

According to Charles Pellat,[54] *manāqib* works in Arabic literary history have taken as their subject a whole spectrum of luminaries—religious dignitar-

51 On the contents, see Cortese, *Manuscripts* 99–100.

52 See below, 2.3.

53 Akkerman, Manuscript treasure 199–200. On the ethnographically *and* culturally informed term and concept of *social codicology* developed by Akkerman in her dissertation, *The Bohra dark archive and the language of secrecy* (2016), as a tense and mutually effective encounter between the world of the social and that of philology, in this case of manuscripts, see Akkerman, Manuscript treasure 183.

54 Pellat, Manāḳib.

ies, scholars, and persons of other professions, as well as entire families and dynasties—all of them distinguished by their deeds and their character traits. Virtues are also honoured in similar genres of works, with titles such as *tarjama*, *taʿrīf*, *sīra*, *akhbār*, *faḍāʾil*. One of the many varieties of the genre is popular hagiography, which can be traced increasingly in the Islamic world from the 5th/11th century. In these works, a (previously orally disseminated) tale of a universally revered ascetic, saint, Sufi, or founder of a Sufi order is cast in the literary form of a portrait of a saint. In this context, *manāqib* can also take on the meaning of "miracle," a concept that also applies to the present work about the *daʿwa* hero from Syria.[55]

In this sense, the eulogy on Rāshid al-Dīn Sinān is to be understood as a collection of popular stories extolling the virtues and miracles of the spiritual and political leader. The most important historical source in this context is the biography of Sinān by the Aleppo historian Kamāl al-Dīn Ibn al-ʿAdīm (d. 660/1262), which was translated and presented by Bernard Lewis. The many details about Sinān's life, actions, and environment contained in Kamāl al-Dīn's biography of the Ismaʿili leader attest to the historical significance of the *Manāqib*, despite its hagiographical character.[56]

The small collection of stories is available, as previously shown, in the London ms. 156/1018 and in Guyard's and Ghālib's editions. All three testimonies mention the date of its compilation shortly after the introduction to the work, given as the end of the month of Shawwāl in 724/October 1324. Only in the colophon of the *Manāqib*, fol. 223[a], as mentioned above, is the name of a compiler listed (*jamaʿahā*), but without mention of the year. For reasons that will become clear, it appears that this is perhaps a second, later compiler or editor.

The name given in this colophon on fol. 223[a] is Abū Firās Shihāb al-Dīn b. al-Qāḍī Naṣr (or Ibrāhīm) b. Dhī l-Jawshan b. al-Ḥusayn al-Daylamī al-Maynaqī, whose father moved from Daylam to Maynaqa, in Syria, in 859/1455, where he was born in 872/1467–8. He was chief *dāʿī* and is also known as the author of a *Kitāb al-Īḍāḥ*. He died in 937/1530–1 or 947/1540–1 in the fortress of Maynaqa.[57]

55 On Sinān's key biographical data: He was born between 527–30/1133–5 to a Shiʿite family in Basra. At a young age he moved to the small Ismaʿili state of Alamūt, where he was educated under Imam Ḥasan II (557–61/1162–6) and received extensive training as a spiritual and military leader. From there he was sent in 557/1162 to the Ismaʿili satellite state in north-western Syria, whose leadership he soon assumed. Sinān died between 588–90/1192–4: Halm, *Die Schia* 228–9.

56 Lewis, Biography; also by Hodgson, *The secret order* 185–92; Poonawala, *Biobibliography* 290.

57 Ibid. 294–5. On Maynaqa (or Manīqa) Castle see Willey, *Eagle's nest* 230–2, map 45; Thorau, Burgen 145, incl. note 76; Guyard, Grand maître 391, incl. note 2.

Since the year and name of the compiler are not mentioned together in any of the three textual witnesses, but separately towards the beginning and in the colophon, it can be assumed that there were multiple redactions (and possibly multiple compilers).

According to this chronology, which is based on the somewhat puzzling evidence found in these *Manāqib* manuscripts, it appears that the compilation of orally circulated stories could have been made by an unnamed compiler in 724/1324, about 130 years after Sinān's death and 50 years after the Mamluk conquest of the region (659/1260). Then in the 15th/16th century, the collection was complemented and edited by Abū Firās.

Marshall G.S. Hodgson devoted a short chapter to the work, foregrounding some specific narrative motifs.[58] Among these is a visit by 40 Sunni *ʿulamāʾ* from Damascus to Sinān's castle of Kahf. Sinān defeats them with his argumentation and convinces them of the right faith; he foresees their collective death on the return journey, whereby the eldest of the group still manages to bring the bad news to the Supreme Qāḍī in Damascus before his own demise.[59] Likewise, Hodgson draws attention to Sinān's touching love of animals. The miracles that the hero performs with particular frequency could be typologised as prophecy, telepathy, or magic. The hagiographic motifs are thus universal, but in the collection of stories they are illustratively embedded in the rocky, mountainous world of Jabal Bahrāʾ. The beneficiaries of the "wondrous miracles" (*ʿajāʾib gharāʾib*) are—how could it be otherwise?—the believing Ismaʿilis (*muʾminūn muwaḥḥidūn*), who are also addressed in the introduction.

Hodgson aptly calls Sinān's mode of representation a "one-man-show."[60] In the *Manāqib* work, the main protagonist is highly active and at times a miracle worker, who travels between his castles, solving problems, caring for the Ismaʿili families, and much involved with foreign policy. With unparalleled arrogance, he rejects Saladin's messenger and defies his siege of Maṣyaf from the neighbouring mountain. Later, having become Saladin's friend, the Lord of the Mountain sends two of his *fidāʾis* out at night; speaking the Frankish language and disguised as monks, they penetrate the tent of a drunkenly sleeping Frankish king and dispatch him with their deadly daggers.[61]

58 Hodgson, *The secret order* 193–7.

59 Guyard, Grand maître, story 12, 421–5.

60 Ibid. 195.

61 In 1192, the Marquis Conrad of Montferrat was assassinated in Tyre shortly before his coronation as King of Jerusalem; historiography disputes whether Rāshid al-Dīn acted in Saladin's interest or whether Richard I the Lionheart was responsible here: Willey, *Eagle's nest* 48; Hodgson, *The secret order* 189; Lewis, Biography 226.

Each story is conveyed by the compiler/editor speaking in the first person, with slight variations, referring to Sinān's close confidants (e.g. *wa-qad ḥakā ilayya baʿḍu l-rufaqāʾi l-umanāʾi ʿani l-mawlā Rāshid al-Dīn*, ms. 156/1018, fol. 189ᵇ). The stories in the compilation are quite different in terms of their length and complexity: extremely simple miracle stories contrast with more complex and stylistically elaborate ones, with interludes in rhyming prose and poetry.[62]

First of all, it is striking that all three textual witnesses have a common core corpus comprising 17 stories, even if the order of the individual stories varies from time to time. But their number, in addition to the 17 core stories, also varies: Guyard's text witness is the most detailed with 31 stories, while the present London manuscript ms. 156/1018 has 21 stories; Ghālib's edition comprises 17 stories.[63] Among the additional stories in the Guyard manuscript is a group of eight consecutive stories. Seven of them deal with the protagonist recognising in wild or even domesticated animals the souls of deceased people or animals and usually reacting compassionately to them.[64]

This group of motifs stands out because the transmigration of souls through different living beings (*tanāsukh*) is not an element of Ismaʿili doctrine. On the other hand, it is a central part of the mythology of their often hostile neighbours and competitors, the Nuṣairis (Alawites).[65] The eighth story that follows here reports on them. In it, a group of ten "chiefs of the Shimālīs and mountain dwellers"[66] seek out the Ismaʿili leader to pay homage to him and his teachings; even a recalcitrant who, as a good Nuṣairi, initially pays reverence to the incoming rays of the sun rather than to Sinān, eventually submits. He ultimately admits (in rhyming prose) that God "reveals to this man what is concealed and discloses the secrets of what is hidden," whereupon Sinān bestows on him, as he has already done for the others of his group, a robe of honour.[67]

As the deputy of Imam Muḥammad II (561–607/1166–1210), who was by then in power in Alamūt, Sinān was actually commissioned to preach in Syria the doctrine of *qiyāma*, the age of the resurrection and return in the flesh of the Imam. Instead, he presented himself as a spiritual leader of cosmic, even divine

62 E.g. story 7, in Guyard, Grand maître 398–408 (translation), 458–63 (edition).

63 Since Ghālib's edition is very unreliable, this cannot be interpreted further.

64 Guyard, Grand maître 437–45, stories 19–27, with the exception of 25.

65 On the influence of Nuṣairi elements on popular Ismaʿili religiosity in the region, see Daftary, *The Ismāʿīlīs* 371–2; Dussaud, Influence.

66 Dussaud, *Histoire* 79 incl. footnote 6, 81–96. The Shimālis are a Nuṣairi clan whose history, teachings, and rites Dussaud describes in detail.

67 Guyard, Grand maître, story 27, 445–8 (translation), 486–8 (edition).

rank.[68] In fact, there is evidence that Sinān had many followers among his former enemies. A treatise attributed to him and published by Guyard shows that he modified the Ismaʿili doctrine of salvation in favour of an approximation of the Nuṣairi doctrine, by declaring himself to be the All-Soul and thus a divine emanation.[69] Sinān's doctrinaire self-promotion had the consequence that the grand master of Alamūt, Imam Muḥammad II, sought to have him killed, and some of the Syrian Ismaʿilis disavowed their allegiance to him.[70]

Thus, the presence or absence of these religiously explosive motifs can be discerned as a reflection of the religio-political dynamics at play, under the influence of which this popular collection of stories was assembled and handed down. The two versions correspond to the controversial positions that could be taken on the doctrinal approach of Nuṣairis and Nizārīs in Syria. The history of tradition and the history of religion are closely intertwined here.

3 Historical Arabic Literary History(s)

Social and political factors, such as mission, emigration, persecution, and diaspora, contributed significantly to the widespread dissemination and diversification of Ismaʿili doctrine and literature. While some richly filled libraries of the Ṭayyibi Bohras have recently been opened in the West Indies, there is still great uncertainty about the literature of the Nizāri Ismaʿilis in Syria, Iran, and Central Asia between the 13th and 20th centuries.[71] One literature that remains almost unknown today is that of the Syrian Ismaʿilis, which is the focus of this article. While the followers of the Ṭayyibi branch of the Ismaʿiliyya see themselves as the proud heirs of the religious and historiographical Fatimid literary tradition,[72] there is a dramatic gap in the tradition in the Nizāri sphere of the

68 On Sinān's career, actions, and transfiguration as imam or god, see Daftary, The *Ismāʿīlīs* 367–73. Sinān's transcendence is also reflected in the dedicated hymns, which are reproduced in ms. 156/1018 following the work. In one of them he is invoked as *khāliq makhlūq*, "created creator," fol. 224[b].

69 In his Fragments relatifs à la doctrine des Ismaélîs, 178–80, Guyard mentions a composite manuscript in the possession of the Societé Asiatique in Paris (Vajda, *Catalogue* 8, no. 21), at the beginning of which is placed a tract entitled *Faṣl min al-faḍ* [sic] *al-sharīf lil-mawlā Rāshid al-Dīn*, which is not identical with the *Manāqib*. In this text, Rāshid al-Dīn presents himself as the incarnation of a number of earlier prophets and Shiʿi spiritual authorities (Guyard, Fragments 178–80, 193–5, 275–84); Dussaud, *Histoire* 23–4, 54; idem, Influence 66, 68–9; Daftary, *The Ismāʿīlīs* 371–2.

70 Guyard, Grand maître 364–5.

71 Virani, *The Ismailis in the Middle Ages* 9–12.

72 Akkerman, Bohras.

Ismaʿiliyya. It can be placed in the context of successive Turco-Mongol waves of attack and conquest, as well as suppression in the subsequent Safavid period. The former Ismaʿili territorial state in Syria apparently became a largely isolated enclave in the course of the history outlined here, up until the late 19th century.

Writing literary history is and remains a core task of Arabic studies. One of its many challenges is to explore, beyond the great monuments, the areas in which literary history takes place under crisis-ridden circumstances that shape its transmission, ways of transmission, and practices. This applies to pre-modern literature as well as—in a renewed age of displacement, flight, and migration—to modern Arabic literature.[73] The exploration of the dispersed, the regional, and the non-conforming contributes significantly to the proportionality of the "big picture" of Arab literary history. This also includes the question of the reasons for and patterns of possible non-transmission.[74]

Taking a closer look at a small, seemingly blank spot on the map of this inexhaustible Arabic-Islamic literary history, we have dealt with a multiply fractured, heterodox literary history in its geographical, political, and social environment. Using the example of a few multiple-text and composite manuscripts and their paratextual contents, we were able to show that the Syrian Ismaʿilis practised a special manuscript culture in their mountainous retreat. Here, away from the cities and the educational institutions, religious experts compiled traditions, text excerpts, *qaṣīda*s, and hymns in thematic anthologies that constituted concise and compact one-volume libraries. These were and are kept and protected in private collections, so that even today they are (intentionally) undocumented and inaccessible to research. Despite their insularity, as the small size of the corpus testifies, some of the ancient Ismaʿili and Fatimid classics reached the Jabal Bahrāʾ, as did textual witnesses from Alamūt and mystical poetry, such as that of Ibn al-ʿArabī. Otherwise, according to the manuscripts, a Syrian-regional religious tradition of thought, text, and poetry developed here. This includes the story collection *Manāqib al-mawlā Rāshid al-Dīn*, whose two variants of transmission—those with and those without the transmigration of souls elements—we have placed in close relation to the interreligious and social dynamics in the remote mountain region.

It is *precisely* in their harsh contrast to the literary high culture at the court of Hama that characteristics and forms of the Ismaʿili tradition in Jabal Bahrāʾ emerge all the more clearly. Nevertheless, this case study naturally leaves quite

73 See Refqa Abu Rumeileh's project: "Country of words: Reading and reception of Palestinian literature from 1948 to the present" (European Research Council, ERC, 2018–23).

74 Cf. Esch, Überlieferungs-Chance 537; Haye, *Verlorenes Mittelalter* 1–4.

a few questions open with regard to the transmission of Ismaʿili doctrine in Syria. One of the most interesting overarching questions may be how to formulate a more precise definition of the so-called "Ismaʿili anthology" here, especially in comparing it with anthologies in other heterodox and Sufi milieus. Further research into the history of transmission would also be promising in the interest of constructing a differentiated literary-historical inventory and analysis. As the preliminary research presented here demonstrates, *majmūʿāt* prove to be productive sources of literary and social historical knowledge.

Acknowledgements

Thanks to: Olly Akkerman, Stefanie Brinkmann, Hülya Çelik, Delia Cortese, Farhad Daftary, Dorothea Günther, Ghazwan Kanbar, Rüdiger Kuhn, Boris Liebrenz, Ulrich Marzolph, Wafi Momen, Nour Nourmamadchoev, Nuha al-Shaʾar, Avi Shivtiel, Ismail Tamir, and for her valuable editorial assistance, Linda George.

Bibliography

Akkerman, O., The Bohra manuscript treasure as a sacred site of philology: A study in social codicology, in *Philological Encounters* 4 (2019), 182–201.

Akkerman, O., The Bohras as neo-Fāṭimids: Documentary remains of a Fāṭimid past in Gujarat, in *Journal of Material Cultures in the Muslim World* 1 (2020), 291–313.

Akkerman, O., *The Bohra dark archive and the language of secrecy: A codicological ethnography of the Royal ʿAlawī Bohra Library in Baroda* (PhD Diss., Freie Universität Berlin, 2016). To be published under the title: *A neo-Fatimid treasury of books: Arabic manuscripts among the Alawi Bohras of Baroda*, Edinburgh 2021.

Amīn, M., *Salamiyya fī khamsīn qarnan*, Salamiyya 1983.

Bauer, T., Jamāl al-Dīn Ibn Nubātah, in J.E. Lowry and D.J. Stewart (eds.), *Essays in Arabic Literary Biography 1350–1850*, Wiesbaden 2010, 184–202.

Bauer, T., Anthologies, Arabic literature (Post-Mongol period), in EI[3], 2007/1, 124–8.

Bauer, T., Literarische Anthologien der Mamlūkenzeit, in S. Conermann and A. Pistor-Hatam (eds.), *Die Mamlūken: Studien zu ihrer Geschichte und Kultur. Zum Gedenken an Ulrich Haarmann (1942–1999)*, Schenefeld 2003, 71–122.

Bausi, A., M. Friedrich, and M. Maniaci (eds.), *The emergence of multiple-text manuscripts*, Berlin/Boston 2019.

Böhme, E., *Die Außenbeziehungen des Königreiches Jerusalem im 12. Jahrhundert: Kontinuität und Wandel im Herrscherwechsel zwischen König Amalich und Balduin IV.*, Berlin/Boston 2019.

Brockelmann, C., *History of the Arabic written tradition*, 2 vols. and 4 suppl. vols., Leiden 2016–18.

Catafago, M., Lettre de M. Catafago a M. Mohl, in *JA*, 4 série, 12 (1848), 485–93.

Cortese, D., *Ismaili and other Arabic manuscripts: A descriptive catalogue of manuscripts in the library of the Institute of Ismaili Studies*, London/New York 2000.

Daftary, F., *The Ismāʿīlīs: Their history and doctrines*, London 1990.

Daftary, F., *The Assassin legends: Myths of the Ismaʿilis*, London 1994.

Douwes, D., Modern history of the Nizari Ismailis of Syria, in F. Daftary (ed.), *A modern history of the Ismailis: Continuity and change in a Muslim community*, London/New York 2011, 19–43.

Douwes, D., and N.N. Lewis, The trials of Syrian Ismailis in the first decade of the 20th century, in *JMES* 21, 2 (1989), 215–32.

Dussaud, R., Influence de la religion Noṣairī sur la doctrine de Rāchid ad-Dīn Sinān, in *JA*, 9 série, 16 (1900), 61–9.

Dussaud, R., *Histoire et religion des Noṣairīs*, Paris 1900.

Elmalı, H., *el-Keşkûl*, in *TDVIA*, xxv, 324–5.

Esch, A., Überlieferungs-Chance und Überlieferungs-Zufall als methodisches Problem des Historikers, in *Historische Zeitschrift* 204 (1985), 529–70.

Friedrich, M., and C. Schwarke (eds.), *One-volume libraries: Composite and multiple-text manuscripts*, Berlin/Boston 2016.

Ghālib, M., *Sinān Rāshid al-Dīn, Shaykh al-jabal al-thālith*, Beirut 1967.

Guyard, M.S., Fragments relatifs à la doctine des Ismaélîs: Texte publié pour la première fois avec une traduction complète et des notes, in *Notices et extraits des manuscrits de la Bibliothèque Nationale et autres bibliothèques*, 2 (1874), 177–428.

Guyard, M.S., Un grand maître des Assassins au temps de Saladin, in *JA*, 7 série, 9 (1877), 324–489.

Halm, H., *Die Schia*, Wiesbaden 1988.

Haye, T., *Verlorenes Mittelalter: Ursachen und Muster der Nichtüberlieferung mittellateinischer Texte*, Leiden 2016.

Hirschler, K., The development of Arabic multiple-text and composite manuscripts: The case of *ḥadīth* manuscripts in Damascus in the late medieval period, in A. Bausi, M. Friedrich and M. Maniaci, *The emergence of multiple-text manuscripts*, Berlin/Boston 2019, 275–304.

Hodgson, M.G.S., *The secret order of Assassins: The struggle of the early Nizārī Ismāʿīlīs against the Islamic world*, Philadelphia 2005 (Erstauflage 1955).

Klein, D. et al. (eds.), *Überlieferungsgeschichte transdisziplinär: Neue Perspektiven auf ein germanistisches Forschungsparadigma*, Wiesbaden 2016.

Lewis, B., Kamāl al-Dīn's biography of Rāšid al-Dīn Sinān, in *Arabica* 13, 3 (1966), 225–67.

Löser, F., Überlieferungsgeschichte(n) schreiben, in D. Klein et al. (eds.), *Überlieferungsgeschichte transdisziplinär*, 1–19.

Merali, A., Fear and violence in late Ottoman Syria: The Ismaʿilis and the School of Agriculture, in *Diyâr* 1 (2020), 58–83.

Metzler Lexikon Literatur, ed. by D. Burdorf, C. Fasbender, and B. Moennighof, 3rd ed., Stuttgart/Weimar 2007.

Pellat, Ch., Manāḳib, in *EI*², vi, 349–57.

Poonawala, I.K., *Biobibliography of Ismaili literature*, Malibu 1977.

Poonawala, I.K., ʿĀmir b. ʿĀmir al-Baṣrī: Ismāʿīlī or unorthodox Twelver Šīʿī-Ṣūfī?, in *Arabica* 66 (2019), 43–81.

Procházka-Eisl, G., and H. Çelik (eds.), *Texts on popular knowledge in early Ottoman times*, vol. 1, Cambridge MA 2015.

Rousseau, J.-B., *Mémoire sur les trois plus fameuses sectes musulmans, les Wahabis, les Nosaïris et les Ismaélis*, Paris 1818.

Schmidt, J., From 'one-volume libraries' to scrapbooks: Ottoman multiple-text and composite manuscripts in the early modern age (1400–1800), in M. Friedrich and C. Schwarke (eds.), *One-volume libraries: Composite and multiple-text manuscripts*, Berlin/Boston 2016, 207–32.

Tāmir, ʿA., *Arbaʿ rasāʾil Ismāʿīliyya*, Salamiyya 1952.

Thorau, P., Die Burgen der Assassinen in Syrien und ihre Einnahme durch Sultan Baibars, in *WO* 18 (1987), 132–58.

Vajda, G., *Catalogue des manuscrits arabes de la Société Asiatique de Paris*, Paris 1950.

Virani, S.N., *The Ismailis in the Middle Ages: A history of survival, a search for salvation*, Oxford 2007.

Walker, P., *Exploring an Islamic empire: Fatimid history and its sources*, London/New York 2002.

Willey, P., *Eagle's nest: Ismaili castles in Iran and Syria*, London/New York 2005.

11

„Betrübte Weisen im Waldrevier“ – Die Taube in Anthologien der Mamlukenzeit

Anke Osigus

Kaum ein Vogel hat in der arabischen Kulturgeschichte eine so große Bedeutung wie die Taube, die sowohl als freilebende Wildform (*barrī*) wie auch als domestizierte Form der Haustaube (*ahlī*) über Jahrhunderte bis in die Gegenwart eng mit dem Alltag der Menschen verbunden war. Ob das ganze Jahr über als Standvögel (*awābid*) oder nur eine Saison als Zugvögel (*qawāṭiʿ*), fast immer gehörten Tauben zur städtischen wie ländlichen Vogelfauna.

Eine Vielzahl von Haustaubenrassen mit unzähligen Farb- und Zeichnungsvarietäten zeugt von einer langen Zuchttradition, die mit großer Akribie gepflegt wurde und die Taubenhaltung außerhalb des orientalischen Kulturraums mitgeprägt hat. Etliche Taubenrassen, die heute in Europa gezüchtet werden, stammen ursprünglich aus der arabischen Region, wie nicht nur die Namen dieser Rassen, sondern oft auch ihrer Farbenschläge erkennen lassen.[1] Das wohl bekannteste Beispiel einer „Einwanderin“ ist die Nürnberger Bagdette (engl. *scandaroon*), eine Warzentaube, die wahrscheinlich im 18. Jahrhundert oder früher von Kaufleuten in die Nürnberger Gegend gebracht wurde und noch heute als „lebendes Denkmal der Taubenzüchterkultur“ von Liebhabern geschätzt wird.[2]

Die Bereiche, in denen die Taube als reales Tier und Kristallisationsfigur in der Literatur der arabischen Vormoderne anzutreffen ist, sind ebenso vielfältig wie verschieden. Keine Rolle für den vorliegenden Beitrag spielen die Nutzeffekte, die mit dem Verzehr von Taubenfleisch[3] – auch zu therapeutischen Zwecken – und der Verwendung von Taubenmist als Heil- und Düngemittel

1 Drei Rassen mögen hier als Beispiele genügen: *Ägyptischer Segler*, Farbenschläge: Abiad, Abrasdel, Rihani (Schmidt/Proll, *Tauben* 38); *Basraer Wammentaube*, Farbenschläge: Abiad, Schrabi, Abrasdel, Rihani (Schmidt/Proll, *Tauben* 47); *Libanontaube*, Farbenschläge: Innabi, Schickli, Mischmischi, Azraq-Achdar, Bayumli, Korunfli, Irgani, Nehasi, Mawardi (Schmidt/Proll, *Tauben* 108).

2 Vgl. Ragheb, *Messagers* 82; Zitat aus Schmidt/Proll, *Tauben* 121.

3 Vgl. Lewicka, *Food* 199–200, 206–7 (Fußnote 352).

 | DOI:10.1163/9789004521780_013

verbunden sind.[4] Für Alltag und Literatur gleichermaßen interessant ist hingegen die Brieftaube, die als Botin politisch und militärisch wichtiger Kurznachrichten seit Beginn des abbasidischen Kalifats (Ende 2./8. Jh.) im Einsatz war.[5] Dank eines engen Netzwerks von Taubenstationen erlebte die Brieftaubenpost in mamlukischer Zeit einen Höhepunkt und wurde – neben *barīd* und *manār* („Leucht-/Feuersignal") – zur dritten Säule der Nachrichtenübermittlung.[6]

In der Poesie ist die Taube einer der beliebtesten, wenn nicht der beliebteste Vogel.[7] Sie gehört zum festen Figureninventar verschiedener Genres, insbesondere der Naturdichtung (*rawḍiyyāt, zahriyyāt, rabīʿiyyāt*) sowie der Liebes- und Trauerdichtung (*ġazal* und *riṯāʾ*), wo sie als Identifikationsfigur des Dichters seine Gefühle anregt und spiegelt.

Angesichts dieser Verbreitung und Beliebtheit überrascht es nicht, dass die Taube auch in Kapitelüberschriften literarischer Anthologien regelmäßig genannt wird, oft sogar als einziges Tier ein eigenes (Unter-)Kapitel einnimmt. Was aber haben die Anthologisten späterer Epochen aus dem reichhaltigen, über Jahrhunderte angewachsenen Fundus der Taubenliteratur ausgesucht? Wie haben sie ihre Auswahl an älteren und jüngeren Texten, an Prosa und Poesie gewichtet, und wie sind jüngere Autoren mit tradierten Topoi und Motiven umgegangen? Dies sind einige Fragen, um die es im vorliegenden Beitrag gehen soll. Als Textgrundlage wurden fünf mamlukenzeitliche Anthologien ausgewählt, die im 8.–9./14.–15. Jahrhundert entstanden sind. Diese sind:

1. Ibn Abī Ḥaǧala (st. 776/1375): *Sulūk as-sanan ilā waṣf as-sakan*[8]
2. ʿAlāʾ ad-Dīn al-Ġuzūlī (st. 815/1411–2): *Maṭāliʿ al-budūr fī manāzil as-surūr*[9]
3. Ibn Ḥiǧǧa al-Ḥamawī (st. 837/1434): *Taʾhīl al-ġarīb*[10]
4. Muḥammad b. Abī Bakr al-Asyūṭī (st. 859 oder 856/1454–5 oder 1452–3): *al-Marǧ an-naḍir wa-l-araǧ al-ʿaṭir*[11]
5. an-Nawāǧī (st. 859/1455): *Ḥalbat al-kumayt*[12]

---

4 Vgl. Viré, Ḥamām 110a.

5 Zur Brieftaube in der arabischen Vormoderne vgl. die Monographie von Ragheb, *Messagers*.

6 Silverstein, *Postal systems* 178.

7 Vgl. v.a. Abū Zayd, *Ḥamām*.

8 Ibn Abī Ḥaǧala, *Sulūk*, fol. 29b–31a; Alev Masarwa hat mir freundlicherweise den Manuskriptauszug und ihre Abschrift zur Verfügung gestellt.

9 Al-Ġuzūlī, *Maṭāliʿ* (Ed. Kairo 1881), i, 66–73 (Kap. 12), ii, 260–4 (Kap. 46); (Ed. Kairo 2000), 81–9 (Kap. 12), 579–82 (Kap. 46).

10 Ibn Ḥiǧǧa, *Taʾhīl al-ġarīb*, 751–69; Ms. Gotha, A 2156, fol. 75b–78a.

11 Al-Asyūṭī, *al-Marǧ an-naḍir*, BN 3385, fol. 113b–115a; BN 3386, fol. 134b–137b.

12 An-Nawāǧī, *Ḥalbat al-kumayt* 323–8.

Was das Verhältnis von Poesie und Prosa (mit und ohne Reim) angeht, so variieren die Werke stark: Ibn Abī Ḥaǧala bietet überwiegend Prosa, bei al-Ġuzūlī und an-Nawāǧī halten sich beide Formen in etwa die Waage, während Ibn Ḥiǧǧa al-Ḥamawī und al-Asyūṭī fast nur Poesie zitieren.

Die beiden ersten Werke sind sich nicht nur zeitlich am nächsten, sie zeigen auch inhaltlich und textlich weitreichende Übereinstimmungen, die sich dadurch erklären, dass Ibn Abī Ḥaǧalas Anthologie al-Ġuzūlī als Vorbild diente, ohne dass dieser darauf hinweist.[13] Ibn Abī Ḥaǧala kann hingegen mit Recht in seiner Einleitung bemerken, dass sein noch nicht ediertes *Sulūk as-sanan ilā waṣf as-sakan* („Der rechte Pfad zur Beschreibung der Wohnsitze“) das erste Werk seiner Art ist.

In 33 kurzen Kapiteln geht es um Themen wie Planung und Kauf eines Hauses, Sehnsucht nach einem eigenen Heim, Nachbarschaft, Belüftungssysteme und Wasserspeicher wie Windturm (*baḏhanǧ* bzw. *bādhanǧ* und *bādanǧ*) und Wasserrad,[14] Badezimmer und Toilette, städtische Fauna, Freizeitbeschäftigungen wie Schach und Musik, Beleuchtung sowie Essen und Trinken. In al-Ġuzūlīs *Maṭāliʿ al-budūr fī manāzil as-surūr* („Aufgänge der Vollmonde über den Wohnsitzen der Freude“) wird die Palette der 50 Kapitel noch um Themen wie Berufsgruppen (Ärzte, Wesire und Kanzleistilisten), Geschenke, Waffen und Bücher erweitert.[15] Die Kapitel, die sich in beiden Werken mit verschiedenen Tieren beschäftigen, spiegeln ihr Verhältnis zueinander wider: Während sich Ibn Abī Ḥaǧala in lediglich drei Kapiteln Vögeln und Kriechtieren (*ḥašarāt*) widmet, behandelt al-Ġuzūlī in sieben Kapiteln die urbane Tierwelt und bezieht dabei auch Tiere mit ein, die man eigentlich nicht in einer Stadt erwartet:

13 Vgl. Masarwa, Urban architecture 110.
14 Ausführlich Masarwa, Urban architecture; ead., Wasser, Wein und Architektur.
15 Vgl. Masarwa, Urban architecture 109–14.

Ibn Abī Ḥağala: *Sulūk as-sanan*	al-Ġuzūlī: *Maṭāliʿ al-budūr*
	12 **Singvögel**
18 Moskitos, Wanzen, Flöhe und andere Kriechtiere	
19 **Tauben**	
20 Papageien, Pfaue, Wachteln und Käfige	
	42 Reittiere
	43 Jagd
	44 Zootiere
	45 Löwen, Giraffen, Elefanten
	46 **Tauben**
	49 Kriechtiere

Beiden Anthologien gemeinsam ist, dass die Taube als einziges Tier ein eigenes Kapitel erhalten hat; im *Maṭāliʿ* ist sie sogar in einem weiteren Kapitel über Singvögel (12) mit Prosa und Poesie prominent vertreten. Wenden wir uns zunächst den in beiden Werken einander entsprechenden Kapiteln zu, welche die Taube allein in den Mittelpunkt stellen.

Wie zu erwarten, baut al-Ġuzūlīs Kapitel 46 auf Ibn Abī Ḥağalas Kapitel 19 auf, das in den gemeinsamen Partien häufig den besseren Text hat.[16] Beide Werke beginnen mit einer weitgehend korrespondierenden Prosaeinleitung, die einen historischen Abriss der arabischen Taubenhaltung bietet. Der Text informiert, dass es unter Angehörigen der Oberschicht ein beliebter Zeitvertreib war, Tauben im Haus zu halten und führt zum Beleg eine Reihe namhafter Taubenliebhaber an. Den Anfang macht der spätabbasidische Kalif an-Nāṣir li-Dīn Allāh (575–622/1180–1225),[17] der von den Vögeln und, so der Text bei Ibn Abī Ḥağala, „dem Spiel mit ihnen" angetan war.[18] Die Wendung *al-laʿb bi-l-ḥamām* steht für ein Vergnügen, das keineswegs ein Privileg von Herrschern und Notablen war, sondern über die Standesgrenzen hinweg besonders Angehörige mittlerer und unterer Schichten ansprach. Die zweckfreie Form des Taubensports

16 Die eingesehenen Editionen haben viele gemeinsame und individuelle Fehler und Lücken.

17 Vgl. zu ihm Hartmann, *an-Nāṣir*, bes. 96–7.

18 Ibn Abī Ḥağala, *Sulūk*, fol. 29^{b}; al-Ġuzūlī, *Maṭāliʿ* (1881) 260, (2000) 579.

unter Mitgliedern der *ʿāmma* war der Obrigkeit oft ein Dorn im Auge, die in wiederkehrenden Säuberungsaktionen versuchte, der Taubenspielerei ein Ende zu bereiten. Als Standardargument wurde angeführt, dass Taubenzüchter unter dem Vorwand, den Flug ihrer Vögel zu verfolgen, auf Dächer stiegen, um fremde Frauen in Innenhöfen und Gärten zu beobachten.[19] Wie tiefverwurzelt diese Ablehnung gegenüber dem Taubensport war, zeigt der (schwache) auf Sufyān aṯ-Ṯawrī (st. 161/778) zurückgeführte *ḥadīṯ*:

كان اللعب بالحمام من عمل قوم لوط

Das Spielen mit Tauben gehört zum Treiben der Leute Lots.[20]

Als Herrscher hätte sich der erwähnte an-Nāṣir kaum um Bedenken dieser Art kümmern müssen; doch galt sein Interesse ohnehin eher der Haltung von Reisetauben, die primär der Briefbeförderung diente und damit gesellschaftlich akzeptierter war als das scheinbar sinnlose Hobby der Taubenspielerei. Der Kalif, der auch ein begeisterter Bogenschütze und Jäger war, soll seinen Tauben so zugetan gewesen sein, dass er wichtige Amtsgeschäfte vernachlässigte, um nicht den Flug seiner Lieblingstaube zu verpassen.[21]

Über zwei Jahrhunderte früher hat der nächste Taubenfreund, in beiden Anthologien als Wesir Abū l-Farağ Yaʿqūb angeführt, gelebt. Es handelt sich um Ibn Killis (318–80/930–91), den mächtigen und kulturbeflissenen ersten Wesir der Fatimidendynastie.[22] Ibn Abī Ḥağala und al-Ġuzūlī überliefern die bekannte Anekdote, nach der ihm das Missgeschick widerfährt, mit seiner Taube die Taube des Kalifen al-ʿAzīz im Wettflug (*musābaqa*) zu besiegen. Als darauf Ibn Killis' Feinde dem Kalifen einreden, dass der „Wesir stets das Beste für sich selber aussuchen" würde, sendet dieser dem Herrscher einen Zweizeiler (unbekannter Herkunft), den beide Anthologien als erstes Taubengedicht anführen:

فكتب إلى الخليفة [من السريع]
قُل لأمير المؤمنين[23] الذي * له العُلا والكَوكَبُ الثاقِبُ
طائِرُكَ السابِقُ لكنّه * جاء وفي خِدْمتِهِ حاجِبُ

19 Vgl. Grotzfeld, al-Laʿb, bes. 193–5.
20 Vgl. Ṣaqr, *Mawsūʿa* vi, 210 (s. auch Grotzfeld, al-Laʿb 194–5).
21 Ibn Taġrībirdī, *Nuğūm* vi, 261–2 (vgl. auch Ragheb, *Messagers* 61).
22 Zu ihm vgl. Canard, Ibn Killis; Saker, *Der Wille zur Macht*.
23 Ibn Abī Ḥağala, *Sulūk*, fol. 29[b]: قل للخليفة.

Da schrieb er an den Kalifen:
Sag dem Beherrscher der Gläubigen, der über Hoheit und einen glänzenden Stern verfügt:
„Dein Vogel hatte den Vorrang, aber er kam an mit einem Kämmerer in seinen Diensten.“

Die Verse verfehlen nicht ihre Wirkung, und das ohnehin gute Verhältnis zwischen Herrscher und Wesir ist wieder ungetrübt, bis dieser, so berichten unsere Texte weiter, stirbt und in Ehren bestattet wird.[24] Keine Erwähnung findet in beiden Anthologien ein zweites Taubenabenteuer Ibn Killis', das als Beispiel für die Vielseitigkeit von Reisetauben in der einschlägigen – arabischen wie europäischen – Literatur oft zitiert wird.[25] Als der Kalif den Wunsch äußert, Kirschen aus Baalbek zu kosten, gelingt es Ibn Killis, die Früchte mit Hilfe von Kairiner Tauben, die sich gerade in Damaskus befinden, nach Kairo zu bringen.

Um eine Vorstellung vom einstigen Marktwert von Spitzenvögeln zu geben, zitieren Ibn Abī Ḥağala und al-Ġuzūlī aus der monumentalen Tiergeschichte *Kitāb al-Ḥayawān* von al-Ğāḥiẓ (st. 255/868–9), nach der die Taube einen Kaufpreis von 500 Dinaren erzielen kann, den kein anderer Vogel erreicht.[26] Wie außergewöhnlich hoch diese Summe auch zu al-Ğāḥiẓ' Zeit war, zeigt die entsprechende Stelle in seinem umfangreichen Taubenkapitel, wo er ausführt, dass nicht nur verschiedene Greifvögel, Pfau, Fasan (*tadruğ*) und Hahn einen geringeren Wert haben, sondern auch Kamel, Esel und Maulesel. Wer einen Bericht prüfen möchte, wonach jemand ein Arbeitspferd (*birḏawn*) oder Reitpferd (*faras*) zu einem Preis von 500 Dinar verkauft hat, könne nur in einer Geschichte aus der nächtlichen Unterhaltung (*ḥadīṯ as-samar*) fündig werden.[27]

Die Reihe der Taubenliebhaber wird fortgeführt mit dem Propheten: Dem unter Einsamkeit (*waḥša*) leidenden ʿAlī b. Abī Ṭālib rät Muḥammad, sich eine Taube zuzulegen, die ihn auch zum Gebet wecken würde. Er empfiehlt den Vogel als Schutz der Knaben vor Dschinnen und soll sogar selbst eine rote Taube mit Namen Wardān in seiner Wohnung gehalten haben.[28]

---

24 Ibn Abī Ḥağala, *Sulūk*, fol. 29b–30a; al-Ġuzūlī, *Maṭāliʿ* (1881) 260, (2000) 579.

25 Vgl. al-Qalqašandī, *Ṣubḥ al-aʿšā* xiv, 391; Abū Zayd, *Ḥamām* 37; Kociejowski, *Pigeon wars* 138–9.

26 Ibn Abī Ḥağala, *Sulūk*, fol. 30a; al-Ġuzūlī, *Maṭāliʿ* (1881) 260, (2000) 579.

27 Al-Ğāḥiẓ, *Hayawān* iii, 212.

28 Ibn Abī Ḥağala, *Sulūk*, fol. 30; al-Ġuzūlī, *Maṭāliʿ* (1881) 261, (2000) 579: Taube in beiden *Maṭāliʿ*-Texten als وردان angeführt.

Ein in Reimprosa verfasstes Loblied auf die Taube von einem gewissen Ibrāhīm b. Baššār preist neben äußerlichen Vorzügen des Vogels auch seine – durch Gesang und Anhänglichkeit – wohltuende Wirkung auf den Menschen. Insbesondere der allein Lebende (*al-waḥīd*) gewöhnt sich schnell an das Verhalten der Taube (*bi-ḥarakātihā*). Gängige Elemente der Taubenbeschreibung unterstreichen ihre Besonderheit: Andere Vögel singen in einer fremden Sprache, sie aber spricht, andere fliehen vor dem Menschen, sie aber wird zahm und sucht seine Nähe. Die Taube hält ihrem Partner über den Tod hinaus die Treue.[29]

Es folgen in beiden Anthologien weitere (Reim-)prosapartien späterer Autoren wie al-Qāḍī al-Fāḍil, Ibn al-Aṯīr und al-Maʿarrī, die sich vor allem auf die Flugtüchtigkeit von Reisetauben beziehen. Al-Qāḍī al-Fāḍils *saǧʿ*-Text über Brieftauben (*ḥamām al-baṭāʾiq*) stammt aus dem Buch *Tamāʾim al-ḥamāʾim* („Talismane der Tauben“) von Ibn ʿAbd aẓ-Ẓāhir (st. 692/1292), das zwar nicht erhalten, aber in einigen Werken ausschnittsweise tradiert wird.[30] Der darin zitierte Leiter des *dīwān al-inšāʾ* und Prosastilist al-Qāḍī al-Fāḍil (st. 596/1200) fühlte sich natürlich besonders angesprochen von Funktionalität und literarischem Reiz der Brieftaubenpost. Da Tauben Botschaften übermitteln und auf den „Kanzeln der Zweige“ sitzen, preist er sie als Propheten und Prediger der Vögel und – wie auch Ibn Abī Ḥaǧala – als „Engel der Fürsten“ (*malāʾikat al-mulūk*). An anderer Stelle formuliert er in Anspielung auf Q 35:1:

وكادتْ تكون ملائكةً لأنّها رُسُلٌ إذا نيطتْ بالرِقاع * طارتْ أُولي أجنحةٍ مَثْنى وثُلاث ورُباع

> Fast sind sie Engel, weil sie doch Gesandte sind: Wenn man ihnen kurze Schreiben anbindet, fliegen sie mit Flügeln, (sogar mit) je zwei, drei oder vier.[31]

Der Briefstilist Tāǧ ad-Dīn Ibn al-Aṯīr (st. 691/1291) wählt für das Flugvermögen der Brieftaube eine naheliegende Hyperbel:[32]

---

29 Al-Ġuzūlī, *Maṭāliʿ* (1881) 261, (2000) 579–80.

30 Vgl. Ragheb, *Messagers* 67–8.

31 Vgl. Q 35:1:
الْحَمْدُ لِلَّهِ فَاطِرِ السَّمَاوَاتِ وَالْأَرْضِ جَاعِلِ الْمَلَائِكَةِ رُسُلًا أُولِي أَجْنِحَةٍ مَثْنَىٰ وَثُلَاثَ وَرُبَاعَ يَزِيدُ فِي الْخَلْقِ مَا يَشَاءُ إِنَّ اللَّهَ عَلَىٰ كُلِّ شَيْءٍ قَدِيرٌ.
Der zitierte Text in Ibn Abī Ḥaǧala, *Sulūk*, fol. 31b; al-Ġuzūlī, *Maṭāliʿ* (1881) 261, (2000) 580.

32 Zu ihm vgl. aṣ-Ṣafadī, *Wāfī* vi, 392–5. Der Text aus Ibn Abī Ḥaǧala, *Sulūk*, fol. 31b; al-Ġuzūlī, *Maṭāliʿ* (1881) 262, (2000) 580.

طالما جارتْها الرياحُ فأصْبحتْ مُخلّفة وراءها تبْكي عليها السُحُبْ * وصدق مَن سمّاها أنْبياء الطيرِ لأنّها مُرْسَلةٌ بالكُتُبْ

Schon lange wetteifern die Winde mit ihnen (den Tauben) und bleiben so weit hinter ihnen zurück, dass die Wolken sie (die Winde) beweinen. Recht hat derjenige, der sie Propheten der Vögel genannt hat, weil sie ausgesandt werden mit Briefen.

Dass die Taubenpost der mit Reittieren betriebenen Landpost ebenbürtig, ja sogar überlegen ist, zeigen die Zeilen des Kanzleistilisten (Ibn Hibatallāh b. Rifāʿa) as-Sadīd (st. 593/1196–7), der die Bezeichnung der Taube als *ayman ṭāʾir* („der am meisten Glück verheißende Vogel") wie folgt begründet:[33]

[...] ولا غرو أن فارق رُسُلَ الأرض وفاتَهم وهو مُرْسلٌ والعَنان عِنانه[34] والجوّ ميدانه والجَناح مَرْكبه والرياح مَوكبه وابتداء الغاية[35] شَوطه والشَوق الى أهله سَوطُه[36]

[...] So ist es kein Wunder, dass sie (die Taube) die Boten der Erde zurückließ und ihnen zuvorkam. Denn wenn sie ausgesendet wird, ist die Wolke ihr Zügel, die Luft ihre Pferderennbahn, die Schwingen ihr Reittier, die Winde ihre Reiterschar, der Startpunkt des Auflassortes ihr Lauf bis ins Ziel und die Sehnsucht nach ihrer Familie ihre Peitsche.

Das letzte Kolon *wa-š-šawq/wa-t-tašawwuq ilā ahlihī sawṭuhū* ist Hinweis darauf, dass der Sexual- und Bruttrieb der Taube zur Motivation für einen schnellen Rückflug in den heimischen Schlag ausgenutzt wird. Das gemeinsame Grundprinzip der zahlreichen Spielarten dieser Methode, die im deutschen Brieftaubenwesen als „Witwerschaft" bezeichnet wird, ist die Trennung verpaarter Tauben – mit und ohne Gelege –, um so den Heimkehrwillen des fliegenden Partners stark zu befördern.[37]

33 Zu ihm vgl. aṣ-Ṣafadī, *Wāfī* xviii, 295–8. Der folgende Text aus Ibn Abī Ḥağala, *Sulūk*, fol. 31ᵇ; al-Ġuzūlī, *Maṭāliʿ* (1881) 262, (2000) 580.

34 Al-Ġuzūlī, *Maṭāliʿ* (1881, 2000): والعيان عيانه.

35 Ibn Abī Ḥağala, *Sulūk*: وابتداء العناية. Man beachte das nicht gemeinte Fachvokabular (Stilmittel *tawǧīh*) in der Formulierung *ibtidāʾ al-ġāya*, die eine Funktion des Genitivs bezeichnet, der durch eine Präposition (*ḥarf al-ǧarr*) bedingt ist (vgl. z.B. Abū Ḥayyān, Ibn Mālik, *Abū Ḥayyān's commentary to the Alfiyya of Ibn Mālik* 238 u.ö.). Mit *ġāya* ist der Ort gemeint, zu dem Brieftauben gebracht und aufgelassen werden (vgl. z.B. Al-Ǧāḥiẓ, *Ḥayawān* iii, 279 u.ö.).

36 Al-Ġuzūlī, *Maṭāliʿ* (1881, 2000): والتشوق إلى أهله.

37 Al-Ǧāḥiẓ, *Ḥayawān* iii, 278–9 beschreibt eine Methode. Zu dieser und einer weiteren, der

Ibn Abī Ḥağala (fol. 31ᵃ) zitiert schließlich einige Zeilen aus seinem nicht erhaltenen Werk *as-Sağʿ al-ḥağalī*. Diese Passage, die al-Ġuzūlī bruchstückhaft wiedergibt,[38] bezieht sich u.a. auf die strittige Frage, ob der Laut der Taube Gesang, Klage oder anderes sei – ein Topos der Taubenliteratur,[39] dem wir in einigen Gedichten wiederbegegnen werden.

Ein anonym überliefertes *mawāliyyā* über ein allzeit klagendes Taubenpaar, das im *Maṭāliʿ* fehlt, beschließt das Kapitel im *Sulūk* (fol. 31ᵃ). Während Ibn Abī Ḥağalas kurzer Artikel überwiegend Prosa enthält, der nur durch vier zweizeilige Gedichte aufgelockert wird, reichert al-Ġuzūlī seinen Text mit weiterer Prosa und Poesie an. Diese Zutaten – darunter sechs weitere Gedichte – finden sich z. T. auch in den Anthologien von Ibn Ḥiğğa al-Ḥamawī, al-Asyūṭī und an-Nawāğī. Al-Ġuzūlīs Kapitel endet mit einem Ausspruch des Damaszener Verwaltungsbeamten und Dichters al-Wadāʿī (st. 716/1316) über die Brieftaube (*barīdiyya*):[40]

قال القاضي علاء الدين الوداعي كان القاضي الفاضل يسمّي الحَمامَ ملائكةَ الملوك فسميتُ أنا البريدية شياطين السلاطين

Der Richter ʿAlāʾ ad-Dīn al-Wadāʿī sagte: „al-Qāḍī al-Fāḍil pflegte die Tauben Engel der Fürsten zu nennen, und ich nenne die Brieftauben Satane der Sultane.“

Die wortspielerische Erweiterung erinnert an einen Prophetenausspruch, der wiederum zeigt, dass eine allzu heftige Passion für Tauben früh abgelehnt wurde: *šayṭānun yatbaʿu šayṭānatan* (Var. *šayṭānan*) soll Muḥammad das Verhalten eines Mannes kommentiert haben, als dieser eine Taube verfolgte.[41]

sogenannten Nestmethode, vgl. auch Ragheb, *Messagers* 124–5. Interessant ist, dass auch im deutschen Brieftaubensport der Begriff des „Spielens“ eine zentrale Bedeutung hat. „(Mit) Männchen/Weibchen spielen“ meint man Tauben für einen erfolgreichen Flug optimal einstellen, z.B. durch Ernährung, Verdunkelung, Flugtraining, Trennung der Geschlechter und kurzzeitige Zusammenführung vor dem Flug (vgl. Kluth, *Züchten, spielen, siegen*). Dass die erzwungene Trennung von verpaarten Vögeln heute von Tierschützern abgelehnt wird, liegt auf der Hand (vgl. z.B. Korte, Brieftaubensport – Gebrauchsanweisung zur Tierquälerei).

38 Al-Ġuzūlī, *Maṭāliʿ* (1881) 262, (2000) 581.

39 Vgl. dazu Abū Zayd, *Ḥamām* 75–120.

40 Al-Ġuzūlī, *Maṭāliʿ* (1881) 264, (2000) 582.

41 Abū Dāwūd as-Siğistānī, *Sunan* vii, 296–7 (Kitāb al-Adab 64: Bāb fī l-laʿb bi-l-ḥamām, Nr. 4940).

Bevor wir uns den weiteren Anthologien zuwenden, soll es zunächst um Kapitel 12 in al-Ġuzūlīs *Maṭāliʿ* gehen, in dem die Taube ebenfalls eine Rolle spielt. Anders als in Kapitel 46 und dem Vorbild in Ibn Abī Ḥağalas *Sulūk* wird in Kapitel 12 auch zoologisches Wissen über die einzelnen Vögel zusammengetragen. Unter dem Titel *fī ṭ-ṭuyūr al-musmiʿa* („Über die Singvögel") werden neben Papagei und Hahn drei Taubenarten vorgestellt, ohne ausdrücklich auf ihre Verwandtschaft untereinander hinzuweisen.[42]

Im ersten Tauben-Artikel *al-qawl ʿalā l-qumrī*[43] erklärt der Text, dass die Turteltaube (*Streptopelia turtur*) ihren Namen der weißen Farbe (ihres Gefieders) verdankt[44] und ihr Laut dem Lachen eines Menschen ähnelt.[45] An Charaktereigenschaften werden ihr Liebe (*mawadda*) und Güte (*raḥma*) zugesprochen: Liebe, weil sie ihre Jungen auf dem Zweig eines Baumes schlüpfen lässt (*yufriḫu ʿalā fanan …*), auf dem auch die Artgenossen ihre Nester haben, und sie sich nicht zurückzieht wie der Rabe. Güte, weil der Tauberich, solange die Küken noch klein sind, sich nicht mit seinem Weibchen paart und die Partner sich gegenseitig füttern. Zu den Gewohnheiten der Turteltaube gehört es, so al-Ġuzūlī weiter, dass sie aus Schutz vor laufenden Tieren (*al-ḥayawān al-māšī*) ihr Nest auf einer Zweigspitze platziert und dabei riskiert, dass die Eier zu Boden fallen und zerbrechen. Von diesem Verhalten berichtet auch ad-Damīrī (st. 808/1405) im *Ḥayāt al-ḥayawān* und führt darauf die Redewendung *aḫraq min ḥamāma* („nachlässiger als eine Taube") zurück.[46] An den kurzen Artikel schließen sich vier Gedichte späterer Autoren an, darunter ein Rätselgedicht aus der Feder des schon erwähnten Ibn ʿAbd aẓ-Ẓāhir.

Als zweite Taubenart führt al-Ġuzūlī unter der Bezeichnung *fāḫit*[47] die Türkentaube (*Streptopelia decaocto*) an, die gleichfalls zur Gattung der Turteltauben gehört[48] und sich als Kulturfolger in Europa im Laufe des 20. Jahrhunderts zum Standvogel entwickelt hat.[49] Der Text hebt ihre schöne, einem *maṯlaṯ* ähnelnde Stimme hervor.[50] Schnell mit den Menschen vertraut, baut

42 Al-Ġuzūlī, *Maṭāliʿ* (1881) 66–75, (2000) 81–9.

43 Al-Ġuzūlī, *Maṭāliʿ* (1881) 68, (2000) 82–3.

44 Zu *aqmar* als Helligkeitsbezeichnung vgl. Fischer, *Farb- und Formbezeichnungen* 266–8; Ullmann, *Flughühner* 5 übersetzt *qumriyyun* mit „hellgrau."

45 Diese Eigenart könnte z.B. auf die Nordafrikanische Lachtaube (*Streptopelia roseogrisea*) hindeuten, die, zur Gattung der Turteltauben gehörig, ein helles Gefieder und einen schwarzen Nackenstreifen hat (Wikipedia).

46 Ad-Damīrī, *Ḥayawān* 41; vgl. auch al-Ǧāḥiẓ, *Ḥayawān* iii, 189.

47 Al-Ġuzūlī, *Maṭāliʿ* (1881) 69, (2000) 83.

48 Viré, Ḥamām 109a.

49 Schletterer, *Taube* 24–5.

50 Mir ist unklar, was genau mit *maṯlaṯ* (oder *muṯallaṯ*) gemeint ist: eine Dreitonreihe, die

sie ihre Nester gerne in Häusern. Da es offenbar an Gedichten zu ihr mangelt, zitiert al-Ġuzūlī zwei weitere Rätsel: ein Gedicht von Amīn ad-Dīn al-Anṣārī (st. 800/1397), dem Leiter der Kanzlei des Sultans in Damaskus (*Dīwān al-inšāʾ aš-šarīf*), und die Antwort darauf von Zayn ad-Dīn Ibn al-ʿAǧamī (st. 795/1393).[51]

Die dritte Taubenspezies führt al-Ġuzūlī als *šifnīn* an,[52] was wiederum für die Turteltaube steht.[53] Das als volkssprachliche Entsprechung genannte *yamām* bezeichnet hingegen die Hohltaube (*Columba oenas*),[54] die zur Gattung der Feldtauben gehört und, wie der deutsche Name sagt, in Baumhöhlen brütet.[55] Der auch in Mitteleuropa heimische Zugvogel hat, so unser Text, einen Laut, der – wie der Klang einer Stockgeige auf den Saiten (*ka-ṣawt ar-rabāb fī l-awtār*) – traurig stimmt und nur im Verein mit anderen Vögeln als schön empfunden wird. Wieder wird auf die lebenslange Treue der Partner verwiesen, die den überlebenden Vogel zwingt, Unterschlupf bei einem seiner Nachkommen zu suchen. Die Hohltaube darf sich nicht satt fressen, weil sie, so der Text, bei Übergewicht ihre Federn verliert und nicht mehr zu einer Begattung imstande ist. Interessant ist die letzte Bemerkung zu ihr, nach der diese ruhige Taubenart sich vor Feinden durch eine Lilie im Nest schützt.[56]

Zu den Quellen dieser drei Artikel macht al-Ġuzūlī keine Angaben; offenkundig ist aber, dass die Texte in enger Verbindung stehen zu dem Werk *Mabāhiǧ al-fikar wa-manāhiǧ al-ʿibar/Manāhiǧ al-fikar wa-mabāhiǧ al-ʿibar* des Prosaautors Ǧamāl ad-Dīn al-Waṭwāṭ (st. 718/1318).[57] Das Werk, das an-Nuwayrī (st. 733/1333) als Vorbild diente für seine Enzyklopädie *Nihāyat al-arab fī funūn al-*

dritte Saite oder ein Akkord einer Laute? Wahrscheinlich ist eine Verbindung zu dem dreitönigen, auf der zweiten Silbe betonten Ruf der Türkentaube, der leicht mit dem der Ringeltaube verwechselt werden kann.

51 Al-Ġuzūlī, *Maṭāliʿ* (1881) 69–70, (2000) 83–4. Al-Ġuzūlī erläutert, dass er al-Anṣārīs Gedicht Ibn al-ʿAǧamī Anfang des Jahres 795/1392–3 in Kairo vorgetragen hat, woraufhin dieser die vorliegende rätselartige Antwort verfasste, die al-Ġuzūlī im *Maṭāliʿ* mit 15 Versen überliefert. Der Austausch wird u.a. zitiert in Ibn Ḥiǧǧa, *Ḫizāna* ii, 792. Zu Amīn ad-Dīn al-Anṣārī vgl. Ibn Ḥaǧar, *Inbāʾ al-ġumr* ii, 31 (unter Muḥammad b. Muḥammad b. ʿAlī al-Anṣārī ad-Dimašqī Amīn ad-Dīn al-Ḥimṣī al-Ḥanafī); zu Zayn ad-Dīn Ibn al-ʿAǧamī vgl. aṣ-Ṣafadī, *Alḥān* i, 224–8.

52 Al-Ġuzūlī, *Maṭāliʿ* (1881) 70, (2000) 84. Beide Drucke des *Maṭāliʿ* schreiben شعين.

53 Dozy, *Supplément* i, 771a: „شَفْنِين signifie selon les uns *alouette*, et selon les autres, *tourterelle* […].“ Nach Viré, Ḥamām 108b ist *šifnīn* der Name der Turteltaube im Irak.

54 Vgl. Viré, Ḥamām 108b.

55 Schletterer, *Tauben* 23.

56 Vgl. Lane, *Lexicon* i, 1466c, der unter dem Lemma *sawsan* angibt, dass die Pflanze u.a. gegen den Stich von giftigen Reptilien und besonders Skorpionen eingesetzt wurde.

57 Aṣ-Ṣafadī, *Aʿyān* iv, 201–7 (der Titel wird dort, 203–4, als *Manāhiǧ al-fikar wa-manāhiǧ al-ʿibar* zitiert); id., *Wāfī* ii, 16–8. Vgl. auch Ghersetti, On Mamluk anthologies again, bes. 78.

adab,[58] stellt eine reizvolle Mischung aus Natur- und Literaturgeschichte dar mit vielen Zitaten aus Dichtung und Philologie. Al-Ġuzūlī hat sich hiervon offenbar zu der Anlage von Kapitel 12 im *Maṭāliʿ* inspirieren lassen; auf jeden Fall stimmen seine Artikel zu *qumrī, fāḫit* und *šifnīn/yamām* über weite Strecken wortwörtlich mit den entsprechenden Texten in al-Waṭwāṭs Buch überein. Diese sind textlich besser und enthalten zusätzliche Angaben, z.B. zum jahreszeitlichen Zugverhalten der Hohltaube (*yamām*).[59]

Nach diesen vogelkundlichen Ausführungen folgt im *Maṭāliʿ* der literarische Teil mit 20 Gedichtzitaten. Das älteste Gedicht stammt von dem Diplomaten und Dichter Aḥmad b. Yūsuf al-Manāzī (st. 437/1045–6),[60] das al-Ġuzūlī zum Anlass nimmt, die Geschichte seiner Begegnung mit Abū l-ʿAlāʾ al-Maʿarrī (st. 449/1058) und al-Manāzīs berühmtes Gedicht über ein Tal (*Wāfī* viii, 285) anzuführen.[61] Die übrigen Dichter, wie al-Arraǧānī (st. 544/1149), Ibn Tamīm (st. 684/1285), Ibn Nubāta (st. 768/1366) und Ibn Ḥiǧǧa al-Ḥamawī (st. 837/1434), stammen überwiegend aus dem 6.–9./12.–15. Jahrhundert und sind nicht chronologisch geordnet. Anders als die Artikel *qumrī* und *fāḫit*, die tatsächlich einige Verse zur Turtel- und Türkentaube zitieren, wird in diesen Gedichten die Spezies *šifnīn* bzw. *yamām* nicht genannt. Mangels geeigneter Gedichte greift al-Ġuzūlī – wie in Kapitel 46 – auf Verse um die poetische Figur der Taube zurück, die meist als *ḥamām(a)* oder seltener *warqāʾ*, pl. *wurq* auftritt.

Ganz auf die Taube in der Dichtung sind die Kapitel in den weiteren zwei Anthologien ausgerichtet. Das Werk von Ibn Ḥiǧǧa al-Ḥamawī *Taʾhīl al-ġarīb* („Freundliche Aufnahme des Fremden/der wunderbaren Poesie"), gegliedert in sechs Kapitel zu den Themen Trauer, Selbstlob, Liebe, Frühling, Wein und Reue, widmet ein Unterkapitel im *bāb ar-rabīʿiyyāt* den Tauben. Der Titel *faṣl fī ḏawāt al-aṭwāq al-muġarrida ʿalā afnān al-adwāḥ wa-furūʿ al-aġṣān* („Abschnitt über diejenigen, die Halsbänder tragen und auf den Ästen der Bäume und Spitzen der Zweige singen") weckt den Anschein, als sei es der Taube wieder gelungen, ein eigenes – wenn auch untergeordnetes – Kapitel einzunehmen, doch enthält nur die erste Hälfte des *faṣl*s Gedichte über Tauben, während die zweite verschiedenen Himmelskörpern gewidmet ist.[62]

58 Vgl. Muhanna, Encyclopaedism in the Mamluk period 160–84.

59 Al-Waṭwāṭ, *Mabāhiǧ* 450–4 (Hg. al-Ḥarbī); id., *Manāhiǧ* ii, 184–7 (Hg. Sezgin).

60 Zu ihm vgl. aṣ-Ṣafadī, *Wāfī* viii, 285–8 (das von al-Ġuzūlī zitierte Taubengedicht in viii, 286).

61 Die Geschichte findet sich z.B. in Abū l-ʿAlāʾ al-Maʿarrī, *Abū l-ʿAlāʾ* 107–8 (mit weiteren Belegen).

62 Ibn Ḥiǧǧa al-Ḥamawī, *Taʾhīl* 751–7 (Tauben), 757–69 (Himmelskörper).

Ibn Ḥiǧǧa (S. 751) leitet das Unterkapitel mit einer – zum Titel passenden – Definition von al-Ǧawharī (st. um 393/1003) ein, die so oder ähnlich von vielen Taubenbeschreibungen zitiert wird:[63]

قال الجوهريّ الحَمامُ عند العَرَبِ هيَ ذواتُ الأطْواقِ كالفَواخِتِ والقَماري وساق حُرٍّ والقطا والوراسين [والوراشين] وأشباه ذلك

Al-Ǧawharī sagte: „Tauben sind bei den Arabern die mit Halsbändern Geschmückten wie Türkentauben, Turteltauben, männliche Turteltauben, das Flughuhn, Ringeltauben[64] und dergleichen mehr.“

Das Flughuhn (*qaṭā*) ist nicht nur durch sein Halsband, sondern auch durch Gemeinsamkeiten in Flugweise und Anatomie mit der Taube verbunden, wird aber heute zu einer eigenen Ordnung gerechnet.[65] *Sāq ḥurr*, der ungewöhnliche Name für die männliche Turteltaube, rührt von der typischen Lautäußerung des Vogels her.[66]

Eine andere Definition der Bezeichnung *ḥamām*, die keine der vorliegenden Quellen überliefert, referiert auf die als Saugtrinken bekannte Fähigkeit: Tauben saugen Wasser auf (*ʿabba*) im Unterschied zu vielen anderen Vögeln, die schlückchenweise trinken und den Kopf dabei anheben:

ونقل الأزهري عن الشافعي أنّ الحمام كلّ ما عبّ وهدر وإن تفرّقتْ أسماؤه والعَبّ بالعين المهملة شدّة جرع الماء من غير تنفّس[67]

Al-Azharī überlieferte nach aš-Šāfiʿī: „Jeder (Vogel), der in einem Zug (Wasser) aufsaugt und gurrt, ist eine Taube, auch wenn sie unterschiedliche Namen hat. Aufsaugen (*ʿabb*) – mit *ʿayn* ohne diakritischen Punkt – bedeutet kräftiges Schlucken von Wasser, ohne dabei zu atmen.“

---

63 Vgl. z.B. ad-Damīrī, *Ḥayawān* 41. Ähnlich mit Nennung der rötlich-schwarzen Taube (*dubsī*), Turteltaube und Ringeltaube in al-Mubarrad, *Kāmil* 503.

64 Die Edition schreibt *warāsīn* (S. 751), das Ms. Gotha 2156, fol. 76ᵃ *warāšīn*. Viré, Ḥamām 108b gibt für *warašān*, aber auch *sāq ḥurr* die Übersetzung „ring-dove or wood-pigeon, (Columba palumbus)“ an.

65 Vgl. de Juana, Order Pterocliformes.

66 Vgl. Ibn Manẓūr, *Lisān al-ʿArab* vii, 306; die Erklärung z.B. in al-Waṭwāṭ, *Mabāhiǧ* 450 (Hg. al-Ḥarbī); id., *Manāhiǧ* ii, 184 (Hg. Sezgin).

67 Ad-Damīrī, *Ḥayawān* 41.

Auch al-Ǧāḥiẓ berichtet, dass ihr anmutiges Trinkverhalten die Taube vor anderen Tieren auszeichnet: Während ein durstiger Mensch nicht mehr trinken will, wenn er sieht, wie ein Hahn hässlich schlürft (*ḥasā*), Hund und Wolf schlabbern (*laʿaṭa*), verspürt er beim Anblick einer trinkenden Taube den Wunsch, mit ihr gemeinsam von demselben Wasser zu trinken, auch wenn sein Durst längst gestillt ist.[68]

Im Anschluss an das Zitat von al-Ǧawharī reiht Ibn Ḥiǧǧa 20 Gedichte – übergangslos ohne Prosaeinschübe – aneinander. Mit Ausnahme eines Gedichts von Ibn Luʾluʾ, das fünf Verse enthält, handelt es sich vorwiegend um Epigramme bzw. Auszüge längerer Gedichte von zwei bis drei Versen. Wie in der Anthologie von al-Ġuzūlī stammen die Dichter aus der Ayyubiden- und Mamlukenzeit, zwei Gedichte hat Ibn Ḥiǧǧa selber beigesteuert.

Etwas jünger als Ibn Ḥiǧǧa ist der Verfasser des nächsten Werks. Es handelt sich um den recht unbekannten Literaten, Kopisten und Gelehrten Muḥammad b. Abī Bakr al-Asyūṭī.[69] Ǧalāl ad-Dīn as-Suyūṭī (st. 911/1515), auch ein Taubenliebhaber, der ein Buch über Tauben mit dem Titel *Ṭawq al-ḥamāma* geschrieben hat, widmet ihm einen Eintrag in der biographischen Sammlung *Naẓm al-ʿiqyān fī aʿyān al-aʿyān*.[70] Danach wurde al-Asyūṭī im Šawwāl 783/1381 geboren und ist 859 oder 856/1454–5 oder 1452–3 gestorben. Als Schüler von Badr ad-Dīn Ibn ad-Damāmīnī (st. 827/1424) soll er ein fleißiger Dichter gewesen sein, der u.a. eine *urǧūza* über das Pferd verfasst hat (*Naẓm* 141). Seine noch nicht edierte Anthologie *al-Marǧ an-naḍir wa-l-araǧ al-ʿaṭir* („Die blühende Aue und der wohlriechende Duft") hat al-Asyūṭī nach Ausweis des Pariser Autographen BN 3385 im Jahr 818/1415 geschrieben. Das Werk gliedert sich in fünf Kapitel mit jeweils fünf Abschnitten (*fuṣūl*) und behandelt die Themen Liebe und Liebesdichtung (Kap. 1–2), Wein- und Gartendichtung (Kap. 3) sowie moralisch-ethische Betrachtungen zur Etikette (*adab*), z.B. für diejenigen, die Königen dienen (Kap. 5,1), zur Bewahrung eines Geheimnisses (Kap. 5,4) und – als *ḫātimat al-kitāb* – zur Askese.

Kapitel 4 stellt unter dem Titel *adabiyyāt* fünf literarische Genres vor, die zu kennen und beherrschen für den Gebildeten jener Zeit als nützlich erachtet wurde:

الباب الرابع في الأدبيّات (113b)

الفصل الأوّل في تغريد الحمامة (113b–115a)

68 Al-Ǧāḥiẓ, *Ḥayawān* iii, 148.

69 Vgl. *GAL* i, 158, Nr. 297; ii, 55, *GALS* ii, 55 (als as-Suyūṭī angeführt).

70 As-Suyūṭī, *Naẓm al-ʿiqyān* 140–2 (Nr. 138).

الفصل الثاني في الموشّحات (115b)

الفصل الثالث في المكاتبات (117b)

الفصل الرابع في لطيف التناجي بالألغاز والأحاجي (133a)

الفصل الخامس في نوادر ونكت (146a)

Mit dem Gesang der Tauben wählt al-Asyūṭī für den ersten *faṣl* einen Topos aus, der bedeutend genug ist, um – stellvertretend für die *qarīḍ*-Poesie – in den Kanon der literarischen Bildung aufgenommen zu werden. Wie Ibn Ḥiǧǧa im *Ta'hīl* hat der Anthologist den rund 30 Gedichten um Tauben keine Prosa beigefügt. Bei den namentlich angeführten Dichtern überwiegen neben wenigen früheren Autoren wie Abū Bakr aš-Šiblī (st. 334/945) und Abū Firās (st. 357/968) Dichter späterer Epochen, darunter mit Ṣadr ad-Dīn ibn al-Muraḥḥil (st. 716/1316) und Yaḥyā b. Salāma al-Ḥaṣkafī (st. ca. 551/1156) auch unbekanntere. Die Gedichte enthalten meist zwei bis drei, maximal acht Verse.

Nur wenige Jahre nach al-Asyūṭīs Werk ist der letzte Textzeuge, die Anthologie *Ḥalbat al-kumayt* („Das Hippodrom des edlen Rennpferdes“/„Das Symposion des Weins“), entstanden.[71] An-Nawāǧīs erfolgreichstes Buch bezieht sich zum Teil explizit auf den Wein, behandelt aber auch Objekte, Akteure und Schauplätze, die mit dem Trinkgenuss verbunden sind, wie Krüge, Kerzen und Sänger. Da Trinkgelage meist in der freien Natur stattfanden, geht es in einigen der insgesamt 25 Kapitel um Gewässer und Wasserräder,[72] Wind und Wolken, Himmelskörper und eben auch Tauben.[73]

Der Titel des hier interessierenden Kapitels 23 *fī ġinā' al-ḥamā'im wa-ḥamā'im ar-rasā'il* („Über den Gesang der Tauben und die Brieftauben“) zeigt seine Zweiteilung an: Der erste Teil präsentiert ausgewählte Poesie zu Tauben allgemein, vereinzelt auch zu anderen Vögeln, der zweite Reimprosa zu Brieftauben.[74] Dieser *saǧ'*-Teil enthält eine ausführlichere Version des Textes von al-Qāḍī al-Fāḍil, den auch Ibn Abī Ḥaǧala und al-Ġuzūlī für ihr Taubenkapitel ausgewählt haben, sowie einen anspielungsreichen Text von Ibn Ḥiǧǧa al-Ḥamawī. Beide Texte, auf die hier nicht näher eingegangen werden kann, sind es wert, in einer eigenen Untersuchung im Hinblick auf ihre wortspielerischen Bezüge zur Brieftaubenpost analysiert zu werden.

---

71 Das Werk wurde zwischen 821–24/1418–21 verfasst (vgl. Masarwa, Wasser, Wein und Architektur 278, Fußnote 9).

72 Das „Wasserkapitel“ 19 wird ausführlich analysiert von Masarwa, Wasser, Wein und Architektur.

73 Zu Autor und Werk vgl. Bauer, al-Nawājī, bes. 326b; zum *Ḥalbat al-kumayt* vgl. van Gelder, A muslim encomium on wine.

74 An-Nawāǧī, *Ḥalba* 322–6 (Poesie), 326–8 (Reimprosa).

Der Strukturierungswille an-Nawāǧīs setzt sich fort im Poesieteil, in dem die fast kommentarlos zitierten 34 Gedichte weitgehend nach Länge und Inhalt angeordnet sind. Während die Zitate der ersten Hälfte fast ausschließlich zwei Verse enthalten, erscheinen in der zweiten Hälfte auch längere Gedichte mit drei bis sechs, einmal sogar zehn Versen (S. 325). Im Hinblick auf die Themen wird in keiner anderen Anthologie so deutlich, dass die Gedichte, wenn sie auch vielleicht keiner bewussten Struktur folgen, so doch in assoziativer Reihung stehen und durch gemeinsame Schlagwörter miteinander verbunden sind. Gut erkennbar sind folgende Motivschwerpunkte:

- Taube in Natur und Garten
- Taube und Wein
- Brieftaube
- Amsel
- Taube als Sängerin
- Halsband der Taube
- Zweifel an Trauer der Taube
- Emotionale Verbundenheit zwischen Taube und Mensch – tatsächlich oder scheinbar?
- Taube in Gefangenschaft

Was die Dichter angeht, so stammen neben einigen anonym überlieferten Versen einzelne Stücke von früheren Dichtern wie Ibn al-Muʿtazz (st. 296/908), die weitaus meisten aber wieder von Autoren aus der Ayyubiden- und Mamlukenzeit, etwa von Ibn Qalāqis (st. 567/1172), Ibn Qurnāṣ (st. 671/1272–3) oder Badr ad-Dīn Ibn aṣ-Ṣāḥib (st. 788/1386).

Die Gedichte

An-Nawāǧīs Eingangsthema ist auch ein guter Ausgangspunkt für den folgenden Rundgang durch die Taubenpoesie der Anthologien. In einer Reihe von Gedichten erscheint die Taube inmitten ihrer natürlichen Umgebung mal alleine, mal in Gesellschaft von Artgenossen oder anderer Vögel noch ohne erkennbaren Kontakt zum Menschen.

Dazu zählen die Verse des Bäckers al-Ḫabbāz al-Baladī (st. ca. 380/990),[75] der, wie aṯ-Ṯaʿālibī in der *Yatīma* betont, ansprechende Poesie verfasst hat, obwohl er *ummī* war, also nicht schreiben konnte:[76]

---

75 Vgl. *GAS* ii, 625–6.

76 Aṯ-Ṯaʿālibī, *Yatīmat ad-dahr* ii, 247 (dort auch das Gedicht). Der folgende Text auch in an-

الخبّاز البلدي [من الطويل]
ذُرى شَجَرٍ للطيْرِ فيه تَشاجرُ * كأنّ صُنوفَ النورِ فيه جَواهِرُ
كأنّ القَماري والبَلابِلَ وَسْطها * قِيانٌ وأوراق الغُصون سَتائِرِ

Die Baumwipfel, in denen sich die Vögel zanken, sind so, als wären die verschiedenen Lichter in ihnen Juwelen,
Die Turteltauben und Nachtigallen in ihrer Mitte Sängerinnen und die Blätter der Zweige Vorhänge.

Die in Vers 1a eingeführten Vögel werden im zweiten Vers als Turteltauben und Nachtigallen benannt, zwei eher unscheinbare Vögel, die durch ihre unterschiedlichen Lautäußerungen auf sich aufmerksam machen. Der Vergleich mit hinter Vorhängen verborgenen Sängerinnen wird häufig von verschiedenen Dichtern in den Anthologien verwendet. Der Beginn des Gedichts erhält durch den *ǧinās* zwischen *šaǧar* und *tašāǧur* eine besondere Betonung und setzt sich von den folgenden, parallel mit *ka'anna* eingeleiteten Vergleichen ab. Ganz ähnlich ist der Beginn in dem schlichten Zweizeiler von Ibn Qalāqis gestaltet:[77]

ابن قلاقس [من الكامل]
والوُرْقُ في الأوْراق قد هتفَتْ على * عَذَبِ الغُصون بأعْذَب الألْحَانِ
فكأنّ أوْراق الغُصون سَتائِرٌ * وكأنّ أصْواتَ الطيور أغاني

Die Tauben in den Blättern gurrten auf den Zweigspitzen die süßesten Klänge.
Als wären die Laute der Vögel Lieder und die Blätter der Zweige Vorhänge.[78]

Auch hier wird der Vergleich einer musikalischen Darbietung bemüht, bei der hinter Vorhängen Gesänge ertönen. In Vers 1 wird in beiden Halbversen ein *ǧinās* verwendet, wobei der erste zwischen *wurq* und *awrāq* so häufig in der Taubenpoesie variiert wird, dass der Beginn formelhaft wirkt. *Wurq* (sg. *warqā'*), nach *ḥamām(a)* die häufigste Bezeichnung für die Taube in der Poe-

---

Nawāǧī, *Ḥalba* 323 (Name des Dichters dort الجناب البلدي; V. 2b statt *satā'ir* wie in der *Yatīma* schlecht zu *qiyān* passendes *manābir*).

77 An-Nawāǧī, *Ḥalba* 323; die beiden Verse stehen am Ende einer Qaṣīde, vgl. Ibn Qalāqis, *Dīwān* 537–8; aṣ-Ṣafadī, *Wāfī* xxvii, 13–4.

78 In der Übersetzung sind die Halbverse von V. 2 miteinander vertauscht.

sie, meint eigentlich eine blaugraue (taubenblaue), aschfarbene Taube.[79] Die Formulierung *wa-l-wurqu fī l-awrāqi* verdeutlicht auf sprachlicher Ebene, wie gut dieser Farbenschlag seiner Umgebung angepasst ist und mit dem Laub fast zu einer Einheit verschmilzt.

Badr ad-Dīn Ibn Lu'lu' (st. 686/1288),[80] ein Favorit der Anthologisten, ist mit ein bis drei Gedichten in vier Werken – *Maṭāliʿ*, *Marǧ*, *Ta'hīl* und *Ḥalba* – vertreten. Im folgenden Gedicht gesellen sich Tauben erst im letzten Halbvers zu Blumen, Windhauch, Morgensonne und Blättern und machen die Gartenidylle perfekt:[81]

وأجاد بدر الدين الذهبي بقوله [من الرمل]
ورياضٍ رقصتْ أزْهارُها * فتمشّتْ نَسْمةُ الريح إليها
طالعتْ شَمْسُ الضُحى أوْراقَها * بعد ما أن وَقَعَ الوُرْقُ عليها

(Da sind) Gärten, deren Blumen tanzen und in die der Windhauch weht.
Die Sonne am späten Morgen scheint auf ihre Blätter, nachdem sich Tauben auf sie gesetzt hatten.

Wie Ibn Lu'lu' verlegt auch Burhān ad-Dīn al-Qīrāṭī (st. 781/1379) sein Epigramm in die Morgenstunden und lenkt die Aufmerksamkeit auf den Ruf einer Turteltaube, der wieder mit Musik, diesmal einer Laute, verglichen wird:

وقال الشيخ برهان الدين القيراطي [من السريع]
تَنفّس الصُبْحُ فجاءتْ لنا * من نَحْوِهِ الأنْفاسُ مِسْكيّه
وأطْرَبَتْ في العُودِ قُمْريّةٌ * وكيف لا تطْربُ عُوديّه[82]

Der frühe Morgen atmete tief, und sein Atemhauch streifte uns moschusduftend.
Auf dem Ast musizierte eine Turteltaube, denn wie kann eine Astbewohnerin/*eine Lautenspielerin* auch nicht musizieren?

79 Vgl. Fischer, *Farb- und Formbezeichnungen* 318–21.
80 Zu ihm vgl. Özkan, Ibn Lu'lu'.
81 An-Nawāǧī, *Ḥalba* 323.
82 Al-Ġuzūlī, *Maṭāliʿ* (1881) 68–9, (2000) 83; Ibn Ḥiǧǧa al-Ḥamawī, *Ta'hīl* 754; an-Nawāǧī, *Ḥalba* 322.

In Vers 2a ist *ʿūd* nur mit „Ast“ zu übersetzen, obwohl die zweite Bedeutung „Laute“ durch das Verb *wa-aṭrabat* evoziert wird, aber nicht intendiert ist. Es liegt also das Stilmittel einer herbeigeführten *tawriya* (*tawriya muhayyaʾa*) vor, während in Vers 2b die Doppelbedeutung von *ʿūdiyya* die Pointe des Gedichts ausmacht.

Nur einzelne Gedichte der vorliegenden Auswahl richten ihr Augenmerk als Vertreter des Genres *waṣf* auf eine mehr oder minder kunstvolle Beschreibung der Taube. Meist werden als Topoi Hals und Füße, kaum je das bei den meisten Arten unauffällige Gefieder bedichtet. Zu den wenigen Ausnahmen zählt ein Naturepigramm des Literaten ʿIzz ad-Dīn al-Mawṣilī (st. 789/1387), das er al-Ġuzūlī vorrezitiert hat:[83]

قلت وأنشدني من لفظه لنفسه الشيخ عزّ الدين الموصليّ رحمه الله تعالى [من الرجز]
مُذ غنّتِ الوُرْقُ على عيدانِها * كم خلع الجوُّ عليها من مِلَحْ
تَدَرَّعَتْ سُحْبًا وخاضتْ شَفَقًا * وطوّقتْ أعْناقَها قوسَ قُزَحْ

Seit die Tauben auf ihren Ästen singen, wie oft haben ihnen da die Lüfte an Schönheiten verliehen ein Ehrengewand.
Sie rüsten sich mit einem Kleid aus Wolken, schreiten in das Abendrot und legen um ihre Nacken einen Regenbogen als Halsband.

Während in Vers 1a *ʿalā ʿīdānihā* wieder das Stilmittel der *tawriya muhayyaʾa* vorliegt (hervorgerufen durch *ġannat*), wählt al-Mawṣilī im zweiten Vers vier Metaphern – Panzerhemd (in *tadarraʿat*) und Wolken, Abendrot und Regenbogen – für die graue Brust- und Rückenpartie, die roten Füße und den farbigen Nackenstreifen. Viele Gedichte in den Anthologien erwähnen das Halsband der Taube, verweisen aber nicht auf seine Mehrfarbigkeit, die zum grauen Federkleid kontrastiert, wie es z.B. bei der Hohltaube oder noch deutlicher bei der Felsentaube, arab. *ṭūrānī* (*Columba livia*), der Stammform der Haustaube, mit ihren breiten grün und purpurn schillernden Halsbändern der Fall ist.

Farblich unscheinbarer ist der Halsstreifen (*ʿilāṭ*) in einem Vers aus einem Lobgedicht von al-Arraǧānī (st. 544/1149):[84]

83 Al-Ġuzūlī, *Maṭāliʿ* (1881) 72, (2000) 87; Ibn Ḥiǧǧa al-Ḥamawī, *Taʾhīl* 756.

84 Al-Ġuzūlī, *Maṭāliʿ* (1881) 72, (2000) 86: in beiden V. 1a *al-ihāb* statt *al-ʿilāṭ* wie in al-Arraǧānī, *Dīwān* i, 402–5 (V. 17). Das Farbadjektiv *aḫṭab* bezeichnet eine Zweifarbigkeit, d.h. die Kombination von einer hellen und einer dunklen Farbe. Im vorliegenden Vers kann *aḫṭab* auch als Elativ zu *ḫaṭaba* in der Bedeutung „Vielredner, Prediger“ gemeint sein (vgl. Fischer, *Farb- und Formbezeichnungen* 321–4). Der Halsstreifen (*ʿilāṭ*) wird in der Dichtung

وقال ناصح الدين الأرّجاني ... [من البسيط]
مِن كلّ أخْطبَ مِسْكيّ العِلاطِ له * في مِنبرِ الأيْكِ تَسْجاعٌ وتَهْدارُ

Von lauter Staubfarbenen mit moschusbraunem Halsstreifen (tönt) auf der Kanzel des Hains ein lautes Gurren und Singen.

Halsband und Farbe der Füße werden nach einer bekannten Überlieferung mit der Geschichte um Noah und die Arche in Zusammenhang gebracht: Als Noah die Taube freilässt, kommt sie mit dem Blatt einer Weinrebe (Var. eines Olivenbaums) zurück, welches das Ende der Sintflut (*ṭūfān*) anzeigt. Für diesen Dienst fordert sie von Gott zur Zierde ein Halsband, das ihr, auf Noahs Fürbitte hin, gewährt wird. Die rote Farbe der Füße erhält sie als Ersatz für ihre nach Rückkehr in die Arche lehmbedeckten Füße.[85]

مُطَوَّقة كساها اللهُ طَوْقًا * ولم يَخْصُصْ به طَيرًا سِواها

(„Eine mit einem Halsband Geschmückte – Gott hat sie mit einem Halsband bekleidet, womit er keinen anderen Vogel ausgezeichnet hat") zitiert al-Ǧāḥiẓ, gibt aber zu bedenken, dass andere Vögel wie Fasane (*tadāriǧ*, sg. *tadruǧ*) mehr Anrecht auf dieses Merkmal hätten, weil ihre Halsbänder schöner seien und auch längst nicht alle Taubenarten ein Halsband trügen.[86]

In den weitaus meisten Gedichten wird das Verhalten der Taube, vor allem ihre Lautäußerung, mit den Gefühlen des Dichters in Beziehung gesetzt. Der tiefe, schnurrende Ton, der je nach Situation und Art variieren kann, wird als Klagelaut gedeutet, der den Dichter rührt, eigene (schmerzvolle) Erinnerungen und Emotionen wachruft und eine Art Leidensgemeinschaft ermöglicht.[87] Da diese Annäherung leichter zu einem Individuum gelingt, ist es meist ein einzelner Vogel, der dem Dichter gegenübersteht. Ein solches Erlebnis beschreibt

häufig als *aḥamm* „schwarz (eines bestimmten Körperteils)" bezeichnet, womit wiederum *ḥamām* „Taube" etymologisch zusammenhängt (Fischer, ibid. 285; 278, Fußnote 3).

85 Al-Ǧāḥiẓ, *Ḥayawān* iii, 195–6. In einer anderen Texttradition lässt Noah wie in Gen 8,7–12 vor der Taube einen Raben ausfliegen, beides Vögel, die einen ausgezeichneten Orientierungssinn haben (vgl. z.B. al-Kisāʾī, *Qiṣaṣ al-anbiyāʾ* 98, wo wiederum von einer Belohnung der Taube nicht die Rede ist).

86 Diesen Einwand lässt al-Ǧāḥiẓ den Besitzer und Fürsprecher des Hahns (*ṣāḥib ad-dīk*) vorbringen (*Ḥayawān* iii, 200). Vgl. dazu auch Miller, *More than the sum of its parts*, bes. 29–53.

87 Eine Vorstellung, die nicht auf den arabischen Sprachraum beschränkt ist. Zur internationalen Erzählliteratur vgl. z.B. Bies, Taube; Schenda, *Who's who der Tiere* (Art. Taube), 362–7.

das folgende Gedicht, das in einigen Quellen dem Mystiker Abū Bakr aš-Šiblī[88] zugesprochen wird:[89]

آخرُ ويقال أنّه للشِبْلِي رحمه الله [من الرمل]
رُبَّ وَرْقَاءَ هَتوفٍ بِالضُحى * ذاتِ شَجْوٍ صَدَحَتْ في فَنَنِ
ذَكَرَتْ إِلْفًا وَدَهْرًا صالِحًا * فبَكَتْ حُزْنًا فهاجَتْ حَزَني
فَبُكائِي رُبَّما أَرَّقَهَا * وبُكاها رُبَّما أَرَّقني
ولقد أَشْكُو فما أُفْهِمُها * ولقدْ تَشْكو فما تُفْهِمُني
غَيْرَ أَنّي بِالجَوَى أَعْرِفُها * وَهي أَيضًا بالجوى تَعْرِفُني

Der Dichter und Sprachgelehrte Friedrich Rückert (1788–1866) hat die Verse 1830 ins Deutsche übersetzt:[90]

> Eine Taube, die am Morgen laut sich macht
> Und betrübte Weisen singt im Waldrevier.
> Ihres Freundes denkt sie und der guten Zeit,
> Weint aus Kummer, und erregt den Kummer mir.
> Und ihr Weinen hat den Schlaf mir oft geraubt,
> Und geraubt hat oft den Schlaf mein Weinen ihr.
> Und ich klag' und sie versteht von mir es nicht,
> Und sie klagt' und ich versteh' es nicht von ihr.
> Aber daß ihr etwas fehlt, das fühl' ich wohl;
> daß mir etwas fehlt, das fühlt sie wohl mit mir.

Während der erste Vers den Blick allein auf die Taube lenkt, erreicht ihre als Wehmut interpretierte Stimmung im zweiten Vers den Dichter. Die folgenden drei Verse sind ganz auf die Identifikation zwischen Taube und Mensch ausgerichtet: in einem Moment der Resonanz weinen und klagen beide wechselweise und fühlen intuitiv das Leid des anderen, ohne dass sie einander verstehen. Die in Wortwahl und Syntax parallel gestalteten Verse (Stilmittel *tarṣīʿ*) spiegeln den emotionalen Gleichklang wider, wie auch die vier letzten Reim-

---

88 Vgl. zu ihm Sobieroj, al-Shiblī.

89 Al-Asyūṭī, *Marǧ*, BN 3385, fol. 113[b]; BN 3386, fol. 135[a].

90 Rückerts Ms. ist aufbewahrt im Nachlass der ULB Münster 5, 050, Bl. 12a. Die Übersetzung wurde erstmals publiziert in *Jahrbücher für wissenschaftliche Kritik* (1830). Rückerts Vorlage ist Kosegarten, *Chrestomathia arabica* 156, die in dieser Partie wiederum auf al-Asyūṭīs Anthologie *al-Marǧ an-naḍir* fußt.

wörter der Übersetzung – „mir,“ „ihr,“ „ihr,“ „mir“ – die Betonung auf das Zwiegespräch unter gleichberechtigten Leidensgenossen legen.

Die Erinnerung an verdrängte Seelenqual kann auch so schmerzhaft sein, dass ihr Auslöser verflucht wird:[91]

أعرابي [من الطويل]
ألا قاتلَ اللهُ الحمامةَ غدْوةً * على الأيْكِ ماذا هيّجتْ يومَ غنّتِ
تغنّتْ بصوتٍ أعْجميٍّ فهيّجتْ * من الشَوقِ ما كانت ضُلوعي أكنّتِ

Ein Beduine
Ach, möge Gott doch die Taube frühmorgens im Baumdickicht verfluchen! Was hat sie (alles) erregt am Tage, als sie sang?
Sie sang mit fremder Stimme und erregte von der Sehnsucht, was meine Brust verborgen hatte.

Wird hier der Ruf der Taube als „fremd, nicht-arabisch“ (*aʿǧamī*) bezeichnet, begegnet man wie in der von Ibn Abī Ḥaǧala und al-Ġuzūlī zitierten Passage (s.o.) bisweilen der Aussage, dass die Taube im Unterschied zu anderen Vögeln spricht – eine Vorstellung, die sich auch der andalusische Dichter Muḥammad ibn al-Ḥusayn aṭ-Ṭubnī (st. 394/1003–4) im folgenden Gedicht zu eigen macht:

وقال محمّد بن الحسين الطبني [من الكامل]
قُمْريّةٌ دَعَتِ الهوى فكأنّما * نَطَقَتْ وليس لها لسانٌ ناطقُ
غنّتْ فحبّبتِ الأراكَ كأنّما * فوق الغُصون حَبابةٌ ومُخارِقُ

Eine hellgraue [Taube], die Liebe hervorgerufen hat; es war, als hätte sie gesprochen, und doch hat sie keine sprechende Zunge.[92]
Sie hat gesungen, da machte sie den Arakbaum verliebt, als ob auf den Zweigen Ḥabāba und Muḫāriq wären.[93]

Der Unglückliche und Liebeskranke sucht häufig Vergessen und Trost im Wein. Deshalb ist es kein Wunder, dass sich in einigen Gedichten zum Ruf der Taube,

91 Al-Asyūṭī, *Marǧ*, BN 3385, fol. 114[b]; BN 3386, fol. 136[b]; Ibn Faḍlallāh al-ʿUmarī, *Masālik al-abṣār* xiv, 264 (hier 9 Verse).

92 Text und Übersetzung von V. 1 zitiert nach Ullmann, *Flughühner* 21. Seine Quelle ist Ibn al-Kattānī, *Kitāb at-Tašbīhāt min ašʿār ahl al-Andalus* 8, 16, 1. Zum Dichter vgl. *GAS* ii, 690.

93 Ḥabāba und Muḫariq sind die Namen einer Sängersklavin (2./8. Jh.) und eines Sängers (st. 230/844–5). Vgl. Pellat, Ḥabāba; Farmer, Mukhāriḳ.

der die Erinnerung heraufbeschwört, der Weingenuss gesellt wie in den folgenden Versen von Ibn al-Muʿtazz:[94]

[من الوافر]
وصَوتِ حَمامةٍ سَجَعتْ بلَيلٍ * وقد حَنّتْ إلى إلْفٍ بعيدِ
فما زِلْنا نقولُ لها أعيدي * وللساقي ألا هلْ من مَزيدِ

(Da ist) ein Ruf der Taube, die in einer Nacht gurrt, weil sie sich nach einem fernen Geliebten sehnt.
Immer wieder sage ich ihr: „Noch einmal!", und zum Schenken: „Gibt es nicht noch mehr?"

Zwei Epigramme von Ibn Nubāta, die in aṣ-Ṣafadīs Briefwechsel mit dem Elitedichter aufgenommen sind, variieren das Motiv auf unterschiedliche Weise. Im ersten Gedicht ist das reale Tier dem schwermütigen Dichter alleinige Gesellschaft in weinseliger Stimmung:[95]

وقال جمال الدين محمّد بن نباتة [من البسيط]
ما لي نَديمٌ سِوَى وَرْقاءَ ساجِعةٍ * مِن بعْدِ مُغْتَبَقي فيكم ومُصْطَبَحي
إذا أدار ادِّكارُ الوَصْلِ لي قدَحًا * مِن أحْمَرِ الدَمْعِ غَنَّتْنِي على قَدَحِي

Mein Zechgenoß blieb allein die Turteltaub, die seufzt,
Seit Morgentrunk, Abendrausch von euren Lippen mich mied.
Und wenn mir nun kreisen läßt Erinnrung eures Vereins
Den Becher voll Thränen roth, singt sie zum Becher das Lied.[96]

Das zweite Gedicht lässt Tauben als Motiv auf Weinbechern erscheinen und bezieht sich auf den Brauch, Trinkgefäße mit Bildern von Herrschern, Tieren,

94 Al-Asyūṭī, *Marǧ*, BN 3385, fol. 115[a]; BN 3386, fol. 136[b]–137[a]; an-Nawāǧī, *Ḥalba* 322; Ibn al-Muʿtazz, *Dīwān* 185. V. 2 spielt an auf Q 50:30: ﴿يَوْمَ نَقُولُ لِجَهَنَّمَ هَلِ امْتَلَأْتِ وَتَقُولُ هَلْ مِن مَّزِيدٍ﴾.

95 Al-Ġuzūlī, *Maṭāliʿ* (1881) 71, (2000) 86: V. 2b in beiden: *ġannānī*; Ibn Ḥiǧǧa al-Ḥamawī, *Taʾhīl* 753; an-Nawāǧī, *Ḥalba* 322; Ibn Nubāta al-Miṣrī, *Dīwān* 119; aṣ-Ṣafadī, *Alḥān as-sawāǧiʿ* ii, 263 mit weiteren Tauben-Epigrammen von aṣ-Ṣafadī und Ibn Nubāta.

96 Der Text der Übersetzung von Friedrich Rückert befindet sich im Nachlass der ULB Münster 5, 038, Bl. 9b–10a. Rückerts Vorlage ist Ibn Ḥiǧǧa al-Ḥamawī, *Taʾhīl al-ġarīb*, Ms. Gotha, A 2156, fol. 76[a].

Pflanzen u. Ä. zu verzieren – ein Topos der Weindichtung, bei dem das gewählte Motiv mit dem Wein und seinen Trinkern in Beziehung gesetzt, manchmal auch ganz abgelehnt wird:[97]

وقال الشيخ جمال الدين محمّد بن نباتة [من البسيط]
وُرْق الحَمام على أقْداح قَهْوَتِنا * قد صُوِّرَتْ فاْسْتَفَزَّتْنا من الفَرَحِ
إذا سَرَتْ أرْيَحِيَّاتُ المُدامِ بنا * كادتْ حَقيقًا تُغَنّينا على القَدَحِ

Tauben, die auf den Bechern unseres Weins gemalt waren, ließen uns vor Freude auffahren.
Als die Großzügigkeit des alten Weins bei uns Wirkung zeigte, sangen sie beinah tatsächlich für uns auf dem/zum Becher.

Eine andere Entstehungsgeschichte des Halsbandes erzählt das folgende Epigramm von Ibn Ḥiǧǧa al-Ḥamawī:[98]

وأنشدني من لفظه لنفسه سيّدي وأخي تقي الدين أبي بكر بن حجّة [من الكامل]
ناحتْ مُطوّقةُ الرياضِ وقد رَأَتْ * دَمْعي تلوّن بَعْد فُرْقة حبّهِ
لكن بتَلْوينِ الدُموعِ تَباخَلَتْ * فغدَتْ مُطَوّقةً بما بَخِلَتْ بهِ

Es klagte die mit einem Halsband geschmückte (Taube) in den Gärten, die einst gesehen hatte, wie sich meine Tränen nach der Trennung von einer Liebe (rot) färbten.
Aber mit der (roten) Farbe der Tränen war sie geizig, und so wurde ihr ein Halsband umgelegt (in der Farbe), mit der sie gegeizt hatte.

Das (rote?) Halsband ist also Ersatz für die Bluttränen des Dichters.[99] Die Pointe in Vers 2 ist ein *iqtibās* aus Q 3:180.

---

97 Vgl. z. B. Ibn Ḥiǧǧa al-Ḥamawī, *Ta'hīl al-ġarīb* 804–7. Das folgende Gedicht aus al-Asyūṭī, *Marǧ*, BN 3385, fol. 114[b] (Rand); BN 3386, fol. 136[b]; aṣ-Ṣafadī, *Alḥān as-sawāǧiʿ* ii, 264.

98 Al-Ġuzūlī, *Maṭāliʿ* (1881) 72, (2000) 87; Ibn Ḥiǧǧa al-Ḥamawī, *Ta'hīl* 755 (V. 2a: لكن به لمّا سَمَحَتْ تباخلت); an-Nawāǧī, *Ḥalba* 323–4. Zu V. 2 vgl. Q 3:180:
﴿وَلَا يَحْسَبَنَّ الَّذِينَ يَبْخَلُونَ بِمَا آتَاهُمُ اللَّهُ مِنْ فَضْلِهِ هُوَ خَيْرًا لَهُمْ بَلْ هُوَ شَرٌّ لَهُمْ سَيُطَوَّقُونَ مَا بَخِلُوا بِهِ يَوْمَ الْقِيَامَةِ وَلِلَّهِ مِيرَاثُ السَّمَاوَاتِ وَالْأَرْضِ وَاللَّهُ بِمَا تَعْمَلُونَ خَبِيرٌ﴾.

99 Vgl. ad-Damīrī, *Ḥayawān* 41, der al-Aṣmaʿī zufolge als mögliche Halsband-Farben Rot, Grün/Dunkelgrau (*ḫudra*) und Schwarz angibt.

Tauben haben eigentlich keinen Anlass, mit Neid auf rotgeweinte Augen zu blicken, haben doch viele Rassen einen roten Augenrand wie etwa die Turteltaube, manche auch eine rote oder orangefarbene Iris wie die in Afrika heimische Halbmondtaube (*Streptopelia semitorquata*), eine Turteltaubenart, die auch Rotaugentaube genannt wird.[100] Dass Tauben zwar schön klagen, aber tatsächlich keine Tränen vergießen, zeigt ein Gedicht von aṣ-Ṣafadī, in dem eine „Aufgabenteilung“ zwischen Vogel und Mensch vorgeschlagen wird:[101]

وقال أيضًا رحمه الله [من الوافر]
وربّ حمامة في الدوح باتت * تجيد النوح فنًّا بعد فنّ
أقاسمها الهوى مهما اجتمعنا * فمنها النوح والعبرات منّي

Manch eine Taube im Gebüsch singt des Nachts schön die Klage Zweig um Zweig.
Ich teile mit ihr die Liebe, wenn wir beisammen sind: Von ihr die Klage, die Tränen von mir.

Badr ad-Dīn Ibn aṣ-Ṣāḥib variiert in zwei Gedichten das Halsband-Motiv und verleiht dem Schmuck eine negative Bedeutung. Im ersten ringt der Dichter um das Verständnis des Klagelauts und findet für die Sprachlosigkeit der Taube eine phantastische Ätiologie (*ḥusn at-taʿlīl*):[102]

وقال الشيخ بدر الدين بن الصاحب [من الرجز]
ناحت حمام البان أم تاهت أسًى * لم أدر ما غناؤها من شوقها
عجماء لا تظهر حرفًا من شجى * لأنها مخنوقة من طوقها

Ob die Taube der Weide klagt oder schwankt vor Leid, ich kenne nicht ihrer Sehnsucht Lied.
Ein stummes Tier, das mit keinem Wort seinen Schmerz offenbart, weil es von seinem Halsband gewürgt wird.

100 Viré, Ḥamām 109a.

101 Al-Asyūṭī, *Marǧ*, BN 3385 fol. 114[b]; BN 3386, fol. 136[a]; as-Ṣafadī, *Alḥān as-sawāǧiʿ* ii, 262.

102 Al-Ġuzūlī, *Maṭāliʿ* (1881) 72, (2000) 87: V. 2b in beiden: مخنوقة بطوقها; Ibn Ḥiǧǧa al-Ḥamawī, *Taʾhīl* 755: V. 1a ناحت حمام البان أم باهت هوًى; 2b مخنوقة بطوقها; id., *Ḫizānat al-adab* ii, 641: V. 2b كأنّها مخنوقة; an-Nawāǧī, *Ḥalba* 324: V. 1a: ناحت حمام البان بائقة الأسى.

Im zweiten ist es nicht das Gurren, sondern offenbar die anmutige Haltung der Taube, die den Geliebten „ins Gedächtniß" ruft:[103]

الشيخ بدر الدين بن الصاحب [من البسيط]
وذات طَوقٍ على الأغْصانِ تُذْكِرُني * قَوامَ قَدِّكَ مَعْ ضَمّي لِمُعْتَنَقَكْ
وسَوّدتْ مُهْجَتي نَوحًا فقُلْتُ لها * سَوادُ قَلْبِي يا وَرْقاءُ في عُنُقِكْ

Nach der Anthologie von Ibn Ḥiğğa al-Ḥamawī hat Friedrich Rückert die Verse etwas freier übertragen:[104]

Die Turteltaub' auf dem Zweig, die ins Gedächtniß mir ruft
Den schlanken Wuchs meines Freunds, den ich umhalst ehemals.
Die Seele macht sie mir schwarz vor Gram, da ruf' ich ihr zu:
O Taub' es liegt alles Schwarz des Lebens dir auf dem Hals.

Auf der lautlichen Ebene dominiert im Gedicht der Buchstabe *qāf*, der in beiden Versen je viermal vorkommt und den klanglich eingängigen Reim auf *-qik* mitbildet. Die Schwärze des Taubenhalses, die mit der Melancholie des lyrischen Ichs korrespondiert, könnte auf den schwarzen Nackenstreifen einiger zur Gattung der Turteltaube gehörenden Arten hindeuten, etwa der Türkentaube oder der Halbmondtaube. Sie erinnert aber auch an die unter Mamluken verbreitete Gewohnheit, Brieftauben zum Zeichen der Niederlage schwarz einzufärben.[105]

Eine Reihe von späteren Dichtern spielen mit dem tradierten Bild der Taube und hinterfragen ihre Rolle als Trauervogel. Um zu „beweisen," dass die Taube nicht annähernd so fühlt, wie ihr Ruf klingt und sie, was die Gefühle des Trauernden angeht, in Wirklichkeit völlig ahnungslos ist, werden allerlei Argumente vorgebracht, die sich an der äußeren Erscheinung, dem Verhalten und Lebensraum des Vogels orientieren. Zu den frühesten Zweiflern der vorliegenden Auswahl zählt der syrische Diplomat und Literat Ibn Sinān al-Ḫafāǧī (st. 466/1074):[106]

---

103 Ibn Ḥiğğa al-Ḥamawī, *Ta'hīl* 755; al-Ġuzūlī, *Maṭāliʿ* (1881) 73, (2000) 87: V. 1b قوام حسنك في ضمّي; V. 2a: قد سودت ... فقلت له.

104 ÜLB Münster, Nachlass Rückert 5, 038, Bl. 9b–10a; Vorlage: Ibn Ḥiğğa al-Ḥamawī, *Ta'hīl al-ġarīb*, Ms. Gotha, A 2156, fol. 76[b].

105 Vgl. Ragheb, *Messagers* 137.

106 An-Nawāǧī, *Ḥalba* 324: V. 2a تتلو, V. 3 aus aṣ-Ṣafadī, *Wāfī* xvii, 507–8 (das Gedicht hat dort 18 Verse).

الأمير أبو محمّد عبد الله بن محمّد الخفاجي عن أبيات [من الطويل]
وهاتفةٍ في البان تُمْلي غَرامَها * علينا وتتْلو من صَبابتِها صُحْفا
عَجِبْتُ لها تشْكو الفِراقَ جَهالةً * وقد جاوبتْ من كلّ ناحيةٍ إلْفا
ويُشْجي قُلوبَ العاشِقين حَنينُها * وما فَهموا ممّا تغنّتْ به حَرْفا
ولو صدقتْ فيما تقول من الأسى * لمَا لَبستْ طَوقًا ولا خضبتْ كَفّا

Eine Rufende in der Weide, die mir ihr Liebesleid diktiert und von ihrer Sehnsucht (ganze) Seiten rezitiert.
Ich wunderte mich über sie, wie sie in (ihrer) Unwissenheit über die Trennung klagt, wo sie aus allen Richtungen einem Freund antwortet.
Ihr Seufzen schmerzt die Herzen der Liebenden, und doch verstehen sie kein Wort von dem, was sie singt.
Wenn sie die Wahrheit spräche über ihr Leid, würde sie kein Halsband tragen und sich nicht die Füße färben.

Der erste Vers folgt der bekannten Vorstellung, wonach der Ruf der Taube ihr Leid auf die Zuhörer überträgt. Die Wortwahl anthropomorphisiert die Taube und versetzt sie in die Berufswelt eines Textarbeiters und Dichters, der „diktiert“ und „rezitiert.“ Die Wehklage scheint nicht vereinbar mit den Antworten des Vogels auf die Rufe eines Freundes, schmerzt aber dennoch „die Herzen der Liebenden,“ auch wenn sie ihnen unverständlich ist. Der hier letzte Vers verstärkt noch einmal den Argwohn und führt als Beweise gegen eine echte Trauer die Schönheitsmerkmale der Taube schlechthin – Halsband und rot gefärbte Füße – an, die an den Schmuck und die hennagefärbten Hände einer Braut erinnern. Ähnlich, aber pointierter dichtet rund zwei Jahrhunderte später Ibn ʿAbd aẓ-Ẓāhir:[107]

وقال القاضي محيي الدين بن عبد الظاهر [من الخفيف]
نَسَبَ الناسُ للحَمامةِ حُزْنًا * وأراها في الحُزْن لَيَسَتْ هُنالكْ
خضبَتْ كَفَّها وطَوَّقَتِ الجِيـ * ـدَ وغَنّتْ وما الحَزين كذلكْ

Die Betrübniß wird zugeschrieben der Taube,
Von Betrübniß an ihr doch find’ ich kein Zeichen.

107 Al-Ġuzūlī, *Maṭāliʿ* (1881) 71, (2000) 86: V. 1a in Ed. 2000 لحمامة, V. 1b in beiden كذلك ; Ibn Ḥiǧǧa al-Ḥamawī, *Taʾhīl* 756 (V. 2a خضّبت); al-Asyūṭī, *Marǧ*, BN 3385, fol. 114[b]: V. 1a نسبوا; BN 3386, fol. 136[a].

Ihre Hand färbt sie, ihren Hals auch beringt sie,
Dazu singt sie; wann thun Betrübte dergleichen?[108]

Wie al-Ġuzūlī im *Maṭāliʿ* überliefert, ist die Taube ein so schneller Flieger, dass selbst Raubvögel sie nur mit List erbeuten können.[109] Diese Flugfreudigkeit einer als Liebesbotin entsandten Taube nimmt Ibn Ṣāḥib Tikrīt (st. 584/1188–9)[110] als Indiz für ihre Seelenlage:[111]

ابن صاحب تكريت [من الطويل]
تحمّلتَ يا بَرْقُ ٱشْتِياقي الى الحِمى * فأنتَ كقَلْبي من غَرامي تُخفّقُ
وما أنتِ يا وَرْقاء مِثْلي حَزِينة * ولو كنْتِ ما كان الجَناح يُصفّقُ

Du hast, o Blitz, meine Sehnsucht in das beschützte Land getragen,
darum zuckst du wie mein Herz vor Liebesschmerz.
Und doch bist du, o Taube, nicht so traurig wie ich; wenn du es wärest,
würden (deine) Flügel nicht so flattern.

Die Schlussverse in einem Gedicht des šāfiʿitischen Rechtsgelehrten und Dichters Ṣadr ad-Dīn Ibn al-Muraḥḥil/Ibn al-Wakīl (st. 716/1316)[112] konzentrieren sich auf die strittige Deutung des Taubenrufs. Ein Experiment verschafft Klarheit:[113]

الشيخ صدر الدين ابن المرحّل [من الكامل]
قالوا الحَمامُ مُعَدِّدٌ فأَجبتُهم * هذا غِناءٌ لا يُعَدُّ نُواحا
أو ما تَراهُ إنْ كَسَرْتَ جَناحَهُ * لَزِمَ السُكوتَ وفي السَلامةِ صاحا

Sie sagten: „Die Taube wehklagt."[114] Da antwortete ich ihnen: „Dies ist
ein Gesang, der nicht gilt als Klage.

---

108 Der Text der Übersetzung von Friedrich Rückert befindet sich in der ULB Münster, Nachlass Rückert 5, 038, Bl. 9b–10a; Vorlage: Ibn Ḥiǧǧa al-Ḥamawī, *Taʾhīl*, Ms. Gotha, A 2156, fol. 76[b].

109 Al-Ġuzūlī, *Maṭāliʿ* (1881) 261, (2000) 580.

110 Zu ihm vgl. Ibn Ḫallikān, *Wafayāt al-aʿyān* iii, 498–500.

111 An-Nawāǧī, *Ḥalba* 324.

112 Vgl. aṣ-Ṣafadī, *Wāfī* iv, 264–84.

113 Mit sechs weiteren Versen in al-Asyūṭī, *Marǧ*, BN 3385, fol. 114[a]; BN 3386, fol. 135[b]; Kosegarten, *Chrestomathia arabica* 156.

114 Zu *ʿadda* II. in der Bedeutung „wie ein Klageweib die Tugenden eines Toten aufzählen;

Oder siehst du nicht, wie sie beharrlich schweigt, wenn du ihr den Flügel brichst, aber ruft, wenn sie gesund ist?“

Die Ansichten im ersten Vers sind konträr, werden aber sprachlich durch ein Wortspiel (*ǧinās* zwischen *muʿaddidun* und *yuʿaddu*) miteinander verbunden. Das abschließende Argument gründet auf einer realen Erfahrung, während Ibn Luʾluʾ und aṣ-Ṣafadī sich literarischer Mittel bedienen, um die Liebes- und Leidensfähigkeit der Taube anzuzweifeln:[115]

وقال بدر الدين يوسف بن لؤلؤ الذهبي [من الكامل]
أنّى تُباريني جَوًى وصَبابةً * وكآبةً وأسًى وفيضَ مآقي
وأنا الّذي أُمْلي الهَوى عن خاطِري * وهْيَ الّتي تُمْلي مِنَ الأوْراقِ

Wie kann sie mit mir wetteifern in Schmerz und Sehnsucht, Betrübnis, Kummer und dem Tränenstrom der Augen,
Wo ich es doch bin, der die Liebe nach seiner Erinnerung diktiert, und sie es, die nur von den Blättern diktiert.

Beinahe erdrückend wirkt in Vers 1 die Aneinanderreihung von fünf Nomina (Stilmittel *taʿdīd*), die der Verzweiflung des lyrischen Ichs Ausdruck verleihen. Die parallel gestalteten Halbverse im zweiten Vers (Stilmittel *tarṣīʿ*) führen den Unterschied zwischen leidendem Dichter und imitierender Taube deutlich vor Augen. Die Doppelbedeutung von *awrāq* – „Pflanzenblätter“ und „Papierblätter“ – bleibt auch in der Übersetzung als Wortspiel erhalten. Derselben *maʿnā* bedient sich aṣ-Ṣafadī in einem Epigramm, das er als Teil der Korrespondenz zwischen ihm und Ibn Nubāta in die *Alḥān as-sawāǧiʿ* aufgenommen hat:[116]

صلاح الدين ابن أيبك [من الخفيف]
لا تقيسوا إلى الحَمامةِ حُزْنًا * إنّ فَضْلي تَدْري به العُشّاقُ
أنا أمْلي الغَرامَ عن ظَهْرِ قلّبٍ * وهْيَ تُمْلي وحَولها الأوْراقُ

einen Toten oder Kranken beweinen“ und „wie ein Vogel kläglich singen“ vgl. Dozy, *Supplément* ii, 100a.

115 Mit insgesamt fünf Versen in al-Ġuzūlī, *Maṭāliʿ* (1881) 72, (2000) 86: V. 1a: انا; Ibn Ḥiǧǧa al-Ḥamawī, *Taʾhīl* 754: V. 2a: أملي الجوى; an-Nawāǧī, *Ḥalba* 326. Dieses und das folgende Epigramm von aṣ-Ṣafadī auch in aṣ-Ṣafadī, *Aʿyān al-ʿaṣr* v, 139.

116 Al-Asyūṭī, *Marǧ*, BN 3385, fol. 114[b]; BN 3386, fol. 136[a]; aṣ-Ṣafadī, *Alḥān as-sawāǧiʿ* ii, 262.

Nehmt für den Kummer die Taube nicht als Maß! Die Liebenden wissen, dass ich darin ihr überlegen bin.
Ich diktiere auswendig den Liebesschmerz, während sie diktiert von Blättern rings umher.

Nach all diesen Zweifeln an ihrer Trauer verdient es die Taube, selbst einmal zu Wort zu kommen. Al-Ġuzūlī zitiert in Kapitel 46 seiner Anthologie einen *inšāʾ*-Text des šāfiʿitischen Rechtsgelehrten und Literaten Zayn ad-Dīn Ibn al-Wardī (st. 749/1349), in dem die Taube einen Monolog anstimmt, als sie auf einen Falken trifft.[117] In Reimprosa verhöhnt sie den Greifvogel als „alten Knochen," der nur als „Werkzeug für Spiel und Jagd" tauge. Sie hingegen – „ein Werkzeug für Ernst und List" rühmt sich ihrer Vorzüge als Briefträgerin, die trotz ihrer Angst vor den „Netzen der Heuchelei und den Schlingen der Lüge" das anvertraute Gut, „das sich Berge geweigert haben zu tragen," zuverlässig (nach Hause) trägt (vgl. Q 33:72). Mit Frohbotschaften und Parfüm (*ḫalūq*) geschmückt, löst sie bei Gelehrten Erstaunen aus über ihre gefärbten Finger und ihr Glück (*yamīn*).[118] *Ḫalūq* ist das bekannte Parfümöl, das aus Safran und Moschus oder anderen Inhaltsstoffen wie Rosen und Sandelholz gemischt und regelmäßig bei frohen Anlässen – wie der Nilschwemme – verwendet wurde. Tauben, die gute Nachrichten brachten – *aṯyār al-bašāʾir* – wurden damit eingerieben und erhielten so eine rote oder gelbe Farbe.[119]

[...] كتمتُ عن الناس سِرّي * وأبهمْتُ في الغِناء والنَوح أمري

„[...] ich verberge vor den Menschen mein Geheimnis und mache in Gesang und Klage meine Sache dunkel," konstatiert die Taube am Ende ihrer Lobrede und dichtet weiter:

[من المجتث]
رأوا[120] خِضابي وطَوقي * فآستنْكفوا من بُكائي
ثمّ آدّعوا أنّ نَوحي * مُناسبٌ لِغنائي

117 Al-Ġuzūlī, *Maṭāliʿ* (1881) 263–4, (2000) 582.

118 Wohl in Anspielung auf den Beinamen *aṭ-ṭāʾir al-maymūn*, der seit der frühen Abbasidenzeit für Tauben verwendet wurde (vgl. al-Ǧāḥiẓ, *Ḥayawān* iii, 147). Vögel mit guten Nachrichten wurden als *ayāmin* „vom Glück Begünstigte" bezeichnet (vgl. Ragheb, *Messagers* 81, 137).

119 Ragheb, *Messagers* 137.

120 Al-Ġuzūlī, *Maṭāliʿ* (1881) 264, (2000) 582: V. 1a: روى خضابي وطرقي.

فقُلْتُ كُفّوا فدَمْعي * بادٍ بغَيرِ ٱخْتِفاءِ
الخَضْبُ من فَيضِ دَمْعي * والطَوق[121] عِقْدُ وَلائي

Sie sahen meine Farbe (der Füße) und mein Halsband; deshalb verachteten sie mein Weinen.
Dann behaupteten sie, dass meine Klage in Wirklichkeit mein Gesang wäre.
Da sagte ich: „Hört auf! Meine Tränen erscheinen, ohne dass ich sie verheimliche.
Die Farbe (der Füße) kommt vom Überfluss meiner Tränen, der Halsring ist das Band meiner Treue.“

Zum Los von domestizierten Tauben gehört es auch, dass sie eine mehr oder weniger lange Zeit in Gefangenschaft verbringen. Dies trifft in besonderer Weise auch auf die Brieftaube zu, die für weite Reisen in einen Käfig oder Korb (beides *qafaṣ*) gesperrt, manchmal sogar (in einer Tasche) am Körper des Trägers verborgen wurde.[122] Mit Sorgfalt ausgesuchte Transporteure reisten mit den Vögeln über Wochen und Monate zu Wasser und zu Lande, um sie von ihren Heimatschlägen zu dem Zielort (*ġāya*) zu bringen, der für die Auflassung (*zaǧl*) der Tauben bestimmt war.[123] Nicht nur die Botentaube, sondern auch der zurückbleibende Partner – meist das Weibchen – musste am Freiflug gehindert werden, da er sonst den Schlag verlassen könnte, wenn die Abwesenheit des fernen Gefährten zu lange währte.[124]

Nur zwei Gedichte aus unserer Auswahl nehmen sich des Themas „Taube im Käfig“ an. Das Epigramm von Sayf ad-Dīn Ibn Qizil al-Mušidd (st. 656/1258)[125] nimmt die Perspektive des Käfigs ein, der sich äußerlich wie innerlich mit einem Menschen identifiziert:[126]

وقال الأمير سيف الدين المشدّ في قفص [من مجزوء الرمل]
أنا للطائرِ سِجْنٌ * أقْتَني كُلَّ مَليح
قُضُبُ البانِ ضُلوعي * وحَمامُ الأيكِ روحي

121 Al-Ġuzūlī, *Maṭāliʿ* (1881) 264, (2000) 582: V. 4b والصبر.

122 Vgl. Ragheb, *Messagers* 127–8.

123 Al-Ǧāḥiẓ, *Ḥayawān* iii, 213–4 beschreibt die Mühen eines solchen Transports, den die Taubenzüchter nur in die Hände besonders vertrauenswürdiger Männer legten.

124 Ragheb, *Messagers* 124.

125 Vgl. *GAL* i, 263–4, *GALS* i, 465.

126 Al-Ġuzūlī, *Maṭāliʿ* (1881) 73, (2000) 87, Überschrift mit Angabe des Dichters von dort; an-Nawāǧī, *Ḥalba* 326 (anonym); aṣ-Ṣafadī, *Wāfī* xxii, 90.

Ich bin für den Vogel ein Gefängnis und erwerbe allerlei Schöne.
Die Zweige der Weide sind meine Rippen und die Taube des Dickichts meine Seele.

Im Gedicht des jüngeren Zeitgenossen Muǧīr ad-Dīn Ibn Tamīm (st. 684/1285) kommt auch die gefangene Taube zu Wort:[127]

وقال الأمير مجير الدين بن تميم [من الكامل]
لم أَنْسَ قَولَ الوُرْقِ وهْيَ حَبيسةٌ * والعَيشُ منها قد أقام مُنغَّصَا
قد كُنْتُ أَلْبَسُ أَخْضرًا من أَغْصُنٍ * فلبِسْتُ منها بَعْدَ ذاك مُقفَّصَا

Nie vergesse ich die Worte der Taube, als ihr Leben in Gefangenschaft trostlos geworden war:
„Einst pflegte ich mich mit einem grünen Zweig zu kleiden, danach kleidete ich mich mit einem zu Gittern geflochtenen/*im Gittermuster*."[128]

Das doppeldeutige Reimwort *muqaffaṣā* (V. 2b) im „Vorher-Nachher-Vergleich" löst die bedrückende Situation humorvoll auf, dennoch zeigen die Verse Mitgefühl für den seiner Freiheit beraubten Vogel. Dass die Turteltaube an ihrer Gefangenschaft nicht unschuldig ist, gibt ein – in den Anthologien fehlender – Vers von Saʿīd b. al-Mubārak Ibn ad-Dahhān an-Naḥwī (st. 569/1174) zu bedenken:

[من الطويل]
كذاك أرى الخفّاشَ يُنْجيه قُبْحُهُ * ويحْتَبِسُ القُمْرِيَّ حُسْنُ التَرَنُّمِ

Genauso sehe ich, daß die Häßlichkeit es ist, die der Fledermaus die Freiheit sichert, und daß der schöne Gesang die hellgraue [Taube] einsperrt.[129]

127 Al-Ġuzūlī, *Maṭāliʿ* (1881) 73, (2000) 87; Ibn Ḥiǧǧa al-Ḥamawī, *Taʾhīl* 756; an-Nawāǧī, *Ḥalba* 326 (anonym): V. 2a من غصوني.

128 Zu V. 2b *muqaffaṣ* in der Bedeutung „kariert, gekästelt (wie ein Käfiggitter)" vgl. al-Ḫafāǧī (st. 1069/1659), *Šifāʾ al-ġalīl* 221 mit Zitat des Gedichts und folgender Erklärung: مقفص: هو نقش في الثياب بالطول والعرض.

129 Text und Übersetzung aus Ullmann, *Flughühner* 16 (Vorlage: al-Qifṭī, *Inbāh* ii, 50).

Die zitierten Epigramme von Ibn al-Mušidd und Ibn Tamīm bilden in an-Nawāǧīs grob nach Themen strukturierter Gedichtauswahl den stimmigen Schlusspunkt. Da dieser Festschrift-Beitrag so düster nicht enden soll, sei es noch einmal einer freilebenden Taube aus Ibn Ḥiǧǧa al-Ḥamawīs Anthologie überlassen, Leser und Zuhörer für sich einzunehmen. In Abwandlung des bekannten Motivs „Taube als Prediger“[130] zeigt Ibn Tamīm (mit Friedrich Rückert), dass der Taubenruf nicht immer für Sehnsucht und Klage steht, sondern auch noch eine andere Bewandtnis haben kann:[131]

مجير الدين بن تميم [من الكامل]
وحَمائِمٍ قد قَصَّرَتْ عن سَجْعِها * فَوقَ الغُصون عِبارةُ الخُطَباءِ
كَرَّرْنَ حَرْفَ الراءِ في أَسْجاعِها * لِتُغيظَ منه واصِلَ بْنَ عَطاءِ
هُوَ لم يَطُقْ بالراءِ نُطْقًا وَهْيَ لم * تَنْطِقْ إذا خَطَبَتْ بِغَيْرِ الراءِ

Die Taube, deren Redekunst auf Aesten
Beschämt die Kanzelredner fern und nah;
Sie häuft den Buchstab Ra in ihren Reden,
Zum Aergernis des Wasil Ben Ata:
Weil er das Ra vermag nicht auszusprechen,
So spricht sie, wenn sie predigt, nichts als Ra.[132]

Danksagung

Mein herzlicher Dank gilt Alev Masarwa, die mich auf mehrere Quellen aufmerksam gemacht und wertvolle Hinweise beigesteuert hat. Sehr dankbar bin ich auch Nefeli Papoutsakis und Hakan Özkan für hilfreiche Korrekturen und Anregungen.

130 Vgl. Abū Zayd, *Ḥamām* 113–20.

131 Ibn Ḥiǧǧa al-Ḥamawī, *Ta'hīl* 752; Ibn Tamīm, *Dīwān* 13, Nr. 1; aṣ-Ṣafadī, *Wāfī* v, 234.

132 ULB Münster, Nachlass Rückert, Arbeitsmanuskript 5, 038, Bl. 9b–10a und Reinschrift 5, 040, Bl. 12b–13a (identisch bis auf Orthographie). Vorlage: Ibn Ḥiǧǧa al-Ḥamawī, *Ta'hīl*, Ms. Gotha, A 2156, fol. 76[a]. Der Theologe und Asket Wāṣil ibn ʿAṭā' (st. 131/748–9) hatte bekanntlich einen Sprachfehler und hat eine Predigt verfasst, in welcher der Buchstabe *rā'* nicht vorkommt (vgl. van Ess, Wāṣil b. ʿAṭā').

Bibliographie

Abū l-ʿAlāʾ al-Maʿarrī, *Abū l-ʿAlāʾ wa-mā ilayhi wa-yalīhi: Risālat al-malāʾika*, Hg. ʿA. al-Hindī, Beirut 1424/2003.

Abū Ḥayyān, Ibn Mālik, *Abū Ḥayyān's commentary to the* Alfiyya *of Ibn Mālik* [*Kitāb Manhaǧ as-sālik fī l-kalām ʿalā Alfiyyat Ibn Mālik*], Hg. S. Glazer, New Haven (Conn.) 1947.

Abū Zayd, ʿA.I., *al-Ḥamām fī š-šiʿr al-ʿarabī*, Kairo 1996.

Abū Dāwūd as-Siǧistānī, *Sunan Abī Dāwūd*, Hg. Š. al-Arnāʾūṭ u.a., 7 Bde., Beirut 2009.

al-Arraǧānī, *Dīwān*, Hg. Q. Māyū, 2 Bde., Beirut 1418/1998.

al-Asyūṭī, Muḥammad Abū Bakr, *al-Marǧ an-naḍir wa-l-araǧ al-ʿaṭir*, Ms. Paris, BN 3385 (Autograph); Ms. Paris, BN 3386.

Bauer, Th., al-Nawājī, in J.E. Lowry und D.J. Stewart (Hgg.), *Essays in Arabic literary biography 1350–1850*, Wiesbaden 2009, 321–31.

Bies, W., Taube, in *Enzyklopädie des Märchens*, Hgg. R.W. Brednich u.a., Bd. 13, Berlin/New York 2010, 240–4.

Canard, M., Ibn Killis, in *EI*², iii, 840–1.

ad-Damīrī, *Ḥayāt al-ḥayawān al-kubrā*, Hg. A. al-Fāris, Damaskus 1992.

de Juana, E., Order Pterocliformes: Family Pteroclidae (sandgrouse), in J. del Hayo, A. Elliot, J. Sargatal (Hgg.), *Handbook of the birds of the world: Sandgrouse to cuckoos*, Bd. 4, Barcelona 1997, 30–59.

Dozy, R., *Supplément aux dictionnaires arabes*, 2 Bde., Leiden/Paris ²1927.

Farmer, H.G., Mukhāriḳ, in *EI*², vii, 518.

Fischer, W., *Farb- und Formbezeichnungen in der Sprache der altarabischen Dichtung: Untersuchungen zur Wortbedeutung und zur Wortbildung*, Wiesbaden 1965.

al-Ǧāḥiẓ, *Kitāb al-Ḥayawān*, Hg. ʿA. Hārūn, Bd. 3, Kairo ²1385/1965.

Ghersetti, A., On Mamluk anthologies again: The case of Jamāl ad-Dīn al-Waṭwāṭ and his *Ghurar al-Khaṣāʾiṣ al-Wāḍihah wa-ʿUrar al-Naqāʾiḍ al-Qābiḥah*, in *MSR* 17 (2013), 72–99.

Grotzfeld, H., al-Laʿb bil-ḥamām, in H.R. Roemer und P. Bachmann (Hgg.), *Die islamische Welt zwischen Mittelalter und Neuzeit: Festschrift für H.R. Roemer zum 65. Geburtstag*, Beirut 1979, 193–7.

al-Ġuzūlī, *Maṭāliʿ al-budūr fī manāzil as-surūr*, 2 Bde., Kairo 1299–1300 [1881/82–83].

al-Ġuzūlī, *Maṭāliʿ al-budūr fī manāzil as-surūr*, Kairo 1419/2000.

al-Ḫafāǧī, *Šifāʾ al-ġalīl fī-mā fī kalām al-ʿarab min ad-daḫīl*, Kairo 1282/1865.

Hartmann, A., *an-Nāṣir li-Dīn Allāh (1180–1225): Politik, Religion, Kultur in der späten ʿAbbāsidenzeit*, Berlin/New York 1975.

Ibn Abī Ḥaǧala, *Sulūk as-sanan ilā waṣf as-sakan*, Ms. İstanbul Üniversitesi 877.

Ibn Faḍlallāh al-ʿUmarī, Šihāb ad-Dīn, *Masālik al-abṣār fī mamālik al-amṣār*, Hg. K.S. al-Ǧabūrī, 15 Bde., Beirut 2010.

Ibn Ḥağar al-ʿAsqalānī, *Inbāʾ al-ġumr bi-abnāʾ al-ʿumr*, Hg. Ḥasan al-Ḥabašī, 4 Bde., Kairo 1969–71.
Ibn Ḫallikān, *Wafayāt al-aʿyān wa-anbāʾ abnāʾ az-zamān*, Hg. I. ʿAbbās, 8 Bde., Beirut 1968–72.
Ibn Ḥiğğa al-Ḥamawī, *Ḫizānat al-adab wa-ġāyat al-arab*, Hg. M.N. Ibn ʿUmar, 2 Bde., Beirut 2008.
Ibn Ḥiğğa al-Ḥamawī, *Taʾhīl al-ġarīb*, Hg. M.Ḥ. al-Miṣrī, Medina 2017.
Ibn Ḥiğğa al-Ḥamawī, *Taʾhīl al-ġarīb*, Ms. Gotha, A 2156.
Ibn al-Kattānī, *Kitāb at-Tašbīhāt min ašʿār ahl al-Andalus*, Hg. ʿA.M.I. Ḥasanayn, Diss. Kiel 1969.
Ibn Manẓūr, *Lisān al-ʿArab*, Bd. 7, Beirut 2000.
Ibn al-Muʿtazz, *Dīwān*, Beirut: Dār Ṣādir o.J.
Ibn Nubāta al-Miṣrī, *Dīwān*, Hg. M. al-Qalqīlī, Kairo 1323/1905.
Ibn Qalāqis, *Dīwān*, Hg. S. al-Furayḥ, al-Kuwayt 1988.
Ibn Tamīm, *Dīwān*, Hgg. H. Nāğī, N. Rašīd, Beirut 1420/1999.
Ibn Taġrībirdī, *an-Nuğūm az-zāhira fī mulūk Miṣr wa-l-Qāhira*, 16 Bde., Hgg. F.M. Šaltūt u.a., Kairo 1929–72.
al-Kisāʾī, *Qiṣaṣ al-anbiyāʾ*, Hg. I. Eisenberg, Leipzig 1922.
Kluth, H.P., *Züchten, spielen, siegen*, Rheda-Wiedenbrück 1986.
Kociejowski, M., *The pigeon wars of Damascus*, Emeryville 2010.
Korte, M., Brieftaubensport – Gebrauchsanweisung zur Tierquälerei, in *Münstier: Das tierische Magazin für's Münsterland* 13 (2019), 2–3.
Kosegarten, J.G.L., *Chrestomathia arabica*, Leipzig 1828.
Lane, E.W., *An Arabic-English lexicon in eight parts*, London/Edinburgh 1863.
Lewicka, P.B., *Food and foodways of medieval Cairines: Aspects of life in an Islamic metropolis of the eastern Mediterranean*, Leiden/Boston 2011.
Masarwa, A., Wasser, Wein und Architektur: Kulissen des Genusses im *Ḥalbat al-kumayt*, in A. Masarwa und H. Özkan (Hgg.), *The Racecourse of literature: an-Nawāğī and his contemporaries*, Baden-Baden 2020, 277–361.
Masarwa, A., Urban architecture and poetry: Two medieval Arabic anthologies as manuals of mapping urban space, in N. Papoutsakis und S. von Hees (Hgg.), *The sultan's anthologist: Ibn Abī Ḥağalah and his work*, Baden-Baden 2017, 101–33.
Miller, J., *More than the sum of its parts: Animal categories and accretive logic in volume one of al-Jāḥiẓ's* Kitāb al-Ḥayawān, Ph.D. diss, New York University 2013.
al-Mubarrad, *Kitāb al-Kāmil*, hg. W. Wright, 2 Bde., Leipzig 1864–92.
Muhanna, E., *Encyclopaedism in the Mamluk period: The composition of Shihāb al-Dīn al-Nuwayrī's (d. 1333)* Nihāyat al-arab fī funūn al-adab, Ph.D. diss., Harvard University 2012.
an-Nawāğī, *Ḥalbat al-kumayt*, Kairo 1357/1938 (Nachdruck der Ausgabe al-ʿĀmiriyya 1276/1859).

Özkan, H., Ibn Luʾluʾ, in *EI*³ (im Druck).

Pellat, Ch., Ḥabāba, in *EI*², iii, 2.

al-Qalqašandī, *Ṣubḥ al-aʿšā fī ṣināʿat al-inšā*, 14 Bde., Kairo 1913–22.

al-Qifṭī, *Kitāb Inbāh ar-ruwāt ʿalā anbāh an-nuḥāt*, Hg. M.A. Ibrāhīm, 2 Bde., Kairo 1952.

Ragheb, Y., *Les messagers volants en terre d'Islam*, Paris 2002.

Rückert, F., [Rezension zu Kosegarten, *Chrestomathia arabica*], in *Jahrbücher für wissenschaftliche Kritik*, Jahrgang 1830, 2, Nr. 26–9, Sp. 205–13, 217–27.

aṣ-Ṣafadī, *Alḥān as-sawāǧiʿ bayna l-bādiʾ wa-l-murāǧiʿ*, Hg. I. Ṣāliḥ, 2 Bde., Damaskus 1425/2004.

aṣ-Ṣafadī, *Aʿyān al-ʿaṣr wa-aʿwān an-naṣr*, Hg. ʿA. Abū Zayd u.a., 6 Bde., Beirut/Damaskus 1997–8.

aṣ-Ṣafadī, *al-Wāfī bi-l-wafayāt. Das biographische Lexikon des Ṣalāḥaddīn Ḫalīl Ibn Aibak aṣ-Ṣafadī*, Hgg. H. Ritter u.a., 30 Bde., Wiesbaden u.a. 1962–2010.

Saker, S., *Der Wille zur Macht: Der fatimidische Wesir Yaʿqūb ibn Killis*, Berlin 2003.

Ṣaqr, ʿA., *Mawsūʿat aḥsan al-kalām fī l-fatāwā wa-l-aḥkām*, 7 Bde., Kairo 1432/2011.

Schenda, R., *Who's who der Tiere: Märchen, Mythen und Geschichten*, München 1998.

Schletterer, M., *Die Taube im Wandel der Zeit: Biologische und historische Variationen*, Osnabrück ²2004.

Schmidt, H. und R. Proll, *Taschenatlas Tauben: 300 Rassen für Zucht und Ausstellung*, Stuttgart 2006.

Silverstein, A.J., *Postal systems in the pre-modern Islamic world*, Cambridge u.a. 2007.

Sobieroj, F., al-Shiblī, in *EI*², ix, 432–3.

as-Suyūṭī, Ǧalāl ad-Dīn, *Naẓm al-ʿiqyān fī aʿyān al-aʿyān*, Hg. Ph. Hitti, London 1927.

aṯ-Ṯaʿālibī, *Yatīmat ad-dahr fī maḥāsin ahl al-ʿaṣr*, Hg. M. Qumayḥa, 4 Bde., Beirut 1983.

Ullmann, M., *Flughühner und Tauben*, München 1982 (Beiträge zur Lexikographie des Klassischen Arabisch Nr. 3).

van Ess, J., Wāṣil b. ʿAṭāʾ, in *EI*², xi, 164–5.

van Gelder, G.J., A muslim encomium on wine: "The racecourse of the bay (Ḥalbat al-kumayt)" by al-Nawāǧī (d. 859/1455) as a post-classical Arabic work, in *Arabica* 42 (1995), 222–34.

al-Waṭwāṭ, *Mabāhiǧ al-fikar wa-manāhiǧ al-ʿibar*, Hg. ʿA. al-Ḥarbī, Beirut 1420/2000.

al-Waṭwāṭ, *Manāhiǧ al-fikar wa-mabāhiǧ al-ʿibar*, 2 Bde., Hg. F. Sezgin, Frankfurt/M. 1990.

Viré, F., Ḥamām, in *EI*², iii, 108–10.

12

The Magic of Books: The Narrative Function of Books in Arabic Popular Epic

Remke Kruk

In 2017, Ghersetti and Metcalfe published *The Book in Fact and Fiction*.[1] In this volume a number of authors approach the topic of books from various angles, but, as Ghersetti remarks in her introduction, the contributions do not nearly exhaust the subject. Many aspects of the role of books are still to be explored. Here I intend to look at one of them, namely the narrative function of books in premodern fictional literature, more specifically the Arabic popular epic.[2] This literary genre flourished particularly in Mamluk times and the topic may thus suitably have a place in Thomas Bauer's congratulatory volume. Contributing to this volume is an honour, for my admiration for Thomas and his work goes a long way back, to his impressive study of Abū Ḥanīfa al-Dīnawarī's *Book on Plants*, which was published in 1988. Whenever I think of him, the words of our dear regretted friend and colleague Wolfhart Heinrichs come to my mind: "That man is a marvel."

That books play a role in *sīra* literature will not come as a surprise. Books, especially books of a magical and mysterious nature, are a widespread element in popular storytelling up to the present day. That includes children's comics. I am thinking in particular of the Donald Duck weekly to which most of the Dutch children I know are addicted.[3] The books in these cases are fictional and often of a magical character. Such books do indeed occur widely in the Arabic popular epic.

The question may be asked, however, whether all the books in *sīra* literature are fictional. Is there ever a book mentioned that actually existed, apart from the Quran, which is a case apart? The issue is connected to the wider question

1 Ghersetti and Metcalfe, *Fact and Fiction*.

2 I am most grateful to Wim Raven (Marburg) for reading and commenting upon a first version of this article.

3 I hope that my learned readership will not be offended by this reference. If so, I may remind them of Aristotle's encouragement to study even the humblest of animals, referring to Heraclitus, who invited guests into the kitchen, saying: "There are gods even here!" (*Parts of Animals*, 645a, 15–24. I cite Peck's translation).

 | DOI:10.1163/9789004521780_014

of the relationship between the popular epic, a type of literature transmitted orally as well as in written form, and the literary tradition of the cultural elite. We can be brief about that: the popular epic was more closely connected to the educated literary tradition than many people realise, and it often shows evidence of that.[4] An example is the episode in *Sīrat ʿAntar* where ʿAntar hangs his *Muʿallaqa* at the Kaʿba.[5] In another episode, ʿAntar is examined about Arabic synonyms.[6]

References to the wider scholarly and scientific literature also occur. In an episode in the long story of King ʿUmar al-Nuʿmān and his sons, a small *sīra* that is incorporated into *1001-Nights* but also circulated in separate MSS,[7] Princess Nuzhat al-Zamān, captured and brought into slavery, is examined to have her knowledge tested—an episode reminiscent of the story of Tawaddud, also in *1001-Nights*. Nuzhat al-Zamān enumerates an extensive series of actually extant books, naming authors and titles. As Littmann pointed out, nearly all of the books belong to the medical tradition: Galen's Hippocratic commentaries, Ibn al-Bayṭār's *Mufradāt* and the *Qānūn* of Ibn Sīnā are some examples. Religious texts just appear in a brief mention at the end: "the books of the Shafiʿites, *ḥadīth* and *naḥw*."[8]

In another *sīra*, *Sīrat al-Ḥākim bi-amrillāh* (more about it later) there is a long episode in which the caliph al-Ḥākim summons various classes of scholars and scientists to his court to let them expound their scholarly views and show their expertise. Religious sciences, such as *tafsīr*, *ḥadīth* and *fiqh*, as well as medicine and related sciences are discussed. This is continued with the sciences of music, poetry and rhetoric. In the course of the discussions a number of authors are mentioned: Greek philosophers and physicians, but also music specialists. Occasionally book titles, too, are mentioned.[9]

In these two cases, the presentation of science, scholarship and books has a very specific purpose. The exposition of Nuzhat al-Zamān's extensive knowledge serves to emphasise her unique qualities, which enhance her value as a slave girl. In the case of *Sīrat al-Ḥākim*, the episode is used to demonstrate the caliph al-Ḥākim's positive attitude to science and scholarship, to which the initial negligence of his son al-Ẓāhir is later contrasted. As opposed to his father al-Ḥākim, al-Ẓāhir does not give remunerations to scholars and scientists. Criti-

4 Cf. Bauer, Misunderstandings 110–1.
5 Heath, *Muʿallaqa*.
6 Chelhod, Sayf 205 n. 2.
7 Paret, *Ritterroman* 4–29.
8 Littmann, *Tausendundein Nächte* i, 2:593–4.
9 Lenora, *Der gefälschte Kalif* 142–5.

cism to that effect from the astronomer Yūnus, author of a work on astronomy, the *Kitāb al-Uṣūl*,[10] is passed on to al-Ẓāhir by the latter's son, upon which the caliph changes his attitude, giving Yūnus and his son Jumhūr prominent positions.[11] In this latter episode, too, book titles are mentioned.[12]

These few examples may serve to demonstrate that actually extant books occasionally do turn up in the epics, with their authors and titles and a specific purpose, but it may not come as a surprise that the majority of books that we encounter are fictional. Here I will largely deal with this latter category, trying to analyse the narrative function of these books in the epics and their possible significance in connection with the wider cultural context.

Why are books introduced in the stories? Are they mentioned just by way of a literary convention? Do they provide an element of prestige? Are they valued for the practical information they have to offer, or revered for the ancient wisdom or hidden knowledge that they contain? Do these books have a function as objects, and if so, how? As we will see, they occur in all these capacities, and what all these functions have in common is that in the epics books are loaded with authority.

For the present purpose, I will look at the genre of the Arabic epic as a whole. The genre is vast and overlaps with others, such as fictional *futūḥ* literature.[13] Not everything is published or even studied, and my approach is by definition eclectic. I will include a representative selection, namely most of the epics treated in Malcolm Lyons' *The Arabian Epic*; the story of King ʿUmar an-Nuʿmān and his sons; *Sīrat al-Iskandar*; *Sīrat al-Ḥākim bi-amrillāh*; and one *Futūḥ* epic. My focus will be more on epics of Arabic origin than on Arabic *sīra*s that have their roots in the Persian *dastān* tradition, such as *Fīrūzshāh*, *Ḥamza*, and *al-Iskandar*, but I will occasionally refer to the latter group. *Sīrat al-amīra Dhāt al-Himma*, the long *sīra* in which the wars with the Byzantines are a leading theme, will be cited fairly often. A number of excellent studies have appeared on this epic, but it leads too far to enumerate and discuss them here.

There are of course substantial differences between the epics, for each of them has its own literary form, background and character. As we will see, however, the very treatment of this theme, the role of books, serves to bring

10 Lenora, *Der gefälschte Kalif* 110, n. 140, referring to B.R. Goldstein, Ibn Yūnus (*EI*², iii, 969), remarks that this is an allusion to the father of Ibn Yūnus al-Ṣafadī, author of the astronomical tables named after al-Ḥākim.

11 Lenora, *Der gefälschte Kalif* 111.

12 Lenora, *Der gefälschte Kalif* 109–10, 119.

13 See Rosenthal's quite valuable chapter "The Historical Novel," in Rosenthal, *Historiography* 186–93.

the differences between the epics into focus. Even a quick glance at the entry 'book' in the narrative index of Malcolm Lyons' *The Arabian Epic* illustrates this: in that entry, references to some epics are far more frequent than to others, and some, such as *ʿAntar*, do not occur at all. This should not be taken to mean that no books are mentioned in those epics: the narrative index refers to Lyons' summaries, not to the epics themselves, where citing unspecified old and venerable books is a standard element. These popular narratives are, after all, presented and experienced, up to modern times, as historical accounts. The question rather is whether books occur that are of more than passing significance in the story and may even play a vital role in it.

The general picture, that much is clear, is that books are a significant element in the epics. They appear in many ways, sometimes in a quite unexpected manner: in *Sīrat Baybars*, a book is plucked out of thin air by Sultan Ṣāliḥ Ayyūb, who appears in the *sīra* as a person with miraculous access to the world of the numinous.[14] The book, *Dalāʾil al-aḥkām*, was magically destined for the vizir Shāhīn.[15]

Books convey prestige to the people connected to them. This may be in a general manner, such as when someone's clothes and the book bag (*maḥfaẓa*) he carries create an impression of respectability.[16] In this case, however, this is window dressing: the man turns out to be a scholar during daytime, but a robber at night. Or the prestige lent by a book may be quite specific: someone is chosen by a Muslim chief to teach martial arts to his young son, and his eligibility for the job is emphasised by pointing out that he is the author of a book on *furūsīya*, chivalrous arts.[17]

References to Islamic religious books apart from the Quran are rare, and if they appear they are very summarily mentioned. This is part of a general trend in the popular epic that also manifested itself in the Nuzhat al-Zamān episode: we seldom come across books of religious learning, while there is frequent mention of books on science and philosophy. These are rarely actually extant books, as opposed to the selection presented in Nuzhat al-Zamān's story. Greek authorities are often mentioned in this context, usually in connection with fictional writings.

To give you an example: In *Sīrat al-Iskandar*, composed probably in the first half of the 8th/14th century,[18] the king of Qayrawān, Hawāsh, arrives at al-

14 Herzog, *Baibars* 140.
15 Herzog, *Baibars* 861, episode 4; *Sīrat Baybars*, i, 55.
16 Herzog, *Baibars* 868, episode 29; *Sīrat Baybars*, i, 481.
17 *Dhāt al-Himma* i, *juz'* 7: 64, 65.
18 Doufikar-Aerts, *Alexander* 275–6.

Iskandar's camp. He poses as a philosopher, speaks in Greek, one of the twelve languages he knows, and "arranges his tent as the place of a scientist, with piles of books, papers and astrolabes." He starts a practice as a soothsayer and astrologer.[19] In the sequel, Hawāsh's daughter Shams al-Barrayn explains to the prophet al-Khiḍr that she has found the true faith by studying books of philosophers, historians and scientists.[20]

Examples from *Sīrat Dhāt al-Himma* show how books fictitiously ascribed to ancient Greek authors are used to solve complicated problems, often of a technical nature: during a siege, the Byzantines manage to cut off the water supply to the city of Amid with the help of information found in a geographical work of Aristotle.[21] Even when a work of narrative fiction is cited as the source for a practical solution there is a Greek connection: al-Baṭṭāl manages to set an enemy castle on fire by throwing walnuts filled with naphta into it, a trick that he knew from *Sīrat al-Iskandar*, where it was suggested to Alexander by the sage Balīnas.[22] Another book in *Sīrat Dhāt al-Himma* also provides practical knowledge, but in this case no source is mentioned, although the subject has a Greek background. It is a lapidary, *kitāb al-aḥjār wa-khaṣāʾiṣihā*, which contains a description of a poisonous stone. Kings wore it in a ring so as to be able to suck its poison if death was their only way out of a difficult situation. The villainous *qāḍī* ʿUqba uses such a stone to poison the water that his Muslim captors use for making bread.[23]

With lapidaries, we are already in the sphere of mysterious knowledge bordering on the occult, knowledge that typically goes back to ancient authorities. Here we touch upon a prominent, not to say essential, aspect of the books, or in general text-bearing objects, that come up in the popular epic. They harbour knowledge, often secret knowledge, going back to ancient times and legendary authorities. If the subject is suitable, ancient Greek philosophers are connected to these writings, as in the case of Aristotle's fictitious book on geography mentioned above. Another example, also from *Sīrat Dhāt al-Himma*, is a golden tablet inscribed with names and charms (*ṭalāsim*) "unknown to anyone," discovered by the Muslims when they were trapped in a cave. It stated that the writer, an astrologer and pupil of Hippocrates who believed in the One God

19 Doufikar-Aerts, *Alexander* 355–6:227 recto and verso.

20 Doufikar-Aerts, *Alexander* 361:243 recto. Balīnas is an alternative spelling of Balīnūs.

21 *Dhāt al Himma* i, *juzʾ* 6: 70, 73.

22 *Dhāt al-Himma* iii, *juzʾ* 23:62.—This is quite an interesting reference in connection with the formative period and dispersion of the Arabic *Sīrat al-Iskandar*. On its wider tradition, see Doufikar-Aerts, *Alexander*.

23 *Dhāt al-Himma* iii, *juzʾ* 21:14.

and in God's messenger Muḥammad, had stored his knowledge on it to be of use to them, providing something for them that would make eating and drinking, as well as other bodily functions, unnecessary for a month. It also put at their disposal a *jinn* that transported them to Constantinople.[24]

Magical tablets of this kind occur throughout the epics. In fact they form a separate area to explore, connected as they are to a whole tradition most prominently represented by the *Tabula Smaragdina*, which according to Pseudo-Apollonius of Tyana (Arabic: Balīnūs or Balīnas), whose *Sirr al-khalīqa* is the oldest known source for it, was discovered in a vault below a statue of Hermes.[25]

"Ancient Books, Histories and *malāḥim*"

Next to the fairly specific examples given above, there is a much wider range of ancient texts that comes up in the epics. As said, referring to ancient books, often of a mysterious nature, is a standard literary device in this kind of literature. It is of course not unique in this particular genre—one regularly comes across it in all kinds of Arabic literature as a common way to lend authority to a statement. In the popular epic, such references to ancient books frequently come up. Unspecified venerable books, histories, and *malāḥim* are cited, in various combinations and under varying titles: *kutub qadīma, kutub ʿaẓīma, al-kutub al-qadīma wa-l-tawārīkh, al-kutub al-aẓīma wa-l-malāḥim al-qadīma. Malāḥim* in this context means prophesies of future events in general, not specifically apocalyptic events.

As to these *malāḥim:* in modern Arabic, *malḥama* (plural *malāḥim*) is the general term for heroic poem or epic, but in premodern times it had a different meaning, as we see, for instance, in Ibn Khaldūn's *Muqaddima*. There, it is connected to a certain kind of popular history: "Later on, works in poetry and prose and in *rajaz* verse dealing with forecasts concerning dynasties were written in considerable quantity. Much of it found its way into the hands of the people. It is called 'predictions' (*malāḥim*). Some of these works concern forecasts about Islam in general. Others are about particular dynasties. All these works are attributed to famous persons. But there is nothing to support ascribing them to the persons on whose authority they are transmitted."[26] Ibn Khaldūn's account

24 *Dhāt al-Himma* vii *juzʾ* 70:133, Lyons *Arabian Epic* ii, *Dhāt al-Himma* episode 170.

25 Weisser, *Geheimnis der Schöpfung* 74–5; Pseudo-Apollonius, *Sirr* Arabic text 5–7.

26 Ibn Khaldūn, *Muqaddima* ii, 219–20 (Rosenthal's translation); *EI*² Ed., *Malāḥim*.

demonstrates once again how intricately the various genres of popular literature of a (semi-)historical nature are intertwined.

Predictions can be used to introduce the appearance of the hero, who is destined to change the course of history, his advent thus being presented as the outcome of a historical development set into motion long ago. An example is found in some versions of *Sīrat ʿAntar*, which start with an introduction going back to Noah and leading up to the appearance of ʿAntar, presenting him as the person predestined to civilise the rough behaviour of the pre-Islamic Arabs and prepare them for the coming of Muḥammad.[27] According to Doufikar-Aerts, in *Sīrat al-Iskandar*, the traditional Alexander romance was transformed into a *sīra* by adding typical *sīra* elements, such as a history of al-Iskandar's descent comprising several generations.[28] Books play a role there: Kaʿb al-Aḥbār studies biographies of kings from the beginning of time to the prophet Muḥammad. He lists 56 kings, among whom he considers al-Iskandar the greatest. He quotes Quran 18:82–98.[29]

In *Qiṣṣat al-amīr Ḥamza al-bahlawān*, we are told that Ḥamza's name was written in "the books of our wise men."[30] And in *Sīrat al-Ḥākim*, the astrologer Yūnus says that he has read in the *malāḥim* that the current ruler will be succeeded by his learned and cultivated son, who will follow in the steps of his grandfather al-Ḥākim.[31] A *sīra* that is particularly rich in such prophesies is *Sīrat Baybars*, to be discussed below.

Not only rulers, but also specific events are announced in various ancient writings. Prominent among those events is the advent of the Prophet Muḥammad and the rise of Islam. In those cases the unspecified 'ancient books' are sometimes combined with holy books such as the Torah and the Bible: "The emperor Nūfīl had been dissuaded from attacking Muḥammad by a sage who had found a description of him in the Bible, the Torah and the old books."[32] Such Biblical descriptions of the Prophet may involve the idea that leaves of the Bible had been folded over, thus concealing the information concerning Muḥammad and Islam.[33]

To give another example from *Sīrat Dhāt al-Himma*: an abbot converts to Islam, saying that the Messiah had spoken about this later prophet *fī kutu-*

27 Heath, *Thirsty Sword* 170–2.
28 Doufikar-Aerts, *Alexander* 275.
29 Doufikar-Aerts, *Alexander* 283:1 verso.
30 Lyons, *Arabian Epic* ii, *Ḥamza* episode 14.
31 Lenora, *Der gefälschte Kalif* 274.
32 *Dhāt al-Himma* i, *juzʾ* 3:55–71.
33 Long, *Futūḥ Ifrīqiya* 91.

bihi wa-tawārīkhihi;[34] and a similar case: a monk who had read all kinds of books, had discovered the hidden secrets and the real truth of religions and had professed the unity of the Retributive (*dayyān*) King, converted to Islam after seeing the prophet Muḥammad in a dream, announcing to him that he would soon die.[35]

An example from *Sīrat Sayf b. Dhī Yazan*: the sage Yathrib tells King Dhū Yazan that a town has to be built at the place where they stand, because he has read in "the old books and histories (*al-kutub al-qadīma wa-l-tawārīkh*) and the great *malāḥim* (*al-malāḥim al-ʿaẓīma*)" that God will send a Hāshimite, Qurayshite prophet named Muḥammad, "the first of the prophets and the seal of the *mursalīn* who will want to move from Mecca to this excellent place and will be buried there."[36]

Not only the appearance of the main hero, but also other events in the epics are said to be predicted in ancient books of various nature. Some examples from *Sīrat Dhāt al-Himma*: The monk Bagh tells the caliph al-Manṣūr that he has read in the books of the wise men (*kutub al-ḥukamāʾ*) and gathered from the *malāḥim* that here, on the location called Dād, a city will be built that will be remembered until the end of times.[37] A monk tells about a prophecy in *Kitāb al-Malāḥim* that ʿAbd al-Wahhāb would take "all these (Byzantine) fortresses."[38] A king's three sons "mixed with monks, read the books of scholars and wise men, learned about all religions," and were eventually moved to convert to Islam.[39]

In *Sīrat Sayf*, in the story leading up to Sayf b. Dhī Yazan's appearance, the sorcerer Saqardīs had read in "the great books (*al-kutub al-ʿaẓīma*) and the old *malāḥim*" that a prince descended from Sem, born from the line of the Tubbaʿ, would appear to fulfil the curse put by Noah on his son Ham, a curse entailing that Ham's black progeny would be servants to the descendants of his brother Sem.[40]

Books Playing a Major Part

In addition, however, there are books that not only receive generic mention, but also play a major part in the narrative. They become, in a way, a narrative agent.

34 *Dhāt al-Himma* ii, *juzʾ* 15:12.
35 *Dhāt al-Himma* vi, *juzʾ* 57:54.
36 *Sīrat Sayf* i, 9.
37 *Dhāt al-Himma*, i, *juzʾ* 6:47.
38 *Dhāt al-Himma* ii, *juzʾ* 12:58.
39 *Dhāt al-Himma* vi, *juzʾ* 58:59.
40 *Sīrat Sayf* i, 32.

Such a case is *Yanbūʿ al-ḥikma*, a book that makes its appearance in *Sīrat Dhāt al-Himma* simultaneously with the trickster-hero Abū Muḥammad al-Baṭṭāl. It is in certain respects symbiotic with the trickster, or Man of Wiles, as he figures in the Arabic epic: an inexhaustible source of solutions for all kinds of problems, for magical tricks, and for profuse knowledge of a variety of languages.

The book is introduced in the episode in which al-Baṭṭāl, a lazy good-for-nothing (but with an excellent memory) of whom his father despairs, is put under the tutorship of qāḍī ʿUqba, a crypto-Christian who is the villain of the *sīra*. Among ʿUqba's students is a Yemeni by the name of Qulayḥ b. Qābūs, who owns a book that is "only found in the treasure stores of kings, containing chapters on difficult judgments and legal questions (*ḥikam mushkilāt wa-masāʾil sharʿiyya*), magical tricks (*nāranjiyyāt*), and various languages." From this book he provides ʿUqba with the answers to many things that he does not know. ʿUqba tells his sister how much he covets this book. Al-Baṭṭāl, having overheard this, disguises himself as ʿUqba's sister and goes to Qulayḥ, asking him for a medicament on ʿUqba's behalf. Qulayḥ, who just happens to be reading in *Yanbūʿ al-ḥikma*, "puts the book down on its cushion" (a valuable reference to actual reading practices) and goes to fetch the medicine. Quick as lightning, al-Baṭṭāl replaces it with a pre-prepared bunch of papers, consisting of rough notes, stories, poetry and suchlike things,[41] papers that contain the very opposite of the intricate type of knowledge that is in the *Yanbūʿ*. When Qulayḥ discovers the theft the following morning, all his anger is directed at ʿUqba and his sister. Nobody suspects al-Baṭṭāl, who after having studied the book for a couple of days knows all the answers to the questions asked in ʿUqba's class and becomes his favourite pupil.[42]

Al-Baṭṭāl keeps the book with him for consultation in difficult situations, such as when he wants to go and steal a lamp from a church in Constantinople.[43] After having studied the book for three days, he knows how to go about it, and having disguised himself as a priest by donning a black robe, a long white beard and a silver cross, he goes on his way. Note how the book again acts as a double of the Man of Wiles, who among other things is also a master of disguise. A monk named Bāḥa possesses a scroll with 500 pictures of al-Baṭṭāl and his *ghilmān* in various disguises, and so manages to unmask the venerable priest who visits his monastery as Abū Muḥammad al-Baṭṭāl.[44]

41 Arabic: *awrāq wa-musawwadāt wa-ḥikāyāt wa-ashʿār wa-ghayr dhālik*.

42 *Dhāt al-Himma* i, *juzʾ* 7:72–4.

43 *Dhāt al-Himma* i, *juzʾ* 8:27.

44 *Dhāt al-Himma* v, *juzʾ* 57:58.

Nothing is said about the authorship of *Yanbūʿ al-ḥikma*, and no emphasis is put on its occult aspects. It just functions as an inexhaustible source of knowledge. In a sense it fulfills the role of the miraculous book probably most widely known in current-day popular literature: the *Junior Woodchucks' Guidebook and Reservoir of Inexhaustible Knowledge* (the *Junior Woodchucks Guidebook* for short) that is consulted all the time by Donald Duck's young nephews Huey, Dewey, and Louie.[45] One might also compare the *Yanbūʿ al-ḥikma* to the Internet, held by many as a miraculous source of by definition trustworthy knowledge.

Yanbūʿ al-ḥikma does not play a pivotal role in the further events of *Sīrat Dhāt al-Himma*. The situation is quite different with the books that figure in the three Mamluk *sīra*s to be discussed next, namely *Sīrat Baybars*, *Sīrat Sayf b. Dhī Yazan* and *Sīrat al-Ḥākim bi-amrillah*. These *sīra*s abound in elements that play only a minor part in the 'Bedouin' *sīra*s such as *Sīrat ʿAntar* and *Sīrat Dhāt al-Himma*: they are full of magic, sorcery and in general the occult. Mythical elements are a prominent feature. Hidden treasures are also a major theme. As such, these *sīras* are representative of the culture of Mamluk Egypt in which they were composed, a culture in which magic and the occult were dominant elements. Two of these *sīra*s have appeared in print, in various editions; monographs have been devoted to all three of them.

Sīrat Baybars

The *Yanbūʿ al-ḥikma*, as a book, plays a significant but minor role in *Sīrat Dhāt al-Himma*. It figures as an object shifting power from the crypto-Christian villain ʿUqba to the Muslim trickster hero al-Baṭṭāl, who makes excellent use of it for practical matters. We encounter these elements on a much wider scale in one of the central Mamluk *sīra*s, namely *Sīrat Baybars*. There, a book of a much more complicated nature, the *Kitāb al-Yūnān*, forms a central element in the *sīra*. 'Yūnān' in this case does not refer to Greece, but to a sage of that name, whose prophesies are laid down in a book that is kept in a monastery, the Monastery of the Pillars. A brief summary of the history and contents of the *K. al-Yūnān* is given by Herzog in his exhaustive study of *Sīrat Baybars*.[46]

In the Arabic text itself, the history of the *K. al-Yūnān* is extensively explained in the episode where Baybars is kidnapped and brought to Genoa. Herzog has

45 Wikipedia, https://en.wikipedia.org/wiki/Junior_Woodchucks, last accessed 2-2-21.

46 Herzog, *Baibars* 873–4, episodes 59–60; Lyons, *Arabian Epic* ii, *Baybars* episode 41.

translated the episode, which he considers as crucial for the narrative.[47] The origin of the *K. al-Yūnān* is very complicated and centres around the struggle (then still in the future) between Christianity and Islam, embodied in the treacherous Christian priest Jawān on the one side and Baybars and his trickster companion Shīḥa on the other. The book was begun by the sage Yūnān and his helpers as a blueprint for the success of the Christian priest Jawān, providing a series of events disastrous for Islam. Yūnān's son 'Inān, however, becomes a Muslim and with his helpers manages to undo these evils by inserting silver pages between the gold ones of the original book, providing support for Shīḥa. All this is embedded in a plethora of *ex eventu* prophesies, apocalyptic texts, secret caves, hidden places, and miraculous pictures of future rulers such as Baybars. Among the events that are predicted is, for instance, Jawān's execution, which is described in detail. At some point in the story, Jawān complains that he has read that he will be crucified, referring not to the *K. al-Yūnān* but to a variety of books: books about spiritual sciences, astrology, philosophy, and geomancy, and also 'Greek books' in general—in short, to the type of books usually cited in *sīra* literature as a source of ancient and powerful knowledge.

This fits in with Herzog's observations: older versions of the *sīra* show that there was an older layer of the story in which the *K. al-Yūnān* did not yet figure as a book. At that stage, various prophetic and apocalyptic texts, consisting of books as well as magical tablets, provided the framework of the story. These were later condensed into the *K. al-Yūnān*. The prophesies of the book would stage by stage be fulfilled by Baybars, whose rulership is thus presented as preordained.[48]

We may note here that this aspect of the *sīra* provides another example of the way in which *sīra* literature and elite literature intertwine: an apocalyptic context is also provided in one of the versions of Ibn an-Nafīs' *Risāla Kāmiliyya* as legitimation of Baybars' rule.[49] It also fits in with Ibn Khaldūn's observations cited earlier.

Herzog has made a thorough analysis of the role which the *K. al-Yūnān* plays in the *sīra*, including what he sees as its function to lift the story from a mere adventure novel to an epic level by adding a mythical and metaphysical layer. While his arguments are quite plausible and well-founded, we should note that

47 Herzog, *Baibars* 68–122.

48 Herzog has also analysed this aspect of the *sīra* in a separate article: see Herzog, Legitimität.

49 Kruk, *History*. Not all MSS of Ibn an-Nafīs' text contain this part, but that is irrelevant for the argument based on this particular version.

they are also part of a wider discussion regarding the popular epic and the question where to place it as a genre. This started already in the 18th century: Caussin de Perceval remarked that *Sīrat ʿAntar* might be seen as the Iliad of the Arabs.[50] There is clearly an urge among Western scholars to fill in what is felt as an unacceptable gap in Arabic literature, namely the absence of epic literature, notably of a great epic. The issue comes up again and again in *sīra* research—the title of Malcolm Lyons' three-volume fundamental work on *sīra* literature, *The Arabian Epic*, sounds like a very definite choice.

The *K. al-Yūnān* certainly has all these metaphysical and mythical connections, but it also plays an important role in *Sīrat Baybars* as in a simple adventure novel. Shīḥa, who knows the *K. al-Yūnān* by heart, often uses it to solve practical problems, such as how to recover the ring stone of the black Ḥākim of the seven islands of al-Thaqaf.[51] This shows that the book also has its *Woodchuck Handbook* aspects.

To summarize: it is noteworthy that the *K. al-Yūnān* as a book has an author; that due to the interference of this fictional author's son it contains conflicting information, making it an exemplar for the strife that is the motor of the story; that next to this mythical level, the book also serves as an inexhaustible source of practical information on the level of the adventure story.

Sīrat al-malik Sayf b. Dhī Yazan

Sīrat al-malik Sayf b. Dhī Yazan is another *sīra* in which a book is a pivotal element. *Sīrat Sayf*, in its currently known form, was composed in Mamluk Cairo, probably around the turn from the 9th/15th to the 10th/16th century.[52] For an up-to-date overview of modern studies on *Sīrat Sayf*, see Blatherwick, notes on pp. 4–6. Several printed versions of the *sīra* exist. In this article I cite the undated Cairo edition of Maktabat al-mashhad al-Ḥusaynī.[53]

Although it contains many elements that connect it to older cultures, among them the South Arabian tradition,[54] the *sīra* in its current form cannot be older than the reign of one of its main protagonists, the Ethiopian king Sayfa Arʿad, who ruled between 1344–72 CE. Norris also points out that the name of al-Qaṣr

50 Heath, Scholarship 25.

51 Lyons, *Arabian Epic* iii, *Baybars* episodes 100–1; Herzog, *Baibars* 887, episode 139; *Sīrat Baybars*, iii 1856–7.

52 Paret, *Saif* 85–9.

53 For details see the bibliography.

54 Norris, Sayf 128; Blatherwick, *Prophets* 6, n. 20.

al-Ablaq in Damascus, which is mentioned in the *sīra*, provides evidence for dating the *sīra*'s core part. Baybars built this castle between 1313–14.[55]

Sīrat Sayf is replete with magic and miraculous events. In fact, it was exactly for that reason that it was disliked by a modern Moroccan audience.[56] Magic and the occult, however, flourished in Mamluk Egypt, and as such the *sīra* gives a good idea of popular Muslim beliefs in Egypt at the time. Chelhod also emphasizes this aspect in his article about *Sīrat Sayf*, adding that the many connections to ancient Egyptian magical lore should not be overlooked.[57] In her monograph on *Sīrat Sayf*, Helen Blatherwick has further explored the connections between ancient Egyptian narrative and *Sīrat Sayf*.[58] She points out that although the *Book of the Nile* is one of many mysterious, magical books in Muslim folklore, it has specific reverberations in pharaonic legend, particularly the ancient Egyptian *Book of Thoth*.[59] This raises the question whether similar connections can fruitfully be explored for major magical books in other Mamluk *sīras*, but this matter falls beyond the scope of this article.

As to the story:[60] Sayf, the son of the Yemenite king Dhū Yazan, is destined to free Yemen from Ethiopian rule. Thus, he would fulfil the curse put by Noah on his son Ham that he and his black progeny would be servants to the descendants of his brother Sem. Sayf's other task was to bring prosperity to the land of Egypt, which until then was a barren waste, because the life-bringing waters of the Nile could no longer reach it, having been blocked in the south by two sorcerers, Jābarṣā and Jābalqā. These sorcerers constantly tried to trick each other about the use of the Nile water, each finding means to divert the river to his own city. Eventually Jābalqā wrote the *Book of the history of the Nile*,[61] or *Book of the Nile*, for short, (like the *K. al-Yūnān* in *Baybars*, this book also has an author) and subsequently hid it, thus gaining power over the river. Jābarṣā, unable to find it, took his revenge by obstructing the course of the river by rocks and cataracts.

Sayf sets out to obtain the book as a wedding gift for his prospective bride.[62] He manages to obtain it after a series of complicated adventures involving

55 Norris, Sayf 129.
56 Kruk and Ott, Popular Manner 189.
57 Chelhod, Geste 181 n. 2; 183–4.
58 Blatherwick, *Prophets* 144–200; 144–8 specifically about the *Book of the Nile*.
59 Blatherwick, *Prophets* 144–8, also 262–3.
60 Extensive summaries of the *sīra* have been given by Paret, *Saif*, and Lyons, *Arabian Epic* ii and iii. Norris, Sayf 144–5, gives a good overview of the origin and role of the *Book of the Nile*. Also useful is Jayyusi, *Adventures* 33–9.
61 *Sīrat Sayf* iii, 162.
62 *Sīrat Sayf* i, 67.

a number of magical beings and supernatural powers.[63] The sorceress ʿĀqila, mother of Sayf's bride Ṭāma, tells him that in addition to the book, which she has kept with her and now brings to him, he needs seven objects and creatures with magical powers, the last of which is Rahq, a powerful black *jinn* who has been enclosed in a pillar.[64] He is freed[65] and with his help the barriers blocking the water are shattered. Then Sayf, carrying the magical book as a breastplate,[66] leads the water to Cairo ("the city of his son Miṣr"), where it forks, bringing the land of the Delta to life. With the water, however, huge crocodiles have also appeared, and Sayf is told that the only way to ward them off is to place the *Book of the Nile* in a pillar from the days of Solomon. Rahq is persuaded to bring over this magical pillar from Ḥawrān in Syria, and a magically created crocodile which has been tricked to swallow the *Book of the history of the Nile* is ordered to enter into it and is sealed in. Subsequently, marks are engraved on the outside of the pillar to indicate the rise of the Nile water, enabling it to serve as a Nilometer.[67]

As we see, the *Book of the Nile* plays a prominent part in the narrative, and as a book it is an actual object, not a vague reference. Its author is mentioned by name, the book is handled, carefully hidden, coveted and carried around. But is it ever read and consulted, like *Yanbūʿ al-ḥikma* in *Sīrat Dhāt al-Himma*? There is no indication of that. After Sayf has managed to get hold of it, it is safely kept by his future mother-in-law for later use, while Sayf engages in a long series of adventures. It is a magical object, serving as a powerful talisman for a very specific use: guiding the water of the Nile back to Egypt and bringing the country to life again. When this is done, it is sealed in to continue its magical guarding of the flow of the Nile.

The situation is different with another magical book in *Sayf*. In this case, it is a book that is carried around and regularly consulted. This book is discovered by Sayf's grandson Damariyāṭ in the magical bag (*jarbandiyya*) of the murdered sorcerer King Hadhād.[68] Hadhād used this bag, for instance, to feed his guests, taking all kinds of utensils, food and drink out of it and later putting everything back again.[69] Damariyāṭ is disappointed when the only thing he finds in it are the substances used for magic and divination, such as date

63 *Sīrat Sayf* i, 67–113; Lyons, *Arabian Epic* ii, *Sayf*, episodes 11–5.
64 *Sīrat Sayf* iii, 163.
65 *Sīrat Sayf* iii, 170.
66 *Sīrat Sayf* iii, 175–9.
67 *Sīrat Sayf* iii, 185–8.
68 *Sīrat Sayf* iv, 100–1.
69 *Sīrat Sayf* iii, 265–6.

kernels, "white peel" (*qishr abyaḍ*), water melon seeds, seeds of green pumpkin (*ʿajjūr*), coarse sand, fine sand, and threads of cotton and flax. He laughs at all this, finding it useless, but then reads "the book," which is apparently also in the bag, and finds it full of magical spells and formulas that can be used for sorcery and divination in combination with the things in the knapsack. Damariyāṭ does not rest before he has read it all and knows everything in it. So here we have a magical book that is actually used for the information which it contains, being carefully studied and kept at hand.

As it turns out later, Hadhād had stolen the book from his master, the sorcerer Yūnān (note the reminiscence of the author of the *K. al-Yūnān* in *Baybars*).[70] The sorceress Rakhma, who had stolen it from the Muslims together with other treasures, brings it to Yūnān. When he sees the book "with its strap"[71] he hems and haws and shakes his head, saying that this book contains powerful secrets and charms. Pointing at it, he makes it fall down like running water.[72]

As was said earlier, references to books of the unspecified type also regularly occur in *Sīrat Sayf*. In the sequel of the episode above, there is frequent mention of such books, among them books connected to the Islamic religion. Rakhma has read in "a book" that her husband is actually her brother and subsequently Sayf and his companions read "books and pages" (*kutub wa-ṣuḥuf*, also *al-ṣuḥuf al-ʿiẓām*) of God's friend Ibrāhīm as part of their appeal to the One God to protect them against magic fires.[73]

Yūnān is not the only element in *Sīrat Sayf* known from other Mamluk *sīras*: A reference is also made to an event involving Baybars' companion Ibrāhīm al-Ḥawrānī.[74] Moreover, the name of Qaṣr al-Halīlaja (Myrobalan Castle), a castle built by the sorcerer al-Hadhād and named after his beloved,[75] as well as the "treasure of Halīlaja," to which Hadhād takes Sayf and his companions,[76] recall the Myrobalan treasure that figures so prominently in *Sīrat al-Ḥākim*, to be dealt with next.

70 *Sīrat Sayf* iv, 238.
71 Text: *bi-niṭāqa*, possibly *bi-niṭāqihi*.
72 *Sīrat Sayf* iv, 236.
73 *Sīrat Sayf* iv, 236–7.
74 Lyons, *Arabian Epic* iii, *Sayf* episode 95; *Sīrat Sayf* iv, 239. The Arabic text says al-Khawrānī.
75 *Sīrat Sayf*, iii, 264–5.
76 *Sīrat Sayf*, iii, 289–90.

Sīrat al-Ḥākim bi-amrillāh

Of the three Mamluk *sīras* discussed here, *Sīrat al-Ḥākim bi-amrillāh* is the one in which books figure most prominently. This *sīra* is not as well-known as the others, because no printed edition of it exists. Claudia Ott has written about it,[77] and Antje Lenora devoted to it her Ph.D. thesis, which resulted in a thorough and valuable monograph.[78] Her research was based on the extant MSS and is provided by a brief plot summary by chapter as well as an extensive summary of the text. Both are based on the Berlin MS of the text. Since I did not have access to any of the MSS when I wrote this article, Lenora's dissertation formed my main source for this *sīra*.

Just as several other *sīras*, the *Sīrat al-Ḥākim* is fictitiously ascribed to a well-known scholar. In the case of *Sīrat al-Ḥākim*, Ibn Khallikān (608–81/1211–82) is presented as the author, and Lenora's opinion on the date of composition of *Sīrat al-Ḥākim*, which she puts between 648/1250 and 736/1335, is partly based on this fictitious authorship.[79]

The story of al-Ḥākim, his coming to power and the end of his reign takes up the first part of the *sīra*. The remaining part deals with his successors, ending with the death of his great-grandson al-Ḥākim al-Manṣūr. Al-Ḥākim is presented as a noble character and an excellent ruler. For a while he is replaced, without people knowing, by a double who takes a number of offensive measures of the kind history ascribes to the real al-Ḥākim.[80] This fits in with Lenora's characterization of the *sīra*: a success story of the expansion of Islamic, more precisely Sunnite, religion.[81] In the *sīra*, al-Ḥākim and his successors have no connection to Shiʿism, and negative aspects historically connected with them are given a positive turn. In this context, it is relevant that the *sīra* regularly pays attention to the extant scholarly tradition, including occasional references to authors and titles, as was mentioned earlier in this article. The books as actual objects, however, were not a crucial element in these cases. In *Sīrat al-Ḥākim*, as in other cases, this latter function is reserved for fictional books. Sometimes such fictional books are mentioned incidentally, such as when a woman is asked how she came to know all these things, to which she answers that her father possessed a book on history which also stated where treasures were hid-

77 Ott, Finally we know; Ott, Wo versteckt.

78 Lenora, *Der gefälschte Kalif*.

79 Lenora, *Der gefälschte Kalif* 140.

80 Lenora, *Der gefälschte Kalif* 38, 159–60.

81 Lenora, *Der gefälschte Kalif* 197.

den.[82] Another case is a book with golden letters, written in Syriac, that was found when a city was looted and contained a description of a wonderful treasure hidden in Constantinople.[83] Occasionally, knowledge from occult books is also used to manipulate people's behaviour, for instance by inciting exclusive love. Such books may also explain how to put magical objects (in this case a magical pearl) to use.[84]

Three books play a major role. Unlike the books in *Sīrat Baybars* and *Sīrat Sayf*, they do not contain messages about pre-ordained events, but overwhelmingly serve to provide access to hidden treasures, frequently sealed by magical means. According to these books, many such treasures were hidden in ancient times in caves under the Muqattam mountains, and sometimes also in the great pyramid. Constantinople, too, is said to contain hidden treasure caves, and one of them actually is the place from which the major books in the *sīra* originate. All this shows the preoccupation with hidden treasures that takes such an important place in Egyptian popular imagination and also manifests itself in books that were written on the subject.[85]

The *sīra* starts with the appearance of al-Abṭan, son of the Fātimid ruler of Qayrawān. He falls into Byzantine captivity and through the favour of the emperor gets access to a treasure cave in Constantinople, from which he obtains three books with occult knowledge.[86] He only opens them later, when he has arrived in Alexandria. The first book describes how to get access to the treasures of Egypt, Syria and Iraq, the second is about alchemy, and the third about magic and other occult sciences. With the help of the first book, al-Abṭan accesses some treasures and uses them to go on pilgrimage to Mecca. Back in Qayrawān, his wisdom and noble personality gain him the respect of the ruler. He acquires a following of adepts and students. Twin sons, ʿAbd al-ʿAzīz and ʿAbd al-Raḥmān, are born to him, to whom he will leave his books. He becomes the mentor of the ruler's nephew Muḥammad,[87] who later travels to Cairo and becomes the successor of the caliph Ismāʿīl b. Muḥammad under the name al-Ḥākim bi-amrillāh. While starting out as a noble and just ruler, Muḥammad increasingly comes under the spell of the limitless possibilities to obtain riches offered by the occult knowledge contained in the books that al-Abṭan and his sons possess. Greed, instigated by his connection with a spirit who serves Sat-

82 Lenora, *Der gefälschte Kalif* 103.
83 Lenora, *Der gefälschte Kalif* 132–3.
84 Lenora, *Der gefälschte Kalif* 113.
85 Lenora, 185; also Braun, *Treasure*.
86 Lenora, *Der gefälschte Kalif* 31–2.
87 Lenora, *Der gefälschte Kalif* 35.

urn, makes him more and more unscrupulous in obtaining riches. This leads to the death of al-Abṭan's son ʿAbd al-Raḥmān.[88] Again and again al-Ḥākim is driven to the treasure caves under the Muqattam mountain, with the ultimate goal of getting access to the Myrobalan treasure, *al-Halīlaja*,[89] one of the two treasures that is forbidden to him (the other is the Treasure of the Bat). ʿAbd al-ʿAzīz b. al-Abṭan finally guides him there with the help of his father's book, urging al-Ḥākim to cross a lake without a way to return. He leaves him there to die, thus avenging his brother, and returning to the city he assumes power over Egypt.

Previously, al-Ḥākim had got hold of another of al-Abṭan's books, inherited by ʿAbd al-Raḥmān. He was, however, unable to read it, and following the advice given in a dream he put it in a safe place so that his as yet unborn son would be able to read it later and use it as a means to avenge his father and to take back his father's lands and riches from ʿAbd al-ʿAzīz.

As we see, these books, two of them in particular, play a dominant part in *Sīrat al-Ḥākim*. One should note that no author of these books is given; that they are of ancient and occult origin; and that they figure in the story as actual books, objects that are handled and consulted all the time. They are not just an inexhaustible source of information, like *Yanbūʿ al-ḥikma* in *Sīrat Dhāt al-Himma;* they do not function as a blueprint for future events, like the *K. al-Yūnān* in *Sīrat Baybars;* and they are not simply used as a magical object, a powerful talisman, like the *K. an-Nīl* in *Sīrat Sayf b. Dhī Yazan.*

Sīrat al-Ḥākim shows obvious links to other Mamluk *sīra*s. A number of its protagonists bear the names of prominent Egyptian locations, sometimes named after them: Miṣr, al-Qāhira, Zuwayla; just as in *Sīrat Sayf b. Dhī Yazan* and in *Sayf*, they are occasionally connected to a founding myth (*al-Qāhira*). The name of ʿArnūs, a Christian ruler threatening the Muslims, connects *Sīrat al-Ḥākim* to *Sīrat Baybars*, where a ruler called ʿArnūs features prominently. The treacherous priest Jawān, one of the main protagonists in *Sīrat Baybars*, also makes his appearance in *Sīrat al-Ḥākim*.[90] And, like in *Sīrat Baybars*, a princess (here named al-Qāhira) is abducted to Genoa.[91]

---

88 Lenora, *Der gefälschte Kalif* 53.
89 For extensive references about this word, see Lenora 160 n. 299.
90 Lenora, *Der gefälschte Kalif* 70.
91 For Lenora's more extensive remarks on this issue, see *Der gefälschte Kalif* 159 and 263.

Concluding

As we see, there is a distinct shift in the role of books in the *sīra*s that are of obvious Mamluk provenance. It starts with the condensation of older prophetic and apocalyptic texts into a prominent leading book, the *K. al-Yūnān*, in *Sīrat Baybars*, as described by Herzog. Subsequent *sīra*s, namely *Sīrat Sayf* and *Sīrat al-Ḥakīm*, also feature books with a major function in the narrative. The question may be asked: why do these substantial books appear in popular literature at this particular time and in this particular context? Are they a sign of a wider interest in books and literature in general among the people, in line with what Thomas Bauer has said about "the blurring of the boundaries between popular and educated literature?"[92] *Sīra* literature regularly shows evidence of such blurring, as was pointed out at the beginning of this article.

A further consideration: the nature of the books differs from *sīra* to *sīra*, but they are all of an occult nature. Did the Mamluk cultural and intellectual climate, in which magical and occult books played such a predominant role, stimulate the introduction of occult books as major agents in popular narrative? We cannot fail to notice that *Yanbūʿ al-ḥikma*, the title of the book featuring in *Sīrat Dhāt al-Himma* (in its present form consolidated in Mamluk times), recalls *Manbaʿ uṣūl al-ḥikma*, a text from the al-Būnī corpus.[93]

And besides all this, what about the Quran? It occurs all over the place in these popular narratives: it is recited, cited, listened to, read, taught in schools, and its message frequently leads to someone's conversion, but does it ever appear as an actual book volume? In the sole case that I have come across, in *Sīrat al-amīra Dhāt al-Himma*, it is very special, namely a Quran in the handwriting of ʿAlī b. Abī Ṭālib. Its function is that of an amulet to protect the party who carries it with them[94]—no better illustration of the fact that books, in the epics, overwhelmingly figure as a manifestation of the mysterious and the occult.

---

92 Bauer, Misunderstandings, 110–1. I owe the reference to Maaike van Berkel (Nijmegen), who discussed the increasing interest in books of "the non-scholarly literati" in Van Berkel, A world of knowledge 374.

93 On this book, see Pielow, *Quellen*; of the many recent publications on the Būnī corpus, I may just refer here to those of Jan Just Witkam (for instance, Witkam, Gazing at the sun), Noah Gardiner (in the context of the present discussion, Gardiner, Forbidden knowledge, is particularly relevant), and especially the ongoing Būnī project of Jean-Charles Coulon.

94 *Dhāt al-Himma* i, *juzʾ* 3:67.

Bibliography

Aristotle, *Parts of animals*, with an English translation by A.L. Peck, London 1968.

Bauer, T., Mamluk literature: Misunderstandings and new approaches, in *MSR* 9, 2 (2005), 105–32.

Bauer, T., In search of "post-classical literature": A review article, in *MSR* 11, 2 (2007), 137–67.

Blatherwick, H., *Prophets, gods and kings in Sīrat Sayf ibn Dhī Yazan: An intertextual reading of an Egyptian popular epic*, Leiden 2016.

Bohas, G. and J.-P. Guillaume, *Le Roman de Baibars traduit de l'arabe et annoté par Georges Bohas et Jean-Patrick Guillaume*, 2nd edition, 10 vols., Paris 1998.

Braun, C., *Treasure hunting and grave robbery in Islamic Egypt*, Ph.D. Thesis, University of London, 2017.

Chelhod, J., La geste du roi Sayf, in *RHR* 161 (1967), 181–205.

Conermann, S. and A. Pistor-Hatam, *Die Mamlūken: Studien zu ihrer Geschichte und Kultur. Zum Gedenken an Ulrich Haarmann (1942–1999)*, Schenefeld 2003.

Dorpmueller, S. (ed.), *Fictionalizing the past: Historical characters in Arabic popular epic, Proceedings of the workshop at the Netherlands-Flemish Institute in Cairo 28th/29th of November 2007 in honor of Remke Kruk*, Leuven 2012.

Doufikar-Aerts, F., *Alexander Magnus Arabicus: A survey of the Alexander tradition through seven centuries: from Pseudo-Callisthenes to Ṣūrī*, Leuven 2010.

EI^2 Ed., Malāḥim, in EI^2, vi, 216–7.

Fahd, T., Malḥama, in EI^2, vi, 247.

Gardiner, N., Forbidden knowledge? Notes on the production, transmission, and reception of the major works of Ahmad al-Būnī, in Ghersetti and Metcalfe (eds.), *The book in fact and fiction*, 81–143.

Ghersetti, A. and A. Metcalfe (eds.), *The book in fact and fiction in pre-modern Arabic literature*, in *JAIS* 12 (2012).

Halm, H., *Die Kalifen von Kairo: Die Fatimiden in Ägypten 973–1074*, Munich 2003.

Heath, P., A critical review of modern scholarship on *Sīrat ʿAntar ibn Shaddād* and the popular *sīra*, in *JAL* 15 (1984), 19–44.

Heath, P., *The thirsty sword. Sīrat ʿAntar and the Arabic popular epic*, Salt Lake City 1996.

Heath, P., ʿAntar hangs his *Muʿallaqa:* History, fiction, and textual conservatism in *Sīrat ʿAntar ibn Shaddād*, in S. Dorpmueller (ed.), *Fictionalizing the past*, 9–24.

Herzog, Th., *Geschichte und Imaginaire: Entstehung, Überlieferung und Bedeutung der Sīrat Baibars in ihrem sozio-politischen Kontext*, Wiesbaden 2006.

Herzog, Th., Legitimität durch Erzählung: Ayyubidische and kalifale Legitimation mamlūkischer Herrschaft in der populären *Sīrat Baybars*, in S. Conermann and A. Pistor-Hatam (eds.), *Die Mamlūken*, 251–68.

Ibn Khaldūn, *The Muqaddimah: An Introduction to History*, translated from the Arabic by F. Rosenthal, 3 vols., London 1967.

Jayyusi, L., *The adventures of Sayf ben Dhi Yazan: An Arab folk epic*, translation & narration by L. Jayyusi, introduction by H. Norris, Bloomington 1996.

Kruk, R., History and apocalypse: Ibn an-Nafīs' justification of Mamlūk rule, in *Der Islam* 72, 2 (1995), 324–37.

Kruk, R. and C. Ott, 'In the Popular Manner': *Sīra*-recitation in Marrakesh anno 1997, in *Edebiyat* 10 (1999), 183–98.

Lenora, A., *Der gefälschte Kalif: Eine Einführung in die Sīrat al-Ḥākim bi-Amrillāh*, University of Halle, Philosophische Fakultät I, Dissertation, 2011 (Online resource) http://dx.doi.org/10.25673/873

Littmann, E., *Die Erzählungen aus den Tausendundein Nächten: Vollständige deutsche Ausgabe in zwölf Teilbänden. Zum ersten Mal nach dem arabischen Urtext der Calcuttaer Ausgabe aus dem Jahre 1839 übertragen von E. Littmann*, 12 vols., 2nd ed., Wiesbaden 1981.

Long, J.E., *Futūḥ Ifrīqiya: Analysis, Arabic text and translation*, Diss. Brandeis, 1978.

Norris, H.T., Sayf ibn Dhī Yazan and the Book of the history of the Nile, in QSA 7 (1989), 125–51.

Ott, C., Finally we know … why, how, and where caliph al-Ḥākim disappeared! Sīrat al-Ḥākim bi-amrillāh and its Berlin manuscript, in S. Dorpmüller (ed.), *Fictionalizing the past*, 63–72.

Ott, C., Wo versteckt sich al-Ḥākim? Eine Spurensuche in der Sīrat al-Ḥākim bi-Amrillāh und ihrer Berliner Handschrift, in H. Biesterfeldt and V. Klemm (eds.), *Differenz und Dynamik im Islam: Festschrift für Heinz Halm zum 70. Geburtstag*, Würzburg 2012, 399–410.

Paret, R., *Sīrat Saif ibn Dhī Jazan: Ein arabischer Volksroman*, Hannover 1924.

Paret, R., *Der Ritter-Roman von ʿUmar an-Nuʿmān und seine Stellung zur Sammlung von tausendundeiner Nacht: Ein Beitrag zur arabischen Literaturgeschichte*, Tübingen 1927.

Paret, R., Sayf b. Dhī Yazan, in EI^1, iv, 74ff.

Pielow, D.A.M., *Die Quellen der Weisheit: Die arabische Magie im Spiegel des Uṣūl al-Ḥikma von Aḥmad Ibn ʿAli* (sic) *al-Būnī*, Hildesheim 1995.

Pseudo-Apollonios, Sirr al-khalīqa wa-ṣanʿat aṭ-ṭabīʿa: Kitāb al-ʿilal li-Balīnūs al-ḥakīm / Buch über das Geheimnis der Schöpfung und die Darstellung der Natur (*Buch der Ursachen*) *von Pseudo-Apollonios von Tyana*, ed. U. Weisser, Aleppo 1979.

Rosenthal, F., *A history of Muslim historiography*, Leiden ^{2}1968.

Sīrat al-amīra Dhāt al-Himma wa-waladihā ʿAbd al-Wahhāb wa-l-amīr Abū Muḥammad al-Baṭṭāl wa-ʿUqba shaykh al-ḍallāl wa-Shūmadris al-muḥtāl: Akbar taʾrīkh li-l-ʿarab wa-khulafaʾ banī Umayya wa-l-khulafāʾ al-ʿabbāsiyya. Jamaʿat hādhihi l-sīra akhbār al-ʿarab wa-ḥurūbihim wa-akhbār mulk Miṣr wa-l-Shām wa-Baghdād wa-ghayrihā min bilād al-Islām wa-bilād al-Ifranj wa-fīhā min al-futūḥāt ma yabharu al-ʿuqūl, 7 vols., Cairo: Maktabat ʿAbd al-Ḥamīd Aḥmad al-Ḥanafī, n.d. (reprint of the edition of 1327/1909, with slight differences in paging).

Sīrat fāris al-Yaman al-malik Sayf b. Dhī Yazan al-baṭal al-karrār wa-l-fāris al-mighwār ṣāḥib al-baṭsh wa-l-iqtidār al-maʿrūf bi-l-ghazawāt al-mashhūra (this is the title as given in vol. i; vols. ii, iii and iv have the following title: *Sīrat fāris al-Yaman al-malik Sayf b. Dhī Yazan ibn Tubbaʿ b. Asad al-Baydāʾ b. fāris al-Natīja b. Waḥsh al-Barr al-fāris al-karrār wa-l-baṭal al-mighwār ṣāḥib al-baṭsh wa-l-iqtidār wa-huwa min sulālat al-tubbaʿ Ḥassān wa-fātiḥ kunūz sayyidinā Sulaymān al-maʿrūf bi-l-ghazawāt al-mashhūra* …), 4 vols., Cairo: Maktabat wa-maṭbaʿat al-mashhad al-Ḥusaynī, n.d.

Sīrat al-Ẓāhir Baybars, Introduction by J. al-Ghiṭānī, 5 vols., Cairo 1996–7 (repr. of the 2nd edition, Cairo 1923–6).

van Berkel, M., Opening up a world of knowledge: Mamluk encyclopaedias and their readers, in J. König and G. Woolf (eds.), *Encyclopaedism from Antiquity to the Renaissance*, Cambridge 2013, 357–76.

[Pseudo-]al-Wāqidī, *Futūḥ Ifrīqiya*, 2 vols., Tunis 1966.

Weisser, U., *Das „Buch über das Geheimnis der Schöpfung" von Pseudo-Apollonius von Tyana*, Berlin 1980.

Witkam, J.J., Gazing at the sun: Remarks on the Egyptian magician al-Būnī and his work, in A. Vrolijk and J.P. Hogendijk (eds.), *O ye gentlemen: Arabic studies on science and literary culture in honour of Remke Kruk*, Leiden 2007, 183–99.

13

Kontrast und Entsprechung – Ibn Ḥiǧǧa al-Ḥamawīs Umgang mit der rhetorischen Standardtheorie aus dem 8./14. Jahrhundert in seinem Kommentar zu seinem Stilmittelgedicht aus dem 9./15. Jahrhundert

Syrinx von Hees

An der Universität Münster gibt es im Masterstudiengang Arabistik/Islamwissenschaft ein Modul mit dem Titel „Sprache und Islam." Dieses Modul ist für Studierende, die sich speziell mit der ‚islamischen Religion' beschäftigen wollen, verpflichtend und wird eigentlich von allen, die den Schwerpunkt ‚arabische Literatur' wählen, ebenfalls belegt, auf jeden Fall ist dies wärmstens empfohlen. Ausgedacht hat sich dieses Modul unser Jubilar Thomas Bauer mit dem Ziel, die außergewöhnlich starke Sprachzentriertheit der arabisch-islamischen Kultur – sowohl in ihren religiösen als auch in ihren profanen Bereichen – als wesentliches Merkmal dieser Kultur in unser aller Bewusstsein zu rücken. Im Mittelpunkt steht seine Vorlesung zur Entwicklung der arabischen Rhetoriktheorie, die für das Verständnis des Korans und der islamischen Koraninterpretation wie auch für die arabische Literaturtheorie grundlegend ist.[1] Möglichkeiten zur Vertiefung dieses Wissens bieten ein begleitendes Seminar verbunden mit einem Lektürekurs. In dieser Form ist dieses Modul einzigartig an einer deutschen Universität. Neben der Grundlagenforschung, die Thomas Bauer zur arabischen Rhetorik geleistet hat, zeugt dieses Unterrichtsangebot in besonderer Weise von seinen didaktischen Fähigkeiten und seinem dezidierten Willen, Wissen zu vermitteln.[2] Seinem Wunsch, dieses Forschungsgebiet zu animieren, versuche ich mit diesem Beitrag ein klein wenig entgegenzukommen.

Thomas Bauer zeichnet in seinem Enzyklopädie-Artikel wie in seiner Vorlesung in deutlichen Schritten die Entwicklung der arabischen Rhetorik hin zur Standardtheorie auf, wie sie sich im 8./14. Jahrhundert im Lehrwerk al-

1 Die Vorlesung basiert auf: Bauer, Rhetorik: Arabische Kultur (Enzyklopädie-Artikel).

2 Zum Beispiel: Bauer, Religion und Klassisch-Arabische Literatur; Bauer, Ambiguität in der klassischen arabischen Rhetoriktheorie.

 | DOI:10.1163/9789004521780_015

Qazwīnīs (666–739/1268–1338), dem Prediger von Damaskus, darstellt.[3] Darüber hinaus verweist er auf zwei Linien, die diese Standardtheorie „in den späteren Jahrhunderten" weiterführen. Wichtig sind hier einerseits die zahlreichen Kommentare und Suprakommentare, die sich auf den knappen Text von al-Qazwīnī beziehen und damit Zeugnis ablegen für dessen kanonische Bedeutung.[4] Ein wichtiger Gegenstand für die zukünftige Forschung ist die Untersuchung dieser Kommentarliteratur, um ihre Funktionen besser zu verstehen und mögliche Weiterentwicklungen bis ins 15./21. Jahrhundert im Nachdenken über die arabische Sprache, Trägerin religiöser wie säkularer Texte, aufzuzeigen.[5] Die andere Linie geht stärker von der literarischen Praxis aus und diskutiert einzelne Stilmittel, wobei eine neue Literaturgattung entstand, die Stilmittelgedichte (*badīʿiyyāt*), welche zum Teil kommentiert werden, so dass wieder ein starker Bezug zur rhetorischen Theorie hergestellt wird.[6] Thomas Bauer hat durch seine Auseinandersetzung mit einem solchen Gedicht aus dem 13./19. Jahrhundert zur Erforschung dieser Stilmittelgedichte einen wichtigen Beitrag geleistet.[7] Für diesen Beitrag habe ich mir vorgenommen, einen Blick auf diesen Entwicklungsstrang zu werfen und dabei der Frage nachzugehen, wie die Verfasser theoretischer Kommentare zu einem Stilmittelgedicht mit dem Text von al-Qazwīnī, dem Prediger von Damaskus, umgehen, der sich ganz schnell als kanonisch durchsetzt. Wird dessen Darstellung als Standard angenommen, auf den man sich bezieht und daran anknüpfend möglicherweise weiterdenkt, und wenn ja, wie? Was passiert im Einzelnen genau?

Als Beispiel habe ich die großartig angelegte *Badīʿiyya* mit Kommentar von Ibn Ḥiǧǧa al-Ḥamawī (767–837/1366–1434) aus dem frühen 9./15. Jahrhundert ausgewählt, um seinen Umgang mit der Standardtheorie zu untersuchen, und zwar anhand eines exemplarisch ausgewählten Stilmittels.[8] Dafür habe ich das erste Stilmittel gewählt, das al-Qazwīnī in seinem dritten Teil der Standardtheorie der arabischen Rhetorik präsentiert, also zu Beginn seiner Abhandlung zur Wissenschaft der Stilmittel (*ʿilm al-badīʿ*).[9] Es handelt sich um ein Stilmit-

3 Vgl. dazu auch Eksell, Figurative speech according to the *Talkhis al-Miftah* by al-Qazwini.

4 Bauer, Rhetorik: Arabische Kultur (2005) 298–9 = (2007) viii, 134–6; siehe auch van Gelder, Badīʿiyya.

5 Kommentarliteratur steht mittlerweile verstärkt im Fokus der Wissenschaft, wobei diese Fragen insbesondere anhand philosophischer und auch juristischer Texte erforscht werden. Für einen ersten Überblick siehe z. B. van Lit, Commentary and commentary tradition; aber auch die Kommentarliteratur zur arabischen Rhetorik ist schon angesprochen worden, z. B. Smyth, Controversy in a tradition of commentary.

6 Bauer, Rhetorik: Arabische Kultur (2005), 297–8 = (2007) viii, 133–4.

7 Bauer, Die *badīʿiyya* des Nāṣīf al-Yāziǧī.

8 Ibn Ḥiǧǧa, *Ḫizānat al-adab*; zu seiner Person siehe: Stewart, Ibn Hijjah al-Hamawī.

9 Al-Qazwīnī, *Matn at-Talḫīṣ* 105–7 = *at-Talḫīṣ* 347–54.

tel mit dem Namen *muṭābaqa*, was meist mit *Antithese* übersetzt wird.[10] Das klingt recht unkompliziert und sollte überschaubar bleiben. Allerdings stellt sich schnell heraus, dass die Diskussionen zu diesem Stilmittel gar nicht so klar daherkommen. Als erstes Hilfsmittel, um arabische Stilmittel zu verstehen, dient uns bislang die (stark) zusammenfassende und systematisierende Übersetzung eines *Badīʿiyya*-Kommentars aus dem frühen 12./18. Jahrhundert von Pierre Cachia, in der er *ṭibāq* mit *parallelism* übersetzt.[11] Als guter Lehrer hat Thomas Bauer immer wieder darauf verwiesen, dass der Begriff *Antithese* im Grunde zu kurz greife, weil das Stilmittel *muṭābaqa* bei den arabischen Rhetorikern umfassender angelegt sei und auch die Verwendung von Farbkontrasten wie rot und grün etwa, dazugehöre und er daher *Kontrast* als adäquatere Übersetzung vorschlage. Das sollte uns eine Warnung sein!

Die Farbkontraste sind nicht weit hergeholt, denn al-Qazwīnī bringt in seinem Lehrbuch zur arabischen Rhetorik im Abschnitt zur *muṭābaqa*, als erstes poetische Beispiel für diese Stilfigur, nachdem er einige Koranverse als Beispiele angeführt hat, folgenden Vers, eingeleitet mit den Worten „zum *ṭibāq* gehört zum Beispiel dieser Vers:“

> Er warf die Gewänder des Todes um sich, rot gefärbt, aber sobald die Nacht über sie hereinbrach, waren sie bereits aus Paradies-Brokat und grün.[12]

Daher wird dieser Beitrag erst einmal nur einen sehr kleinen Aspekt – speziell den der Farbkontraste – herausgreifen, anhand dessen schließlich weitere Fragen aufgeworfen werden.

Das Besondere an den Stilmittelgedichten mit Kommentar ist, dass ein Autor nicht nur eine theoretische Definition und/oder Diskussion des Stilmittels zu liefern hat, sondern in seinem Lobgedicht auf den Propheten auch selbst einen Beispielvers dichten muss, der das zu besprechende Stilmittel exemplarisch und natürlich auch vorbildlich beinhaltet. Ibn Ḥiǧǧa al-Ḥamawī hat sich außerdem zur Aufgabe gemacht, dem Beispiel eines seiner Vorgänger, nämlich ʿIzz ad-Dīn al-Mawṣilī (st. 780/1337) zu folgen und den Namen des Stilmittels auch noch in diesen Beispielvers zu integrieren.[13] Zur *muṭābaqa* dichtet er folgenden Vers – der elfte Vers seines Lobgedichts auf den Propheten Muḥammad:

10 Heinrichs, Ṭibāḳ.

11 Cachia, *Arch rhetorician* 51 (das Werk stammt aus der Feder des palästinensischen Gelehrten ʿAbd al-Ġanī an-Nābulusī, st. 1143/1731).

12 Al-Qazwīnī, *Matn at-Talḫīṣ* 106 = *at-Talḫīṣ* 350.

13 Bauer, ʿIzz al-Dīn al-Mawṣilī.

> *bi-waḥšatin baddalū ʾunsī wa-qad ḫafaḍū qadrī wa-zādū ʿuluwwan fī ṭibāqihimī*
>
> Sie tauschten die Vertrautheit mit mir gegen Fremdheit ein, indem sie meinen Rang herabsetzten und an Höhe ihrem Rang (*ṭibāqihimī*) hinzufügten.[14]

Seinen Kommentar zum Stilmittel *muṭābaqa* beginnt Ibn Ḥiǧǧa al-Ḥamawī mit einer lexikographischen Diskussion des Begriffes.[15] Das ist nicht neu, findet sich aber nicht im Lehrbuch des Predigers von Damaskus, auch nicht in dessen eigenem Kommentar, den er *al-Īḍāḥ*, „die Verdeutlichung," nennt.[16] Ibn Ḥiǧǧa al-Ḥamawī greift also als allererstes weiter zurück und präsentiert eine Diskussion zur Wortbedeutung, mit der bereits Ibn al-Muʿtazz (247–96/861–908), Dichter und Kalif sowie der erste Autor eines spezifischen Werkes über Stilmittel, seine Präsentation der *muṭābaqa* begann.[17] Ibn Ḥiǧǧa al-Ḥamawī weist nun seinerseits mit deutlichen Worten darauf hin, dass die Bedeutung von *muṭābaqa* laut sprachlicher Konvention – nämlich in Übersetzung am ehesten „die Übereinstimmung" – keinen Bezug zum Fachausdruck habe, bei dem es um das Zusammenbringen von zwei Gegensätzen gehe, wie z.B. Tag und Nacht oder weiß und schwarz.[18] Das ist alles nicht neu, nur bei al-Qazwīnī nicht zu lesen.[19]

---

14 Ibn Ḥiǧǧa, *Ḫizānat al-adab* (1987) i, 156 = (2005) ii, 71.

15 Ibn Ḥiǧǧa, *Ḫizānat al-adab* (1987) i, 156 = (2005) ii, 71: „Laut Lexikographie (*fī l-luġa*, also im konventionell festgelegten Sprachgebrauch, wie ihn die Lexikographen beschreiben) heißt *muṭābaqa*, dass das Kamel seinen Hinterlauf an den Ort seines Vorderlaufs setzt; denn, wenn es das macht, dann sagt man „das Kamel macht *ṭibāq*"." Er führt dann noch zwei Zitate ganz früher Lexikographen an: „Al-Aṣmaʿī (gest. 213/828) sagte: „Der Ursprung von *al-muṭābaqa* ist das Setzen des Hinterlaufs an den Ort des Vorderlaufs beim Lauf der Vierbeiner," und al-Ḫalīl b. Aḥmad (gest. 170/786 o. 175/791) sagte: „Man sagt: Mit zwei Dingen wird *ṭibāq* gemacht, wenn man sie an einer Stelle vereint"."

16 Al-Qazwīnī, *al-Īḍāḥ* 255–60.

17 Ibn al-Muʿtazz, *Kitāb al-Badīʿ* 36; Ibn Ḥiǧǧas Formulierung ist beinahe identisch mit derjenigen von ar-Ruʿaynī (st. 779/1377), der ebenfalls einen ausführlichen Badīʿiyya-Kommentar verfasst hat, siehe ar-Ruʿaynī, *Ṭirāz al-Ḥulla* 356; die beiden Zitate der frühen Lexikographen finden sich dagegen so bei Ibn Rašīq, *al-ʿUmda* (1925) 565 = (1988) 576.

18 Ibn Ḥiǧǧa, *Ḫizānat al-adab* (1987) i, 156 = (2005) ii, 71: „Zwischen der sprachlichen Konvention (also der lexikographischen Definition) und dem Fachausdruck (*iṣṭilāḥ*) besteht (allerdings) keine Beziehung, weil *muṭābaqa* als Fachausdruck das Versammeln von zwei Gegensätzen in einer Redesequenz oder einem Gedichtsvers meint, wie z.B. Ein- und Ausfuhr, Nacht und Tag, weiß und schwarz."

19 Über die Entwicklung der Diskussionen dieses Begriffs bis hin zu dieser Einsicht ließe sich ausführlicher berichten, was ich aber hier bewusst ausklammere. Ibn Ḥiǧǧa al-Ḥamawī ist auf jeden Fall nicht der erste, der diese Einsicht hat.

An dieser Stelle, an das genannte Gegensatzpaar „weiß und schwarz“ anschließend, führt Ibn Ḥiǧǧa al-Ḥamawī mit Verweis auf ar-Rummānī (296–384/909–94), den Autor eines frühen Werkes über die sprachliche Unnachahmbarkeit des Korans, „und andere“ an, dass nur Weiß und Schwarz wirkliche Gegensätze sind, im Unterschied zu den restlichen Farben:

> Bei den Farben tritt überhaupt nur bei diesen beiden, also dem Weißen und dem Schwarzen eine *muṭābaqa* ein. Ar-Rummānī und andere sagten: Das Weiße und das Schwarze sind ein Gegensatzpaar im Unterschied zu den restlichen Farben, und zwar, weil diese beiden ineinander übergehen können.[20]

Dieser Hinweis auf eine Diskussion, ob Farbkontraste als Gegensätze angesehen werden können, oder nicht, ist im Vergleich zu vielen anderen Autoren nun gar nicht üblich.[21] Unter den vielen Autoren, die ich zum Vergleich herangezogen habe, sind es überhaupt nur zwei, die darauf eingehen.

Im 5./11. Jahrhundert ist es Ibn Rašīq (390–456 o. 463/1000–63 o. 1071),[22] einer der frühen Literaturtheoretiker, der in Nordafrika wirkte, der in seiner Diskussion zur *muṭābaqa*, nachdem er eine ausführliche Diskussion über die Begrifflichkeit(en) bringt, gefolgt von einer Vielzahl von Beispielen, eine Warnung vorträgt, dass manche Verse als Beispiele für die *muṭābaqa* angeführt werden, die aber gar keine echten Gegensätze beinhalten, wie etwa *ḥilm* (Einsicht) und *ǧahl* (Dummheit), deren echte Gegenätze jeweils anders lauten würden, nämlich *safah* (Torheit) oder *ṭayš* (Leichtsinn), beziehungsweise *ʿilm* (Wissen) oder *maʿrifa* (Kenntnis).[23] Solch ein Vers gehöre daher besser in das Kapitel zur *muqābala*,[24] eine Stilfigur, die von den meisten Autoren separat von der

---

20 Ibn Ḥiǧǧa, *Ḫizānat al-adab* (1987) i, 156 = (2005) ii, 71.

21 Verglichen habe ich bislang mit folgenden Werken, die vor al-Qazwīnīs Lehrbuch entstanden, (in chronologischer Reihenfolge): Ibn al-Muʿtazz, *Kitāb al-Badīʿ*; Qudāma Ibn Ǧaʿfar, *Kitāb Naqd aš-šiʿr*; al-Qāḍī al-Ǧurǧānī, *al-Wasāṭa*; Abū Hilāl al-ʿAskarī, *Kitāb aṣ-Ṣināʿatayn*; al-Bāqillānī, *Iʿǧāz al-Qurʾān*; Ibn Rašīq, *al-ʿUmda*; Ibn Sinān al-Ḫafāǧī, *Sirr al-faṣāḥa*; Usāma Ibn Munqiḏ, *al-Badīʿ fī naqd aš-šiʿr*; al-Baġdādī, *Qānūn al-balāġa*; ar-Rāzī, *Nihāyat al-īǧāz*; al-Muṭarrizī, *al-Īḍāḥ fī šarḥ al-Maqāmāt*; as-Sakkākī, *Miftāḥ al-ʿulūm*; Ibn al-Aṯīr, *al-Maṯal as-sāʾir*; Ibn Abī l-Iṣbaʿ, *Taḥrīr at-taḥbīr*; az-Zanǧānī, *Kitāb Miʿyār an-nuẓẓār*; al-Qarṭāǧannī, *Minhāǧ al-bulaġāʾ*; Ibn Mālik, *al-Miṣbāḥ*; Ibn an-Naqīb, *Muqaddima*; Ibn az-Zamlakānī, *at-Tibyān fī ʿilm al-bayān*; an-Nuwayrī, *Nihāyat al-arab*; Naǧm ad-Dīn Ibn al-Aṯīr, *Ǧawhar al-kanz*.

22 Van Gelder, Ibn Rashīq.

23 Ibn Rašīq, *al-ʿUmda* (1925) 572–3 = (1988) 582–3; Ibn Rašīq verweist dabei auf al-Qāḍī al-Ǧurǧānī, der diese Warnung bereits ausspricht, al-Qāḍī al-Ǧurǧānī, *al-Wasāṭa* 45–6.

24 Ibn Rašīq, *al-ʿUmda* (1925) 573 = (1988) 582.

muṭābaqa diskutiert wird (dazu später mehr). Als weiteres Beispiel zitiert Ibn Rašīq in diesem Zusammenhang ein Versbeispiel, in dem die Farben Schwarz, Rot, Gelb und Weiß vorkommen:

> Schwarz ihre Locken, rot ihre Handflächen, gelb ihre Schlüsselbeine und weiß ihre Wangen.[25]

und bringt im Anschluss daran das Zitat von „ar-Rummānī und anderen," die sagen, dass nur Schwarz und Weiß echte Gegensätze sind, im Unterschied zu den restlichen Farben, auf die das nicht zutrifft.[26] Dieses Zitat hat Ibn Ḥiǧǧa al-Ḥamawī höchstwahrscheinlich von ihm übernommen, wobei er es gekürzt hat.[27] Ibn Rašīq meint dazu:

> Dies zeigt sich ganz deutlich und bleibt niemandem verborgen. Ich habe es hier nur angeführt, um die Behauptung von einigen zu entkräften, die beste *muṭābaqa* sei der Vers von ʿAmr b. Kulṯūm:
> Wir brachten weiße Banner und holten sie rot zurück, nachdem sie sich satt getrunken hatten.[28]

Es ist klar, dass Ibn Rašīq diese Verse, in denen verschiedene Farben kontrastiert werden, als Beispiele anführt, um zu argumentieren, dass sie nicht richtig zum Stilmittel der *muṭābaqa* passen, und zwar, weil sie nicht mit echten Gegensätzen arbeiten.

---

25 Ibn Rašīq, *al-ʿUmda* (1925) 574–5 = (1988) 583–4, ein Gedicht, das er auch noch in anderer Reihenfolge kennt: Gelb ihre Schlüsselbeine, rot ihre Handflächen, schwarz ihre Locken und weiß ihre Wangen.

26 Ibn Rašīq, *al-ʿUmda* (1925) 575 = (1988) 584: „Ar-Rummānī und andere sagen: Das Weiße und das Schwarze sind ein Gegensatzpaar. Die restlichen Farben bilden zwar einen Gegensatz jeweils mit ihrem Gegenpart, aber nur Weiß ist in Wirklichkeit das Gegenteil von Schwarz; denn, immer wenn man davon etwas verstärkt, vergrößert sich die Entfernung zum Gegenpart. Dagegen verhält es sich bei den anderen Farben so, dass, wenn man sie verstärkt, vergrößert sich dadurch die Nähe zum Schwarz und wenn man sie schwächer macht, vergrößert sich die Nähe zum Weiß. Außerdem ist es so, dass das Weiße gefärbt werden kann, aber nicht färbt, und das Schwarze färbt, aber nicht gefärbt werden kann, was bei den anderen Farben nicht so ist, weil sie alle färben und gefärbt werden können. Ende ihrer Rede."

27 In dem Werk *an-Nukat fī iʿǧāz al-Qurʾān* von ar-Rummānī kommt dieser Hinweis gar nicht vor, s. Ibn Rašīq, *al-ʿUmda* (1925) 575, Fußnote, was auch ich nochmals bestätigen kann.

28 Ibn Rašīq, *al-ʿUmda* (1925) 575 = (1988) 584.

Diese Diskussion, inwiefern Farben als Gegensätze verstanden werden können, findet sich aber bei der Mehrheit der vielen Autoren, die sich mit Stilmitteln befasst haben, überhaupt nicht.[29]

Warum also ist es Ibn Ḥiǧǧa al-Ḥamawī überhaupt ein Anliegen, auf diese Aussage, dass Farben nämlich eigentlich nicht als Gegensätze anzusehen sind (außer schwarz und weiß), sofort am Anfang seiner Präsentation des Stilmittels *al-muṭābaqa* einzugehen? Er selbst erklärt dies folgendermaßen:

> Wenn sie die restlichen Farben zur *muṭābaqa* hinzufügen – was korrekterweise als *tadbīǧ* (Verzierung) zu bezeichnen ist – dann führen sie damit den *tadbīǧ* in die *muṭābaqa* ein, wie die Verse von Ibn Ḥayyūs (syrischer Dichter, 394–473/1003–81), der in Form einer *kināya* (eine Stilfigur, die die Wirkung nennt und damit die Ursache meint) sagte:
>
> Sei stolz auf einen Onkel väterlicherseits – die Großzügigkeit seiner rechten Hand umfasst alle –, und auf einen Vater, der schändliche Taten ablehnt!
>
> Mit weißer Ehre/Weite, roten Schärfen (also Schwertern), schwarzem Kampfesstaub und grüner Weitherzigkeit/Weiträumigkeit.[30]

Ibn Ḥiǧǧa al-Ḥamawī spricht also in anonymer Form von Leuten, die das Phänomen ‚Farbkontraste' unter dem Stichwort *muṭābaqa* eingeführt haben, was seiner Meinung nach nicht so passend ist, sondern besser unter dem Stichwort *tadbīǧ* abgehandelt werden sollte, losgelöst von der Diskussion über Gegensätze, der Antithese. Dies ist eine versteckte, aber deutliche Kritik an der Standardtheorie, denn al-Qazwīnī ist genau derjenige, der den Farbkontrast in seine Präsentation der *muṭābaqa* einbaut (dazu gleich noch mehr).[31]

---

29 Bislang habe ich diese Diskussion nur noch bei Naǧm ad-Dīn Ibn al-Aṯīr (st. 737/1336) gefunden, einem Autor, der Anfang des 8./14. Jahrhunderts in Syrien lebte und also Zeitgenosse von al-Qazwīnī war, allerdings nicht in seinem Abschnitt zur *muṭābaqa*. Vielmehr führt er das letztgenannte Versbeispiel als eine Art der *muqābala* an, die gerade nicht mit Gegensätzen arbeitet. In seinem Kommentar zu diesem Vers führt er aus, dass die Verben „bringen" und „holen" echte Gegensätze seien, „weiß" und „rot" dagegen nicht und mithin diese spezielle Art der *muqābala* hier vorläge. Als Erklärung führt er an dieser Stelle dann aus (ohne dabei auf eine Autorität zu verweisen), dass Weiß keinen anderen Gegensatz habe als Schwarz und dass die restlichen Farben im Unterschied dazu nicht als Gegensatz gelten, weil sie sich färben lassen und auch selbst färben, Naǧm ad-Dīn Ibn al-Aṯīr, *Ǧawhar al-kanz* 87–8.

30 Ibn Ḥiǧǧa, *Ḫizānat al-adab* (1987) i, 156 = (2005) ii, 71–2.

31 Al-Qazwīnī, *Matn at-Talḫīṣ* 106 = *at-Talḫīṣ* 350; al-Qazwīnī, *al-Īḍāḥ* 257–8.

Dass das Spiel mit Farbkontrasten aber im Unterschied zur Standardtheorie unter dem Begriff *tadbīǧ* als selbständiges Stilmittel gewürdigt werden soll, macht Ibn Ḥiǧǧa al-Ḥamawī in seiner *Badīʿiyya* mit Kommentar deutlich, indem er ihm einen eigenen Eintrag und damit auch einen eigenen Beispielvers – mit Integration des Namens – widmet.[32] Dieses Stilmittel hat einen anderen Stellenwert: Ibn Ḥiǧǧa al-Ḥamawī baut es in den 123. Vers seines Prophetenlobs ein. Er erklärt dazu, dass dieses Stilmittel als eigene Art von Ibn Abī l-Iṣbaʿ (585 o. 589–654/1189 o. 1193–1256) beschrieben wurde, einem Literaten, der noch unter ayyubidischer Herrschaft in Ägypten wirkte.[33] Ibn Ḥiǧǧa al-Ḥamawī sieht in ihm eine zentrale Bezugsautorität, wie es sich hier, aber auch schon in seinem Vorwort zeigt und darüber hinaus noch an vielen weiteren Stellen. In dem recht überschaubaren Vorwort etwa, nennt Ibn Ḥiǧǧa al-Ḥamawī neben seinem Mäzen, dem Obersten Staatssekretär Nāṣir ad-Dīn al-Bārizī,[34] seine Vorläufer in der Gattung des Stilmittelgedichts, nämlich Ṣafī ad-Dīn al-Ḥillī (677 o. 678–749/1278 o. 1279–1348)[35] und ʿIzz ad-Dīn al-Mawṣilī, der den ersteren überbieten wollte, unter anderem durch die Integration des Stilmittelnamens, aber laut Ibn Ḥiǧǧa al-Ḥamawī dabei keine schöne Poesie verfasste und sich außerdem auch nicht nach Ibn Abī l-Iṣbaʿ gerichtet habe.[36] Es ist klar, dass Ibn Ḥiǧǧa al-Ḥamawī dies besser machen möchte. Hier, in seinem Abschnitt über *tadbīǧ* hebt er Ibn Abī l-Iṣbaʿ als „Entdecker" dieses Stilmittels hervor und in der Tat ist Ibn Abī l-Iṣbaʿ wohl der erste, der das Spiel mit Farbkontrasten gesondert betrachtet und unter der Bezeichnung „Verzierung" (*tadbīǧ*) als eigenes Stilmittel würdigt.[37]

Ibn Abī l-Iṣbaʿ erklärt, dass es bei diesem Stilmittel darum gehe, dass der Dichter oder auch der Prosaschriftsteller Farben verwendet, und zwar mit dem Ziel, damit eine *kināya* oder *tawriya* (Mehrdeutigkeit) zu bilden.[38] Nach dieser Definition geht es bei dem Einsatz der Farben also vor allem darum, dass damit etwas anderes als die Farbe selbst zum Ausdruck gebracht werden soll. Das Interesse des Kritikers wird darauf gelenkt, wie diese anderen Stilfiguren das Farbspiel beeinflussen. Dagegen diskutiert Ibn Abī l-Iṣbaʿ hier überhaupt nicht die Tatsache, dass dabei verschiedene Farbbegriffe in einem Vers zusam-

32 Ibn Ḥiǧǧa, *Ḫizānat al-adab* (1987) i, 453–4 = (2005) iv, 353–6.

33 Zu diesem Autor siehe Bauer, Ambiguität in der klassischen arabischen Rhetoriktheorie 21–47; und Harb, Ibn Abī l-Iṣbaʿ.

34 Siehe zu ihm auch meinen Aufsatz, Ein Lobgedicht auf den Obersten Staatssekretär 219–24, in dem es zwar um dessen Sohn geht, aber auch um den Vater Nāṣir ad-Dīn al-Bārizī.

35 Heinrichs, Ṣafī ad-Dīn ʿAbd al-ʿAzīz b. Sarāyā al-Ḥillī.

36 Ibn Ḥiǧǧa, *Ḫizānat al-adab* (1987) i, 17–8 = (2005) i, 304–5.

37 Ibn Abī l-Iṣbaʿ, *Taḥrīr at-taḥbīr* 532–5.

38 Ibn Abī l-Iṣbaʿ, *Taḥrīr at-taḥbīr* 532.

mengebracht werden und dadurch eine Art Gegensatz entsteht, auf jeden Fall eine Gegenüberstellung, die man im Zusammenhang mit Farben gut als Kontrast bezeichnen könnte. Als erstes Versbeispiel bringt Ibn Abī l-Iṣbaʿ zwei Verse des syrischen Dichters Ibn Ḥayyūs, den ja auch Ibn Ḥiǧǧa al-Ḥamawī in seinem Abschnitt zur *muṭābaqa* erwähnt. Allerdings hat Ibn Abī l-Iṣbaʿ zur Veranschaulichung seines neu definierten Stilmittels zwei andere Verse von Ibn Ḥayyūs ausgewählt:

> Willst du etwas Sicheres über sie erfahren, dann triff sie am Tag des Gewinns oder Kampfs.
>
> Du wirst das Weiß der Gesichter finden, das Schwarz des aufgewühlten Staubs, das Grün der Flanken und das Rot der Klingen.[39]

Diese Verse führt Ibn Hiǧǧa al-Ḥamawī dann auch in seinem Abschnitt zum *tadbīǧ* als erstes Beispiel an.[40] Ibn Abī l-Iṣbaʿ bringt nach weiteren Beispielen und Erläuterungen zu diesem Stilmittel am Ende seines Abschnitts noch ein einschlägiges Beispiel, nämlich einen Vers aus einem Trauergedicht von Abū Tammām:

> Er warf die Gewänder des Todes um sich, rot gefärbt, aber sobald die Nacht über sie hereinbrach, waren sie bereits aus Paradies-Brokat und grün.[41]

Ibn Abī l-Iṣbaʿ kommentiert diesen Vers nicht weiter, etwa wo und wie hier eines der anderen Stilmittel integriert ist und welche Wirkung das hat. Ibn Ḥiǧǧa al-Ḥamawī greift diesen Vers nicht auf, weder in seinem Abschnitt über die *muṭābaqa*, noch in seinem Abschnitt über den *tadbīǧ*, obwohl es genau das Versbeispiel ist, das al-Qazwīnī auswählt und in seine Darstellung der *muṭābaqa* integriert.[42] Dieses Gedicht, in dem die Farben rot und grün kontrastiv gegenübergestellt werden (auch wenn Ibn Abī l-Iṣbaʿ dies so nicht formuliert), ist überhaupt das erste Gedichtbeispiel, das al-Qazwīnī in seinem Lehrbuch zur *muṭābaqa* anführt! Es drängt sich nun die Frage auf, warum al-Qazwīnī das gemacht hat? Wie ist seine Darstellung der *muṭābaqa* zustande gekommen? Damit sind wir zwar wieder bei der Entstehungserzählung der Standardtheorie, die obwohl im Groben erzählt, im Einzelnen jedoch immer

39 Ibn Abī l-Iṣbaʿ, *Taḥrīr at-taḥbīr* 533.

40 Ibn Ḥiǧǧa, *Ḫizānat al-adab* (1987) i, 453 = (2005) iv, 354.

41 Ibn Abī l-Iṣbaʿ, *Taḥrīr at-taḥbīr* 535.

42 Al-Qazwīnī, *Matn at-Talḫīṣ* 106 = *at-Talḫīṣ* 350; al-Qazwīnī, *al-Īḍāḥ*, 257–8.

noch aufgeklärt werden kann und zum Verständnis der Autoren der „späteren Jahrhunderte“ und ihrem Umgang mit dem Lehrwerk sogar aufgeklärt werden muss.

Wir haben schon darauf hingewiesen, dass Ibn Rašīq bereits im 5./11. Jahrhundert das Thema Farben im Rahmen seiner Diskussion der *muṭābaqa* anspricht, worauf Ibn Ḥiǧǧa al-Ḥamawī ja auch zurückgreift, aber mit dem Ziel, diese Farbspiele nicht wirklich als *muṭābaqa* anzusehen, sondern besser unter das Stilmittel der *muqābala* einzuordnen, auch wenn er dies selbst noch nicht vollzieht.[43] Es ist dann Ibn Abī l-Iṣbaʿ, der im frühen 7./13. Jahrhundert, dieses Farbspiel als eigenständige Stilfigur ausweist und dabei die Verbindung mit anderen Stilmitteln in den Vordergrund rückt und sich überhaupt nicht mehr für das Phänomen „Gegensatz“ im Zusammenhang mit den Farben interessiert.

Auch das Versbeispiel von Abū Tammām findet sich gar nicht bei früheren Autoren in ihrer Diskussion der *muṭābaqa*. Eine Ausnahme stellt Ibn Sinān al-Ḫafāǧī (422–66/1031–73) dar, der diesen Vers allerdings nicht als Beispiel einer *muṭābaqa*, sondern – wie von Ibn Rašīq vorbereitet – als Beispiel einer *muqābala* präsentiert.[44] Entsprechend hebt er in seiner Diskussion dieses Verses nicht das Phänomen des Farbkontrasts hervor oder die Kombination mit anderen Stilfiguren, sondern diskutiert dies als Beispiel von einer „Gegenüberstellung“ (*muqābala*), die aber nicht mit einem echten Gegensatz (*taḍādd*) arbeitet, sondern nur mit einem Widerspruch (*muḫālif*), was von vielen Autoren als ein wichtiges Unterscheidungsmerkmal zwischen *muṭābaqa* und *muqābala* angeführt wird.[45] Ibn Sinān al-Ḫafāǧī erwähnt an dieser Stelle, dass es aber andere Autoren gebe, die dieses Beispiel dem *ṭibāq* zuordnen.[46] Ibn Abī l-Iṣbaʿ auf jeden Fall fand, dass dieser Vers ein gutes Beispiel für sein neues Stilmittel sei.

Das neu entdeckte Stilmittel mit dem Namen *tadbīǧ* wird in der Nachfolge von einem wichtigen Autor zwischen Ibn Abī l-Iṣbaʿ und al-Qazwīnī durchaus aufgegriffen und dabei auch der Beispielvers von Abū Tammām zitiert. Der in Damaskus wirkende Sprachgelehrte Badr ad-Dīn Ibn Mālik (ca. 645–86/ca. 1245–87)[47] präsentiert dieses wie auch die beiden Stilmittel *muṭābaqa*

43 Ein Autor, der dies dann genau so durchführt, ist Naǧm ad-Dīn Ibn al-Aṯīr, der sein Buch erst nach Ibn Abī l-Iṣbaʿ verfasst, s. o. Fn 29.

44 Ibn Sinān al-Ḫafāǧī, *Sirr al-faṣāḥa* 195.

45 Diese Diskussionen über die Unterschiede zwischen *muṭābaqa* und *muqābala*, beziehungsweise ihre gegenseitigen Unterordnungen würden in diesem Beitrag zu weit führen und werden daher hier nicht weiter diskutiert, auch wenn sie interessante Einblicke in die Entwicklungsgeschichte der arabischen Rhetorik liefern.

46 Dies trifft allerdings auf alle von mir zum Vergleich herangezogenen Autoren nicht zu.

47 Simon, Badr al-Dīn Ibn Mālik.

und *muqābala* sehr deutlich nach der Systematik, die Ibn Abī l-Iṣbaʿ entwickelt hatte, nur dass Badr ad-Dīn Ibn Mālik noch systematischer vorgeht und damit für diese drei Stilfiguren eine in herausgehobener Weise prägnante Darstellung bietet.[48] Eigentlich erfüllt seine Darstellung in höherem Maße den Charakter eines Lehrbuchs als die Darstellung von al-Qazwīnī, zumindest dieser drei Stilmittel, die al-Qazwīnī nämlich unter einen Hut packt und gemeinsam vorstellt und damit im Grunde einen recht verworrenen Beitrag zur Darstellung der Antithese leistet. Das Werk von Badr ad-Dīn Ibn Mālik tritt mit dem gleichen Anspruch wie al-Qazwīnī auf, nämlich eine zusammenfassende Darstellung der rhetorischen Lehren von as-Sakkākī (555–626/1160–1229) zu sein,[49] wobei Badr ad-Dīn Ibn Mālik zu den von as-Sakkākī präsentierten Wissenschaften der Bedeutungen und der Deutlichkeit der erste ist, der diese um die Wissenschaft der Stilmittel erweitert und auf diese Wissenschaft auch deutlich mehr Gewicht legt, was al-Qazwīnī von ihm übernimmt.[50] An unserem Beispiel der *muṭābaqa* (ausgewählt nach dem Standardtext von al-Qazwīnī), welches, wie wir mittlerweile verstanden haben oder auch nur erahnen, eigentlich auch die Stilfiguren *tadbīǧ* und *muqābala* umfasst, stellt sich eine neue Frage: Wieso und wie hat sich eigentlich das Werk von al-Qazwīnī als einschlägiges Lehrwerk durchgesetzt, das so häufig kommentiert wurde?

Deutlich zeigt sich im Fall des Literaten und Staatskanzlisten Ibn Ḥiǧǧa al-Ḥamawī, dass er sich mit der Standardtheorie auseinandersetzt, wenn auch in unserem Beispielfall bislang nur anonym. Im 9./15. Jahrhundert kann Ibn Ḥiǧǧa al-Ḥamawī den kanonischen Text also nicht einfach ignorieren, auch wenn er sich wie in unserem Beispiel bei der Einordnung und Diskussion des Phänomens der Farbkontraste gegen die Lehrmeinung und Systematik von al-Qazwīnī wendet und sich stattdessen ganz bewusst auf Ibn Abī l-Iṣbaʿ bezieht, dessen Namen er deutlich nennt und immer wieder lobend herausstellt, ja manchmal sogar von dessen „Schule" (*maḏhab*) spricht.[51] Wieso erwähnt er aber Badr ad-Dīn Ibn Mālik in diesen Zusammenhängen gar nicht, der ja zu dieser Schule zu gehören scheint, zumindest was unser Beispiel betrifft?

---

48 Ibn Mālik, *al-Miṣbāḥ* 191–6; Badr ad-Dīn Ibn Mālik bringt diese drei Stilmittel wirklich in direkter Folge, zuerst *muṭābaqa* (191–2), dann *muqābala* (192–5) und schließlich *tadbīǧ* (195–6). – Vgl. dies mit Ibn Abī l-Iṣbaʿ, *Taḥrīr at-taḥbīr*, *Bāb aṭ-Ṭibāq* (111–5); *Bāb Ṣiḥḥat al-muqābalāt* (179–84); und *Bāb at-Tadbīǧ* (532–5).

49 Heinrichs, as-Sakkākī.

50 Simon, Badr al-Dīn Ibn Mālik.

51 So etwa in seiner Präsentation des Stilmittels der *muqābala*, Ibn Ḥiǧǧa, *Ḫizānat al-adab* (1987) i, 129 = (2005) ii, 24, wo er stark gegen die Lehrmeinung von al-Qazwīnī (allerdings wieder ohne ihn zu nennen) argumentiert, dass die *muqābala* eben getrennt von der *muṭābaqa* zu behandeln sei.

Gleichzeitig bleibt die Frage, wieso al-Qazwīnī dieser Schule zumindest im Hinblick auf eine getrennte Präsentation von *muṭābaqa, muqābala* und *tadbīǧ* nicht gefolgt ist. Wie sich an unserem Beispiel, spezifisch an der Diskussion zu den Farbkontrasten, zeigen lässt, kannte al-Qazwīnī diese Schule. In seinem Lehrwerk, dem *Talḫīṣ*, erscheint das Versbeispiel von Abū Tammām nur mit den einleitenden Worten: „Zum *ṭibāq* gehört," mehr wird dazu nicht ausgeführt.[52] Da es außerdem ja das erste Versbeispiel ist, erscheint es so unkommentiert an dieser Stelle wie das normalste Beispiel für eine *muṭābaqa*. Allerdings versteht man dies schon anders nach dem Studium des Kommentars, den al-Qazwīnī selbst zu seinem Lehrbuch verfasst hat.[53] Erstens bringt er dort vor Abū Tammāms Vers bereits eine Menge einschlägiger Versbeispiele für das Spiel mit Gegensätzen, sodass der Vers mit den Farbkontrasten von Abū Tammām nicht mehr das erste Gedichtbeispiel für eine *muṭābaqa* ist. Außerdem fügt er dort die beiden Verse von Ibn Ḥayyūs sowie ein Zitat aus den Makamen des al-Ḥarīrī als weitere Beispiele hinzu, die mit Farben spielen:

> Seitdem der gelbe Freund (gemeint ist hier in der Form einer *tawriya* das Gold) abtrünnig und das grüne Leben staubgrau wurde, wurde mein weißer Tag schwarz und mein schwarzer Scheitel weiß, sodass selbst der blauäugige Feind um mich trauerte, wie liebenswert ist da der rote Tod![54]

Diese Passage von al-Ḥarīrī hatte auch Ibn Abī l-Iṣbaʿ neben weiteren Beispielen gebracht und ebenso führt sie Ibn Ḥiǧǧa al-Ḥamawī neben anderen (auch eigenen) Beispielen in seinem Abschnitt zum *tadbīǧ* an.[55] Bemerkenswert ist meines Erachtens nun die Tatsache, dass Badr ad-Dīn Ibn Mālik genau diese drei Beispiele (den Vers von Abū Tammām, das Verspaar von Ibn Ḥayyūs und das Prosazitat von al-Ḥarīrī), in genau dieser Reihenfolge und keine weiteren zum *tadbīǧ* präsentiert.[56] Dies sind genau die drei Beispiele, die al-Qazwīnī in genau dieser Reihenfolge in seinem Kommentarwerk zitiert und dann erklärt:

> Es gibt Leute, die das, was wir hier angeführt haben, *at-tadbīǧ* (die Verzierung) nennen. Es wird damit erklärt, dass in einem Denkinhalt, der Lob oder etwas anderes zum Ausdruck bringen soll, Farben verwendet wer-

52 Al-Qazwīnī, *Matn at-Talḫīṣ* 106 = *at-Talḫīṣ* 350.

53 Al-Qazwīnī, *al-Īḍāḥ* 255–60.

54 Al-Qazwīnī, *al-Īḍāḥ* 258.

55 Ibn Abī l-Iṣbaʿ, *Taḥrīr at-taḥbīr* 533; Ibn Ḥiǧǧa, *Ḫizānat al-adab* (1987) i, 453 = (2005) iv, 353.

56 Ibn Mālik, *al-Miṣbāḥ* 195–6.

> den, und zwar mit dem Ziel, eine *kināya* oder eine *tawriya* zu bilden. Was nun den *tadbīǧ al-kināya* (die Verzierung in Form einer *kināya*) betrifft, so sind der Vers von Abū Tammām und die beiden Verse von Ibn Ḥayyūs dafür ein Beispiel. Was den *tadbīǧ at-tawriya* (die Verzierung in Form einer *tawriya*) betrifft, so ist der Wortlaut *al-aṣfar* im Prosatext von al-Ḥarīrī ein Beispiel.[57]

Es ist also klar, dass al-Qazwīnī diese „Schule," wie es Ibn Ḥiǧǧa al-Ḥamawī ausdrückt, sehr wohl kannte, und hier höchstwahrscheinlich auch nicht auf Ibn Abī l-Iṣbaʿ, sondern direkt auf Badr ad-Dīn Ibn Mālik zurückgreift. Wieso kam er dann auf die Idee, dieses bis dahin immer noch „neue" Stilmittel einfach in den Eintrag zum „alten" Stilmittel der *muṭābaqa* einzugliedern, zumal auch schon früher argumentiert wurde, dass diese Farbspiele nicht recht zur *muṭābaqa* passen würden? Möglicherweise ist es al-Qazwīnī in diesem Fall ein Anliegen gewesen, sich von Ibn Mālik abzuheben. Das wäre ein erster Erklärungsversuch für die Unterschiede, der aber natürlich mit weiteren Detailuntersuchungen abgeklärt werden müsste. Wenn das der Fall wäre, sieht es aber so aus, dass er damit nicht immer in den Jahrhunderten nach ihm auf Verständnis stieß. Ibn Ḥiǧǧa al-Ḥamawī ist ihm darin auf jeden Fall nicht gefolgt, sondern der „Schule" des Ibn Abī l-Iṣbaʿ.

Ibn Ḥiǧǧa al-Ḥamawī steht darin unter den *Badīʿiyyāt*-Verfassern nicht allein. Zumindest weist auch das erste dieser Stilmittelgedichte von Ṣafī ad-Dīn al-Ḥillī einen eigenen Vers zum Stilmittel *tadbīǧ* auf und der Autor verweist in seinem, im Vergleich zu Ibn Ḥiǧǧa al-Ḥamawī knapper angelegten, Kommentar eindeutig auf Ibn Abī l-Iṣbaʿ als Erfinder dieses Stilmittels und präsentiert neben dem Verspaar von Ibn Ḥayyūs auch das koranische Beispiel, das Ibn Abī l-Iṣbaʿ für diese Stilfigur heranzieht und auch ausführlich kommentiert (35:27):

> In den Bergen sind weiße und rote Adern, buntfarbige und rabenschwarze.[58]

Aus der Perspektive von Ibn Ḥiǧǧa al-Ḥamawī gehört also auch Ṣafī ad-Dīn al-Ḥillī – zumindest im Hinblick auf unser Farbbeispiel – zur „Schule" des Ibn Abī l-Iṣbaʿ. Dies trifft höchstwahrscheinlich auch auf ʿIzz ad-Dīn al-Mawṣilī zu,

57 Al-Qazwīnī, *al-Īḍāḥ* 258.

58 Übersetzungen dieser Passage fallen unterschiedlich aus. Oben habe ich die Übersetzung der Ahmadiyya ausgewählt; Rudi Paret übersetzt: „Bei den Bergen gibt es verschiedenartige Schichten, weiße, rote und kohlschwarze;" und die Azhar-Übersetzung hat: „Die Berge sind weiß- oder rotgestreift und rabenschwarz in verschiedenen Tönungen."

obwohl ihn Ibn Ḥiǧǧa al-Ḥamawī dafür kritisiert, sich nicht nach Ibn Abī l-Iṣbaʿ gerichtet zu haben.[59] Anders steht es dagegen mit der *Badīʿiyya* von Ibn Ǧābir (698–780/1298–1378), die zwischen Ṣafī ad-Dīn und ʿIzz ad-Dīn entstanden ist.[60]

Wenn wir zur Darstellung des Stilmittels *al-muṭābaqa* bei Ibn Ḥiǧǧa al-Ḥamawī zurückkehren, können wir festhalten, dass sein Einwurf zu den Farbkontrasten relativ zu Beginn seiner Diskussion der *muṭābaqa*, der die Überzeugung zum Ausdruck bringt, diese besser losgelöst vom Phänomen des Spiels mit Gegensätzen zu betrachten, von seiner kritischen Auseinandersetzung mit al-Qazwīnīs Lehrbuch zeugt und gleichzeitig Zeugnis ablegt von seinem Lob der Art der Systematik, die Ibn Abī l-Iṣbaʿ entwickelt hat. In seiner Diskussion der *muṭābaqa* bleibt dies aber nicht das einzige Zeugnis dieser kritischen Haltung gegenüber der Standardtheorie und gleichzeitiger Hervorhebung der Leistungen von Ibn Abī l-Iṣbaʿ. Ibn Ḥiǧǧa al-Ḥamawī lehnt zum Beispiel mit noch stärkeren Worten das Vorgehen von al-Qazwīnī ab, die *muqābala* unter dem Oberbegriff der *muṭābaqa* zu subsumieren.[61] In seinem Abschnitt zur *muqābala* zitiert Ibn Ḥiǧǧa al-Ḥamawī zum Teil seitenweise aus dem Werk von Ibn Abī l-Iṣbaʿ.[62] Ganz besonders aber lobt er dessen systematische Unterteilung der *muṭābaqa* in ein Spiel von Gegensätzen, bei dem einerseits die Gegensatzpaare wörtlich (*bi-alfāẓ al-ḥaqīqa*) zu verstehen sind und andererseits im übertragenen Sinn (*bi-alfāẓ al-maǧāz*).[63] Er schreibt, dass Ibn Abī l-Iṣbaʿ damit „die Herzen heile."[64] In der Tat ist dies wahrscheinlich eine zentrale Unterscheidung in Bezug auf das Stilmittel der *muṭābaqa*, die Ibn Abī l-Iṣbaʿ deutlich formuliert. Wie Ibn Abī l-Iṣbaʿ dazu kommt, ist in sich eine interessante Geschichte, die hier aber nicht weiter ausgebreitet werden soll. Erstaunlich ist allerdings, dass al-Qazwīnī diese Unterscheidung ganz und gar ausblendet. Für die Frage nach dem Umgang von Ibn Ḥiǧǧa al-Ḥamawī mit der Standardtheorie reicht

59 Die Badīʿiyya von ʿIzz ad-Dīn al-Mawṣilī weist ebenfalls einen Vers zum *tadbīǧ* auf, den Ibn Ḥiǧǧa al-Ḥamawī in seinem Abschnitt zum *tadbīǧ* auch zitiert. Allerdings habe ich leider keinen Zugang zu dessen eigenem Kommentar *at-Tawaṣṣul bi-l-badīʿ ilā at-tawassul bi-š-šafīʿ*.

60 Ibn Ǧābir – und mit ihm sein Kommentator ar-Ruʿaynī – orientiert sich in diesem Zusammenhang zumindest stärker an der Standardtheorie. Was sie zur *muṭābaqa* genau sagen und wie sie dabei die Farbspiele unterbringen, soll an einem anderen Ort dargestellt werden.

61 Ibn Ḥiǧǧa, *Ḫizānat al-adab* (1987) i, 157 = (2005) ii, 72.

62 Ibn Ḥiǧǧa, *Ḫizānat al-adab* (1987) i, 129–130 = (2005) ii, 24–6; vgl. Ibn Abī l-Iṣbaʿ, *Taḥrīr at-taḥbīr* 179–84.

63 Ibn Ḥiǧǧa, *Ḫizānat al-adab* (1987) i, 157 = (2005) ii, 73; vgl. Ibn Abī l-Iṣbaʿ, *Taḥrīr at-taḥbīr* 111.

64 Ibn Ḥiǧǧa, *Ḫizānat al-adab* (1987) i, 157 = (2005) ii, 73: *šafā l-qulūb*.

es hier festzuhalten, dass er diese eben immer wieder deutlich kritisiert und sich seine Ablehnung der Kategorisierungen von al-Qazwīnī nicht etwa nur auf ein „neu erfundenes Stilmittel der Verzierung durch Farbkontraste" beschränkt, sondern viel tiefer geht und wesentliche Punkte der Darstellung betrifft, auch des so grundlegenden Stilmittels der *muṭābaqa* im engeren Sinn.

Bei aller Kritik an al-Qazwīnī ist aber auch deutlich, dass sich Ibn Ḥiǧǧa al-Ḥamawī in seiner gesamten Diskussion zur *muṭābaqa* an dessen Lehrbuch ausrichtet. Der kanonische Text von al-Qazwīnī ist permanenter Bezugspunkt, selbst wenn dies in anonymisierter Form geschieht. So fasst Ibn Ḥiǧǧa al-Ḥamawī zum Beispiel nach seinem kurzen Hinweis auf das Phänomen der Farbkontraste noch einmal zusammen, um was es bei der *muṭābaqa* grundsätzlich geht:

> Es steht fest, dass bei den meisten Leuten die *muṭābaqa* das Versammeln von zwei Gegensätzen ist, bestehend entweder aus zwei Nomina oder zwei Verben oder anderem.[65]

Die Definition „das Versammeln von zwei Gegensätzen" wird auch von al-Qazwīnī vorgetragen und findet sich so bei eigentlich allen Autoren, die sich mit der *muṭābaqa* beschäftigen.[66] Die Ergänzung „bestehend entweder aus zwei Nomina oder zwei Verben oder anderem" ist dagegen relativ neu, denn sie basiert auf der Systematik von al-Qazwīnī. In der Tat systematisiert al-Qazwīnī als allererstes die *muṭābaqa* nach diesen grammatikalischen Kriterien, dass sie nämlich entweder aus zwei Nomina, oder zwei Verben, oder zwei Partikeln, oder auch aus Wörtern unterschiedlicher Klasse gebildet werde.[67] Diese Klassifizierung basiert auf der Beobachtung, die von einigen der früheren Autoren immer wieder auch wiederholt wird, dass eine gute *muṭābaqa* „nicht Nomen und Verb oder Verb und Nomen zusammenbringt."[68] Wie die früheren Autoren belässt es Ibn Ḥiǧǧa al-Ḥamawī hier bei der Erwähnung von Nomina und Verben, auch wenn er dies nun wie al-Qazwīnī formuliert. Im Lehrbuch von al-Qazwīnī erscheint dies als wichtiges Einteilungskriterium, dem er entsprechend auch Beispiele zuordnet. Ibn Ḥiǧǧa al-Ḥamawī lässt es wie die früheren Autoren bei dieser Bemerkung, ganz ohne Beispiele.

---

65 Ibn Ḥiǧǧa, *Ḫizānat al-adab* (1987) i, 157 = (2005) ii, 72.

66 Al-Qazwīnī, *Matn at-Talḫīṣ* 105 = *at-Talḫīṣ* 348.

67 Al-Qazwīnī, *Matn at-Talḫīṣ* 105 = *at-Talḫīṣ* 348–9; al-Qazwīnī, *al-Īḍāḥ* 255–6.

68 Vgl. etwa (in chronologischer Reihenfolge): al-Baġdādī, *Qānūn al-balāġa* 86; ar-Rāzī, *Nihāyat al-īǧāz* 110; al-Muṭarrizī, *al-Īḍāḥ fī šarḥ al-Maqāmāt* 78; az-Zanǧānī, *Kitāb Miʿyār an-nuẓẓār* ii, 93; Ibn an-Naqīb, *Muqaddima* 302; an-Nuwayrī, *Nihāyat al-arab* vii, 83.

Ibn Ḥiǧǧa al-Ḥamawī setzt also den Lehrbuchtext von al-Qazwīnī voraus und hangelt sich auch in der Anordnung seines eigenen Beitrags daran entlang. Er setzt sich dabei immer wieder davon ab und bringt dies mal subtiler und mal stärker zum Ausdruck. Es gibt aber auch Passagen, in denen er al-Qazwīnī folgt wie etwa in der Übernahme der Kategorien einer *muṭābaqa*, die durch Verneinung entsteht (wobei dies eine schon länger diskutierte Art ist), sowie in der Kategorie einer „vorgetäuschten *muṭābaqa*“ (*īhām al-muṭābaqa*), ein Begriff, der interessant ist und den wahrscheinlich al-Qazwīnī hervorbrachte. Ibn Ḥiǧǧa al-Ḥamawī hat auch lobende Worte für den Prediger von Damaskus übrig. In seinem Abschnitt über die *muṭābaqa* lobt er ihn für die Auswahl eines moderneren Beispielverses in seinem Kommentar, der aus der Feder des seldschukenzeitlichen Dichterjuristen al-Arraǧānī (460–544/1067-1149-50) stammt:

> Ich stieg ab bei einem der Herrschenden mit Ruhm – Die Bedürftigkeit der Männer danach ist der Schlüssel zum Reichtum.[69]

An dieser Stelle nennt er den Autor des kanonischen Texts für das Studium der arabischen Rhetorik dann auch mit vollem Namen, al-Qāḍī Ǧalāl ad-Dīn al-Qazwīnī und nennt auch die Titel beider Werke, nämlich aus „seiner Verdeutlichung seiner Zusammenfassung.“ Ibn Ḥiǧǧa al-Ḥamawī weiß also auch al-Qazwīnī zu schätzen.

Dieser kleine Einblick in den Umgang mit der Standardtheorie in den späteren Jahrhunderten und dies insbesondere in dem Entwicklungsstrang, der stärker mit der poetischen Praxis in Verbindung steht, konnte bereits sehr deutlich machen, dass der kanonische Text, der sich so schnell als Grundlagentext in allen höheren Bildungseinrichtungen durchsetzt, wirklich ein zentraler Bezugstext ist, auch in diesem von der Theorie weiter entfernten Entwicklungsstrang der Stilmittelgedichte mit ihren Kommentaren. Gleichzeitig konnten wir auch sehr deutlich sehen, dass dieser kanonische Text dabei keinesfalls zu einem dogmatischen Text wird in dem Sinne, dass man ihm nicht widersprechen dürfe. Das trifft überhaupt nicht zu, wie wir zeigen konnten. Am Ende bleiben trotzdem noch viele Fragen und Wünsche offen. Auf die nächsten sechzig Jahre!

69 Ibn Ḥiǧǧa, *Ḫizānat al-adab* (1987) i, 160 = (2005) ii, 77–8.

Bibliographie

al-ʿAskarī, Abū Hilāl, *Kitāb as-Ṣināʿatayn al-kitāba wa-š-šiʿr*, Hgg. ʿA.M. al-Biǧāwī und M.A. Ibrāhīm, Kairo 1952.

al-Baġdādī, *Qānūn al-balāġa fī naqd an-naṯr wa-š-šiʿr*, Hg. M.Ġ. ʿAǧīl, o.O. ca. 1980.

al-Bāqillānī, *Iʿǧāz al-Qurʾān*, Hg. aṣ-Ṣ.A. Ṣaqr, Kairo 1963.

Bauer, T., Rhetorik: Arabische Kultur, in G. Ueding (Hg.), *Rhetorik. Begriff – Geschichte – Internationalität*, Tübingen 2005, 283–300 = G. Ueding (Hg.), *Historisches Wörterbuch der Rhetorik*, viii, Tübingen 2007, 111–37.

Bauer, T., Religion und Klassisch-Arabische Literatur, in A. Pflitsch und B. Winckler (Hgg.), *Poetry's voice – society's norms*, Wiesbaden 2006, 13–29.

Bauer, T., Die *badīʿiyya* des Nāṣīf al-Yāziǧī und das Problem der spätosmanischen arabischen Literatur, in A. Neuwirth und A.C. Islebe (Hgg.), *Reflections on reflections: Near Eastern writers reading literature*, Wiesbaden 2006, 49–118.

Bauer, T., Ambiguität in der klassischen arabischen Rhetoriktheorie, in O. Auge und C. Witthöft (Hgg.), *Ambiguität im Mittelalter*, Berlin 2016, 21–47.

Bauer, T., ʿIzz al-Dīn al-Mawṣilī, in *EI*[3], first published online: 2018; first print edition 2018–3 (110–1).

Cachia, P., *The arch rhetorician or the schemer's skimmer: A handbook of the late Arabic badīʿ drawn from ʿAbd al-Ghanī an-Nābulsī's Nafaḥāt al-azhār ʿalā nasamāt al-asḥār*, Wiesbaden 1998.

Eksell, K., Figurative speech according to the *Talkhis al-Miftah* by al-Qazwini. With an excursus on A.F. van Mehren's *Die Rhetorik der Araber*, in: K. Eksell und G. Lindberg-Wada (Hgg.), *Studies of imagery in early Mediterranean and East Asian poetry*, Frankfurt 2017, 195–231.

Heinrichs, W.P., Ṭibāḳ, in *EI*[2], x, 450–2.

Heinrichs, W.P., Ṣafī ad-Dīn ʿAbd al-ʿAzīz b. Sarāyā al-Ḥillī, in *EI*[2], viii, 801–5.

Heinrichs, W.P., as-Sakkākī, in *EI*[2], viii, 893–4.

Harb, L., Ibn Abī l-Iṣbaʿ, in *EI*[3], first published online: 2017; first print edition 2017–3.

Ibn Abī l-Iṣbaʿ, *Taḥrīr at-taḥbīr fī ṣināʿat aš-šiʿr wa-n-naṯr*, Hg. Ḥ.M. Šaraf, Kairo 1963.

Ibn al-Aṯīr, Ḍiyāʾ ad-Dīn, *al-Maṯal as-sāʾir fī adab al-kātib wa-š-šāʿir*, Hg. K.M.M. ʿAwīḍa, Beirut 1998.

Ibn al-Aṯīr, Naǧm ad-Dīn, *Ǧawhar al-kanz: Talḫīṣ Kanz al-barāʿa fī adawāt ḏawī l-yarāʿa*, ed. M.Z. Salām, Alexandria 1974.

Ibn Mālik, Badr ad-Dīn, *al-Miṣbāḥ fī l-maʿānī wa-l-bayān wa-l-badīʿ*, Hg. Ḥ.ʿA. Yūsuf, Kairo 1989.

Ibn Sinān al-Ḫafāǧī, *Sirr al-faṣāḥa*, Hg. D.Ġ. aš-Šawābika, Kairo 2006.

Ibn Ḥiǧǧa al-Ḥamawī, *Ḫizānat al-adab wa-ġāyat al-arab*, Hg. ʿI. Šaʿītū, 2 Bde., Beirut 1987; Hg. K. Diyāb, 5 Bde., Beirut [2]2005.

Ibn al-Muʿtazz, ʿAbdallāh, *Kitāb al-Badīʿ*, Hg. I. Kratchkowsky, London 1935.

Ibn an-Naqīb, *Muqaddimat Tafsīr Ibn an-Naqīb fī ʿilm al-bayān wa-l-maʿānī wa-l-badīʿ wa-iʿǧāz al-Qurʾān*, ed. Z.S. ʿAlī, Kairo 1995.

Ibn Rašīq, *al-ʿUmda fī ṣināʿat aš-šiʿr wa-naqdihi*, Kairo 1925; *al-ʿUmda fī maḥāsin aš-šiʿr wa-ādābihi*, Hg. M. Qarqazān, Beirut 1988.

Ibn az-Zamlakānī, *at-Tibyān fī ʿilm al-bayān al-muṭliʿ ʿalā iʿǧāz al-Qurʾān*, Hgg. A. Maṭlūb und H. al-Ḥadīṯī, Bagdad 1964.

an-Nuwayrī, *Nihāyat al-arab fī funūn al-adab*, Bd. 7, Hg. ʿA. Būmalḥim, Beirut o.J.

al-Muṭarrizī, *al-Īḍāḥ fī šarḥ Maqāmāt al-Ḥarīrī*, Hg. M.N. ar-Raḥīl, Riad 1402.

al-Qarṭāǧannī, Ḥāzim, *Minhāǧ al-bulaġāʾ wa-sirāǧ al-udabāʾ*, ed. M.Ḥ. Ibn al-Ḫūǧa, Tunis [3]1986.

al-Qazwīnī, Ǧalāl ad-Dīn, *Matn at-Talḫīṣ*, Hg. M.ʿA. Ḫafāǧī, Beirut 1934; *at-Talḫīṣ fī ʿulūm al-balāġa*, Hg. ʿA. al-Barqūqī, Beirut o.J.

al-Qazwīnī, Ǧalāl ad-Dīn, *al-Īḍāḥ fī ʿulūm al-balāġa: al-Maʿānī wa-l-bayān wa-l-badīʿ*, Hg. I. Šams ad-Dīn, Beirut 2003.

Qudāma Ibn Ǧaʿfar, *Kitāb Naqd aš-šiʿr*, Konstantinopel 1302.

al-Qāḍī al-Ǧurǧānī, *al-Wasāṭa bayn al-Mutanabbī wa-ḫuṣūmih*, Hgg. M.A. Ibrāhīm und ʿA.M. al-Biǧāwī, Kairo o.J.

ar-Rāzī, Faḫr ad-dīn, *Nihāyat al-īǧāz fī dirāyat al-iʿǧāz*, Kairo 1317.

ar-Ruʿaynī, Abū Ǧaʿfar, *Ṭirāz al-Ḥulla wa-šifāʾ al-ġulla*, Hg. R. as-Sayyid al-Ǧawharī, Alexandria, o.J.

Simon, U., Badr al-Dīn Ibn Mālik, in *EI*[3], first published online: 2009; first print edition 2009–1.

Smyth, W., Controversy in a tradition of commentary: The academic legacy of al-Sakkākī's *Miftāḥ al-ʿulūm*, in *JAOS* 112, 4 (1992), 589–97.

as-Sakkākī, Y.b.A.B., *Miftaḥ al-ʿulūm*, Hg. N. Zarzūr, 2. Auflage, Beirut 1987.

Stewart, D.J., Ibn Hijjah al-Hamawī, in J.E. Lowry and D.J. Stewart (Hgg.), *Essays in Arabic literary biography 1350–1850*, Wiesbaden 2009, 137–46.

Usāma Ibn Munqiḏ, *al-Badīʿ fī naqd aš-šiʿr*, Hgg. A.A. Badawī u.a., Abu Dhabi o.J.

van Gelder, G.J., Badīʿiyya, in *EI*[3], first published online: 2009; first print edition 2009–4 (94–6).

van Gelder, G.J., Ibn Rashīq, in *EI*[3], first published online: 2018; first print edition 2018–2.

van Lit, L.W.C., Commentary and commentary tradition: The basic terms for understanding Islamic intellectual history, in *MIDEO* 32 (2017), 3–26.

von Hees, Syrinx, Ein Lobgedicht auf den Obersten Staatssekretär zum Anlass eines „house-sitting" – Überschneidungen von Herrschaftshof und Bildungsbürgertum und ihre Reflexion bei an-Nawāǧī, in A. Masarwa und H. Özkan (Hgg.), *The racecourse of literature: an-Nawāǧī and his contemporaries*, Baden-Baden 2020, 213–62.

az-Zanǧānī al-Ḫazraǧī, *Kitāb Miʿyār an-nuẓẓār fī ʿulūm al-ašʿār*, Hg. M.ʿA.R. al-Ḫafāǧī, Kairo o.J.

14

ʿAbd ar-Raḥīm al-Buraʿī: Eine Spurensuche

Ines Weinrich

بالأبرق الفرد أطلال قديمات　　لآل هند عفتهنّ الغمامات
وملعب لعبت هوج الرياح به　　كأنّهم فيه ما ظلّوا ولا باتوا

Auf der einsamen mit Geröll bedeckten Anhöhe sind alte Spuren
von der Sippe Hinds, verwittert vom Regen
Ein Ort, mit dem die Sturmwinde ihr Spiel trieben
als ob sie dort nie abgestiegen wären oder gehaust hätten[1]

Über die Literatur der lange von der Forschung vernachlässigten Jahrhunderte, also der Zeitspanne **A**rabische **L**iteratur **E**lfhundert bis **A**chtzehnhundert (ALEA), wissen wir, nicht zuletzt aufgrund der Forschungen von Thomas Bauer, zwar inzwischen sehr viel mehr als vor einigen Jahrzehnten, doch ist unser Bild weit davon entfernt vollständig zu sein. Als Verfasser obiger Verse ist recht bald der jemenitische Dichter ʿAbd ar-Raḥīm al-Buraʿī identifiziert. Beim Versuch, sich ein näheres Bild von ihm zu machen, fühlt man sich jedoch mehr als einmal wie über verwitterte Spuren gebeugt, die von immer neuen Schichten überlagert werden (fast so vielen, wie es im Arabischen Begriffe für Bodenformen gibt). Der vorliegende Beitrag versteht sich also als Spurensuche zu Leben und Werk des Dichters, und das sowohl in den Gedichten selbst als auch in historischen Quellen und in Sekundärliteratur.

Die Person: Zahlen und Namen

ʿAbd ar-Raḥīm al-Buraʿī ist ein ebenso bekannter wie unbekannter Dichter. Seine Gedichte sind heute buchstäblich in aller Munde. Nicht nur sind sie mir während meiner Feldforschung zu muslimischen Gesängen in Syrien und

1 Pet. 641 fol. 42a; al-Buraʿī, *Dīwān* 2006, 50. Gedichte zitiere ich nach Pet. 641 und dem Druck von 2006; die Divergenz einzelner Handschriften und Drucke wird unten ausführlich behandelt. Die unterschiedlichen Erscheinungsformen des *Dīwān* erfordern in diesem Fall eine Abweichung in der Zitierweise, indem hier jeweils auch das Erscheinungsjahr angegeben wird.

 | DOI:10.1163/9789004521780_016

Libanon begegnet, sondern sie gehören auch in das Repertoire von Prophetenlobsängern (*munšidūn, maddāḥūn*) in Ägypten, Marokko, Palästina, Jemen und Oman.[2] Entsprechend finden sich seine Gedichte auch in zeitgenössischen Sammlungen von Liedtexten, die von ägyptischen und syrischen *munšidūn* benutzt werden, sowie in Sammlungen, die stärker der Dokumentation des benutzten Repertoires als dem täglichen Gebrauch dienen.[3] Auch Yūsuf b. Ismāʿīl an-Nabhānī (st. 1932) hat zwanzig seiner Gedichte in seine vierbändige Sammlung von Prophetenlob aufgenommen.[4] Al-Buraʿīs Gedichte sind überdies häufig in Kompilationen performativer liturgischer Texte – Gedichte, Gebete (*duʿāʾ*), Bittgebete für den Propheten (*aṣ-ṣalāt ʿalā n-nabī*), *mawlid*, *taḏkīr* – enthalten, und dies weit über die arabische Welt hinaus.[5] Es gibt aber auch Anzeichen, dass seine Kompositionen nicht allein auf das Umfeld religiöser Spezialisten beschränkt sind. So werden Verse von ihm als Belegverse in Rhetorikwerken verwendet, und vereinzelt sind Gedichte auch ohne religiösen Kontext online zu finden.[6]

Sucht man jedoch in den einschlägigen arabistischen und islamwissenschaftlichen Nachschlagewerken nach dem Dichter, so steht die dünne Ausbeute durchaus in Diskrepanz zur beschriebenen Verbreitung der Gedichte. Lediglich Carl Brockelmann hat einen kurzen Eintrag zu ihm. Dort ordnet er ihn in das 5./11. Jahrhundert ein („um das Jahr 450/1058 blühte“).[7] Auch die erste wissenschaftlich begleitete Ausgabe seines *Dīwān* bezeichnet al-Buraʿī in der Titelei als Gelehrten des 5./11. Jahrhunderts (*min ʿulamāʾ al-qarn al-ḫāmis*

---

2 Abdel-Malek, *Muḥammad* 30 und Frishkopf, Inshad 77 (dort als al-Burʿī) für Ägypten; Waugh, *Memory* 163 für Marokko; Knappert, Mawlid 213 (dort als al-Barʿī) für Palästina; Dafari, *Ḥumainī* 216 für Jemen; Moustafa und al-Shīdī, Al-Huwāmah 111 für Oman. Zu Syrien außerdem Dalāl, *al-ʿĀlim* 38.

3 Bei ersteren handelt es sich um kleine handliche Formate im preiswerten Pappeinband mit portablem Charakter (z.B. al-Ḥalabī, *Anāšīd*; Anon., *al-Qāmūs*); Dokumentationssammlungen sind aufwendiger in der Gestaltung, häufig größer, schwerer und im Hardcover gebunden (z.B. Abū l-Fatḥ, *al-Mutāḥ*; Abū l-Makārim, *Maǧmūʿat al-madāʾiḥ*; al-Qabbānī, *Ǧāmiʿ*). Alle genannten Sammlungen enthalten Gedichte von al-Buraʿī.

4 An-Nabhānī, *al-Maǧmūʿa*.

5 Neben al-Buraʿī sind hier besonders häufig Gedichte von Yaḥyā b. Yūsuf aṣ-Ṣarṣarī (st. 656/1258) und Šaraf ad-Dīn al-Būṣīrī (st. 694–7/1294–7) enthalten. Siehe für Gedichte von al-Buraʿī, *inter alia*, al-Mālikī, *al-Bāqa* (aus Saudi-Arabien); al-Qāhirī, *Madāʾiḥ* (aus Indien); *Various devotional texts*, British Library EAP466/1/18 (https://eap.bl.uk/archive-file/EAP466-1-18) (aus Kenia).

6 Z.B. Bilgrāmī, *Ṣubḥat* 449, 490–1; https://www.youtube.com/watch?v=GK-tO5HAewQ.

7 *GAL* I, 259, *GALS* I, 459. In einem Nachdruck hat sich ein Zahlendreher eingeschlichen, 1085 anstatt 1058. Während Brockelmann lediglich von einer ungefähren Lebenszeit spricht, wird später häufig 1058 als Sterbejahr genommen.

al-hiǧrī).[8] Die Literaturgeschichte von Ǧurǧī Zaydān, deren Erstdruck 1910–3 erschien, enthält nur einen knappen Satz und keinerlei Datum zu al-Buraʿī. Er ordnet ihn aber insgesamt in die letzte abbasidische Phase und damit unter die Dichter von Mitte 5./11. bis Mitte 7./13. Jahrhundert ein.[9] Die Formulierung „aus dem 5. Jahrhundert" findet sich auch in *al-Maǧmūʿa an-nabhāniyya* sowie in al-Baġdādīs *Hadiyyat al-ʿārifīn*.[10] Die neueren arabischsprachigen Nachschlagewerke geben ein Sterbedatum, das zweieinhalb Jahrhunderte später liegt, nämlich 803/1400–1.[11] Muḥammad Qadrī Dalāl gibt 1495 als Sterbejahr an, das Nachwort eines gedruckten *Dīwān* aus dem Jahr 1994 favorisiert die späte Mamlukenzeit als Lebenszeit, und das Nachwort eines Drucks aus dem Jahr 1967 hält das 10./16. Jahrhundert als Lebenszeit für wahrscheinlich.[12] Tatsächlich ist al-Buraʿī in keinem der bekannten biographischen Lexika der mamlukenzeitlichen Epoche enthalten. Das spricht auf den ersten Blick dafür, dass er tatsächlich später als im 5./11. Jahrhundert gelebt haben mag. Vielleicht war Jemen aber auch zu weit weg von Zentren wie Kairo und Damaskus, so dass Werk und Name nicht dorthin vordrangen, auch nicht in die spätmamlukischen Werke.

Das Datum 803/1400–1 scheint auf ein lokalhistorisches Werk über jemenitische *ṣulaḥāʾ* (fromme und gelehrte Männer) zurückzugehen. Es enthält einen Eintrag unter dem Namen ʿAfīf ad-Dīn ʿAbd ar-Raḥīm b. ʿAlī al-Muhāǧirī.[13] Der Autor, ʿAbd al-Wahhāb b. ʿAbd ar-Raḥmān al-Burayhī, über den nicht viel bekannt ist, starb 904/1499, also nur hundert Jahre nach 803/1400–1, was er als Sterbedatum angibt für die Person, die unser gesuchter al-Buraʿī sein kann.[14] Sein Werk, ediert unter dem Titel *Ṭabaqāt ṣulaḥāʾ al-Yaman al-maʿrūf bi-Tārīḫ al-Burayhī*, ist wie ihm vorangehende Werke anderer jemenitischer Gelehrter nicht chronologisch, sondern nach Regionen angeordnet. Dort führt er den Namen unter *min ahl Buraʿ* an, was die *nisba* al-Buraʿī erklärt. Bei Buraʿ handelt es sich um eine Bergregion in der Tihāma. Im *Tāǧ al-ʿarūs* beschreibt Muḥammad Murtaḍā az-Zabīdī (st. 1205/1791) „Buraʿ" als einen Berg (*ǧabal*) in der Tihāma in der Nähe von Wādī Sihām mit einer Festung, einigen Dörfern und

8 Al-Buraʿī, *Dīwān* 1950.

9 Zaydān, *Tārīḫ* 821, zur Zeitspanne 798.

10 An-Nabhānī, *al-Maǧmūʿa* i, 119; al-Baġdādī, *Hadiyya* 559.

11 Kaḥḥāla, *Muʿǧam* v, 202; az-Ziriklī, *al-Aʿlām* iii, 343; al-Munaǧǧid, *Muʿǧam* 322; Durnayqa, *Muʿǧam* 202; Abū l-Fatḥ, *al-Mutāḥ* ii, 345.

12 Dalāl, *al-ʿĀlim* 38; al-Buraʿī, *Dīwān* 1994, Nachwort 173; al-Buraʿī, *Šarḥ* 300.

13 Al-Burayhī, *Ṭabaqāt* 43–4. Zu einer alternativen Vokalisierung s. u.

14 Lange Zeit war die Zuschreibung des lediglich unter *Tārīḫ al-Burayhī* zirkulierenden Werks widersprüchlich, da die Gelehrtenfamilie Burayhī mehrere Generationen umfasst; zur Identifizierung des Autors siehe die Einleitung des Herausgebers in al-Burayhī, *Ṭabaqāt*, bes. 7–10.

einem Markt. Er erklärt weiterhin, dass die Historiker ihn als *nisba* dem versierten Dichter ʿAbd ar-Raḥīm al-Buraʿī zugeordnet hätten, bekannt für seine Prophetenlobgedichte und hoch geschätzt bei den Menschen seines Heimatorts.[15] Für die Übereinstimmung des in al-Burayhī genannten Namens mit dem hier behandelten Dichter, der ganz offensichtlich derselbe ist, den az-Zabīdī nennt, spricht weiterhin, dass al-Burayhī als Versbeispiel den ersten der eingangs zitierten Verse anführt, der tatsächlich in mehreren Handschriften seines *Dīwān* enthalten ist.[16] Schließlich wird die Übereinstimmung dadurch untermauert, dass al-Buraʿī, der häufig seinen Namen in seine Gedichte einflicht, von sich zuweilen auch als „al-Muhāǧirī" spricht. So findet sich am Ende eines Prophetenlobs folgender Vers:

أزح مِحَن الدارين بعطف منك عن   مولّفها عبد الرحيم المهاجري

Nimm hinweg durch deine Gnade die Plagen des Diesseits und des Jenseits
vom Verfasser ʿAbd ar-Raḥīm al-Muhāǧirī.[17]

Zwar wird al-Burayhī in keinem der genannten arabischsprachigen Nachschlagewerke als Quelle angegeben, wohl aber enthalten sie indirekt einen Verweis auf ihn. Der von ihnen als Beleg genannte *Mulḥaq* des *al-Badr aṭ-ṭāliʿ bi-maḥāsin man baʿd al-qarn at-tāsiʿ* von Muḥammad b. ʿAlī aš-Šawkānī (st. 1250/1834–5), ein auf Jemen zentriertes biographisches Lexikon, wiederholt nämlich nahezu wörtlich den knappen Eintrag zu al-Buraʿī in al-Burayhīs *Ṭabaqāt*. Im *Mulḥaq* lautet der Name leicht abgeändert ʿAbd ar-Raḥīm b. ʿAlī al-Buraʿī al-Hāǧirī al-Yamanī.[18] Es gibt allerdings keinen Verweis auf al-Burayhī, so dass theoretisch auch andere Werke als Quelle in Frage kommen. Übereinstimmend geben al-Burayhī und aš-Šawkānīs *Mulḥaq* den Ort an-Nayyābatayn als Ort seiner Herkunft an. Dort soll al-Buraʿī Recht und Grammatik studiert haben, bis er schließlich selbst unterrichtete und Rechtsgutachten erteilte. Er muss es bereits zu Lebzeiten zu einem bestimmten Bekanntheitsgrad gebracht haben, denn es erreichten ihn Anfragen aus vielen Regionen, und er galt als großer Gelehrter. Nach al-Burayhī hat er seine Heimat nicht verlassen; es gibt

15 Az-Zabīdī, *Tāǧ* xx, 318.

16 Pet. 641 fol. 42[a]; Pet. 649 fol. 47[b]; Riyad fol. 31[b]; Gotha fol. 29[b].

17 Pet. 641 fol. 20[a]; al-Buraʿī, *Dīwān* 2006, 105. Ein weiteres Beispiel findet sich Pet. 641 fol. 83[b]; al-Buraʿī, *Dīwān* 2006, 96.

18 Aš-Šawkānī, *al-Badr* ii, 120. Der *Mulḥaq* ist hier mit neuer Paginierung eingebunden. Der Anhang wurde im Jahr 1348/1929 durch Muḥammad b. Muḥammad b. Yaḥyā b. Zubāra zusammengestellt (*Badr* ii, 1). Die *nisba* al-Yamanī findet sich gelegentlich auch als „al-Yamānī."

allerdings Hinweise darauf, dass er die Pilgerfahrt unternahm und sogar einige Zeit im Ḥiǧāz verbrachte. Die Vita, die Nawwāl Abū l-Fatḥ – nur in einer Fußnote – anführt, trägt stark hagiographische Züge und ist in dieser Hinsicht von nur geringem Nutzen.[19] Doch der Dichter spricht in mindestens einem Gedicht von seiner Pilgerfahrt, und ʿAbd al-Munʿim Ḫafāǧī sieht in einem weiteren Gedicht, das die Sehnsucht nach seinen Kindern thematisiert, einen Hinweis auf einen längeren Aufenthalt im Ḥiǧāz (*muǧāwara*).[20] Mehrere Autoren geben an, er sei bei Yanbuʿ, einem Ort an der Küste zum Roten Meer im heutigen Saudi-Arabien, etwa 200 Kilometer von Medina entfernt, verstorben. Der englische Reisende Eldon Rutter erwähnt die Grabmoschee eines ʿAbd ar-Raḥīm al-Buraʿī, die er 1925 auf dem Weg von Medina nach Yanbuʿ passierte.[21]

Das Vorgehen, auch die Gedichte auf Hinweise auf biographische Daten zu untersuchen, setzt voraus, dass diese auch tatsächlich von al-Buraʿī stammen, was nicht immer zweifelsfrei vorausgesetzt werden kann. Daher sollen zunächst die zahlreichen Ausgaben der unter dem Namen al-Buraʿī zirkulierenden Werke und ihr Verhältnis zueinander beschrieben werden.

Erscheinungsformen des *Dīwān*

Brockelmann verzeichnet 26 Handschriften von al-Buraʿīs *Dīwān* sowie weitere 14 Manuskripte, die einzelne Gedichte von al-Buraʿī enthalten. Zu ergänzen sind eine von Wagner erwähnte Handschrift in der Aḥqāf Bibliothek in Tarīm (Hadramaut) sowie eine Handschrift in Sankt Petersburg.[22] Es ist davon auszugehen, dass durchaus weitere Handschriften existieren. Die älteste unter den mir im Jahr 2020 stark eingeschränkten Forschungsbedingungen zugängliche Handschrift stammt aus dem Jahr 999/1591. Dabei handelt es sich um Peter-

19 Demnach soll er 130 Jahre gelebt haben, neben dem Ḥiǧāz auch Syrien, Irak und den Maghreb zu Studienzwecken bereist und 99 Mal die Pilgerfahrt verrichtet haben (Abū l-Fatḥ, *al-Mutāḥ* ii, 345, Fn. 1). Eine leicht modifizierte Fassung dieser Vita gibt auch Šubayb (*Fann* 152). Beide beziehen sich dabei auf dasselbe Werk, das mir in Deutschland nicht zugänglich war: Ǧawād Murābiṭ, *al-Buraʿī al-Yamanī, aš-šāʿir wa-l-faqīh*, Beirut 1978.

20 Pet. 641 fol. 41ᵃ, fol. 11ᵃ; al-Buraʿī, *Dīwān* 2006, 101, 89; al-Buraʿī, *Dīwān* 1994, Nachwort, 173.

21 Durnayqa, *Muʿǧam* 202; al-Buraʿī, *Dīwān* 1994, Nachwort, 173 (spricht lediglich von „in der Nähe von Medina"); Rutter, *Holy cities* ii, 270.

22 *GAL* i, 259, *GALS* i, 459; Wagner, *Poetics* 299 Fn. 126; Salemann, *Indices* Nr. 741. Al-Munaǧǧid, *Muʿǧam* 322, erwähnt lediglich mehrere frühe Drucke und keine Handschrift, was in Diskrepanz zu den ansonsten zahlreich bei ihm aufgeführten Handschriften von *madīḥ nabawī* steht.

mann I 641 in der Staatsbibliothek Berlin.[23] Sie enthält 85 Gedichte, die thematisch geordnet sind. Wilhelm Ahlwardts ausführliche Beschreibungen erlauben einen vergleichenden Blick auf die übrigen Handschriften:

- Wetzstein 249 enthält dieselben Gedichte, deren Reihenfolge im zweiten Teil von Pet. 641 abweicht. Die Abschrift wurde im Jahr 1080/1669 von einem Muḥammad zum eigenen Gebrauch getätigt.
- Wetzstein 247 stimmt im Anfang mit Pet. 641 überein und enthält etwa 4.000 Verse; 19 Blätter fehlen. Die Abschrift stammt aus dem Jahr 1091/1680.
- Landberg 996 stimmt in Anfang und Ende mit Wetzstein 247 überein und stammt aus dem Jahr 1067/1656.
- Petermann I 649 beginnt wie Pet. I 641, weicht aber ansonsten stark ab, indem einige Gedichte daraus nicht vorhanden sind, andere enthaltene Gedichte wiederum befinden sich nicht in Pet. 641. Die Handschrift wurde 1129/1717 verfasst.
- Wetzstein 248, 1 bezeichnet Ahlwardt als „Bruchstück" des *Dīwān*, dessen Reihenfolge sich in etwa an Wetzstein 249 orientiert. Am Ende fehlen acht Blätter; er datiert die Abschrift auf ca. 1750.

Der Eintrag Nr. 7618 führt sieben Handschriften auf, die eines oder mehrere Gedichte von al-Buraʿī enthalten, sowie Querverweise zu weiteren Handschriften mit denselben Gedichten.[24] Es würde den Rahmen dieses Beitrags sprengen, sämtliche bekannte Handschriften seiner Gedichte zu vergleichen. Die auf Ahlwardt beruhende Schilderung vermittelt einen ersten Eindruck von den unterschiedlichen Erscheinungsformen von Handschriften mit dem Titel *Dīwān al-Buraʿī*. Es gibt allerdings auch ein Kontinuum: die meisten Handschriften sprechen übereinstimmend von ʿAbd ar-Raḥīm al-Buraʿī im Titel, so dass dies der gängige Name gewesen sein muss, unter dem seine Gedichte zirkulierten.

Im 19. Jahrhundert wurden die Werke von al-Buraʿī vielfach gedruckt. Allein die in Brockelmann aufgeführten Exemplare seines *Dīwān* umfassen Lithographien aus Kairo (1282/1865, 1288/1871) und Bombay (1291/1874, 1301/1884) sowie acht Drucke aus Kairo zwischen den Jahren 1280/1863 und 1319/1901. Zu ergänzen sind unter anderem die von J.A. Dafari erwähnten Drucke[25] sowie die Drucke Mumbai 1875 und Bombay 1884, die sich in der British Library befinden. Von diesen frühen Drucken liegen mir drei vor (Mumbai 1875, Kairo 1880, Bombay 1884). Sie enthalten keinerlei Angabe zu einer Druckvorlage.

23 Ahlwardt 7616 (*Verzeichniss* vi, 589–90), dort ebenfalls mit Sterbedatum um 450/1058.

24 Ahlwardt 7617 und 7618 (*Verzeichniss* vi, 590–91).

25 Dafari, *Ḥumainī* 215.

In der ersten Hälfte des 20. Jahrhunderts erschien eine Ausgabe des *Dīwān* durch den Azhar-Gelehrten Ḥāfiẓ Ḥusayn al-Masʿūdī. Mir liegt davon nur die zweite Auflage von 1950 vor.[26] Dort ist kein Hinweis auf eine Handschrift enthalten. *Šarḥ* und *ḍabṭ*, die in der Titelei als Tätigkeiten des Herausgebers genannt werden, scheinen sich lediglich auf die Vokalisierung des Textes und die Erklärung ausgewählter Lexeme in Fußnoten zu beziehen. Gelegentlich erfolgen Verweise auf Koranverse oder Erläuterungen zur Morphologie, aber nur selten finden sich mehr als ein bis zwei Fußnoten pro Seite. Al-Masʿūdī erklärt, er habe in der zweiten Auflage vor allem die Verse kommentiert, die in der ersten ohne Anmerkungen geblieben waren.[27]

Parallel dazu erschienen immer wieder Drucke, die nicht diese Ausgabe als Vorlage nahmen, sondern wie die Drucke aus dem 19. Jahrhundert lediglich die Gedichte abdrucken (z. B. al-Buraʿī, *Dīwān* 1994). Auch mit der 1967 in vierter Auflage erschienenen und als *Šarḥ* (Kommentar) betitelten Ausgabe liegt letztlich solch ein Fall vor.[28] Hier beschränkt sich der Kommentar ebenfalls auf gelegentliche Fußnoten, die in unterschiedlicher Dichte anfallen. Sie sind nicht identisch mit den Anmerkungen durch al-Masʿūdī; ein namentlicher Hinweis auf Personen, die für diese Ausgabe verantwortlich zeichnen, fehlt ebenso wie eine Angabe zur Druckvorlage.

Im Jahr 2006 schließlich erschien eine weitere Ausgabe, die auf einem Manuskript der Azhariyya Bibliothek in Kairo beruht.[29] Der Herausgeber, ʿĀṣim Ibrāhīm al-Kayyālī, macht allerdings keinerlei Angaben zu seiner Tätigkeit oder zur Handschrift; sein Vorwort beschränkt sich darauf, die Bedeutung al-Buraʿīs als Mystikers hervorzuheben, sowie auf einige Zeilen zu seinem Leben. Hier schreibt er lediglich, dass „die meisten“ darin übereinstimmen, al-Buraʿī sei 803/1400 (sic) gestorben, allerdings gebe es abweichende Meinungen.[30] Dass das Manuskript der Azhariyya Bibliothek die Vorlage zum Druck bildete, wird lediglich durch den Abdruck einiger seiner Seiten als Faksimile ersichtlich.[31] Dort ist eine Widmung mit dem Datum Ǧumādā I 1200/1786 zu erkennen.

Um meine Einordnung des Dichters nicht auf eine einzige Handschrift basieren zu müssen, habe ich eine Auswahl an Handschriften und Drucken getroffen, auf der die folgenden Ausführungen basieren. Diese umfassen

26 Al-Buraʿī, *Dīwān* 1950; nach Šubayb, *Fann* 154 Fn. 1, erschien die erste Auflage 1934.

27 Al-Buraʿī, *Dīwān* 1950, 4.

28 Al-Buraʿī, *Šarḥ*.

29 Al-Buraʿī, *Dīwān* 2006.

30 Al-Buraʿī, Dīwān 2006, Vorwort 3–8.

31 al-Maktaba al-Azhariyya, Adab 5752 (ʿāmm), 62371 (ḫāṣṣ): laut dem Stempel der ersten Seite.

- Pet. 641, verfasst 999/1591[32]
- Pet. 649, verfasst 1129/1717
- Riyad 149, verfasst 1129/1717
- Gotha Hs. Orient. A 2239, ohne Jahr
- Druck Mumbai 1875
- Druck Kairo 1880
- Druck Bombay 1884
- Druck Kairo 1950
- Šarḥ Kairo 1967
- Druck Beirut 1994
- Druck Beirut 2006 (= Azhariyya, geschrieben vor 1200/1786)

Die Handschrift Pet. 641 besteht aus 118 Folios und enthält 85 Gedichte. Vorne mit eingebunden sind einige vermutlich vormals leere Seiten, die zahlreiche Lese- und Besitzvermerke aus dem 12./18. und 13./19. Jahrhundert sowie drei zusätzliche Gedichte in anderer, ungelenker Schrift enthalten. Die Gedichte sind unvokalisiert, deutlich geschrieben und mit Überschriften in Rot versehen. Auch die Halbverse sind durch Trennzeichen (drei Punkte oder geschwungene Striche) in Rot abgeteilt, einige Gedichte sind auch zu Beginn und Ende jeder Zeile so gerahmt. Der *Dīwān* beginnt mit einer kurzen Einleitung bestehend aus Gotteslob, erweitertem Glaubensbekenntnis und Segensbitte für den Propheten und seine Gefährten. Der charakteristische erste Satz ist auch in einigen anderen Handschriften vorhanden, nämlich Pet. 649, Riyad und Azhariyya:

الحمد لله الذي اختصّ حبيبه الأسنى[33] بمقام قاب قوسين أو أدنى * وقرن اسمه الشريف بأعظم أسمائه الحسنى *

> Preis sei Gott, der seinen strahlenden Geliebten mit dem Rang von zwei Bogenlängen oder näher ausgezeichnet hat[34] * Und seinen ehrwürdigen Namen mit dem großartigsten Seiner schönen Namen verknüpft hat *

Dann folgt hier der Hinweis auf den *Dīwān*, der in einem einzigen Satz die Programmatik seiner Anordnung erläutert, nämlich eine dreiteilige Gliederung in Prophetenlob, an Gott gerichtete Gedichte sowie Gedichte, die er im Austausch

---

32 Nahezu identisch mit Pet. 641 ist die Handschrift Paris 3113, verfasst 1025/1616. Sie wird daher nicht in die ausführlichen Beschreibungen aufgenommen.

33 *Al-asnā* fehlt in Pet. 641.

34 Ein Verweis auf Koran 53:9, wo Muḥammad bis auf etwa zwei Bogenlängen Entfernung Gott nahe sein durfte, um mit ihm zu kommunizieren.

mit seinen Kollegen und mystischen Gefährten schrieb: *fa-hāḏā dīwānun laṭīfun ǧāmiʿun li-mā qālahu š-šayḫu ʿAbdu r-Raḥīmi l-Buraʿiyyu r yamtadiḥu fīhi sayyidanā Muḥammadan ṣ wa-baʿḍi tawassulātin ilāhiyyātin yatawassalu bihā ilā mawlāhu wa-baʿḍi qaṣāʾida fī l-waʿẓi wa-yatlū ḏālika qaṣāʾidu fī madḥi s-sādati ṣ-ṣūfiyya r.*

Der Teil mit Prophetenlob – er wird am Ende als *nabawiyyāt* bezeichnet (fol. 68ᵇ–69ᵃ) – enthält 44 Gedichte. Ihm folgt ein verhältnismäßig kurzer Teil (bis fol. 80ᵇ) mit zwölf Gedichten, die als *ilāhiyyāt wa-t-tawassulāt* bezeichnet werden. Der dritte Teil umfasst 28 Gedichte, bezeichnet als *qaṣāʾid ṣūfiyya* (fol. 80ᵇ–81ᵃ). Den Abschluss bildet eine *qaṣīda*, die der Dichter während seiner Krankheit kurz vor seinem Tod verfasste (*Lī fī nawālika yā mawlāya āmālū*, fol. 117ᵃ).

Der erste Teil beginnt mit folgendem Gedicht: *A min taḏakkuri ahli l-bāni wa-l-bānī / am min tabadduli ǧīrānin bi-ǧīrānī.* Hier sticht sofort die frappierende Ähnlichkeit mit al-Būṣīrīs Mantelgedicht (*Qaṣīdat al-Burda*) ins Auge, und darauf wird noch zu kommen sein. Die Prophetenlobgedichte werden in der Regel nicht durch besondere Überschriften eingeleitet, sondern zumeist durch *yamdaḥuhu.* Neben gängigen Themen wie Lob, Verweis auf Wunder (*muʿǧizāt*), Dank, Liebe und Bitte um Beistand sind Gedichte enthalten, die Mekka und Medina zum Thema haben und als Sehnsuchtsgedichte (*tašawwuq*) gewertet werden können (z. B. fol. 14ᵇ; fol. 69ᵃ).[35] Ein Gedicht wurde anlässlich der Genesung seines Sohnes nach schwerer Krankheit verfasst (fol. 45ᵃ), ein anderes als Bitte um die Genesung seines Sohnes (fol. 46ᵃ).

Die unter *ilāhiyyāt* aufgeführten Gedichte im zweiten Teil umfassen Themen wie die Bitte um Vergebung, das Eingeständnis von Schuld und Fehlerhaftigkeit, Selbsttadel, Preis und Dank für erwiesene Gnade und Aufruf zu Demut. Er schließt mit drei Mahngedichten (*fī l-waʿẓ*) ab.

Im dritten Teil ist jedes der Gedichte einer Person zugeordnet, eingeleitet in der Regel durch *qāla fī* oder *yamdaḥu.* Es handelt sich um Lob seiner Gefährten sowie überregional bekannter Gelehrter und Mystiker. Mit einigen von ihnen pflegte er regelmäßig Austausch (*muʿātaba wa-murāsala,* fol. 103ᵃ). Zuweilen enthalten sie auch Tadel oder Entschuldigung. Die genannten Personen werden als *faqīh, ṣāliḥ, šayḫ,* selten als *faqīr* oder *al-ʿārif bi-llāh* bezeichnet. Die Namen sind nicht immer eindeutig einer historischen Person zuzuordnen. Der überwiegende Teil verweist auf ein jemenitisches Umfeld. Es sind Namen loka-

35 Zum Sehnsuchts-Topos in der Prophetenlobdichtung siehe Diem und Schöller, *Living* ii, 56–8; Makkī, *al-Madāʾiḥ* 119–24; Muḥammad, *al-Madāʾiḥ* 171–85, 316–9; ʿUmrānī, *al-Madāʾiḥ* 126–34.

ler Persönlichkeiten aus Familien, die in der Tihāma und besonders in Zabīd ansässig sind, wie die Ahdal oder Nahārī Familie.[36]

Die Handschrift Pet. 649 enthält 69 Gedichte auf 123 Blättern. Hier fehlen die Überschriften wie auch sämtliche Zusatzzeichen zu Schmuck oder Abtrennung von Halbversen. Die dreiteilige Struktur klingt entfernt an, doch die Vorlage der Abschrift scheint unvollständig gewesen zu sein. Das würde die kryptische Zwischenüberschrift erklären, die zum dritten Teil überleitet und mitten im Satz beginnt (fol. 76[b]). Dort ist von den *ilāhiyyāt* die Rede, obgleich diese hier weitgehend fehlen. Der *Dīwān* beginnt ebenfalls mit *A min taḏakkuri ahli l-bāni wa-l-bānī*, und der erste Teil stimmt bis auf das Fehlen einiger Gedichte weitgehend mit Pet. 641 überein. Von den *ilāhiyyāt* aber sind lediglich Selbsttadel und *waʿẓ*, d.h. der letzte Part aus Pet. 641, enthalten. Der dritte Teil stimmt dann wieder bis auf einige Lücken mit Pet. 641 überein. Doch am Ende fehlt das Abschlussgedicht (*Lī fī nawālika yā mawlāya āmālū*), stattdessen folgen sieben Gedichte, die in keiner anderen Handschrift und keinem Druck enthalten sind.

Die Handschrift Riyad besteht aus 60 Blättern und enthält 57 Gedichte, ohne Vokalisierung und mit Überschriften in Rot. Hier fehlen sämtliche Gedichte aus dem dritten Teil, während die Gedichte des ersten und zweiten Teils nahezu vollständig mit Pet. 641 übereinstimmen. Am Ende ist ein weiteres Gedicht angefügt, welches nicht in Pet. 641 und 649 enthalten ist: *Yā rāḥilīna ilā Minā bi-qiyādī.*

Die Handschrift Gotha enthält nur 29 Gedichte, ebenfalls unvokalisiert und mit Überschriften in Rot. Die Einleitung beginnt nicht wie in den übrigen Handschriften, und der *Dīwān* wird hier etwas diffus als bestehend aus Gotteslob, Prophetenlob, Mystik und Anderem bezeichnet (*minhā ilāhiyyātun wa-minhā nabawātun* (sic) *wa-minhā ṣūfiyyātun wa-minhā ġayru ḏālika*) (fol. 1[b]). Der *Dīwān* eröffnet mit einem prägnanten Vertreter der *ilāhiyyāt*, *Taǧallat li-waḥdāniyyati l-ḥaqqi anwārū*. Dann folgt eine Auswahl von Gedichten aus dem ersten und zweiten Teil, die in ihrer Abfolge mit Pet. 641 weitgehend übereinstimmen. Auch hier fehlt der dritte Teil, was in Diskrepanz zur Einleitung steht, in der *ṣūfiyyāt* angekündigt werden. Am Ende befindet sich das Gedicht *Lī fī nawālika yā mawlāya āmālū*, welches als das letzte Gedicht des *Dīwān* bezeichnet wird. Doch hier wechselt die Handschrift, und angefügt wird in ungelenker Schrift *Laka l-ḥamdu ḥamdan nastaliḏḏu bihī ḏikrā*, welches nicht in Pet. 641 und 649, wohl aber in den meisten anderen hier besprochenen *Dīwān*-Versionen vorhanden ist.

---

36 Ho, *Graves*; Voll, al-Ahdal; sowie entsprechende Einträge in al-Burayhī, *Ṭabaqāt*; al-ʿAydarūs, *an-Nūr*.

Die Ausgabe durch al-Masʿūdī enthält 92 Gedichte, die voll vokalisiert sind. Sie beginnt mit *Taǧallat li-waḥdāniyyati l-ḥaqqi anwārū*, und hier ist die dreiteilige Anordnung nur in Ansätzen vorhanden. Zwar ist die ungefähre Abfolge *ilāhiyyāt* /*nabawiyyāt* / *ṣūfiyyāt* zu erkennen, doch sind die Gedichte der drei Sektionen aus Pet. 641 immer mal wieder vermischt. Das letzte Gedicht ist *Yā rāḥilīna ilā Minā bi-qiyādī*, mit dem Zusatz „mit diesem Gedicht endet der *Dīwān* (*wa-qad ḫutima bihā d-dīwān*)."

Der als *šarḥ* bezeichnete Druck von 1967 enthält 90 Gedichte. Er beginnt mit Gotteslob und endet mit den Mahngedichten, gefolgt von *Yā rāḥilīna ilā Minā bi-qiyādī* und *Lī fī nawālika yā mawlāya āmālū*. In den Gedichten dazwischen schimmert gelegentlich die Reihenfolge von Pet. 641 durch. Tatsächlich findet sich auf Seite 199 eine Zwischenüberschrift, die das Ende der *ilāhiyyāt* (hier *qaṣāʾid rabbāniyya* genannt) und *nabawiyyāt* anzeigt und den letzten Teil als *qaṣāʾid ṣūfiyya* ankündigt.

Der Druck Beirut 1994 enthält 89 Gedichte ohne Einleitung und ohne Vokalisierung, Er beginnt mit *Taǧallat li-waḥdāniyyati l-ḥaqqi anwārū* und endet wie Pet. 641 mit *Lī fī nawālika yā mawlāya āmālū*. *Ilāhiyyāt* und *nabawiyyāt* sind vermischt, dafür ist der dritte Teil relativ stabil. Dieser Druck hat vor allem zu den *ilāhiyyāt* und *nabawiyyāt*, die in den Handschriften nur knapp eingeleitet werden, ausführliche Überschriften, bei denen nicht hervorgeht, woher sie stammen.

Die Ausgabe von 2006 schließlich enthält 97 Gedichte. Die Einleitung beginnt wie in den vorgestellten Handschriften, verweist dann aber wie Pet. 649 und Riyad nur auf „Prophetenlob und Anderes" (*al-qaṣāʾid an-nabawiyya wa-ġayruhā*). Die Gedichte sind vokalisiert und im Druck anders angeordnet als in der Handschrift, nämlich nach Reimbuchstaben. Die Handschrift beginnt mit *Ḫalli l-ġarāma li-ṣabbin damʿuhū damuhū*, einem Prophetenlob. Die Zwischenüberschrift, die das Ende der *qaṣāʾid rabbāniyya* und *nabawiyya* anzeigt und die *ṣūfiyya* und Selbsttadel ankündigt, wurde kurioserweise beibehalten (S. 99). Diese Zwischenüberschrift ergibt bei Anordnung nach Reim natürlich keinerlei Sinn; sie zeigt aber, dass die Vorlage thematisch angeordnet war.

Die Drucke Mumbai 1875 und Bombay 1884 stimmen hinsichtlich Anordnung, Zwischentitel und Überschriften überein, lediglich das Layout weist leichte Unterschiede auf. Die Gedichte sind unvokalisiert, eine Einleitung fehlt, und die Überschriften weichen zum Teil ab von Pet. 641. Beide enthalten einen Anhang mit einem Prophetenlobgedicht, das unter dem Namen *al-Qaṣīda al-ǧinniyya* bekannt sei. Der Druck Kairo 1880 ist dagegen vokalisiert. Er hat weder Einleitung noch Anhang, doch ist sein Inhalt ansonsten im großen und ganzen identisch mit den beiden anderen Drucken.

Alle drei Drucke enthalten 89 Gedichte und beginnen mit *Taǧallat li-waḥdāniyyati l-ḥaqqi anwārū*. Die Reihenfolge der Gedichte ist insgesamt anders als in den beschriebenen Handschriften, aber die bekannte Einteilung ist noch zu erkennen, da viel Prophetenlob zusammenhängend hintereinander erscheint und am Ende die Gedichte für die *ṣulaḥā'* weitgehend *en bloc* auftauchen. Am Ende stehen die drei Mahngedichte und ein Prophetenlob, bevor der *Dīwān* wie Pet. 641 mit *Lī fī nawālika yā mawlāya āmālū* abschließt.

Der Vergleich der hier benutzten Erscheinungsformen des *Dīwān* zeigt durchaus mehr auf als lediglich die Erkenntnis, dass alle Versionen sich voneinander unterscheiden. Wir können festhalten: Die Handschrift Pet. 641, zugleich die älteste der zugänglichen Handschriften, ist am klarsten in der Anordnung und deren Präsentation. Hier werden die *nabawiyyāt*, die *ilāhiyyāt* und die *ṣūfiyyāt* deutlich voneinander abgetrennt und benannt. Diese Einteilung lässt sich in unterschiedlichen Graden auch in anderen Handschriften erkennen. Sie liegt im großen und ganzen Pet. 649 zugrunde, auch wenn dort insgesamt 22 Gedichte aus allen drei Teilen fehlen und neun Gedichte zusätzlich enthalten sind. Die Handschrift Riyad enthält nur *nabawiyyāt* und *ilāhiyyāt*, die in Reihenfolge weitgehend mit Pet. 641 übereinstimmen. Auch der Auszug Gotha enthält nur *nabawiyyāt* und *ilāhiyyāt*, beginnt allerdings nicht mit *A min taḏakkuri ahli l-bāni wa-l-bānī* (Prophetenlob) wie die bisher genannten Handschriften, sondern mit *Taǧallat li-waḥdāniyyati l-ḥaqqi anwārū* (Gotteslob). Dieses Gedicht steht auch in den frühen Drucken (Mumbai 1875, Kairo 1880, Bombay 1884) sowie den Drucken von 1950, 1967 und 1994 an erster Stelle. Aufschlussreich in diesem Zusammenhang ist eine weitere recht frühe Handschrift aus dem Jahr 1038/1629, welche Otto Loth beschreibt. Sie hat dieselbe dreiteilige Anordnung, nur dass hier die *ilāhiyyāt* den ersten Teil ausmachen, gefolgt von den *nabawiyyāt* und *ṣūfiyyāt*.[37] Diese Befunde verweisen auf eine relativ stabile Konzeption des *Dīwān* in drei Teilen, die in zwei Varianten im Umlauf war, einmal mit Prophetenlob am Beginn und einmal mit Gotteslob am Beginn. Die thematische Dreiteilung lässt sich auch in späteren Handschriften erkennen, auch wenn es gelegentlich zu Aufweichungen in der Anordnung gekommen ist.

Darüber hinaus legt der Vergleich nahe, dass al-Buraʿī nicht selbst einen *Dīwān* zusammengestellt hat. Darauf deuten auch die Formulierungen „*mā wuǧida*" und die Tatsache, dass spätere Handschriften immer wieder Gedichte aufweisen, die nicht in früheren enthalten sind. Dabei kann es sich natürlich um fälschliche Zuordnungen handeln, doch müssten in diesem Fall auch die Verse, die Verweise auf Name oder geographische Herkunft enthalten,

---

37 Loth, *Catalogue* 239.

gefälscht worden sein (s.u.). Vielmehr scheinen seine Anhänger oder Schüler die Gedichte gesammelt und verbreitet zu haben. Wer eine Handschrift in die Hand bekam und noch zusätzlich ein Gedicht wusste, hat es angefügt, wie im Fall von *Yā rāḥilīna ilā Minā bi-qiyādī* am Ende der Abschrift mit der Anmerkung versehen, dass es noch diese großartige *qaṣīda* aus der Feder al-Buraʿīs gebe, oder im Fall von *Laka l-ḥamdu ḥamdan nastaliḏḏu bihī ḏikrā*, das in anderer Schrift nach dem eigentlichen Abschlussgedicht angefügt wurde.[38] Alle Handschriften und Drucke zeigen überdies einen hohen Variantenreichtum in den einzelnen Gedichten auf; dabei handelt es sich um den Austausch einzelner Lexeme oder schlichtweg um Fehler.

Reihenfolge: (1) *nabawiyyāt (erstes Gedicht A min taḏakkur)* (2) *ilāhiyyāt* (3) *ṣūfiyyāt*
Pet. 641; Paris 3113; Pet. 649 (von *ilāhiyyāt* nur Selbsttadel und *waʿẓ*); Riyad (ohne *ṣūfiyyāt*)
nach Ahlwardt auch Wetzstein 249, 247 (unvoll.), 248 (unvoll.); Landberg 996

Reihenfolge: (1) *ilāhiyyāt (erstes Gedicht Taǧallat)* (2) *nabawiyyāt* (3) *ṣūfiyyāt*
India Office (nach Loth); Gotha (ohne *ṣūfiyyāt*); Drucke 1875; 1880; 1884; 1950; 1967 grob; 1994 grob
(alle Drucke mit unterschiedlichen Abweichungen in der Reihenfolge)

Der *mawlid*-Text

Abschließend seien einige Worte zum *mawlid* gesagt, dem nach bisherigem Forschungsstand neben dem *Dīwān* einzigen anderen erhaltenen Werk von al-Buraʿī. Brockelmann verzeichnet keine Handschrift von al-Buraʿīs *mawlid*, sondern lediglich einen Kairoer Druck von 1280/1863.[39] Weitere Drucke aus dem späten 19. Jahrhundert werden von Dafari und al-Kayyālī erwähnt.[40] Ahmed Salmi führt einen al-Barʿī aus dem 5./11. Jahrhundert als Verfasser von *mawlidiyya* Gedichten auf.[41] Dies beruht anscheinend auf einer Gleichsetzung von *mawlidiyya* als Gedichtform und *mawlid*, prosimetrischen kürzeren Werken mit der Geburt und frühen Lebensspanne Muḥammads im Zentrum. Eine *mawlidiyya*, ein Gedicht, das anlässlich der Geburt komponiert und zum Jah-

38 Riyad fol. 59[b]; Gotha fol. 47[a].
39 *GALS* i, 459.
40 Dafari, *Ḥumainī* 90; al-Buraʿī, *Dīwān* 2006, Vorwort 8.
41 Salmi, Mawlidiyya.

restag der Geburt feierlich vorgetragen wurde und im engeren Sinne der Definition in das Milieu der andalusischen und nordafrikanischen Fürstenhöfe des 8./14. bis 10./16. Jahrhundert fällt, ist im Werk von al-Buraʿī nicht verzeichnet.[42] Zwar besteht ein Großteil seiner Gedichte aus Prophetenlob, aber keines wurde explizit anlässlich des Prophetengeburtstages verfasst. Vielmehr nehmen Nachtreise und Himmelfahrt (*al-isrāʾ wa-l-miʿrāǧ*) einen deutlich prominenteren Rang als *mawlid* in den Gedichten ein.

Von al-Buraʿīs *mawlid* liegt mir ein Druck aus Kairo um das Jahr 1880 vor,[43] bei dem es sich um eine ähnliche Ausgabe wie bei Brockelmann erwähnt zu handeln scheint, denn beide tragen den Zusatz *aš-šahīr bi-l-ʿArūs*. Dieser Namenszusatz, „bekannt als [*Mawlid*] *al-ʿArūs*," verweist auf die Problematik vieler *mawlid*-Texte vor allem aus der Phase vom späten 6./12. bis ins 8./14. Jahrhundert, als die ersten kürzeren, zur Lesung in einer Sitzung geeigneten Texte entstanden.[44] Besonders populäre Texte unter ihnen zeichnen sich durch eine Einleitung in Kunstprosa (*saǧʿ*), ein unmittelbar gestaltetes Narrativ der Ereignisse vor und nach der Geburt ohne erklärende oder Details diskutierende Zusätze und eine hohe Frequenz von Gedichten aus. Dabei kommt es auch zu Überschneidungen und Erweiterungen einzelner Texte, die ihrerseits bereits vorliegendes Material wie Prophetenbiographien (*siyar*) und Zusammenstellungen über die Eigenschaften des Propheten und Beweise seiner Prophetenschaft (*šamāʾil, ḫaṣāʾiṣ, faḍāʾil, dalāʾil*) verarbeiten oder zitieren. Auch scheinen besonders beliebte Gedichte zwischen einzelnen Texten gewandert zu sein. Wir haben es hier also mit fluiden Texten zu tun, bei denen eine Autorenschaft nicht immer eindeutig zu bestimmen ist, respektive mit Texten, die über die Jahrhunderte nicht stabil bleiben.

Einer davon trägt den Titel *Mawlid al-ʿArūs* und wird dem hanbalitischen Gelehrten Ibn al-Ǧawzī (st. 597/1200) zugeschrieben.[45] Dass die Kairoer Drucke den Zusatz *aš-šahīr bi-l-ʿArūs* tragen, legt eine Verwechslung beider Texte nahe. Dass al-Buraʿīs *mawlid* von einem Kopisten oder Druckverantwortlichen mit *Mawlid al-ʿArūs* gleichgesetzt wurde, ist nicht weiter verwunderlich, da beide Texte sich in Aufbau, Stil und hinsichtlich der verwendeten Gedichtformen ähneln. Umgekehrt nämlich führt Ahlwardt zwei Manuskripte mit Ibn al-Ǧawzī als Verfasser auf, die in weiten Passagen mit dem frühen, al-Buraʿī zugeschriebenen Druck sowie einem Abdruck von „Mawlid al-Buraʿī" in einer zeitgenössischen Sammlung von *mawlid*-Texten übereinstimmen.[46]

42 Zu *mawlid*-Texten siehe Katz, *Birth*; zur *mawlidiyya* Weinrich, Mawlidiyya.

43 Al-Buraʿī, *Mawlid ar-rasūl*.

44 Zu dieser Phase und ihren Texten siehe Katz, *Birth* 6–62.

45 Katz, *Birth* 51–3; Ibn al-Ǧawzī, *Mawlid*.

46 Ahlwardt, *Verzeichniss* ix, 114–5; al-Buraʿī, *Mawlid ar-rasūl*; al-Buraʿī, Mawlid.

Beide Texte, *Mawlid al-Buraʿī* und *Mawlid al-ʿArūs*, sind trotz aller Ähnlichkeiten aber keinesfalls identisch.[47] Die tatsächliche Autorenschaft von al-Buraʿī kann an dieser Stelle nicht ausführlich diskutiert werden. Die Tatsache, dass einige Gedichte aus al-Buraʿīs *Dīwān* prominent in einem *mawlid*-Text vertreten sind, scheint in jedem Fall ausgereicht zu haben, dass dieser unter dem Namen al-Buraʿī zirkulierte und mindestens bis ins 20. Jahrhundert hinein auch in Gebrauch war.[48]

Die Gedichte im *Dīwān*: Formen und Themen

Bei den Gedichten handelt es sich überwiegend um Langgedichte in *qaṣīda*-Form. Die Länge liegt bis auf wenige Ausnahmen deutlich über 20 Versen pro Gedicht; durchschnittlich sind es etwa 60 Verse. Viele haben um die 40 oder um die 80 Verse, das längste Gedicht hat 118 Verse. Einige wenige Gedichte sind Vierzeiler oder Sechszeiler, wobei hier auffällt, dass diese nicht in allen hier verwendeten Handschriften enthalten sind. Dazu zählt beispielsweise *Ǧawāmiʿu l-ḫayri fī d-dārayni tābiʿatun*, eine Ermahnung zu Gehorsam gegenüber Koran und Sunna, die laut Überschrift dem, der sie befolgt, zur Glückseligkeit verhilft und der in einer Version geradezu apotropäische Funktionen zugewiesen wird: „ihm soll nicht länger Schlimmes widerfahren, weder im Diesseits noch im Jenseits“ (*wa-kafāhu šarrahimā*).[49] Al-Buraʿīs Autorenschaft solcher Verse ist nicht auszuschließen, kann aber hier auch nicht bewiesen werden.

Aus den Gedichten stechen drei Langgedichte in *muḫammas*-Form hervor.[50] Bei zweien davon handelt es sich um Prophetenlob, das dritte ist ein Lobgedicht auf einen Yaḥyā b. Aḥmad al-Ahdal. Al-Buraʿī hat darüber hinaus einen *taḫmīs* auf Verse von Muḥammad b. ʿUmar an-Nahārī verfasst.[51] Bei den strophischen Prophetenlobgedichten besteht der fünfte Halbvers jeweils gleichbleibend aus einer Aufforderung zum Bittgebet für den Propheten (*taṣliya*):

47 Beide Texte werden ausführlich im Rahmen meines von der DFG finanzierten Projekts „*mawlid*-Texte aus dem 13. bis 18. Jahrhundert: Prophetenfrömmigkeit als rituelles Ereignis?“ (Referenznummer 389265477) behandelt.

48 Dafari, *Ḥumainī* 216; Knappert, Mawlid 213.

49 Al-Buraʿī, *Dīwān* 2006, 195.

50 Ich benutze *muḫammas* in Abgrenzung zu *taḫmīs* als allgemeine Bezeichnung für ein Gedicht mit fünfzeiligen Strophen und *taḫmīs* für die poetische Erweiterung einer *qaṣīda* durch das Einfügen von drei weiteren Halbversen pro Vers.

51 Al-Buraʿī, *Dīwān* 2006, 101 (nicht in Pet. 641). Der Herausgeber von al-Burayhīs *Ṭabaqāt* erwähnt einen Muḥammad b. ʿUmar an-Nahārī, der 747/1346–7 starb und damit gut der Verfasser jener Verse sein könnte (al-Burayhī, *Ṭabaqāt* 70 Fn. 6).

بمحمّد خطر المحامد يعظم وعقود تيجان القبول تنظّم
وله الشفاعة والمقام الأعظم يوم القلوب لدى الحناجر كظّم
فبحقّه صلّوا عليه وسلّموا

Durch Muḥammad wird die Bedeutsamkeit der Lobpreisungen gewaltig
und die Krone der Gunst wird mit Perlen versehen
Ihm sind Fürsprache und der höchste Rang zuteil
am Tage, da die Herzen der Gläubigen in banger Erwartung des Urteils verharren[52]
Um seiner Wahrheit willen, sprecht das Bittgebet und grüßt ihn[53]

Das zweite, etwas schlichter in der Sprache, beginnt folgendermaßen:

أعلمت من ركب البراق عتيما وتلاه جبريل الأمين نديما
حتّى سما فوق السماء قدوما ودنا فكلّم ربّه تكليما
صلّوا عليه وسلّموا تسليما

Weißt du, wer in tiefschwarzer Nacht auf Burāq ritt
gefolgt von Ǧibrīl, dem Vertrauten, als Begleiter
Bis er schließlich hoch über dem Himmel stand,
nahe war und mit seinem Herrn sprach
Sprecht das Bittgebet für ihn und grüßt ihn[54]

Diese Formen fallen im Repertoire von al-Buraʿī zwar auf, sind in ihrer Form aber insgesamt nicht außergewöhnlich. Strophische Formen mit einer *taṣliya* als Kehrvers sind auch aus Andalusien und Nordafrika belegt. Al-Maqqarī nennt hierunter besonders die Gedichte von Ibn al-Ǧannān (st. 646–48/1248–50) oder Abū Isḥāq Ibn Sahl al-Išbīlī (st. zwischen 643/1245 und 659/1260) und bringt auch anonyme Beispiele.[55] Darüber hinaus existiert eine starke jemenitische Tradition der Strophendichtung mit einer lokalen Variante, genannt *ḥumaynī*. In der *ḥumaynī*-Dichtung sind die Wörter in der Regel nicht flek-

52 Mit Bezug auf ein *ḥadīṯ*, nach dem die Herzen am Jüngsten Tag aus Furcht in die Kehle steigen (Ibn al-Aṯīr, *an-Nihāya* 237).

53 Pet. 641 fol. 59[b]; al-Buraʿī, *Dīwān* 2006, 151. Dieses ist mit 40 Strophen das längste der Strophengedichte, die beiden anderen beiden haben 22 respektive 26 Strophen.

54 Pet. 641 fol. 69[a]; al-Buraʿī, *Dīwān* 2006, 165.

55 Al-Maqqarī, *Nafḥ* vii, 431–70; Ibn al-Ǧannān, *Dīwān* 149–55 (28 Strophen). Solche Gedichte wurden beispielsweise zum Gedenken an den Prophetengeburtstag (*mawlid*) oder aber auch zum Abschluss von Unterrichtssitzungen vorgetragen.

tiert, sondern enden mit *sukūn*; und es werden Ausdrücke verwendet, die lokal geprägt sind und die Umgangssprache evozieren. Die *ḥumaynī*-Dichtung entstand im 8./14. Jahrhundert. Eine wichtige Rolle wird dabei den Zusammenkünften der Mystiker zugeschrieben, bei denen gesungene Poesie eine tragende Rolle spielte. Mit der Eroberung der Tihāma und Teile des südlichen Hochlands durch die Ayyubiden im späten 6./12. Jahrhundert wurde nicht nur der sunnitische Islam gestärkt, sondern parallel entstand auch eine breite Anhängerschaft der islamischen Mystik. Einen nicht unerheblichen Einfluss auf die Verbreitung von Strophendichtung im Jemen könnte die strophische Poesie Ibn ʿArabīs (st. 638/1240) gespielt haben, dessen Werke im Jemen und gerade in Zabīd stark rezipiert wurden.[56] Dafari erwähnt darüber hinaus den andalusischen Mystiker Abū l-Ḥasan aš-Šuštarī (st. 668/1269), der für seine mystischen Strophengedichte – sowohl in der Hoch- als auch in der Umgangssprache – bekannt ist, als möglichen Einflussgeber und sieht in Mekka einen wichtigen Umschlagsort für Poesie.[57] *Ḥumaynī*-Poesie ist aber keinesfalls ausschließlich religiös. Sie wurde auch an den Höfen der rasulidischen Herrscher gepflegt, die ab 632/1235 die Region beherrschten. Spätere Darstellungen der Frühgeschichte von *ḥumaynī* haben vor dem Hintergrund politisch-ideologischer Auseinandersetzungen die Rolle der mystischen Praxis bei der Entstehung von *ḥumaynī* heruntergespielt oder sogar gänzlich ausgeblendet und stattdessen das Umfeld der höfischen Kultur betont.[58] Es ist also durchaus wahrscheinlich, dass al-Buraʿī die strophische Dichtung des arabischen Westens gekannt hat. Mark S. Wagner nennt al-Buraʿī sogar als wichtigen Dichter von *ḥumaynī*, doch Dafari bezweifelt, dass al-Buraʿī andere als hochsprachliche Gedichte verfasst hat.[59] Tatsächlich sind zwar einige seiner Gedichte in einfacher Sprache und mit kurzen Halbversen, aber es findet sich keine strophische unflektierte Dichtung.

Musikalische Elemente wie Echo, die Wiederkehr von Klang und ein ausgeprägter Rhythmus durch Wiederholung und syntaktische Parallelismen sind auch in nicht-strophischen-Gedichten zu finden. Ein prägnantes Beispiel ist *Laka l-ḥamdu ḥamdan nastaliḏḏu bihī ḏikrā*. Hier wiederholt der Dichter zu Beginn von 18 Zeilen die Worte *Laka l-ḥamdu ḥamdan*. Dieses Gedicht ist zwar nicht in Pet. 691 und 649 vorhanden, aber es enthält eine Namenserwäh-

56 Knysh, *Ibn ʿArabi* 227, 232–3.

57 Dafari, *Ḥumainī* 44–5.

58 Zur jemenitischen Strophendichtung siehe Dafari, *Ḥumainī*; Wagner, *Poetics*; Wagner, *Joseph*; zur frühen Geschichte von *ḥumaynī* besonders Dafari, *Ḥumainī* 39–59; Wagner, *Joseph* 11–28.

59 Wagner, *Poetics* 299; Wagner, *Joseph* 170 Fn. 117 (dort als al-Burʿī); Dafari, *Ḥumainī* 216.

nung in Vers 31, wie wir sie auch in anderen Gedichten von ihm antreffen.[60] Ein anderes Beispiel ist *Yā rabbi ṣalli ʿalā n-nabiyyi l-muǧtabā*. Von insgesamt 17 Versen beginnen sieben mit *Yā rabbi ṣalli ʿalā n-nabī* und neun mit *ṣallū* respektive *ṣallā*.[61] Auch hierzu finden wir Beispiele in der Dichtung von Ibn al-Ǧannān, der die ersten sieben Zeilen eines Gedichts mit *Ṣallū ʿalā* beginnen lässt.[62] Wiederholung und Parallelismen treten nicht immer zu Beginn oder als durchgehendes Strukturmerkmal auf, sondern auch punktuell in der Mitte eines Gedichts.[63] Für beides finden sich auch bekannte Beispiele bei al-Būṣīrī, so in *al-Qaṣīda al-Muḥammadiyya* (jeder ihrer 16 Verse beginnt mit *Muḥammadun* und ordnet dem Propheten eine Eigenschaft zu) oder in *al-Qaṣīda al-Muḍariyya*.[64]

Ein Großteil der Langgedichte weist die für die *qaṣīda* typische Einteilung in *nasīb*, *raḥīl* und *madīḥ* auf. Darüber hinaus finden sich Motive der altarabischen Dichtung wie die Spuren der verlassenen Lagerstatt, topographische Markierungen des Ḥiǧāz, die materielle Kultur der Karawanenreise oder der Tadler. Die Sehnsucht nach Mekka und Medina ist in einigen Gedichten zentrales Thema, in anderen Subthema von *nasīb* und *madīḥ*. Dabei geht es weniger um die Pilgerfahrt als vielmehr um die Liebe zum Propheten und den Wunsch, ihm nahe zu sein. Öfter also steht das Grab (*qabr*, *ḥimā*) im Mittelpunkt und nicht die Kaaba. Neben die genannten Motive treten das Bild der fortziehenden Karawane und des zurückgelassenen lyrischen Ich, die Brise des Windes und der Auftrag an den Karawanenführer respektive den Wind, Grüße an den Propheten zu übermitteln. Ein anderes häufiges Thema ist die Unzulänglichkeit des Menschen und die daraus resultierende angemessene Haltung der Demut (*ḫuḍūʿ*, *taḍarruʿ*) sowie die Vergänglichkeit des Menschen und Gottes weises Wirken in der Schöpfung. Form und Inhalt können hier nur angerissen werden, da Gedichte zunächst zur Klärung von al-Buraʿīs Identität und Lebenszeit betrachtet werden müssen.

Namen und Orte in Gedichten

Wir haben bereits gesehen, dass der Dichter sich häufig selbst am Ende eines Gedichts nennt, in der Regel in Verbindung mit der Bitte um Vergebung. Am

60 Al-Buraʿī, *Dīwān* 2006, 93 (26 Verse).

61 Pet. 641 fol. 4[b]; al-Buraʿī, *Dīwān* 2006, 19.

62 Ibn al-Ǧannān, *Dīwān* 148–9 (22 Verse).

63 Beispielsweise Pet. 641 fol. 21[a–b]; al-Buraʿī, *Dīwān* 2006, 76–7.

64 Al-Būṣīrī, *Dīwān* 224–7.

häufigsten verwendet er den Namen ʿAbd ar-Raḥīm, der zu einem Wortspiel mit der Gotteseigenschaft *raḥīm* geradezu einlädt. Ein hübsches Beispiel ist folgender Vers, der gleichzeitig Beispiel für die direkte Zwiesprache mit Gott ist, die einige der Gedichte auszeichnet:

إن قال عبد الرحيم ذنبي فقُل أنا المشفق الرحيم

> Wenn ʿAbd ar-Raḥīm sagt: Meine Schuld! / dann sag du: Ich bin der Gütige und Barmherzige.[65]

Nahezu ebenso häufig wie die Erwähnung seines Namens sind geographische Markierungen seiner Heimat, am häufigsten Buraʿ. Daneben tritt sein Heimatort an-Nayyābatayn auf. In einem Gedicht beschreibt er die Sehnsucht nach seinen beiden Kindern, während er sich auf Pilgerfahrt befindet, und beginnt mit folgendem Vers:

طيف الخيال من النيّابتين سرى إلى الحجاز فوافى مضجعي سحرا

> Das Phantombild aus an-Nayyābatayn[66] reiste des Nachts / in den Ḥiǧāz, wo es am frühen Morgen meine Schlafstatt erreichte.[67]

Namen und geographische Markierungen untermauern die Identifizierung des namentlichen Eintrags in al-Burayhī als Autor der meisten Gedichte im *Dīwān*. Auch die Identifizierung namentlich genannter Persönlichkeiten deutet auf eine Lebenszeit im 8./14. Jahrhundert. Bei diesen Personen handelt es sich entweder um Zeitgenossen, die al-Buraʿī lobt, oder um solche, in deren Namen er Gedichte verfasst hat (*ʿalā lisān*).[68] Wie erwähnt, verweisen die Namen auf ein jemenitisches Umfeld, doch eine genaue Identifizierung wird erschwert durch die Tatsache, dass die Namen aus den einzelnen Familien sich stark ähneln, so dass nicht immer zweifelsfrei bestimmt werden kann, um welche Person es sich handelt. Auch ist zuweilen nur von einem „Sulaymān" oder „Šayḫ ʿUmar" die Rede.[69] Einige bekanntere Personen habe ich folgendermaßen identifiziert: Bei ʿUmar b. Muḥammad al-ʿUrābī handelt es sich um den Gelehrten und Sufi

65 Pet. 641 fol. 78ᵃ; al-Buraʿī, *Dīwān* 2006, 151.
66 Ich folge hier al-Burayhī in der Vokalisierung; die meisten Drucke haben an-Niyyābatayn.
67 Pet. 641 fol. 11ᵃ; al-Buraʿī, *Dīwān* 2006, 89.
68 Gedichte *ʿalā lisān* kommen insgesamt sechs Mal vor, zweimal in den *nabawiyyāt* und vier Mal in den *ṣūfiyyāt*.
69 Pet. 641 fol. 102ᵇ; fol. 106ᵇ.

ʿUmar b. Muḥammad, bekannt als al-ʿUrābī, der aus der näheren Umgebung der Bergregion Buraʿ stammt und im Jahr 811/1408–9 nach Mekka übersiedelte. Dort starb er 16 Jahre später im Ramadan 827/April 1424.[70] Ebenfalls aus der Nähe von Buraʿ stammt Muḥammad b. Yaḥyā aš-Šāriqī, ein zu seiner Zeit bekannter Koranleser und Gelehrter, der neben seinem Heimatort aš-Šāriqa auch in Taʿizz und Zabīd wirkte. Er starb im Jahr 820/1418.[71] Schließlich wird Aḥmad b. Abī Bakr ar-Raddād genannt, der schafiitische Gelehrte, Mystiker und Oberrichter Aḥmad b. Abī Bakr al-Qurašī, bekannt als Ibn ar-Raddād. Er starb im Ḏū l-Qaʿda 821/Dezember 1418.[72]

Indirekt verweist auch das Gedicht mit Bezug zur *Burda* auf eine historische Persönlichkeit, nämlich auf al-Būṣīrī und die Tatsache, dass al-Buraʿī später als im 7./13. Jahrhundert gelebt haben muss. Das Gedicht folgt zwar im Reim nicht der *Burda*, doch stimmen Syntax und Vokabular der jeweils ersten Verse auffällig überein.[73] Von den Autoren, die sich mit al-Buraʿī beschäftigen, thematisiert dies lediglich Muḥammad Fatḥ Allāh Miṣbāḥ.[74] Miṣbāḥ beschreibt die Dichtung al-Buraʿīs insgesamt als von der *Burda* beeinflusst.[75] Gewiss sind strukturelle Ähnlichkeiten bemerkbar; auf der anderen Seite hatte sich aber im 8./14. Jahrhundert längst ein Repertoire an gängigen Motiven und Strukturen des *madīḥ nabawī* herausgebildet. Die *Burda* hatte hierbei durchaus Einfluss, doch gehen ihr wiederum die Entwicklungen des *madīḥ nabawī* ab dem 5./11. bis Mitte 7./13. Jahrhundert voraus.[76]

Lebenszeit und Umfeld

Die kombinierte Analyse historischer Quellen und der Gedichte selbst zeigt, dass eine Lebenszeit al-Buraʿīs im 5./11. Jahrhundert endgültig *ad acta* gelegt

70 Pet. 641 fol. 100[b]; fol. 101[a] ggf. derselbe als Šuǧāʿ ad-Dīn ʿUmar al-ʿUrābī; fol. 105[a] als Šuǧāʿ ad-Dīn ʿUmar b. Muḥammad al-ʿUrābī al-Kinānī; zu ihm al-Burayhī, *Ṭabaqāt* 41; as-Saḫāwī, *Ḍawʾ* vi, 131–2.

71 Pet. 641 fol. 93[b]; al-Burayhī, *Ṭabaqāt* 42–3.

72 Pet. 641 fol. 91[a]; fol. 98[a] derselbe als Aḥmad b. Abī Bakr al-Qurašī; zu ihm al-Burayhī, *Ṭabaqāt* 299–302; Ibn Ḥaǧar al-ʿAsqalānī, *Inbāʾ* iii, 177–8; as-Saḫāwī, *Ḍawʾ* i, 260–3.

73 Al-Būṣīrī, *Dīwān* 190–201; zur *Burda* siehe Stetkevych, *Mantle Odes*; Thomas Bauer hat eine deutsche Übersetzung vorgelegt (https://www.uni-muenster.de/imperia/md/content/alea/busiri.pdf).

74 Miṣbāḥ, *Burda* 360–2. Knapp erwähnt wird die *Burda* nur noch in al-Buraʿī, *Šarḥ*, Nachwort 299.

75 Miṣbāḥ, *Burda* 432–3.

76 Zu Entwicklungen im *madīḥ nabawī* ab dem 5./11. Jahrhundert siehe beispielsweise Bāšā, *al-Adab* 335–7, 410–2; Muḥammad, *al-Madāʾiḥ*; Makkī, *al-Madāʾiḥ* 101–7, 119–24.

werden kann. Namen und Orte in Gedichten weisen vielmehr auf die Person hin, die von al-Burayhī beschrieben wird. Darüber hinaus lassen allgemeine formal-ästhetische Kennzeichen der Gedichte und genannte lokale Persönlichkeiten als Adressaten oder Auftraggeber von Gedichten eine Lebensspanne im 8./14. Jahrhundert bis zum frühen 9./15. Jahrhundert als gesichert gelten. Eine kleinere Irritation ist in diesem Zusammenhang allerdings noch zu verzeichnen, und zwar in Form des Eintrags in einem modernen bio-bibliographischen Werk von Ismāʿīl b. Muḥammad al-Wašalī, *Našr aṯ-ṯanāʾ al-ḥasan ʿalā baʿḍ arbāb al-faḍl wa-l-kamāl min ahl al-Yaman wa-ḏikr al-ḥawādiṯ al-wāqiʿa fī hāḏā z-zaman.*[77] Dort findet sich eine ausgesprochen lange Fassung von al-Buraʿīs Namen, in der „al-Mihāǧirī" vokalisiert wird, nach einem Stamm der Region Buraʿ: *ʿAbd ar-Raḥīm b. Aḥmad b. ʿAbd ar-Raḥīm b. Ismāʿīl b. Ibrāhīm b. Ismāʿīl b. Muslim b. Qays b. al-Ḥāriṯ al-Buraʿī al-Mihāǧirī* (sic) *nisbatan ilā Mihāǧir qabīla min ǧabal Buraʿ*. Diesen Hinweis auf den Stamm habe ich in keinem anderen Nachschlagewerk gefunden. Entscheidender ist allerdings das Todesjahr, welches mit Verweis auf al-Burayhī als „nach 830/1426" gegeben wird. Al-Wašalī hat dieses Datum nicht direkt von al-Burayhī übernommen, sondern aus einem genealogischen Werk über die Ahdal Familie von Abū Bakr b. Abī l-Qāsim b. Aḥmad al-Ahdal (st. 1035/1626), *al-Aḥsāb al-ʿaliyya fī l-ansāb al-Ahdaliyya.*[78] Dort wird al-Buraʿī als Verfasser von Lobgedichten auf mehrere Mitglieder der Familie erwähnt. Tatsächlich bezieht sich al-Ahdal auf al-Burayhī, nennt aber „nach 836" als Todesjahr.[79] Die Ziffer sechs kann leicht als Lesefehler beruhend auf der Verwechslung von *sitta*/*sana* erklärt werden; bei dem Austausch von 3 durch 30 müsste schon ein gravierenderer Schreibfehler vorliegen. Der Edition von al-Burayhī mit der Zahl 803 liegen vier Handschriften zugrunde; al-Ahdal müsste damit eine andere Handschrift von al-Burayhī benutzt haben, oder in der Abschrift seines Werkes ist ein Fehler unterlaufen. Der Sachverhalt kann ohne weitere Handschriften von al-Ahdal und al-Burayhī nicht endgültig geklärt werden.

Die Evidenz für das Sterbejahr 803/1400–1 ist damit relativ dünn; sie beruht bisher letztendlich auf vier Handschriften von al-Burayhīs *Ṭabaqāt*. Dessen ungeachtet bleibt das frühe 9./15. Jahrhundert als letzte Lebensspanne anhand

---

77 Al-Wašalī, *Našr* iii, 165–70 (mit vollständiger Wiedergabe zweier Gedichte). Der Verfasser starb 1356/1937.

78 *Wa-kānat wafātuhu baʿda ṯalāṯīna wa-ṯamānimiʾatin kamā ḏakarahu fī l-Aḥsābi l-ʿaliyyati li-s-sayyidi l-ʿallāmati Abī Bakrin b. Abī l-Qāsimi l-Ahdali naqlan ʿan Tārīḫi l-Burayhī* (al-Wašalī, *Našr* iii, 170).

79 *Wa-tuwuffiya ʿAbdu r-Raḥīmi l-maḏkūru kamā fī Tārīḫi l-Burayhiyyi baʿda sittatin wa-ṯalāṯīna wa-ṯamānimiʾatin hiǧriyya*. Dieses Zitat, das ich nur online einsehen konnte, kann zu diesem Zeitpunkt nicht weiter überprüft werden.

formal-ästhetischer Kriterien und genannter Persönlichkeiten gesichert. Al-Buraʿīs Sterbedatum würde damit in die Zeitspanne von as-Saḫāwīs *Ḍaw'* fallen, das Gelehrte des 9./15. Jahrhunderts behandelt. Dass al-Buraʿī dort nicht enthalten ist, würde zunächst nur bedeuten, dass er zu as-Saḫāwīs Lebzeiten nicht zu den weithin überregional bekannten und bedeutenden Gelehrten zählte. Dass al-Buraʿī nicht in *an-Nūr as-sāfir ʿan aḫbār al-qarn al-ʿāšir* von ʿAbd al-Qādir b. Šayḫ al-Aydarūs (st. 1038/1628) enthalten ist, der ja nun auf jemenitische Persönlichkeiten fokussiert, spricht hingegen dafür, dass er vor dem 10./16. Jahrhundert starb.

Damit hat al-Buraʿī in der späten Rasulidenzeit gelebt. Unter den Rasuliden (632–858/1235–1454) setzten sich Entwicklungen fort, die mit der ayyubidischen Eroberung weiter Teile des Jemen im Jahr 569/1173 begonnen hatten, nämlich die Stärkung des Sunnitentums und Schwächung der Ismailiyya sowie der zaiditischen Imame. Die Ayyubiden beherrschten die Tihāma und das südliche Hochland; unter den Rasuliden kamen das nördliche Hochland mit Sanaa, der Hadramaut und südliche Teile der Arabischen Halbinsel hinzu. Besonders Aden entwickelte sich zu einem wichtigen Handelshafen und Garant für eine florierende Wirtschaft. Die rasulidischen Herrscher taten sich als Förderer von Kunst und Wissenschaft hervor, gründeten Bildungsinstitutionen und Bibliotheken und finanzierten Studienreisen. Gelehrte, Dichter und Mystiker waren gern gesehene Gäste am Hof, und Städte wie Zabīd oder Aden entwickelten sich zu Zentren schafiitischer Gelehrsamkeit.[80] Aufenthalte von aufstrebenden oder hochrangigen Gelehrten aus Damaskus und Kairo wie des *ḥadīṯ*-Spezialisten Ibn Ḥaǧar al-ʿAsqalānī (st. 852/1449) oder des Experten in Koranlesarten Muḥammad Ibn al-Ǧazarī (st. 833/1429) sind belegt.[81] Solche Lehraufenthalte können neben den bereits genannten Einflüssen eine weitere Quelle zur Verbreitung von strophischer Dichtung und *mawlid* gewesen sein.

Al-Buraʿī lebte zu einer Zeit, in der die Mystik eine breite Resonanz in der Bevölkerung erfuhr. Besonders unter al-Ašraf Ismāʿīl (reg. 778–803/1377–1401) wuchsen sufische Gemeinden stark an, denn er patronisierte sie stärker als seine Vorgänger.[82] Zwar kann man durchaus von einer Massenbewegung sprechen, aber dies war keine zentral organisierte Bewegung mit klar voneinander abgegrenzten Orden und straff organisierten Riten. Vielmehr waren Mystiker in lokalen Gemeinschaften und weitgehend dezentral organisiert; viele Niederlassungen gab es auf dem Land und besonders in der Tihāma.[83] Die Ent-

80 Knysh, *Ibn ʿArabi* 227–33; Margariti, *Aden*.

81 Knysh, *Ibn ʿArabi* 232; al-Burayhī, *Ṭabaqāt* 334–52.

82 Knysh, *Ibn ʿArabi* 241.

83 Knysh, *Ibn ʿArabi* 228.

wicklung der islamischen Mystik befand sich in einem Stadium, das man mit Bezug auf Denis Gril die *ḫirqa*-Periode respektive prä-Orden-Periode nennen kann.[84] Al-Buraʿī war Zeitgenosse einiger einflussreicher Mystiker im Jemen. So war er Zeitgenosse des bekanntesten lokalen Mystikers, Ismāʿīl al-Ǧabartī (st. 806/1403), auch wenn er ihn nicht erwähnt.[85] Der einflussreichste Mystiker, zu dem al-Buraʿī Kontakt hatte, war sicherlich Ibn ar-Raddād (st. 821/1418). Ibn ar-Raddād stammte aus einer bedeutenden Familie in Mekka, wo er Recht studierte. Mit etwa 20 Jahren ging er in den Jemen, wo er al-Ǧabartī traf, dessen Anhänger wurde und bis zu seinem Tod blieb. Er war ein enger Vertrauter von Sultan al-Ašraf Ismāʿīl, der ihn 817/1415 zum schafiitischen Oberrichter in Zabīd ernannte. Diese Ernennung bedeutete gleichzeitig eine Stärkung der Fraktion, die zugunsten der Lehre Ibn ʿArabīs argumentierte.[86] Alexander Knysh hat gezeigt, dass die Lehren Ibn ʿArabīs in der späten ayyubidischen und frühen rasulidischen Zeit durch jemenitische Sufis eingeführt und vor allem im 8./14. Jahrhundert durch al-Ǧabartī verbreitet wurden. Gleichzeitig formierte sich unter einigen Gelehrten eine starke Opposition, die allerdings erst nach dem Tod von Ibn ar-Raddād unter der Führung von Ibn al-Muqriʾ (st. 837/1444) die Oberhand gewann.[87] Den Höhepunkt der Rezeption der Schriften Ibn ʿArabīs im Jemen datiert Knysh ins späte 8./14. und frühe 9./15. Jahrhundert, was mit der späten Lebensphase al-Buraʿīs zusammenfällt.[88] Für al-Buraʿī scheint die ʿUrābī Familie der wichtigste Bezugspunkt gewesen zu sein, was die Mystik betrifft. Er kann ʿUmar b. Muḥammad al-ʿUrābī (st. 827/1424), der als wandernder Mystiker im Jemen eine große Anzahl von Anhängern um sich zog, noch persönlich getroffen haben, bevor dieser 811/1408–9 nach Mekka ging. Ihm widmet al-Buraʿī mehrere Lobgedichte (s. o. Fn. 70). Den *šayḫs* der ʿUrābī-Familie widmet er darüber hinaus ein 83 Verse langes Gedicht, in dem er chronologisch die spirituellen Meister der Familie erwähnt (*qaṣīdatun … yuḏakkiru fīhā mašāyiḫa l-Aʿrābiyyi min ahli l-ḫirqati ʿalā tartībi l-iǧāza*).[89]

Parallel zu der Auseinandersetzung mit den Schriften Ibn ʿArabīs verlief die in *samāʿ* und *ḏikr* praktizierte Mystik. *Ḏikr* fand vor Sonnenaufgang oder

---

84 Gril, Khirqa.

85 Zu al-Ǧabartī siehe Gril, Khirqa 64–6; Knysh, *Ibn ʿArabi* 241–6; as-Saḫāwī, *Ḍawʾ* ii, 282–4.

86 Zur Biographie siehe die in Fn. 72 genannten Quellen; zu seiner Rolle in Zabīd zusätzlich Knysh, *Ibn ʿArabi* 246–52.

87 Knysh, *Ibn ʿArabi* 225–69.

88 Knysh, *Ibn ʿArabi* 233.

89 Al-Buraʿī, *Dīwān* 2006, 25. Das Gedicht ist nicht in Pet. 641 enthalten, in Vers 78 aber nennt der Dichter sich selbst. Dennoch bleibt festzuhalten, dass das Gedicht ansonsten nur in den drei frühen Drucken sowie zwei weiteren Drucken (*Dīwān* 1994, 17 und *Šarḥ* 35) enthalten ist.

zwischen dem Abend- und Nachtgebet statt, und *munšidūn* sangen Gedichte von Ibn ʿArabī, Ibn al-Fāriḍ (st. 632/1235) und Ibn ar-Raddād.[90] Es ist mehr als wahrscheinlich, dass auch Gedichte von al-Buraʿī gesungen wurden. Einige Formen, beispielsweise solche mit Strophen und Wiederholungen, eignen sich besonders für gemeinschaftlich ausgeführten Gesang. Vereinzelt finden sich bereits aus der Zeit vor dem 20. Jahrhundert Hinweise auf die Verbreitung seiner Gedichte, auch durch *munšidūn*.[91] Dafür gibt es meines Erachtens auch materielle Evidenz, nämlich in den Handschriften selbst in Form von Hinzufügungen und Weglassungen, Konzentration auf die *nabawiyyāt*, Neuarrangement der Gedichte und Umdeutungen. Aufweichungen in der Anordnung des *Dīwān* und Varianten scheinen nämlich nicht zuletzt hervorgerufen durch den häufigen Gebrauch der Gedichte und durchgeführt von denjenigen, die al-Buraʿīs Gedichte benutzten, sprich die *munšidūn*. Dazu zählt nicht allein, dass einzelne Personen Gedichte in Handschriften hinzugefügt haben, die sie als Gedichte al-Buraʿīs aus einem anderen Zusammenhang kannten. Auch Weglassungen sind relevant: Die Handschriften Gotha und Riyad bestehen aus nur zwei Teilen. Eine mögliche Erklärung ist, dass die *munšidūn* auswählten, was sie in der Praxis brauchten, und das waren in diesem Fall nicht die *ṣūfiyyāt*, wo viele Gedichte personen- und situationsgebunden sind. Der Fokus auf *nabawiyyāt* zeigt sich auch darin, dass ein *Dīwān* öfter als „Prophetenlob und Anderes" bezeichnet wird; auch charakterisiert az-Zabīdī al-Buraʿī als „Prophetenlobdichter" (*mādiḥ al-Muṣṭafā*).[92]

Es lässt sich in dieser Hinsicht eine Veränderung in der Definition *ṣūfiyyāt* beobachten. In den Handschriften Pet. 641 und 649 werden als *ṣūfiyyāt* die Gedichte bezeichnet, die an die *ṣulaḥāʾ* gerichtet sind.[93] Diese umfassen neben Lob auch Ermahnung oder Entschuldigungen, in denen auf konkrete Ereignisse Bezug genommen wird. Andere Handschriften scheinen auch *ilāhiyyāt* und *nabawiyyāt* als *ṣūfiyya* zu verstehen. Dort ist nur noch von *qaṣāʾid ṣūfiyya* die Rede, ohne Erwähnung der *ṣulaḥāʾ*, und die Überschriften dazu fehlen zum Teil; dafür wird ein Selbsttadel in diese Sektion aufgenommen, der in den frühen Handschriften zu den *ilāhiyyāt* zählt.[94] Umgekehrt konnten Gedichte ihre Relevanz auch behalten, wenn ihr ursprünglicher Kontext nicht mehr bekannt

90 Al-Burayhī, *Ṭabaqāt* 41, 100, 300–1; Ibn Ḥaǧar al-ʿAsqalānī, *Inbāʾ* iii, 178; Knysh, *Ibn ʿArabi* 233–4; as-Saḫāwī, *Ḍawʾ* i, 261.

91 Az-Zabīdī, *Tāǧ* xx, 318; al-Wašalī, *Našr* iii, 166.

92 Az-Zabīdī, *Tāǧ* xx, 318.

93 *Wa-huwa mā qālahu fī s-sādati ṣ-ṣāliḥīna mina l-madḥ* (Pet. 641 fol. 80b–81a; Pet. 649 fol. 76b).

94 Z. B. al-Buraʿī, *Dīwān* 2006, 99; al-Buraʿī, *Dīwān* 1884, 100, al-Buraʿī, *Šarḥ* 199.

war, oder sie wurden umgedeutet: Das Gedicht, das al-Buraʿī nach überstandener schwerer Krankheit seines Sohnes komponierte, wird in einer Fassung lediglich zu einem Liebesgedicht an den Propheten (*qaṣīdatun fī t-taġazzuli bih*).[95] In einem anderen Fall wird ein auf seine Gefährten bezogenes Gedicht zur allgemeinen Bitte.

Schließlich sticht die Anordnung des *Šarḥ* von 1967 hervor: er beginnt wie andere Versionen mit *Taǧallat li-waḥdāniyyati l-ḥaqqi anwārū*, doch in der Sektion Prophetenlob wird dem sonst üblichen Anfangsgedicht (*A min taḏakkuri ahli l-bāni wa-l-bānī*) ein *muḫammas* (*Bi-Muḥammadin*, s.o.) vorgeschaltet. In beiden Sektionen folgen dann zunächst Gedichte ohne *nasīb* und mit vielen Parallelismen und Wiederholungen: Hier hat jemand die Gedichte neu arrangiert, und zwar mit bekannten und leicht singbaren Gedichten an erster Stelle.

Die bisherige Spurensuche hat zu mehreren Ergebnissen und Überlegungen geführt. Auch wenn Jemen nicht immer im Blickfeld der mamlukenzeitlichen Gelehrten und ihrer biographischen Lexika lag: al-Buraʿīs Lebenszeit fällt mit der Mamlukenherrschaft zusammen, und seine Gedichte sind heute weit über den Jemen hinaus verbreitet, von Marokko bis Indien. Was im einzelnen die Verbreitungswege seines Werks waren, muss noch näher untersucht werden. Die engen Verbindungen zwischen Südarabien und Indien, insbesondere Gujarat und die östliche wie westliche Südküste, die zum Ziel von Migration von Familien aus dem Hadramaut und der Tihāma wurden, trugen zur Rezeption von al-Buraʿīs Poesie in Indien bei.[96] Nicht zuletzt stammt fast ein Drittel der bei Brockelmann aufgezählten Manuskripte vom indischen Subkontinent.[97]

Al-Buraʿī hat in der späten Rasulidenzeit gelebt, überwiegend in seiner Heimatregion in der Tihāma, aber auch einige Zeit im Ḥiǧāz verbracht, wo er allem Anschein nach auch gestorben ist. Er war zu Lebzeiten sowohl als Jurist als auch als Dichter bekannt, denn es erreichten ihn juristische Anfragen und kompositorische Auftragsarbeiten. Er pflegte Kontakte mit Mitgliedern aus bedeutenden Gelehrtenfamilien und einflussreichen Sufis im Jemen und Ḥiǧāz, besonders Zabīd und Mekka.

Einen *Dīwān* hat er wohl nicht selbst zusammengestellt, doch seine Gedichte waren spätestens im 10./16. Jahrhundert in einer dreiteiligen themati-

95 Pet. 641 fol. 45[a]; al-Buraʿī, *Dīwān* 1994, 93.

96 Bilgrāmī, *Ṣubḥat*; Ho, *Graves*; Margariti, *Aden*; al-Qāhirī, *Madāʾiḥ*; aš-Širwānī, *Nafḥat*.

97 Dabei handelt es sich um Bibliotheken im Norden. Die Erschließung der arabischen Handschriften im stärker arabisierten Südindien (Kerala, Tamil Nadu) steht noch in den Anfängen; die in einem Pilotprojekt meiner Kollegin Ophira Gamliel dokumentierten Kompilationen performativer Texte mit Poesie und *mawlid* lassen vermuten, dass al-Buraʿīs Gedichte auch hier vertreten sind (*Locating and Sampling Arabic and Arabic-Malayalam Manuscripts in Kerala, South India*, EAP1228).

schen Anordnung im Umlauf, die entweder mit Gotteslob oder mit Prophetenlob begann. Eine nicht unbedeutende Rolle haben *munšidūn* bei der Verbreitung und schriftlichen Bewahrung seiner Poesie gespielt. Dabei kam es zu Veränderungen im Arrangement der Gedichte und in Kontextzuschreibungen. Darüber hinaus ist ein ihm zugeordneter *mawlid*-Text im Umlauf.

Während al-Burayhī in seinen *Ṭabaqāt* aus dem 9./15. Jahrhundert al-Buraʿī als Juristen und Gelehrten (*al-faqīh al-ʿālim*) beschreibt, titulieren spätere Handschriften und Drucke ihn als *al-ʿārif bi-llāh*, *sayyidī* oder *al-mutaṣawwif*. Al-Buraʿī wird in Vor- und Nachworten von Drucken als herausragender Sufi und demutsvolle Persönlichkeit gepriesen, das heißt, er gerät selbst zum Verehrten.[98] Auch ihm zugeschriebene *karāmāt* (Huldwunder) sind belegt.[99] Es scheint, als habe al-Buraʿī, der zwar im 8./14. und 9./15. Jahrhundert über einen gewissen lokalen Bekanntheitsstatus verfügte, erst in spätosmanischer Zeit Karriere gemacht, und das weniger als Gelehrter und Jurist, sondern in erster Linie als Sufi und Dichter.

Bibliographie

Quellen

Anon., *al-Qāmūs al-ǧadīd fī l-qaṣāʾid wa-l-anāšīd li-s-sāda aš-Šāḏiliyya ʿalā tartīb al-ḥurūf al-abǧadiyya*, Kairo ²1972.

al-Aydarūs, ʿA. b. Š. b. ʿA., *an-Nūr as-sāfir ʿan aḫbār al-qarn al-ʿāšir*, Hgg. A. Ḥālū et al., Beirut 2001.

al-Baġdādī, I.B., *Hadiyyat al-ʿārifīn: Asmāʾ al-muʾallifīn wa-āṯār al-muṣannifīn*, Istanbul 1951.

Bilgrāmī, Ġ.ʿA.Ā., *Subḥat al-marǧān fī āṯār Hindustān*, Hg. M.F. an-Nadawī as-Sīwānī, Aligarh 1972.

al-Buraʿī, ʿA., *Dīwān*, Hs. Staatsbibliothek Berlin, Orientabteilung, Petermann I 641.

al-Buraʿī, ʿA., *Dīwān*, Hs. Staatsbibliothek Berlin, Orientabteilung, Petermann I 649.

al-Buraʿī, ʿA., *Dīwān*, Hs. Gotha, Orient. A 2239.

al-Buraʿī, ʿA., *Dīwān*, Hs. Universität Riyad 149.

al-Buraʿī, ʿA., *Dīwān*, Hs. Paris 3113.

al-Buraʿī, ʿA., *Dīwān*, Mumbai 1291/1875.

al-Buraʿī, ʿA., *Dīwān*, Kairo 1297/1880.

al-Buraʿī, ʿA., *Dīwān*, Bombay 1301/1884.

98 Al-Buraʿī, *Šarḥ*, Vorwort; *Dīwān* 1994, Nachwort; *Dīwān* 2006, Vorwort.

99 Al-Wašalī, *Našr* iii, 170.

al-Buraʿī, ʿA., *Dīwān*, Hg. Ḥ.Ḥ. al-Masʿūdī, Kairo [2]1369/1950.

al-Buraʿī, ʿA., *Šarḥ Dīwān al-Buraʿī*, Kairo [4]1386/1967.

al-Buraʿī, ʿA., *Dīwān*, Beirut 1994.

al-Buraʿī, A. b. ʿA. al-Hāǧirī al-Yamānī (sic), *Dīwān*, Hg. ʿĀ.I. al-Kayyālī, Beirut 2006.

al-Buraʿī, ʿA., *Mawlid ar-rasūl aš-šahīr bi-l-ʿArūs*, o.O. [1880?].

al-Buraʿī, ʿA., Mawlid al-Buraʿī, in Ṣ. Hawwārī (Hg.), *al-Mawlid an-nabawī aš-šarīf*, Beirut 2003, 13–50.

al-Burayhī, ʿA. b. ʿA., *Ṭabaqāt ṣulaḥāʾ al-Yaman al-maʿrūf bi-Tārīḫ al-Burayhī*, Hg. ʿA.M. al-Ḥibšī, Sanaa [2]1414/1983.

al-Būṣīrī, Š. A. ʿA. b. S., *Dīwān al-Būṣīrī*, Hg. M.S. al-Kīlānī, Kairo 1955.

al-Ḥalabī, M.T. und M.ʿI. Daqqāq (Hg.), *Anāšīd aṣ-ṣafā fī madīḥ al-Muṣṭafā wa-mawlid al-ʿAlamī*, Damaskus [5]1992.

Ibn Aṯīr, M., *an-Nihāya fī ġarīb al-ḥadīṯ wa-l-aṯar*, Hg. ʿA. b. Ḥ. b. ʿA. al-Ḥalabī al-Aṯarī, Dammam 1421/2000.

Ibn al-Ǧawzī, *Mawlid al-Ǧawzī aš-šahīr bi-l-ʿArūs*, Beirut o.D.

Ibn al-Ǧannān al-Anṣārī al-Andalusī, *Dīwān Ibn al-Ǧannān*, Hg. M.M. Bahǧat, [Mosul?] 1410/1990.

Ibn Ḥaǧar al-ʿAsqalānī, *Inbāʾ al-ġumr fī abnāʾ al-ʿumr*, Hg. Ḥ. Ḥibšī, 4 Bde., Kairo 1389–1419/1969–98.

al-Maqqarī at-Tilimsānī, Š. A. b. M., *Nafḥ aṭ-ṭīb fī ġuṣn al-Andalus ar-raṭīb*, Hg. I. ʿAbbās, vii, Beirut 1968.

an-Nabhānī, Y. b. I., *al-Maǧmūʿa an-nabhāniyya fī l-madāʾiḥ an-nabawiyya*, 4 Bde., Beirut 1320/1902.

al-Qabbānī, M.ʿA., *Ǧāmiʿ an-nafaḥāt al-qudsīya fī l-anāšīd ad-dīniyya wa-l-qaṣāʾid al-ʿirfāniyya wa-l-muwaššaḥāt al-andalusiyya*, Beirut 1992.

al-Qāhirī, Ḥ.M., *Madāʾiḥ al-Muṣṭafā wa-manāqib al-ḫulafā* (sic), Bombay 1297/1880.

Rutter, E., *The Holy Cities of Arabia*, ii, London 1928.

as-Saḫāwī, Š. M. b. ʿA., *aḍ-Ḍawʾ al-lāmiʿ li-ahl al-qarn al-tāsiʿ*, 12 Bde., Beirut o.J.

aš-Šawkānī, M. b. ʿA., *al-Badr aṭ-ṭāliʿ bi-maḥāsin man baʿd al-qarn at-tāsiʿ*, 2 Bde., Kairo o.J.

aš-Širwānī, A. b. M., *Nafḥat al-Yaman fīmā yazūlu bi-ḏikrihi aš-šaǧan*, Calcutta 1811.

al-Wašalī, I. b. M.: *Našr aṯ-ṯanāʾ al-ḥasan ʿalā baʿḍ arbāb al-faḍl wa-l-kamāl min ahl al-Yaman wa-ḏikr al-ḥawādiṯ al-wāqiʿiyya fī hāḏā z-zaman*, Hg. I.A. al-Maqḥafī, 4 Bde. & Suppl., Sanaa [2]1429/2008.

az-Zabīdī, M.M., *Tāǧ al-ʿarūs min ǧawāhir al-Qāmūs*, Bd. xx, Hgg. ʿA. al-ʿIzbāwā, Kuwait 1403/1983.

Sekundärliteratur

Abū l-Makārim, ʿA. aš-Šayḫ ʿAlī (Hg.), *Maǧmūʿat al-madāʾiḥ an-nabawiyya*, 20 Bde., Beirut 2004.

Abdel-Malek, K., *Muḥammad in the modern Egyptian popular ballad*, Leiden 1995.

Ahlwardt, W., *Verzeichniss der arabischen Handschriften*, 10 Bde., Berlin 1887–99.

Abū l-Fatḥ, N., *al-Mutāḥ min al-mawālid wa-l-anāšīd al-milāḥ*, 3 Bde., o.O. [Damaskus] 1995.

Bāšā, ʿU.M., *al-Adab fī bilād aš-Šām: ʿUṣūr al-Zankiyyīn wa-l-Ayyūbiyyīn wa-l-Mamālīk*, Damaskus 1972.

Dafari, J.A., *Ḥumainī poetry in South Arabia*, PhD dissertation, University of London, 1966.

Dalāl, M.Q., *al-ʿĀlim ar-raḥḥāla aš-šayḫ ʿAlī ad-Darwīš al-Ḥalabī*, Damaskus 2008.

Diem, W. und M. Schöller, *The living and the dead in Islam: Studies in Arabic epitaphs*, 3 Bde., Wiesbaden 2004.

Durnayqa, M.A., *Muʿǧam aʿlām šuʿarāʾ al-madḥ al-nabawī*, Beirut 2003.

Frishkopf, M., Inshad dini and aghani diniyya in twentieth-century Egypt: A review of styles, genres, and available recordings, *MESA Bulletin* 34, 2 (2000), 167–83.

Gril, D., De la *khirqa* à la *ṭarīqa:* Continuité et évolution dans l'identification et la classification des voies, in R. Chih und C. Mayeur-Jaouen (Hgg.), *Le soufisme à l'époque ottomane, XVIe–XVIIIe siècle*, Kairo 2010, 57–82.

Ho, E., *The graves of Tarim: Genealogy and mobility across the Indian Ocean*, Berkeley 2006.

Kaḥḥāla, ʿU.R., *Muʿǧam al-muʾallifīn*, 15 Bde., Damaskus 1957–61.

Katz, M.H., *The birth of the Prophet Muḥammad: Devotional piety in Sunni Islam*, London 2007.

Knappert, J., The Mawlid, in *Orientalia Lovaniensia Periodica* 19 (1988), 209–15.

Knysh, A.D., *Ibn ʿArabi in the later Islamic tradition: The making of a polemical image in medieval Islam*, Albany 1999.

Loth, O., *A catalogue of the Arabic manuscripts in the Library of the India Office*, London 1877.

Makkī, M.ʿA., *al-Madāʾiḥ an-nabawiyya*, Kairo 1991.

al-Mālikī, M. b. ʿAlawī al-Ḥusaynī (Hg.), *Bāqa ʿaṭira min ṣiyaġ al-mawlid wa-l-madāʾiḥ an-nabawiyya al-karīma*, o. O. 1983.

Margariti, R.E., *Aden & the Indian Ocean trade*, Chapel Hill 2007.

Miṣbāḥ, M.F., *Burdat al-Būṣīrī wa-aṯaruhā fī l-adab al-ʿarabī al-qadīm*, Beirut 2011.

Moustafa, Y.Sh. und Ǧ. b. Kh. al-Shīdī, Al-Huwāmah and at-Tawḥīd in the Mālid: A comparative study conducted in some Wilāyāt of the Bāṭinah Region, in I. El-Mallah (Hg.), *The complete documents of the international symposium on the traditional music in Oman: October 6–16, 1985*, i, Wilhelmshaven 1995, 109–18.

Muḥammad, M.S., *al-Madāʾiḥ an-nabawiyya ḥattā nihāyat al-ʿaṣr an-mamlūkī*, Beirut 1996.

al-Munaǧǧid, Ṣ., *Muʿǧam mā ullifa ʿan rasūl allāh*, Beirut 1982.

Salemann, C., *Indices alphabetici codicum manuscriptorum persicorum, turcicorum, arabicorum, qui in Bibliotheca Imperialis Literarum Universitatis Petropolitanae adservantur*, o. O. 1888.

Salmi, A., Mawlidiyya, in *EI*², vi, 897–8.

Stetkevych, S.P., *The mantle odes: Arabic praise poems to the prophet Muḥammad*, Bloomington 2010.

Šubayb, Ġ., *Fann al-madīḥ an-nabawī fī l-ʿaṣr al-mamlūkī*, Saida 1998.

ʿUmrānī, F., *al-Madāʾiḥ an-nabawiyya fī š-šiʿr al-andalusī*, Qum 1438/2007.

Voll, J.O., al-Ahdal family, in *EI*³, first published online: 2010; first print edition 2010–1.

Wagner, M.S., *The poetics of* ḥumaynī *verse: Language and meaning in the Arab and Jewish vernacular poetry of Yemen*, PhD dissertation, New York University 2004.

Wagner, M.S., *Like Joseph in beauty: Yemeni vernacular poetry and Arab-Jewish symbiosis*, Leiden 2009.

Waugh, E.H., *Memory, music, and religion: Morocco's mystical chanters*, Columbia, SC 2005.

Weinrich, I., Mawlidiyya, in *EI*³, first published online: 2022; first print edition 2022–5.

Zaydān, Ǧ., *Tārīḫ ādāb al-luġa al-ʿarabiyya*, Kairo 2013 [1910–13].

az-Ziriklī, Ḫ., *al-Aʿlām*, 8 Bde., Beirut ¹⁵2002.

15

Orpheus zwischen Kāf und Nūn: Ein Ausflug in die arabische Unterwelt

Claudia Ott

Was haben Claudio Monteverdi, Christoph Willibald Gluck und Wolfgang Amadeus Mozart mit Reinhard Mey und der Progressive-Metal-Band Voyager gemeinsam?* Die Komponisten vom Frühbarock bis zur Klassik, der deutsche Liedermacher und die australische Gruppe haben wie viele andere Musiker quer durch die Musikgeschichte berühmte Werke zum Thema *Orpheus* geschaffen. Insbesondere Monteverdis Oper *L'Orfeo* (Uraufführung 1607) begeisterte in hunderten festlichen Aufführungen bis in die jüngste Vergangenheit ein riesiges Publikum, zu dem mit an Sicherheit grenzender Wahrscheinlichkeit auch Thomas Bauer schon einmal gezählt hat. In Mozarts *Zauberflöte* (UA 1791), der meistgespielten Oper aller Zeiten, ist der Orpheusmythos unüberhörbar, wenn auch im Gewande der freimaurerischen Initiationsriten. Mozart kam im Rahmen der Wiener Loge *Zur Wohltätigkeit,* in die er 1784 eintrat, mit diesen Riten in Berührung, die sich als die „legitime Fortführung oder Wiederaufnahme der Egyptischen Geheimnisse"[1] verstanden. In der befreundeten Loge *Zur Wahren Eintracht,* in der Mozart oft zu Gast war, bildete die Erforschung der antiken – altägyptischen und altgriechischen – Mysterien gar das zentrale Forschungsprogramm. Und Emanuel Schikaneder, der Librettist der *Zauberflöte,* hatte 1780 die Oper *Orfeo ed Euridice* von Christoph Willibald Gluck aufgeführt.[2] Aber auch zahllose andere Künstler – Dramatiker, Dichter, Maler, Bildhauer, Filmemacher – haben die Figur des Orpheus in den Mittelpunkt eines ihrer Werke gestellt. Der mythische Sänger Orpheus ist für die Künste vielleicht eine der inspirierendsten Figuren überhaupt. Nach dem antiken Mythos musste Orpheus, dessen Gesang Götter, Menschen, Tiere und

* Nach Drucklegung dieses Artikels erschien Tausendundeine Nacht. Das Buch der Liebe (München 2022), in dem die Geschichte von Sul und Schumul erstmals aus den ältesten Quellen übersetzt wurde. Im Nachwort ab Seite 489 wird ausführlich über die Themen des vorliegenden Artikels gehandelt. Zu einigen Aspekten gibt es dort auch neuere und vollständigere Informationen nachzulesen.

1 Assmann, *Zauberflöte* 375.

2 Assmann, *Zauberflöte* 400.

 | DOI:10.1163/9789004521780_017

Pflanzen, ja sogar Steine erweichen konnte, in die Unterwelt hinabsteigen, um seine Ehefrau Eurydike, die an einem Schlangenbiss gestorben war, zu befreien. Es gelang ihm, den Gott der Unterwelt zu überzeugen, seine Frau freizugeben, jedoch unter der Bedingung, dass auf dem Rückweg Orpheus vorangehen müsse, ohne sich umzudrehen, andernfalls Eurydike endgültig ins Totenreich verbannt würde. Es ist wohlbekannt, wie tragisch diese Prüfung ausgeht, und es ist sicher dieses tragische Ende, das die Künste aller Zeiten und aller Disziplinen so fasziniert hat.

Ein fernes Echo des Mythos von Orpheus in der Unterwelt ist möglicherweise aus *Tausendundeine Nacht* zu vernehmen. Auch in der Liebesgeschichte von *Sūl und Šumūl*[3] muss der Held seine Geliebte aus der Unterwelt zurückholen, zwar nicht genau auf dieselbe Art wie Orpheus, und zum Glück für beide auch ohne den Fluch des Umwendens. Dafür kommen andere Elemente ins Spiel, die für Unterhaltung und Spannung sorgen, wie Zaubervorführungen oder Flüge mit Dschinnen und Ifriten. Eine weitere Besonderheit ist die starke Betonung christlicher Elemente ohne den geringsten Hintergedanken einer Hierarchie der Religionen oder gar einer Konversion zum Islam oder zum Christentum. Im Gegenteil ist hier ein äußerst respektvoller Umgang mit der jeweils anderen Religion zu beobachten.

Auffällig ist außerdem die herausragende Rolle des Singens und der Rezitation von Gedichten. Kaum eine zweite Geschichte aus *Tausendundeine Nacht* legt einen so großen Wert auf die poetische Dimension wie *Sūl und Šumūl*. Die verschiedenen Textfassungen enthalten bis zu 120 Gedichte – für eine einzige Geschichte eine enorme Anzahl, verglichen mit den 1250 Gedichten in der Ägyptischen Rezension, die nach der Zählung von Grotzfeld 180 Geschichten beinhaltet,[4] den 253 Gedichten in der Galland-Handschrift, die mit 36 Geschichten mehr als ein Viertel des Gesamttexts von *Tausendundeine Nacht* umfasst[5] und den nur 45 Gedichten in den 69 Geschichten der Kayseri-Handschrift,[6] viele davon nur Ein- oder Zweizeiler. Die Gedichte in *Sūl und Šumūl* dagegen sind nicht nur zahlreich, sondern zumeist auch viele Verse lang. Im Gegensatz zu vielen Gedichten in anderen Teilen von *Tausendundeine Nacht*[7] sind sie offensichtlich für die Situationen verfasst worden, in denen sie ein-

3 In ihrem Forschungsband über arabische *Tausendundeine Nacht*-Handschriften behandeln Ibrahim Akel und Abubakr Chraïbi die Geschichte von Sūl und Šumūl ausführlich. Chraïbi verdanken wir auch den Brückenschlag zum Mythos von Orpheus: Chraïbi, Presentation 135.

4 Vgl. Grotzfeld, *Erzählungen* 131–43.

5 Vgl. Ott, *Wie alles begann* 670.

6 Vgl. Ott, *Das glückliche Ende*.

7 Vgl. Heinrichs, Function(s).

gesetzt werden. Sie sind also keine poetischen Zitate, sondern Unikate und Originale. Zudem sind die meisten davon handlungsrelevant, sie enthalten also Informationen, die andernfalls in der Geschichte fehlen würden. In der Regel werden die Gedichte auf dem Höhepunkt einer Rede zur Bekräftigung des Gesagten eingefügt. Manche Dialoge bestehen aber auch ganz aus Gedichten. In besonders kunstvoll komponierten Dialogen wird im Reim und Metrum aufeinander geantwortet. Ein Beispiel hierfür wird weiter unten ausführlich zitiert. Wie sehr die Geschichte von den Gedichten lebt, wissen sogar ihre Protagonisten selbst, wenn sie ihre eigene Liebesgeschichte weitererzählen: „Daraufhin erzählte ich ihm meine Geschichte, trug ihm auch die dazugehörigen Gedichte vor, und er bekam Mitleid mit mir … ."[8]

Hier – und an vielen anderen Stellen – drängt sich die Frage nach der Vortragsweise der Gedichte auf. Wie dürfen wir uns deren klangliche Realisierung vorstellen? Und welche Hinweise darauf gibt uns der Text selbst? Vor jedem Gedicht steht in den Handschriften der Hinweis auf das poetische Genre (*šiʿr*), das den Erzählfluss unterbricht, sowie die Bemerkung, dass es mit „erhobener Stimme" vorgetragen wurde (*anšada wa-ǧaʿala yaqūl*). Sicher sind die Musikalität der Sprache, das rhythmisch artikulierte Metrum und der melodiöse Klang der Stimme Hauptelemente dieses Vortrags. Auch wird ein zusätzlicher Akzent dadurch gesetzt, dass den Gedichten Segenswünsche für den Propheten vorgeschaltet werden, die man sich durchaus vom Publikum der Geschichte respondiert vorstellen darf: (*baʿd aṣ-ṣalāt ʿalā Muḥammad ar-rasūl*), wie es für Vorträge arabischer Epik belegt ist.[9] Jedoch im Unterschied zu manchen anderen Gedichten in *Tausendundeine Nacht*, die mit Instrumentalbegleitung, etwa zur Laute, gesungen werden,[10] bleibt bei *Sūl und Šumūl* die genaue Vortragsweise unerwähnt und bis auf das klösterliche Klangholz werden keine Musikinstrumente erwähnt. Die Frage nach der Vortragsweise kann also aus dem Text heraus nicht mit Sicherheit beantwortet werden. Aber eines ist sicher: Auf die Gedichte in *Tausendundeine Nacht* wartete das Publikum wie auf die Arien in einer Oper. Und speziell *Sūl und Šumūl* hat außer Arien auch noch Rezitative, Duette und Lamentos zu bieten! Die Einführungstexte in arabischen Liedersammlungen wie dem *Kitāb al-Aġānī* oder den *Masālik al-abṣār*, in denen an manchen Stellen recht ausführlich über die Aufführungspraxis von gesungenen Gedichten (hier *ṣawt* „Lied" genannt) gehandelt wird,[11] könnten demge-

8 MS Kairo Taymūriyya qiṣaṣ 15, p. 28.

9 Vgl. Ott, *Metamorphosen* 208.

10 Beispielsweise in der Geschichte *Nuraddin Ibn Bakkar und die Sklavin Schamsannahar*, vgl. Ott, *Tausendundeine Nacht – Wie alles begann* 429–37.

11 Vgl. Gökpinar, *Musikkultur*. Ich danke Yasemin Gökpinar für diese Anregung.

genüber als eine Art Opernführer gelesen werden. *Sūl und Šumūl* aber ist fast so etwas wie eine Opernlibretto, auch wenn wir den performativen Aspekt heute nur noch erahnen können.

Kommen wir zum Inhalt der Geschichte. Die Eigennamen der Liebenden deuten auf den Gang der Handlung bereits hin: Sūl (aus *su'l*) „Verlangen" und Šumūl (*šumūl*) „Zusammenführen" sind praktisch Personifikationen von Suchen und Wiederfinden. Am Vorabend ihrer Hochzeit wird die schöne Šumūl von einem schlangenartigen Drachen entführt, und Sūl macht sich auf die Suche nach ihr. Seine Suche führt Sūl vom Stammeslager der Banū Saʿd im Jemen oder im Irak, je nach der Manuskriptvorlage, durch Jordanien, Syrien und Palästina bis nach Ägypten. Auf der langen Reiseroute reiht sich Kloster an Kloster, und Sūl fragt stets die dort wohnenden Mönche um Rat und Wegweisung. Die Dialoge, die sich daraus entspinnen, sind wie Duette auskomponiert. Sie sind nicht nur poetisch äußerst ausdruckskräftig, sondern auch stärker als in allen anderen Geschichten aus *Tausendundeine Nacht* von christlichen Formeln und Themen geprägt und so ist es vielleicht kein Zufall, dass die älteste Handschrift der Geschichte von *Sūl und Šumūl* zumindest zeitweise in christlichem Besitz war (s.u.).

Gleichzeitig bewegt sich die Reise von der Welt der Beduinen über eine magische Gemeinschaft von Zauberern bis in die Sphäre der Dschinnen. Einer der Mönche, bei dem Sūl etwas länger zu Gast ist, vermittelt ihm die Bekanntschaft mit einem prominenten Zauberer, der ihn mithilfe des Königs der Zauberer schließlich in einem atemberaubenden Flug hinab in die Unterwelt bringt, wo die Reise vor dem Thron des Teufels endet. Bemerkenswert ist die Fairness, mit der der Teufel Sūl behandelt, obwohl sich dieser weigert, sich vor ihm zu verneigen. Diese gewissermaßen sympathische Version einer arabischen Teufelsgestalt ist in der Literatur wohl einmalig. Auch Sūl kann, wie Orpheus, den Herrn der Unterwelt davon überzeugen, ihm seine Frau wiederzugeben, allerdings reicht hierfür seine Gesangskunst nicht alleine aus: Neben einem besonders langen und eindrucksvollen Lied werden auch noch einige Verhandlungen und die Fürsprache von Zauberern, Dschinnen und Ifriten notwendig. Zurück geht es auf dem Landweg per Dschinn und Ifrit; hierfür wird sich die Dschinnenkönigin in ein Reitpferd für Sūl verwandeln, ein Ifrit in eines für Šumūl. Doch Sūl kehrt mit zwei Frauen aus der Unterwelt zurück – wie wird das enden?

Sūl und Šumūl ist aber auch die Geschichte eines arabischen Pantoffelhelden. Der Held der Geschichte handelt nämlich nicht aus eigenem Antrieb, sondern folgt stets den Anweisungen seiner weiblichen Vorgesetzten, erst seiner Mutter, später seiner Amme und endlich seiner Ehefrau. Sogar die doppelte Ehe, in die die Geschichte schließlich mündet, ist nicht seinem eigenen

Wunsch entsprungen, sondern wurde von seiner Frau und deren Freundin von langer Hand eingefädelt; bis hin zur Ausstattung der Paläste mit einem unterirdischen Verbindungsgang, durch den er zwischen den beiden Ehelagern hin und her wechseln kann, ist alles von den Frauen eingerichtet worden. Im Unterschied zu manchen anderen Geschichten in *Tausendundeine Nacht* sind die weiblichen Protagonistinnen auch alle mit Namen ausgestattet und agieren ebenbürtig mit ihren männlichen Partnern. Liest man die Geschichte unter diesem Vorzeichen – im aktuellen Band der Neuübersetzung von *Tausendundeine Nacht*[12] ist sie in deutscher Übertragung zu lesen, so wird sie auch als Parodie auf eine weibliche Art des Umgangs mit Macht und Patriarchat verständlich.

Die bei weitem älteste erhaltene Handschrift der Geschichte von *Sūl und Šumūl* wurde zwischen 1860 und 1862 durch den preußischen Konsul Johann Gottfried Wetzstein in Damaskus erworben und 1864 nach Tübingen verkauft, wo sie bis heute in der Universitätsbibliothek aufbewahrt wird.[13] Die Handschrift dürfte in Ägypten hergestellt worden sein, nicht nur die koptische Seitenzählung, sondern auch Ägypten als Ziel der Reise Sūls und die herausragende positive Rolle des ägyptischen Mönchs weisen darauf hin. Wie viele andere Handschriften von *Tausendundeine Nacht* gelangte sie irgendwann im Verlauf ihrer Sammelgeschichte nach Syrien, wurde dort weiter verkauft und vererbt, bis Wetzstein sie in Damaskus kaufte.[14] Die Handschrift weist nur wenige Lesernotizen am Rande auf, darunter die eines christlichen Lesers oder Besitzers (fol. 15[a]); das separate Blatt mit Leser- und Studiennotizen (fol. 85) gehört zu einem anderen Buch und ist fälschlich in die Handschrift von Sūl und Šumūl geraten. Schon Wetzstein datierte die Handschrift in seinem Katalog ins 14. Jahrhundert;[15] die späteren Kataloge und auch jüngere Forschungen zu Papier- und Schriftqualität bestätigen diese frühe Datierung.[16] Vergleiche mit datierten Handschriften des epischen Genres legen eine Datierung „um 1400" nahe. Die Handschrift ist somit die älteste in substantiellem Umfang erhaltene *Tausendundeine Nacht*-Handschrift überhaupt und bis zu 100 Jahre älter als

12 Bisher erschienen *Tausendundeine Nacht – Wie alles begann* (2004) und *Tausendundeine Nacht – Das glückliche Ende* (2016). Der Band *Tausendundeine Nacht – Das Buch der Liebe* (2022) ist kürzlich erschienen. Ich danke Ulrich Nolte, meinem langjährigen Lektor im Verlag C.H. Beck, für wertvolle Gedankenanstöße nicht nur zu diesem Artikel.

13 Tübingen, Universitätsbibliothek, Ma VI 33.

14 Vgl. Ott, Wonderland 171.

15 Wetzstein, *Catalog* 6: „Die ca. 500 J. alte HS ist vielleicht die älteste existierende, da 1001 Nacht nur für den Gebrauch in Kaffeehäusern copirt und daher bald abgenutzt wird."

16 Vgl. Chraïbi, Presentation 117.

die berühmte Galland-Handschrift, die bisher als die älteste *Tausendundeine Nacht*-Handschrift galt.[17]

Die Tübinger Handschrift enthält mehrere umfangreiche Fragmente der Geschichte von *Sūl und Šumūl* in einer für die Aufnahme in *Tausendundeine Nacht* vorbereiteten Fassung. Hierfür wurde die Geschichte in Nächte eingeteilt und an den Nachtgrenzen wurde die Nachtformel eingeschoben, allerdings fehlen die Überschriften und Zählungen der Nächte; die betreffenden Zeilen sind frei geblieben. Ganz ähnlich wie im Fall der Kayseri-Handschrift[18] heißt es in der Tübinger Handschrift von *Sūl und Šumūl* einfach „Und als die nächste Nacht gekommen war …“:

> Da erreichte das Morgengrauen Schahrasad und sie hörte auf zu erzählen. „Wie schön und wie spannend ist deine Geschichte!,“ sagte ihre Schwester. „In der nächsten Nacht,“ erwiderte sie, „erzähle ich euch etwas noch Spannenderes und noch viel Aufregenderes als das!“
>
> [Und als] die nächste Nacht [gekommen war], sagte Dunyasad zu ihrer Schwester Schahrasad: „Ach, Schwester, ich beschwöre dich bei Gott! Wenn du nicht schläfst, so erzähle dem König die Geschichte von Sūl und Šumūl zu Ende!“ – „Mit Vergnügen und Hochachtung,“ antwortete sie.
>
> Es ist mir zu Ohren gekommen, o glücklicher König, dass, nachdem Sūl sein Gedicht zu Ende gesprochen hatte, der Mönch aus seiner Klause schaute. […]

Die Tübinger Handschrift von *Sūl und Šumūl* enthält insgesamt zwölf solcher Nachtzäsuren, von denen elf auf den ersten Seiten der Handschrift recht regelmäßig aufeinanderfolgen, während die zwölfte erst ganz zum Schluss steht. Es scheint, als wäre die Aufbereitung für *Tausendundeine Nacht* unvollständig geblieben, vielleicht war die Handschrift auch niemals tatsächlich Teil einer vollständigen Tausendundeine Nacht-Ausgabe, sondern wurde nur für eine solche vorbereitet.

Interessanterweise trägt das Werk noch einige markante Spuren seiner Vorgeschichte als arabisches Beduinenepos: Die Einschübe des „virtuellen Erzählers“ richten sich an ein typisches Publikum von Vorlesestunden mit arabischer Epik, zum Beispiel in der mehrfach wiederkehrenden Formulierung: „Der

17 Der Herausgeber Muhsin Mahdi selbst ist ein Vertreter der Theorie, daß die „Galland-Handschrift“ schon aus dem 14. Jahrhundert stammt. Er geht dabei von einer anderen Deutung des Münznamens Ašrafī aus. Folgt man aber Heinz Grotzfelds These, kann die „Galland-Handschrift“ erst um 1450 entstanden sein. Vgl. Grotzfeld, Numismatic.

18 MS Kayseri Râşit Ef. 614, vgl. Ott, *Das glückliche Ende* 379–85.

وأدرك شهرزاد الصبح فسكتت عن الحديث. قالت
أختها ما أحسن حديثك وأعجبه. قالت الليلة القا[بلة]
أحدثكم بأعجب وأغرب

الليلة القابلة قالت دنيازاد لأختها شهرزاد
بالله عليك يا أختاه إن كنتي غير نايمة فاتمي للملك
حديث السول والشمول. قالت حبا وكرامة زعموا
أيها الملك السعيد أن السول لما فرغ من شعره كبر
الراهب من صومعته. وقدس وسبح ومجد وكبر
وأجاب السول على شعره. يقول
أهلا وسهلا بشخص جل خالقه أعطاه حسنا به يزهو
على البشر
أراك تسأل عن أمر ذهبت به وأنت من أجله بالهم
أنت تسأل عن بدر على غصن وقد تكامل منسوب
إلى البشر
لا والذي رفع السبع الشداد ومن سقى البلاد وأروى
بساير القطر

ABB. 1 Tübinger Handschrift von Sūl und Šumūl, Ma. VI 33, fol. 7b

Erzähler spricht: Ihr edlen Herren!" (*qāla r-rāwī: Yā sāda, yā kirām*).[19] Und in der Schlusspassage wird die ganze Geschichte selbst als „Epos" (arab. *sīra*) bezeichnet. Auch dies erinnert an den Schluss der Kayseri-Handschrift, wo das „Epos von Tausendundeiner Nacht" (*sīrat alf layla wa-layla*) als Titel gesetzt ist.[20]

Die Tübinger Handschrift von *Sūl und Šumūl* ist jedoch, wie erwähnt, nur bruchstückhaft erhalten. Die graeco-koptische Blattzählung beginnt mit Blatt 35. Es fehlen also 34 Blätter, fast 70 Seiten, des Anfangs und weitere Blätter im Textverlauf, die sich auf einige Dutzend summieren. Alle erhaltenen Fragmente sind schon 1902 durch den Tübinger Orientalisten Christian Friedrich Seybold ins Deutsche übertragen und in einer arabischen Textedition herausgegeben worden,[21] 2016 erschien eine Neuedition durch Ibrahim Akel und Aboubakr Chraïbi.[22]

Ebenso bruchstückhaft – und wohl ebenso alt – ist eine Handschrift mit dem Anfang der Geschichte von *Sūl und Šumūl*, die lange in der Sammlung des Verlags E.J. Brill in Leiden aufbewahrt und von dort vor einigen Jahren an das King Faysal Centre for Research and Islamic Studies in Riyad verkauft wurde.[23] Auch dieses Fragment, das etwa ein Drittel des Texts enthält, ist in Nächte eingeteilt, die sogar numeriert sind: erhalten sind die Nächte 274 bis 283. Dieses Fragment war also bereits Teil einer vollständigen *Tausendundeine Nacht*-Fassung. Die erhaltenen Textteile wurden ebenfalls 2016 durch Ibrahim Akel und Aboubakr Chraïbi ediert.

In der Sammlung des ägyptischen Intellektuellen Ahmad Pascha Taymūr (1871–1930), die unter dem Namen „Taymūriyya" in der Nationalbibliothek in Kairo aufbewahrt wird, befindet sich eine dritte Version der Geschichte, und zwar in einer Handschrift in mehreren Teilen, die mindestens neun *Tausendundeine Nacht*-Geschichten enthält. Die „Taymūriyya-Handschrift" wurde in Fachkreisen durch die Dissertation von Sophia Schwab, später Grotzfeld, bekannt, die sie zusammen mit Heinz Grotzfeld dann auch in ihrer Einführung zu *Tausendundeine Nacht* beschrieb.[24] Eine Mikrofilmkopie der Handschrift liegt im Institut für Arabistik und Islamwissenschaft der Universität Münster.[25] Als Sammelhandschrift ist die „Taymūriyya-Handschrift" durch ihren Mittelteil, die Geschichte von Zayd und al-Kaḥlā, datierbar auf das islamische Jahr

19 Tübingen, M.A. VI 33, fol. 66a und weitere Stellen. Vgl. Ott, Coffeehouse 446.
20 Vgl. Ott, *Ende* 368.
21 Seybold, *Geschichte*.
22 Akel und Chraïbi, Texts.
23 Vgl. Akel, Liste 69–70.
24 Grotzfeld und Grotzfeld, Erzählungen 44.
25 Mein Dank gilt Hakan Özkan für die Erschließung der Mikrofilmkopie; eine Seite daraus ist unten abgebildet (Abb.3).

ABB. 2 Erste Seite der Geschichte von Sūl und Šumūl in der Riyader Handschrift, KFCRIS 2415, fol. 1ª

1002, das dem Jahr 1594 christlicher Zählung entspricht. Geschrieben wurde dieser Teil laut Kolophon von Muḥammad b. aš-Šayḫ Muḥammad b. Zaytūn. Obwohl der Duktus der Schrift nahelegt, dass auch die anderen Handschriftenteile offensichtlich vom selben Schreiber geschrieben wurden, ist dies nicht eindeutig beweisbar. Dennoch darf „um 1600" als Datierung gelten.

Die Kairoer Handschrift von *Sūl und Šumūl* umfasst im Original 38 Seiten[26] und ist damit erheblich kürzer als die Tübinger und auch die Riyader Version einmal gewesen sein müssen. Wir haben hier also eine Kurzfassung der Geschichte vor uns. Da sie nicht als Teil von *Tausendundeine Nacht* präpariert ist, können wir an dieser Geschichte nachvollziehen, wie eine parallele Überlieferung gleichzeitig innerhalb und außerhalb von *Tausendundeine Nacht* lebendig sein konnte.

Eine vierte Textfassung liegt in der Sammlung *Kitāb al-Ḥikāyāt al-ʿağība* vor, deren Text von Hans Wehr herausgegeben wurde. Ulrich Marzolph hat Sophia Grotzfelds Übersetzung dieser Geschichte in seine Ausgabe „Das Buch der

26 Die Handschrift ist ausnahmsweise nicht nach Blättern, sondern nach Seiten gezählt. Daher die Seitenangaben mit p. statt fol.

wundersamen Geschichten" übernommen.[27] Auch diese Fassung, eine Handschrift der Hagia-Sophia-Bibliothek in Istanbul, wurde, wie die Kairoer Fassung, 2016 durch Ibrahim Akel und Aboubakr Chraïbi in einer synoptischen Edition herausgegeben, der diese auch die fünfte erhaltene Fassung, ein Londoner Manuskript, hinzufügten.[28]

Doch zurück zur Geschichte von *Sūl und Šumūl*. Auf seiner Suche nach seiner Braut Šumūl zieht Sūl von Kloster zu Kloster; die Mönche, die er dort antrifft, antworten auf seine in Gedicht- bzw. Liedform vorgetragene Frage stets mit einem entsprechenden Gedicht oder Lied. Beide Gesprächspartner dieser poetischen Dialoge beziehen sich in ausgesprochen höflicher Weise auf die Religion des anderen, indem sie ihn an dessen Autoritäten, liturgische Gewohnheiten, Feste oder Heiligen gemahnen. So beschwört Sūl die Mönche „beim Pfingstfest," „beim Klangholz" oder „bei Simeon, dem Säulenheiligen," die Mönche antworten mit Schwüren auf koranische Gottesnamen oder mit der Redewendung, auf die im Titel dieses Artikels Bezug genommen wird: *wa-ḥaqqi man yaqḍi bayna l-kāfi wa-n-nūni*.[29]

(*basīṭ*)
aqsamtu bi-llāhi aymānan mu'akkadatan
fa-sma' maqāliya yā man qad yunādīnī

mā in ra'aytu wa-lā abṣartu min aḥadin
wa-ḥaqqi man yaqḍi bayna l-kāfi wa-n-nūnī

mimmā dahāka fa-ḫabbirnī wa-anta bihī
bi-ṣ-ṣidqi minka wa-fīhi lā turāyīnī[30]

An dieser Stelle sei ein Einblick in die *Tausendundeine Nacht*-Übersetzerwerkstatt gestattet, der immer auch ein Einblick in das tägliche Scheitern und Verbessern sein muss. Der erste Versuch einer metrisch getreuen Übersetzung der drei Verse lautete:

27 Marzolph, *Geschichten* 328–60.

28 Chraïbi, Presentation; Akel und Chraïbi, Texts.

29 Der Halbvers findet sich in der Kairoer Handschrift auf S. 23, Zeile 4, in der Tübinger Handschrift gleichlautend auf fol. 19[b], die Londoner Handschrift bietet denselben Wortlaut auf fol. 241[a]. Die Riyader und die Istanbuler Handschrift enthalten diese Passage des Textes nicht. In der Edition von Akel und Chraïbi stehen die Kairoer und Londoner Fassungen auf S. 228, die Tübinger auf S. 162.

30 MS Kairo Taymūriyya qiṣaṣ 15, p. 23, Z. 4–6 (siehe Abb. 3).

ABB. 3 Kairoer Handschrift, Taymūriyya qiṣaṣ 15, p. 23. Die Handschrift trägt eine pagina- statt folio-Zählung

Ich schwöre heilige Eide, höre, was ich dir sag',
Du, der mich mit deinem Rufen aus dem Kloster gehetzt:

Ich habe niemand gesehen und von keinem gehört,
So wahr der Herr zwischen Kāf und Nūn sein Urteil gesetzt!

Doch du erzähle mir alles, was dir ist widerfahr'n,
Spiel mir nichts vor, sondern sag die reine Wahrheit jetzt!

Doch was bedeutet dieses „Urteil" zwischen den Buchstaben Kāf und Nūn? Was für ein Konflikt mag zwischen zwei Buchstaben schwelen, so dass man zwischen ihnen „richten" (*yaqḍī*) müsste? Besteht hier ein Zusammenhang mit der Buchstabenmagie oder Onomatomantik (*sīmiyā'*), etwa mit dem Zahlenwert der Buchstaben und seiner Berechnung (*ḥisāb al-ǧummal, kasr* und *basṭ*) – als Gimatria auch aus der jüdischen Kabbala bekannt –, der divinatorischen Bedeutung von Buchstaben (*'ilm al-ǧafr*), ihren astrologischen Verbindungen (*qirānāt*) oder einer anderen geheimen, magischen Eigenschaft (*ḫawāṣṣ al-ḥurūf*)?[31]

Nach einigem Knobeln wurde klar: Die Lösung des Rätsels ist viel einfacher. Arabischkundige denken bei den beiden Buchstaben *Kāf* und *nūn* sofort an den Imperativ *kun!*, den göttlichen Schöpfungsbefehl. Der Wortlaut *kun fa-yakūn*, der Befehl „Sei!" und dessen sofortige Erfüllung, steht zweimal im Koran, einmal sogar in Verbindung mit dem Lexem *qaḍā*.[32] Die Redewendung *bayna l-kāfi wa-n-nūni* „zwischen *kāf* und *nūn*" bezeichnet die Zeit, die zwischen diesen beiden Buchstaben verstreicht, also die Dauer, die der kurze Vokal *u* beansprucht, während der Schöpfungsbefehl *kun!* ausgesprochen wird. Nämlich Null. In einem Nichts an Zeit kann Gott alles „ausrichten," er kann „es richten" im Sinne von „beschließen" bzw. „ins Werk setzen." Da dieses abstrakte zeitliche Nichts dem menschlichen Verstand schwer begreiflich ist, wird der Zeitabstand zwischen *Kāf* und *Nūn* im Wörtchen *kun*, den sich jeder Sprecher leicht vorstellen kann, zur Veranschaulichung eingesetzt. So jedenfalls erklärt es ein Korankommentar.[33] Auch in Predigten wird dieser Verweis auf den Koran

---

31 „Die Magie der *sīmiyā* betrachtet die Worte als Ausschüttungen der göttlichen Energie und erkennt speziell jeden einzelnen Buchstaben dieser koranischen Worte als Konzentration derselben, die unmittelbar an der göttlichen Segenskraft partizipiert." Dorpmüller, *Magie* 31.

32 Q 2:117 kombiniert hier mit dem Verb *qaḍā*: „Beschließt er eine Sache, spricht er zu ihr: Sei! Und dann ist sie." (Ü Bobzin); Q 6:14 mit *aradnā*: „Vielmehr ist unsere Rede, wenn wir irgendetwas wollen, dass wir zu ihm sagen: Sei! und dann ist es." (Ü Bobzin).

33 *wa-kawnu amrihī bayna l-kāfi wa-n-nūni kināyatun 'ani s-sur'ati wa-illā fa-lā yaḥtāǧu ilā*

und auf Gottes Wirken häufig zitiert,[34] und auch die Übersetzung Seybolds zur fraglichen Stelle: „Bei dem, der da spricht und es geschieht!"[35] weist darauf hin, auch wenn in Seybolds Formulierung das entscheidende Element, nämlich der direkte Bezug auf ein Koranwort und dessen Deutung in der Redewendung, völlig fehlt.

Daher der zweite Übersetzungsversuch:

> Ich schwöre heilige Eide, höre, was ich dir sag',
> Du, der mich herausruft aus meinem klösterlichen Tun:
>
> Ich habe niemand gesehen und von keinem gehört,
> So wahr der Schöpfer es richtet zwischen Kaf und Nun!
>
> Doch du erzähle mir alles, was dir ist widerfahr'n,
> Spiel mir nichts vor, sondern sprich die reine Wahrheit nun!

Mit seiner Antwort an den muslimischen Fragesteller stellt sich unser christlicher Mönch in eine äußerst interessante poetische Tradition. Schwüre bei religiösen Autoriäten des angesprochenen Partners sind in der arabischen Dichtung sowohl bei Gedichten an christliche als auch an zoroastrische Gesprächsbzw. Liebespartner belegt, etwa bei Abū Nuwās (gest. um 200/815) oder Mudrik aš-Šaybāni (3.–4./9.–10. Jh). Geert Jan van Gelder bietet eine einfache Erklärung, wie sie auch auf die Schwurgedichte in *Sūl und Šumūl* zutreffen dürfte: „It is obviously far more effective, when adressing someone, to swear by things that are holy to the addressee than by things that he would reject or find meaningless."[36] Für Gregor Schoeler hingegen dürfen beim Sprecher des Gedichts in seinem Fall – es geht um eine Liebeswerbung zwischen Männern – gewisse Hintergedanken vorausgesetzt werden: „Concealed behind this is of course nothing other than the endeavor to win the young man over and make him submit to the poet's wishes. Thus, the oaths are purely rhetoric."[37] Im Vergleich mit den von van Gelder und Schoeler vorgestellten Gedichten haben wir in *Sūl und Šumūl* eine erheblich erweiterte Ausformung der Szene vor uns. Hier werden nicht nur Schwüre eines Muslims bei christlichen Autoritäten, sondern

---

lafẓi kun bal mahmā arāda šay'an aẓharahu, aqraba min laḥẓi l-ʿuyūni wa-innamā ǧā'ati l-ʿibāratu ʿalā qadri mā tafhamu l-ʿuqūlu: Ibn ʿAǧība, *Baḥr* iv, 24, zu Q 16:40.

34 Siehe beispielsweise Franklin Lewis in seinem Artikel in der *EQ*, s. v. Persian Literature and the Qur'an, hier in bezug auf die persische Literatur. Ich danke Hakan Özkan und Nefeli Papoutsakis für diesen Beleg und weitere wertvolle Hinweise.

35 Seybold, *Sul und Schumul* 23.

36 Van Gelder, Christian Boy 58.

37 Schoeler, Zoroastrian Boy 76.

im Gegenzug auch Schwüre christlicher Sprecher unter Berufung auf die dem Islam heiligen Namen und Dinge zitiert. Beide Seiten beschwören durch den Rekurs auf die religiöse Autorität des jeweils anderen umso wirkungsvoller ihre Aussagen.

Aber es ist nicht die Aussage selbst, die zählt. „Ich habe Šumūl nicht gesehen," könnte der Mönch auch in zwei oder drei Worten sagen. Auf den kargen Informationswert kommt es nur insofern an, als der Mönch damit den Helden eine Station weiterschickt, wo der nächste Mönch mit dem nächsten Gedicht schon auf ihn wartet. Solche Elemente haben mithin eine performative Dimension.

Wenn der Vergleich zu einer wohlbekannten, wenn auch auf den ersten Blick recht weit entfernten europäischen Tradition gestattet ist, so wäre die Rolle des Mönches hier mit der der Herbergswirte im weihnachtlichen Krippenspiel zu vergleichen. Auch die Wirte – bis auf den letzten – haben jeweils dasselbe zu sagen, nämlich: „Wir haben keinen Platz in der Herberge." Aber auch sie sagen es jeder mit anderen Worten, und der Unterhaltungswert eines Krippenspiels bemisst sich auch und gerade in der Variationsvielfalt und der Phantasie, mit der diese Nebenrollen, die für den Gang der Handlung aber doch essentiell wichtig sind, ausgearbeitet sind. Ähnlich die Mönche in *Sūl und Šumūl*. Bis auf den letzten Mönch, der Sūl zu sich hineinbittet und ihm den Übergang in die Welt der Zauberer vermittelt, haben alle Mönche exakt dieselbe Botschaft: „Wir haben Šumūl nicht gesehen," und der künstlerische Wert dieser Dialoge und damit der ganzen Geschichte steckt eben in der Variationsbreite der poetischen Ausformung dieser Aussage. Nicht umsonst werden die Gedichte nur so weit so variiert, dass der Wiedererkennungswert der Szenen immer noch im Vordergrund steht; davon abgesehen sind sie sorgfältig nach den Regeln des *ʿarūḍ* gestaltet; in zwei Fällen sind die Dialoge sogar im selben Reim und Metrum gehalten, das heißt, der Mönch antwortet auf die Frage Sūls mit einem klanglich exakt entsprechenden Gedicht. Hier wird die performative Dimension ganz deutlich. Sūl und die Mönche singen quasi jeweils ein Duett. Im folgenden Fall ist das ganze Duett im Metrum *basīṭ* (⏓–⏑– | ⏓⏑– | ⏓–⏑– | ⏓(⏑)–) gehalten:

O Klostermönch, der du Psalter und Evangelium aufschlägst,
Und daraus schöne und melodiöse Suren vorträgst!

Im Namen Simeons bitt' ich dich, der auf seiner Säule
Saß, daß du mir die Bitte, die ich hab, nicht abschlägst.

Ich frag' dich bei des Messias menschlicher Natur,
Beim Patriarchen und bei dem Priesterkreuz, das du trägst,

Bei König Saul und bei jenem Holzbrett, das vor dem Tor
Des Klosters hängt und das du, sooft der Morgen graut, schlägst:

O Mönch des Klosters! Hast du den Mond vorbeikommen seh'n,
Der näher als Ohr und Aug dem Herzen war allernächst,

Und der mein Freund und Gefährte war, mein Labsal und Freud,
Bevor das Schicksal mir diesen Freund hat fortgehext?

Ich lebte ständig in Angst und Schrecken vor diesem Fall:
Das Schicksal straft dich genau mit dem, wovor du dich schreckst.

Bei Gott beschwöre ich dich, dass du mir Auskunft erteilst,
Sobald du nur die geringste Spur des Mondes entdeckst.

O sag es mir, lieber Mönch, und dafür gebe dir Gott,
Dass stets das Glück dir sei hold in allem, was du bezweckst!

Als Sūl sein Gedicht beendet hatte, schaute der Mönch zu ihm heraus. Er trug prächtige weiße Haare und einen langen weißen Bart und war eine ehrfurchtgebietende Erscheinung. Es war, als läge ein Lichtglanz auf ihm, wenn er das „Dreimal Heilig!" anstimmte und seine Litaneien sang. Der Mönch antwortete ihm mit diesen Versen:

Ahlan wa-Sahlan! Willkommen dem ratsuchenden Gast,
Der du in meinen Gedanken längst schon Raum gefasst hast.

Du kamst und fragtest nach einem Vollmond, dessen Natur
Kaum in die menschliche Hülle, die ihn eingezwängt, passt.

Den Vollmond habe ich weder selbst geseh'n noch gehört
Nicht in der finstersten Nacht, noch, wenn ihr Dunkel verblasst.

Doch komm herein und erzähl mir alles, was du erlebt
Und welche Wechsel des Schicksals du schon durchgemacht hast.

Mein Gast, erzähle mir, wer du bist und woher du kommst,
Und Gott gewähre dir dafür ein Glas Regen zur Rast.

Darauf entgegnete ihm Sūl:

O Klostermönch! Ich bin der berühmte Liebende, der
In die verliebt ist, die seinen Kummer offengelegt.

Ich liebte sie, so wie sie mich liebte, und diese Lieb'
Saß tief in unseren Leibern, wo die Herzkammer schlägt.

Doch als ich mich sicher wähnte, dass ich sie hätt' gekriegt,
Da hab ich nur das Frohlocken meiner Neider erregt.

O führ uns schnellstens zusammen, weil mein Herz diese Kluft
– Sie an dem einen, ich an dem andren Ort – nicht erträgt!

Als er mit seinem Gedicht zuende war, sprach der Mönch die Verse:

Gott sei gelobt und gepriesen, der sich uns eingeprägt
Als einz'ger Herr aller Menschen, ewig und unbewegt.

Du hast mit deiner Geschichte meinen Kummer vermehrt.
Doch hab Geduld, denn Geduld ist's, was den Kummer zerschlägt![38]

Die Mönche in der Liebesgeschichte von *Sūl und Šumūl* spielen mithin äußerst bedeutsame Rollen: Sie sind Wegweiser in einem Mysterienspiel, das Sūl immer weiter Richtung Unterwelt und durch die Begegnung mit dem Teufel in eine Art Initiation führen und zu einem neuen Menschen lassen wird. Zumindest der letzte Mönch entpuppt sich geradezu als Mystagoge, und auch die anderen haben im Grunde wie die Klöster mystagogische Funktionen, weil der Protagonist (der Myste) durch sie immer weiter in eine religiöse Sphäre eintaucht. Die Elemente Tod, Liebe und Musik verbinden sich dabei zu einer Art Mysterienspiel, wie es in Mozarts Oper *Die Zauberflöte* meisterhaft vorgeführt wird. Und so dürfen wir wohl auch *Sūl und Šumūl* als eine Art Mysterienspiel vor unserem inneren Ohr und Auge ablaufen lassen – gewissermaßen ein Unterweltsfahrt-Spiel mit musikalischer Dimension in religiöser Crossover-Landschaft.

38 Kairo Taymūriyya qiṣaṣ 15, pp. 20–1.

Liste zitierter Literatur

Akel, I. und Chraïbi, A., The tale of Sul and Shumul – Texts, in A. Chraïbi (Hg.), *Arabic manuscripts of the Thousand and One Nights: Presentation and critical editions of four noteworthy texts; observations on some Osmanli translations*, Paris 2016, 137–260.

Akel, I., Liste des manuscrits arabes des Nuits, in A. Chraïbi (Hg.), *Arabic manuscripts of the Thousand and One Nights: Presentation and critical editions of four noteworthy texts; observations on some Osmanli translations*, Paris 2016, 65–114.

Assmann, J., *Die Zauberflöte: Ein literarischer Opernbegleiter mit dem Libretto Emanuel Schikaneders und verwandten Dingen*, Zürich 2012

Chraïbi, A., The tale of Sul and Shumul – Presentation, in A. Chraïbi (Hg.), *Arabic manuscripts of the Thousand and One Nights: Presentation and critical editions of four noteworthy texts; observations on some Osmanli translations*, Paris 2016, 115–36.

Dorpmüller, S., *Religiöse Magie im „Buch der probaten Mittel": Analyse, kritische Edition und Übersetzung des Kitāb al-Muǧarrabāt von Muḥammad Ibn Yūsuf as-Sanūsī (gest. um 895/1490)*, Wiesbaden 2005.

Gökpinar, Y., *Höfische Musikkultur im klassischen Islam: Ibn Faḍlallāh al-ʿUmarī (gest. 749/1349) über die dichterische und musikalische Kunst der Sängersklavinnen*, Leiden 2020.

Grotzfeld, H., The age of the Galland manuscript of the Nights: Numismatic evidence for dating a manuscript?, in *JAIS* 1 (1996), 50–67.

Grotzfeld, H. und Grotzfeld, S., *Die Erzählungen aus Tausendundeiner Nacht*, Dortmund 2012.

Heinrichs, W., The function(s) of poetry in the Arabian Nights: Some observations, in A. Vrolijk und J.P. Hogendijk (Hgg.), *O ye gentlemen: Arabic studies on science and literary culture in honour of Remke Kruk*, Leiden 2007.

Ibn ʿAǧība, A., *al-Baḥr al-madīd fī tafsīr al-Qurʾān al-maǧīd*, Hg. ʿU.A. al-Rāwī, Beirut 2015.

Ott, C., From the coffeehouse into the manuscript: The storyteller and his audience in the manuscripts of an Arabian epic, in *Oriente Moderno* N.S. (LXXXIII), 2 (2003), 443–51.

Ott, C., *Metamorphosen des Epos: Sīrat al-Muǧāhidīn (al-Amīra Ḏāt al-Himma) zwischen Mündlichkeit und Schriftlichkeit*, Leiden 2003.

Ott, C., *Tausendundeine Nacht – Wie alles begann: Tausendundeine Nacht. Nach der ältesten arabischen Handschrift in der Ausgabe von Muhsin Mahdi erstmals ins Deutsche übertragen*, München 2004.

Ott, C., *Tausendundeine Nacht – Das glückliche Ende: Nach der Handschrift der Raşit-Efendi-Bibliothek Kayseri erstmals ins Deutsche übersetzt*, München 2016.

Ott, C., Wetzstein in Wonderland: Arabian epic manuscripts in the Wetzstein Collections, in B. Liebrenz und C. Rauch (Hgg.), *Manuscripts, politics and Oriental studies: Life and collections of Johann Gottfried Wetzstein (1815–1905) in context*, Leiden 2019, 162–73.

Marzolph, U. (Hg.), *Das Buch der wundersamen Geschichten. Erzählungen aus der Welt von Tausendundeine Nacht: Unter Verwendung der Übersetzungen von Hans Wehr, Otto Spies, Max Weisweiler und Sophia Grotzfeld zusammengestellt, kommentiert und herausgegeben*, München 1999.

Seybold, C.F., *Geschichte von Sul und Schumul: Unbekannte Erzählung aus Tausend und Einer Nacht*, aus dem Arabischen übersetzt von C.F. Seybold, Leipzig 1902; *Geschichte von Sul und Schumul, unbekannte Erzählung aus Tausend und einer Nacht*, nach dem Tübinger Unikum herausgegeben von Dr. C.F. Seybold, mit Handschrift-Facsimile, Leipzig 1902.

Schoeler, G., *Abū Nuwās' poem to the Zoroastrian boy Bihrūz: an Arabic 'sawgand-nāma' with a Persian 'kharja'*, in A. Talib, M. Hammond und A. Schippers (Hgg.), *The rude, the bad and the bawdy: essays in honour of Professor Geert Jan van Gelder*, Cambridge 2014, 66–79.

van Gelder, G.J., Mudrik al-Shaybânî's poem on a christian boy: Bad taste or harmless wit?, in E. de Moor und G. Borg (Hgg.), *Representations of the divine in Arabic poetry*, Amsterdam 2001, 49–70.

Wetzstein, J.G., *Catalog Arabischer Manuscripte / In Damascus gesammelt*, Berlin 1863.

16

Poetisch wider Willen: Der Koran im Vers Māmayhs – Über poetische Verfahren der Doppel- bzw. Mehrfachcodierung und des Code-Switching in *iqtibās*-Epigrammen

Alev Masarwa

Die Inkorporation koranischer Aussagen in künstlerische Texte (*iqtibās*, wörtl. das Feuerholen am fremden Herd; Entlehnen) ist gängige intertextuelle Praxis. Doch als literar-ästhetisches Wunder mit einer negativen Intertextualität,[1] wie es Thomas Bauer im Vergleich mit der zeitgenössischen arabischen Poesie hervorgehoben hat, ist der koranische Text weder Prosa noch Poesie. Stenggenommen übersteigt der Koran als ästhetischer und zugleich autoritativer Offenbarungstext mit seinen strukturellen und narrativen Eigenarten auch das gewöhnliche Verständnis von Textkohärenz und Textgrenze. Damit sind der Einspielung einer Koranstelle in die Domäne der Dichtung als poetisches Verfahren einige Grenzen gesetzt. Einerseits darf der Offenbarungstext nicht oder nur geringfügig verändert werden, andererseits müssen unter Einsatz adäquater rhetorischer Figuren Reim und Metrum eingehalten werden. Darüber hinaus muss je nach Gattungszugehörigkeit die poetische Aussage überzeugen und originell sein. Über Jahrhunderte hinweg haben Dichter Möglichkeiten gefunden, mit diesen Einschränkungen meisterhaft und spielerisch umzugehen, sie als Herausforderung zu nehmen und sich sogar an die Grenzen des noch Erlaubten zu wagen oder diese zu übertreten. So kommen Koranzitate in religiöser und profaner Dichtung ebenso vor, wie in Wein- oder *muǧūn*-Epigrammen. Einer, der mit besonderer Vorliebe Epigramme mit eigebauten Koranversen schrieb und somit ‚mit dem Feuer spielte', war der syrische Dichter Māmayh (altern. Māmāy) ar-Rūmī (gest. ca. 987/1579).[2] Sein umfangreicher *Dīwān* (*Rawḍat al-muštāq wa-bahǧat al-ʿuššāq*) umfasst mehrere Hundert Epi-

1 Bauer, The relevance of early Arabic poetry for Qurʾanic studies 706.

2 Mit vollem Namen Muḥammad b. Aḥmad b. ʿAbdallāh (Ibn) ar-Rūmī ad-Dimašqī. Māmayh, Māmay oder Māmīh war sein Spitz-/Kosename, den er neben Ibn ar-Rūmī als *maḫlaṣ* verwendete, siehe Masarwa, Māmayh ar-Rūmī, in EI[3] (eingereicht). In einigen Quellen lautet sein Ehrenname Šams ad-Dīn, siehe u.a. *Fihris* al-Azhar [*maǧāmīʿ* 829/40060].

DOI:10.1163/9789004521780_018

gramme, von denen – ungeachtet einer beachtlichen Anzahl an nicht markierten – 51 in ihren Überschriften explizit als *iqtibās*-Epigramme markiert sind. Das Textkorpus dieser *muqtabasāt*[3] umfasst Themen der Liebes-, Wein- und Spottdichtung zu unterschiedlichsten poetischen Anlässen. Unter dem Aspekt der Doppel- bzw. Mehrfachcodierung[4] werden in diesem Beitrag die Formen und Resultate des Aufeinandertreffens zweier Textsorten und damit einhergehend ihre latenten und manifesten semantischen Codes näher analysiert. Da koranische Textfragmente, wie überhaupt die meisten Zitate in diesen Gattungen, ohne graphemische oder syntaktische Zitatsignale, somit auch ohne offensichtliche Störung der Textisotopie in den Vers eingefügt werden, interessieren vor allem die formal unsichtbaren Zäsurstellen, an denen ein solcher Codewechsel (Code-Switching) realisiert wird.

Code-Switching bezeichnet zunächst primär den Wechsel zwischen zwei oder mehr Sprachen innerhalb einer kommunikativen Situation. Māmayh verfasste eine Reihe von (*mulammaʿ*-) Gedichten, in denen er abwechselnd und ohne prosodische Einbußen versweise oder halbversweise Arabisch und Türkisch schrieb – somit *mulammaʿ*-Gedichte mit einer *mulammaʿ*-Struktur.[5] In solchen Gedichten ist der Codewechsel ein offensichtliches Verfahren der ‚interlinguaren Interferenz'.[6] Etwas komplexer gestaltet sich dies im Wechsel zwischen den Varietäten einer Sprache, was ebenfalls als Code-Switching bezeichnet wird und in Bezug auf die vorliegenden Koranzitate Anwendung finden soll.[7] In Abgrenzung zu expliziten Markierungsformen unterteilt Plett als linguistische Interferenz die impliziten Signale der Intertextualität. Codewechsel ist demnach auch dann gegeben, wenn das Zitat u.a. einer anderen Sprachstufe (diachrone Interferenz), einem anderen Soziolekt (diastrati-

3 Alternativer Plural für VIII. q-b-s *iqtibāsāt*.

4 Für die elementaren Verfahren, die Kontaktbeziehungen von Texten darzustellen, werden in der Intertextualitätsforschung verschiedene Beschreibungshilfen wie Palimpsest, Anagramm, Überdeterminierung, Doppelkodierung verwendet (siehe Lachmann, *Gedächtnis* 57–8). Nach Lachmann bedeutet Doppel- bzw. Mehrfachkodierung – an sich je nach Fachdisziplin ein vielschichtiger Begriff –, „dass die Sinnherstellung nicht durch den Zeichenvorrat des gegebenen Textes programmiert ist, sondern auf den eines anderen verweist." Siehe ebd. 58, vgl. 59–60, 78.

5 Zur Gattung siehe Harb, Macaronic Arabic poetry.

6 Terminus nach Plett, Sprachliche Konstituenten 85; vgl. Broich, Formen der Markierung 31–47.

7 Code-Switching bezeichnet nicht nur den Wechsel zwischen Sprachen, sondern auch den Wechsel zwischen Varietäten einer Sprache, siehe Riehl, Code-Switching. Zu den Diskursfunktionen von Code-Switching zählt Gumperz auch das Zitat, siehe ders., *Discourse strategies* 75.

sche Interferenz), einem anderen Sprachregister (diatypische Interferenz) und einer anderen Schriftart (graphemische Interferenz) unterteilt werden kann.[8]

Lexikalisch ein Verbalnomen von VIII. q-b-s, bedeutet *iqtibās* im übertragenen Sinne: sich unterrichten lassen, Nutzen ziehen, sich eine Wissenschaft aneignen, Kenntnis erwerben. Als rhetorischer Terminus steht er für das Zitat (Entlehnung, Einfügung) in Prosa und Dichtung, nicht nur aus dem Koran, sondern auch aus der *ḥadīṯ*-Literatur. Hingegen bezeichnet *taḍmīn* überwiegend die Einfügung eines fremden Verses, eines *ḥadīṯs* oder aber einer bekannten Redewendung (*qawl*, *maṯal*) in das eigene Gedicht. Nach der arabischen Rhetoriklehre unterliegt die Einfügung einer Koranstelle jedoch gewissen Konventionen, wie sie u.a. im *al-Muṭawwal* von at-Taftazānī (st. 792/1390) beschrieben sind: „Der *iqtibās* ist die Einbettung der Rede, sei es in Prosa oder Dichtung, aus dem Koran oder *ḥadīṯ*, ohne dass sie [die Einbettung] sich als eine solche [Rede aus dem Koran oder *ḥadīṯ*] gibt, d.h. in der sie nicht explizit darauf hinweist, dass sie aus dem Koran oder *ḥadīṯ* stammt. So sind Phrasen, mit denen üblicherweise die Rede eingeleitet wird, wie „So sagte Gott, der Erhabene," oder „So sagte der Prophet, Segen und Friede seien mit ihm," oder „nach der Überlieferung" oder dergleichen, zu vermeiden."[9] Daneben behandeln Rhetorikbücher auch den Modus des Zitats, in welchem der ursprüngliche koranische Bedeutungsgehalt im eigenen Vers beibehalten oder im Verskontext verändert wird,[10] sowie die Lizenzen, mit denen gewisse Änderungen im Wortlaut durchgeführt werden bzw. erforderlich sind.[11] Damit steht die Definition des *iqtibās*

---

8 Plett, Sprachliche Konstituenten 85.

9 At-Taftazānī, *al-Muṭawwal* 723:
وأما الاقتباس فهو أن يضمّن الكلام نثرًا كان أو نظمًا شيئًا من القرآن والحديث لا على أنه منه أي: لا على طريقة أن ذلك الشيء من القرآن أو الحديث، يعني: على وجه لا يكون فيه إشعار بأنه من القرآن أو الحديث، وهذا احتراز عمّا يقال في أثناء الكلام قال الله تعالى، أو قال النبي - عليه الصلاة والسلام - كذا، أو في الحديث كذا، ونحو ذلك.
Für eine jüngere Schrift siehe Ibn Maʿṣūm, *Anwār* ii, 217–9; vgl. an-Nābulusī, *Nafaḥāt* Nr. 169 (Übers. Cachia, *Arch Rhetorician*): „The introduction into one's prose or verse from the Qur'ān or the Traditions of the Prophet with only minor alterations and without obvious indication that they are drawn from those sources."

10 At-Taftazānī, *al-Muṭawwal* 724; Ibn Ḥiǧǧa, *Ḫizāna* iv, 359:
واعلم أن الاقتباس على نوعين نوع لا يخرج به المقتبس منه عن معناه. [كقول ...] ونوع يخرج به المقتبس عن معناه.

11 Es handelt sich hierbei überwiegend um die Transformationsoperatoren wie in der klassischen Rhetorik: Addition, Subtraktion, Substitution, Permutation, siehe z.B. Ibn Ḥiǧǧa, *Ḫizāna* iv, 359:
ثم اعلم أنه يجوز أن يغيّر لفظ المقتبس منه، بزيادة أو نقصان أو تقديم أو تأخير أو إبدال الظاهر من المضمر أو غير ذلك.

im Gegensatz zum modernsprachlichen und wissenschaftlichen Gebrauch des Zitats, das durch optische oder zumindest semantische Signale (*signa citationis*) dezidiert markiert werden muss.[12]

Zu den Phänomenen der Adaptation fremder Rede in die eigene entwickelte die arabische Literaturtheorie eine feinteilige Nomenklatur, die sie u.a. unter Konzepten des Plagiats (*sariqa*), Unterschlagung/Diebstahl (*iḫtilās*), Einbettung (*taḍmīn*), Anleihe (hier *istiʿāra*), Über-/Entnahme (*aḫḏ*), Nachweis/Referenz (*istišhād*) und Anspielung (*talmīḥ*) mit zahlreichen Subkategorien bespricht.[13] Werke, die sich speziell mit der Wiedergabe koranischen Wortlauts auseinandersetzen,[14] bilden mit der Zeit eine Art Normpoetik des koranischen Zitats, das sich immer mehr im Terminus *iqtibās* verdichtet und als Stilmittel und Redeschmuck auch in Rhetorikhandbücher eingeht.[15]

Obwohl der Disput über die Frage nach der Zulässigkeit und dem *aptum* (Angemessenheit) des *iqtibās* älter ist,[16] scheint sich erst ab dem 8./14. Jh. eine wertende Klassifikation zu etablieren. Ṣafī ad-Dīn al-Ḥillī (st. 750/1349) – wie nach ihm Ibn Ḥiǧǧa (st. 837/1434) – unterscheidet hierbei zwischen koranischen Zitaten, die *maqbūl* (erlaubt), *mubāḥ* (annehmbar, nicht verwerflich), *mardūd* (anstößig, verwerflich) sind[17] und teilt sie den gattungsbezogenen, literarischen und außerliterarischen Orten des Zitats, seinem neuen ‚Milieu' in den verschiedenen Künsten zu. In Predigten, Kanzelreden, Staatsschreiben/Bestallungsurkunden,[18] im Prophetenlob und dem Lob auf die Prophetenfamilie gelten Koranzitate als *maqbūl*, in der *ġazal*-Dichtung, in Erzählungen (*qiṣaṣ*), *aṣ-ṣifāt*,[19] in der Epistolographie und dergleichen als *mubāḥ*. Als verwerflich

---

12 Vgl. Helmstetter, Zitat iii, 896–9, und Simon, Zitat iv, 1049–81.

13 Feinsinnige Unterschiede dieser Terminologie besprechen Sanni, *The Arabic theory*; ders., Again on taḍmīn 7–17, mit Verweisen zum Gebrauch des *taḍmīn* als koranisches Zitat; von Grunebaum, Plagiarism, insb. 238–45 und Qāḍī, Literature and the Qurʾān 214–5.

14 Ausgiebig hierzu Orfali, In defense of the use of Qurʾān in adab, mit einer Edition des *Rafʿ al-iltibās ʿan munkir al-iqtibās* von Ibn Abī Luṭf (st. 993/1585), einem Zeitgenossen Māmayhs; ders., "I see a distant fire", zum frühesten erhaltenen und eigenständigen Werk zum *iqtibās* von aṯ-Ṯaʿālibī (*K. al-iqtibās min al-Qurʾān al-karīm*); ders., Kitāb Intizāʿāt al-Qurʾān al-ʿaẓīm, und ders., Iqtibās.

15 Siehe MacDonald und Bonebakker, Iḳtibās: „The practice of using Ḳurʾānic expressions is often mentioned in works on literary theory, but rules for it and the specific term iḳtibās, instead of the more general taḍmīn [q.v.], may not have existed earlier than the 6th/12th century."

16 Siehe Qāḍī, Literature and Qurʾān 214b.

17 Ṣafī ad-Dīn al-Ḥillī, *Šarḥ al-Kāfiyya* 326.

18 Hier für *ʿuhūd*, Sg. *ʿahd*.

19 In der Aufzählung wird nicht besonders deutlich, was al-Ḥillī mit *aṣ-ṣifāt* bezeichnet. Vermutlich meint er allgemein Beschreibungen. Bei Ibn Ḥiǧǧa, der al-Ḥillīs Klassifizierungen fast wörtlich übernimmt, fehlt dieser Terminus.

gelten ihm solche *muqtabasāt*, die einen koranischen Auszug in einen frivolen oder scherzhaft-obszönen Kontext einbauen,[20] oder aber auch solche, in denen Passagen zitiert werden, in denen Gott von sich selbst spricht. Die literarische Praxis unterschied sich jedoch von diesen Normvorgaben, wie dies van Gelder am Beispiel der *muǧūn*-Dichtung dargelegt hat.[21] Als erhabenes Wort Gottes, rhetorisch-stilistisches und sinnstiftendes Wunder ist der Koran für die Dichtung Schwelle und Potenzial gleichzeitig. Die gesamte Spannweite der Funktionen des *iqtibās* einzufassen, ist hier nicht der Ort, zumal die Text-Text- und Kontext-Beziehung immer beidseitig und in Wechselwirkung untersucht werden muss, und Autoren jeweils unterschiedliche Vertextungspraktiken und Motivierungen haben. Gleichwohl ist anhand der vorliegenden Epigramme Māmayhs unter (text-)pragmatischen Gesichtspunkten zu untersuchen, auf welche Funktionen die bewusst gestaltete Kollision zweier Textsorten von äußerstem Deutungspotenzial verweist und welche Rückschlüsse eine solche intertextuelle Praxis hinsichtlich des Verständnisses von der poetischen Vers- und der koranischen Textgrenze erlaubt. Der *iqtibās* kann zur Erhöhung der Stilebene, als Amplifikation oder Antithese zur literarischen Aussage, wie auch zur Bedeutungskomplexion herangeführt werden – was dem ‚Feuerfangen' des Verses, wenn man das „Feuerholen" des *iqtibās* metaphorisch auf die literarische Praxis überträgt, gleichkommt. In vielen Fällen, so hält Thomas Bauer fest, hat der *iqtibās* ‚keinen anderen Sinn, als den Effekt der Inkongruenz zwischen Pathos und Heiligkeit des zitierten Wortes einerseits und Trivialität und Profanität des Anlasses des Zitats [andererseits] zu erzielen.'[22] Dies steht beispielsweise ganz im Gegensatz zu appellativen, moralisch und politisch motivierten Reden, die ein anderes Kommunikationsziel als die Dichtung verfolgen. Hier hat die kontextuelle Symmetrie von Referenztext und dem aufnehmenden Text eine über Emotion und Erinnerung, die *persuasio* verstärkende Rolle.[23] Folgende Parameter lassen sich für das koranische Zitat als poetisches Element hervorheben: a) Umfang/Explizitheit des Zitats, b) Ort und Milieu

---

20 Dasselbe scheint auch für die Einspielung biblischer Zitate in profane Literatur gegolten zu haben, wie Metschies für die manieristische Stilistik Baltasar Graciáns (st. 1658) herausgearbeitet hat: „Der religiöse Bezirk ist dem ‚genus sublime' zugeordnet: Zitate aus der Bibel dürfen nicht auf „niedrige Dinge" („cosas humildes"), Zitate aus der profanen Literatur nicht ohne Einschränkung auf „heilige Dinge" („cosas sagradas") bezogen werden." [Hervorhebungen im Original] Siehe Metschies, „Concepto" und Zitat 155 (nach dem Traktat *Agudeza y arte de ingenio*).

21 Van Gelder, Forbidden firebrands.

22 Bauer, *Liebe und Liebesdichtung* 444.

23 Vgl. hierzu Dähne, Context equivalence 12–3.

des Zitats, c) Funktion des Zitats und d) Sichtbarkeit/Unsichtbarkeit/Grad der Markierung des Zitats.

Der Aspekt der Markiertheit bzw. der expliziten Nicht-Markiertheit, wie sie in den Kommentarwerken zum *Talḫīs Miftāḥ* als Stilprinzip hervortritt, erlangte in der Forschung bislang wenig Aufmerksamkeit. Das (theoretische) Gebot, *inquit*-Formeln nicht zu nutzen, um die Gleichstellung des koranischen Textes mit dem poetischen zu vermeiden, schützt unverkennbar sowohl den koranischen Text in seiner Domäne als auch den Dichter. Zunächst muss an der literarischen Praxis erhoben werden, ob diese Norm umgesetzt wurde und in den Fällen, bei denen das explizite Referenzsignal fehlt, welche differenzierten Techniken zur Einleitung des Zitats (lexikalische, semantische oder stilistische Signale) durch die Dichter verwendet wurden, die auf das Zitatsegment verweisen. Denn ein künstlerischer Text will als ein solcher, stets als Kunst, erkannt werden, indem er seine Verfahren im Latenten oder Manifesten bloßlegt. Außer in wenigen Fällen, in denen sich das koranische Zitat aus Auszügen zusammensetzt, die für sich genommen keine Sinneinheit bilden, ist aber davon auszugehen, dass der koranische Wortlaut durch die Leserschaft erkannt wurde. In vielen Fällen gibt sich der koranische Text aber selbst zu erkennen, weil das Wort Gottes im Koran durch verschiedene Redeinstanzen (Gott über sich selbst, Engel über Gott, Figurenreden, Dialoge etc.) wiedergegeben ist. Das koranische Zitat, das in den aufnehmenden Text ohne offensichtlichen semantischen Bruch eingesetzt wird, ist somit durch seinen eigenen lexikalischen und semantischen Code in der Skala der Markiertheit, eines mit einer mehr oder minder offensichtlichen Grundmarkierung.[24] Im *taḍmīn* gestaltet sich das Zitat im Gegensatz dazu sehr viel subtiler und seine Wiedererkennung ist im hohen Maße mit dem literarischen Bildungshorizont des Lesers verbunden, sofern nicht alltagssprachlich gebräuchliche Redewendungen oder Sprichwörter benutzt werden. Dafür spielt sich der ursprüngliche Verskontext des *taḍmīn* im neuen Umfeld aber nicht automatisch ein und ist auch für die Sinnerschließung meist nicht erforderlich.

Eine weitere latente Grundmarkierung ist der Gattung der Epigramme inhärent, da in ihnen besonders häufig Adaptionstechniken zur Anwendung kommen, insbesondere im zweiten Halbvers der zweiten Verszeile,[25] insofern ist der Leser von Epigrammen ohnehin in der Erwartung eines pointierten Abschlusses. Wenn darüber hinaus noch durch Paratexte wie Überschriften eindeutig

24 Generell zur Markierung von Intertextualität siehe Pfister, Konzepte insb. 25–30.

25 Von zweizeiligen Epigrammen ausgehend steht im Folgenden II-b für den *ʿağuz*-Halbvers der zweiten Zeile und II-a für den *ṣadr*-Halbvers; alternativ I-a und I-b, wenn es sich um einzeilige Epigramme handelt.

auf einen *iqtibās* (z.B. durch Formulierungen wie *wa-lahū qtibās*; *wa-qāla muqtabisan* etc.) referiert wird, liegt der Fokus des Lesers unausweichlich auf der Ausführung des *iqtibās* im Kontext des Epigrammthemas. Wie im Folgenden versucht wird darzulegen, bedeuten all diese Determinierungen aber nicht, dass die Tiefenschichtigkeit der Epigrammkunst allein in der *anagnorisis* ihr Ende findet.

Iqtibās-Korpus

Das Korpus der *iqtibās*-Epigramme umfasst 63 Gedichte im *Dīwān*,[26] die verschiedene Intertextualitätsmarker vorweisen und die im Folgenden nach paratextuellen und intratextuellen Referenzsignalen unterteilt werden. Da Māmayh in allen poetischen Formen exzessiven Gebrauch vom Korantext macht, beschränke ich mich hier aus pragmatischen Gründen überwiegend auf die zweizeilige Epigrammform.[27] Technisch gehören zu diesem Korpus auch die Chronogramme, da von den 77 im *Dīwān* enthaltenen Chronogrammen die überwiegende Mehrheit einen *iqtibās* oder eine koranische Allusion (hier *talmīḥ*) enthält. Doch müssten diese im erweiterten Kontext ihres poetischen Anlasses berücksichtigt werden, um die Funktionen der Zitateinspielung innerhalb des *abǧad*-Verses besser herauszuarbeiten, zumal Chronogramme ohnehin unmissverständlich durch spezifische Signalworte den Codewechsel anzeigen, um damit auf den mit Buchstabenwerten zusätzlich codierten Vers (vielfach ein *iqtibās*, *taḍmīn*, ein Motto oder eine Formel) zu verweisen.[28]

Paratextuelle Referenzsignale

51 Epigramme sind in ihren Überschriften markiert durch Formulierungen wie *qāla muqtabisan*, *wa-lahū qtibās* (43x) oder durch strukturelle Verweise wie *lahū ayḍan*, *wa-miṯluhū* (8x). 12 Epigramme sind nicht explizit als *iqtibās*-Gedichte markiert, sondern unter anderen Versgattungen oder -themen benannt, oder tragen keinen expliziten Titel. Je nach Handschrift variieren die von Kopisten hinzugesetzten Überschriften vor allem in der Zuordnung der Terminologie, wenn es sich um ein *ḥadīṯ*-Zitat handelt. Auffällig ist, dass die

26 Siehe tabellarische Übersicht im Anhang.

27 Der zum Korpus gehörende Einzeiler (*mufrad*) und der Vierzeiler sind in der tabellarischen Übersicht angegeben.

28 Zu den Chronogrammen im *Dīwān* Māmayhs siehe Masarwa, Performing the occasion.

Handschriften bei den *iqtibās*-Epigrammen wenige Varianten aufweisen, im Gegensatz zu vielen anderen Gattungen im *Dīwān*, deren Variantenapparat die Umfänge der Gedichte um ein Mehrfaches übersteigt.

Metrische Einbettung

Māmayh schöpft bei diesen Epigrammen nicht das gesamte Spektrum klassischer Metren aus, doch von den 16 Metren sind 10 vertreten: 1x *kāmil*; 1x *muǧtaṯṯ*; 1x *mutadārik*; 1x *ṭawīl*; 3x *ḫāfīf*; 4x *sarīʿ*; 6x *wāfīr*; 8x *basīṭ*; 12x *ramal*; 19x *raǧaz*. Zu diesen klassischen Versmaßen kommt ein Gedicht hinzu, das metrisch doppelt codiert ist, indem es zwei Metren (hier *sarīʿ* und *raǧaz*) gleichzeitig enthält und in den Rhetorikbüchern als *maǧmaʿ al-baḥrayn* bezeichnet wird. Daneben verwendet Māmayh die *iqtibās*-Technik auch in nachklassischen Formen, in einer *mawāliyā* und fünf Mal im *ḏūbayt*. Welche Implikationen die Häufigkeit der Metren in Bezug auf Rhythmus, Musikalität und eventuell Tonalität hat, kann hier nicht erfasst werden, wohl aber spiegelt die Häufigkeit der benutzen Metren Māmayhs Vorliebe für musikalische Gattungen der Dichtung wider. Andererseits ist zu bedenken, dass nicht jedes koranische Segment, das sich als Zitat für ein Epigrammmotiv angeboten hätte, auch prosodisch einbetten ließ.

Ort der Einbettung

Bei der Mehrheit der Gedichte ist der Ort der Einbettung in II-b, wobei das Zitatsegment nicht immer die gesamte Halbverslänge ausschöpft. In zwei Gedichten erstreckt sich das Zitatsegment auf den gesamten Vers II, und in zwei Gedichten verteilt es sich auf den ersten Vers.

Intratextuelle Markierungen und Zäsurstellen – Beispiele

Das Korpus der *iqtibās*-Epigramme teilt sich hinsichtlich der Markierung in drei Gruppen auf: in explizit markierte (+++), in nicht markierte (-) und in implizit markierte Zitate, mit divergierendem Deutlichkeitsgrad (+)/(++). [〉〈] markiert das Zitatsegment, das Modulationen unterworfen sein kann.

Explizite Markierungen

Im folgenden Epigramm #365[29] erstreckt sich das Zitatsegment auf den gesamten Vers II (a–b):

#365 اقتباس[30] [بحر مجزوء الرجز]

1 كَيْفَ الضَّلَالُ يَا مَنْ ضَلُّوا بِقَوْلِ اللهِ
2 ⟩وَأَيْنَمَا تَوَلُّوا فَثَمَّ وَجْهُ اللهِ⟨

Wie ist denn Irr[leit]ung möglich, oh ihr, die ihr abgeirrt seid? Wo doch Gottes Wort lautet:
⟩Wohin ihr euch wendet, dort ist Gottes Angesicht.⟨ [Q 2:115]

Die *inquit*-Formel markiert die Zäsurstelle (am Ende von 1–b), an der das Zitatsegment eingeführt wird. Der Leser hat somit zwei Halbverse lang Zeit, das Zitat wahrzunehmen. Mit der rhetorischen Frage bereitet Māmayh den Leser lexikalisch (*ḍālla*, *ḍalāl*) und semantisch auf das Zitatsegment vor. Einer solchen Formulierung, wo Gottes Wort als nächstes erwartet wird, folgen gewöhnlich keine dem koranischen Wortlaut widersprechenden Inhalte. Māmayh bleibt sowohl im kontextuellen Thema des Korans als auch seines Verses: die Irrleitung der Menschen gegenüber der allpräsenten Rechtleitung Gottes. Ähnlich explizit ist in #854 das Zitat mit der Redeeinleitung („Gesandte wie Engel sprachen"):

#854 دوبيت اقتباس واكتفا [ذوبيت]

1 إِيَّاكَ مِنَ الدَّعْوَى وَقِرْ إِنْعَامَا بِالْعَجْزِ وَقُلْ لِلْمُدَّعِي إِنْ عَامَا
2 الرُّسْلُ مَعَ الْأَمْلَاكِ جَمْعًا نَطَقُوا ⟩سُبْحَانَكَ لَا عِلْمَ لَنَا إِلَّا مَا⟨

Hüte dich vor der Anklage (dem Anspruch) und gib in der Schwäche (dem Unvermögen) eine Wohltat (Gottes) zu und sage dem Ankläger, wenn er obsiegt (für ʿ-w-m) [oder: wenn es ihm heftig danach dürstet; für ʿ-y-m]:

29 Die Gedicht-Nummern verweisen auf die Nummerierung der Leithandschrift Ms. Berlin We II 243, weitere benutzte Ms. und die Folionummern finden sich im Anhang.

30 Strenggenommen wäre dieses Verfahren als *ʿaqd* (Versifikation) zu bezeichnen. Siehe Sanni, *The Arabic theory of prosification* bes. 152, 159.

Gesandte wie Engel sprachen vereint aus: / ›Gepriesen seist du! Kein Wissen haben wir – nur das ...‹ [Jenseits der Zeile mitgedacht (*iktifāʾ*): ... was du uns lehrtest. Du bist der Wissende und Weise. Q 2:32]

Hier zitiert Māmayh eine Sequenz aus Q 2:32, die mit *naṭaqū* in Position II-a eine direkte Rede, somit ein Doppel-Zitat (Zitat im Zitat) einleitet und Gott anspricht. Dass an dieser Stelle der Codewechsel eintritt, signalisiert unzweideutig das Wort *subḥānaka*, das nur in Bezug auf Gott verwendet wird. Ferner kündigt sich bereits in I-b mit dem Imperativ (*wa-qul*) ein Zitatsegment an. Eine weitere Ebene erhält die poetische Aussage durch die rhetorische Figur der Aposiopese (*iktifāʾ*).[31] In der Oberflächenstruktur der ersten semantischen Reihe (ohne koranischen Kontextbezug) soll man keine Ansprüche einklagen und seine Schwäche als einen Segen (*niʿma*)[32] sehen. Māmayh platziert den Versanlass lexikalisch in eine Gerichtssituation[33] (*daʿwā*, *qarra* und *muddaʿī*) und substituiert für die Erweiterung der lexikalischen Dichte die im koranischen Kontext sprechenden Engel *malāʾika* mit *amlāk*.[34] Das Koranzitat, das dem Kläger zur Einsicht vorgehalten werden soll, dient als Exempel, Zeuge und Vergleich, da bereits Gesandte vor Gott bestätigten, nicht mehr zu wissen bzw. zu haben. In diesem Kontext versteht sich *ʿağz* neben Schwäche auch als Armut. In der zweiten semantischen Reihe, die das koranische Versende mitberücksichtigt, ist das *ʿağz* jedoch gottgewollt, weshalb einerseits eine Klage obsolet ist, andererseits – berücksichtigt man die Klasse der Zeugenschaft – die anfängliche Schwäche/Armut in der Tat ein Gnadenerweis Gottes ist. Damit sind die Anspielungskünste Māmayhs und die Sinnaureolen von *ʿağz* aber noch nicht erschöpft. *Al-ʿağuz* bezeichnet zudem den zweiten Halbvers, auf den Māmayh hier als (unvollständigen) Zitatträger verweist, mit dessen Umfang man sich zufriedengeben soll.

---

31 Cachia, *The arch rhetorician* 54.

32 Hier mit der Wort- und Klangfigur (*al-ğinās al-mafrūq al-malfūf*) zu *niʿma* in der graphemischen Aufspaltung von *inʿāmā* zu *in*+*ʿāmā*.

33 Die Gerichtsthematik liegt für Māmayh auch biographisch nahe, da er sich seinen Lebensunterhalt phasenweise als Dragoman an verschiedenen Gerichten in Damaskus sicherte. Siehe GAL ii, 271 und GALS ii, 382.

34 Im Vers davor (Q 2:31): *malāʾika*. Im Epigramm fungiert *amlāk* in Nachbarschaft zu *rusl* zwar als Pluralform von Engel (*malak*) und König (*malik*, Pl. *mulūk* und *amlāk*), lässt sich aber im *tawğīh* zur Gerichtslexik verwenden, wo es Eigentum und Besitz (*milk*, *mulk*, Pl. *amlāk*) heißt.

Nichtmarkierte *muqtabasāt*

Die nichtmarkierten Epigramme sind diversen Themen gewidmet. In unserem Korpus sind Spott-, Liebes- und Weinepigramme genauso vertreten wie explizit religiös-moralisierende. Einem Biotop in Sottobosco-Gemälden ähnelnd, beschreibt Māmayh im folgenden Spott-Epigramm einen auswuchernden Bart. Formal findet sich keine Zitat-Markierung. Auch der Zäsurstelle, die mit *ǧahannam fīhā* markiert ist und eine Höllenbeschreibung erwarten lässt, muss nicht zwangsläufig etwas Koranisches folgen. Dennoch findet sich genug lexikalische Dichte, die auf den Koran hinweist:

#615 وله هجوًا في شعر الذقن [بحر مجزوء الرجز]

1 حيّاتُ شَعْرِ ذَقْنِهِ   فِـي خَـدِّهِ إِنْتَشَـرَتْ
2 وَقَعْـرُهُ جَهَنَّـمُ   فِيهَا ›وُحُوشٌ حُشِرَتْ‹

A: حياة:
Das Barthaarleben (das lebendige Barthaar) breitete sich auf seiner Wange aus.
oder B: حيات:
Die Schlangen seines Barthaares breiteten sich auf seiner Wange aus.
Und sein Grund (Boden) ist die (reinste) Hölle, wo: ›wilde Tiere versammelt werden.‹ [Q 81:5]

Māmayh nutzt für das Zitat nicht die gesamte Breite von II-b aus, weil er diesen Platz braucht, um den in dieser Sure typischen Konditionalsatz (*iḏā* + Subjekt + Verb) an die eigene Syntax anzupassen.[35] Die *Dīwān*-Handschriften geben für dieses Epigramm sowohl die Schreibung mit حياة (Leben) als auch mit حيّات (Schlangen) an. Nimmt man die lectio difficilior als Textgrundlage (Variante A), tritt eine kunstvolle Tiefenschicht hervor, wobei die Formulierung *ḥayātu šaʿri ḏaqnihī* etwas sperrig wirkt. Der erste Vers ließe sich zunächst ohne Spott als lebendige Beschreibung des Barthaars, das sprießt und gedeiht (*intašarat*), lesen. Eine Störung des ersten Bildes bietet dann der zweite Vers mit einer überraschenden lexikalischen Wendung zu *ǧahannam* und den *wuḥūš* im Zitatsegment. Allein das Wort (*ḏaqn*) in I-a, häufig in Spottversen verwendet, korrespondiert mit der Schmähung in II. Die Versgestaltung fordert den Leser zur Re-

35 Zur Sure und Übers. siehe Corpus Coranicum: [https://corpuscoranicum.de/kommentar/index/sure/81/vers/5/#koran.]

Lektüre des Epigramms und zur Rekapitulation des koranischen Kontextes der Sure *at-Takwīr* (Verhüllung) auf. Was vorher lebte und sich ausbreitete, steht dann im Kontrast (lexikalisch im *ṭibāq* ausgedrückt: *intašarat* – *ḥuširat*; *ḥayāt* – *ǧahannam*) zum koranischen Kontext der Sure, in deren erster Hälfte es um die Apokalyptik verheißenden Vorgänge geht. Dieser Kontrast löst sich schließlich auf, wenn Vers I im Lichte des Untergangsszenarios gelesen wird. Zutage tritt der verstärkte Spott auf den unsauberen, wilden Haarwuchs, dessen Grund/Boden (dessen Träger) auf einen noch schlimmeren Zustand verweist.

Die zweite Lesart mit „Schlangen" ist in Kombination mit *ḏaqn* und *ǧahannam* vergleichsweise unzweideutig: sie kennzeichnet von vornherein das Spottepigramm auf einen ungepflegten Bart und dessen Träger. Das koranische Untergangsszenario amplifiziert in beiden Lesarten des Epigramms den Spott, vor allem, weil am Boden des Barthaars (hier *ǧahannam*) selbst mehr lauert (*wuḥūš*) als die „Schlangen" oben in I-a vermuten lassen.

Ein weiteres, scherzhaftes Epigramm ohne offensichtliche Markierung handelt von einem Mädchen, das Asmāʾ heißt.

#645 وقال في مليحة اسمها أسما [بحر الرجز]

1 قَالَ عَوَاذِلِي بِدَعْدٍ فِي الْهَوَى   فُتِنْتَ أَمْ بِزَيْنَبٍ وَسَلْمَى
2 أَمِ الرَّبَابِ أَمْ سُعَادَ قُلْ لَنَا   أَجَبْتُهُمْ ⟨إِنْ هِيَ إِلَّا أَسْمَا⟩

Meine Zensoren fragten: Bist du in Daʿad verliebt, oder bist du von Zaynab oder Salmā entzückt?
Oder von ar-Rabāb oder Suʿād? Sag es uns! / Da antwortete ich ihnen: ⟩Keine, außer Asmāʾ!⟨ [und koranisch: ⟩Das sind nur Namen!⟨] [Q 53:23]

Die Zäsurstelle befindet sich diesmal in II-b und leitet im Vers Māmayhs nach *aǧabtuhum* eine direkte Rede ein, während der mitimplizierte koranische Wortlaut eine Antwort auf eine Aufforderung ist. Der Oberflächensinn in der ersten semantischen Reihe ergibt Asmāʾ als Auserwählte, wobei die Preisgabe des Namens der Geliebten sich nicht gehört und den Leser sicherlich zunächst erstaunt. In der zweiten Reihe mit *tawriya* kümmert sich der Getadelte nicht weiter um die Frauen („es sind doch nur Namen!") um nicht getadelt zu werden. Eine Irritation baut Māmayh jedoch dadurch ein, dass er die Zensoren gleich nach fünf Frauen fragen lässt, die vordergründig den Getadelten als Aufreißer darstellen. Damit lenkt der Dichter den Leser aber auf die lüsterne Neugier der Zensoren selbst, die schließlich als die dritte Ebene mit dem koranischen Verskontext von 53:23 („Das sind bloße Namen, die ihr und eure Väter aufgebracht habt, und wozu Gott keine Vollmacht herabgesandt hat. Sie (d.h. diejenigen, die derartige Wesen als göttlich verehren) gehen nur Vermutungen nach und dem, wonach (ihnen) der Sinn steht, wo doch die Rechtleitung von ihrem Herrn zu ihnen gekommen ist“)[36] die Tadler im Epigramm entblößt. Sodann erhält auch die Antwort eine weitere scharfsinnige Dimension, die diesmal mit dem koranischen Inhalt antwortet. Letztlich verdeutlicht Māmayh dem Leser durch die Auswahl der Frauennamen, welche typische altarabische Namen der Dichter-Geliebten (*maʿšūqāt*; *maḥbūbāt*) sind, das fiktive Szenario des Tadels. Damit unterstreicht er den spielerischen, aber kunstreichen Aspekt des *iqtibās* mit dem er seine anfänglich provokante und unmoralische Preisgabe der Geliebten mit Namen auflöst und als eine dritte Antwort, diesmal im Einklang mit der koranischen Botschaft, in den Tadel der Tadler überführt.

Eine Trennung, die den Liebenden verarmt hat, ist das Thema des nächsten Epigramms ohne explizite Zitatmarkierung:

#1254 وله اقتباس [بحر الرجز]

1 \281ب\ إِنَّ الَّذِي قَاطَعَنِي صُدُودَا صَيَّرَنِي بَعْدَ الغِنَى فَقِيرَا

2 كَمْ بِعْتُ فِي جَمَالِهِ جِمَالًا ›وَالْخَيْلَ وَالْبِغَالَ وَالْحَمِيرَا‹

Wahrlich derjenige, der sich von mir trennte und abwandte, / trieb mich, nach dem ich reich war, in den Ruin.

Wie viele Kamele verkaufte ich wegen seiner Schönheit: ›und Reittiere, und Rinder und Esel.‹ [Q 16:8]

Die Zäsurstelle in II-b ist vorbereitet mit dem *ǧinās* (*ǧamāl*/Schönheit – *ǧimāl*/ Kamele als wertvoller Besitz) und letzteres dient ihm als Brückenwort und *apex* der Verkettung für das anschließende Zitatsegment, das in absteigender Folge der Tiere bis hin zum Esel veranschaulicht, wie der Liebende beinahe in den Ruin getrieben wird. Im Kontext der Sure *an-Naḥl* (die Bienen) werden die Nutztiere aufgezählt, die dem Menschen als Reittiere dienstbar gemacht wurden, während hingegen bei Māmayh der Liebende diese nacheinander verliert. Das Zitat verwendet Māmayh somit zweifach metaphorisch. In der Szenerie eines finanziellen Fiaskos dient die absteigende Folge der Tiere zur Amplifikation des Verlustes. Dies wiederum steht metaphorisch für die Verausgabung des Liebenden für einen unempfänglichen Geliebten, wobei die absteigende Folge

36 Hervorbebungen durch die Verfasserin; zur Sure und Übers. siehe Corpus Coranicum: [https://corpuscoranicum.de/index/index/sure/53/vers/23].

mit dem Esel als letztem Glied sowohl als Vorwurf an den Geliebten als auch für eine resignierte Selbstevaluation des Liebenden über dem Vers schwebt.

Implizit markierte *muqtabasāt*

In diese durchaus tentative Einteilung gehören solche Epigramme aus dem Korpus, deren Intertextualitätssignal etwas stärker hervortritt als in den zuvor besprochenen Beispielen und mit denen sich das künstlerische Verfahren zu erkennen gibt – und das ist schließlich auch das Ziel des Dichters, vor allem in der Epigrammkunst. Unter diese Kategorie fallen beispielsweise solche Gedichte, in denen Gottesnamen, Propheten oder koranische Narrative genannt werden, oder solche, die vordergründig religiös-moralisierende und koranische Inhalte thematisieren. Dennoch ist es keine Regel, dass überall, wo Gott oder einer der Propheten vorkommt, ein *iqtibās* folgen muss. Im folgenden Epigramm bietet Māmayh eine Art Umkehrung der religiösen Lexik, damit auch des *iqtibās*:

\# 366 وله مثله [بحر السريع]

1 بَدَا نَبِيُّ الْحُسْنِ فِي فَتْرَةٍ مِنْ لَحْظِهِ وَالْجَفْنَ قَدْ سَنَّا

2 أَسْلَمَتِ الأَعْجَامُ أَرْوَاحَهَا 〉وَقَالَتِ الأَعْرَابُ آمَنَّا〈

> Der Prophet der Schönheit erschien mit mattem Blick und geschärften Augenlidern (als Waffe).
> Die Nichtaraber ergaben sich ihm (wörtl. lieferten ihm ihre Seelen/ihren Geist aus) und 〉die Beduinen sagten: „Wir glauben!“〈 [Q 49:14]

Zunächst liest sich das Epigramm als Prophetenlob und Polemik gegen die Wüstenaraber mit ihrem Lippenbekenntnis zum Glauben (*qālat+āmannā*) in Kontrast zu den Nichtarabern, die mit ihrer ganzen Seele den Islam (*aslamat+arwāḥuhā*) angenommen haben. Das Thema dürfte Māmayh persönlich betroffen haben, da er wegen seiner nichtarabischen Abstammung (und vermutlich auch seiner Lebensführung) von seinen Zeitgenossen bissige Spottverse erhielt. In der Oberflächenstruktur liest sich der zweite Vers daher als Konversion (*aslama*, den Islam annehmen) zweier Völkerschaften, weil lexikalische Signalwörter aus dem gleichen semantischen Feld (*nabiyy* und *fatra*) zuvor platziert wurden und die Perzeption lenken. Die Zäsurstelle ist lexikalisch mit *arwāḥuhā* nicht besonders markiert, so dass man hier glauben kann, die Motivation des Dichters durchschaut zu haben. Doch birgt der zweite Vers einige Störungen, die zur Rekapitulation des Epigramms auffordern. II-a bildet die erste Hälfte eines koordinierten Adversativsatzes, so dass der beabsichtigte Kontrast zur Geltung kommt. Die Modalität des Satztyps erfordert zudem eine Sprechpause (nach *arwāḥuhā*), der eine zweite im Zitatsegment selbst folgt (Sprechpause durch direkte Rede mit Einleitung *wa-qālat*).[37] Nachdem der Leser mühelos den ersten Vers lesen konnte, wird er im zweiten Vers gleich zwei Mal gebremst, um an dieser Stelle das koranische Zitat und Māmayhs Polemik wahrzunehmen. Das Zitatsegment selbst wiederum erfüllt im Kontext der Sure eine der Polemik ganz gegensätzliche Funktion: in der Botschaft der Sure (Q 49:1–13) soll gegenseitiger Spott, Argwohn und Streit gerade unterlassen werden. Schließlich kommt hiernach mit dem Begriff *fatra*[38] der Anachronismus der Konversionsgeschichte im Epigramm zu Tage, das den Widerspruch Māmayhs zur koranischen Aussage Spott zu unterlassen, in zweifacher Hinsicht aufhebt. Zum einen spottet Māmayh formal nicht, da er auf dieser Ebene nur beschreibt, dass die Nichtaraber (nicht der arabischen Sprache mächtig) mit ihren Seelen den Islam angenommen haben, während die Beduinen/Wüstenaraber, der Sprache mächtig, ihren Glauben aussprachen. Zum anderen tritt zu Tage, dass die verehrte Person nicht der Prophet, sondern die geliebte Person ist (als ein Prophet der Schönheit). Māmayh kleidet mit dem Stilmittel des *tawǧīh* sein schlichtes Liebesepigramm in eine religiöse Lexik. Entsprechend geht es mit *aslama* (hier nicht religiös gelesen) bei den beiden Völkern nicht mehr darum, in welcher Form sie den Islam annahmen, sondern dass alle Menschen der Schönheit des Geliebten ergeben waren. Ob nun für den Leser im Nachklang dieser Versgestaltung eher der versöhnliche oder der polemische Ton überwiegt, ist unerheblich.

Gewöhnlich betten sich alle Zitate harmonisch in den Redefluss des Verses ein und nur lexikalische Besonderheiten, kleinere syntaktische Störungen oder ein allzu kontrastiver Satzbau signalisieren mehr oder minder stark ein folgendes koranisches Zitat. Zuweilen signalisiert das Zitatsegment selbst seinen ursprünglichen Kontext (Selbstreferentialität), wie im folgenden Epigramm.

---

37 Grundsätzlich wäre anzunehmen, dass nach der Wiedererkennung des Koranzitats, die Betonung eine andere ist als bei der Erstlektüre.

38 *Fatra* (Mattheit, Zeitraum, Phase) bezeichnet u. a. den Zeitraum zwischen der Sendung von zwei Propheten (insbesondere zwischen Jesus und Muḥammad), in dem die Befolgung der prophetischen Lehren nachgelassen habe (vgl. Pellat, Fatra). In Bezug auf das Berufungserlebnis des Propheten bezeichnet *fatra* gewöhnlich die Periode des Ausbleibens göttlicher Offenbarung (*fatrat al-waḥy*) zwischen der ersten und zweiten Offenbarung, in der der Prophet formal *nabiyy* und noch nicht *rasūl* ist; siehe Madigan, Revelation 447b und Fulton, Fatra.

Hier geht die Signalstärke von der Phrase *wa-min āyātihī* (bereits in II-a beginnend) aus, das in dieser Wortfolge 22 Mal im Koran vorkommt, ein Großteil davon in der zitierten Sure *ar-Rūm*.

#373 اقتباس أيضًا [بحر السريع]

1 يَـا عُصْبَـةَ الْعِشْـقِ هَلُمُّـوا إِلَـى   رُؤْيَا مُحَيًّا زَادَنِي عِشْقَا
2 وَقَدْ حَوَى مُعْجِزَ عِيسَى ›وَمِنْ   آيَاتِـهِ يُرِيكُـمُ الْبَرْقَـا‹

Oh, Bund der Liebe! Los, auf zum Anblick eines Gesichts, das mir die Liebe zu ihm gesteigert (vermehrt) hat.
Denn es (bzw. der Geliebte) birgt (besitzt) das Wunder Jesu (d.h. kann Tote auferwecken) ›und es gehört zu seinen Zeichen, dass er (es) euch den Blitz zeigt.‹ [Q 30:24]

Das Epigramm beginnt wie ein typisches Liebesepigramm und endet mit dem Koranzitat, das mit Blitzen die Reize des Geliebten beschreibt. Das Wunder Jesu bereitet den Codewechsel zudem in II-a vor. Doch die Blitze sind im koranischen Zusammenhang die Zeichen Gottes,[39] und gehören nicht zu den – zumindest kodifizierten – Wundern, die Jesus vollbracht hat. Genau an diesem Punkt baut Māmayh aber die Störung ein, die er syntaktisch kaschiert (das Poss.-Pron. von *āya* verweist hier separat betrachtet auf Jesus, nicht auf Gott) mit dem Effekt, dass der Vers nach außen hin offensichtlich falsch, wenn nicht gar blasphemisch ist. Ein weiteres Störsignal bettet Māmayh – praktisch als Hilfe für den Leser – durch ‚falsche' Montagetechnik ein, die eine fingierte Ähnlichkeitsbeziehung zwischen Gottes Tat und Jesus herstellt, denn in der Sure *ar-Rūm* ist von den Wundern Jesus nicht die Rede. Māmayh verweist auf Jesus als einen Propheten der Liebe, der Tote auferwecken konnte. Somit geht die Ähnlichkeitsbeziehung wieder auf, weil in Vers I der Liebende nach dem Geliebten strebt, der ihn in Vers II wie Jesus wiederbelebt und sich die

39 Zur Sure und Übers. siehe Corpus Coranicum: [https://corpuscoranicum.de/index/index/sure/30/vers/24]
„Und zu seinen Zeichen gehört es, dass er euch (wenn es gewittert) den Blitz sehen lässt. (Dann seid ihr) in Furcht (vom Blitz erschlagen oder sonstwie geschädigt zu werden) und (zugleich) in Verlangen (nach dem Regen, den das Gewitter mit sich zu bringen pflegt). Und er lässt vom Himmel Wasser herabkommen und belebt damit die Erde (wieder) nachdem sie abgestorben war. Darin liegen Zeichen für Leute, die Verstand haben."

„Zeichen" im Zitatsegment (*wa-min āyātihī …*) auf den Geliebten und dessen Schönheitsfunken, beziehen.

Zu dieser Gruppe der etwas stärker markierten Zitate gehören solche, die in der Literaturtradition besonders häufig als *iqtibās* verwendet wurden und die dort ein Eigenleben fortführen. Zu diesen, die im poetischen Raum eine Karriere gemacht haben, gehört beispielsweise Q 36:40 [لَا الشَّمْسُ يَنبَغِي لَهَا أَن تُدْرِكَ الْقَمَرَ] wobei die Dichter im Vers die Verneinungspartikel umstellen, und das Präpositionalgefüge streichen [وَالشَّمْسُ لَا يَنبَغِي أَنْ تُدْرِكَ الْقَمَرَا], um syntaktisch freier anbinden zu können.

#903 اقتباس أيضًا [بحر البسيط]

1 لَمَّا تَبَدَّا وَكَاسُ الرَّاحِ فِي يَدِهِ وَلِلْعُقُولِ بِحُسْنِ الْوَجْهِ قَدْ قَمَرَا
2 شَبَّهْتُهُ قَمَرًا وَالرَّاحَ شَمْسَ ضُحًى ›وَالشَّمْسُ لَا يَنبَغِي أَنْ تُدْرِكَ الْقَمَرَا‹

Als er mit dem Weinpokal in der Hand erschien und mit der Schönheit seines Gesichts den Verstand (der Anwesenden) überwältigte,
verglich ich ihn mit dem Mond und den Wein mit der Sonne des Vormittags und ›es ziemt der Sonne nicht, den Mond einzuholen.‹
[Q 36:40: „Und weder steht es der Sonne an, den Mond einzuholen, noch kommt die Nacht dem Tag zuvor. Alle (Gestirne) schweben an einem Himmelsgewölbe (w. schwimmen in einem Himmelsgewölbe)."[40]]

Dass Māmayh hier nicht nur seine Kunstfertigkeit im *iqtibās* zeigen will, sondern ebenfalls an die *iqtibās*-Tradition[41] zu diesem Vers anknüpft, und sich mit meinen Vorgängern misst, signalisiert er mit *lil-ʿuqūl* (hier im Sinne von: für die Verständigen). Er wendet sich damit an die Leserschaft, die einen Rückbezug zu seinen Vorgängern herstellen sollen, die ebenfalls dieses Koranzitat in ihre Epigramme aufgenommen haben.

Eine stärkere koranische Markierung weist das folgende Bartepigramm auf, das neben dem *iqtibās* aus der bezeichnenden Sure *an-Naml* (Ameise) noch einen *tawǧīh* mit grammatikalischer Lexik aufweist:

40 Übers. nach Paret, vgl. Corpus Coranicum: [https://corpuscoranicum.de/de/verse-navigator/sura/36/verse/40/commentary].

41 An-Nawāǧī ordnet ein solches Epigramm mit gleichem Koranzitat, Reim und Metrum im *Ḥalbat al-kumayt* 146 (im 12. Kapitel) wohl fälschlich Ibn Nubāta (st. 768/1366) zu und zitiert im Anschluss daran sein eigenes. Im *Dīwān* Ibn Nubātas konnte ich das Epigramm nicht finden. Aṣ-Ṣafadī und Ibn Taġrībirdī ordnen es dem Dichter Ibn Qizil zu, in dessen

#271 اقتباس أيضًا [بحر مجزوء الرجز]

1 لَمَّا سَكَنْتُ مُهْجَتِي   بِعَارِضٍ لَا يُهْمَلُ
2 فَأَنْشَدَتْ مِنْ فَرْحَةٍ   〉يَا أَيُّهَا النَّمْلُ ادْخُلُوا〈

Als ich mein Herz an einer Wange wohnen ließ [gram. mit *sukūn*, ohne Vokal aussprach], die nicht vernachlässigt ist – oder: die man nicht übersieht/vergisst [gram. die nicht unpunktiert ist],
da rief es voller Freude 〉Ameisen! Tretet ein!〈 [Q 27:18]

Die Zäsurstelle, an der der Codewechsel eintritt, wird markiert durch *fa-anšadat*, allerdings signalisiert der Vokativ (*yā+ayyuhā*) eine recht typische koranische Einleitung. In dieser Szenerie freut sich der Dichter, einen schönen belebten Ort gefunden zu haben und ruft die Ameisen als Gäste auf, einzutreten. In der zweiten semantischen Reihe beschreibt der Dichter den aufkommenden Wangenflaum (hier stehen die Ameisen metaphorisch für den Bartflaum) seines Geliebten. Doch die Freude darüber liest sich zunächst als ein Widerspruch, da er ja nicht den Bart wollen kann. Der Widerspruch löst sich jedoch auf, wenn das koranische Zitat weiter und im Kontext mitberücksichtigt wird.[42] Was im Vers als explizite Einladung ausgedrückt ist, wird implizit umgekehrt. Die Ameisen sollen sich in ihre Behausungen zurückziehen und nicht auf der Wange erscheinen.[43] Somit wird der Koranvers selbst ebenfalls als *tawriya* gelesen. Eine dritte semantische Reihe arbeitet im Hintergrund mit der Terminologie der Grammatik (*tawǧīh*) zur Verstärkung der *imaginatio*. Liest man *sakkana* (vokallos aussprechen) statt *sakana*; *muhaǧǧī* (von *h-ǧ-w*: in der Bedeutung buchstabierend) statt *muhǧah* (von *m-h-ǧ*); *ahmala* (unpunktiert schreiben) statt *yuhmalu* zusammen mit *ʿāraḍa* (kollationieren) und folgt diesem Bild, dann drückt *lā yuhmalu* litotisch die Punktiertheit der Buchstaben, also den Bartwuchs aus, und die Ameisen stehen für die Punkte, die sich

Dīwān sich dieses Epigramm auch findet. Siehe Ibn Qizil, *Dīwān* 461 No. 708; vgl. auch Ibn Maʿṣūm, *Sulāfa* ii, 274.

42 *Sūrat an-Naml*: „(17) Die Heerscharen Salomons, aus Dschinnen, Vögeln, Menschen, / wurden versammelt und aufgestellt in Reih und Glied, (18) bis sie in das Tal der Ameisen kamen. Da sprach eine Ameise: Ameisen! Geht hinein in eure Wohnungen, / auf dass Euch Salomo und seine Heerscharen nicht zertreten, / ohne es zu bemerken!" Zitiert nach Bobzin, *Der Koran*.

43 Eine weitere, die *imaginatio* verstärkende Bildebene liefert die Wortwahl Māmayhs im ersten Vers. Mit metrischen und semantischen Konzessionen gelesen, würde analog zur (koranischen) Aufforderung an die Ameisen in die Behausungen reinzugehen, der Vers mit *sakana*+*ʿāriḍ* (Wolke)+*yahmilu* (ohne *lā*) auch heißen: *Als sich mein Herz an einer Regenwolke, aus der es reichlich regnete, beruhigte, da rief es vor Freude:* [...].

zurückziehen sollen. Māmayh verwendet hier das koranische Zitatsegment nicht allein als graphemisches oder lexikalisches Material. Die Sinnerschließung der poetischen Aussage erfolgt unter Einbezug des koranischen Kontextes, wofür Māmayh seine eigenen Verse kodiert – und dies mehrfach! Dabei dient ihm der *iqtibās* als ein Kontrasttext, dessen Aussage etappenweise seiner eigenen widerspricht, dann aber wieder mit der koranischen Aussage übereinstimmt. Der Leser kann auf jeder der dargebotenen Ebenen des Epigramms eine denkwürdige und sinntragende Aussage mitnehmen und nach jeder praktisch auch den ‚Platz verlassen.' Welche Sinnebene vom Leser zuerst erfasst wird, unterliegt nicht einer vorgegebenen Reihenfolge und ist vom Wissen und der Empfänglichkeit für bestimmte sprachliche Signale abhängig. Geht der Leser allerdings zu früh, verpasst er das kunstreiche Spektakel, das ihm Māmayh anbietet.

Fazit

Die vorgestellten Beispiele geben nur einen Auszug dessen, mit welchen poetischen Verfahren Māmayh gearbeitet hat. Ungeachtet der gebotenen Stilnorm, Koranzitate nicht zu markieren, bietet das Korpus Māmayhs gleich eine Bandbreite von explizit markierten bis hin zu nichtmarkierten Koranzitaten. Hatte sich der Koran gegenüber der altarabischen Poesie gerade durch seine negative Intertextualität ausgezeichnet, war er doch nicht davor gefeit, dass nachfolgende Dichtergenerationen sich ihn ausgiebig als Prätext zunutze machten. Wie an den Beispielen dargelegt wurde, dient der *iqtibās* als eines der vielfältigen Instrumente der Sinnkomplexierung des poetischen Textes, bei dem ein ungestörter linearer Oberflächensinn mit der Einbettung des Koranzitats (durch Ähnlichkeitsrelation) hergestellt wird, auf dessen Präsenz und Fremdartigkeit (Differenzrelation) im neuen Umfeld der Epigrammtext aber in den meisten Fällen selbst verweist. Neben der Zäsurstelle, die offen (durch Figurenrede, verba dicendi u.a.) oder verdeckt auf dieses Spannungsverhältnis (zwischen der Differenz- und Äquivalenzrelation) verweist, sind es kleinere motivische, lexikalische oder syntaktische Anomalien, Wort- oder Lauthäufungen, die Signale der Intertextualität aussenden und den Leser zur wiederholten Evaluierung der Lektüre anregen. Die Signale werden aber nicht ausgesendet, um allein wiedererkannt zu werden, sondern vielmehr, weil sie Kreuzungen zwischen dem Koransegment und dem poetischen Text herstellen, mit denen die Ausgestaltung der tieferen Ebene durch Tropen mit hoher Ambiguitätspotenz erfasst werden soll. Der *iqtibās* ist für Māmayh somit nicht vorrangig ein Element des Redeschmucks oder ein Behelfsmittel, das allein von sich aus neben seinen eigenen Versen pulsiert. Im Gegenteil, das koranische Zitat erhöht die Vielschichtigkeit, weil es unweigerlich mit seiner eigenen Vielschichtigkeit in einen poetischen Kontext transferiert wird. Da dies ein bewusster Akt ist, kommt Māmayh die Rolle des Feuerbändigers zu. Seine Kunstfertigkeit kontrolliert in welchem Ausmaß das semantische Feuer in seine Verse greift.

Handschriften

Ms. Berlin We II 243

#270[86a]; #271[86a]; #304[97b]; #364[134a]; #365[134a]; #366[134a]; #367[134a]; #368[134a,134b]; #372[134b]; #373[134b]; #389[136b]; #410[138b]; #439[142a]; #446[142b,143a]; #448[143a]; #449[143a]; #466[144b]; #469[145b];#487[146b,147a]; #497[148a]; #498[148a]; #499[148a]; #500[148a]; #501[148a,148b]; #505[148b]; #506[148b]; #507[149a]; #508[149a]; #531[151b]; #561[154a]; #567[154b]; #573[155a]; #576[155b]; #577[155b]; #580[155b]; #615[159a]; #621[160a]; #640[162a]; #645[163a]; #646[163a]; #672[165b]; #706[168b]; #711[169a]; #712[169a]; #723[170a]; #753[173a]; #780[175a,175b]; #797[177b]; #819[180a]; #848[185b]; #854[186a]; #858[186b]; #901[190a,190b]; #902[190b]; #903[190b]; #910[191a]; #929[192b];#938[194a]; #942[195b]; #1067[306a]; #1079[309b]

Ms. Berlin We 163

#1254[281b]; #1255[281b]

Ms. Petersburg 1105

#1254[212b]; #1255[213a]

Übersicht *Iqtibās*-Korpus

* Intratextuelle Markierungen: (+++) explizit markierte Zitate; (++) und (+) implizit markierte Zitate mit divergierendem Deutlichkeitsgrad; (-) keine Markierung.

** Paratextuelle Markierungen, die einen *iqtibās* kennzeichnen: m für Überschriften; (m) für strukturelle Verweise wie *lahū ayḍan*, etc.; – paratextuell nicht markiert; +/++ paratextuell mit einem Thema, einer Gattung oder einer Stilfigur markiert.

	Dīwān Nr.	Metrum	Markierung*	Paratextuelle Markierung **		Zitatposition	Zitatumfang/Worttreue	Zitatquelle	*inquit*-Formen; Signalverstärker
1	#270	*rağaz*	+ +	*wa-lahū min al-isti*ʿ*ārati wa-l-iqtibās*	m+	II-b	›أَشْرَقَتِ الأَرْضُ بِنُورِ رَبِّهَا‹	Q 39:69	*anšadtu*
2	#271	*rağaz*	+ +	*lahū qtibās*	m	II-b	›يَا أَيُّهَا النَّمْلُ ادْخُلُوا‹	Q 27:18	*qāla*
3	#304	*ramal* (4 Zeilen)	+	*wa-qāla muqtabisan*	m	II-b	›كُونُوا قِرَدَةً‹	Q 2:65	*qultu*
4	#364	*rağaz*	-	*iqtibas*	m	II-b	›وَأُوتِيَتْ مِنْ كُلِّ شَيْءٍ وَلَهَا‹	Q 27:23	
5	#365	*rağaz*	+++	*iqtibas*	m	II a–b	›وَأَيْنَمَا تُوَلُّوا ... فَثَمَّ وَجْهُ اللّٰهِ‹	Q 2:115	*bi-qawli llāhi*
6	#366	*sarī*ʿ	+	(*iqtibās*) *wa-lahū miṯ-luhū*	(m)	II-b	›وَقَالَتِ الأَعْرَابُ آمَنَّا‹	Q 49:14	*kontextuelle Kongruenz*
7	#367	*rağaz*	-	(*iqtibās*) *wa-ayḍan*	(m)	II-b	›مَا كُنْتَ تَدْرِي مَا الْكِتَابُ‹	Q 42:52	
8	#368	*wāfir*	++	(*iqtibās*) *wa fī l-ma*ʿ*nā*	(m)	II-b	›فَإِنْ عُدْنَا فَإِنَّا ظَالِمُونَا‹ *fa- ergänzt*	Q 23:107	*Stilebene*
9	#372	*sarī*ʿ	++	*wa-lahū qtibās*	m	II-b	›الْحَمْدُ لِلّٰهِ الَّذِي هَدَانَا‹	Q 7:43	*selbstreferentiell*
10	#373	*sarī*ʿ	++	*iqtibās ayḍan*	m	II-b	›وَمِنْ آيَاتِهِ يُرِيكُمُ الْبَرْقَا‹	Q 30:24	„*wa-min* (*āyātihī*)“

(*fortges.*)

	Dīwān Nr.	Metrum	Markierung*	Paratextuelle Markierung **		Zitatposition	Zitatumfang/Worttreue	Zitatquelle	*inquit*-Formen; Signalverstärker
11	#389	*wāfir*	-	*wa-min al-iqtibās*	m	II-b	حَكَى حَجَرًا 〉وَإِنَّ مِنَ الْحِجَارَهْ〈 *koran.: ka-l-ḥiǧāratī > ḥakā ḥaǧaran*	Q 2:74	
12	#410	*ḫafīf*	-	*wa-qāla muqtabisan*	m	II-b	〉سَلَقُوكُمْ بِأَلْسِنَهْ〈	Q 33:19	
13	#439	*ramal*	+ +	*wa-lahū qtibās*	m	II-b	〉اخْسَئُوا فِيهَا وَلَا〈	Q 23:108	*sa-yunādūna ġadan … iḫsaʾū* selbstrefenziell
14	#446	*ḫafīf*	+ +	*wa-lahū qtibās*	m	II-b	〉إِنَّ كَيْدَ الشَّيْطَانِ كَانَ ضَعِيفًا〈	Q 4:76	*lexikalische Häufung bi-kaydi raǧīmin + inna kayda š-šayṭān …*
15	#448	*sarīʿ+raǧaz (mufrad)*	++	*mufrad*	-	II-b	〉يُدْخِلُ مَنْ يَشَاءُ فِي رَحْمَتِهْ〈	Q 76:31	*selbstreferentiell*
16	#449	*ramal*	+	*iqtibās*	m	II-b	〉لَا يَكَادُونَ يَفْقَهُونَ حَدِيثًا〈	Q 4:78	*qul li-qawmī* (*in I-a*)

(*fortges.*)

	Dīwān Nr.	Metrum	Markierung*	Paratextuelle Markierung **		Zitatposition	Zitatumfang/Worttreue	Zitatquelle	*inquit*-Formen; Signalverstärker
17	#466	*raǧaz*	+	*wa-lahū muqtabisan*	m	II-b	〉مَا أَمْرُنَا إِلَّا كَلَمْحٍ بِالبَصَرْ〈 Auslassung von *wāhidatun*	Q 54:50	
18	#469	*raǧaz*	+++	*wa-qāla muḍamminan*	m	II-b	〉مَنْ غَشَّنَا لَيْسَ مِنَّا〈	*ḥadīṯ*	*qawl Ṭāhā: …*
19	#487	*raǧaz*	+	*wa-lahū muqtabisan*	m	II-b	〉المَالُ وَالْبَنُونَ زِينَةُ الْحَيَاهْ〈	Q 18:46	*qul li-man*
20	#497	*ramal*	-	*wa-lahū qtibās*	m (*tawǧīh*)	II-b	〉وَرَفَعْنَاهُ مَكَانَا〈	Q 19:57	
21	#498	*raǧaz*	-	(*iqtibās*) *wa-lahū miṯluhū*	(m)	II-b	〉وَيَسْفِكُ الدِّمَاءَ〈	Q 2:30	
22	#499	*raǧaz*	++	*iqtibās ayḍan*	m	II-b	〉إِنَّا هَدَيْنَاهُ السَّبِيلْ〈	Q 76:3	*qālat li+ innā hadaynāhu …*
23	#500	*raǧaz*	+++	*miṯluhū*	(m)	II-b	〉مَا فِي السَّمَوَاتِ وَمَا فِي الأَرْضِ〈	Q 2:284	*wa-saḫḫara llāhu lakum …*
24	#501	*ramal*	+	*iqtibās ayḍan*	m	II-b	〉لَيْسَ لِلإِنْسَانِ إِلَّا مَا سَعَى〈	Q 53:39,40	*ayyuhā + Imperativsatz*
25	#505	*ḫafīf*	+	*wa-lahū qtibās*	m	II-b	〉إِنَّمَا أَنْتَ مُنْذِرُ〈	Q 79:45	*arsala … qāʾilan – munḏir*

(*fortges.*)

	Dīwān Nr.	Metrum	Markierung*	Paratextuelle Markierung **		Zitatposition	Zitatumfang/Worttreue	Zitatquelle	*inquit*-Formen; Signalverstärker
26	#506	*ramal*	+++	*wa-lahū miṯluhū*	(m)	II-b	⟩وَقَضَى رَبُّكَ أَنْ لَا⟨ *illā > an lā*	Q 17:23	*selbstreferentiell*
27	#507	*raǧaz*	+++	*wa-qāla ayḍan*	(m)	II-b	⟩يُثَبِّتُ اللّٰهُ الَّذِينَ آمَنُوا⟨	Q 14:27	*wa-l-Ḥaqqu … bi-qawlihī: … selbstreferentiell*
28	#508	*ramal*	++	*wa-lahū qtibās*	m	II-b	⟩يَوْمَ لَا يَنْفَعُ مَالٌ⟨	Q 26:88	*lexikalische und semantische Kongruenz yawma ḥisāb*
29	#531	*ramal*	-	*wa-lahū qtibās*	m	II-b	⟩قَالَ كَلَّا لَنْ تَرَانِي⟨	Q 17:143	*qāla im Zitatsegment*
30	#561	*mutadārik*	-	*wa-lahū min al-iqtibās*	m	II-b	مِنْ رِيقَتِهِ ⟩فَرِحِينَ بِمَا⟨	Q 3:170	
31	#567	*ramal*	++	*wa-lahū haǧwan*	- Spott	II-b	⟩بَعَثَ اللّٰهُ غُرَابًا⟨	Q 5:31	*baʿaṯa llāhu + qultu*
32	#573	*basīṭ*	+	*wa-lahū muwarriyan iqtibās*	m	II-b	⟩وَزَادَهُ بَسْطَةً فِي الْعِلْمِ وَالْجِسْمِ⟨	Q 2:247	*rabbu l-ʿarš*

(*fortges.*)

	Dīwān Nr.	Metrum	Markierung*	Paratextuelle Markierung **		Zitatposition	Zitatumfang/Worttreue	Zitatquelle	*inquit*-Formen; Signalverstärker
33	#576	*mawāliyā*	-	-	- *iktifāʾ*	II-b	يَا مَنْ يَظُنُّوا سلوى [سوايَ!] ›إِنَّ بَعْضَ الظَّنِّ‹ *koran.:* *yā-ayyuhā llaḏīna āmanū ǧtanibū kaṯīran mina ẓ-ẓanni inna baʿḍa ẓ-ẓanni iṯmun*	Q 49:12	
34	#577	*ḏūbayt*	++	*dūbayt*	- metr. Gattung	II-b	قَدْ ›أَنبَتَهُ اللَّهُ نَبَاتًا حَسَنًا‹ *wa>qad*	Q 3:37	*selbstreferentiell*
35	#580	*basīṭ*	++	*wa-lahū fī l-kīmiyā ayḍan*	- Thema	II-b	›فَذُوقُوا عَذَابَ الْحَرِيقْ‹	Q 22:22	*selbstreferentiell; Höllenbeschreibung*
36	#615	*raǧaz*	-	*wa-lahū haǧwan fī šaʿri ḏ-ḏaqni*	- Gattung +Thema	II-b	›فِيهَا وُحُوشٌ حُشِرَتْ‹	Q 81:5	*ǧahannam, ḥuširat*

(*fortges.*)

	Dīwān Nr.	Metrum	Markierung*	Paratextuelle Markierung **		Zitatposition	Zitatumfang/Worttreue	Zitatquelle	*inquit*-Formen; Signalverstärker
37	#621	*sarīʿ*	+	*wa-lahū qtibās*	m	II-b	〈وَكَانَ أَمْرُ اللهِ مَفْعُولَا〉	Q 33:37 vgl. Q 4:47 vgl. Q 8: 42; 44	*selbstreferentiell und mehrfach als iqtibās verwendet* *vgl. #902*
38	#640	*rağaz*	-	*wa-qāla muqtabisan*	m	II-b	〈لِأَنَّهُمْ أَعْجَازُ نَخْلٍ خَاوِيَهْ〉 *koran.: ka-ʾannahum aʿǧāzu naḫlin ḫāwiyatin*	Q 69:7	
39	#645	*rağaz*	-	*wa-qāla fī malīḥatin ismuhā asmāʾ*	- Thema	II-b	〈أَجَبْتُهُمْ إِنْ هِيَ إِلَّا أَسْمَا〉	Q 53:23	*ağabtuhum im Zitatsegment*
40	#646	*basīṭ*	-	*wa-min al-iqtibās*	m	II-b	〈وَلَا تُحَرِّكْ بِهِ لِسَانَكْ〉	Q 75:16	
41	#672	*wāfir*	-	*wa-qāla*	-	II-b	〈كَفَى بِالْمَرْءِ إِثْمًا〉	*ḥadīṯ*	-
42	#706	*rağaz*	-	*wa-qāla qtibās(an)*	m	II-b	تُنْكِرُهَا 〈إِنْ هِيَ إِلَّا فِتْنَتُكْ〉	Q 7:155	*qāla l-qalbu*
43	#711	*rağaz*	+	*wa-lahū qtibās*	m	II-b	〈وَمَا رَمَيْتَ إِذْ رَمَيْتْ〉	Q 8:17	*qāla qalbī + munšidan: … enigmatische Lexik*

(*fortges.*)

	Dīwān Nr.	Metrum	Markierung*	Paratextuelle Markierung **		Zitatposition	Zitatumfang/Worttreue	Zitatquelle	*inquit*-Formen; Signalverstärker
44	#712	*d̲ūbayt*	-	*wa-lahū dubayt*	- metr. Gattung	II-b	›لَا تُدْرِكُهُ مِنَ السَّنَا الأَبْصَارُ‹	Q 6:103	
							Ergänzung zu koran.: *lā tudrikuhū l-abṣāru*		
45	#723	*wāfir*	++	*wa-lahū qtibās*	m	II-b	›وَيَبْقَى وَجْهُ رَبِّكَ ذُو الْجَلَالِ‹	Q 55:27	*selbstreferentiell*
46	#753	*ramal*	-	*iqtibās*	m	II-b	›وَإِنَّهَا لَكَبِيرَةٌ‹	Q 2:45	
47	#780	*wāfir*	-	*wa-min hağwin, iqtibās*	m+ Gattung	II-b	›وَمَا مِنْ دَابَّةٍ فِي الأَرْضِ إِلَّا‹	Q 11:6 Q 6:38	*qultu ...:*
48	#797	*rağaz*	-	*wa-lahū qtibās*	m	II-b	›يَكَادُ زَيْتُهَا يُضِيءُ‹	Q 24:35	
49	#819	*basīṭ*	++	*qāla: iqtibās wa-ktifā'*	m+	(I-b) + II-b	تَحْتَ طِبَاقِ الثَّرَى I-a ergänzt ›فَأَصْبَحُوا لَا تُرَى‹	Q 20:6 Q 46:25	*semantische Kongruenz*
50	#848	*basīṭ*	+	*wa-min al-iqtibās*	m	II-b	›وَكُلُّ حِزْبٍ بِمَا لَدَيْهِمْ‹	Q 30:32 Q 23:53	*semantische Kongruenz*

(*fortges.*)

	Dīwān Nr.	Metrum	Markierung*	Paratextuelle Markierung **		Zitatposition	Zitatumfang/Worttreue	Zitatquelle	*inquit*-Formen; Signalverstärker
51	#854	*ḏūbayt*	+++	*ḏūbayt, iqtibās wa-ktifā᾽*	m++	II-b	›سُبْحَانَكَ لَا عِلْمَ لَنَا إِلَّا مَا‹	Q 2:32	*naṭaqū und subḥāna selbstreferentiell*
52	#858	*basīṭ*	+++	*wa-min al-iqtibās*	m	II-b	فَاللّٰهُ قَالَ لَهُمْ ›حَتَّى إِذَا فَرِحُوا‹	Q 6:44	*qāla llāhu lahum: …*
53	#901	*kāmil*	++	*wa-qāla, madḥ šarīf, iqtibās*	m+	I-a + II-b	›يَا أَيُّهَا النَّاسُ اتَّقُوا‹ ›صَلُّوا عَلَيْهِ وَسَلِّمُوا تَسْلِيمًا‹	Q 4:1 Q 33:56	*Markierung durch Häufung (zwei Zitate) und Position selbstreferentiell*
54	#902	*basīṭ*	++	*wa-lahū qtibās*	m	II-b	›لِيَقْضِيَ اللّٰهُ أَمْرًا كَانَ مَفْعُولًا‹	Q 8:44 (vgl. Q 8:42 und Q 4:47)	*siehe #621*
55	#903	*basīṭ*	+	*iqtibās ayḍan*	m	II-b	›وَالشَّمْسُ لَا يَنْبَغِي أَنْ تُدْرِكَ الْقَمَرَا‹	Q 36:40	*bekannter Vers*

(*fortges.*)

	Dīwān Nr.	Metrum	Markierung*	Paratextuelle Markierung **		Zitatposition	Zitatumfang/Worttreue	Zitatquelle	*inquit*-Formen; Signalverstärker
56	#910	*ramal*	++	*wa-lahū fī l-iflās*	- Thema	II-b	›فَتَرَى الْمُفْلِسَ غَيْظًا ... لَمْ يَزَلْ يَتْلُو عَبَسَ‹ *Umkehrung: ʿabasa wa-tawallā*	Q 80:1	
57	#929	*dūbayt*	-	*wa-lahū qtibās*	m	II-b	سَمِعْتُ لِسَانَ الْحَالِ قَالَ ›اهْبِطُوا مِصْرًا‹	Q 2:61	*relativiert die Aneignung der koranischen Redeinstanz zweifach: „hörte", „meinen Zustand sagen" (lisān al-ḥāl, Zustandssprache)*
58	#938	*ṭawīl*	-	*wa-lahū fī Sulaymān*	(m)+	II-b	وَقَدْ عَصَى النَّمْلُ سُلَيْمَانَا	*talmīḥ Q*	*Sulaymān, naml und ʿaṣā (Epigramm für einen Jüngling namens Sulaymān)* *vgl. #271*

(*fortges.*)

	Dīwān Nr.	Metrum	Markierung*	Paratextuelle Markierung **		Zitatposition	Zitatumfang/Worttreue	Zitatquelle	*inquit*-Formen; Signalverstärker
59	#942	*ramal*	+++	*wa-qāla*	- *ḥādīṯ*	II a–b	›يُوسُفُ أَحْسَنُ مِنِّي وَأَنَا أَمْلَحُ مِنْهُ‹	*ḥadīṯ*	*qāla ḫayru l-ḫalqi …* *yunqalu ʿanhū*
60	#1067	*dūbayt*	+++	*wa-lahū qtibās*	m	II-b	›وَالْكَاظِمِينَ الْغَيْظْ‹	Q 3:134	*kalāmu llāhi*
61	#1079	*ramal*	++	*wa-lahū fī tawḥīd*	- Thema	II-b	›فَلَا إِلَهَ سِوَاهُ‹	Q 2:255	*selbstreferentiell*
62	#1254	*rağaz*	-	*wa-lahū qtibās*	m	II-b	›وَالخَيْلَ وَالْبِغَالَ وَالْحَمِيرَا‹	Q 16:8	
63	#1255	*muğtaṯṯ*	-	*wa-lahū qtibās*	m	II-b	›وَمَا أُبَرِّئُ نَفْسِي‹	Q 12:53	

Bibliographie

[al-Azhar] *Fihris al-kutub al-mawǧūda bi-l-Maktaba al-Azhariyya*, 8 Bde., Kairo 1945–68.

Badrī, Ḥ.F., *Muʿǧam āyāt al-iqtibās*, Bagdad 1400/1980.

Bauer, T., Formel und Zitat: Zwei Spielarten von Intertextualität in der altarabischen Dichtung, in *JAL* 24 (1993), 117–38

Bauer, T., *Liebe und Liebesdichtung in der arabischen Welt des 9. und 10. Jahrhunderts. Eine literatur- und mentalitätsgeschichtliche Studie des arabischen Ġazal*, Wiesbaden 1998.

Bauer, T., The relevance of early Arabic poetry for Qurʾanic studies: Including observations on *kull* and on Q 22:27, 26:225, and 52:31, in A. Neuwirth, N. Sinai und M. Marx (Hgg.), *The Qurʾān in context: Historical and literary investigations into the Qurʾānic milieu*, Leiden 2010, 699–732.

Bauer, T., Wie fängt man eine Qaṣīde an? Formelhafte und nichtformelhafte Nasīb-Einleitungsverse, in *ZAL* 25 (1993), 50–75.

Bobzin, H., *Der Koran*, München 2012.

Broich, U., Formen der Markierung von Intertextualität, in ders. und M. Pfister (Hgg.), *Intertextualität. Formen, Funktionen, anglistische Fallstudien*, Tübingen 1985, 31–47.

Cachia, P., *The arch rhetorician or the schemer's skimmer: A handbook of late Arabic badīʿ drawn from ʿAbd al-Ghanī an-Nābulsī's* Nafaḥāt al-azhār ʿalā nasamāt al-asḥār, *summarized and systematized*, Wiesbaden 1998.

Dähne, S., Context equivalence: A hitherto insufficiently studied use of the Qurʾān in political speeches from the early period of Islam, in S. Günther (Hg.), *Ideas, images, and methods of portrayal: Insights into classical Arabic literature and Islam*, Leiden 2005, 1–16.

al-Fukaykī, ʿA., *al-Iqtibās min al-Qurʾān al-karīm fī š-šiʿr al-ʿarabī*, Damaskus 1996.

Fulton, A.S., Fatra, in *EI*[1], ii, 92.

Gumperz, J., *Discourse strategies*, Cambridge 1982.

Harb, L., Macaronic Arabic poetry, in *EI*[3], first published online: 2020; first print edition: 2021–3.

Heinrichs, W., An evaluation of sariqa, in *QSA* 5–6 (1987–8), 357–68.

Helbig, J., *Intertextualität und Markierung: Untersuchungen zur Systematik und Funktion der Signalisierung von Intertextualität*, Heidelberg 1996.

Helmstetter, R., Zitat, in *Reallexikon der deutschen Literaturwissenschaft*, 3 Bde., Berlin, New York 2003, iii, 896–9.

Ibn Ḥiǧǧa, *Ḫizānat al-adab wa-ġāyat al-arab*, Hg. K. Diyāb, 5 Bde., [2]Beirut 1425/2005.

Ibn Maʿṣūm al-Madanī, *Kitāb Anwār ar-rabīʿ fī anwāʿ al-badīʿ*, Hg. Š.H. Šukr, 7 Bde., Naǧaf 1388–9/1968–9.

Ibn Qizil, *Dīwān*, Hg. M. al-Ḥabbāzī, Jerusalem 1423/2002.

Lachmann, R. *Gedächtnis und Literatur*, Frankfurt a.M. 1990.

Macdonald, D.B., and S.A. Bonebakker, Iḳtibās, in *EI*², iii, 1091–2.

Madigan, D.A., Revelation, in *EQ*, iv, 437–48.

Masarwa, A., Māmayh ar-Rūmī, in *EI*³ (eingereicht).

Masarwa, A., Performing the occasion: The chronograms of Māmayya ar-Rūmī, in S. Conermann und G. Şen (Hgg.), *The Mamluk-Ottoman transition: Continuity and change in Egypt and Bilād al-Shām in the sixteenth century*, Göttingen 2017, 177–206.

Mehren, A., *Die Rhetorik der Araber*, Kopenhagen/Wien 1853.

Metschies, M., „Concepto" und Zitat, in *Romanistische Forschungen* 79 (1967), 152–7.

an-Nawāǧī, Šams ad-Dīn, *Ḥalbat al-kumayt*, 1357/1938 (Nachdruck der Ausgabe al-ʿĀmiriyya 1276/1859).

Orfali, B., In defense of the use of Qurʾān in Adab: Ibn Abī l-Luṭf's Rafʿ al-iltibās ʿan munkir al-iqtibās, in M. Pomerantz und A. Shahin (Hgg.), *The heritage of Arabo-Islamic learning: Studies presented to Wadad Kadi*, Leiden 2015, 498–527.

Orfali, B., Kitāb intizāʿāt al-Qurʾān al-ʿaẓīm: A compendium of Quranic quotations attributed to the Fatimid Secretary Abū l-Qāsim ʿAlī Ibn al-Ṣayrafī (d. 542/1147), in J. Elias und B. Orfali (Hgg.), *Light upon light; Essays in Islamic thought and history in honor of Gerhard Bowering*, Leiden 2019, 91–135.

Orfali, B., Iqtibās, in *EI*³, first published online: 2018; first print edition: 2019–1.

Orfali, B., und Pomerantz, M., "I see a distant fire": al-Thaʿālibī's Kitāb al-Iqtibās min al-Qurʾān al-karīm, in N. al-Shaar (Hg.), *Qurʾan and adab*, Oxford 2017, 191–215.

Pellat, Ch., Fatra, in *EI*², ii, 865.

Pfister, M., Konzepte der Intertextualität, in U. Broich und ders. (Hgg.), *Intertextualität: Formen, Funktionen, anglistische Fallstudien*, Tübingen 1985, 1–30.

Plett, H.F., Sprachliche Konstituenten einer intertextuellen Poetik, in U. Broich und M. Pfister (Hgg.), *Intertextualität. Formen, Funktionen, anglistische Fallstudien*, Tübingen 1985, 78–98.

Qāḍī (Kadi), W., und Mir, M., Literature and the Qurʾān, in *EQ*, iii, 205–27.

Riehl, C.M., Code-Switching, in *Sprache im Fach*, München; Eichstätt (1. Mai 2019) [https://epub.ub.uni-muenchen.de/61752/]

Ṣafī ad-Dīn al-Ḥillī, *Šarḥ al-Kāfiyya al-badīʿiyya fī ʿulūm al-balāġa wa maḥāsin al-badīʿ*, Hg. N. Našāwī, ²Beirut 1412/1992.

Sanni, A., *The Arabic theory of prosification and versification*, Stuttgart 1998.

Sanni, A., Again on taḍmīn in Arabic theoretical discourse, in *BSOAS* 61 (1998), 1–19.

Simon H.-U., Zitat, in *Reallexikon der deutschen Literaturgeschichte*, 5 Bde., ²Berlin u.a. 1984, iv, 1049–81.

at-Taftazānī, *al-Muṭawwal: Šarḥ Talḫīṣ Miftāḥ al-ʿulūm*, Hg. ʿA. al-Hindāwī, Beirut 1428/2007.

van Gelder, G.J., Forbidden firebrands: Frivolous iqtibās (quotation from the Quran) according to medieval Arab critics, in *QSA* 20–21 (2002–3), 3–16.

von Grunebaum, G., The concept of plagiarism in Arabic theory, in *JNES* 3 (1944), 234–53.

17

Ibrāhīm Ibn al-Mullā's (d. 1032/1623) *Ḥalbat al-mufāḍala wa-ḥilyat al-munāḍala*: The Correspondence of an Ottoman-Era Aleppine Littérateur

Nefeli Papoutsakis

Ibrāhīm Ibn al-Mullā is one of many Ottoman-era Arabic littérateurs whose extant oeuvre has not received any scholarly attention so far.[1] His *Ḥalbat al-mufāḍala wa-ḥilyat al-munāḍala fī l-muṭāraḥa wa-l-murāsala wa-l-musājala* (The Racecourse of Competition and the Ornament of Contest: Exchanges, Correspondences and Repartees) is a selection of his correspondence and literary exchanges with contemporary notables, littérateurs and scholars. Apart from letters to family members and to Ottoman dignitaries and potential patrons, a few documents composed on behalf of others as well as poems extemporized at meetings between Ibrāhīm and his friends, the bulk of this work consists of riddle exchanges. This paper discusses Ibrāhīm's life and work and assesses the importance of the *Ḥalbat al-mufāḍala* as a source for the history of the Arabic literary riddle.

The Banū l-Mullā

Ibrāhīm was born in Aleppo around 967/1560.[2] On his father's side, he was descended from a Kurdish family of Shāfiʿite scholars hailing from Ḥiṣn Kayfā in Northern Mesopotamia—hence his nisba al-Ḥaṣkafī.[3] It is worth looking briefly at the history of this family as it shows the continuities in the life

1 See al-Būrīnī, *Tarājim* ii, 14–29; al-Khafājī, *Rayḥāna* i, 97–8; *idem, Khabāyā* 143–6; al-ʿUrḍī, *Maʿādin* 216–24; Ḥājjī Khalīfa, *Sullam* i, 23; al-Muḥibbī, *Khulāṣa* i, 11–2; al-Baġdādī, *Hadiyya* i, 30; al-Ṭabbākh, *Iʿlām* vi, 200–3; al-Tunkī, *Muʿjam* iii, 45–8; Ziriklī, *al-Aʿlām* i, 30; Kaḥḥāla, *Muʿjam* i, 10–1; GAL ii, 274, GALS ii, 385.

2 967/1560 is the year in which Ibrāhīm's brother Muḥammad was born. It is not known who the elder was, but when the two are mentioned together in the sources, Muḥammad normally comes first, which fact suggests his seniority.

3 Al-Būrīnī, *Tarājim* ii, 27.

 | DOI:10.1163/9789004521780_019

of scholarly households between pre-Ottoman and Ottoman times and puts Ibrāhīm's social position in perspective. Ibrāhīm's great-great-grandfather, Aḥmad b. Yūsuf, known as Mullā Ḥājj, a native of Sind (a village north of Mosul), had studied for twelve years in Tabriz before settling at Ḥiṣn Kayfā, where he served as *qāḍī* and mufti until his death in 894/1489 or 895/1490.[4] Mullā Ḥājj penned several commentaries and glosses on important works of religious literature (*fiqh*, *ʿaqāʾid*, *qirāʾāt*, sufism). His commentary on ʿAbd al-Karīm ar-Rāfiʿī's (555–623/1160–1226) *al-Muḥarrar*, a manual of Shāfiʿī law, is often singled out for praise in the sources.[5] Mullā Ḥājj's grandson, Muḥammad b. ʿAlī al-Ḥaṣkafī (891–971/1486–1564), who witnessed the transition from Mamluk to Ottoman rule, had been born in Aleppo and held several important and prestigious posts there (administrator of the Umayyad mosque and inspector of the pious endowments of the Holy Cities), in Damascus (administrator of the *takiyya* Salīmiyya in al-Ṣāliḥiyya and inspector of the shrine of Ibn Adham) and in Irak (inspector of the shrines of ʿAlī and al-Ḥusayn).[6] Muḥammad had married a daughter of Sharaf al-Dīn Yaḥyā b. ʿAbd al-Wahhāb (d. 935/1528–9),[7] the nephew and right-hand man of Muḥibb al-Dīn Ibn Ājā (854–925/1450–1519), the head of the chancery of the Mamluk Sultan Qanṣūh al-Ghawrī (r. 906–22/1501–16), and thus acquired considerable fortune in form of pious endowments (*awqāf*) in the area of Maʿarrat Miṣrīn, south-west of Aleppo, that had belonged to the wealthy and powerful Banū Ājā family.

Ibrāhīm's father, Aḥmad b. Muḥammad Ibn al-Mullā al-Ḥaṣkafī, was a known historian, philologist and littérateur of Aleppo.[8] Born there in 937/1530–1, he studied philology, rhetoric, religious sciences, law, mathematics, logic and

4 Ibn al-Ḥanbalī, *Durr* i, 201–5; Ziriklī, *al-Aʿlām* i, 275; Kaḥḥāla, *Muʿjam* i, 328.

5 Al-Muḥibbī, *Khulāṣa* i, 12; Ḥājjī Khalīfa, *Kashf* ii, 1613.

6 Ibn al-Ḥanbalī, *Durr* ii, 393–4; al-Ṭabbākh, *Iʿlām* vi, 53–4.

7 Ibn al-Ḥanbalī, *Durr* ii, 554–5.

8 Ibn al-Ḥanbalī, *Durr* i, 239–68; al-Būrīnī, *Tarājim* i, 180–5; al-Khafājī, *Rayḥāna* i 97–8; *idem*, *Khabāyā* 143–8; al-Ghazzī, *al-Kawākib* iii, 99–101; *idem*, *Luṭf* i, 289–92; Ḥājjī Khalīfa, *Sullam* i, 221–2 (both entries nos. 602 and 603 refer to him; the death year is wrong in both entries); al-Muḥibbī, *Khulāṣa* i, 277–80; *idem*, *Nafḥa* ii, 655–61; Ibn al-ʿImād, *Shadharāt* x, 650–2; al-Baġdādī, *Hadiyya* i, 151; cf. al-Ṭabbākh, *Iʿlām* vi, 135–48; Ziriklī, *al-Aʿlām* i, 235. As becomes clear from the entry on his father, the addition in *Durr* of the name Muḥammad in Aḥmad's genealogy after his grandfather's name on the authority of al-Ghazzī's *Kawākib* is erroneous; Ibn al-Ḥanbalī was better informed about the history of this family; the correct genealogy can also be found in Aḥmad's entry in *Luṭf* and in Ibrāhīm's entry in the *Khulāṣa*. See also Martel-Thoumian, De curieux notables; *pace* Martel-Thoumian, who has overlooked the relevant entries in *Durr*, Aḥmad's great-grandfather had never been *qāḍī* of Tabrīz; even though he studied there for twelve years, he held, as said, the judgeship of Ḥiṣn Kayfā. The sources, however, mostly dub him *qāḍī quḍāt Tabrīz* to honour him. During that period there was an

philosophy under several prominent scholars in Aleppo, Damascus and Istanbul, including Badr al-Dīn al-Ghazzī (d. 984/1577), ʿAbd al-Raḥīm al-ʿAbbāsī (869–963/1463–1556) and Raḍī al-Dīn Ibn al-Ḥanbalī (908–71/1502-3-63), a renowned Aleppine polyhistor, who was his principal mentor.[9] As was customary by then for aspiring Arab scholars, in 958/1551 Aḥmad travelled to Istanbul in an attempt to develop his contacts and advance his career; he later described that trip in a travelogue entitled *al-Rawḍa al-wardiyya fī l-riḥla al-Rūmiyya*.[10] Returning to Aleppo in the same year and presumably as a result of his networking activities at the capital, he obtained a teaching post at the Bulāṭiyya madrasa. In 976/1568–9 he was further appointed to a post at the Ḥijāziyya madrasa.[11] But, as al-Būrīnī (963–1024/1556–1615) remarks, Aḥmad soon became disappointed by the unfair way appointments were made and therefore abandoned teaching and contented himself with the presumably substantial income of his family *awqāf*, spending most of his time in the *waqf* villages studying and writing.[12] Nevertheless, he regularly came to Aleppo and hosted literary gatherings to which all learned Aleppines flocked. Al-Būrīnī

inflationary use of titles; thus, Ibrāhīm constantly dubs his father *shaykh al-Islām*; the same title is assigned by Najm al-Dīn al-Ghazzī to his own father; likewise, the sources refer to Ṣalāḥ al-Dīn al-Kurānī (see below), a legal witness, as *qāḍī*. Martel-Thoumian mistook Aḥmad's great-grandfather for his grandfather; she therefore failed to identify the Muḥammad b. ʿAlī mentioned in al-Ṭabbākh, *Iʿlām* vi, 53–4, as his father. Sharaf al-Dīn b. Yaḥyā was not a son, but a nephew of Muḥibb al-Dīn Ibn Ājā.

9 Ibn al-Ḥanbalī gives a very detailed list of the subjects and works that Aḥmad had studied with him and other teachers in *Durr* i, 239–48.

10 According to the online catalogue of the Juma Almajid Center for Culture and Heritage (Dubai), this work is extant in Maktabat Makka al-Mukarrama (Taʾrīkh 118; title: *Riḥlat Ibn al-Mullā al-Ḥaṣkafī*). Several Arab scholars travelled to Istanbul and attached themselves to powerful Ottoman dignitaries that could procure for them appointments in their homelands. Apparently the first to write a travelogue describing such a trip was Badr al-Dīn al-Ghazzī. On suchlike travelogues, see Elger, *Istanbul-Reisende*.

11 Ibn al-Mullā, *Ḥalba* MS Berlin, 36v: a poem by ʿUmar b. ʿAbd al-Wahhāb al-ʿUrḍī praising and congratulating Aḥmad on this appointment. According to an excerpt from the rough copy (*musawwada*) of ʿUmar al-ʿUrḍī's *Tārīkh Ḥalab* (*al-Muntuqā* 40), Aḥmad was dismissed from his teaching positions in the Ṣalāḥiyya and the Ḥijāziyya madrasas in 981/1573–4. This means that he had held a further position in the Ṣalāḥiyya.

12 The reason for his disappointment may well have been his dismissal from his teaching posts in 981/1573–4 (see previous note). Al-Ṭabbākh, *Iʿlām* vi, 145, cites an excerpt from a *majmūʿa* by Muḥammad b. ʿUmar al-ʿUrḍī (d. 1071/1660, see al-Muḥibbī, *Khulāṣa* iv, 89–103) to the effect that Aḥmad chose to live at his country estate due to his strained relationships to his peers, whom he often lampooned. Be this as it may, the fierce competition for the now much fewer salaried posts strained the relationships among Arab scholars; retreat and seclusion had thus become a common occurrence—if not a trend—in this milieu in Ottoman times: see Meier, Perceptions 430–3.

gives a detailed and vivid account of his murder at his cottage (in 1000, 1002 or 1003/1594–5)[13] at the hands of a farmer—the embittered cousin of a woman who had been married to another man due to Aḥmad's intervention with her father. Al-Būrīnī adds that his two sons avenged his death promptly, with God's help, and that the murderer and his accomplices were killed in retaliation. Apart from poetry (his *Dīwān*, collected by his son Ibrāhīm, is not extant), Aḥmad authored a number of now lost literary works. Ibn al-Ḥanbalī and al-Muḥibbī mention the titles of two *rasāʾil* on love (*Risālat ṭālibat al-wiṣāl min maqām dhāk al-ghazāl*, patterned after al-Ṣafadī's *ʿAbrat al-kaʾīb*; and *Shakwā l-damʿ al-murāq min sihām al-firāq*), as well as *ʿUqūd al-jumān fī waṣf nubdha min al-ghilmān*, a collection of epigrams on handsome youths patterned after Ibn al-Ḥanbalī's *Martaʿ al-ẓibā wa-marbaʿ dhawī l-ṣibā*. Among other things, Aḥmad also abridged and updated the following historical works: al-Dhahabī's *Taʾrīkh al-Islām* (*al-Muntaqā min Taʾrīkh al-Islām li-l-Dhahabī*), Ibn al-ʿAdīm's *Bughyat al-ṭalab*, and Ṭashköprüzāde's *al-Shaqāʾiq al-Nuʿmāniyya* (*al-Nashr al-ʿābiq min iqtiṭāf al-Shaqāʾiq*).[14] The only published work of his is *Muʿtat al-adhhān min al-Tamattuʿ bi-l-iqrān*, an abridgment and continuation of Ibn Ṭūlūn's (d. 955/1548) lost *al-Tamattuʿ bi-l-iqrān bayna tarājim al-shuyūkh wa-l-aqrān*.[15] His abridgment of al-Jannābī's (d. 999/1590) world history *al-ʿAylam al-zākhir fī ʿilm al-awāʾil wa-l-awākhir*, entitled *al-Muntakhab min Taʾrikh al-Jannābī*, was published as part of an Arabic MA thesis in 2010.[16] It notably consists in an abridgment of only the last part of that work, which deals with the history of the Ottoman dynasty. In addition, Aḥmad produced commentaries on several works on grammar and syntax,[17] the most acclaimed of which

13 Al-Ghazzī, *al-Kawākib* iii, 101 and *Luṭf* i, 292 gives as his death year 1000 or 1003, commending that the latter date is more probable. The colophon of MS Feyzullah 1999 of his *Muntahā amal al-arīb* (see below) dates his death in 1002 and cites a chronogram commemorating it. The place in which he died should be Bātantā, a village north of Idlib which exists to the present day (online: Batenta or Batitiya; the name is corrupted in the sources) and is often mentioned by Ibrāhīm as his father's residence in the *Ḥalba*.

14 All three works survive in manuscript form: Ziriklī, *al-Aʿlām* i, 235; al-Ṭabbākh, *Iʿlām* i, 41–3; vi, 148; al-Ṭabbākh and Ziriklī give the title of the second work as *Mukhtaṣar al-Durr al-muntakhab*, which suggests that it is an abridgment of Ibn al-Shiḥna's *al-Durr al-muntakhab*, but in a passage from the introduction cited in *Iʿlām* i, 42, Aḥmad states clearly that it is an abridgment and update of *Bughyat al-ṭalab*.

15 See Martel-Thoumian, De curieux notables.

16 Shākir, *al-Muntakhab*. On al-Jannābī, see Ziriklī, *al-Aʿlām* vii, 231 (additional sources); *GAL* ii, 300, *GALS* ii, 411–2, and iii, 1281; Rosenthal, al-Djannābī.

17 See al-Ṭabbākh, *Iʿlām* vi 148; Shākir, *al-Muntakhab*, 16. His and Ibn al-Ḥanbalī's glosses to ʿAḍud al-Dīn al-Ījī's *Mukhtaṣar al-muntahā*, a work on *uṣūl al-fiqh* and juridical disputation (*jadal*) and al-Jurjānī's glosses to it, were edited by Ibrāhīm and survive in MS

is *Muntahā amal al-arīb min al-kalām ʿalā Mughnī al-labīb*, his commentary on *Mughnī al-labīb*, Ibn Hishām's (708–761/1310–60) famous treatise on syntax, which survives in numerous manuscripts.[18]

Ibrāhīm's brother, Muḥammad b. Aḥmad Ibn al-Mullā (967–1010/1560–1602), too, was a littérateur and historian.[19] He studied various philological and religious disciplines as well as jurisprudence and astronomy under his father and ʿUmar b. ʿAbd al-Wahhāb al-ʿUrḍī (950–1024/1543–1615), another distinguished scholar of Aleppo, *ḥadīṯ* expert and mufti of the Shāfiʿites there.[20] It is unclear whether he ever held a judgeship or other posts, but he is known to have travelled to Istanbul, as his father had done before him, presumably with a view to obtaining one, in 999/1590.[21] Al-ʿUrḍī praises his acumen, piety and amiability and commends his *Nihāyat al-arab min dhikr wulāt Ḥalab*, a still extant biographical work on the Muslim governors of Aleppo that closes with al-Ḥājj Ibrāhīm Pasha (gov. 1008/1599–1600). Among other things, Muḥammad, who was much admired as a poet, also authored a now lost treatise on whether the Prophet's parents can be counted as Muslims,[22] a commentary on the *ḥadīṯ* collection of Muslim, a treatise on hashish and *banj*, one on the name Muḥammad, and one on the sprouting beard (*ʿidhār*) of youths and its depiction in literature.[23]

Gotha orient. A 1048. A further work of Aḥmad treating questions pertaining to 20 different sciences patterned after Ibn al-Ḥanbalī's *Unmūḏaj al-ʿulūm li-ḏawī l-baṣāʾir wa-l-ʿulūm* is mentioned in *Durr* i, 248.

18 The online catalogue of the Juma Almajid Center for Culture and Heritage lists 13 MSS of this work. The *Muntahā amal al-arīb* has been the subject of three Arabic university theses to date.

19 Al-Khafājī, *Rayḥāna* i, 197–8; al-Muḥibbī, *Khulāṣa* iii, 348–50; al-Ṭabbākh, *Iʿlām* vi, 163–7 (both this and al-Muḥibbī's entry on Muḥammad are based on a report by ʿUmar al-ʿUrḍī); Ziriklī, *al-Aʿlām* vi, 8; *GALS* ii 407.

20 Al-Khafājī, *Rayḥāna* i, 279–80; al-Ghazzī, *Luṭf* ii, 587–90 and the sources given there. Among other things ʿUmar al-ʿUrḍī composed commentaries on al-Qāḍī ʿIyāḍ's *Shifāʾ*, Jāmī's *Kāfiya* and al-Qushayrī's *Risāla*.

21 Ibn al-Mullā, *Ḥalba* fol. 7r; *idem*, *Abkār* fol. 105r.

22 See a *taqrīẓ* on this work by his brother Ibrāhīm in *Ḥalba* fol. 35v–36r.

23 MS Oxford Laud.Or. 206 preserves an abridgment of *Rawḍat al-manāẓir fī ʿilm al-awāʾil wa-l-awākhir*, a history by Ibn al-Shiḥna the father (d. 814/1412), and an extract from a commentary on a poem on the Prophet titled *al-Mughnī li-khātimat al-mutaʾakhkhirīn*, attributing both to Muḥammad. At the end of his entry on him, al-Ṭabbākh edits the introduction of his treatise *Dalālat al-athar fī ṭahārat al-shaʿar*. His work on the sprouting beard gave rise to a long poetic exchange between him and Ṣalāḥ al-Dīn al-Kūrānī: see the latter's *Dīwān* 185–96.

Ibrāhīm's Life and Works

Ibrāhīm received his first education from his father, who also taught him literature and served him as a model in his scholarly and literary endeavours. He further studied *ḥadīṯ*, Quran exegesis, rhetoric, logic and theology under ʿUmar al-ʿUrḍī, and studied syntax and Shāfiʿī law under Maḥmūd al-Baylūnī (d. 1006/1598), a pious Aleppine scholar, expert in *ḥadīṯ* and *qirāʾāt*.[24] He spoke Turkish and Persian and had some knowledge of Persian literature. Thanks to the eminence of his family, he had a broad circle of acquaintances among the elites of Aleppo and other Syrian towns.[25] From early on Ibrāhīm also tried to establish contacts to the Ottoman scholarly establishment. His *dīwān* preserves several eulogies on Ottoman dignitaries that were currently serving or had served in Aleppo, the earliest of which date from the early 980s and address two incumbent Ottoman *qāḍī*s of Aleppo; likewise, the *Ḥalba* preserves some epistles addressed to Ottoman notables. Obviously Ibrāhīm cultivated these contacts with a view to advancing his career. Nevertheless, he did not travel to Istanbul, as his father and brother had done, until very late in his life. His biographer Abū l-Wafāʾ al-ʿUrḍī (993–1071/1584–1660), who knew him personally, comments that although he was very ambitious, he did not pursue his aims with resolve. In fact, we know of only three posts that he held for unknown periods of time: around 995/1587 he taught at the Qurnāṣiyya madrasa, but had to compete for this post with Abū l-Yumn al-Batrūnī (d. 1046/1636–7), a Ḥanafī scholar;[26] in 1007/1598–9 he was appointed *qāḍī* (apparently deputy *qāḍī*) of the district of Shughr, a small town close to Antakya;[27] and at the beginning of 1013/1604 he briefly occupied the post of Abū l-Jūd al-Batrūnī (mufti of the Ḥanafīs, d. 1039/1629) at the Muqaddamiyya madrasa in Aleppo.[28] Al-ʿUrḍī

---

24 Al-Ghazzī, *Luṭf* ii, 628–37 and the sources given there; Sellheim, al-Bailūnī 570–4, 579–82.

25 In some cases, Aḥmad ordered Ibrāhīm to answer his correspondent on his behalf, whereas sometimes Ibrāhīm engaged his father's friends or acquaintances in correspondence.

26 Ibn al-Mullā, *Ḥalba* fol. 59^{v} marginal note; on his quarrel with Abū l-Yumn, see al-ʿUrḍī, *Maʿādin* 222. On Abū l-Yumn, see al-Būrīnī, *Tarājim* i, 263–5; al-Muḥibbī, *Khulāṣa* i, 156–7.

27 Ibn al-Mullā, *Abkār* fol. 85^{r} (a rubric mentioning that he was *qāḍī* of Shughr in Rajab 1007) and 111v (a couplet describing the district of Shughr as a desolate place). In Rabīʿ II 1006/Dec 1597 he addressed a poem to Kamāl al-Dīn Ṭāshköprüzāde (*Abkār* fol. 87^{r-v}) complaining about the *shadāʾid al-ʿazl* and imploring him to help him. Kamāl al-Dīn may have procured him the position at Shughr or it was his nephew Ibrāhīm b. ʿUmar al-Marʿashī (d. ca. 1017/1608–9), *qāḍī* of Antakya at the time, who appointed him to that job.

28 Ibn al-Mullā, *Abkār* fol. 101^{v}–102^{r} (a poem on the occasion of his appointment). On the feud he had with Abū l-Jūd al-Batrūnī because of this and other matters see al-ʿUrḍī, *Maʿādin* 222–4. On Abū l-Jūd al-Batrūnī, see al-Būrīnī, *Tarājim* i, 260–2; al-Muḥibbī, *Khulāṣa* i, 114–6.

ascribes arrogance to Ibrāhīm and relates a few incidents that should exemplify his haughtiness in his dealings with peers and Ottoman dignitaries, but perhaps his judgment was influenced by his partisanship for Abū l-Jūd. Be this as it may, Ibrāhīm did not travel outside Northern Syria, except in 1020/1612 when he performed the pilgrimage. During that voyage, he renewed his ties to Ḥasan al-Būrīnī, who was *qāḍī* of the Syrian pilgrims in that year and whom Ibrāhīm had first met in Aleppo in 1017/1608. Al-Būrīnī notes that soon after Ibrāhīm's return to Aleppo news reached him that he had secluded himself and avoided human company. Eventually, however, Ibrāhīm embarked on a trip to Istanbul to promote his interests, but died on the way.[29]

Ibrāhīm adhered to the Qādiriyya and the Bakriyya ṣūfī orders and regularly attended their ceremonies. His *dīwān* comprises several poems praising Muḥammad b. Abī l-Ḥasan al-Bakrī (d. 994/1586), who was the head of the Bakriyya at the time and was hailed as an axial saint, and the Bakriyya in general.[30]

His bulky *dīwān*, entitled *Abkār al-maʿānī l-mukhaddara wa-asrār al-mabānī l-muddakhara* (Secluded Virgin Meanings and Hoarded Superb Forms), survives in a 265-folio long autograph MS, which Ibrāhīm started writing on 28 Rajab 1014 / 9 Dec 1605. The earliest poem dates from 979/1571–2 and the last dated entry is from Ramaḍān 1018 / November–December 1609. Genre, chronology, the principle of variation and the association of ideas—all played a role in the arrangement of the poems. At the volume's beginning, after a two-and-a-half-folio introduction, stand a few *tawassulāt* (entreaties to God), a genre of religious poetry that thrived in Ottoman times. These are followed by a ca. 300-verse long praise poem on the prophet patterned after al-Būṣīrī's *Hamziyya* but rhyming in *-āmū*, and two praise poems on Muḥammad al-Bakrī. Thereupon follow poems that belong to very diverse genres and are very roughly chronologically arranged: love poetry of various forms (epigrams, *dūbayt*s, *mawāliyā*s, and long poems); eulogies addressed to state officials, scholars and littérateurs, incl. congratulatory poems on various occasions; elegies; poems composed as openings of prose epistles (*ṣadr muṭālaʿa*); *tawassulāt*, ṣūfī poetry and *zuhdiyyāt*, additional praise poems on Muḥammad al-Bakrī (incl. an elegy on his death) and the Bakriyya; blame of the times (*ḏamm al-zamān*) and his contemporaries; *takhmīsāt* of various genres and lengths; epigrams to be inscribed on objects or buildings, epigrams on books he had read, satiric epigrams, epigrams on contemporary events, incl. chronograms, epigrams incorporating Quran

29 Al-ʿUrḍī, *Maʿādin* 218.
30 See Sabra, al-Bakrîya; *idem*, al-Bakrī.

verses, proverbs or verses by other poets; *muwashshaḥāt*, esp. in imitation of *muwashshaḥāt* by his father, Ibn al-Ḥanbalī and others, incl. a *muwashshaḥa* in praise of coffee; *musājalāt* (poems on various topics extemporized at meetings between Ibrāhīm and his friends, each party composing a verse or two alternately), invitations, reproofs, pleasantries, and poems expressing longing for friends and relatives; *dūbayts* and *mawāliyās* on various themes; riddles and replies to riddles. According to Ibrāhīm's own testimony, a highlight of the *dīwān* is a panegyric ode he addressed to the grand vizier Kuyucu Murād Pasha (d. 1020/1611) during the latter's stay in Aleppo in 1016/1607; the ode so pleased the recipient that he had it copied and sent to Sultan Ahmed (r. 1011–26/1603–17), who is also praised in the poem.[31] These are the highest authorities ever praised by Ibrāhīm, who however eulogized several Ottoman *ʿulamāʾ*. Towards the end of the *dīwān* (fol. 229^{v}), in an entry dated Shawwāl 1016 / February 1608, Ibrāhīm declares that he henceforth will only compose poems patterned after the poetry of the ṣūfīs to atone for the other poetry he had produced that far and hoping for God's forgiveness. The last 35 folios of the *dīwān* indeed mostly contain poems on pious topics but there are also some pieces on mundane issues.

The following works by Ibrāhīm are apparently lost: a versification of *Durar al-ḥukkām fī sharḥ ghurar al-aḥkām* (short title: *al-Durar wa-l-ghurar*), the famous compendium of Ḥanafi law by the Ottoman jurist Mollā Khosrew (d. 885/1480) commented upon by the author himself, in more than 5,000 *rajaz*-couplets;[32] three commentaries on al-Juwaynī's (d. 478/1085–6) *al-Waraqāt* (*uṣūl al-fiqh*);[33] two *ḥāshiyas* on al-Taftazānī's (722–93/1322–90) *Mukhtaṣar al-maʿānī* (rhetoric);[34] commentaries on three didactic poems (on grammar, syntax and logic) by ʿAbd al-ʿAzīz b. ʿAbd al-Wāḥid al-Miknāsī (d. 964/1557);[35] a collection of fatwas concerning ecstatic utterances entitled *Mustawfā l-naṣr fī fatāwā ʿulamāʾ al-ʿaṣr*;[36] a volume on *tafsīr* (possibly the same work as *Shifāʾ al-saqīm fī āyāt Ibrāhīm*);[37] *Inʿāsh al-rūḥ bi-maʾāthir Naṣūḥ*, an epistle in rhymed prose on the conflict between the Janissaries of Damascus and Naṣūḥ Pasha,

---

31 Ibn al-Mullā, *Abkār* fol. 223^{v}–226^{r}. On Murād Pasha see de Groot, Murād Pasha Kuyudju.

32 Al-Būrīnī, *Tarājim* 21–4 (al-Būrīnī's *taqrīẓ* on Ibrāhīm's versification), 29; al-ʿUrḍī, *Maʿādin* 219.

33 Ḥājjī Khalīfa, *Kashf* ii, 2006.

34 Ḥājjī Khalīfa, *Kashf* i, 476.

35 Ḥājjī Khalīfa, *Kashf* i, 361, 751, and ii, 1210.

36 Ḥājjī Khalīfa, *Kashf* ii, 1676.

37 Ḥājjī Khalīfa, *Sullam* i, 23, and *Kashf* ii, 1050. *Pace* al-Ṭabbākh, *Iʿlām* i, 47, the *Shifāʾ al-saqīm* is a work on *tafsīr*, as noted in *Sullam* i, 23, not on history, and should not be confused with Muḥammad Ibn al-Mullā's *Nihāyat al-arab min dhikr wulāt Ḥalab*.

the wali of Aleppo in 1011–3/1602–4;[38] *Tanwīr al-baṣīra wa-taʿmīr al-sarīra bi-l-adʿiya al-maʾthūra*, presumably on prayers;[39] and an epistle in defence of Ibn al-Ḥanbalī.[40]

The *Ḥalbat al-mufāḍala*

Numerous collections of private letters by distinguished prosaists survive since Būyid times. The *Ḥalba*, however, rather belongs to a much rarer type of works, exemplified by Ṣalāḥ al-Dīn al-Ṣafadī's *Alḥān al-sawājiʿ bayn al-bādī wa-l-murājiʿ*, that preserve both sides of a littérateur's correspondence, namely both his letters and poems and those by his correspondents to which his own pieces relate. Ibrāhīm mentions the *Ḥalba* in the introduction to his *dīwān* stating that he chose to publish his prose letters and poetic exchanges with friends and acquaintances separately in that work. The *dīwān* includes all of Ibrāhīm's poems prior to 1019/1610 found in the *Ḥalba* but cites only his side of the exchange; in the introductory rubrics Ibrāhīm regularly refers the reader to the *Ḥalba*, where he could find both sides of the exchange. An exception was made for the *musājalāt* that cannot be split apart and are therefore included in both works. Ibrāhīm started writing the 115-folio long autograph MS of the *Ḥalba* (MS Gotha), obviously a fair copy, at the beginning of Dhū l-Qaʿda 1017 / June 1609.[41] The earliest dated piece is an epistle to his father from 980/1572–3; the latest dated entry is from the end of Shaʿbān 1031 / beginning of July 1622.[42]

---

38 Ḥājjī Khalīfa, *Kashf* i, 183.

39 Ḥājjī Khalīfa, *Kashf* i, 501.

40 *An-Naṣr al-raḍī al-munjalī* etc.: Ḥājjī Khalīfa, *Kashf* ii, 1956. An abridgement he did of al-Ṣafadī's *al-Wāfī* entitled *Iqtiṭāf shaqāʾiq al-Nuʿmān min riyāḍ al-Wāfī bi-wafayāt al-aʿyān* is extant in the Library of al-Azhar (Taʾrīkh 479, Abāẓa 6774). A short anthology (eight-folio long, an excerpt?) by Ibrāhīm, entitled *Ḥilyat al-ādāb* and featuring poems from the Abbasid period to his own times, survives in a manuscript in the Ẓāhiriyya: see Murād and Sawwās, *Fihris* i, 187.

41 A different hand has written fol. 70^{v}–71^{v}, 89^{r-v}, 106^{v}–108^{r}, 114v–115^{r-v} on behalf of Ibrāhīm.

42 To judge by its title, MS Berlin Wetzstein 1886,2 (Ahlwardt 7959), which is partly an autograph, should be a further copy of the *Ḥalba*, but actually only the first seven folios are from this work; fol. 8–13 presumably derive from Ibrāhīm's commonplace book and contain poetry by his friend Ibn Qaḍīb al-Bān (d. ca. 1040/1630—see Ziriklī, *al-Aʿlām* iv, 44); fol. 14–32 contain poems from Ibrāhīm's *dīwān* written by at least three different hands (incl. Ibrāhīm's), some of which are crossed out; finally, folia 33–8 also derive from Ibrāhīm's commonplace book and preserve poetry by his teacher ʿUmar al-ʿUrḍī. Four out of eight entries preserved in the first seven folia are missing from MS Gotha; these should be pieces that Ibrāhīm chose not to include in the *Ḥalba*.

Apart from a few epigrams scribbled on the first two and the last folio, the *Ḥalba* contains 103 entries that can be grouped into the following categories: riddle exchanges (40 items, all but one in verse); epistles (24 items, all but one in prose); poetic exchanges other than riddles (19 items); *musājalāt* (twelve items); legal documents (petitions for formal appointment) composed on request of involved persons (four pieces, prose); two commendations (*taqrīẓ*, one in prose, one in verse) and two *ijāza*s (prose). Apparently, this is a selection of Ibrāhīm's correspondence, given that the volume covers a fifty-year period. With one notable exception, all prose pieces (epistles, commendations, petitions and an *ijāza*) are by Ibrāhīm; the other side of the exchange, actually relevant only for epistles, is not included. The exception is Muḥammad al-Bakrī's *ijāza* to Ibrāhīm permitting him to transmit *ḥadīṯ* and religious disciplines (*al-ʿulūm al-sharʿiyya*) on his authority and admitting him as a member of the Bakriyya, which is preceded by Ibrāhīm's letter to the master praising him and asking for the *ijāza*. With very few exceptions, riddle and other poetic exchanges are preserved in full, that is to say, both sides of the exchange are cited (I count each exchange as one entry, regardless of the number of poems exchanged—usually two). Ibrāhīm orders the entries in blocks of similar materials—for example, entries 1–12, 39–46, 48–9, 76, 78–9 (my numeration) are prose pieces; entries 50–5, 57–8, 60–5, 69–75 are riddle exchanges, and entries 19–22, 28, 30–2 are *musājalāt*—but the principle of variation and to a lesser degree chronology also played a role in the arrangement of the material.

Only four of Ibrāhīm's forty correspondents (excl. three unnamed addressees) have left no trace in the sources. The remaining 36 men fall into three main categories: relatives (five); Ottoman dignitaries (seven); friends and acquaintances, most of whom were known littérateurs and scholars (28). Family members and Ottoman dignitaries are the primary recipients of Ibrāhīm's letters. His father, who spent much time at the *waqf* villages, is the recipient of six letters expressing longing; another four letters of this sort are addressed to his brother (two pieces), to a cousin and to the cousin's son. Ibrāhīm's brother was also involved in several poetic exchanges. He participated in ten *musājalāt*, six of which were composed by the two brothers and their friend Fatḥ Allāh al-Baylūnī (977–1042/1570–1632), another Aleppine littérateur,[43] and three by the two brothers alone. Muḥammad, who engaged in four riddle exchanges with Ibrāhīm, also answered two poems by his brother, in which the latter was asking him why it is that Time wrongs the virtuous and why a lover becomes dazed upon seeing his beloved.

---

43 See Schwartz, al-Bailūnī, and the sources given there.

The Ottoman dignitaries to whom Ibrāhīm wrote were men that he knew from the time they had served in Aleppo and who had meanwhile been promoted to higher posts. These include such prominent figures as Yaḥyā Efendi b. Zakariyyā (d. 1053/1644),[44] ʿAlī Efendī b. Sinān (d. 1005/1596–7),[45] Kamāl ad-Dīn Ṭāshköprüzāde (959–1030/1552–1621),[46] Jushamī Mehmed Efendī (d. 1044/1634–5),[47] and Akhīzāde Ḥusayn Efendi (980–1043/1553–1634).[48] Besides, the *Ḥalba* preserves a 'poetic epistle' (actually a poem) that Ibrāhīm addressed to all three: *şeyhülislam* Asʿad Efendi (d. 1034/1625),[49] then *qāḍī l-quḍāt* of Istanbul Kamāl ad-Dīn Ṭāshköprüzāde and then *kazasker* Yaḥyā b. Zakariyyā, in 1027/1618, complaining about the extortion suffered by the locals from the Janissaries. All these men took an active interest in Arabic culture and were courted by Arab littérateurs.[50]

Ibrāhīm engaged the majority of his correspondents, those falling into the category 'friends and acquaintances,' in poetic—not prose—correspondence (only two prose epistles are addressed to men belonging to this group), which fact shows the importance of poetry in learned communication (most of Ibrāhīm's epistles, too, open with a short poem (*ṣadr muṭālaʿa*)) and accounts for the high percentage of poetic texts in the *Ḥalba* (72 of the 103 entries). Some of these men, such as the Damascenes Yūsuf al-ʿAlmawī (d. 1006/1597), a poet,[51] jurist Shams al-Dīn Ibn al-Minqār (d. 1005/1596)[52] and judge Muḥibb al-Dīn al-

44 See Kaya, Yahyâ Efendi; Ziriklī, *al-Aʿlām* viii, 145; Ibn Ayyūb, *Rawḍ* i, 554–5; al-Muḥibbī, *Khulāṣa* iv, 467–72. Ibrāhīm addressed to him two epistles, in 1005 and 1024. He had also addressed a poem to his father, Zakariyyā Efendi, in 981, when he was *qāḍī* of Aleppo.

45 See Ibn Ayyūb, *Rawḍ* ii, 807–8; al-Bakrī, *Rawḍa* 174; *idem*, *Nuzha* 159. Ibrāhīm addressed to him two poems in 985, when he was *qāḍī* of Aleppo, and an epistle and a poem in 999, to congratulate him on becoming *kazasker*.

46 See İpşirli, Taşköprizâde; al-Ghazzī, *Lutf* ii, 607–10 and the sources given there. Ibrāhīm addressed to him two poems (in 1006, asking for help; and in 1012 congratulating him on becoming *kazasker*) and an epistle in 1024.

47 See Ḥājjī Khalīfa, *Fadhlaka* 444. Ibrāhīm addressed to him two eulogies in 1017 and 1018, when he was *qāḍī* of Aleppo, and a letter congratulating him for being appointed *qāḍī* of Bursa in 1019.

48 See İpşirli, Ahîzâde; al-Muḥibbī, *Khulāṣa* ii, 109–11. Ibrāhīm sent to him a letter expressing longing in 1024, when he was *qāḍī* of Istanbul.

49 See Aktepe, Esad Efendi; al-Būrīnī, *Tarājim* ii, 49–51; al-Muḥibbī, *Khulāṣa* i, 396–8; *idem*, *Nafḥa* iii, 76–8. Ibrāhīm probably did not know him personally.

50 On the relationship between Ottoman dignitaries serving in the Arab provinces and the local scholars and littérateurs, see Pfeifer, Encounter.

51 See Ibn Ayyūb, *Rawḍ* ii, 1087–8, al-Ghazzī, *Lutf* ii, 708–11; al-Muḥibbī, *Khulāṣa* vi, 500; Ziriklī, *al-Aʿlām* viii, 215.

52 See Ibn al-Ḥanbalī, *Durr* ii, 418–24; Ibn Ayyūb, *Rawḍ* ii, 1004–5; al-Khafājī, *Rayḥāna* i, 128–30; al-Ghazzī, *Lutf* i, 143–51; al-Muḥibbī, *Khulāṣa* vi, 115–21.

Ḥamawī (949–1016/1542–1610)[53] were acquaintances of his father and Ibrāhīm first contacted them in that capacity while they were on visits to Aleppo. Others were men of his own generation or younger: Egyptian poets ʿAbdallāh al-Danawsharī (d. 1025/1616)[54] and Muḥammad al-Ḥattātī (d. 1051/1641),[55] Damascene poet Aḥmad Ibn al-Minqār (d. 1032/1623)[56] and Ḥasan al-Būrīnī were also first contacted while on visits to Aleppo. But most of Ibrāhīm's correspondents were fellow Aleppines, for example, jurists and littérateurs Najmaddīn Ibn al-Ḥalfā (d. 1054/1644–5)[57] and Ibrāhīm b. Abī l-Yumn al-Batrūnī (d. 1053/1643),[58] and poets Ṣalāḥ al-Dīn al-Kūrānī (see below), Yūsuf b. ʿImrān (d. 1074/1663)[59] and Ḥusayn Ibn al-Jazarī (997–1033/1589–1624),[60] who was Ibrāhīm's pupil.

Poetic exchanges other than riddles arose from various occasions: a feast day, an invitation, a scholar's visit to Aleppo, the return of a book, a grievance, etc., or were simply initiated for pleasure and entertainment. Questions such as those posed by Ibrāhīm to his brother (about the reason of Time's unfairness or a lover's befuddlement) were patently an excuse for engaging somebody in playful communication. Riddle exchanges, too, by far the commonest type of entries in the *Ḥalba*, often sprang from a need to communicate with friends or else a wish to approach a respectable scholar or littérateur with grace and wit. This was common practice among Arab littérateurs and scholars from Ayyubid times on. Riddle exchanges are often cited in Ottoman-era Arabic biographical dictionaries, too, attesting to the continuation of this tradition. Ibrāhīm exchanged riddles with 24 of his 33 Arab correspondents. With 15 of them he either only exchanged riddles or he chose to solely cite his riddle exchanges with them in the *Ḥalba*. The sheer amount of relevant entries suggests that Ibrāhīm was particularly fond of the genre. His *dīwān* actually preserves additional riddles, incl. juridical riddles, *aḥājī* (charades) and a few *muʿammayāt* (logogriphs)—all riddle kinds absent from the *Ḥalba*.[61]

53 See Elger, *Istanbul-Reisende* 73–112, and the sources given there.

54 See al-Khafājī, *Rayḥāna* ii, 85–7; al-Muḥibbī, *Khulāṣa* iii, 53–6; Ziriklī, *al-Aʿlām* iv, 97.

55 See al-Khafājī, *Rayḥāna* ii, 74–6; *idem*, *Khabāyā*, 457–70; al-Muḥibbī, *Khulāṣa* iii, 366–75; Ziriklī, *al-Aʿlām* vi, 9–10, *GAL* ii, 370, *GALS* ii, 497.

56 The son of jurist Shams al-Dīn: al-Būrīnī, *Tarājim* i, 163–77; al-Muḥibbī, *Khulāṣa* i, 296–7; *idem*, *Nafḥa* i, 360–4.

57 See al-Khafājī, *Khabāyā* 285–7; al-Muḥibbī, *Khulāṣa* iv, 181–4; al-Ṭabbākh, *Iʿlām* vi, 263–6.

58 See al-ʿUrḍī, *Maʿādin* 233–8; al-Muḥibbī, *Khulāṣa* i, 10–11; *idem*, *Nafḥa* ii, 651–4, al-Ṭabbākh, *Iʿlām* vi, 257–9; Ziriklī, *al-Aʿlām* i, 81.

59 See al-Khafājī, *Rayḥāna* i, 104–9; *idem*, *Khabāyā* 149–55; al-Muḥibbī, *Khulāṣa* vi, 506–7; al-Ṭabbākh, *Iʿlām* vi, 318–22.

60 See al-Khafājī, *Rayḥāna* i, 113–25; *idem*, *Khabāyā* 161–71; al-Muḥibbī, *Khulāṣa* ii, 81–4; al-Ṭabbākh, *Iʿlām* vi, 209–13. His *dīwān* has been edited by al-Ṭabbākh in *al-ʿUqūd al-durriyya* 2–231.

61 On these riddle kinds see Papoutsakis, al-Ḥaẓīrī; *eadem*, Muʿammā.

Ibrāhīm initiated riddle exchanges equally often as his correspondents (21 out of 40 cases). A typical entry consists of two pieces, a poem containing a riddle and an answer poem composed in the same metre and rhyme. In three out of four cases in which the recipient reciprocated by adding a riddle of his own to the answer poem, there follows a third poem as a reply to this. More often than not, the riddles are embedded in longer odes that include praise of the addressee, expressions of affection and longing for him, complaints of neglect, etc., and, occasionally, by way of an introduction, other themes as well, e.g. nostalgic recollection of one's youth, complaint about the times, or the coming of spring. The replies normally contain extensive praise of the received poem and the correspondent and do not normally disclose the solution; instead they offer a riddling description of the sought notion/word—this being the rule in riddle correspondences—and may drop the solution word as if by chance once or twice. Apologies for the supposed bad quality of one's poem or one's daring to engage the addressee in a riddle exchange and similar expressions of modesty are also very common, as are elaborate good wishes at the poem's closure. Thus, while in some entries the poems are relatively short (three to eleven verses), the majority of them are much longer (up to 38 lines, eleven poems being between 42- and 63-line long). At times there is a discrepancy in the length of the riddle and the answer poem, answer poems being as a rule longer that those containing the riddle. Ibrāhīm often included a riddle in welcome poems that he addressed to scholars and littérateurs visiting Aleppo—men to whom he apparently wrote for the very first time. Besides, his riddles are often about the recipient's name (six of the 21 riddles by Ibrāhīm), which obviously constituted an honour for the addressee.

The majority of the riddles in this corpus are 'mixed,' that is to say, they give both semantic clues, referring to the meaning of a given word (in Saussurian terms, the signified) and clues regarding the way of writing it (in Saussurian terms, the signifier), but there are also a few purely 'notional' riddles (riddles that give semantic clues only—see an example below). Therefore, they are relatively easy and entertaining.

In all the above respects, Ibrāhīm's riddle correspondence resembles the riddle correspondences of Mamluk littérateurs and scholars and, especially, that of Shihāb al-Dīn al-Ḥijāzī (790–875/1388–1471), who also exploited the genre to involve his learned contemporaries in playful communication.[62] This is indicative of the continuities in literary trends between Mamluk and Ottoman times. Elsewhere I have tried to show that the logogriph ('word riddle,'

62 See Papoutsakis, Literary riddle.

offering clues as to the signifier only) as was shaped by Timurid-Persian littérateurs in the 9th/15th century (the 'new *muʿammā*'), gradually became the most popular kind of riddle with Ottoman-era Arabic littérateurs.[63] This was apparently not yet the case in Ibrāhīm's times.[64] What is more, the 'new *muʿammā*', an epigram of no more than tree lines, was not suitable for literary correspondences and the cultivation of relationships. Therefore, notional and mixed riddles, which could be integrated in longer poems expressing deference for the correspondent, apparently remained prevalent in them.

In closing, I should like to cite an example of such a riddle exchange. In this case, Ibrāhīm engaged his friend Ṣalāḥ al-Dīn b. Muḥyī l-Dīn Muḥammad al-Kūrānī (d. 1049/1639), a legal witness at Aleppo's main court,[65] who was his most frequent correspondent (eleven exchanges, seven of which on riddles, and one *musājala*). Al-Kūrānī is an interesting littérateur in his own right and a riddle aficionado at that. Apart from three *dīwāns* (partly extant),[66] he authored a treatise on riddles entitled *Nūr maṣābiḥ al-dayājī fī l-muʿammā wa-l-aḥājī* (extant);[67] a *badīʿiyya* with commentary; a *muʿāraḍa* to al-Būṣīrī's *Hamziyya*; *maqāmāt* treating scientific issues (relating to *tafsīr*, *ḥadīth*, and *uṣūl al-fiqh*); an epistle on the antinomian ṣūfī (*majdhūb*) Abū Bakr b. Abī l-Wafāʾ (d. 991/1583)[68] (extant); as well as *Maṭlaʿ al-nayyirayn fī manāqib al-shaykhayn*, a work on ʿUmar al-ʿUrḍī and Abū l-Jūd al-Batrūnī, incl. some of their relatives and his own literary exchanges with them. It appears that al-Kūrānī composed several witty epigrams on smoking and the water pipe, a theme that was beginning to catch on in Arabic poetry at that time.[69] Possibly as a reaction to these poems, Ibrāhīm sent to al-Kūrānī a riddle on the water pipe. Some of the motifs found in al-Kūrānī's reply poem were also exploited in his epigrams.[70]

---

63 See Papoutsakis, Muʿammā.

64 He only has five *muʿammayāt* of the new type cited at the very end of his *dīwān* (fol. 262ᵃ–263ᵇ).

65 Al-Būrīnī, *Tarājim* ii, 243–53; al-Khafājī, *Rayḥāna* i, 281–3; *idem*, *Khabāyā* 277–80; al-Muḥibbī, *Khulāṣa* ii, 252–6; al-Ṭabbākh, *Iʿlām* vi, 238–252; Kaḥḥāla, *Muʿjam* i, 842.

66 Al-Ṭabbākh, *Iʿlām* vi, 244. I only had access to his *dīwān* MS Cairo, that contains poems composed prior to 1009. This *dīwān* includes, among other things, two *badīʿiyyas* on Ottoman dignitaries, two collections of epigrams: on handsome youths and on beautiful girls, and a long 'zoopoetic' poem patterned after Ibn al-Ghānim al-Maqdisī's (d. 678/1279) *Kashf al-asrār ʿan ḥikam al-ṭuyūr wa-l-azhār*. Al-Ṭabbākh had found 30 folios of another *dīwān* of his (*Iʿlām* vi, 246), possibly the same as *Salāsil al-nuḍār* (or *al-qarār*) *fī taqyīd al-firār* (or *al-ghirār*: obviously a mistake for *al-firār*) that exists in four MSS (online Catalogue of the Juma Almajid Center).

67 See Papoutsakis, Muʿammā 83.

68 See Watenpaugh, Deviant dervishes.

69 Al-Khafājī, *Rayḥāna* i, 283; *idem*, *Khabāyā* 277–8; al-Ṭabbākh, *Iʿlām* vi, 246, 247.

70 MS Gotha, fol. 105ᵛ–106ʳ; MS Berlin, fol. 3ᵛ–4ʳ. The few textual variants are given in the footnotes to the translation.

بتاريخ أوايل ذي القعدة سنة سبع وعشرين وألف أرسلت إلى صاحبنا الفاضل اللبيب واللوذعي الأريب القاضي صلاح الدين بن القاضي محمد الشهير بابن الكوراني أحد شهود المحكمة الكبرى بحلب ملغزًا له من نظمي عن غليون الذي يشرب فيه التتن [من الطويل]

صلاحي فلاحي مَن به أتجمّلُ – أجِبْني فما في المصر غيرُك يُسأَلُ
فما اسمُ لنوعٍ من جَوارٍ ويُشْتَهى – يُقَبَّلُ بالأفواه شوقًا ويُقبَلُ
ويجري بلا ماءٍ معَ الريح حاملًا – ومن عجبٍ بالنار يؤذى ويُشعَلُ
محبٌّ ترى في قلبه حُرقةَ الجوى – وبالكسر قد يُبلى وللهجر يُحمَلُ
يقود بذوقٍ نافرَ الطبعِ للوفا – ويُفضي إلى قرب الحبيب ويُوصلُ
ولو كنتُ ذا حُكمٍ أُولّى ولايةً – وقولي مسموعٌ وبالحقّ يُعمَلُ
خصصتُ به ثغرَ الحبيب ومبسمَ الـ – شنيبِ فلا يُعطى لغيرٍ ويُبذَلُ
فحُلّ لنا إشكالَ ذاك مفصّلًا – فإنّيَ فيما قد سألتُك مجمِلُ

وكتب لي الجواب القاضي صلاح الدين من الوزن والقافية

إليك أخا العلياء إنّي مفصّلُ – كما فصّل الدُّرَّ الوشاحُ المفصّلُ
فقد قُلتَ إنّي سائلٌ لك مُجمِلٌ – وفي ذلك الإجمالِ قولُكَ أجملُ
وهل يُسأَلُ التفصيلُ عمّا تَخالُهُ – شهيرًا وفي أيدي الحبائب يُنقَلُ
يدورُ على ثغر الملاح مسلسلًا – وقد صحّ فيها دورُهُ والتسلسلُ
وعهدي به في البحر يجري وإنّه – بأيديك فُلكٌ وَهْيَ بالبحر أمثلُ
وأنت به أدرَى خبيرٍ ومثله – ألا فاسقِني خمرًا به الخمس تكملُ
وقد قلتمُ لو كنتُ أُعطى ولايةً – وقولي مسموعٌ وبالحقّ يُعمَلُ
خصصتُ به ثغرَ الحبيب ومبسمَ الـ – شنيبِ فلا يُعطى لغيرٍ ويُبذَلُ
كأنّكم جوّزتم ظلمَ عاشقٍ – يشاهده والنار في القلب تَشعَلُ
ويرجو به رَشفًا ليُطفي أُوامَهُ – بموضع مصِّ الثغر منه ويأمُلُ
نعم إن رضيتم منعه عن رضابه – فليس لأهل العشق إلّا التحمّلُ
أما جعلوه حيلةً وحبائلًا – يُصاد به رشفُ الثغور فيحصُلُ
منافع ما فيه لدينا كثيرةٌ – وأعظمُها يلقى به الهضمَ مأكلُ
على أنّهم قد حرّموه تحكُّمًا – بغير دليلٍ والمحرِّمُ أجهلُ

فقل جملة الأشياء في الأصل حلُّها   قديمٌ ولم يحرمْ علينا المحلَّلُ
على طُوره آنستُ نارًا كأنّني   كليمٌ على أنوارها أنا مُقبِلُ
أنادَى بها أقبِلْ علينا ولا تخف   ولم يَدْعُني إلّا الحبيبُ المدلَّلُ
أناوِلُهُ إيّاه حيث دخانُهُ   على وجه بدرٍ منه كالغيم يُسبَلُ
فيُحجَبُ عن عين الرقيب فأرتمي   على قدميه خِيفةً وأُقبِّلُ
وعنه غليظُ الطبعِ يُعرِض نافراً   إلى حيث ألقتْ وهو للرحل يُحمَلُ
وهذا جوابي قد أتاك مفصَّلًا   ولكنّه إن لوحظ الحقُّ مجمَلُ
فإنّ الذي فيه منافعُ جمّةٌ   يُقصّر عنه الوصفُ والشرحُ يُشكِلُ
وإنّي على الحالين فيه مقصِّرٌ   وفضلُك ممدودٌ وطَولُك أطولُ
ولست بهذا في الحقيقة سائلًا   ولكن عن الآداب والفضل تُسألُ
فطارحتَ مطروحًا له الدهرُ طارحٌ   وحيدُ بني الآدابِ فيه معطَّلُ
ألم تدر أنّ النظم باللطم مُشعَرٌ   على أنّ بابَ الشعر والسعر مقفَلُ
ولكنّنا نتلوه أُسوةَ من مضى   ونحن على آثارهم نترسّلُ
وحسبُ الفتى خِلٌّ صدوقٌ يحثّه   على باعث الذكر الجميل ويفعلُ
فلا زلت محفوفًا بأنوار شمعه   ومجلِسُكَ العالي به يتهلَّلُ

At the beginning of Dhū l-Qaʿda 1027 (= end of October 1618) I sent to my excellent and sagacious friend, the ingenious and resourceful judge Ṣalāḥ al-Dīn b. Muḥammad, known as Ibn al-Kūrānī, one of the notaries at the high court of Aleppo, a riddle poem of mine on the water pipe which is used to smoke tobacco:[71]

My Ṣalāḥ (*lit.* welfare), my prosperity, he who helps me bear (difficulties) patiently, answer me, for there is nobody else in town whom one may ask!
What is a kind of running beings (young women / ships)[72] that is desired and taken with the mouth and kissed longingly?

---

71 The introductory notes in MS Berlin are somewhat differently phrased. There Ibrāhīm notes that the use of the water pipe spread after the year 1000 and that it was unknown before that.

72 *Jawārin* is the plural of *jāriya*, *lit.* "running" (fm., active participle of the verb "to run"), that may mean, among other things, a ship or a young woman, a female slave. In this verse the context suggests that the meaning is "young women," but *yajrī bilā māʾin maʿa l-rīḥi ḥā-*

It runs with the wind, not with water, and carries / is pregnant—the strange thing about it is that it is kindled and molested with fire.
(It is) a lover in whose heart burns passionate love[73]—breaking may afflict it and it is carried along when parting.
Through taste it makes the naturally shy show fidelity—it attains nearness to the beloved and is united with him.
Had I authority, were I a wali and were my word heard and implemented,
I would assign it to the exclusive use of the beloved's mouth, the mouth of one with cool and sweet front teeth, and would not grant and waste it on anybody else.
Clear, please, the obscurity of this in all detail!—for I have phrased my question succinctly indeed.

Judge Ṣalāḥ al-Dīn sent to me the answer using the same metre and rhyme:

Exalted man, I shall detail my answer to you distinctly, the way pearls are distinctly lined on an ornamental belt.
You said "I've phrased my question succinctly"—succinctness has indeed beautified your word!
One needs not ask for details concerning what I think is well-known and is passed on among the beloveds' hands.
It circulates in the mouths of handsome youths and it is fine that it does so.
I've seen it running in the sea and it's indeed a ship in your hands that are so much like sea![74]
You are most knowledgeable about it and similar things—oh, do serve me wine to drink with it, a five-year-old wine!
You said: "Were I appointed as a wali and were my word heard and implemented,

milan in the next verse should evoke the meaning "ship." *Ḥāmilan*, "carrying," also means "pregnant" and aims at misleading one to think of a young woman again. In both cases, while hinting at the water pipe (the desired "young woman," a metaphor), Ibrāhīm also alludes to the second meaning of the word *ghalyūn*, namely "galleon," a type of sailing ship ("it runs with the wind").

73 Both MSS have *ḥurqata l-nawā*, but Gotha corrects to *al-jawā* in the margin.

74 Al-Kūrānī refers here to both meanings of *ghalyūn*, galleon and water pipe. He exploits the trite comparison of a patron's hands with rivers or seas (of bounties) to praise Ibrāhīm, whose hands are the sea in which the "ship" runs.

I would assign it to the exclusive use of the beloved's mouth, the mouth of one with cool and sweet front teeth, and would not grant and waste it on anybody else."

As if you granted that a lover be wronged[75]—a lover that observes it and a fire is kindled in his heart.

He hopes and expects to get a sip from it, at the place where the (beloved's) mouth sucks it, to quench his burning thirst.

Sure, if it pleases you that he is prevented from (sucking) his (the beloved's) saliva, the lovelorn cannot but endure this.

Have they not made it a subterfuge and a snare to catch (*lit.* hunt) and obtain a sip from the mouths?

In my opinion it has numerous benefits, the greatest of which is that it eases the digestion of food.

They have forbidden it, however, arbitrarily, without any proof, but those who forbid it are most ignorant.

Say, therefore: All things are basically allowed since olden times and what is lawful to us has not been made forbidden.

I observed a fire on its mountain—as if I were Moses—and advanced towards its light,[76]

being summoned by it: "Approach and fear not!"—None but my spoiled beloved called me.

I gave him it while its smoke screened his full moon-like face like a cloud.

It concealed it[77] from the eyes of his guardian and I threw myself in fear at his feet and kissed them.

Boors turn away from it and shun it, but travellers take it with them wherever they go.[78]

That's my answer: it came to you detailed, but in actual fact it's concise.

For what has numerous benefits can hardly be described and is difficult to explain.

I fall short in both respects, but your kindness is stretched out and your bounty('s reach) is even longer.

---

75 Both MSS have *jawwaztum jawr*(*a*), but Gotha corrects to *ẓulm*(*a*) in the margin.

76 This and the next verse refer to Q 20:10–1 (on Moses and the burning bush; *ānastu nāran* is a quotation). Vv. 16–9 offer an additional, erotic argument that illustrates the benefits of the water pipe: the smoke screens the beloved from the guardian's eyes giving the lover the opportunity to approach and kiss him.

77 Instead of *fa-yuḥjabu* MS Gotha reads *yuḥjabu* (the poetic license called *kharm* or a mistake).

78 Conjectural translation; I don't know what *ilā ḥayṯu alqat* refers to (possibly to *raḥl*?).

But I don't actually ask for your bounty; rather I ask for learnedness and virtue.
You have engaged in correspondence a man cast out, whom Time has discarded, and who alone is unemployed among littérateurs.
Don't you know that slapping cleaves to poetry? But still, the doors to both poetry and the price (i.e. reward) (for it) are closed.[79]
Yet we recite it, as people have done before us, and exchange poems, following in their footsteps.
It suffices one to have a veracious friend that spurs him on to what creates good repute and acts (accordingly).
Never cease to be surrounded by the lights of its candle and the noble meetings that you host may never cease to rejoice at it![80]

Bibliography

Primary Sources

al-Baghdādī, I., *Hadiyyat al-ʿārifīn: Asmāʾ al-muʾallifīn wa-āthār al-muṣannifīn*, 2 vols., Istanbul 1951.

al-Bakrī, M., *al-Rawḍa al-maʾnūsa fī akhbār Miṣr al-maḥrūsa*, ed. ʿA. ʿĪsā, Cairo 1997.

al-Bakrī, M., *al-Nuzha al-zahiyya fī dhikr wulāt Miṣr wa-l-Qāhira al-Muʿizziyya*, ed. ʿA. ʿĪsā, Cairo 1998.

al-Būrīnī, Ḥ., *Tarājim al-aʿyān min abnāʾ al-zamān*, ed. Ṣ. al-Munjid, 2 vols., Damascus 1959–63.

al-Ghazzī, N.M., *al-Kawākib al-sāʾira bi-aʿyān al-miʾa al-ʿāshira*, ed. Kh. al-Manṣūr, 3 vols., Beirut 1997.

al-Ghazzī, N.M., *Luṭf al-samar wa-qaṭf al-thamar min tarājim aʿyān al-ṭabaqa al-ūlā min al-qarn al-ḥādī ʿashar*, ed. M. al-Shaykh, 2 vols., Damascus 1981–2.

Ḥājjī Khalīfa, *Sullam al-wuṣūl ilā ṭabaqāt al-fuḥūl*, ed. E. İhsanoğlu et al., 6 vols., Istanbul 2010.

Ḥājjī Khalīfa, *Kashf al-ẓunūn ʿan asmāʾ al-kutub wa-l-funūn*, 2 vols., Beirut [?].

Ḥājjī Khalīfa, *Fadhlakat aqwāl al-akhyār fī ʿilm al-tārīkh wa-l-akhbār*, ed. M. al-Sayyid, (s.l.) 2003.

al-Khafājī, A., *Rayḥānat al-alibbā wa-zahrat al-ḥayāh al-dunyā*, ed. ʿA.M. al-Ḥulw, 2 vols., Cairo 1967.

79 The unsaleability of poetry is a common motif of littérateurs' complaints about their times.

80 The pronouns refer to the water pipe.

al-Khafājī, A., *Khabāyā al-zawāyā fī-mā fī l-rijāl min al-baqāyā*, ed. M.M. Arkīn, Damascus 2015.

Ibn Ayyūb, M., *Kitāb ar-Rawḍ al-ʿāṭir fī-mā tayassara min akhbār ahl al-qarn al-sābiʿ ilā khitām al-qarn al-ʿāshir*, ed. M. al-Ḥabbāzī, 2 vols., Beirut 2020.

Ibn al-Ḥanbalī, R.M., *Durr al-ḥabab fī ta'rīkh aʿyān Ḥalab*, ed. M.M. al-Fakhūrī and Y.Z. ʿAbbāra, 2 vols., Damascus 1972.

Ibn al-ʿImād, *Shaḏarāt al-dhahab fī akhbār man dhahab*, ed. ʿA. al-Arnā'ūṭ and M. al-Arnā'ūṭ, 10 vols., Damascus 1986–93.

Ibn al-Mullā, I., *Abkār al-maʿānī l-mukhaddara wa-asrār al-mabānī l-muddakhara*, MS Paris, Bibliothèque Nationale, Arabe 3239 (autograph).

Ibn al-Mullā, I., *Ḥalbat al-mufāḍala wa-ḥilyat al-munāḍala fī l-muṭāraḥa wa-l-murāsala wa-l-musājala*, MS Gotha, Orient-A-02323 (autograph—all references are to this MS unless otherwise stated).

Ibn al-Mullā, I., *Ḥalbat al-mufāḍala wa-ḥilyat al-munāḍala fī l-muṭāraḥa wa-l-murāsala wa-l-musājala*, MS Berlin, Wetzstein 1886,2 (Ahlwardt 7959) (partly autograph).

al-Kūrānī, Ṣ., *Dīwān*, MS Cairo, Dār al-Kutub, Taymūr Shiʿr 246 (pages numbered).

al-Muḥibbī, M.A., *Khulāṣat al-athar fī aʿyān al-qarn al-ḥādī ʿashar*, 4 vols., Beirut [1966], repr. Cairo 1868.

al-Muḥibbī, M.A., *Nafḥat al-rayḥāna wa-rashḥat ṭilā' al-ḥāna*, ed. ʿA.M. al-Ḥulw, 5 vols., Cairo 1968.

al-ʿUrḍī, A., *Maʿādin al-dhahab fī aʿyān al-musharrafa bihim Ḥalab*, ed. M. Altūnjī, [Aleppo] 1987.

al-ʿUrḍī, ʿU., *al-Muntaqā min muswaddat Tārīkh Ḥalab—ḥawādiṯ sanawāt 981–986 h. / 1573–1578 m., li-muntaqī Shāmī majhūl*, ed. M.J.Ḥ. al-Shūrbajī, Damascus 2020.

Secondary Sources

Aktepe M., Esad Efendi, in *TDVIA*, ii, 340–1.

De Groot, A.H., Murād Pasha Kuyudju, in *EI*², vii, 600–1.

Elger, R., *Glaube, Skepsis, Poesie: Arabische Istanbul-Reisende im 16. und 17. Jahrhundert*, Würzburg 2011.

İpşirli, M., Taşköprizâde Kemâleddin Efendi, in *TDVIA*, xl, 152–4.

İpşirli, M., Ahîzâde Hüseyin Efendi, in *TDVIA*, i, 548–9.

Kaḥḥāla, ʿU.R., *Muʿjam al-mu'allifīn*, 4 vols., Damascus 1958.

Kaya, B.A., Yahyâ Efendi Zekeriyyâzâde, in *TDVIA*, xliii, 245–6.

Martel-Thoumian, B., Des curieux notables: Étude sur le Muʿtat al-adhhān d'Ibn al-Mallā (937–1003/1530–1595), in A. Pellitteri et al. (eds.), *Re-defining a space of encounter. Islam and Mediterranean: Identity, alterity and interactions. Proceedings of the 28th Congress of the Union Européenne des Arabisants et Islamisants, Palermo 2016*, Leuven 2019, 133–40.

Meier, A., Perceptions of a new era? Historical writing in early Ottoman Damascus, in *Arabica* 51 (2004), 419–34.

Murād, R.ʿA., and Y.M. al-Sawās, *Fihris makhṭūṭāt Dār al-Kutub al-Ẓāhiriyya: Qism al-adab*, 2 vols., Damascus 1402/1982.

Papoutsakis, N., Abū l-Maʿālī al-Ḥaẓīrī (d. 568/1172) and his *Inimitable book on quizzes and riddles*, in *WZKM* 109 (2019), 251–69.

Papoutsakis, N., Quṭbaddīn an-Nahrawālī's (917–990/1511–1582) *Treasure of names* and other Ottoman-era Arabic treatises on the art of the *muʿammā*, in *JAIS* 20 (2020), 53–89.

Papoutsakis, N., The literary riddle in the age of an-Nawāǧī: The riddles of Ibn Ḥaǧar al-ʿAsqalānī and Šihābaddīn al-Ḥiǧāzī, in A. Masarwa and H. Özkan (eds.), *The racecourse of literature: an-Nawāǧī and his contemporaries*, Baden-Baden 2020, 147–68.

Pfeifer, H., Encounter after the conquest: Scholarly gatherings in 16th-century Ottoman Damascus, in *IJMES* 47 (2015), 219–39.

Rosenthal, F., al-Dj̲annābī, *EI*², iii, 452.

Sabra, A., Household sufism in sixteenth-century Egypt: The rise of al-Sâda al-Bakrîya, in R. Chih and C. Mayeur-Jaouen (eds.), *Le soufisme à l'époque ottomane, XVIe–XVIIIe siècle*, Cairo 2010, 101–18.

Sabra, A., al-Bakrī, Muḥammad b. Abī l-Ḥasan, in *EI*³, first published online: 2019; first print edition 2019–4.

Sellheim, R., Die Gelehrtenfamilie Ibn al-Bailūnī, in U. Haarmann and P. Bachmann (eds.), *Die islamische Welt zwischen Mittelalter und Neuzeit: Festschrift für Hans Robert Römer zum 65. Geburtstag*, Beirut 1979, 562–82.

Schwarz, F., „Ich erzähle nichts als die Wahrheit!" Erlebnis und Erinnerung im Notizheft und im Dīwān von Muḥammad Fatḥallāh al-Bailūnī aus Aleppo (gest. 1632), in S. Reichmuth and F. Schwarz (eds.), *Zwischen Alltag und Schriftkultur: Horizonten des Individuellen in der arabischen Literatur des 17. und 18. Jahrhunderts*, Beirut 2008, 81–99.

Shākir, R.M., *al-Muntakhab min Taʾrīkh al-Jannābī, ikhtiṣār Aḥmad b. Muḥammad b. Mullā: Dirāsa wa-taḥqīq*, MA Thesis, al-Jāmiʿa al-Urdunniyya, [Amman] 2010.

al-Ṭabbākh, M.R., *Iʿlām al-nubalāʾ bi-tārīkh Ḥalab al-shahbāʾ*, ed. M. Kamāl, 8 vols., 2nd ed., Aleppo 1988.

al-Ṭabbākh, M.R., *al-ʿUqūd al-durriyya fī l-dawāwīn al-Ḥalabiyya*, Aleppo 1929.

al-Tūnkī, M., *Muʿjam al-muṣannifīn*, 4 vols., Beirut 1344(/1925–6).

Watenpaugh, H.Z., Deviant dervishes: Space, gender, and the construction of antinomian piety in Ottoman Aleppo, in *IJMES* 37 (2005), 535–65.

Ziriklī, Kh., *al-Aʿlām: Qāmūs tarājim li-ashhar al-rijāl wa-l-nisāʾ min al-ʿarab wa-l-mustaʿribīn wa-l-mustashriqīn*, 8 vols., Beirut 1969–70.

Index of Arabic Terms

Index of Names

The Arabic article (al-) is ignored for alphabetical purposes.

al-ʿAbbāsī, ʿAbd al-Raḥīm (d. 963/1556) 368
ʿAbd al-ʿAzīz 263–4
ʿAbd al-Majīd I (d. 1277/1861) 195
ʿAbd al-Raḥmān 263–4
al-Abṭan 263–4
Abū l-ʿAmaythal (d. 240/854) 164
Abū Bakr b. Abī l-Wafāʾ (d. 991/1583) 379
Abū Bakr al-Ṣiddīq (r. 11–13/632–634) 3–4
Abū Firās (d. 357/968) 199, 225
Abū Ḥayyān al-Gharnāṭī (d. 745/1345) 52
Abū Hilāl al-ʿAskarī (d. ca. 400/1010) 273n21
Abū Muḥammad al-Baṭṭāl 251, 255–6
Abū Nuwās (d. ca. 200/815) 2, 83, 113, 163n70, 328
Abū l-Raddād (d. 279/892–3) 171
Abū Shāma (d. 665/1267) 7–8
Abū Tammām (d. ca. 231/845) 27–9, 79n60, 277–81
al-Ahdal, Abū Bakr b. Abī l-Qāsim (d. 1035/1626) 307
al-Ahdal, Yaḥyā b. Aḥmad (8th/14th century) 301
ʿĀʾisha al-Bāʿūniyya (d. 923/1517) 158, 162
Akhīzāde Ḥusayn Efendi (d. 1043/1634) 376
ʿAlī b. Abī Ṭālib (r. 35–40/656–661) 216, 265
ʿAlī Efendī b. Sinān (d. 1005/1596–7) 376
al-ʿĀmilī, Bahāʾ al-Dīn (d. 1031/1622) 197
ʿAmr b. Kulthūm (6th century CE) 274
al-Amshāṭī (d. 725/1325) 52
al-Anṣārī, Amīn al-Dīn (d. 800/1397) 221
al-Anṣārī, Jābir b. ʿAbdallāh (d. 78/697) 199
ʿAntar 248, 250, 253, 256
(Pseudo-)Apollonius of Tyana 251–2
Apostles 161
ʿĀqila 260
Aristotle 111n39, 247n3, 251
ʿArnūs 264
Ashʿab 55, 58
Asʿad Efendi (d. 1034/1625) 376
Asmāʾ (6th century CE) 11–24, 31–3
al-Aṣmaʿī (d. 213/828) 234n99, 272n15
al-Ashraf Ismāʿīl (r. 778–803/1377–1401) 308–9
al-Asyūṭī, Jalāl ad-Dīn *see* al-Suyūṭī
al-Asyūṭī, Muḥammad b. Abī Bakr (d. 859 or 856/1454–5 or 1452–3) 212–3, 219, 224–5, 231–9
al-Aydarūs, ʿAbd al-Qādir b. Shaykh (d. 1038/1628) 296n, 308

Bagh 254
Baḥā 255
al-Bakrajī, Qāsim b. Muḥammad (d. 1169/1756) 161–2
al-Bakrī, Muḥammad b. Abī l-Ḥasan (d. 994/1586) 372, 375–6
Balīnas, Balīnūs *see* (Pseudo-)Apollonius of Tyana
al-Banawānī, ʿAbd al-Wahhāb b. Yūsuf (d. ca. 860/1456) 61, 63–4
al-Bāqillānī, Abū Bakr Muḥammad (d. 403/1013) 153, 273n21
al-Bārizī, Nāṣir al-Dīn (d. 823/1420) 276
al-Baṣrī, ʿĀmir b. al-ʿĀmir (d. after 700/1300–1) 196n23, 199
al-Batrūnī, Abū l-Jūd (d. 1039/1629) 371, 379
al-Batrūnī, Abū l-Yumn (d. 1046/1636–7) 371
al-Batrūnī, Ibrāhīm b. Abī l-Yumn (d. 1053/1643) 377
Baybars, al-Ẓāhir (d. 659/1260) 253, 256–65
al-Baylūnī, Fatḥ Allāh (977–1042/1570–1632) 375
al-Baylūnī, Maḥmūd (d. 1006/1598) 371
al-Bilgrāmī (d. 1200/1786) 159, 288, 311
al-Bisṭāmī, Abū Yazīd (d. ca. 261/875) 21
al-Bulqīnī, Sirāj al-Dīn ʿUmar (d. 805/1403) 172
al-Buraʿī, ʿAbd al-Raḥīm (d. 803/1400–1) 287–312
al-Burayhī, ʿAbd al-Wahhāb (d. 904/1499) 289–90, 301n51, 305–8, 312
al-Būrīnī (d. 1024/1615) 366–73, 377
al-Būṣīrī, Sharaf al-Dīn (d. 694–7/1294–7) 157n44, 288n5, 304, 306, 372

Caussin de Perceval 258
Christ 161

al-Dādīkhī, Qays b. Manṣūr (d. 655/1257) 200n40
al-Dhahabī (d. 748/1348 or 753/1352) 2
Damariyāt 260–1
al-Danawsharī, ʿAbdallāh (d. 1025/1616) 377
Dhāt al-Ḥimma 249–65
Diʿbil (d. 245/860) 164
al-Dīnawarī, Abū Ḥanīfa (d. 282/895) 247

Fīrūzshāh 249

Galen 248
al-Ghazzī, Badr al-Dīn (d. 984/1577) 367–71
al-Ghuzūlī, ʿAlāʾ al-Dīn (d. 815/1411–2) 174, 212–44

Hadhād 260–1
al-Ḥājj Ibrāhīm Pasha (gov. 1008/1599–1600) 370
al-Ḥākim (r. 386–411/996–1021) 248–9, 253, 256, 258, 261–5
al-Ḥākim al-Manṣūr (d. 386/996) 262
al-Ḥalabī, Shihāb al-Dīn Maḥmūd (d. 725/1325) 155
Ham 254, 259
al-Ḥamawī, Muḥibb al-Dīn (d. 1016/1610) 376–7
al-Ḥamdānī, Abū Firās (d. 357/968) 199
Ḥammād al-Rāwiya (d. 155/771) 183–4
Ḥamza 253
al-Ḥarīrī, Abū Muḥammad al-Qāsim (d. 516/1122) 280–1
al-Ḥaṣkafī, Muḥammad b. ʿAlī (d. 971/1564) 367
al-Ḥaṣkafī, Yaḥyā b. Salāma (d. 551/1156) 225
al-Ḥattātī, Muḥammad (d. 1051/1641) 377
Hawāsh 250–1
Heraclitus 247n3
al-Ḥijāzī, Shihāb al-Dīn (d. 875/1471) 65, 170, 173, 378
al-Ḥillī, Ḥaydar (d. 1304/1887) 155n36
Hippocrates 251

Ibn ʿAbd al-Ẓāhir (d. 692/1293) 179n80, 183n106, 184n117, 185n119, 217, 220, 237
Ibn Abī Ḥajala (d. 776/1375) 173–89, 212–20, 225, 232
Ibn Abī l-Iṣbaʿ (d. 654/1256) 151–6, 162–3, 276–82
Ibn al-ʿAdīm, Kamāl al-Dīn (d. 660/1262) 203, 369
Ibn Ājā, Muḥibb al-Dīn (d. 925/1519) 367
Ibn al-ʿAjamī, Zayn al-Dīn (d. 795/1393) 221
Ibn al-ʿArabī, Muḥyī l-Dīn (d. 636/1240) 199, 207, 303, 307–10
Ibn al-Athīr, Ḍiyāʾ al-Dīn (d. 637/1239) 153
Ibn al-Athīr, Najm ad-Dīn (d. 737/1336) 155, 273n21, 275n29, 278n43
Ibn al-Athīr, Tāj al-Dīn (d. 691/1291) 217
Ibn al-Bayṭār (d. 646/1248) 248
Ibn al-Dahhān, Saʿid b. al-Mubārak (d. 569/1174) 242
Ibn al-Damāmīnī, Badr al-Dīn (d. 827/1424) 224
Ibn al-Fāriḍ (d. 632/1235) 110, 176
Ibn Ḥajar al-ʿAsqalānī (d. 852/1449) 51, 86, 308
Ibn al-Ḥalfā, Najm al-Dīn (d. 1054/1644–5) 377
Ibn al-Ḥanbalī, Raḍī al-Dīn (d. 971/1563) 367–70, 373–4
Ibn Ḥayyūs (d. 473/1081) 275, 277, 280–1
Ibn Ḥazm (d. 456/1064) 162
Ibn Ḥijja al-Ḥamawī (d. 837/1434) 60, 63–4, 157–8, 162, 179n76, 186, 212–3, 219, 222–5, 234–9, 243, 269–84
Ibn Iyās (d. 929/1523) 64, 170–4, 176
Ibn Jābir (d. 780/1378) 159, 282
Ibn al-Jannān (d. 646–48/1248–50) 302, 304
Ibn al-Jawzī (d. 597/1200) 4, 300
Ibn al-Jazarī, Ḥusayn (d. 1033/1624) 377
Ibn al-Jazarī, Muḥammad (d. 833/1429) 308
Ibn Jubayr (d. 614/1217) 2
Ibn Khallikān (d. 681/1282) 262
Ibn Killīs, Abū l-Faraj Yaʿqūb (380/991) 215–6
Ibn Luʾluʾ, Badr al-Dīn (st. 686/1288) 224, 228, 239
Ibn Makānis (d. 794/1392) 179n80
Ibn Mālik, Badr al-Dīn (d. 686/d. 1287) 278–81
Ibn Maʿṣūm, ʿAlī Khān Ṣadr al-Dīn (d. 1120/1708) 159–60, 336, 350
Ibn al-Minqār, Aḥmad (d. 1032/1623) 377
Ibn al-Minqār, Shams al-Dīn (d. 1005/1596) 376
Ibn al-Mullā, Ibrāhīm (d. 1032/1623) 366–84

Ibn al-Mullā al-Ḥaṣkafī, Aḥmad b. Muḥammad (b. 937/1530–1) 367–8
Ibn al-Mullā, Muḥammad b. Aḥmad (d. 1010/1602) 367
Ibn al-Muqaffaʿ (d. ca. 139/757) 119–45
Ibn Muqātil (d. 761/1359) 50–69
Ibn al-Muqriʾ (d. 837/1444) 309
Ibn al-Muraḥḥil, Ṣadr ad-Dīn (d. 716/1316) 225, 238
Ibn al-Muʿtazz, ʿAbdallāh (d. 296/908) 148, 226, 233, 272
Ibn Nubāta al-Miṣrī (d. 768/1366) 52, 60, 71–89
Ibn Qaḍīb al-Bān (d. ca. 1040/1630) 374n42
Ibn Qalāqis (d. 567/1172) 226–7
Ibn Qizil al-Mushidd, Sayf al-Dīn (d. 656/1258) 241, 243
Ibn Qurnāṣ (d. 671/1272–3) 226
Ibn Quzmān (d. 555/1160) 51, 102
Ibn al-Raddād, Aḥmad b. Abī Bakr (d. 821/1418) 306, 309–10
Ibn Rashīq (d. 456/1065 or 463/1071) 148–55, 272–4, 278
Ibn al-Ṣāḥib, Badr al-Dīn (d. 788/1386) 177, 226, 235
Ibn Ṣāḥib Tikrīt (d. 584/1188–9) 238
Ibn Sahl al-Ishbīlī, Abū Isḥāq (d. between 643/1245 and 659/1260) 302
Ibn al-Ṣāʾigh (d. 720/1320) 177
Ibn Sayyid al-Nās (d. 734/1334) 52
Ibn al-Shiḥna (d. 814/1412) 369–70
Ibn Sīnā (d. 428/1037) 248
Ibn Ṭabāṭabā (d. 322/934) 148
Ibn Taghrībirdī, Yūsuf (d. 874/1470) 86, 170, 173, 350n41
Ibn Tamīm, Mujīr al-Dīn (d. 684/1285) 222, 242–3
Ibn ʿUṣfūr al-Ishbīlī (d. 669/1270) 182–3, 188
Ibn al-Wakīl, Ṣadr al-Dīn (d. 716/1316) *see* Ibn al-Muraḥḥil
Ibn al-Wardī, Zayn al-Dīn ʿUmar (d. 749/1349) 177, 240
Ibrāhīm b. Bashshār (ca. 8th/14th century) 217
Ibrāhīm al-Ḥawrānī 261
Ibrāhīm al-Miʿmār (d. 749/1348–9) 50, 60, 90–116
ʿImād al-Dīn al-Kātib al-Iṣfahānī (d. 597/1201) 7, 9, 163n70
Imam ʿAlāʾ al-Dīn Muḥammad III (d. 653/1255) 199–200
Imam Ḥasan II (r. 557–61/1162–6) 203n55
Imam Ḥasan ʿAlī Shāh Maḥallatī (d. 1298/1881) 191
Imam Muḥammad II (d. 607/1210) 205–6
ʿInān 257
al-Iskandar 249–53
Ittifāq (fl. 8th/14th century) 109–10
ʿIzz al-Dīn b. Munqidh (ca. 6th/12th century) 4
ʿIzz al-Dīn al-Mawṣilī (d. 789/1387) 157–8, 162, 229, 271, 276, 281, 282n59

Jābalqā 259
Jābarṣā 259
al-Jabartī, Ismāʿīl (d. 806/1403) 309
al-Jāḥiẓ (d. 255/868–9) 216, 224, 230, 240, 241n123
Jarīr (d. ca. 110/728–9) 27
Jawān 257, 264
al-Jazzār, Abū l-Ḥusayn (d. 679/1281) 177
Jesus *see* Christ
Jumhūr 249
al-Junayd (d. 297/910) 21
al-Jurjānī, ʿAbd al-Qāhir (d. 471/1078) 153–4
al-Jurjānī, Muḥammad b. ʿAlī (d. 729/1329) 153
al-Jurjānī, Qāḍī Abū l-Ḥasan ʿAlī (d. 392/1001) 369n17
Jushamī Mehmed Efendī (d. 1044/1634–5) 376
al-Juwaynī (d. 478/1085–6) 373

Kaʿb al-Aḥbār 253
al-Khabbāz al-Baladī (d. ca. 380/990) 226
al-Khafājī, Ibn Sinān (d. 466/1074) 152–3, 236–7, 242n128, 278
al-Kaftī, Khalīl al-Hamdānī (unidentified) 177
Kāfūr (d. 357/968) 150
Khalaf al-Aḥmar (d. 180/796) 83
al-Khalīl b. Aḥmad (d. 160/776 or 170/786 or 175/791) 182n99, 272n15
Kāshifī, Ḥusayn Wāʿiẓ (d. 910/1504–5) 150–1
al-Khiḍr (prophet) 251
al-Kirmānī, Ḥamīd al-Dīn (d. after 411/1020–1) 196n23, 199

al-Kūrānī, Ṣalāḥ al-Dīn Muḥammad (d. 1049/1639) 368, 370n23, 377, 379, 381–2
Kürenberger (ca. 12th century) 114
Kuyucu Murād Pasha (d. 1020/1611) 373

al-Maʿarrī (d. 449/1058) 217, 222
al-Malik al-Ashraf (d. 635/1237) 154
al-Malik al-Mu'ayyad, Abū l-Fidā' (r. 710–31/1310–31) 51, 190
al-Malik al-Nāṣir, Ḥasan b. Muḥammad b. Qalāwūn (r. 748–52/1347–51 and 755–62/1354–61) 172
al-Malik al-Nāṣir, Muḥammad b. Qalāwūn (r. 693–4/1293–4, 698–708/1299–1309, 709–41/1310–41) 51–2
al-Malik al-Ṣāliḥ, Ismāʿīl b. Muḥammad b. Qalāwūn (r. 743–6/1342–5) 79n62, 85
Māmayh al-Rūmī (d. ca. 987/1579) 334–63
al-Manṣūr, Abū Jaʿfar ʿAbd Allāh (r. 136–58/754–75) 254
Manṭiqī Rāzī (d. between 367/976 and 380/990) 150
al-Maqdisī, Ibn al-Ghānim (d. 678/1279) 379n66
al-Maqqarī (d. 1041/1631) 302
al-Maqrīzī, Taqī al-Dīn Aḥmad (d. 845/1441–2) 85–7, 170–5
Marcabru (d. ca. 1150) 104n20
al-Marghīnānī, Naṣr b. al-Ḥasan (5th/11th century) 149
Marquis Conrad of Montferrat (d. 1192) 201n61
Mary (the Virgin Mary) 61
al-Masʿūdī (d. 346/957) 199, 293, 297
al-Miknāsī, ʿAbd al-ʿAzīz (d. 964/1557) 373
al-Minūfī (d. 927/1521) 169, 174–5, 177
Mollā Khosrew (d. 885/1480) 373
Montez, Lola (d. 1861) 109
al-Muʿaddil (d. 658/1259–60) 199
Muʿāwiya b. Abī Sufyān (r. 41–60/661–80) 3–4
al-Muhājirī, ʿAbd al-Raḥīm (ca. 15th century) 289–90
Muḥammad (the Prophet) 8, 123, 152, 155–7, 161–2, 199, 216–9, 253–4, 271, 278, 287–312, 318, 336–7, 347–9, 370, 372
Muḥammad b. al-Ḥusayn (unidentified) 177
Muhammad Shah Agha Khan III (d. 1957) 195–7
Muʿīn al-Dīn Unur (r. 534–44/1140–9) 4
Muʿīn al-Dīn, Hibat Allāh b. Masʿūd (d. 739/1338–9) 176n46
Mujīr al-Dīn, Abū Saʿīd Abak (d. 564/1169) 4
Mullā Ḥājj, Aḥmad b. Yūsuf (d. 894/1489 or 895/1490) 367
al-Muqaddasī (al-Maqdisī), ʿĪsā (d. after 878/1473) 61, 63
Muraqqish the Elder (d. ca. 552 CE) 13
Muṣṭafā Tāmir Mīrzā (end of 19th century) 197
al-Mustanṣir (d. 487/1094) 191
al-Mutanabbī (d. 354/965) 79n60, 150, 155, 164

al-Nabhānī, Yūsuf b. Ismāʿīl (d. 1932) 288–9
al-Nābigha al-Dhubyānī (fl. 570–600 CE) 27
al-Nābulusī, ʿAbd al-Ghanī (d. 1143/1731) 152, 158–62, 271n11, 336n9
al-Nahārī, Muḥammad b. ʿUmar (8th/14th century) 301
Nāṣīf al-Yāzijī (d. 1287/1871) 161
al-Nāṣir li-Dīn Allāh (r. 575–622/1180–1225) 214
al-Nawājī (d. 859/1455) 52, 64, 212–3, 219, 225–8, 243, 350n41
al-Naysābūrī, Aḥmad b. Ibrāhīm (fl. 4th/10th or 5th/11th century) 199
Noah 152, 230, 253–4, 259
Nūfīl 253
Nūr al-Dīn, grandson of Ibn al-Fāriḍ (end of 8th/14th century) 176
Nūr al-Dīn Zangī (d. 565/1174) 5, 7–8
Nuzhat al-Zamān 248, 250

Orpheus 316–9

al-Qāḍī al-Fāḍil (d. 596/1200) 217, 219, 225
al-Qāḍī al-Nuʿmān (d. 363/974) 199
al-Qalqashandī, Shihāb al-Dīn Aḥmad (d. 821/1418) 73, 82
Qanṣūh al-Ghawrī (r. 906–22/1501–16) 367
al-Qarṭājannī, Ḥāzim (d. 684/1285) 149
al-Qazwīnī, Jalāl al-Dīn (d. 739/1338) 81, 153, 165, 269–84
al-Qīrāṭī, Burhān al-Dīn (d. 781/1379) 185–86, 228

Qiwāmī Ganjawī (6th/12th-century) 155n41
Qulayḥ b. Qābūs 255
al-Qushayrī, ʿAbd al-Karīm (d. 465/1073) 21

al-Rabbāṭ, Aḥmad (d. 1246/1830) 129
al-Raddād, Aḥmad b. Abī Bakr *see* Ibn al-Raddād
al-Rādūyānī, Muḥammad b. ʿUmar (5th–6th/11th–12th century) 149, 151, 155
al-Rāfiʿī, ʿAbd al-Karīm (d. 623/1226) 367
Rahq 260
Rakhma 261
Rāshid al-Dīn Sinān (d. ca. 589/1193) 190–1, 194, 199–207
Rashīd al-Dīn Waṭwāṭ (d. 573/1177) 149–51
Richard I the Lionheart 204n61
al-Ruʿaynī, Abū Jaʿfar (d. 779/1377) 272, 282n60
Rückert, Friedrich (1788–1866) 231, 233, 236, 238n108, 243
Rūdakī (d. 329/940–1) 150
al-Rummānī (d. 384/994) 273–4

al-Shābb al-Ẓarīf (661–88/1263–89) 36–48
al-Sadīd, Ibn Hibatallāh b. Rifāʿa (d. 593/1196–7) 218
al-Ṣafadī (d. 764/1363) 37, 51, 61–3, 176, 179n80, 183n106, 233, 235
Ṣafī al-Dīn al-Ḥillī (d. 750/1349) 155–7, 162–5, 276, 281, 337
Sheherazad 321
Sāʿida b. Juʾayya (1st/7th century) 179n79
al-Sakkākī (d. 626/1229) 153, 166, 279
Saladin (d. 589/1193) 7–8, 194–5, 204, 209
Ṣāliḥ Ayyūb (d. 647/1249) 250
Salmān al-Fārisī (1st/7th century) 199
Shams al-Barrayn 251
Sharaf al-Dīn Rāmī (middle of 8th/14th century) 150
Sharaf al-Dīn Yaḥyā b. ʿAbd al-Wahhāb (d. 935/1528–9) 367–8
Ṣarīʿ al-Dilāʾ (d. 412/1021) 183–5
al-Shāriqī, Muḥammad b. Yaḥyā (d. 820/1418) 306
al-Ṣarṣarī, Yaḥyā b. Yūsuf (d. 656/1258) 288n5
al-Shawkānī, Muḥammad b. ʿAlī (d. 1250/1834–5) 290
al-Shaybānī, Mudrik (3rd–4th/9th–10th century) 328
Sayf b. Dhī Yazan 256, 258–68
Sayf al-Dawla (d. 356/967) 150, 155
Sayfa Arʿad 258
al-Sayyid Sharaf al-Dīn (unidentified) 176
al-Shayzarī, Abū l-Thanāʾ Maḥmūd b. Niʿma (d. after 565/1169) 163n70
Sem 254, 259
al-Shiblī, Abū Bakr (d. 334/945) 225, 231
Shīḥa 257–8
Solomon 79, 351n42–3
Sufyān al-Thawrī (d. 161/778) 215
Sūl 316–31
Sultan Ahmed (r. 1011–26/1603–17) 373
Shumūl 316–31
al-Shushtarī, Abū l-Ḥasan (d. 668/1269) 303
al-Suyūṭī (d. 911/1505) 155, 159, 169–74, 187, 224

al-Thaʿālibī (d. 961/1038) 7n26, 226, 337n14
al-Taftazānī (d. 793/1390) 336, 365, 373
al-Tahānawī (d. unknown) 151
Ṭāhir al-Jazāʾirī (d. 1338/1920) 164–5
Tāj al-Dīn ʿAbd al-Raḥīm al-Qazwīnī (8th/14th century) 81n68
Ṭalāʾiʿ b. Ruzzīk, al-Malik al-Ṣāliḥ (d. 556/1161) 3
Ṭāma 260
Tamīm b. al-Muʿizz (d. 374/984) 177
Ṭāshköprüzāde, Kamāl al-Dīn (d. 1030/1621) 369, 371n27, 376
al-Ṭayyib b. al-Āmir (d. 526/1132) 192
al-Ṭayyibī, Shams al-Dīn (b. 592/1195) 196n23, 199
al-Ṭībī, Ḥusayn b. Muḥammad (d. 743/1343) 155
al-Tilimsānī, Shams al-Dīn Muḥammad *see* al-Shābb al-Ẓarīf
al-Tilimsānī, ʿAfīf al-Dīn (d. 690/1291) 10–29
al-Ṭubnī, Muḥammad b. al-Ḥusayn (d. 394/1003–4) 232

ʿUmar b. ʿAbd al-ʿAzīz (r. 99–101/717–20) 3–4
ʿUmar b. al-Khaṭṭāb (r. 13–23/634–44) 4
ʿUmar al-Nuʿmān 248–9
ʿUnṣurī, Abū l-Qāsim Ḥasan Aḥmad (d. ca. 431/1039–40) 150

'Uqba 251, 255–6
al-'Urābī, 'Umar b. Muḥammad (d. 827/1424) 305–6, 309
al-'Urḍī, Muḥammad b. 'Umar (d. 1071/1660) 368n12
al-'Urḍī, Abū l-Wafā' b. 'Umar (d. 1071/1660) 162, 371
al-'Urḍī, 'Umar b. 'Abd al-Wahhāb (d. 1024/1615) 368n11, 370–1, 374n42, 379
Usāma b. Munqidh (d. 584/1188) 1–8
'Uthmān b. 'Affān (r. 23–35/644–55) 3

al-Wadā'ī, 'Alā' al-Dīn (d. 716/1316) 219
Walter von der Vogelweide 114
al-Warrāq, Sirāj al-Dīn (d. 695/1296) 177
al-Washalī, Ismā'īl b. Muḥammad (d. 1356/1937) 307
al-Wa'wā' al-Dimashqī (d. between 370–390/980–1000) 163n70
William of Tyre (1130–86) 190n2

Yaḥyā Efendi b. Zakariyyā (d. 1053/1644) 376
Yaḥyā Ibn Abī Ṭayyi' (d. 627/1230) 2
Yūnān 256–61, 264–5
Yūsuf b. 'Imrān (d. 1074/1663) 377
Yūnus 249, 253

al-Zabīdī, Murtaḍā (d. 1205/1791) 289–90, 310
al-Ẓāhir li-I'zāz Dīn Allāh (r. 411–27/1021–36) 248–9
Zakariyyā Efendi (ca. 11th/17th century) 376n44
Zayd b. Muḥammad al-Ḥusaynī, Abū 'Abdallāh (6th/12th century) 3

Printed in the United States
by Baker & Taylor Publisher Services